D1187189

ETHICS

KARL BARTH

——ETHICS——

Edited by
DIETRICH BRAUN

Translated by
GEOFFREY W. BROMILEY

T. & T. CLARK
36 GEORGE STREET, EDINBURGH

Originally published in a two-volume edition as *Ethik* I 1928 © 1973
Theologischer Verlag Zürich and *Ethik* II 1928/1929 © 1978
Theologischer Verlag Zürich.

Printed in the U.S.A. by Vail-Ballou Press, Inc.
for
T. & T. Clark Ltd., Edinburgh

0 567 09319 0

First printed 1981

Contents

Translator's Preface

Karl Barth would never publish in his lifetime the lectures on ethics which the editors of the Swiss *Gesamtausgabe* have now presented in two volumes that are condensed into one in this translation. Nevertheless the lectures are of considerable interest for all who have a concern for theology in general and the theology of Barth in particular. There are three reasons why this is so.

First, they form an essential link in the development of Barth's own thinking as an ethicist. When he delivered them, Barth was at a crucial point in the movement from earlier ethical concerns to the larger theological conception which underlies the ethical chapters in the *Church Dogmatics*. As he understood it, dogmatic theology included ethics within its compass. Hence the demand arose for a rethinking of ethical foundations. Yet Barth retained a highly practical ethical interest and with his special concern to avoid legalism and yet to maintain a structured divine command he saw himself committed to an exploration of the implications of his dogmatics for actual Christian conduct both personal and social.

Second, the lectures clearly came to serve as a first draft of the ethical section of the *Church Dogmatics*. Already the outline is clear: an introductory chapter (cf. *Church Dogmatics* II, 2), then successive chapters on the command of God the Creator (cf. III, 4), God the Reconciler (cf. IV, 4 Fragment and the unfinished and unrevised *Christian Life*), and God the Redeemer (cf. the chapter projected for V). When the lectures are compared in detail with the available material in *Church Dogmatics*, it will be seen that Barth also made considerable use of the contents of these earlier discussions. He was to revise, expand, rearrange, and alter, and especially to drop the concept of the orders of creation, but the positive relation should not be minimized on account of the changes.

Third, the lectures have interest in their own right. Even Barth's attempt to work with a doctrine of the orders calls for attention. The comparatively stronger influence of his Social Democratic leanings, e.g., in the criticism of competitiveness, is also significant. The emphasis on collective pressures, e.g., that of developing technology, answers in advance a later criticism of Jacques Ellul in his *Ethics of Freedom*. Many of his themes, problems, and conclusions are astonishingly relevant today even though the lectures were given fifty years ago and the topical allusions and illustrations have obviously dated. Above all, his general rooting of ethics in dogmatics still calls for one consideration in antithesis to the inveterate tendency either to base it on law and tradition on the one side or on pragmatic concerns and changing mores and circumstances on the other.

It should perhaps be pointed out to readers that the notes and textual markings in this translation have been taken over from the original Swiss edition. For an explanation of the critical apparatus readers should consult the Editor's Preface which follows.

GEOFFREY W. BROMILEY

Editor's Preface

What shall we do? In the summer and winter semesters of 1928, a year after the publication of Martin Heidegger's *Sein und Zeit* and Carl Schmitt's *Der Begriff des Politischen*, the same year that Eberhard Grisebach brought out his work *Gegenwart*, the Kierkegaard renaissance reached its height, and the word "decision" was on the lips of all, Karl Barth at Münster put to himself for the first time, in a series of academic lectures, the fundamental question of ethics. The Christian form of this question is: What is commanded of us by God? Not man but the Word of God as the commanding and claiming of man is, as the acting subject, the theme of theological ethics. It would be a misunderstanding to conceive of this Word as an abiding objective truth which is inscribed somewhere and formulated in some way, which man may know or not and acknowledge or not, and over which he can gain the mastery by insight or act. Instead, it is expressly understood as the revelation of the command of God, as a present event in the midst of the reality of our life which he who hears God's Word cannot overlook.

The ethical lectures of 1928 were not printed during the lifetime of Karl Barth because the author, as he confessed to his friend Eduard Thurneysen, appears in them as still an advocate of the doctrine of the orders of creation which later he passionately rejected. Nevertheless, this circumstance and explanation should not cause us to lose sight of the fact that in these 1928 lectures, notwithstanding their borrowing of a bit of debatable tradition, there did in fact take place a fresh grounding of the materials of general and special ethics which was generated by the rediscovery of the Word and which resembles what may be seen in respect of God's Word in the *Christian Dogmatics in Outline*, which had been published in the early autumn of 1927. In those Münster years Karl Barth found himself in lively debate with his brother, the philosopher Heinrich Barth, with the religious philosopher Heinrich Scholz, who later became professor of mathematical logic and basic research, with the philosopher Heinrich Knittermeyer, and also with leading representatives of the Roman Catholic theology of the day. In part the ethical lectures arose under the impression of the impulses received in these discussions. In a strict sense they do not belong to the dialectical phase of the development of Barth's theology, that of the *Romans* and the works of reforming revolt at the beginning of the twenties. On the other hand they are also not an expression of the new principle of analogy. Instead, the present work forms part of a bridge for the road which leads from the 1922 essay *Das Problem der Ethik in der Gegenwart* (Ges. *Vorträge* I, pp. 125ff.) to the ethics of the *Church Dogmatics*. In the 1928 lectures Barth offered a general sketch of theological ethics in which he anticipated what would be developed in the *Church Dogmatics* at the end of each volume as the doctrine of the command of God. While this chief theological work of his remained a fragment—apart from the basis of ethics in II, 2 and the chapter of special ethics in the doctrine of creation which deals with the command of God the Creator in III, 4, the author has left behind only his doctrine of baptism (IV, 4) and some sections of the ethics of reconciliation—the 1928 outline is undoubtedly of particular interest not only because it is the only complete sketch of a detailed elucidation of the doctine of sanctification but also because it represents the first structured lectures of Barth that we have.

The text of the lectures was available for this edition in two forms. On the basis of a manuscript that has not survived, we have first the original which was typed at Barth's dictation by Charlotte von Kirschbaum, his assistant for many years; we then have a copy which Rudolf Pestalozzi, a Zürich merchant who was a friend of the author's, had duplicated and which in 1929 was distributed by the SCM in Geneva in two volumes, *Ethics* I (254 pages) and *Ethics* II (301 pages).

The author expanded the original with a series of additions written partly in ink and partly in pencil in the margins. Among these, two groups may be distinguished. First we have those which were put in the text at once, and presumably before the course began, since the Pestalozzi version includes them. The text containing these additions represents the lectures as Barth delivered them in 1928/1929. In this edition it is called Text A. Then there are the additions which were obviously made later, since they are not in the Pestalozzi copy of 1929. When Barth moved from Münster to Bonn he repeated the lectures to his students there in the summer of 1930 and the winter of 1930/1931. It may be conjectured that the second group of additions to the original arose on the occasion of this repetition. A comparison with the notebooks which two of the Bonn audience, Pastor Helmut Traub and Professor Helmut Gollwitzer, have kindly placed at my disposal strengthens this conjecture. The basis of the present edition, then, is Text B, the full text of the lectures of 1928/1929 supplemented by the additions of 1930/1931. The marks ⌐ ¬ are used in this edition to denote these additions. As a rule we have refrained from reproducing single words from the first version when these had to be excised or changed by the author in order to fit in the extensions. On the other hand, an excised word or phrase or sentence is given in the notes as Text A when a new version has replaced it in Text B to expand the sense or to make it more precise.

In reproducing the text I have kept to the guidelines laid down by the Conference of Editors of the Barth *Gesamtausgabe*. Incomplete sentences have been completed according to sense, and missing words have been added, in angular brackets. Grammatical mistakes have been corrected, repetitions excised, and spelling slips put right, without being noted. The author's style of spelling has been adjusted in principle to modern usage and kept only where it is especially characteristic of Barth, e,g,, in the use of capitals for *Alle, Viele, Jeder,* and *Andere.* The punctuation has also been improved and completed in accordance with modern rules. In doubtful cases I have kept to the general trend in the *Church Dogmatics.* The underlinings of words and sentences in Text A have been indicated by italics. But before beginning his lectures in Münster, and two years later in preparing Text B, Barth introduced additional underlinings, partly for oral delivery and partly to emphasize more the material importance of certain words and phrases. Naturally it has not been possible in every case to distinguish clearly between the two intentions. Hence the additional underlinings have not been introduced into the present text in cases where the choice of words in the sentence as a whole seems to make them superfluous. In the interests of greater perspicuity the text has also been given a tighter structure by the introduction of new divisions. Sometimes the author prepared the way for these either by a dot and dash or by a simple slanting line, which in many cases, of course, simply indicates the end of a lecture. It has been thought necessary and helpful, at times, to tie the text together by additional sentences. These are indicated by a vertical line after the period. Sections that Barth cut out of the first version and marginal notes in the Ms which are notes on the text but not true corrections or necessary additions are dealt with in the footnotes. When the author simply cites or alludes to a biblical verse the reference has been supplied by the editor in angular brackets. Works by other authors which are given only abbreviated titles in the main body of the text are given their full titles in the notes along with the place and year of publication and the numbers of the pages in the edition used by Barth. Reference is also made to more recent editions of these works. Quotations from books and writings are given in full wherever possible. When there is divergence from the original wording the note is introduced by a "cf." and when the quotations are incomplete or there is obviously a formal mistake in the author's version, the correct text is given in the footnote. Some special difficulties arose in the final chapter when the semester was reaching its close and Barth did not always succeed in expressing his thoughts precisely in the decreasing time available. In one or two instances the editor has here taken the liberty of interpreting grammatically complicated sentences, and in a few others attention is drawn in the notes to obvious errors of grammar, fact, or syntax.

Indexes of scripture references, names, and subjects have been supplied with the help of Sebastian Barth, Gerhard Siegert, and Reiner Marquard, whose cooperation I am glad to acknowledge.

Thanks are also due to Professor Markus Barth, who did valuable preliminary work for this edition and in particular gave me essential help in deciphering one part of his father's handwritten marginal notes. I must also thank Pastor Dieter Zellweger, Mr. Siegfried Müller, and Mrs. Else Koch for their help in establishing the titles of some older works and their researches in some historical questions. I am especially indebted to Dr. Heinrich Stoevesandt for his expert advice in the grammatical and syntactical clarification of various passages, for his help in verifying not a few dicta whose elucidation demanded skill in detection, and also for many important pointers. He gave me powerful support in preparing this edition, especially in its final phase. Finally, I owe a debt of gratitude to Dr. Fritz Schröter, who read the proofs and here and there suggested improvements in the Ms, and also to the Theologischer Verlag Zürich for its kindness and friendly cooperation.

DIETRICH BRAUN

Abbreviations

Anfänge I	*Anfänge der dialektischen Theologie*, Part I: Karl Barth, Heinrich Barth, Emil Brunner, ed. J. Moltmann (Theol. Bücherei 17), Munich 1962, 1966²
Anfänge II	*Anfänge der dialektischen Theologie*, Part II: Rudolf Bultmann, Friedrich Gogarten, Eduard Thurneysen, ed. J. Moltmann (Theol. Bücherei 17), Munich 1963, 1967²
CA	Confession of Augsburg (1530), (T.G. Tappert, *The Book of Concord*, Philadelphia 1959, pp. 23ff.)
CChrL	Corpus Christianorum, series Latina
CR	Corpus Reformatorum
CSEL	Corpus scriptorum ecclesiasticorum Latinorum
CW	*Die Christliche Welt*
Denz.	H. Denzinger, Enchiridion Symbolorum 30th ed., Freiburg 1955
EA (o), e.1.	M. Luther, *Werke* (Erlangen Edition), 1826ff., rev. E.L. Enders, 1862ff., (opera) exegetica latina
EKG	*Evangelisches Kirchengesangbuch*
Ges. Vorträge I	K. Barth, *Das Wort Gottes und die Theologie, Gesammelte Vorträge*, Munich 1924 (ET: *The Word of God and the Word of Man*, London 1928)
GuV I−IV	R. Bultmann, *Glaube und Verstehen, Gesammelte Aufsätze*, vols. I−IV, Tübingen 1933−1965 (ET: *Faith and Understanding*, vol. I, London 1969)
Inst.	*J. Calvin, Christianae Religionis Institutio 1559*
KD	*K. Barth, Die Kirchliche Dogmatik*, 1932ff. (ET: *CD-Church Dogmatics*, 195−96)
MPG	J.P. Migne, Patrologiae cursus completus, series Graeca
MPL	J.P. Migne, Patrologiae cursus completus, series Latina
*RGG*³	*Die Religion in Geschichte und Gegenwart*, 3rd ed.
WA	M. Luther, *Werke. Kritische Gesamtausgabe* (Weimar Edition), 1883ff.
ZdZ	*Zwischen den Zeiten*
ZSTh	*Zeitschrift für systematische Theologie*
ZThK	*Zeitschrift für Theologie und Kirche*

ETHICS I

Lectures at Summer Semesters at Münster (1928) and Bonn (1930)

Introduction

§1

ETHICS AND DOGMATICS

Ethics as a theological discipline is the auxiliary science in which an answer is sought ⌜in the Word of God to the question of the goodness of human conduct. As a special elucidation of the doctrine of sanctification it is reflection on⌝[1] how far the Word of God proclaimed and accepted in Christian preaching effects a definite claiming of man.

1

Ethics (from *ēthos*) is equivalent to morals (from *mos*). Both are the philosophy of customs (*Sitten*). The German *Sitte* (from the Old German *situ*) denotes a mode of human conduct, a constancy of human action. In general, then, ethics or morals is the philosophy, science, or discipline of modes of human conduct or constancies of human action. As generally defined in this way, however, ethics is not yet distinguished from three other sciences: 1. The psychology of the will investigates the natural constancies of human action; 2. the study of habits, the statistics of morality, or the history of culture enquires into the same constancies as they have achieved freedom and continue freely in history; and 3. the science of law studies them as they have received the guarantee and sanction of political society. Whenever the task of ethics is undertaken as a real task, however, it is understood as one that differs from the tasks of these other disciplines.|

Custom in the sense of the ethical or moral question is something

---

[1]Text A: "in which, in elucidation of the doctrine of sanctification, there is reflection on."

3

other than the congruence of a mode of conduct with a discoverable natural law of human volition and action. Even the naive identification of natural law and moral law as this may be seen in Rousseau, L. Feuerbach, and E. Haeckel does not pretend merely to describe but also lays claim upon human volition and action.[2] Among these three, and even more so among the true perfecters of ethical naturalism, M. Stirner and F. Nietzsche, this identification is a matter of passionate proclamation.[3] One does not preach a natural law as the identity of natural and moral law was continually preached from Rousseau to Nietzsche. Where this is preached, identification in fact obviously means predication, which means that the distinction between the two is abandoned.|

Custom in the sense of the ethical question also differs from the congruence of human action with what is ordinarily called habit, i.e., with a more or less widespread usage. Though this congruence may exist to some degree, and though an ethical trend characterized by the names of Höffding and Paulsen[4] has now and then nourished the identification of the two concepts, nevertheless no one has seriously attempted to dissolve moral philosophy in the study of custom or to contest that immoral customs on the one side and the moral breach of custom on the other are possibilities with which ethics has to reckon.|

Morality in the sense of the ethical question differs thirdly from congruence with existing state law or legislation. If state law with its palpable general validity is for Jeremy Bentham (d.1832) the most pregnant expression of the constancy of human action which ethics seeks;[5] if morality according to H. Cohen may try to view itself as the power of legislation;[6] and if an unending affinity between morality and law is the concept of many positivistic and idealistic ethicists, no one thus far has been able to establish a simple equation of ethics and jurisprudence.|

The ethical question would be at an end, or would not yet have begun, if we really tried and were able to unite it fully with the psychological, historical, and legal inquiries to which human action is

---

[2]Cf, J. J. Rousseau, *Discours sur l'origine et les fondements de l'inégalité parmi les hommes*, 1754 (*Oeuvres*, XXII vols. Paris 1819–1820, IV, pp. 201–373); L. Feuerbach, *Über Spiritualismus und Materialismus*, 1866 (*Sämtliche Werke*, new ed. W. Bolin and F. Jodl, Stuttgart, 1960², vol. X, pp. 91–220; E. Haeckel, *Die Welträtsel*, 1899, chap. 19: "Monistische Sittenlehre" (*Gemeinverständliche Werke*, ed. H. Schmidt-Jena, Leipzig, 1924, vol. 3, pp. 358ff.).

[3]Cf. M. Stirner, *Der Einziger und sein Eigentum*, Leipzig 1845, 1901³; F. Nietzsche, *Jenseits von Gut und Böse*, 1866, and *Zur Genealogie der Moral*, 1887 (Nietzsche Werke, *Kritische Gesamtausgabe*, ed. G. Colli and M. Montinari, VI, 2, Berlin 1968).

[4]H. Höffding (1843–1931), a Danish philosopher, wrote his *Ethics* in 1887 and is often associated with the German philosopher F. Paulsen (1846–1908), whose *System der Ethik* (Berlin 1889; Stuttgart and Berlin 1921¹²) uses a similar psychologico-historical method.

[5]Cf. J. Bentham, *An Introduction to the Principles of Morals and Legislation*, 1780 (Works, 11 vols. 1838–1843, new impr. New York 1962, vol. 1, pp. 1–54).

[6]H. Cohen, *Ethik des reinen Willens*, Berlin 1904, 1907,² 1921³.

also subject. The ethical question cannot in fact be asked without some attention being paid to the constancies of human behavior which these other sciences investigate. ⌐But it is the knowledge of the natural, historical, and legal constancies which can become a problem and call for ethical knowledge. The ethical problem cannot begin where the natural, historical, and legal constancy of human action has not become a problem. As this comes about, however, the question reaches fundamentally beyond natural, historical, and legal possibility and reality.⌐ It becomes the ethical question as the question of the origin of this constancy, of the correctness of the natural, historical, and legal rule, of the worth which makes a human action a style of action, which gives it a claim to be normative, to ask for repetition, to be a model for others. This question is not set aside by the reference to those other constancies but is posed precisely by the insight into them. Are they valid? That is the ethical question. The morality or goodness of human conduct which ethics investigates has to do with the validity of what is valid for all human action, the origin of all constancies, the worth of everything universal, the rightness of all rules. ⌐With such concepts as validity, origin, worth, and rightness we denote provisionally and generally that which transcends the inquiries of psychology, cultural history, and jurisprudence—the transcendent factor which in contrast is the theme of ethical inquiry.⌐

In this first section we have to make it clear in what specific sense we have to deal with ethics in the sphere of theology.

2

It is not self-evident that there is in theology a particular discipline which bears the name of ethics and addresses itself to the ethical task. It is not self-evident that in theology we have to pursue ethics as well as dogmatics. The question whether and in what sense this is to be established encyclopedically does not merely belong, as E. W. Mayer (*Ethik*, p. 192)[7] rather disparagingly thinks, "to the ancient inventory of theological and ethical literature," but as it is answered it is so significant for the character and direction of the handling of the discipline that we cannot avoid discussing it. We shall first learn and test the answers that have been given to the question in the past.

There has not always been theological ethics. It is true that in hints and directions on detailed and concrete problems, in exegetical and homiletical excursuses, at specific points in dogmatic investigations and presentations, the question of the goodness of human conduct has been raised and answered by theologians from the very first. ⌐Yet well into the second century there seem to have been obstacles to making this an

[7]E. W. Mayer, *Ethik*, Giessen 1922, p. 192.

independent question in theological thought and utterance. It is worth noting that one of the first from whom we have particular ethical tractates was the later Montanist Tertullian.[8] And the author of the supposedly oldest Christian *ēthika* or collection of Christian rules of life was none other than the great theoretician and organizer of Eastern monasticism, Basil of Caesarea.⌐9 As a systematic work, kept separate from the development of the Christian creed, we may then mention Ambrose's writing *De officiis* (c. 391).[10] A feature of this is that in title, form, and content it is fairly close to the pagan classical model of Cicero. Another feature is that it offers direction not so much for the Christian as such and in general but rather for the future clergyman, so that we find in it (I, 73f.) such admonitions as that one should not dawdle along the street with the slowness of a transported idol nor rush along it with the speed of a startled deer. The presupposition on which an independent Christian ethics arose is obviously the concept of the possibility and reality of an evident human holiness, of a perfect Christian life which could be demanded from and ⌐realized by all Christians according to Tertullian and by the clergy and especially the monks according to Basil and Ambrose,⌐ and then of the need to describe this holiness and supply its norm. It is materially significant that in doing this there was a by no means arbitrary compulsion to follow the familiar channels of thought of Aristotle and Stoicism, ⌐a resultant phenomenon represented by the name of Gregory the Great, who could expressly work the four cardinal virtues of antiquity into his exposition of the Book of Job.⌐11|

Medieval Christian ethics may be found in brief, not in a textbook, but in the famous rule of Benedict of Nursia (the end of the sixth century)[12] or at the end of the Middle Ages in the *Imitation of Christ* ascribed to Thomas à Kempis.[13] Even a comprehensive and purely scientific account of ethics such as one finds in the second part of the *Summa theologica* of Thomas Aquinas under the title of "Human Acts in General and in Particular" unambiguously has its basis in Aristotle and its crown and true scope in the religious life in the narrowest sense of the term, namely, the life of the clergyman and the monk.[14] The tendency to raise the ethical question independently is undoubtedly present in Thomas but in him, too, there still seem to be obstacles to doing this, for in fact he presented it within and not outside his dogmatics and in subordination to the dogmatic inquiry.|

[8]Cf. CSEL 20, 70, 76; CChrL 1 and 2.
[9]Cf. MPG 31, 619−1428.
[10]Cf. MPL 16, 25−194.
[11]Cf. MPL 75, 509−1162; 76, 9−782.
[12]Cf. CSEL 75.
[13]Opera omnia, 7 vols., ed. M. J. Pohl, Freiburg 1902−1922, vol. 2: *De imitatione Christi quae dicitur libri IV*, Freiburg 1904.
[14]*Summa theologica*, Salzburg 1933ff. vols. 9−14 (*Prima Secundae*) and 15−24 (*Secunda Secundae*).

Luther with his *Sermon on Good Works* (1520)[15] could hardly be claimed as a reformation example of independent ethics; and Calvin's strong interest in the ethical question did not prevent him from embodying in his dogmatics his discussions of the regenerative significance of the Holy Spirit and faith and of the law and obedience to it.[16] ⌐From Melanchthon, it is true, we have two versions of a philosophical ethics (1538, 1550, Corp. Ref. 16),[17] but in his case, too, the Loci leave us in no doubt as to the systematic place of theological ethics.⌐[18]

It was the followers of the reformers who began gradually to see things differently. The Lutheran Thomas Venatorius with his *Three Books on Christian Virtue* (1529)[19] may be mentioned first. He belonged to Nuremberg, was obviously influenced by Andreas Osiander, and thus described faith as the love, power, and virtue imparted to man in Christ (W. Gass, II, 107).[20] Calvinism became Puritanism on the fatal slope on which Lambert Danaeus in Geneva wrote his *Three Books on Christian Ethics*.[21] The Lutheran George Calixt followed him with his *Epitome of Moral Theology* (1634).[22] In the seventeenth century, the age of the Jesuits in the Roman Catholic church, the Pietists in the Protestant church, the coming of Cartesianism into philosophy with its rediscovery of the creative role of the human subject, and the development of the baroque in art with the Faustian fervor of its will to express itself, interest in Christian morality begins to acquire a new importance among Roman Catholic, Lutheran, and Reformed theologians. ⌐The dogmaticians now protest what the reformers had taken for granted, namely, that theology is not just a theoretical but also a practical discipline, indeed, that it is even more practical than speculative (F. Turrettini, 1, 7, 15),[23] and as the result of many discussions⌐ the distinction between dogmatic and moral theology begins to be gradually accepted. |

In the eighteenth century moral theology unmistakably took over the lead. In Schleiermacher we again find doctrinal and moral teaching brought into a certain balance and mutual relation, but it should not be overlooked that this took place in the framework and on the basis of a

---

[15]WA 6, 202−76 (*Works* 44, pp. 21ff.).

[16]*Inst.* III, 1−3, 6−10, also 11−18, 19, and II, 6−8.

[17]*Epitome philosophiae moralis*, 1538 (CR XVI, 21−163; *Ethicae doctrinae elementa*, 1550 (CR XVI, 165−276).

[18]For the gradual development of the link between dogmatics and the topics of theological ethics (the divine law, the Decalogue, natural law, etc.), cf. the 1521 ed. of the Loci in CR XXI, 81−227, the 1533 ed. in CR XXI, 253−332, and the 1541 ed. in CR XXI, 601−1050.

[19]T. Venatorius, *De virtute Christiana libri tres*, Norinbergae 1529.

[20]W. Gass, *Geschichte der christlichen Ethik*, 2 vols., Berlin 1886.

[21]L. Danaeus, *Ethices Christianae libri tres*, Genevae 1577, 1640[7].

[22]G. Calixt, *Epitome theologiae moralis*, pars prima, Helmstedt 1634.

[23]F. Turrettinus, *Institutio Theologiae Elencticae . . .*, Genevae 1679−85, 1688[2], 1847. In the first locus on theology, question VII, section XV says literally that theology is more practical than speculative in relation to its *final end*, which is practice.

fundamentally superior discipline which Schleiermacher again calls ethics,[24] a view which a hundred years later is confirmed and readopted with some modifications by W. Herrmann[25] and E. Troeltsch.[26] By means of some simple comparisons K.I. Nitzsch and later Martin Kähler and H.H. Wendt, also in the nineteenth century, renewed the attempt to integrate ethics into dogmatics after the pattern of Thomas and the reformers.[27] More typical of the thrust of the age was the reverse attempt of R. Rothe, in accordance with his theory of the gradual disappearance of the church in the state, to swallow up dogmatics totally in ethics apart from assigning to it the miserable role of presenting a theology of the confessional writings.[28] It has yet to be seen—I have in mind E. Hirsch on the one side[29] and F. Gogarten and R. Bultmann on the other[30]—whether the renewal of interest in the ethical task and determination of theology resulting from the Kierkegaard renaissance of the last ten years will not finally work itself out in the direction of R. Rothe.[31]

[24]Cf. F. Schleiermacher, *Kurze Darstellung des theologischen Studiums*, Berlin 1811, 1830², §§29, 35 (ed. H. Scholz, Leipzig 1935, pp. 12, 15) (E. T. Richmond 1966).
[25]Cf. W. Herrmann, *Ethik*, Tübingen 1901, 1909⁴, 1913⁵, (1921), pp. 1ff.
[26]Cf. E. Troeltsch, "Grundprobleme der Ethik," *ZThK* 12 (1902), 125—78 (*Ges. Schriften*, II, Tübingen 1913, pp. 552ff.).
[27]C. J. Nitzsch, *System der christlichen Lehre*, Bonn 1829, 1851⁶, pp. 3ff.; M. Kähler, *Die Wissenschaft der christlichen Lehre von dem Grundartikel aus*, Erlangen 1883—1887, pp. 467ff. (reprinted Neukirchen 1966, pp. 467ff.); H. H. Wendt, *System der christlichen Lehre*, Göttingen 1906, pp. 12ff.
[28]R. Rothe, *Theologische Ethik*, I—III, Wittenberg 1845—1848, I—V, Wittenberg 1867—1871². For the theory of the dissolution of the church in the state cf. the earlier work *Die Anfänge der christlichen Kirche und ihrer Verfassung*, Wittenberg 1837.
[29]E. Hirsch (1888—1972), Professor of Church History (1921), then Systematic Theology (1935) at Göttingen, who stood at the opposite pole to Barth when the latter was the first holder of the chair of Reformed Theology at Göttingen from 1921 to 1925.
[30]F. Gogarten (1887—1967), who stood by Barth in 1921—1922 and helped to found the journal *Zwischen den Zeiten*, which was for a decade the organ of the Dialectical Theology and took its title from Gogarten's article. in *CW* 34 (1920), 374—78 (*Anfänge* II, pp. 95—101); R. Bultmann, Professor in Breslau (1916), Giessen (1920), and Marburg (1921); cf. K. Barth and R. Bultmann *Briefwechsel* 1922—1966, ed. B. Jaspert, Zürich 1971 (vol. V, 1 of this complete ed. of Barth's works).
[31]Barth has in view the tendency which he saw in these theologians, in their different ways, to concentrate theology on anthropology. Cf. E. Hirsch, "Jesus Christus der Herr," *Theologische Vorlesungen*, Göttingen 1926; "Antwort an R. Bultmann," *ZSTh* 4 (1927), 631—61; *Kierkegaard Studien*, I—III, Gütersloh 1930—1933. G. Gogarten, *Die religiöse Entscheidung*, Jena 1921; *Von Glaube und Offenbarung*, Jena 1923; *Ich glaube an den dreieinigen Gott*, Jena 1926; *Die Schuld der Kirche gegen die Welt*, Jena 1928; "Das Problem einer theologischen Anthropologie," *ZdZ* 7 (1929), 439—511. R. Bultmann, "Das Problem einer theologischen Exegese des Neuen Testaments," *ZdZ* 3 (1925). 334—57 (*Anfänge* II, pp. 47—72); "Welchen Sinn hat es, von Gott zu reden?" *ThBl* 4 (1925), 129—35 (*GuV* I, pp. 26—37; ET, pp. 53ff.); *Jesus*, Berlin 1926; "Die Frage der 'dialektischen' Theologie," *ZdZ* 4 (1926), 40—59 (*Anfänge* II, pp, 72—92); "Zur Frage der Christologie," *ZdZ* 5 (1927), 41—69 (*GuV* I, pp. 85—113; ET, pp. 116ff.); "Die Bedeutung der 'dialektischen Theologie' für die neutestamentliche Wissenschaft," *ThBl* (1928), 57—67 (*GuV* I, pp. 114—33; ET, pp. 145ff.).

So much, then, for our sketch of the *history* of the problem. For the relative newness of the independence of ethics in theology and the ensuing tendency to swallow up dogmatics in it points to a *problem*. Assuming that in some sense and context theology has to discuss the goodness of human conduct, is it appropriate or advisable to do this in the form of a separate discipline from dogmatics?

First, the *negative* accent which dogmatics acquires with this distinction, as though it did not deal also and precisely with the goodness of human conduct, could very well mean an emptying out of the task of dogmatics against which the latter ought to appeal in all earnest. It was an insidious move when already in the middle of the seventeenth century theologians began to speak of the two "parts" of theology: first the knowledge (*agnitio*) of God and then the service (*cultus*) of God (Wendelinus, Prolegomena IV, p. 38).[32] Those theologians showed more tact who did not work out this division in the form of giving dogmatics two main sections (so Wendelinus, P. van Mastricht[33] et al.) but like the Lutheran J. Gerhard tried to make it fruitful point by point.[34] What does it mean for dogmatics if De Wette (*Lehrbuch*, p. 1)[35] is right when he says that in doctrine our knowledge soars up in faith and surmise to eternal truth while in morality the law is expounded by which our power of action achieves goals in life? Or if A. Schlatter (*Ethik*, p. 30)[36] is right when he says that the dogmatician illumines our consciousness but the ethicist sheds light on our will? Or if G. Wünsch (*Theologische Ethik*, p. 66)[37] is right when he says that dogmatics shows how we believe while ethics should show how we should act on the basis of the holy? If ⌐the knowledge of God is not in itself the service of God,¬ if eternal truth does not include goals, if illumined consciousness is not in itself will and faith act—then what are they? Does not all this bring dogmatics under the suspicion of being an idle intellectual game? If it really accepts these and similar disjunctions, it has good reason to abdicate in favor of ethics. But it might well be that it cannot do so because it has to carry out a task which ethics with its question of the goodness of human conduct cannot take from it but which wholly and at every point embraces this concern of ethics, so that with Thomas and the reformers, and some more recent scholars who have followed them,

[32]M. F. Wendelinus, *Christianae Theologiae libri II* . . ., Hanover 1634, 1641[3]: Proleg IV: "On the Division of Christian Theology."

[33]P. van Mastricht, *Theoretico-Practica Theologia*, 1698[2], where in bk I, pt. I chap. 3, he refers to the two divisions of faith and observance (based on 2 Tim. 1:13).

[34]J. Gerhard, *Loci theologici* . . ., 9 vols., Jena 1610–1625, 1657[2] (new ed. Preuss, Berlin 1863ff., and F. Frank, Leipzig 1885). In this work Gerhard has a practical application at the end of each locus.

[35]W. M. L. de Wette, *Lehrbuch der christlichen Sittenlehre und der Geschichte derselben*, Berlin 1833, p. 1.

[36]A. Schlatter, *Die christliche Ethik*, Stuttgart 1914, p. 30; 1929[3] (1961), p. 35.

[37]G. Wünsch, *Theologische Ethik*, Berlin and Leipzig 1925, p. 66.

it must resolutely contest the necessity and possibility of a theological ethics independent of dogmatics.

Second and conversely the *positive* accent which ethics acquires with the distinction can from the very outset prove to be a source of error for the way in which the goodness of human conduct can be a theme in theology. Those who radically distinguish dogmatics and ethics undertake to show how far different inquiries and methodologies really underlie the two. But so far as one can see, the result of this is highly suspect. ⌐I will give some illustrations from the more recent history of theological ethics.¬

According to Schleiermacher (*Chr. Sitte*, p. 23)[38] dogmatics has to ask what *has to be* because the religious form of the self-consciousness, the religious frame of mind, *is*, while ethics has to ask what *must become* of, and through, the religious self-consciousness because the religious self-consciousness *is*. We in contrast ask how it is possible in theology to posit the religious self-consciousness as being, as a given entity, as a given methodological starting point. And if this is done, will the description of what should become of and through the religious self-consciousness become theological ethics, the theological determination of the goodness of human conduct, or will it become something entirely different?

⌐According to Christian Palmer (*Die Moral d. Chrts.*, p. 21f.)[39] the difference between dogmatics and ethics is simply that between the divine and the human. Doctrine sets before us what God has done and achieved for us by his saving revelation, so that we do not first have to act, to bring offerings, or to do works in order to save our souls, but may simply accept what has already been fully done, placing ourselves and grounding ourselves on the foundation that has already been laid for all eternity. But the kingdom of God is also at the same time the result of human and morally free activity, every true moral act being just as much the work of man as of God. Ethics has to do with the human side of the kingdom of God mediated through the human will, i.e., through free human action. We ask whether the kingdom of God is really manifest to us in this sense as the act of man, or whether the shift of glance from the acts of God to the act of man does not necessarily signify a change to another genre which subsequently raises the question whether doctrine as thus coordinated is really dealing with the acts of God and not in the last resort with the Schleiermacherian analysis of the human self-consciousness.¬

According to A. Ritschl (*Rechtf. u. Vers*, III⁴, p. 14)[40] dogmatics covers all the stipulations of Christianity in the schema of God's work, while

---

[38]F. Schleiermacher, *Die christliche Sitte nach den Grundsätzen der evangelischer Kirche im Zusammenhang dargestellt*, ed. L. Jonas, Berlin 1843, 1884² (*Sämtliche Werke* I, 12), p. 23.
[39]C. Palmer, *Die Moral des Christentums*, Stuttgart 1864, pp. 21ff.
[40]A. Ritschl, *Die christliche Lehre von der Rechtfertigung und Versöhnung*, vols. I−III, Bonn 1870−1874, vol. III, 1895⁴, p. 14.

ethics, presupposing knowledge of these, embraces the sphere of personal and corporate Christian life in the schema of personal activity. We ask how one can manage to embrace the Christian life as such in theology. We also ask in what sense human activity deserves to be called the theme of a true theological ethics.

According to T. Haering (*D. Chr. L.*, p. 9f.)[41] doctrine shows how the kingdom of God as God's gift becomes a kind of personal possession by faith in Christ, while morals shows us that as this faith is a spur and power enabling us to work at the task enclosed in the gift, the kingdom of God will be realized, coming increasingly to us and through us, "here in time and then eternally." We ask how it can be "shown" in theology that faith in Christ is a power and spur enabling us to cooperate in the actualization of the kingdom of God. Will not the spur and power which can be "shown" be something quite other than faith, and will not the ethics which confidently thinks it can "show" them be something other than theological ethics?

According to O. Kirn (*Grundr. d. E.*, p. 1)[42] dogmatics looks at the Christian life in terms of its foundation on God's saving revelation and therefore from the standpoint of "believing receptivity," while ethics looks at it in terms of its active development and therefore from the standpoint of "believing spontaneity." We ask how either dogmatics or ethics can look at the Christian life which, according to Colossians 3:3, is hidden in God, and whether a presentation of what we can indeed look at in the form of "believing spontaneity" really deserves to be called theological ethics. ⌐All these conceptions are variations on the old Augustinian theme that we must view together divine and human action in grace as two sides of one and the same event. The possibility of doing this, however, is more problematical than is conceded here.⌐

According to Schlatter (p. 30) the relation is as follows. We do dogmatics when we take note of what we have become and of what we perceive in us, while we do ethics when we clarify what we are to become and to make of ourselves. When the dogmatician has shown us God's work that has taken place for and in us, the ethicist shows us our own work that is apportioned to us because we are God's work. We ask what it means in theology to take note of, to perceive, to clarify, or to show. Does not the particularity of theological perceiving and showing mean that there can be no question of this kind of binding division of the problem into God's work and ours, that the perception of what we are to become and to make of ourselves, the displaying of our own work (notwithstanding all the protestations that we ourselves are God's work) can never lead to a theological ethics?

According to Carl Stange (*Dogm.* I, pp. 50ff.) [43] dogmatics considers

[41]T. Haering, *Das christliche Leben. Ethik*, Stuttgart 1902, 1907², p. 9 (1926³).
[42]O. Kirn, *Grundriss der Theologischen Ethik*, Leipzig 1906, p. 1, 1936⁷, pp. 1f.
[43]Cf. C. Stange, *Dogmatik*, vol. 1: *Einleitung in die Dogmatik*, Gütersloh 1927, pp. 49ff., 53.

all the detailed statements of the Christian faith and shows that the essence of Christianity established in the symbols corresponds to the ideal that religious philosophy has generally demonstrated to be the nature of religion, thus indicating that Christianity is a religion of revelation. Ethics offers a similar proof in relation to the effect of Christianity on the shaping of historical life. A historical manifestation of a particular form of historical life must always represent the outworking of the nature or essence proper to this form. As ethics describes these outworkings, which can be understood only as outworkings of the essence of Christianity, and as it thus describes the essence of the Christianity that produces them, it, too, shows that Christianity is the religion of revelation. Now even assuming that this demonstration is a meaningful enterprise, and even assuming that it is possible to place oneself with Schleiermacher on the elevated platform from which Christianity can be seen as a specific form of historical life and by means of an ideal concept of religion measured against other such forms of historical life, we ask how one can establish in theology—our objection to Stange is the same as to all the rest—the continuity between the "manifestation" and the "essence" of this particular form of historical life. Does the revelational nature of Christianity transfer itself so naturally to the manifestation, to its historical outworking, that without further ado one can simply read off the former from the latter? How can an ethics which turns truly and honestly to the manifestation establish any claims to be called theological ethics?

We regard all these attempts at a methodological distinction between dogmatics and ethics as ethically suspect because with great regularity there takes place in all of them a suspicious change in direction, a suspicious exchange of subjects, namely, of God and man, as may be seen at its crassest in the formula of Schlatter. This suspicious exchange, however, rests on the suspicious hypothesis that revelation puts theology in a position to speak of God and man in one and the same breath, and to do so wholly to man's advantage, a glance at the holy God being followed by a second glance at holy man. On the basis of this presupposition the early church, as we have seen, did achieve a theological ethics, although not without borrowing from Cicero and Aristotle. But this hypothesis and the exchange based upon it involve quite simply the surrender of theology, ⌐at any rate of Christian theology.⌐ Theology is ⌐Christian⌐ theology when and so far as its statements relate to revelation. Revelation, however, is the revelation of God and not of pious man. If there is a shift of direction, even with an appeal to revelation, so that theology is suddenly looking at believing spontaneity, at what we are to become and to make of ourselves, at the outworking of the essence of Christianity, or however the formula runs, then there is in reality a turning away from revelation and it ceases to be theology. The supposed expansion of the subject means in fact its loss. This is illustrated by the incidental definitions of dogmatics, which we cannot go into here but which may be shown to be just as mistaken as those of ethics. Inevitably when ethics is defined as it is, it drags dogmatics and all the rest of theology down into the same plight as itself.

Theology is a presentation of the reality of the Word of God directed to man. This presentation involves it in three different tasks. As exegesis theology investigates the revelation of this Word in holy scripture. As dogmatics it investigates the relation of the content of the modern preaching of the church to this Word revealed in scripture; as homiletics it investigates the necessary relation of the form of modern preaching to this Word. The tasks of these three theological disciplines differ. The first has an essentially historical character, the second an essentially dialectico-critical, and the third an essentially technological. But the orientation and subject are the same. Exegesis whose theme is the pious personalities of the prophets and apostles, or even of Jesus himself, and dogmatics whose object has really become the piety of the preacher and his congregation, have ceased to be theology. They have lost from under their feet the ground on which theology is given a special theme in a special .way. For the definition of theology cannot equally well be reversed.│

Theology is not the presentation of the reality of the Word of God addressed to man *and also* the presentation of the reality of the man to whom God's Word is addressed. This is also a reality, of course, and it need hardly be said that in none of its main disciplines can theology ignore it. Theology knows the reality of the Word of God only as that of the Word of God addressed to man and it cannot for a moment abstract itself away from this determination of its theme. One may thus say that not just dogmatics but theology in general includes from the very first and at every point the problem of ethics. But the man to whom God's Word is directed can never become the theme or subject of theology. He is not in any sense a second subject of theology which must be approached with a shift of focus. When this transition takes place, when such questions can be asked as what we are to become and to make of ourselves, death is in the pot (cf. 2 Kings 4:40). For even though theology neither can nor should lose sight of it for a single moment, the reality of the man whom God's Word addresses is not at all on the same plane as the reality of the Word of God, so that there cannot be that coordination of looking upward and downward which is envisaged in the above-mentioned formulae of modern writers. Receptivity and spontaneity, gift and task, the inward and the outward, being and becoming can certainly be coordinated, but not God and God's Word on the one side and man on the other. It is not true that this second reality stands like a second pole over against the first and in a certain tension with it. It is not true that pious man has to work at the coming of the kingdom of God. [He has to pray for the coming of the kingdom of God—but this is something different.] It is not true that he is related to God's Word as subject is to object. All these are notions that are possible only on the basis of the idea of a synthesis and continuity between nature and supernature—an idea which ruined the ancient Catholic Church and which signified a repenetration of the church by paganism.

The reality of the man who is addressed by God's Word relates to the reality of God's Word itself as predicate relates to subject. Never in any respect is it this reality in itself. It is it only as posited along with the reality of God's Word. It may be discovered only in terms of that reality and discussed only as that reality is discussed. There are Christians only in Christ and not in themselves, only as seen from above and not from below, only in faith and not in sight, and not therefore as there are Mohammedans, Buddhists, and atheists, or Roman Catholics and Protestants.

When we speak of Christians and Christianity and Christendom in the latter sense—and if only for the sake of brevity we often cannot avoid doing so—we should always be aware that we are speaking of the Christian *world*, which is truly world or cosmos (in the sense of John's Gospel) as the rest of the world is. We are then speaking in typically untheological fashion. Why should we not speak untheologically of Christianity instead of Christ? Undoubtedly the pious man, even the Christian, can be in himself a rewarding, interesting, and instructive object of academic research. There is even a whole series of auxiliary theological disciplines, and one that is indispensable to exegesis, dogmatics, and homiletics, namely, church history, in which the Christian as such is ostensibly, dialectically, and for the sake of instruction the theme of theological research as well. But willynilly church history makes it truly evident that the Christian as such is not the man addressed by the Word of God and that there can never really be any talk of his patent holiness even though he be an Augustine or a Luther. This discipline is precisely the one which shows that the Christian and Christianity are phenomena in the cosmos alongside many other phenomena. Precisely with its dialectically intended untheological questions, it makes it clear that there have to be theological questions and answers if the Christian is to be understood as something other than a portion and bearer of the cosmos.

This is what obviously happens when the question of the goodness of human conduct is raised in theology. In the first part of the section we saw that this question radically transcends the questions of psychology, history, and law. It obviously has to do this in theology too, where goodness must be understood along the lines of the concept of conformity to God. For in theology too, in methodological continuation of the line in church history and in analogy to the profane disciplines referred to in the first subsection, we also find the auxiliary disciplines of religious psychology, folklore, and church law. If there is to be ethics in theology, if in some sense the question of the goodness of human conduct has to be put here, this question cannot be the same as that of religious psychology, folklore, or church law, nor, even methodologically, can it be put side by side with that of church history. Its object cannot be the Christain life as such, which is good because of its conformity to God. Instead, to take up again the concepts of the first subsection, its theme is the *correctness* of the Christian's Christianity, its *validiy, origin,* and *worth.* The goodness of human conduct can be sought only in the goodness of the Word addressed to man. We should be doing neither theology nor ethics if we related the question to dogmatics, and let it be determined in the same way as the theological authors adduced—a way which is at all events readily suggested by the unfortunate history of the problem.

3

According to what is perhaps a more appropriate encyclopedic integration of ethics into theology, we find it best to answer the question by attempting an independent discussion of how and how far ethics really constitutes one of the tasks of theology.

We have defined theology as a presentation of the reality of the Word of God addressed to man. We have seen that this theme cannot be divided into the two themes of God *and* man and that theological ethics cannot be grounded in such a way that when enough has been said about what God has done for and to and in us we have then to speak about a second topic, namely, what we have to do. We do not reject this second question out of indifference to what it has in view but because, when it is put in this abstraction as a second question over against the first, we cannot take it seriously either as a theological question nor indeed, as we have seen, as an ethical question. Yet we have to deal more fully with what it has in view.

Within theology the concern of ethics obviously emerges in relation to dogmatics. Dogmatics is the science of the content of Christian preaching, i.e., of the relation of preaching to God's revealed Word. The concern of dogmatics is that God's Word be heard in Christian preaching. It thus presents the reality of God's Word, not directly, but as it is reflected in the many ways that the word of pious man is moved by its theme, in the dogmatic dialectic whose intentional point of origin, relation, and goal is the reality of God's Word. Since the human word of preaching is also directed to man, how can it ever lose sight of the reality of the Word which at every point must finally speak for itself, the reality which is really heard by man, which really addresses and claims and seizes him?—not just thinking man but existing man, man who even as he thinks lives and acts and is caught in the act of his being. Only the doer of the Word, i.e., the hearer who is grasped by God's Word in the very act, is its true hearer. Because it is God's Word to real man, and because real man is man caught at work, in the act of his being, he hears it[44] in and not apart from his act, and not in any act, but in the life-act,

---

[44]Text A has *"man hört es . . . ."* for *"hört man es . . . ."*

the act of his existence, or he does not hear it at all. He does not hear it in the distraction, be it ever so profound and spiritual, in which he imagines that, while it may be true, it does not apply to him, the reference being to some other or others and not to himself. Other than in this actuality of the Word that is truly spoken and accepted dogmatics cannot at any point on its long way present its object, although many times it must apparently (but only apparently) go far astray from the concrete reality and situation of man.|

Necessarily this topic must be expressly dealt with at a specific point on the path of dogmatics, namely, where dogmatics as the doctrine of reconciliation in particular has also to say that the event of the reconciliation of sinful man by God and to God is a real event which is effected on this man as he is, that God's grace comes to him. If anybody—and this would be very suspicious—has not noted it already in the rest of dogmatics, ⌐in the doctrine of God or creation or christology,¬ then at the very latest he must pay regard to it here where it has a personal application, or all the rest is nonsense. The Word of God whose reality we are trying to describe is not just spoken but is spoken ⌐for you,¬ to you. You cannot think or say or do anything, you cannot draw a single breath, without a decision of some kind being made in relation to the Word of God that is spoken to you.|

In dogmatics we give the name of sanctification to this claiming of man as such ⌐which is basically fulfilled in God's revelation, attested to in holy scripture, and promulgated in Christian preaching.¬ As we understand the Word not only as the Word of God, not only as the Word of our Creator, not only as the Word of His faithfulness and mercy, not only as the Word that calls and justifies us, and not only as the Word that establishes the church and promises our redemption, as we understand it—all this ought to be enough, one might think—expressly and emphatically as the sanctifying Word, we have the right to state that the reality of the Word of God embraces the reality of the man who receives it and therefore gives the Christian answer to the question of the goodness of human conduct.

Good means *sanctified by God*. This is how we may briefly formulate the answer, bluntly challenging the need for special ethics in theology as we recall the strong total content of the concept of sanctification. To remember not only the ethical character of dogmatics in general but also the express answer to the ethical question that is given in the doctrine of sanctification is to ensure that ethics is not possible as an independent discipline alongside dogmatics. Not just in general, but also in particular, the concern of ethics is a proper concern of dogmatics.

It would be inadvisable, however, simply to accept this assertion and not proceed further. The ethical question is obviously not just one question among many others but is in an eminent sense the question of human *existence*. As we will, we *are*. What we do, we *are*. Man does not exist and also act. He exists as he acts. His action, his stepping forth or appearance (*existere*), is his existence. The question whether and how far he acts rightly is thus none other than the question whether he exists rightly. If, then, ethics inquires into the goodness of human action and dogmatics both as a whole and in detail aims at the statement that human action is good in so far as God sanctifies it, this point of coincidence is of very special significance for both parts. Let us first leave it undecided what it might mean for an ethics that is not radically and naturally theological ethics that here in dogmatics it is confronted by theology, by the voice of the church. For dogmatics, at any rate, it cannot be a matter of indifference that here in the concern of ethics as its own proper concern it comes up against the question of human existence. It is not at all true—I cannot approve of this intrusion of Kierkegaard into theology as it may be seen, if I am right, in Bultmann[45]—that the question of human existence is as much the theme of theology and dogmatics too. The theme of theology and dogmatics is the Word of God, nothing else, but the Word of God is not merely the answer to the question of human existence but also its origin. The question of human good which transcends all psychology, custom, and law arises, and arises with such sinister urgency, and arises like any genuine question out of a secretly preceding answer, because the Word of God is spoken to man, because the Word of God lays claim to his life.

The theme of dogmatics is simply the Word of God, but the theme of the Word of God is simply human existence, life, or conduct. Obviously this can be for dogmatics no more than a relational point, one locus among others, from which it can move on in the agenda once it has dealt with it and has said what is to be said about the doctrine of sanctification. For on the fact that it really has this point of relation depends the whole answer to the question whether its presentation of the reality of the Word of God will differ from a metaphysics which, developed in the attitude of a spectator, and depicting a reality that is not heard existentially, that does not come home to man or claim him or make him responsible, cannot possibly be the reality of the Word of God no matter how rich or profound its content might be. If God be understood apart from the relation to our existence, then even though he be the triune God of Nicaea or the God so fully described by Luther and Calvin, he is not God but a human idol, a mere concept of God.

Naturally it is not in our own power to give dogmatics this relation to the reality of man just as it is not in our own power to make dogmatics a depiction of the reality of the Word of God. God alone does these things at his own sovereign good pleasure. But here as everywhere it is fitting that theological scholarship should be ready to serve God as he wills. As

---

[45]Cf. n. 31. Cf. Bultmann's concept of dialectical theology as insight into the dialectic of human existence, *Faith and Understanding* I, pp. 152ff., a point on which he and Barth disagreed, cf. Barth-Bultmann *Briefwechsel*, letters 39, 40, 47, 48. On the problem of Bultmann's understanding of Kierkegaard and Barth's attitude to Kierkegaard cf. H. Diem, "Methoden der Kierkegaardforschung," *ZdZ* 6 (1928), pp. 165 ff., 170.

dogmatics can and does take measures to guard at least to some degree against the distraction of human thought which is constantly trying to avoid paying attention to the Word, so it can take measures to guard at least to some degree against the same distraction when it wants to forget that we are dealing with the Word that is addressed to man. First, it can make some effort to resist this distraction ⌐by always avoiding all pure speculation and positively by constantly observing and emphasizing that all its statements bear the character of decision.⌐ Second, it will not fail to present the doctrine of sanctification with the emphasis it deserves, for here the question of the theme of the Word of God is a burning one. Third, it will do well to remember that it is a human work, and to recall the classical model of the transition from Romans 11 to Romans 12, and therefore not to insist that all that is necessary has been said, but rather to leave room precisely at this point for an auxiliary discipline which independently can take up the doctrine of sanctification again and in its own context work out all its implications. |

Recognition of the need for this auxiliary discipline entails a practical confession of humility on the part of theology which is most appropriate at this specific point. In actually saying again, as though it had not already said it, its own decisive word about the hearing of the Word, it acknowledges that *its* decisive word is not *the* decisive word. By this repetition it shows that precisely at this decisive point all theology is not a masterwork but at very best an associate work, so that there can be no question of a dogmatic system that is in itself an adequate presentation of this lofty subject. However good it may be, it has not spoken from heaven but on earth, and therefore it must say again what only God himself can have said once and for all. |

The theological encyclopedia knows auxiliary disciplines at other points as well and it may be shown that all of them imply a similar reservation of theology in relation to itself. Thus we find that Old Testament and New Testament introduction, the history of Near Eastern and Hellenistic religion, and Palestinian studies are all auxiliary to exegesis; liturgical and catechetic studies to homiletics; historical and confessional history to dogmatics; and church history to all three theological disciplines. |

Ethics is an auxiliary discipline of this kind in relation to dogmatics. There must be no change into another genre here. We have seen that this is the error in the usual distinction between dogmatics and ethics and we must avoid it. Theological ethics is itself dogmatics, not an independent discipline alongside it. We obey only an academic necessity in treating it separately. Ethics, too, reflects on the Word of God as the transcendent meaning, theme, and bearer of Christian preaching in the form of criticism of the pious human word. It reflects especially on the fact that this Word of God which is to be proclaimed and received in Christian preaching claims man in a very particular way. It was most fitting—we are again thinking of the Pauline epistles and especially of

Romans—when the early church devoted that qualified attention to the problem of ethics. Even in the modern emancipation of ethics from dogmatics there lay a justifiable concern, and in its overdevelopment a nemesis and historically understandable reaction to the fall against which no dogmatics is secure, a fall into spectator-metaphysics, into the luxury of an idle worldview. But it is high time to move away from this historically justifiable but materially very dangerous reaction against an unethical dogmatics. It is high time to try to do justice to that concern as can be properly done only in the sphere of the reformation churches, i.e., in such a way that the ultimately pagan introduction of a second standpoint, which will unavoidably result in the loss of the first and true one, is reversed, and in ethics, too, the sole inquiry, even if it has a specific edge, is not into a second thing but into the one and only thing that is necessary. Conducted in any other way the enterprise of theological ethics will finally mean the destroying and not the upbuilding of the church.

§2

THEOLOGICAL AND PHILOSOPHICAL ETHICS

Ethics is theological ethics to the extent that it sees the goodness of human conduct in the reality of the Word of God that sanctifies man. As on this presupposition it confesses the concrete revelation of God in Christ by the Holy Spirit, it acknowledges the validity of another ethics which on the basis of the same Christian confession will as philosophical ethics seek and find the goodness of human conduct in the possibility, grounded in that reality, of human action that is rightly claimed by one's fellowman.[1]

1

We have already said that ethics is not originally or self-evidently theological ethics. Always and still today the question of the goodness of human conduct arises in other contexts than that of theology. Historically considered, theological ethics undoubtedly signifies a kind of annexation comparable to the entry of the children of Israel, against which objections can obviously be made, into the land of Canaan, where other nations claimed to have, if not an original, at least a very ancient right of domicile. On the field of ethical deliberation, which is apparently open to all kinds of other possible investigations, and which has

---

[1]Text A: "in the possibility corresponding to that reality." In this section Barth is in tacit conversation with his brother, the philosopher Heinrich Barth (1890–1965). Cf. §2, subsection 4c (pp. 67ff.) of the latter's work *Philosophie der praktischen Vernunft*, Tübingen 1927.

been long since lit up and worked over by a whole series of what are often very serious investigations, there takes place the entry, or, one might almost say, the invasion of a rival whose investigation differs in such an extraordinary way from all other possible and actual investigations that on their part doubt as to the legitimacy of this act seems almost unavoidable, especially as this rival is in no position to behave peacefully as one partner in discussion among many others. But, modest though its entry may be formally, and primitive though its intellectual equipment may perhaps appear, it advances the claim that it is the one that with its investigation has the last word which absorbs all others.

When, as sometimes happens, the philosophical ethicist of any trend pays attention to theological ethics, he finds himself set in a strange world. What is alien to him here is a presumed and puzzling knowledge of the whence and whither of every ethical question and answer. What is a problem to him, the law or goodness or value which the philosophical ethicist seeks as a standard by which to measure human conduct, the problem of the truth of the good, seems to be no problem at all here. Instead, in the concept of God of a proper theological ethics, in the concept of the reality of the God who has dealings with man through his Word, this problem is the inwardly secure and presupposed starting point of every question and answer. Conversely, what is no problem for him, the real situation of man in the light of the ethical question and answer, his real commitment to the norm of the good, his real distance from any achieving of this norm, and the real overcoming of this distance, not by man, but by the truth of the good itself known as a reality, all this is here an acute problem, the goal of every ethical question and answer. What relation is there between an inquiry that is ruled by knowledge of the whence and the whither and that which he knows as ethics, no matter whether he espouses naturalism, positivism, or idealism? In the light of any system of philosophical ethics, will not the definition of the good that we gave in the first section, namely, conduct sanctified by God's Word, cause him to shake his head? Can the philosophical ethicist fail to see that even though the same question of the goodness of human conduct is in some way at issue here as in the inquiry that he calls ethics, nevertheless the "in some way" is calculated to lead him to the decision that what is attempted is both impossible on the one side and insignificant on the other. It is impossible because a suspension of the fundamental rules of human thought is entailed if we simply start with the concept of God as the quintessance of the good, with the truth, regarded as a reality, of an absolutely transcendent and decisive Word of God addressed to man. It is insignificant because the question of the real situation of man, and concepts like conscience, sin, and grace, although they may have psychological and historical importance, can only hamper and confuse the question of ethics, the question of the true law, value, or good, the question of the quality of human conduct to be deduced from these criteria. This decision, the summary rejection of theological ethics as such, is at least a very natural one for the philosophical ethicist as such. |

This being so, it is on the other hand very natural for the theological ethicist to forget that he is in the situation of the attacker and not the attacked, that if he understands his own work he cannot stop to justify himself, that ipso facto as a theologian he enters the sphere of ethical reflection and cannot regard the supposedly original inhabitants of the land as a court to which he is commanded or is even able to give account. |

The protest or disregard with which philosophical ethics usually rejects theological ethics carries with it for the latter the temptation to enter into debate with the former in the form of apologetics. This is the first possibility that we must oppose here. Apologetics is the attempt to establish and justify theological thinking in the context of philosophical, or, more generally and precisely, nontheological thinking. In our own case it is the attempt to establish and justify the approach of theological ethics in the context of philosophical ethics.

Schleiermacher does apologetics when he maintains that, if not the Christian self-consciousness, at least the general religious self-consciousness which underlies it, is with its moral content or orientation an unavoidable element even in the inquiry of philosophical ethics, and when he thus aims at least indirectly to justify Christian ethics at the bar of philosophical ethics (*Chr. Sitte*, pp. 29, 75). De Wette does apologetics when he extols the Christian revelation from which Christian ethics derives as manifested and actualized reason (*Lehrbuch*, p. 2). Hagenbach does apologetics when he has philosophical ethics aiming at Christianity, in which alone it finds its fulfillment because belief in God is the supreme shoot of the moral life (*Enzykl.* 12th ed., p. 436).[2] W. Herrmann does apologetics when he thinks that without further ado he can claim that every ethics that wants to deal not only with the concept of the good but also with its achievement by man must see to it that the Christian religion is understood as a morally liberating power and must itself at its peak become Christian ethics (*Ethik*, 4th ed., p. 3). G. Wünsch does apologetics when he wants Christian ethics to be understood as a possibility, foreseen in philosophical ethics, of reflection on values, as the affirmation of a particular position on values, namely, that the really acknowledged holy in the form of the personality is the chief value anchored in the transcendent, Christian ethics also commending itself to philosophical ethics because its formal criteria are identical with those of the latter (*Theol. Eth.*, p. 59f.).[3] Finally A. Schweitzer does apologetics when with reference to Indian ethics he thinks he can trace back the distinction between religious and

---

[2] K.R. Hagenbach, *Encyclopädie und Methodologie der Theologischen Wissenschaft*, Leipzig 1833, 12th ed., revised, expanded, and edited by M. Reischle, Leipzig 1889, p. 436 (E.T. New York 1894).

[3] Cf. G. Wünsch, op. cit., pp. 59ff., 61f.

philosophical thinking to the relative distinction between a more intuitive and a more analytical knowledge of the basic moral principle (*Kult. u. Ethik*, p. 24f.).[4]

These and similar linkages cannot achieve what explicitly or implicitly they are meant to achieve, namely, the establishment and justification of theological ethics in the framework of the inquiry of philosophical ethics. Two possibilities exist.

First, the linkages may be taken seriously on the assumption that it is fitting to measure theological ethics by philosophical ethics as its appointed judge, as the court where the question of truth must be answered, because from the very first the distinctive content of the inquiry of theological ethics, or the empty space for it, is contained in a superior and original way in philosophical ethics, and has to be brought to conscious development—this is the business of apologetic argumentation—in order that the desired validation of its existence might be thereby achieved. If the linkages are intended in this way, they simply mean that the distinctive content of the inquiry of theological ethics is surrendered from the very outset. What is intended, established, and justified is something other than this inquiry with its distinctive content. Apologetics may then succeed, but it has become irrelevant before it has even commenced. The philosopher who really thinks he knows a higher principle by which to ask and answer the question of the whence and whither, and who thinks he can meet the theologian as a judge in the question of truth, is absolutely right when he feels that in a true theological ethics he is in an alien world. He can really be annoyed here. Theological ethics is no longer a proper theological ethics when it falls into the disorder in which it can no longer irritate such a philosopher. The theological question of the whence and whither, and the answer to it, consists neither of a necessary moment in our spiritual life, nor of the actualization of human reason, nor of the achievement of the good by man, nor of even the highest position on values, even though it acknowledges the holy in the form of personality and anchors the latter in the transcendent, nor of the moral principle known intuitively for a change instead of analytically. It consists of the truth of the Word of God, which as such cannot be derived from any other word, nor measured by any other word, nor tested as to its validity, nor spoken by man to himself, but which can only be spoken to him, which perhaps he may not hear, but which, if he has heard it, he can have heard only in obedience, without being in any position to find out why he must obey. The enterprise of a real theological ethics would not be vindicated in relation to philosophical ethics by the proof that philosophical ethics in some way contains it in itself. The principle of a real theological ethics would be concealed by this proof. Working with

---

[4]Cf. A. Schweitzer, *Kultur und Ethik*, Munich 1923, 1958[11], pp. 23ff. (*Kulturphilosophie*, pt. 2) (E.T. London 1932, 1946).

this principle, it would still be irritating to the philosopher. Philosophical ethics could accept that apology, ⌐be satisfied with those conditions of its existence,⌐ and give to a ⌐pseudo-⌐theological ethics the desired license without for a single moment feeling disturbed in its verdict that a true and proper theological ethics, which the apologetic renounces as such, is something impossible and insignificant.

The second possibility is that the linkages ⌐between the problem of philosophical ethics and that of theological ethics⌐ are not meant in such a way ⌐that the latter must be given a basis in the former but⌐ rest on the very different assumption that the philosophical inquiry contains the theological inquiry within itself to the extent that philosophizing takes place on the premise of the knowledge that characterizes theology, namely, knowledge of the revelation of God's Word. Philosophy has here come down from its judicial throne and set itself and its questions and answers on the same ground as theology—the conflict of the faculties is childishness—sharing the whence and the whither with theology and yet not ceasing on this account to be philosophy. On this assumption all the linkages might be more or less significant, not as an apology for theological ethics—philosophy itself would decree that such an apology is not needed—but rather to show clearly the justification and even the necessity of philosophical ethics alongside theological ethics. A philosophy which with theology and just as well as theology— for why should theology have any precedence or advantage in this respect, since it, too, is a human work?—has the hearing of the Word of God as its presupposition, can come to the side of theology as an equal partner, and in regard to these and similar linkages can raise the question and offer some indication of the possibility of the concept with whose reality theology methodologically starts. Often, too, it may perhaps be its living conscience, e.g., when recollection of the possibility of this concept ought to be calculated to invite to knowledge, to new knowledge of the constantly forgotten reality. This is the definition of the relation between theological and philosophical ethics that we actually have in view here. But when the linkages are meant in this way, they cannot signify a grounding and justifying of theological ethics in the sphere of philosophical ethics. It is admitted on both sides that the annexation is right. How can the distinctive starting point and goal of theological ethics be grounded or justified in terms of philosophy when with theology, philosophy itself, as in its own way Christian knowledge, is not rebellion but obedience? The result of our first discussion, then, is that in no case can a serious debate between theological and philosophical ethics have anything whatever to do with apologetics. Theological ethics cannot spare the philosopher vexation at its own conduct, for it will always be strange enough even to itself. From the philosopher's standpoint it is an unheard-of annexation. It cannot please him as though there were no danger in it. It cannot make its distinctive whence and whither innocuous in order to ensure for itself a place in the sun. By its existence as true theological ethics it has to put the philosopher, like the theologian, like everybody, before the decision whether its enterprise is to be rejected as impossible and insignificant or whether he will adopt the presupposition on which this enterprise rests. It can come to a meaningful and mutually fruitful agreement with him only when it is and remains determined to show its colors as true theological ethics. ⌐There can be no apologetic of theological ethics in relation to a philosophical ethics that sets itself with it on the ground of its own presupposition. A philosophy that does this does not ask for any such apologetic. Whatever philosophy may say to its efforts, from the standpoint of theology apologetic means a veiling of the decision in which alone theological statements can and will be valid.⌐

2

The apologetic attitude of theological ethics vis-à-vis philosophical ethics is not the only one against which we must safeguard ourselves. Alongside apologetics, there has commended itself to theology, in the attempt to maintain its own existence, the method of isolation, diastasis rather than synthesis. This does not come alone, but forms a kind of expansion, continuation, and crowning of apologetics in much the same way as war is the continuation of politics with other means. In spite of apologetics, theology has never so fully lost its recollection of the uniqueness of its task and activity that it does not somewhere suddenly rediscover its self-awareness, that the proof of the philosophical basis of its task and activity is not in some way completed in the proof of its independence, its distinction, its special character as compared with the task and activity of the philosopher. What is thought to be the need to give an account to philosophy would have succeeded all too well if its result were that theological ethics ceases to be something other than philosophical ethics. It obviously cannot lead to this, as it came close to doing in, e.g., W. Herrmann,[5] but when the theologian has validated himself to the philosopher, he must now for good or ill show also at some point that he is not a superfluous figure, a mere alter ego of the philosopher. With some fervor a little superiority is now maintained in relation to the philosopher, a little extra and better knowledge, and some attempt is made to define this. To this extent we have to do here with a second attitude of theological ethics that differs from the first. Covered by the linkages, theological ethics must and will demonstrate its uniqueness, particularity, and independence. What needs to be said in this regard may be summed up in four trains of thought.|

1. With E. W. Mayer (p. 191) the so-called Christian religious consciousness may be laid down as the source of theological ethics and with F. Schleiermacher its task may be defined as the description of the

---

[5]W. Herrmann, op.cit., pp. 1ff.

mode of action that arises out of the dominion of the self-consciousness with a Christian determination (*Chr. Sitte*, p. 33). Instead of the Christian religious consciouess De Wette (*Lehrbuch*, p. 2), Kirn (*Grundr. d. E.*, p. 2),[6] and Wünsch (*Theolog. Eth.*, p. 64) can also speak of revelation. In contrast, De Wette, I. A. Dorner (*Chr. Sittenlehre*, p. 21),[7] and E. W. Mayer name reason as the source of philosophical ethics, Kirn names experience, and Wünsch names reason and empirical experience. In all these cases what is obviously meant is not the self-consciousness with a Christian determination.|

2. The place of theological morals, as Schleiermacher in particular sharply emphasizes (pp. 33f.), is the church understood as the fellowship of those who share a Christian disposition. The ethical subject of theological ethics according to Wünsch (loc. cit.) is the man who has been born again by conversion and to whom the knowledge of God has been imparted by illumination. Hence according to Schleiermacher (p. 29) theological ethics lacks a "universal historical tendency." Its relation to philosophical ethics is to be defined as follows: What Christian morality requires is binding only for Christians; philosophical ethics makes a general claim, for it seeks to be binding for everyone who can raise himself up to perception of the philosophical principles from which it derives (p. 2). According to Wünsch the ethical subject of philosophical ethics is the rational man.[8]|

3. The presupposition of theological ethics is to be found with I. A. Dorner and Hagenbach (*Enzykl.*, p. 436) in the Spirit of God or Christ as the power that works in believers,[9] or with Kirn (p. 3) in "the vital energy of the personality that is filled with the Spirit of God," while the same authors find the presupposition of philosophical ethics in the moral or rational self-determination of man.[10] According to Wünsch this ethics asks: "What must I do because the categorical imperative commands?" but theological ethics asks: "What must I do because God is?"[11]|

4. The content of theological ethics may be found with Hagenbach (p. 435) in historically determined moral perceptions, especially in the personal divine-human manifestation of the life of the Redeemer, or with De Wette (p. 3f.) in positive laws,[12] or with Kirn (p. 3) in the idea of the kingdom of God,[13] whereas that of philosophical ethics is for Hagenbach the idea of moral personality which is valid for everyone who

---

[6]O. Kirn, op.cit., 1936[7], p. 3.

[7]I. A. Dorner, *System der christlichen Sittenlehre*, ed. A. Dorner, Berlin 1885, p. 21 (E.T. New York 1887).

[8]G. Wünsch, loc. cit.

[9]Cf. K. R. Hagenbach, op.cit., p. 436; the text has "the believer."

[10]Cf. O. Kirn, op.cit., p. 3; Kirn does not actually use the phrase ascribed to him by Barth.

[11]G. Wünsch, loc. cit.

[12]Cf. W. M. L. de Wette, op.cit., p. 3.

[13]Cf. O. Kirn, loc. cit.

would be a rational being.[14] ⌐According to I. A. Dorner the inner being, the individual personality, is the special stuff of theological ethics, whereas the universal side of ethics, social relations etc., are the special stuff of philosophical ethics (p. 22)⌐[15] and so on. This is the position of diastasis.|

But is this not perhaps just as suspicious as the attitude of synthesis previously depicted? For what really happens under the sign of this ⌐more or less illuminating and⌐ ingenious antithesis? Again there obviously exists a double possibility.|

First, the intentional division of roles between the two partners is carried through seriously. The idea is that there is a serious theological ethics which in fact investigates only the conduct that arises under the rule of the Christian religious self-consciousness and in the sphere of the corresponding historical outlook, its norms being binding only for members of the church who are, of course, assumed to be believers in whom the Spirit of God is an effective force. There is also a serious philosophical ethics which can be traced back abstractly to reason and experience, which is satisfied with the idea of the moral whose final word is man's self-determination, and which can make a claim as such to universal validity.|

We have two questions to put to this: (1) Can the theology of reason or experience or both together recognize an abstract content of truth, with universal validity, and then as theology, concerned equally abstractly with revelation or the expectorations of the religious self-consciousness, not worry about it any more but confidently commit it to its philosophical neighbor, "guarding its ancient traditions in dark caves like the condor," as Christian Palmer mockingly put it (*Die Moral d. Chrts.*, p. 18)? ⌐Is it really adequate as the doctrine of the cultivation of the individual personality?⌐ Is revelation the revelation of truth and the religious self-consciousness the consciousness of truth? Or are they something different, such as obscure sources of all kinds of religious notions which philosophy may confidently pass by and perhaps has to do so in a compact with theologians? Are they or are they not indispensable to the knowledge of truth? If theology is serious with its supposed knowledge of a whence and whither of all ethical questions and answers that is superior to all reason and empiricism, how can it take seriously a philosophy that lacks and even denies this knowledge? Instead of concluding with it a shameful peace should it not have the courage to call immoral a philosophical morality which is not just as much Christian morality as it is itself?|

We also ask (2) what happens if philosophy will not in the long run let itself be relegated to that airless sphere of the idea in which we theologians would like to put it? If it will not in the long run allow

[14]K. R. Hagenbach, loc. cit.
[15]I. A. Dorner, op. cit., p. 21.

theologians to take from it the problem of actualization, of the concrete, of the factual situation of man, along with the problem of the transcendent presupposition of all actualization? Is it really part of the nature of philosophy that it usually takes evil, and therefore reconciliation, too lightly? (I. A. Dorner, p. 24)? If positivism and to a large extent Kantian idealism have left the sphere of this problem unoccupied, this does not prove by a long way that philosophy always does so. With what right may theologians forbid any crossing of the frontier presupposed in this antithesis? Or do they propose to greet philosophy on what they think is their own special territory with the attitude of the elder brother in the parable of the prodigal son? Do they secretly live by the fact that philosophy espouses the crassest Pelagianism and even atheism and by the desire that it will always be content with this so as not to make theology itself superfluous? These are the two questions that must be put to the first possibility. |

The second possibility is that the division of roles will not be meant so strictly. There is awareness here that all truth is enclosed in God's Word and that whether it be rational or historical, secular or religious, ecclesiastical or social, it concerns theology and must be the theme of theology and cannot be accessible to philosophy either except through the same Word of God. Theology, then, does not refrain from speaking with the same universal validity as philosophy, and philosophy speaks as Christian philosophy. As a result theology loses the secret or open advantage with which it usually safeguards itself in that antithesis as though it were in a sanctuary from which philosophy is excluded. It will no longer pass on to philosophy tasks which it must itself reject as wrongly formulated, e.g., development of the false doctrine of the moral self-determination of man (as though what is wrong in theology could be right in philosophy), just as it will itself decline tasks that are passed on to it by philosophy. It will not look on askance and bewail the omission of its own terminology when a philosophy of practical reason may perhaps in its own way, without ceasing to be philosophy, make fruitful instead of rejecting the superior knowledge that characterizes itself. At a single word this means the end of the glory of a theological standpoint that is safeguarded against philosophy, but theology with its direct link with the church can again draw alongside philosophy with its indirect link. If proposals for the division of roles aim at fixing the relation between a Christian *theological* ethics and a *Christian* philosophical ethics, then they might not be without importance as proposals and pointers. But the attitude of isolation, as though theology knew secrets which philosophy, to be serious philosophy, neither knows nor ought to know—this attitude must be abandoned no less than that of apologetics.

If all this and all apologetics is set aside, if theology as such relentlessly fulfills its office, then its independence is thereby ensured and demonstrated and it need not be concerned any more to assert it. If it is sure of its subject, the transcendent Word of God, it cannot be upset if the same Word of God is also in another way the subject of philosophy. The distinction that as a science of the church's witness it sees it under the category of reality, while philosophy as the epitome of the science of man sees it and makes it a criterion under the category of possibility, has no more significance than the difference in the colors of professorial robes about which it is inappropriate to enter into a battle of prestige. The burden of diastasis is bearable if it is perceived that the true diastasis is not between theology and philosophy but between both of them and their genuine subject and that they themselves stand alongside one another in the church and must not basically or finally reproach one another. There is no place left at all for the game of Pharisee and publican with which theology finds compensation for its disparagement by worldly wisdom, or for the mysterious insistence on a special relation of theology to the good Lord, whereas only the categorical imperative remains for philosophy, for the rational man. That this should be eliminated is a not unimportant ethical presupposition for the success of theological or any other real ethics.

3

We have still to come to an understanding about a third possibility in the relation between theological and philosophical ethics—a possibility which we have not discussed so far but which historically and materially merits the closest attention before we strike out on our own. I have in mind the Roman Catholic view of the matter.

To anticipate, we must praise this view at least for seeing the error of the attitudes of apologetics and isolation and for successfully avoiding them, notwithstanding all the ambiguities on both sides, and even within the great ambivalence of the Roman Catholic system as such. One cannot fundamentally accuse this view[16] of either handing over theology to a philosophy that is recognized as a supreme norm in and in spite of its secularity or of arrogantly and inopportunely setting theology at a distance from philosophy. Here philosophical morals—the human soul is by nature Christian—is resolutely claimed, not as theological, but as Christian morals. It is recognized as such. It is treated as in its own way an equal partner of theological morals, whose voice is to be heard and which is not for a moment to be neglected, although it is also not for a single moment to be given the precedence. |

Moral philosophy and moral theology are mutually related to one another, presuppose one another, and are always basically united in the person of the Roman Catholic theological ethicist, but in such a way that moral theology forms from the very first the fulcrum of the eccentric wheel and can never lose this position. The problem of the relation of the two sciences is solved by a simple but consistent establishment of

[16]Lit. "blame it for."

two different but equally valid spheres of problems which necessarily follow one another in a specific order, moral philosophy being on the lower rung and moral theology on the upper. Willingly letting itself be taught by experience and history, moral philosophy perceives the basic principles of moral action with the light of natural reason. Yet while these are rational principles like the laws of logic, the imperative being rooted in the being of man as such, it still derives them from revelation, since they would otherwise be subject to error. Finding it to be man's determination to glorify the *Creator* by his existence as a creature, and thereby to prepare himself for eternal felicity, it also finds the moral good that is to be done in the four Aristotelian virtues of wisdom, justice, courage, and moderation. Adapted to the rational nature of man, this is the *relative* good, relative, that is, to the absolute good of the divine essence which is the idea of the good. In contrast moral theology draws directly on scripture, tradition, and the source of the church's living teaching office. It thus makes the elevation of fallen man to the order of grace its presupposition. Its task is to depict the supernatural morality which alone can actually lead man to this goal, to unfold the positive Christian moral law and its implied duties, and at the peak to develop the three theological virtues of faith, love, and hope. According to Roman Catholic teaching, grace is a higher element in life, differing from man's natural state. Its effect is sanctification, the renewal of nature from the disruption of sin, and the elevation of nature to the mysterious image and likeness of God (Mausbach, *Kult. d. Geg.*, II, p. 540).[17] Grace does not destroy nature but annexes and perfects it. The law of the new covenant which regulates the renewal is understood from the very outset as an excellent parallel of the law of nature (p. 523).|

When faced with this construction, this bold union of Aristotle and Augustine (p. 527), which was undoubtedly intimated in the early church, developed in basic outline by Thomas Aquinas, and in the course of the centuries constantly refined by the Roman Catholic church, we do not have to compare it with the confusion of the corresponding Protestant conceptions and in this way be forced to acknowledge that it is a classical, and as, we might calmly say, one of the most grandiose achievements in this whole field. What we have to learn from it is perfectly clear. In model fashion it states (1) that the final and true presupposition of theological and philosophical ethics, seen from the standpoint of the former, has to be one and the same, namely, the knowledge of God; (2) that theological ethics cannot in any sense take its questions and answers from philosophical ethics, with which it has a common origin in the same answer of truth; (3) that it cannot recognize as ethics a philosophical ethics that either lacks or totally denies this presupposition, but in view of what will always be at least some

---

[17]Cf. J. Mausbach, "Christlich-katholische Ethik" in *Die Kultur der Gegenwart*, ed. P. Hinnenberg, I, IV, 2: *Systematische christliche Theologie*, Berlin and Leipzig 1906, p. 540.

remnants of the presupposition it must claim all ethics, not as theological, but as Christian ethics, recognizing and taking it seriously as ethics
in accordance with its own presupposition; and (4) that there can be only
a relative and methodological but not a material antithesis between
theological ethics and a theological ethics based on this presupposition.
This form and these main features of the Roman Catholic construction
correspond so closely to the results of our own discussions in subsections
1 and 2 that we cannot but regard them as normative for what follows. |

Nevertheless there can also be no doubt that the same theses
necessarily have a different sense for us from that which they have in
Roman Catholicism. Between the Roman Catholic view and our own
stands a difference in the concept of God, of man, of the sin of man, and
of the grace which comes to him. On this basis the intention and the
whole character of the definition of the relation between the two
disciplines are materially very different for all the formal agreement. |

The Roman Catholic view of the mutual relation between moral
philosophy and moral theology rests on the fundamental Roman
Catholic conception of the harmony, rooted in the concept of being,
between nature and supernature, nature and grace, reason and revelation, man and God. The order of obligation is built on the order of
being, ethics on metaphysics, which forms the common presupposition
of philosophy and theology. In spite of the fall, imitative human
knowledge is fundamentally able to master true being, the supreme
good, i.e., God, even though because of the fall it needs special
illumination by revelation to keep it from error. The fall has so
hampered the knowledge of God that usually it cannot arise without
God's grace, at least in any depth. But it has not made it impossible.
There is still a relic of man's relation by creation to God. Fundamentally, even in the state of sin, man can still have without grace a
knowledge of the existence, unity, spirituality, and personality of God.
In relation to obligation and volition his free will in relation to God has
only been weakened by sin. The soul is thus Christian and the light of
natural reason is claimed as the principle of moral philosophy. The
created order which remains in spite of sin is then the point of contact to
which moral theology, which is founded on grace and draws on scripture
and dogma, must orient itself, the only thing being that it is this which
finally justifies that claim, which finally executes it, which has thus to
precede it in rank, and for which, as the superstructure, it can only be
the foundation. |

These presuppositions of the Roman Catholic construction, which G.
Wünsch seems to have taken over unsuspectingly as the final conclusion
of his theological ethics (§32, pp. 122f.), are at every point suspect and
even unacceptable from our own standpoint. This is not the place to do
more than sketch in short strokes the objection which even in this part of
the problem Protestantism directs against Roman Catholicism as a
whole. |

This objection necessarily starts already with the definition of God as the supreme being. For where and how is God knowable and given to us in his being and not in and as his act? If the God grasped in his being is an entity that man can master, with what right does this entity deserve to be called God? Is not this ambiguity suspiciously betrayed in the idea that on the assumption of a natural source of knowledge there is a partial and quantitative knowledge of God whose object is, e.g., the personality and not the triunity of God, ⌐creation and not reconciliation⌐? Does man really know God when he admittedly does not know him totally, in his nature, as the Lord in the pregnant ⌐and comprehensive⌐ biblical sense of the term? Is not metaphysics viewed as a basic discipline superior to both philosophy and theology, a relapse into apologetics in which both theology and philosophy can only lose their true origin and subject matter? As is well known, even the theology of the early church was to a large extent apologetically oriented. Later, of course, the Roman Catholic teaching on principles became infinitely more assured and refined. But when we measure it by the measure of what is described as the knowledge of God in the biblical documents, we are forced to regard it as a deviation in which we cannot participate.|

For this reason the construction of the order of moral obligation on the order of being is also for us an impermissible beginning. From what standpoint can we men verify this construction? When we who are not God but men accomplish this derivation of obligation from being, does it not entail a weakening and indeed a destroying of obligation as such? If there is a divinely ordered obligation, how can it be grounded for us except in itself? Does not its command have to be one and the same as the divine act of commanding; indeed, as the divine commanding itself? How can we look beyond this to an underlying divine being, and if we do, have we taken it seriously as obligation?|

If we are asked why we cannot unite the definition of God as being and the derivation of moral obligation from being with the seriousness of the concept of God and his command, we can only reply that it is because we can understand all man's fellowship with God only as grace. Grace, however, rules out any attempt to snatch at God's being beyond his act. Grace says that only by and in the divine act do we have fellowship with God and also knowledge of God. We could no longer understand grace as grace, i.e., we could only understand the event in which God meets us and gives us his command as actually another act which has nothing directly to do with God, if grace really shared its power with a capacity of our own nature and reason, if an ascent of man to God were really possible, and an order of obligation could exist, on the basis of a direct relation of man to God which grasps the divine being and thus bypasses his grace. If we thus divide the relation between the two factors of ⌐essence and grace⌐, grace as the supposedly second divine factor becomes a subject that we can master as we master subjects for which the concept of the divine is necessarily too good in our eyes.

God's grace—this is the Protestant axiom behind which we cannot let ourselves be pushed—is either full, total, and exclusive grace or it is not divine but at best a demonic power and wisdom. In the idea of a grace that can be bypassed and that serves only to kindle a previously existing light, we do not recognize the serious exclusiveness of the biblical concept of revelation and reconciliation in its analogy to the creation of the world out of nothing. |

With this insight, in the light of the sole efficacy and sufficiency of grace, we must also view—naturally as the second thing, not the first—the corresponding negation, the concept of sin, much more sharply than this Roman Catholic doctrine does. We cannot accept a purely relative, quantitative, and factual significance of the fall for the capacity of man in relation to God. Without being in Manichean fashion unmindful of the creation of man by God and man's determination, by creation, for God, we must reject any fitness of man for cooperation with God on the basis of this orientation to him. This side of the fall, that orientation in itself and as such produces no possibility or reality of even a restricted fellowship with the living and true God. If, as we shall see later, grace and the divine command have an implication for the pure creatureliness of man as such, this is an implication of grace and not a presupposition of nature and reason. It was again an aberration when the early church from at least the second half of the first century[18] began to seek and find the sources of Christian morality and moral teaching in both reason *and* revelation and consequently in both Cicero, etc., *and* the Gospels. The obvious reason for this aberration was that grace began to be understood as no longer grace and sin as no longer sin, and the reign began of an idea of the perfect Christian state which in §1, 2 we came upon with regret at the cradle of emancipated Christian morals. |

Justification and also sanctification are not the work of both God and man but of God alone, and theology cannot unite with a philosophy which would have things different in order that it may itself follow the same path as Roman Catholic theology does. The distinction between philosophical and theological ethics cannot mean that the two draw on different sources and even if in mutual fulfillment rest in different ways on the knowledge of God. For philosophy, too, grace cannot be a mere illumination and direction of human thought that in itself is already on the way to God. On the other hand, for theology, too, grace is not something that it can handle as its special preserve even if in only a relative antithesis to philosophy, so that on the basis of its special relation to it—mark well, on the basis of its special relation to God's *grace*—it can and should claim precedence over philosophy. |

Is not this distinction of two different sources of ethics, and the resultant ranking of theology and philosophy, simply another relapse into the isolation of theology which in what is perhaps a fateful way

[18]More accurately the second.

compromises the strict validity of its own principle by passing on to philosophy another valid principle, and which will not satisfy philosophy itself, perhaps, and rightly so? If the "wisest of all intermediaries," as Mausbach (p. 527) calls Thomas, cleverly avoided in fact the crass errors of apologetics and isolation which recent Protestant ethics has committed, does not the basic error which seems to be present in him frighten us all the more? What are finally the Protestant mistakes but coarser forms of the refined error that we must see in the union of Aristotle and Augustine as such? If formally and in its main structural outlines we accept the Roman Catholic definition of the relation between philosophical and theological ethics as a model, we must at least give to it a different basis and content corresponding to the Protestant view of God, man, sin, and grace.

4

The debate with the most important definitions of the relation between philosophical and theological ethics is now behind us. We have conducted it from a specific point assigned to us by our task, the task of theological ethics. It is obvious that when conducted from the standpoint of philosophy the debate would have other aspects. But if it were a matter of the philosophy which is alone at issue here, namely, that which shares with theology the latter's final knowledge, the material result could not possibly be any different. In the rejection of the method of apologetics and isolation, and in the material rejection of the Roman Catholic construction along with an acknowledgment of its great formal significance, philosophy might argue differently but could only agree with us. With the same proviso and the same expectation we now address the task of giving our own answer to the problem indicated in the title of the present section. The proviso is that we do not presume to speak in the name of both theology and philosophy but are fundamentally leaving it to philosophy to speak the word that it ought to speak here. The expectation is that philosophy will speak very differently but will not in fact have anything different to say.[19]

a

The Common Christianity of Philosophical and Theological Ethics

Among the results of our deliberations thus far the concept of a Christian philosophy must have proved especially strange from more

---

[19]Text A had here an additional passage which Barth later excised: "In the thesis I mentioned as the common presupposition of theological and philosophical ethics the confession of the concrete revelation of God in Christ by the Holy Spirit, and as the marks of distinction, for theological ethics the question of the reality of the Word of God that sanctifies man, and for philosophical ethics the question of the possibility corresponding to that reality. The common basis and the differences are obviously the three points which we must now elucidate and define." (Cf. p. 30).

than one standpoint. In explanation we may observe primarily that "Christian theology," if the term Christian is to have any significance, is a concept which is not in any sense any more self-evident. Just as well and just as badly as philosophy, theology is a human science. It knows, understands, and speaks on earth and not in heaven. If the word "Christian" is not to be simply a historical differentiation of *this* theology from similar phenomena in Buddhism or Islam, if the thought behind it is Christ, and therefore the revelation of the living and true God to man, and therefore a science that has as its theme, not one of the revelations of the demonic, which also exist, but the revelation of this the living God, then the question how this science acquires the predicate "Christian" is no less apposite than the question how philosophy, the science of man's understanding of himself, comes to presuppose God's revelation and therefore to have a claim to be called "Christian." One might even consider whether theology's claim to be Christian is not even bolder than raising such a claim for philosophy, whether the Christian element in philosophy, the revelation of God, cannot have at least the less striking significance of a decisive but unexpressed *presupposition*, and might not be applied to science as a whole, to art, to education, and finally indeed to any practical area, whereas the Christian element in theology, which is perilously isolated compared to all these fields, claims to arise precisely as the *theme* of human investigation, assertion, and presentation. Might it not be that for serious reasons there are more objections against the Christianity of theology than that of philosophy?|

We will begin with three negative statements: (1) If the Christian element is understood seriously as the Word of God, it cannot have even for the theologian the significance of a first and basic principle, a definition, which is then adapted to be the principle of further definitions and supposedly guarantees the Christianity of the whole. (2) The Christian element, seriously understood, cannot consist even for the theologian in a specific method, in the deduction of all statements from holy scripture or dogma, or even in the candid and sincere expression of the religious consciousness. (3) Again the Christian element cannot lie in the degree of depth and force of the personal Christian piety of the theologian concerned. Sought in any of these three directions, the Christian element would obviously be under man's control and it need hardly be shown that it would then no longer be taken seriously as the Christian element, and in spite of the presence of perhaps all the qualities we should constantly have to reckon with the possibility that the theology is not Christian at all.|

Taken seriously, the concept "Christian," even when applied to theology, can be no more than a pointer to the testimony: "*I* am the way, the truth, and the life" [John 14:6]. The Christianity of theology does not in any way rest upon itself but upon the revelation that is its theme. In this regard it should be remembered that the revelation is God himself. But God himself is our Lord from and by and to whom we are what we are. In an absolute sense we can have the way, the truth, and the life, the Christian element, only as and to the extent that it has us. "Not that I have already attained this or am already perfect; but I press on to make it my own, because Christ Jesus has made me his own." The one who speaks here is not a philosopher who, as we theologians like to think, has no knowledge as such of the joyful possession of salvation. It is the apostle of Jesus Christ who in Philippians 3:12 speaks thus of that joyful possession. It is thus that the possession takes place. Knowledge of God, as it takes place, is an absolute reality on its own, distinguished by the fact that it cannot be elucidated in any of the forms of human perception even though it always takes place in such forms. It itself apprehends man, not without human receptivity and even spontaneity, but precisely not in such a way that human receptivity and spontaneity take place on the same plane as its own action and might claim to be correlative with it, so that it would then make sense to talk of a religio-psychological circle, but rather in such a way that it can only be believed by man—the same apostle would rather talk of being known than of knowing [cf. Gal. 4:9]—and *witness* can then be given to it in obedience ("I believe and so I speak" [2 Cor. 4:13]).

This is how it is with the Christianity of theology. To repeat our polemic against the Roman Catholic view, it is grace. Being identical with God's Word and therefore with God himself, it is precisely not an instrument that is put in the hand of man. It can be real only in the reality of the act of the living and true God himself. Man can only bear witness to it in faith and obedience and the power of this witness is again that of God and not of man. Bearing witness to this reality of God which reveals itself and makes itself present to us is the office of the church and of theological science in the service of the church. Seen from above, its Christianity, its relation to God's Word, is with God, while seen from below it stands in the faith and obedience of those who discharge this ministry. On both sides this means that the Christianity of theology is *divinely* certain but humanly *un*certain. The Christianity of theological ethics lies, then, in the reality of God's commanding, of God's Word so far as it claims us men and finds our faith and obedience.

Theological ethics confesses God's revelation in Christ through the Holy Spirit. In accordance with what has been said, this obviously does not refer to the content and form and religious fervor of any confessional formula. Nor is its Christianity guaranteed thereby. It cannot itself guarantee its own Christianity. It can only confess by its act its faith and obedience and its knowledge of God's revelation. It can only bear witness to the Christian element. It does this when as theological ethics it presents the reality of the Word of God sanctifying and claiming man as God's command. When it has done this which is its duty to do, then as a discipline auxiliary to dogmatics it must confess with all dogmatics that it is an unprofitable servant [cf. Luke 17:10]. The truth itself must then impress the seal of truth on its presentation. The Christian element must then speak for itself. But the truth is free and the Christian element is free, for the truth and the Christian element are not distinct from God. God, however, is the Lord who in the church and theology as well as his whole creation can be served only by those who *are* appropriated without being able to boast of *having* appropriated to themselves what is worth boasting about.

If we have first put theology in its proper place so far as its Christianity is concerned, it should not be hard to see that ⌐under the same conditions⌐ a Christian philosophy cannot be impossible. Again we do not seek its Christianity, or the Christian confession that we have expressly assigned to it in the thesis,[20] in the content or form of fervor of a confessional formula. Indeed, we must explicitly say of philosophy in distinction from theology that if it is to be science in the strict sense it must fundamentally refrain from confessing whenever this possibility arises. We commend the celebrated passages in which even the sober Kant could not help preaching in his own way about the starry heavens above and the moral law within.[21] But in such passages, even he, not to speak of someone like Fichte, transgresses the limits of philosophy. For the theme of philosophy in contrast to theology is not the Word of God that is to be proclaimed but thinking, willing, and feeling man that is to be understood. Philosophy would be guilty of shifting into another genre and neglecting its own proper function if more than very occasionally it were to become proclamation of the Christian element, which is the business of the church, and of theology within it. |

Philosophy is, of course, called to bear witness to Christian truth, which is truth itself. Nor is it called to do so, indeed, at a lower level than theology. Within the church there is no human activity that is not called to bear witness to Christian truth alongside the church's proclamation, and again not at a lower level than this. All human action that has God's Word as its presupposition is witness in this broader and no lesser sense. This applies to philosophy as a self-understanding of man in which man is not seen apart or in eminent abstraction from God's Word, but in determination by it as the man who confronts and is apprehended and seized by its claim and promise; in which he is not seen and understood in general but specifically in the sphere of the church of pardoned sinners which has been instituted by Christ and is united in him; in which it is constantly noted that man belongs to God, not by nature and as a general truth, but on the basis of God's manifested grace, and that in ethics he is thus to be measured by the standard of what is heard from God. A Christian philosophy of this kind will not have to

[20]Cf. p. 30 and n. 19.
[21]*Kritik der praktischen Vernunft* 1788 (*Gesammelte Schriften*, pt. 1, vol. 5, Berlin 1908, p. 161), ET tr. L. W. Beck, Library of Liberal Arts, Indianapolis 1956, p. 166.

utter a single statement of explicitly Christian content or speak any dogmatic or biblical word, just as Christian art does not have to produce only portrayals of Christ, oratorios, Christian novels, and the like. Knowing the witness of the Bible and dogma, it simply has to fashion its own statements according to the laws of its own subject, and in this way, with this indirectness, it will bear witness to the Christian element. It has a theme which expressly differs from that of theology. What is the theme of theology is for it merely (though what does merely mean here?) a presupposition. Yet this does not make it a secular discipline. A discipline is secular only to the extent that it departs from that knowledge. Theology itself can be secular. No discipline is secular that has that knowledge as its presupposition.|

One may well ask whether there can be a philosophy that shares with theology the latter's final word. What are we to say to this question? Above all that on the basis of theology one has the right to put it only when it is directed with even greater sharpness to what is now called theology in our midst. There is Christian philosophy in the same sense as there is Christian theology, justified not by its works but by faith. The presence of Christianity in philosophy, too, is ultimately a question of the grace of God. Knowledge of the presupposition of a meaningful understanding of man by himself is in the last analysis a being known rather than a knowing and it again rests with God whether he will give the power of witness to the witness of a philosophy grounded in this knowledge. We are saying precisely the same thing when we call the presence of Christianity a question of faith and obedience.|

In relation to this side of the matter, to the human decision in which the grace of God can be seen, we may and must put to all philosophy the question whether it realizes how strongly "it is drawn into a deeper responsibility by the existence of the Christian revelation" (Knitter-meyer, *D. Phil. u. d. Chrt.*, p. 7), that "from the moment when a truth was proclaimed in Palestine which ousted the Greek Logos from its place of power in western culture and revealed a new salvation to man" it has been confronted by a force "of which we know that it has power over life and death and can kill off philosophy" (pp. 16f.). "The reality is now fundamentally different. World history is no longer world judgment by the idea but it stands in the reality of the Word which is proclaimed in the gospel of Jesus Christ and which means God and the neighbor" (p. 27). "In the place of man and reason comes Jesus Christ the Lord and the faith that frees" (p. 27), an experience which philosophy cannot evade "any more than the whole life of man can evade the experience that the Word of Jesus Christ is proclaimed as the Word of salvation" (pp. 30f.). "To be able to maintain the claim of philosophy at all it is necessary continually to relate it afresh to man in his real state and that means primarily and finally to adjust it to the total change that has taken place with the proclamation of the Word of

Christ" (pp. 35f., cf. 50).[22] This is the question, the question of repentance, which the church cannot cease to put to philosophy, especially when it hears it in this way from within itself. This question, the question of Christ, *is* put to philosophy, because, as Knittermeyer rightly stresses,[23] it is put to man as such. How can a scientific self-understanding on man's part fail to take a very different direction when the seriousness of this question has been perceived?

Here as elsewhere, however, we must be careful to say the right thing about whether this or that man, in this case this or that philosopher, is really a hearer and therefore a witness of the Word. We should again be misconstruing world judgment as world judgment by the idea that Christ has set aside, and instituting ourselves as judges of the world, if we were to arm ourselves with some norm of what is Christian and survey philosophical ethicists with a view to saying which of them belong to the sheep and which to the goats. In theology and philosophy, as everywhere where human work is done, the judgment whether human work has been done in God [cf. John. 3:21] is in God's hands. Fundamentally we cannot press on beyond the questions that we have everywhere to put to its authors, and even when they cannot perhaps give satisfactory answers, we cannot arrive at a definitive statement whether a work is valid for us as witness or not. It might be that in one case we have evaded a witness by not hearing it as such and in another that we have wrongly lent our ears to the voice of a demon. The Christian and its opposite never meet us anywhere with the clearcut distinction of black and white but both of them broken up a hundredfold in both philosophy and theology. Our own deciding and dividing can take place only in faith and can be justified only in faith. It is enough for philosophy, as for theology too, that there is a grace of God and a space in the church of Christ for it, that it is summoned thereby to reflect on whether the object of its reflection is real man, i.e., man set in the light of revelation, and that the truth-content in any philosophy depends on how far it is indirect witness to revelation on the basis of this reflection. We do not really need to judge the servants of another [cf. Rom. 14:4] in order to achieve critical scientific certainty as to our own path.

b
The Word of God as Reality and Theological Ethics

We may be brief here, for we shall have to deal expressly with this matter in the third subsection of the Introduction when unfolding the task of theological ethics, and then again in the first chapter of our exposition in the strict and proper sense. It interests us here only by way of contrast to the issue of philosophical ethics.

[22]Cf. H. Knittermeyer, *Die Philosophie und das Christentum*, Jena 1927. There are minor inaccuracies in Barth's quotations from p. 7, p. 27, and pp. 35f.
[23]Op. cit., pp. 31f.

Theology, too, is an act of human reflection and understanding. Unlike philosophy, however, it is not man's reflection on and understanding of himself. In basic analogy to jurisprudence, natural and historical science, and medicine, it is reflection on and understanding of an object that is to be distinguished methodologically from inquiring man who is the subject of the science. Like all these sciences, theology has the object of its research and instruction contingently given to it. Among all sciences only philosophy (perhaps including mathematics) is pure self-reflection and self-understanding, inquiry and instruction "without an object." In distinction from it theology is one of the positive sciences (or one of the three higher faculties as they used to put it). It arises in a very simple and earthly way out of the concrete demands of a specific sphere of human purpose, namely, the church, which does not want to teach without also learning and therefore does not want to take away the education of its ministers from the university, just as thus far the university has obviously not wanted to lose from the circle of its scientific investigations and answers the reflection and understanding demanded by this sphere. |

The basic object which characterizes the reflection demanded in the sphere of the church is the Word of God, God's revelation to man. This object constitutes and validates the existence of the church and of theological science (as the function of both the church and the university). The existence of this science is on the one hand a confession of the church that it regards *scientific* questions and answers as necessary in relation to this object while on the other hand it is a confession of the university that it regards scientific questions and answers as possible in relation to *this* object. It would be all up with theology, ⌐and the abolition of the theological faculty would demand serious consideration⌐, if either the church could seriously lose interest in *science* or the university in *this* science. |

For philosophy the object of theology is fundamentally in *question* like the objects of all human thought and volition along with the man as such to which it directs its attention. It is one of the possible objects whose reality philosophy, which reckons only with the reality of man himself, does not have to deny but also does not consider—except, perhaps, as the presupposition of man himself, which is another matter. A theology which wants to follow it in this, treating the Word of God as a possibility that has still to be discussed, would obviously be just as pointless an enterprise as a jurisprudence that tried to treat as a problem that factual and necessary existence of the state and its laws, or a medicine that did the same with the fact and necessity of man's physical life. The lawyer or doctor may perhaps do this to the extent that he has also minored in philosophy, but once he begins to think in terms of law or medicine the problem can no longer exist for him. Theology too, presupposing the reality of its object, may be only a possibility for philosophy, but it proceeds like any other positive science in its adoption of the church's concern for truth. In the self-evident sense in which the same is true for jurisprudence and medicine and natural and historical science, its thought is tied to the reality of its object. If the theologian thinks freely as though he were a philospher—and even if he does so in a secondary way, then like the lawyer and doctor he must see to it how far this is compatible with his main function—he no longer thinks theologically and he can no longer demand that what he says from this angle, ⌜e.g., from the spectator standpoint of a historian or psychologist,⌝ enjoys any right of participation in the theological dialogue.

If he wants to be a theological scholar and teacher, faithful to his office both in the church *and* in the university, he cannot wander at large among all kinds of other subjects (as has happened very widely, for example, in the last decades or centuries with respect to the reality of ⌜human piety and its⌝ history, as though ⌜something of this nature⌝ could just as well be its object as the Word of God). He cannot abstract away from this object. He cannot act as though God had not spoken, or perhaps had not spoken, or as though it had first to be investigated whether he had really done so. He cannot permit theological thinking to be at root anything but thinking about this object (as object!). He must form its concepts as predicates of this subject and not (we have already had to guard against this possibility in the discussion in the first section) as a presentation of the pious Christian man who receives the Word of God. If with this alteration of the object it can undoubtedly be a science too, it ceases therewith to be theology. Above the demand that it be scientific, i.e., that it follow a method appropriate to a specific object, there stands for positive science, and therefore for theology, the demand that it be objective, i.e., that it be faithful to its particular object, for concretely it is only on this basis that it may be scientific. |

If theology is to include ethics, or a definition of the good in human conduct, we must not fail to note that God has spoken, speaks, and will speak to man, so that man is told what is good (Mic. 6:8). In no way, however, can this sanctifying reality of God's Word be a problem here. In no way, again, can there by any question of listening to some other reality of nature and history instead of to this reality. In no way, as has been said, can obedient or disobedient man become the theme of the presentation. Without denying that scientific problems and, in their own way, urgent concerns are present here, we have to say that the existence of the church is constituted and validated by an object, indeed, by this specific object, so that theology, in so far as there is such, and with it theological ethics, must inquire into the relation of this object to human conduct, into the sanctifying reality of God's Word, and not into anything else. According to the proclamation of the Christian church the true good of human conduct is this reality. Theological ethics, not in the least ashamed of being tied in this way, not departing for a single moment from this standpoint, nor replacing it by another, nor changing it into another, has the task of showing how far this is so. If it fails in this task, if it simply prolongs its existence by changing into another genre, e.g., that of religious science, then its enterprise as such, and the enterprise of theology as a whole, must be regarded as shattered. In such a case the church would do well to renounce the claim to science and the university would do well to renounce the claim to *this* science. ⌜The time for dissolving the theological faculty would then have come.⌝ So long and so far as theology takes itself seriously, it can set itself no other task than this, and so long and so far as theology is taken seriously as such, neither philosophy nor any other science can demand that it set itself any other task than this.

c

The Word of God as Possibility and Philosophical Ethics

A self-aware theology which bears strongly in mind its objective and scientific nature will be the very last to set itself its own task in such a way as to deny all other sciences, to view them as impossible, or even to discredit them as less valuable, and to condemn them from its own standpoint to a mere appearance of existence under the suspicion of pagan ungodliness. Theology does not really need to safeguard its own rank among the other sciences by a frenzied posture of absoluteness or by allotting to the others roles which it regards as less valuable in relation to its own. If Paul in Philippians 3:4ff. regarded all else as refuse in order that he might win Christ, it should be recalled that he did not say this against the usual intellectual arrogance of the children of the world but against the much more dangerous spiritual arrogance of Pharisaism. He certainly did not want to replace Jewish Pharisaism by a Christian and, more specifically, a theological Pharisaism. A theology that is set on its own feet can unreservedly acknowledge the justification and even the equal justification of other sciences. Human thought is necessarily shown its limits by the particular object of theology, by the Word of God. It is [reminded] how conditioned it is. It is thus liberated from the illusion of self-justification. It is also fundamentally liberated for an understanding of other tasks whose *objects* cannot be compared with *this* object, the object of theology, but which as human *tasks*, set for *men* by other spheres of human ends alongside the church, are to be tackled by *men* with the same seriousness and in the same weakness as theology displays in discharging its own office, so that they do not really fall behind the task of theology in worth. God's Word does at any rate tell man also that he is a man, i.e., that he is a creature committed to different human ends and as a thinker to different objects. He who has learned from God's Word what hard, the very hardest, objectivity is, cannot possibly—according to the principle that he who is faithful in big things will also be faithful in little things [cf. Luke 16:10]—fail to take other objects seriously, and no less so even though this object cannot be mentioned in the same breath with them.

This recognition of nontheological sciences by theology cannot extend only to the positive sciences. If it lies in the nature of the human search for truth that in contrast to the positive, object-oriented sciences which are demanded by the various ends of human life, there should also be the disinterested self-reflection and self-understanding of thinking man without an object, namely, philosophy, theology will say, not last of all but first of all, that this is there by fundamental right. Or is theology to let itself be overtaken by natural and historical science in perceiving that man, who inquires into objective truth in the positive sciences, must always become a primary question to himself? Will not the seriousness of "know thyself," which stands at the beginning of philosophy, be especially and with a very different urgency perceived by this positive science, in which man is confronted by God's Word, than in those in which commitment to the object is accompanied by forgetfulness that knowledge without *knowledge* of knowledge is *no* knowledge? How can this be forgotten in theology with its commitment to *this* object and how can philosophy not be recognized and even demanded by it?|

Naturally it is a very definite philosophy, not that of a particular school or tendency, but one determined by its presupposition, that will be demanded by theology and acknowledged by it to be justified, to be equally justified. We have already said that the concept of a Christian philosophy, like that of a Christian theology, cannot be determined by any special material principle or any special epistemological principle or any special fervor—otherwise the Christian element in it would again be understood as a possibility at man's disposal. It can be determined absolutely only by the knowledge of the Christian element, the Word of God, that precedes its self-reflection (which always in itself observes the limits of humanity). Its self-reflection will always be determined by this knowledge. This type of philosophy, no matter what philosophical school it might follow, will be distinguished primarily from every non-Christian philosophy by its awareness that in practicing that reflection it cannot say the last word that solves the question of man but that the question can be put in merely penultimate words only after and as the last word has been and is spoken. On the presupposition of the answer that has been given, not by theology or the church but by God in Jesus Christ through the Holy Spirit, it cannot evade but has to broach the real question, the problem of man's questionability in his real life-situation. In this regard it is no less but more real philosophy than a non-Christian philosophy which betrays itself constantly by not staying with the question of man, but at some point, even if it be in a little apotheosis of the question, moving on to an answer, propounding a final reality in an absolutizing of thought or thinking or even thinking man, and thus pacifying both itself and man, so that instead of a philosophy it becomes a theology, albeit a pagan one.|

Christian philosophy, which starts by hearing God's Word, can wait. It knows, as theology must also know, that the final reality cannot be posited by man as a means to answer himself and pacify himself. It sees that the egocentricity of all human attempts to posit a final reality is an error, or what theology would call a sin. Factually, of course, it is unable simply to get rid of the error, just as theology cannot get rid of the sin. Hence it cannot get by without a thesis, and as philosophical ethics it cannot get by without positive concepts such as goodness, value, purpose, duty, virtue, freedom, or idea. Without these it could only say nothing at all or pass over from self-reflection to proclamation, to theology (and then the "know thyself" would not be discussed as it ought to be). If, however, it performs its reflection in the form of *self*-reflection, as though the principle and reality of the good were man himself, or were in man himself, it realizes that this is not so, for it recognizes the limits of humanity and is thus aware that all such positings are provisional and relative and simply point to the good whose principle and reality are not really man and are not really in man. It takes and presents what is posited as a possible and not the real answer to man's questions as to the goodness of his conduct and in so doing it is the science which first raises the question in all its seriousness.|

It cannot indeed view the good other than as obedience. An action is obedience, however, when its goodness obviously lies not in doing it or in doing it in a particular way but in doing what is commanded because it is commanded, only that being obedient ⌐which is done according to the command.⌐ It has perceived that that man is a liar and a ghost who by means of self-reflection, self-understanding, and self-responsibility wants to tell himself what is good. It is a summons to the real man who is addressed and *contradicted* in all the glory of his egocentricity, who may begin to speak but cannot finish, whose speech about himself can have truth only as broken speech, as a confession of its brokenness. It is a summons to the I which no longer thinks it can master the claim that encounters it, or that it can misuse this claim to strengthen itself—the last and greatest triumph of pagan philosophy—but which is set aside by this claim and only thus can find its true basis. It is a claim to responsibility in which man recognizes and confesses that he himself always falls short of what is required and is justified, not on account of his achievement, but only in the decision of obedience for him who requires it and for what is required.|

It is to be noted that philosophy cannot issue this summons by itself, representing and activating the reality of the Word and confronting the I of man with the Thou that lays this claim to him. Not even theology can do this, nor the proclaiming church, nor any man. Only God the Lord himself reads ethics in *this* sense ⌐and not *either* the philosopher *or* the theologian.⌐ Nor is it even the office of philosophical ethics to *proclaim* this reality as such. In this regard it differs from theological ethics. It shares with the church and theology the task of simply confronting man's unprofitable and dangerous recollection of himself with the recollection of the wholly other who stands over against him, of pointing out that this wholly other himself speaks to man. For it, however, this wholly other cannot be God himself—it differs in this from the church and theology. Theology, of course, cannot proclaim the Word of God without recalling the *neighbor*, the brother, in whose claim upon us the Word of God comes to us. But one could not call this reminder the true task of theology. It is simply the great instrument that it uses when and so far as it is a matter of defining the Word of God as the Word that comes to us. This recollection, the changing of self-responsibility into responsibility to the Thou of the other man, is the true and concretely specific task of *philosophy*. To the extent that self-reflection, the "know thyself," is at issue, the fellowman is the representative and bearer of the divine Logos who must call man away from all his dreams to reality.

Where the Word of God is heard, there this self-reflection takes place, and there the other *man* must be heard. His voice is the one that is missed in all *pagan* philosophy. Philosophy which will hear this word cannot possibly want to be a pagan theology positing ultimate reality. The claim of the fellowman, however, relates to God's claim as possibility does to reality. The same Word of God is heard in both. In its reality the Word of God obviously cannot be the object of human self-reflection, but only the object of God's self-revelation and therefore the object of faith and obedience, and in faith and obedience the object of proclamation. Men can only serve when and where God really speaks. But this human service is the *possibility* corresponding to the divine reality, posited with it, ⌐and grounded in it.⌐ Because the reality of the Word is not without this possibility, Christ is not without his church. Service of the Word is the human activity which is the essence of the church. The possibility of God's Word coming to us is the fellowman who is commissioned by God and who serves his Word. This applies not merely to ecclesiastical office in the narrower sense but to the church as such. This is the new meaning, actualized in Christ, of the fellowman as brother and neighbor. The fellowman *can* bring God's Word to us when God wills to speak his Word ⌐through him.⌐ We have to receive him because of this possibility.|

Philosophy cannot go beyond this possibility that is posited with the reality of God's Word if it is not to go beyond the Word of God itself, if it is to be true to its own task, if it is not to become theology. It can no longer summon man to self-responsibility except as it teaches him to understand himself as standing in the responsibility which he owes to his fellowman *when* the latter is set before him as the bearer and representative of the divine Logos. That he *is* this belongs to another book and is not as self-evidently and directly true as Gogarten, for example, seems to assume.[24] ⌐It *becomes* true whenever God causes it to become true.⌐ Philosophy can as little demonstrate the Thou that captures my I for God as theology can demonstrate the Word of God itself. Both can only

[24]Cf. F. Gogarten, *Ich glaube an den dreieinigen Gott*, Jena 1926, pp. 60ff.

bear witness, and the power of their witness is the power of the free God. Nevertheless, philosophy *can bear witness* when and so far as it has as its presupposition real knowledge of man, knowledge of the church, and knowledge of the fellowman who draws man to responsibility. With this presupposition it does not bear witness to the law but to the gospel and the grace which, of course, encloses the law. For it is grace if we have the fellowman who with his claim represents the divine claim, just as the law is also established hereby.

Undoubtedly we are on different levels of intellectual activity when theology speaks about God but not without reference to the brother, and philosophy speaks about the fellowman for God's sake, when the reality of God's Word on the one side and its possibility on the other side is the object of investigation, when the same Word of God is the theme here and the presupposition there. These differences are necessary differences in human conceptuality. As such they are rightly the principle of a sober distinction between theology and philosophy. But they are not more than that. They are not the principle of a distinction of rank and value. Philosophy is *not* ancillary to theology. With philosophy, theology can only want to be ancillary to the church and to Christ.

§3

THE WAY OF THEOLOGICAL ETHICS

The task of theological ethics is that of presenting the claiming of man by the Word of God. It has to depict (1) the event of the claiming as such and then its significance for man, i.e., (2) his claiming as God's creature, (3) his claiming as a pardoned sinner, and (4) his claiming as an heir of the kingdom of God. Under 2−4 it must consider in each case (a) the uniqueness of the ethical standpoint, (b) the normative form of the noetic basis, (c) the decisive content of the ethical demand, and (d) the fulfilment of the ethical demand.

1

In relation to the results of the work to be done in theological ethics it is obviously not a matter of indifference that we should expressly discuss first the way in which questions are to be raised and answered. The matter of finding the right way or the right division is not just a formal one. Here as elsewhere it is no more and no less than the matter of finding the right basic concepts without which one may in some circumstances live well and happily but one cannot achieve a coherent thought and understanding when they are needed. Here as elsewhere, however, the criterion whether the concepts are right or not has to be that of appropriateness to the particular theme which seems to be at issue in theological ethics.

In the light of the conclusion reached in our first two sections we no longer need to explain but simply to state by way of demarcation what lines of inquiry and consequent divisions of theological ethics we must set aside.

On the basis of the relation that we have established between theological and philosophical ethics, we regard as useless all attempts to build the former on the latter or to derive it from it. Apart from the great classical example of Roman Catholic ethics, this is the way taken by W. Herrmann, O. Kirn, E. W. Mayer, G. Wünsch, at the start De Wette, and, in the form of express apologetics, T. Haering. It leads to a twofold division: e.g., 1. Natural Moral Life and Moral Thought, 2. Christian Moral Life (W. Herrmann);[1] or 1. Ethical Principles, 2. Systematic Presentation of the Christian Moral Life (Kirn);[2] or 1. Moral Philosophy, 2. Moral Teaching (Mayer);[3] or 1. The Nature of Morals, 2. The Nature of Christian Morals (Wünsch).[4] According to what has been said already we cannot approve either the methodological subordination of Christian morals to morals in general, the independence of morals in general alongside and over against Christian morals, or the assumed superiority of a theological moral teaching that draws from a special source. Hence we must reject this whole method. |

Looking back to what has been said about the relation between dogmatics and ethics we also cannot agree with ordinary theological ethics about the actual questions which usually underlie it either with or without a philosophical substructure. According to Schleiermacher's ingenious conception theological ethics has to speak about the "purifying" action that takes place in the discipline of church and home and also in the state, about the "disseminating" action that takes place in marriage and both extensively and intensively in the church, and finally about the "representative" action that takes place in church worship, social life, art, and play.[5] According to Hofmann it is a matter of the Christian disposition and its actualization in moral action in the relation to God, in the church, in the family, in the state, and in society.[6] According to Herrmann it is a matter of the rise and development of the Christian life.[7] According to Kirn it is a matter of the rise and development of Christian personality on the one hand and the practice of morality in society on the other.[8] According to Haering it is a matter of

---

[1] W. Herrmann, op. cit., pp. 18−85, 86−227; 1913[5] (1921), pp. 12−87, 88−237. Under 1. Herrmann has "Natural Life and Moral Thought."
[2] O. Kirn, op. cit., pp. 9−27, 28−69; 1936[7], pp. 9−34, 35−94.
[3] E.W. Mayer, op. cit., pp. 14−70, 173−314.
[4] G. Wünsch, op. cit., pp. 29−58, 59−126.
[5] F. Schleiermacher, op. cit., pp. 30−75, 97−290, 291−501, 502−705.
[6] J.C. v. Hofmann, Theologische Ethik (1874), Nördlingen 1878, pp. 98−129 and 129−350.
[7] W. Herrmann, op. cit., pp. 86−162, 163−227; 1913[5] (1921), pp. 88−170, 170−237.
[8] O. Kirn, op. cit., pp. 32−47, 47−69; 1936[7], pp. 40−60, 61−94.

the new life of the Christian as personality and of the Christian life in social circles.[9] According to E. W. Mayer it is a matter of moral character, the nature of Christian conduct in the various forms of action and social life, its order and structure, and finally its result, the kingdom of God.[10] According to Wünsch's not wholly clear arrangement it is a matter (1) of the nature of God, (2) of the moral outcome of experience of God, (3) of Christian character, and (4) of some residual problems, among which Wünsch places the ethics of the Sermon on the Mount![11] An original and powerful approach is that of Schlatter, for whom the four Platonic virtues of justice, truth, happiness, and strength, related to the communion of will, knowledge, feeling, and life, constitute the schema of inquiry and presentation.[12]

We cannot go along here (even with Schlatter) because, as has been shown, there occurs a distinction between theology and ethics and a shift of focus from God to man which we cannot endorse. Against all these divisions we have to bring the objection that they are derived from something other than the matter itself and that they are not therefore brought and applied to the matter to its advantage. Schleiermacher certainly makes an acute observation when he discerns elements of criticism, construction, and play in human conduct, but does this really grasp and describe Christian conduct as such? That the fact of the Christian life confronts us with the problem of its rise and development (Herrmann, Kirn), or with the antithesis of disposition and activity (Hofmann), is certainly true in its own place, but are these distinctions really denotative of the Christian life?

The favorite distinction between individual and social ethics, which may be seen in varying degrees in Hofmann, Martensen, Haering, Kirn, and Mayer,[13] may pass as possible and meaningful. (Schlatter in his *Ethics*, 1914, pp. 53f. had some noteworthy things to say against it, and it would hardly be commended to us by a good philosophical ethics.) In any case, however, one has to say that it carries with it the self-evident presupposition that Christian conduct is simply a special instance of conduct in general, so that if the correlation of individual and society is constitutive for the latter it must be for the former too. Similarly Schlatter's derivation of Christian moral teaching from will, knowledge, feeling, and life, refreshing though it is alongside the rather arid

[9]T. Haering, op. cit., pp. 200−314, 315−454; 1926[3], pp. 230−360, 361−536.

[10]E. W. Mayer, op. cit., pp. 194−245, 245−308, 308−13, 313f.

[11]G. Wünsch, op. cit., pp. 70−82, 82−112, 112−18, 118−26.

[12]A. Schlatter, op. cit., pp. 47−56, 57ff.; 1923[3] (1961[4]), pp. 54−57, 58ff.

[13]J. C. v. Hofmann, op. cit., pp. 129−64, 164−350; H. Martensen, *Den christelige Ethik*, 1871−1878, which has a first part on general ethics and two special parts on individual and social ethics; T. Haering, op. cit., pp. 200−314, 315−455; 1926[3], pp. 230−360, 361−536; O. Kirn, op. cit., pp. 32−47, 47−69; 1936[7], pp. 40−60, 61−94; E. W. Mayer, op. cit., pp. 246−65, 265−308.

dispositions of the Ritschlians, entails a simplistic adoption of what is perhaps a correct and perhaps also an arbitrary definition of human conduct as the schema for a presentation of Christian conduct.[14]

All these divisions and classifications are nontheological to the extent that according to the same methods (even presupposing that they are right) they could obviously apply just as well to a Buddhist, Socialist, or Anthroposophical ethics as to a Christian ethics when the same concepts are filled out in different ways. What we miss in them is a specific congruence with the specific matter at issue here, namely, the Christian understanding of the goodness of human conduct. To explain this do not things have to be said that cannot be said in the framework of a concept of human conduct in general? Is not a distinctive mode of understanding essential to this understanding? Are not severe truncations of this understanding unavoidable if we take it for granted, as is plainly done all the way from Schleiermacher to Schlatter, that we may enter and follow paths that can obviously lead us to other places too? Does there not avenge itself here the fateful distinction between ethics and dogmatics, the fateful shift of focus from God to man?|

If that distinction and shift are right, then in ethics man himself, or in this case the problem of human action, will have to be the measure of all things, the theme, and the framework within which the inquiry must take place. On this assumption it may and must be, as is clearly presupposed in those divisions and classifications, that man has to pose certain questions: How can he become and be a Christian? What does it mean to act as such? What is meant by Christian willing, knowing, and feeling? What does Christian conduct imply for human aspirations in life and culture, for society, state, and church, for marriage and family, for art and science, for work and recreation? Theological ethics supposedly has to answer these questions which are not *raised* responsibly in decision vis-à-vis the divine command that has really been *issued*. It supposedly has to say something to man when he himself can say the one thing that has to be said only with the act of his decision vis-à-vis the Word of God that has really come to him. At this point there can be no agreement.

Undoubtedly, as may abundantly be seen in the authors quoted, many profound, true, serious, and fruitful things, even things that call for decision, may be said in an ethics that replies in this way to man. But no less undoubtedly a basically untheological ethics which replies in this way to man throws a veil by its whole attitude over the true whence and whither of a theological ethics, over its relation to the Word of God which is really published—a veil which can only be regarded as impossible when the damage it does is perceived. Why should theological ethics accept the invitation to take up the position of a center of information on every possible subject? Why should it not put its own

[14] Cf. A. Schlatter, op. cit., pp. 53−56; 1929³ (1961⁴), pp. 61−63.

questions instead of having put to it from outside questions which theology does not really have to answer and concerning which it does not have, and out of its own resources obviously cannot fashion, any guarantee that philosophical ethics, to whose sphere of competence these questions plainly belong, can even acknowledge them to be correctly put? Why should it let itself be forced into the position and attitude of having to answer when even the most profound and true and serious and fruitful things it can produce are from the very first put on the wrong track and cannot be heard as a summons to decision, or can be heard as such only in spite of the untheological beginning?|

If, however, theology is fundamentally the science of Christian *proclamation*, then it does not have to reply to man's questions in its statements but man himself is questioned by these statements. Its theme is God's Word, not the Word of God that is claimed by man but the Word that claims him. It certainly claims man in the whole problem of his conduct. But the problem and the contribution that Christianity has to make to it cannot be the theme. It cannot let its questions be framed by the problem, just as it is a perversion if Christian proclamation does this. It cannot derive and divide them and achieve its basic concepts thus, unless it is content to be merely an inferior replica of philosophical ethics. Justice will be done to the special problem of Christian ethics which must occupy us here when we do not regard the Christian element as just a predicate but as the subject, as is appropriate in a discipline auxiliary to dogmatics; when we do not let human conduct as such be the center, the beginning, and the end of theological ethics, but allot this position instead to man's claiming by the Word of God, to his sanctification, to God's action in and on his own action.

2

If this determination of the way that lies ahead of us is right, the further question arises how we are to handle and structure in detail the task that is thereby set for us. A first step is fairly simply and self-evidently shown to be necessary. The Word of God must first be indicated and presented as the subject of the claiming of man, as the command that sanctifies him. We believe that in theological ethics we have to seek and find the goodness of human conduct in the event of an act of God himself toward man, namely, the act of his speech and self-revelation to him. Man does good acts when he acts as a hearer of God's Word, and obedience is the good. Thus the good arises out of hearing and therefore out of the divine speaking. One may also put it in this way. Man does good acts when he is led by God to responsibility. To act in and out of responsibility to God is to act in a committed way. In this commitment the good is done. Thus the good arises out of responsibility and therefore out of the divine speaking to which man responds with his acts. One may also put it in this way. Man does good acts when he acts as a Christian. Theologically this means when he acts as one whom God encounters in his revelation in Christ through the Holy Spirit, so that his action takes place in this encounter or confrontation. To act in this confrontation is to act as one who is addressed. In this being addressed the good is done. Thus the good arises out of the encounter and therefore out of God's speaking and the encounter in which the confrontation takes place. This is fundamentally the theological answer to the ethical question. Its characteristic feature is that in asking about the goodness of human conduct it understands man as one who is addressed by God and it thus points away from man to God and his speaking, or, more accurately, his commanding. The good in human conduct is its determination by the divine commanding. We shall have to consider more closely what this determination implies. But at all events a theological ethics can seek the good only in this determination of human conduct and therefore only in the divine commanding which produces it. It cannot seek it in human conduct itself and as such. Why not? For the moment we can only state the answer. The concept of the God who confronts man in absolute supremacy, the fact that God speaks to man and man is spoken to by him, is here taken so seriously that the question of the goodness of human conduct can be answered only with a reference to him who alone is good [cf. Mark 10:18], with an assertion of the absolute transcendence of him who is good, except that recognition that the God who alone is good is the one who commands, as an act relative to us and not as a transcendent being, means that his immanence, a highly actual immanence, is also perceived, and therewith, but only therewith, a positive answer to the ethical question is made possible. |

Thus the claiming and sanctifying of man by God, and therefore the goodness of his conduct, really lies in the reality of the divine *commanding*. How far this divine commanding is an event is the first thing a theological ethics will have to show and develop as a basic and comprehensive principle. In accordance with the doctrine of revelation in the prolegomena to dogmatics we cannot lay too much stress on the fact that the dominant principle of theological ethics, the sanctifying Word of God, is to be understood as an *event*, a reality which is not seen at all unless it is seen as a reality that takes place. In ethics no less than dogmatics God's Word is not a general truth which can be generally perceived from the safe harbor of theoretical contemplation. Nor is it a being from which an imperative may be comfortably deduced. God's Word *gives* itself to be known, and in so doing it is heard, man is made responsible, and his acts take place in that confrontation. The Word of God is the Word of God only in act. The Word of God is *decision*. God *acts*. Only with reference to this reality which is not general but highly specific can theological ethics venture to answer the ethical question. Its theory is meant only as the theory of this *practice*. But this practice presupposes that it is taking place and only on this presupposition does it dare to give an answer. In the same divine decision, in the same actuality, in the same knowledge of revelation, the knowledge which is itself revelation, the Christian church exists and there is faith and obedience in it. As this decision is taken man acts as a hearer and with responsibility, and to that extent he does good acts. For the decision is that God gives his command to him, the lawless one, and thus calls him out of darkness into his wonderful light [cf. 1 Pet. 2:9].

To understand things in this way is our first task. It will logically take the form of three questions concerning the occurrence, the context, and the significance or force of this commanding. This is the totally different material which in our first chapter must replace the doctrine of philosophical principles so beloved in modern theological ethics.

Obviously, however, this can be only the foundation, the general thesis. How shall we then proceed? When the reality of the divine commanding is presupposed, it has to be made clear how far this commanding applies to *man*, how far the divine decision about *man* takes place. The question suggests itself whether, when justice is done in the foundation to the concern for a theocentric orientation of ethics, it might not be appropriate to adopt as a framework for the necessary detailed demonstration one of the schematisms already mentioned, e.g., individual and social ethics, or the rise and development of the Christian life, or will, knowledge, and feeling. Might it not be in place to pick up the concept of personality and character on the one side, or sociological concepts on the other, as empty vessels into which the Christian element is to be poured? Might not the task of theological ethics have to be sought in a Christian illumination of the human microcosm and macrocosm, in a Christian answer to the questions of human life? If it is only a rather headstrong concern for a strictly theological orientation that stands in our way, or if it is in the interests of an attainable clarity to do so, why should we not yield, or at least be able to yield, and put our further questions in terms of the concept of man, especially if the possibilities of putting them in terms of the sanctifying Word of God seem to be already exhausted? But this is not at all the case.|

It is no mere matter of formal interest in a theocentric theology. If it were, then we could take a different course as Schaeder has long since shown that he can do.[15] The simple question is whether theological ethics would really act even in the interests of man and his questions about life if it were to give up its birthright and abandon the standpoint which it has the task of making fruitful in the field of ethics. If it has rightly understood itself and its principle, the sanctifying Word of God understood as event, can it wrest the word from this Word and begin to

---

[15]Cf. E. Schaeder, *Theozentrische Theologie*, vol. I: Historical Part, Leipzig 1909; vol. II: Systematic Part, 1914, I³ 1925 and II² 1928, pp. 1–75. Schaeder's *Das Geistproblem der Theologie*, Leipzig and Erlangen 1924, forms a transition to the revised and expanded third edition of I and second and reconstructed edition of II. For criticism, cf. Brunner's review in *ZdZ* 2 (1926), 182f. and Barth: *Die Christliche Dogmatik im Entwurf*, Munich 1927, pp. 92ff.

speak about the Word in all kinds of applications? Must it not take seriously the fact that this Word itself will see to its application and above all that it wills to be heard to the very last? So far as their Christian illumination is concerned, will not personality and science and the state and any other conceivable area of human action fare much better if we give the word to the Word, if we let things work themselves out naturally in these areas as the Word is allowed to speak according to its own logic? It cannot serve the cause of clarity if we begin with the concept of the divine command and then try to continue with thoughts about the individual and society or the unrolling of a psychological schema or the variation of a table of Christian duties and virtues. For our basis of ethics can hardly serve as a basis for this, and the concept of the divine command as the basis of ethics can only be obscured by entry upon divergent paths of this kind. Nor are we compelled to take such paths as though we had said all that can be said about the Word of God when we have asserted its actuality. So far we have not even approached its content, so how can we have said all that there is to say about it? Precisely in relation to man, the theme of our present investigation, does it not have a specific and very rich content in virtue of which it may perhaps grasp and comprehend the whole problem of human conduct in a much more powerful and profound way than if we venture to move on to those applications and illuminations with the help of an alien schematism attached to it?—a content that we have simply to allow to speak if we are to come in the easiest and most appropriate way to the path that is needed for a perspicuous and truly exhaustive presentation of our theme.|

What, then, does God's Word say? It is the Word of the divine *creation*, the divine *reconciliation*, and the divine *redemption*. One may also say that it reveals the kingdom of Christ the Lord as that of nature, grace, and glory. One may also say that it speaks to us about our *determination* for God, about the event of our *relation* to God, and about the goal of our *fulfillment* in God. These are not accidentally or arbitrarily chosen standpoints. As may be seen, they are the great orientation points of the whole course of Christian dogmatics. To build on them in an auxiliary discipline like ethics, which deals with the whole and recapitulates the whole, obviously makes sense. On the basis and presupposition of the development of the concept of God, which might be a better parallel for our first chapter of ethics than dogmatic prolegomena, dogmatics shows (1) how God the Lord is the *Creator* of all that is not himself and therefore [the Lord] of man, the epitome of all that he himself [is] not. It regards the world and man from the standpoint of this original divine lordship which is understood to be original and therefore absolutely superior to man's own being. It shows (2) how God the Lord is the *Reconciler* of man, the God of the convenant whose faithfulness cannot be broken but only set in a clearer light by man's unfaithfulness, whose majesty in face of man's sin proves itself to be all the more powerful as grace. It thus sees man from the standpoint of this divine lordship which is maintained in spite of the reality of man. It sees him in the paradox of one who has fallen but is still upheld, who is an enemy but is still loved, who is a rebel and yet still a servant. It shows (3) how God the Lord is the *Redeemer* of man, the First who is also the Last, whose kingdom comes, the kingdom of the rift that has been bridged, of the new heaven and the new earth, of glory. It thus views man eschatologically, i.e., from the standpoint of this eternal divine lordship that has been promised and fulfilled to man as one who lives in time, who waits and hastens onward within a positive limit that is full of hope, who is both overshadowed by death as the removal of everything in this world and also illumined by the resurrection of the dead in which everything will be made new. It is only in appearance that we are indicating herewith three parts or steps of truth or knowledge. For in reality, just as in the doctrine of the divine triunity, which is the secret root of this order, here, too, the one total thing is said three times, and Jesus Christ, who is the very Word of God, stands at the controlling center of the thought of reconciliation, and is thus also the presupposition and quintessence of the thought of creation and the thought of redemption.

We are obviously in no position, however, to waive this threefold movement of our Christian knowledge or to state this thrice-determined Christian truth in a single word. The one Word is God's own Word which we cannot speak but can only hear spoken to us. And what we hear is threefold. This is why we cannot make of it a system. If it were a system, we should have to be able to trace it back to *one* word. A system has a central point or cardinal statement from which all the rest can be deduced. The reality of God's Word is, of course, the central point on which everything turns here. We, however, have no word for this reality. Naturally we can and must recognize it as such but we have only words relating to it and not a word for it. ⌐Exclusive of the statement "God is the Lord,"⌐ these words are creation, reconciliation, and redemption. They do not denote a system but a way. We have certainly not sought this way but found it with unfathomable contingency in God's revelation, in its attestation by holy scripture, and in the dogma of the church. If we may assume that it has been correctly described, then we must naturally keep to it in ethics too, without trying to work with unguaranteed concepts borrowed from psychology and logic. |

The concept of man contained in God's own Word understands him as God's creature, as God's pardoned sinner, and as God's future redeemed. We see ourselves in these relations when and insofar as we see ourselves in God's Word. In these relations we obviously have to ask about our sanctification, about the significance of the divine decision, of the event of God's commanding. In these three relations we see ourselves as claimed by God's Word. This is man—and we take as a basis, not a general and abstract concept of man, but the concrete

Christian concept, when we say that this is *sanctified* man, who is the predicate and not the subject of the statements of theological ethics. Man is God's creature, a sinner pardoned in Christ, the heir of God's kingdom, because and to the extent that God claims him as such. In all these relations the divine commanding is the principle of the goodness of his conduct. It is plain that these relations, too, do not denote stages or parts of man's being, and that these understandings of sanctification are not different stages or parts of God's commanding, but that we are always dealing with the one whole man and the one whole command of God as this is given to him in God's revelation. Here too, then, the differentiation can only be intended logically and not ontologically. It can denote only various points on the way of knowledge, only various angles from which to understand what is intrinsically one whole reality, not a division within this reality. But this one whole reality is God's own reality whose unity we do not control and which as an absolutely actual reality cannot be used by us to form the unity of a system. The distinction is thus necessary as a logical distinction. We do not have at our disposal the synthesis which would remove it. God is the synthesis, but not a synthesis that we have made or can make. Thus the significance of the divine commanding is necessarily different as we understand it as that of God the Creator, God the Reconciler, and God the Redeemer, although these three are not three but one. How can we possibly understand his command in one word without that distinction if we can understand God himself only in the denoted movement of knowledge?

The history of Christian ethics with its innumerable conflicts between types of thinking oriented to creation, reconciliation, or redemption, to nature, grace, or glory, shows us that in fact this movement has taken place in the ethical thinking of Christianity. If we understand that the Word of God is moral truth, we understand that the distinction which underlies this movement is necessary and cannot be evaded. Hence we not only see that the historical conflicts in their own way make sense but we can also express in the proper place the different concerns obviously intimated by them. In the proper place! We shall thus be able to avoid the rigidity with which one or other of the possible and justifiable standpoints has been adopted and treated as the one absolute standpoint. Yet we also cannot unite these different standpoints into a single one. This would be to forget the need to distinguish them and the fact that their unity only lies in the reality of God, which is not at our command. One can establish the validity of the different standpoints only as stations on a *way*. Thus the nature of Christian moral knowledge is to be sought and found neither in isolated preference for one or the other standpoint, nor in a construction that unites and harmonizes all three, but in the *treading* of this way in accordance with the divine act of revelation, in the act of *traversing* the three standpoints, in the basically single circle of the *movement* of knowledge described.

To make this movement of knowledge is the task of the second special part of ethics, of our second, third, and fourth chapters, an exact repetition on a small scale of the same movement that dogmatics makes on a big scale, with the practical, not methodological, difference that ethics pays particular attention to the question of the claiming of man as such. Again, everything depends here, as in dogmatics, on whether or not we understand the relation between the three successive developments kinetically and not statically, just as the picture of a movement can be presented only in the sequence of all three stages and not by a delineation of the first or second or third stage nor by a recapitulatory depiction or grouping together of all three. We are asking about the good. We cannot expect to see the good, however, in the second, third, or fourth chapter, and even less in a summary of their conclusions, but if at all only in the act of thinking structured according to these chapters. The good is what is commanded me, a man, as God's creature, pardoned sinner, and heir of his kingdom. As I myself as this man see myself set under God's command, I know the good. Hence I cannot know it except as I do it. And as I do it I know myself as this man: "from him, by him, to him" [cf. 1 Cor. 8:6]. Claimed by the divine self, I know myself in that cycle of knowledge, I see myself thrice claimed. My conduct in this thrice-understood claim is the conduct commanded me, my good conduct. In the second chapter, then, we shall speak of the commanding of God the Creator, in the third of the commanding of God the Reconciler, and in the fourth of the commanding of God the Redeemer, but never intending to say three different things, since the Creator, Reconciler, and Redeemer are one and the same God and "from him, by him, to him" denotes one and the same claiming by God. We have simply to say the same things three times in fundamentally different ways. In detail then, in the ordering of the content of the three chapters, the way to be taken has to be three times fundamentally the same, though different thoughts will have to be expressed at the different points. Here again, however, four elements seem to force themselves upon us with a certain materially grounded necessity and not without some support at least from classical models.|

It is clear first that at the beginning of each chapter it will be necessary to work out the *uniqueness of the specific ethical standpoint*, showing how far human action as divinely commanded in one sense or the other really does come each time under a special light that cannot be exchanged for that of the other standpoints, how far precisely from this standpoint it is claimed and therefore sanctified by God's Word in an indissolubly distinctive way.|

Thus when we think of the special features of the command of the *Creator* as we need to do at the beginning of the second chapter, the particular aspect of the divine commanding is to be understood as the necessity of the *life* that is given us. As in the light of creation we understand the necessity under which we are set by the divine claim as the necessity of life, we are saying that what is commanded us, the good, is to be sought first in the reality of human existénce because and in so far as this existence rests on God's creation and therefore on his will. Where the divine claiming is known at all it truly wills to be known as one that begins with the fact that we are. We are not except as we are the Lord's. As we live, we stand under the necessity of living to him. He is the necessity of our lives. We have simply to understand what life is and we shall also understand what is commanded us. |

The same claiming takes on a very different aspect when we view it from the standpoint of *reconciliation*. The same reality at the beginning of the third chapter has to be described as the necessity of *law*. We now see ourselves in our contradiction of God as sinners and also, of course, in the contradiction which God victoriously and supremely contradicts, as sinners, then, whom God in his grace has accepted in spite of their sin. Here the command, the good, obviously does not coincide any longer with our existing. It is set for us and opposed to us. It strives against our life because we are sinners. The reverse side of the grace that comes to us sinners is the judgment on us which precisely as recipients of grace we cannot evade. The crucial thing is that we should now understand the good in this strife against us, as the judgment on us that it signifies, as the law in its necessity. Over against us enemies to whom God has shown mercy, the divine claiming necessarily means the law whose validity cannot in any circumstances be called into question by our corruption, and which cannot be twisted or explained away no matter what may become of us.[16] |

Finally the same reality, seen from the standpoint of *redemption*, is the necessity of *promise*. We not only have life as God's creatures and law as members of the covenant of grace, but also as such we have promise. Our first point in the last chapter is that as God really claims us we are addressed as heirs of his eternal kingdom. The promise is the goal of our life which may be seen in and with the divine claiming. The promise is the consummation which is held out before us, pledged to us, and allotted to us in advance. As such it, too, is in its own way the divine claim. From this point, too, from the eschatological boundary, God meets us as the one who commands. The promise, too, sets our conduct under necessity. This is the same divine necessity that we also know as the necessity of life and the necessity of law, and it must never be absent for a single moment. We would not know the necessity of life and law if we did not know the necessity of promise, if, in addition to bidding us live and humbling us, the divine claim did not also summon us to consider a truly better future, if it did not mean also goal, fulfillment, and perfection.

To this first question of the distinctiveness of the specific ethical question there must then be added in all three areas the question of the

---

[16]Marginal note by Barth: "Word of God = command, 3 forms: life, law, and promise."

distinctiveness of the specific *knowledge* of the divine claim, or, as we might put it, of the form of the divine command.|

We know the commanding of the *Creator*, the necessity of life, to the extent that we know our *calling*, not understood, of course, in the narrowest sense, but as the epitome of the necessity, the "commandedness," of the concrete reality in which each individual exists as such. We do not live any kind of life according to our own caprice. As we know ourselves in God's Word, we are oriented to our fellows and we live a life whose specific ends are totally determined and which actualizes that orientation in a particular way. As thus determined our life has a necessity by creation. Our life itself then becomes for us the divine command.|

Second, we know the commanding of the *Reconciler*, the necessity of *law*, to the extent that, biblically speaking, we encounter Moses, the divinely *commissioned fellowman* who is set before us in this sense, or, more generally, to the extent that human *authority* encounters us. The brokenness in which we [are] set under God's judgment because of our sin and the reconciliation in which we exist by his grace mean concretely that our conduct, in so far as we know ourselves in God's Word, is done on all sides not merely in that orientation to our fellows in the form of our calling, but under the contradiction, direction, and instruction of fellowmen who are superior to us because they meet us with authority, so that it is always conduct in specific forms of subjection and under an alien human law. As thus determined, the law of the good is necessarily the divine command which strives against us and which we cannot refuse to respect as such.|

Third, we know the commanding of the *Redeemer*, the necessity of *promise*, in the voice of our own *conscience*. Our determination for the life of the world to come, our eschatological determination, means concretely that the obligation resting on my conduct covers more than its determination by my calling and by the authority that encounters me. Beyond both of these there is in us recollection of the perfect as the measure of the good in relative independence of the command of calling and the command of the commissioned fellowman. As thus determined, the promise is necessarily the divine command for the final and eternal goal of our conduct.——These are the deliberations on the ground of knowledge or the form of the divine command which in all three chapters will form the second development in our train of thought.|

A third development will clearly have to take place as we answer the question of the content of the divine commanding. *What* does God want in claiming us for himself? At this point we can turn at once into a well-known path of reformation theology, namely, the doctrine of the threefold use of the law in which not only Christian necessity but also the Christian content of God's law can be very fully described.|

The command of God the *Creator*, the necessity of *life* to which we subject ourselves in obedience to our calling, is obviously in content the necessity and command of *order*. There is a political or civil use of the law, as earlier thinkers put it. In this sense the command means the external order of our life by which we are disciplined and human life is possible as life together. As we live according to our calling we recognize that we live in orientation to our fellows. We recognize that the necessity of our life is the community of life. We recognize that our conduct is bound by the fact that it takes place with this reference, by a rule which is valid both for my fellows and me and me and my fellows, which precedes in dignity both his ends and mine, both my ends and his. This obligation of an order of life is the necessity of life properly understood. It is what God first wants from us. What occupies us here is materially the problem of the law of nature which is not set aside but confirmed and reestablished by revelation. |

The command of God the *Reconciler*, the necessity of *law* under which we stand as pardoned sinners in that concrete subjection to the commissioned fellowman, is in content the necessity or command of *humility*. The older writers spoke of the pedagogic use of the law. The law must put us where we belong. It is meant to lead us to repentance and faith where we can know only our own sin and God's judgment and grace. As we subject ourselves, as we act as those who must be told something, we recognize that we have deserved to be contradicted and that we are helped by being contradicted. We recognize the alien majesty of the law in our life as our judgment and salvation. Our salvation is that we have been disturbed and attacked in our possession, our security, our self, and to grasp our salvation means yielding to the attack. This humbling, this dispossession, this giving up to death of the old man is what God the Reconciler wants of us when he sanctifies us. What meets us here is the specifically Old Testament side of the revealed command but one which forms an integral part of the New Testament witness too. |

The command of God the *Redeemer*, the necessity of *promise* under which we stand as heirs of God's kingdom as we hear the voice of conscience with its witness to coming perfection, is in content the command of the necessity of *gratitude*. Earlier scholars spoke of a third use of the law, the didactic or normative use. Only as the recipient of the Holy Spirit does man really come under God's command. As our conscience makes the perfect present, we recognize the necessity of free action in faith and obedience, the command of gratitude as the Heidelberg Catechism called this principle of the new Christian life oriented to God's future. God's command is not content to order our going and to push us into and keep us in the corner in which we can live only by God's grace. As it does this it speaks to us as to God's elect from and to all eternity. It demands our gratitude, or, very simply, ourselves. For obviously the only possible thanks for God's election is that we should recognize our obligation, indeed, our having fallen forfeit to him. If it is not in our power to grasp the perfect, to put ourselves in God's hand as he takes us in his hand, the point of our existence should now be that of sacrifice, of witness and demonstration that we have heard, that we have heard this last and strongest meaning of his Word. What we have to deal with in this context is the specifically New Testament side of the command of God to which witness is borne in the Sermon on the Mount and the ethics of Paul and John but which is also not unknown to the witness of the Old Testament as well.——This, then, will be the third development in our train of thought in all three areas. In what will have to be said along these lines a certain resemblance may be seen to what is worked out in many ethical systems as a doctrine of "duties." |

Finally, along a fourth line of thought, we shall be concerned to understand as truly *good* conduct the human conduct which is thus understood to be set under God's command. We cannot forget that sanctification as well as justification is God's *grace*, total, real and effective grace. The one to whom God is gracious, i.e., to whom he not only promises forgiveness of sin in Christ but whom he also claims for himself in Christ, whom he both justifies *and* sanctifies (and grace would not be grace were it not grace in this totality), this person—and we should not shrink from saying this even though we must weigh its meaning very carefully—this person does *good* acts. What will have to be shown at the fourth point in each area is how far a *fulfillment* of God's command takes place in virtue of the same divine act of sanctification in which the command of God is set before man as a demand and in which man himself is set under the command. Again we can adopt a classical, and in this case a biblical, triad of concepts which seems to be ready to hand for this purpose. I have in mind the Pauline sequence of faith, love, and hope. All three of these are characterized by the fact that they describe a real attitude and action on man's part, yet one which is in no sense man's own achievment, but which—as man certainly stands or falls by his believing, loving, and hoping, as he is certainly called to do this—is in the strictest sense a work, or rather *the* work of God on man: *faith* (πίστις), God's being faithful to himself; *love* (ἀγάπη), God's free good will, as the one he is, to his own, no matter who or how they are, his free good will not to withhold but to give himself and all his benefits; and finally *hope* (ἐλπίς), the perfect comfort of the same God, as the eternal goal of their temporal existence, that God in all this fullness of his truth is our God. This is the subjective meaning of these three concepts. In this way they describe the fulfillment of the commands. |

Faith is the fulfillment of the necessity of life. God is the necessity of life. It is from God that we proceed, for he is the Creator of our existence, its Creator out of nothing. To do justice to the necessity of life is to do God's will. It is to put ourselves under the order of his creation according to and in our calling. This takes place only so far as and as we believe, affirming without either knowing or seeing, but simply because it is said to us by God's Word in Jesus Christ, that he is our Creator and the Lord of our life, that we belong to him, and that that is no life, therefore, which is not ready to be life under his command. This affirmation, this Yes, is the miracle of faith. Without faith we can only rebel. Without faith we live without necessity, we have no calling, we know of no order. If God decides for us in sanctifying us, claiming us, and putting us under his command, then faith is his inexpressible gift. |

Love is the fulfillment of law [cf. Rom. 13:10]. God judges and pardons us as he opposes the law to us like a rock on which we are inevitably broken, as he subjects us to human authority exercised in his name, as he forces us into humility. But this humbling of us is not an end in itself. The law is not fulfilled by our recognition that we are sinners who live by grace. In this plight God wills to be loved by us. In this plight which he prepares for us his love for us is concealed. Our humbling is complete only when we love him in return. Concretely the command which puts us there must also be the fulfillment. Again our fellowman is the specific other that is to be loved by us for God's sake, in God's place, and in demonstration of our love for God. The law would not have been fulfilled in us, it would not have discharged its deathdealing office, if love had not been spoken to us by it. Nor could we ourselves have fulfilled the law if we thought that we should be like God in holding up before our neighbor the law that judges him. In so doing we should simply show that we ourselves still stand under the unfulfilled law, that our contradicting of God is still unbroken, that our love for God has not yet awakened. That this happens, that we can love our neighbor instead of judging him, this Yes to God is again his miracle to us. If God decides for us, if he sets us under his command, this miracle takes place and love, our love, is his gift, just as faith is. We would love neither him nor our neighbor if he had not first loved us [cf. 1 John 4:19]. When, indeed, can our love be anything other than our *being* loved? |

Finally *hope* is the fulfillment of the necessity of promise. If it is true that God by the voice of conscience claims our gratitude and freedom, then beyond every existing order and in spite of the humility that we are given, our conduct acquires an orientation toward coming perfection. Faith affirms God, love rejoices in God, and hope seeks him. Beyond all that is present, hope expects everything from him. To that extent faith and love also live by hope. Hope would, of course, be mere fantasy and fanaticism if it were just an unrest of spirit. It is the fulfillment of the command, real gratitude, to the degree that it is not our own unrest but that of the Holy Spirit who as the Spirit of prayer will lead us into all truth [cf. John 16:13] and in whom, as the pledge of our inheritance [cf. Eph. 1:14], the eternal future is already present. Again this Yes to God, with which we seek God after and because we have already found him, after and because we are already found by him, is God's own miracle to us. If God decides for us and sanctifies us by his command, it is his gift to us that we are those who hope.——Thus faith, love, and hope are the good in human conduct and are therewith the answer of theological ethics to the ethical question—the goal that we have to reach in this last development of our thinking. Understood with a pinch of salt, this is our equivalent of teaching about "virtues." After this brief preliminary notice we shall now address ourselves to the matter itself.

	The Word of God as the *Command of*		
	the *Creator*	the *Reconciler*	the *Redeemer*
means (standpoint)	life	law	promise
is revealed as (knowledge)	calling	authority	conscience
demands (content)	order	humility	gratitude
gives (fulfillment)	faith	love	hope

CHAPTER ONE

The Reality of the Divine Command

§4

THE REVELATION OF THE COMMAND

The truth of God is not a general and theoretical and consequently a conditioned truth. It reveals itself in the concrete event of our own conduct as our decision for or against the command of the good that is given to us.

1

If according to Pythagoras it is true that in a right triangle the sum of the squares of the two shorter sides equals the square of the longest side, this is a general and theoretical and consequently a conditioned truth. If it is true that the earth is a sphere slightly flattened at the two poles, or that the German Empire was founded in 1871, or that there has been an intermediate biological stage between man and a superior chimpanzee, or that we may shortly expect a revolutionary change in the whole surface of the earth which will necessarily have the most serious consequences for all of us, or that our life is determined at its most important points by the conjunction of the planets on our birthday, or that the whole cosmos is evolving from matter to spirit and God has achieved self-awareness in this process, then all these empirically demonstrable facts of nature and history, all these scientific hypotheses, all these speculative, metaphysical constructions, no matter how strict might be the differentiation between them, are both corporately and individually general and theoretical and consequently conditioned truths, like all other acknowledged or alleged truths on this level. They are *general* truths to the extent that I can assert them as such without the fact of my being this specific person having any significance; to the extent that in asserting them I must consciously ignore as far as possible my own subjectivity, which could only disrupt the objectivity of my knowledge. They are *theoretical* truths to the extent that I can best assert them with the participation of one who is as far as possible a nonparticipant, an onlooker, a spectator, a spectator even of my own life if they affect my own life; to the extent that in asserting them no act of my own is needed but that of calculation, observation, and syllogistic combination along with a bit of experience and intuition; to the extent that my own action consists only in contemplation and the actual assertion itself. They are consequently *conditioned* truths to the extent that their assertion is reached on the presupposition that I am "born to observe and ordained to see,"[1] that the criteria of truth that I use in this act are true criteria of truth, that the significance of my assertion of these truths will not be hurt if it is conditioned by myself, by the ineradicable remnant of subjectivity without which there can be no objectivity, conditioned by my practice (as which even the purest and most passive *theōrein* must finally be claimed), conditioned by the question of truth which is obviously put to me and which challenges my knowledge of truth as such. There is no doubt that even in the shadow of this last question of truth which we ourselves link with its being conditioned, we can to a large extent be glad about our knowledge of general and theoretical truths, so glad that it might seem to be unprofitably scrupulous of us even to think of the shadow. But no matter what our view of it may be, all these truths are in fact challenged as such by the question of truth, the question of ourselves and what we do, the question which we would like to exclude as much as possible when we think generally and theoretically but which itself includes within itself our general and theoretical thinking. Whether we pay attention to it or not, this question is posed and it is the *ethical* question. |

The superior truth in question here, the truth of my conduct (including my *theōrein* and therefore the condition on which my assertions are assertions of truth), the truth of my life and existence is the truth of the good. All general or theoretical truth, from the truth that two and two make four to the boldest achievable knowledge of higher worlds,[2] and no matter how clear and certain they may be in themselves, stand in the brackets of the question whether my life and therefore my action and therefore my *theōrein* has a part in the truth of a basically different and higher order, in the truth of the good. They thus stand in the brackets of the ethical question. It is so much a matter of the truth of another order that the inquiry which it implies in relation to the bracketed general and theoretical truths does not relate to their content

---

[1] Cf. Goethe, *Faust* II, Act 5: Song of Lynceus the look-out: "born to see, ordained to observe."
[2] Cf. the title of R. Steiner's book, *Wie erlangt man Erkenntnisse der höheren Welten?* Berlin 1909, Dornach 1961[20].

(how two and two make four or how it stands with the final question that is directed to me as the one who asserts this truth). It is so much a matter of another order that a removal of the brackets in the sense of a general and theoretical answer to the question, in the sense of an extension of our general and theoretical knowledge by knowledge of this supreme truth is ruled out in advance. From the very outset those who deal with it with this in view deal with it in vain. With what right, however, do we refer here to the truth of a *higher* order? Because at best all general and theoretical truth cannot be more than clearly and certainly asserted *being*. But all being—no clear and certain assertion can evade this condition, as is most evident in the case of mathematics as perhaps the clearest and most certain of all the sciences—all being, as true being, as *ontos einai*,[3] if we are not content merely to assert it, is not grounded in itself but in a hypothesis or presupposition of being which itself, if the same question is not to repeat itself *ad infinitum*, cannot be thought of as being but only as not being, cannot be thought of as the beginning or source or mother-ground of being but only as its negation and position, as the pure *origin* of its being which as that of Creator to creature stands in no continuity with it and which cannot possibly be sought on the level of general and theoretical, mathematical and physical, historical and psychological, or metaphysical and metapsychological truths, on the empirical or the speculative way. If it is sought there, no matter how sublimely, something other will always be found, perhaps another theoretical and general truth, but another truth which, significant though it may be, and absolute though it may be in our own thinking, is still a truth of being which stands in the same need of regress, of validation by another criterion, as all other truths of being, all other truths sought and found at this point. |

The question of origin shows itself to be such, to be the question of truth in truth, of superior, unconditional truth, not by the fact that we ascribe to its object this character of general and theoretical absoluteness—for in so doing we should admit that we do not know what we are about and show how unattainable this superiority is—but by the fact that it is understood as the question that is primarily put by the *object* to us, to our action, and undoubtedly to our *theōrein*, though not to a *theōrein* abstracted from our existence as contemplation, but to our existential *theōrein*, and beyond that to the fact of our existence in general, to our life-act. We are asking about the unconditional when we ask unconditionally as we do not do in general and theoretical asking, i.e., when our asking expresses the basic acknowledgment that we *are asked*. We see it as the question of the origin that precedes all being when we see it as being prior in order to the questions of our general and theoretical thinking. But we see it as being genuinely prior in order to

[3]In the typescript Barth transliterated this, so that it is not clear whether he has in view the ontological *ontos einai* or the Platonic *ontōs einai*.

these questions when we do not see it as our question—as such it could only be general and theoretical again—but when we understand and accept it as the question that is put to us, as the question which we *cannot* answer incidentally from the safe harbor of our self-consciousness as spectators of our own life, but which we can, which, indeed, whether we like it or not, we *must* answer only with our life itself, to which our whole active life and each of our individual acts, whatever it may be, must be viewed as the answer, in relation to which our whole existence takes on the character of *answerability*. The very thing, then, which general and theoretical thinking as such would rather hurry past, my very existence as an individual, as this or that person, the very subjectivity of my conduct, becomes important, becomes *the* important thing, the only important thing, when it is a matter of the unique knowledge of the unique truth of origin. It becomes important because this truth *applies* to me and at every moment I have to understand my existence in relation to it as responsibility and decision, whether the decision be for it or against it or be left open. It is *decision* and as such the revelation of this truth to us for good or ill. Knowledge of the good occurs as we do it or not. Ethics is understanding of the good, not as it is known to us as a general and theoretical truth, but insofar as it reveals itself to us in our doing of it or not, insofar as the concrete reality of our life-situation is decision for or against it. All ethics which tries to look beyond this revelation of the good in our own decision, this active revelation, to a *being* of the good or a goodness of being, and which tries to define good actions and duties and virtues on this basis, might in some circumstances kindle our interest in the same way as higher physics or metaphysics; but beyond what it can itself achieve it would at once make necessary an authentic ethics which has to ask about the origin of this being of the good or this good being, and to do so in relation to our own decision, to our existence in decision. |

The ethical problem is not a problem, i.e., not a general theoretical question to which a general theoretical answer can be given. The reality of ethical science—science presupposes the possibility of common knowledge—makes sense only when there is fellowship in this supremely special knowledge, a knowledge of the good which reveals itself for good or ill in our decision. Thus theological as well as philosophical ethics—the former directly, the latter, as we have seen, indirectly—presupposes the church, the church as the place where the common presupposition is the givenness of the question of unconditional truth that is put to man, and therefore the fact that man is questioned, and therefore the revelation of this truth in his existential decision. The truth is the fellowship of individuals precisely in and not in spite of their individuality, the particularity in which the good is known here. |

On the presupposition of the church, on whose basis alone ethical knowledge is possible, what is thought and said in common about the ethical problem cannot consist of its recognition as a problem, of making it general and theoretical, of treating it as one of the many human questions, of treating the answer to it as an evident truth. It can only aim at showing us how far the meaning of our life-situation, of the wholly unproblematical reality of our existence, can be the revelation, the *becoming* evident, of the good. This becoming evident of the good in the reality of our own existence is the divine act of sanctification. It is the thing from which we must not abstract in any way if we are to pursue theological ethics and not theological physics. The latter would happen if the extension of our general and theoretical knowledge were secretly or openly to control our ethical inquiry, if we were to ask about the unconditioned without wanting to ask unconditionally, i.e., with the strictest attention to our *being asked,* if we were to try to deduce what being ought to be from being itself, if we were thus to try to understand God as the supreme being instead of in the way that he reveals himself, i.e., in the act of his divine being. The place where God is revealed as the quintessence of the good, where the knowledge of God thus becomes the knowledge of the good or theological ethics, is the divine act of *sanctification.* It is thus the reality of our existence or our decision to the extent that in it, no matter how the decision may go, God has decided on our *salvation.*

As God sanctifies us, the truth becomes unconditioned special truth applying to you and me today and tomorrow, not the truth which I maintain but the truth which maintains itself over against me, which fulfills itself in me. We must not leave this place, or stop considering the answerability of our life-situation, if we are to know how far God's command is real, how far, as we have been asking in this first section, it is revealed to us. It is revealed to us in the event of our own conduct understood as responsibility. We must now ask how far this is so.

2

The common formula for the ethical problem, and one which does justice to the depth of the matter, runs as follows: "What shall we do?" The question, then, is that of human *conduct.* The questioning "what" seems to indicate that the sought content of this conduct is not to be found self-evidently in our own range of vision. The concept "shall" implies that the good is this content that is sought. Since it is "we" who ask, we confess that this question applies to all of us and we must work together to find an answer. We thus find that we have to take very seriously both the terms which constitute the formula and with them the formula itself. We are thus directed at once by the problem to the reality of our existence as the source of knowledge of the divine command.

a. Is the *"what?"* in this question meant seriously? Are we as ready as it suggests to will what we should, not seeking the apparent glory of the "should" for what we ourselves will? It is not wholly self-evident that as we ask what we should do we are not long since bound by what we want to do, so that our ethical question will lead to self-demonstration which is not, of course, necessarily meant to be base or bad. Especially in times of a single, strong, and definite cultural will, as in the period from the beginning of the century to the first world war and well into the war itself, ethical reflection can easily not be meant very seriously in the sense that in it—one has only to think of the products of war theology in all countries—the content of the imperative that is apparently sought is fixed from the very outset in the form of specific practices whose goodness is no longer open to discussion, being known only too well, so that the factual result of ethical reflection is obviously the ethical justifying of a more or less compact: *"This* is what we will do." A similar self-assurance on the part of the actual ethos might well have been the secret of the ethics of Thomas Aquinas. Times and people who know all too well what they want must accept it if we accompany their ethical work relatively rather than absolutely from this standpoint, and with a certain mistrust whether they have properly investigated *what* we should do. The less this mistrust is in place, the more open the relation is between ethics and the actual ethos, and the more seriously the *what?* is meant, the more it means that a vacuum is created in the whole state of actual willing and doing, that there has to be questioning though not necessarily rejection. It was this vacuum that cost Socrates his life as an enemy of religion and morality—what was meant, of course, was the self-assurance of Athens after the age of Pericles. Between our self-evident desires and our self-evident action in their naive or ideologically enlightened givenness there comes the doubt whether *this* really is after all the good.

If the ethical question is serious in this sense, it means at once and automatically that ethics becomes *critical* in another sense. We no longer have the time to wander in distant metaphysical regions in search of the good. We no longer have the time to try to *contemplate it as being.* This *being* somewhere above the "ought" is the infallible mark of an ethics that does not quite take the "what?" of the ethical question seriously, that gets its knowledge elsewhere from the actual ethos of the ethicist and his time and background, and that is really making no more than an appearance of asking. In a seriously questioning "what?" we confess that we ourselves are scrutinized in our own being or existence, that an eternal eye is focused on our acts, that what we will and do are measured. If we put the question: *"What* shall we do?" as those who really do not know and really need instruction, then we confess that we are attacked and questioned and laid in the balances in the reality of our own existence, in our own most proper *this.* The attacker who has come into the midst of our life and under whose criticism our *this* is set is the good itself, the command which is issued to us. A seriously meant *"what* shall we do?"—and it is for us to be clear whether and how far we know a seriously meant "what shall we do?"—is already a witness that we know the command. Only where the command reveals itself does there come about the shattering of the self-assurance of our ethos which is the presupposition of a critical ethics. Only there does the seriously meant question arise.

b. "What *shall* we do?" is the question. Are we seriously asking what we *should* do? It might be that here, too, a substitute has to be set aside before we can say that the question is seriously meant. It might be that we have not yet heard the metallic ring of the "shall," that we have openly or secretly clothed this concept with the very different concepts of what is *convenient* or *useful* or *valuable* to us. From the hedonists of antiquity to Max Scheler, as is well known, the ethical question has often been put in this way and answered with an imperative that is formulated accordingly. There can be no doubt that the question of the orientation of our conduct, in virtue of which it is meant to be directed toward what is convenient, useful, or valuable, is not only a possible, and even in its own way serious question but also that its concern ought to be expressed in a comprehensive discussion of the concept of command and of what is commanded. (There will be an opportunity for such a discussion in the second chapter on the command of God the Creator.) It may be asked, however, whether we have really reached the concept of command at all, whether we may legitimately formulate imperatives at all, if, like Scheler, we simply ascribe to the concept of value a necessity that claims our conduct. For the highest value [is] seen being and the highest being has seen value.[4] If we have this necessity in view, have we really asked what we ought to do? For in the concept of the "ought" do we not recognize again the concept of origin which fundamentally transcends being? Can we not talk of an "ought" only when it is a question of unconditional truth and not merely of truth that is or that is seen? No *value,* not even the highest, can claim to be *unconditional* truth, and least of all, one might think, when this highest value is to be found, as Scheler believes, in human personhood,[5] since the concepts value, seeing, and being are all on the same level, the level where there is only conditional and not unconditional truth. How else can a value be validated but by being seen, experienced, asserted, and estimated by us as a value? Is it too much to demand that if an imperative or command is understood as a claiming of our existence, of our life, of the only life we have, it must qualify as such in some *better* way than this?

We are perhaps not challenging too sharply the seriousness that an ethics of material values, a kind of higher physics, might have as such, if we state that we cannot be content with *this* kind of seriousness when it is a matter of the concept of the "ought," if we say that we can speak of

---

[4]M. Scheler, *Der Formalismus in der Ethik und die materiale Wertethik*, Pt. I, 1913; Pt. II, 1916; Halle 1921[2], 1927[3]; Bern 1954[4] (*Gesammelte Werke*, II), pp. 95f., 129, 302f., 306ff.
[5]Op. cit., pp. 14ff., 120, 360, 381ff., etc.

an "ought" only when unconditional truth—truth of the first degree and not the second, like seen truth or the truth of being—is the necessity which impinges on human willing and doing, when by such an "ought" we understand a claim which does not need to be validated by my seeing and experiencing its validity but which is grounded in itself and comes to me in such fashion that without asking about what I see or experience I have to validate myself *before it* in respect of the question how far *I* can meet *it*. Assuming that I must take the concept of the "ought" more seriously than is possible in the framework of an ethics of values, and assuming further that I ask only on the presupposition of the serious content of the concept: "What *shall* we do?", it is plain that my serious question is a radiant witness that I know the "ought." But how? How indeed? Not from an experience of value, for in such a case I should not know it and my question would not be serious in the stricter sense. Obviously, then, from the fact that the "ought" *has* made itself known to me, that the self-grounded claim *has* come to me, and I *have been* placed under its standard. As I cannot *ask* about God, but only about an idol of my own heart, without confessing, not that I have seen, experienced, and grasped God, but that God has *spoken* to me, that I *am* known by him, so—and we are speaking here of one and the same reality—I cannot *ask* about the "ought," but only about the substitute of a being of value or value of being, without confessing that I *ought*, that the command has been spoken to me and has been accepted by me. If I seriously ask: "What *shall* I do?", I have already understood that my existence is claimed by the good and that this claim, the command of the good, is *given* to me. My question, then, does not mean that I am raising a theoretical problem, as the rich young ruler obviously did [cf. Mark 10:17–31 par.], but that I see that a practical problem has already been raised whose problem is my problem, so that I present and clarify it to myself and others, which is clearly the point of ethical reflection. Seriously asking: "What *shall* I do?", I have directed myself away from general and theoretical problems to my own practical reality. It is here that the truth of the good is known or it is not known to all. It reveals itself to me in my own decision as I do it or not, as I am judged by it or saved.

c. "What shall we *do?*" is the ethical question. We shall now consider whether we mean it seriously when we ask about what we should *do*. This again is not self-evident. The question: "What shall we *do?*" can also be a question of curiosity which does not have to be an ignoble curiosity. Practice, too, can legitimately become the subject of theoretical interest. This happens in psychology. And psychology is not in itself a disreputable matter. It becomes this, as happens, only when it confuses itself with ethics or even with theology. Ethics, ethical reflection as theoretical inquiry for the sake of inquiry, with no orientation to what ought to be done, is, of course, an impossibility. We cannot simply want to *know* what is good. One wants to know with a view to doing it or not doing it the very next moment, with reference to the total seriousness of the decision that has to be taken the very next moment. Hence one cannot learn to know the good merely in order to form a judgment about it or to take up an attitude toward it. Often enough we all of us seem to be asking about the good, but we only seem to be doing so. We ask: "What shall we do?", but again like the rich young ruler we do so with certain practical presuppositions which we do not regard as open to question, which we are resolved not to give up in any circumstances, and in relation to which we would rather restrict our freedom. We have not thought of asking about that whose doing or nondoing will at once mean our salvation or damnation. We ask frequently and attentively but we really ask, not "what *shall* we do" but "what *can* we do." We ask so as to supply material for the second question whether we will do anything at all or whether we would rather do this or that. This ethical investigation, which may sometimes be conducted very carefully, this abstract reflection and consultation with others, takes place under the proviso that we may take a very different view from that corresponding to the results of the investigation, and on the assumption that it does not finally matter much what view we take, it will probably be the everyday ethics familiar to everybody. Why should not this type of inquiry find its right and seriousness along the lines of psychological research? The only thing is that we must have no illusions about its theoretical character, about the fact that fundamentally it is not ethics, and that we must not exchange its seriousness for that event of the literally intended question: "What shall we *do?*"

If we take this question literally, we do not have in mind what we *might* do after an *intervening* moment of free reflection but what we *will* in all circumstances do the *very next* moment—or what we will perhaps not do, but then under the whole judgment of nonfulfillment or transgression of the command. I have again no time at my disposal, no intervening moment, no neutral place in time where I might first consider the good in its being and take up an attitude toward it. I cannot put off the decisive decision, but it stands directly at the door. I know that I will now decisively decide. It is a matter of doing what I *should*. What I should, however, is the claim directed to me, not the good in essence but the good in act, the good that comes to me, in relation to which I must reply the very next moment and not the one after, in relation to which my next step will bring to light my adequacy or inadequacy. Asking what I should do, I know that it is not in my choice to give my act the character of decision but that whatever I do it *always has this to my salvation or damnation*, that my existence is the answer to the question, not a question that I put, but the question that is put to me. Here again, then, there is no room for the discussion of theoretical problems. If I ask what I should *do*, then I know that the very next moment I myself am the answer to this question. My putting of the question can again have only the point of making clear to me this situation of mine, of making me aware of the decisive character of the very next moment. Again, then, I have directed myself out of general and theoretical inquiry to the very practical reality of my decision. In it, in my doing or not doing of what I should do, I see the unconditioned truth that saves or judges me, the truth of the good. In it the revelation of the command takes place. If a purely theoretical interest in practice is forbidden me, if I can ask only with this seriousness, then that is a witness that this revelation has in fact taken place.

d. We can now briefly investigate the seriousness of the question by means of the emphasis: "What shall *we* do?" When I as an individual put the ethical question in the plural, then if I mean what I obviously say I confess that by the responsibility which I have to accept in my decision I understand the measurement of my action by a claim that is not valid for me alone but universally valid. The crisis of the "what?", the seriousness of the "ought," the urgency of the deed would not be perceived and the whole question would clearly be something other than the ethical question if the "what shall *we* do?" were merely a rhetorical cloak for a secret "what shall *I* do?" For although the good, when it reveals itself, undoubtedly reveals itself to *me*, in the event of my conduct, not to a collective we, not in the form of a mass experience; although it undoubtedly comes to *me* questioning everything, making an imperious demand, pointing to the very next moment; although no other and no society can take from me my own responsibility, nevertheless I have no less indisputably failed to see and hear its presence if my ethical reflection does not take my real situation into account, if I am not fully clear that the individual element which is the goal and to which there is a summons, my naked existence, is again something that I do not have for myself alone but in fellowship with all men, and that the summons, even as it comes very directly and specifically to *me*, sets me materially in a series with all others, that it aims at me and reaches me not merely as this particular person but as man. A demand is made on me, not as a personality or individual, nor as a member of this or that natural or historical collective, but as *man*.

Otherwise there would again be the threat that I might view the good as being, this time from the distance of my particularity, of my isolated case; that I might protect my individuality against the crisis in face of which there can be no assured "this," against the seriousness for which the seriousness of my own special case is not really a match and over against the urgency which can know no distinctions between some people and others. There would again be the threat that I might make a conditioned truth out of unconditioned truth—a truth conditioned by my personal distinctiveness, by the special concerns which distinguish me from others. That unconditioned truth comes to me in a distinctive way, as it really does come to me, does not mean that I may treat it as conditioned by my distinctiveness. If it comes to me, I may not hide behind my distinctiveness but must confess that I am one among many others, simply man, so that my question—*mine*—can only run: "What shall *we* do?"—yes, in all the singularity of my person and case: "What shall *we* do?" If I seriously ask thus, I bear witness in so doing that I have given up the least possibility of trying to see the good as being, even this last and perhaps the most dangerous because the most natural and apparently the most honorable concealment. The "we" points to the inescapable decision which I must take—a decision which even my distinctiveness and that of my special case do not enable me to evade. In the very distinctiveness of my special case the command comes to *man*. *It* determines the special element in my special practical situation, whereas the assertion of my distinctiveness can only be again abstraction and theory. If I know this, if I know that everything depends on my doing or nondoing and not on whether I am this or that person, then I ask seriously: "What shall *we* do?" and I say therewith that I really know the command issued to me, that it *revealed* to me.

§5

THE COMMAND AS THE COMMAND OF GOD

The truth of the good that reveals itself in our conduct is the truth of the concretely given command which as such is the command of God.

1

We have shown in §4 how it is and must be with the revelation or knowledge of the truth of the good if there is such a thing, if the question: "What shall we do?" is seriously meant and put in all its parts. *If* there is such a thing —- ?! So long as we ask generally and theoretically whether there is such a thing, we can in fact only ask hypothetically. But the hypothesis ventured here is the thesis of the original unconditioned truth which, since it can appear only on the surface of general hypothetical thinking, indicates the limit of this thinking and also its own superiority. Hence the question whether there is such a thing cannot be answered generally and theoretically because, if it exists, it is not a general theoretical truth. How can anything general and theoretical be said, then, about its revelation and knowledge? The universal validity of this revelation and knowledge is the universal validity of the task and proclamation of the church, of the church in which there should be agreement that *this* truth, as the unconditioned truth which alone is universally valid, is not general and theoretical but practical truth, and that its revelation and knowledge can and will become real only in the event of man's *action*. If there is a truth of the good in this sense, its revelation and knowledge cannot be the result of our reflection. We have not found *it*, for what we find is conditioned truth, conditioned by ourselves and having neither the right to raise a claim to our existence nor the strength to enforce such a claim. No, it has found *us*. The point of ethical reflection, then, cannot be to try to find the truth of the good but to give an account of what it means that we *are* found by it, to give an account of the character of responsibility that our conduct will always have in face of it. The moment of reflection can be filled only by preparation for the moment of action that immediately follows. It has no independent worth—a point overlooked in all ethics oriented to a supposed being of the good. Its worth, the worth of all ethical theory, can lie only in its relation to the very next moment. The worth of any ethical theory can lie only in its relation to practice. It is there that revelation and knowledge of the good take place. It is there that the good is real as the crisis of our willing and doing, whether good or evil [cf. 2 Cor. 5:10]. It is there in our decision that the good finds us and is then also found by us as one finds a judge. Knowledge of the good is knowledge of the judge who, as we decide, declares salvation or perdition to be our eternal destiny. |

One must say the same thing in reverse or negatively. Knowledge of the good is the self-knowledge in which we see that in our reflection on the good which precedes decision we are *not ourselves judges* and are in no position, through a choice of this or that act preceding our decision, to pronounce judgment on ourselves or to bring about our own determination for salvation or perdition. The image of Hercules at the crossroads which often forms a model even for Christian morality is a pagan image for a pagan thing. It presupposes that man possesses a standard for the goodness of the commanded good and the badness of its opposite. The application of this standard is then the business that occupies the moment of reflection. But how in the world can we acquire such a standard if the goodness to be measured is that of unconditioned truth? Like Hercules at the crossroads we could obviously consider, measure, compare, and choose only if it were not a matter of the unconditioned truth of the good but of the conditioned truth which we have power to establish as such. If, however, it is a matter of the unconditioned truth of the good in what man does, then man is precisely *not* Hercules. When the good reveals itself in his conduct, whether it be good or bad, he knows that he himself *has* not measured and chosen but instead he *has been* measured and either chosen or rejected, that his existence has been placed and weighed on the scales. He then knows that he is not at all his own judge of virtue and vice but has found his judge in the good. How could he ever dream, then, of occupying a superior throne from which he might recognize and choose the good as the good? How could he ever reach such an exalted place? The worth and point of the ethical reflection that precedes decision cannot be the pagan and irreverent illusion of a free choice on the basis of "you will be like God, knowing good and evil" [Gen. 3:5], but rather a readiness to recognize the good in what is absolutely commanded us in the choice that takes place in our act, no matter what the choice may be or how the act may be qualified by it. |

The righteousness that may be seen in our decision is that of a court against which there can be no appeal. Before we obey or disobey we are in no position to test the rightness of the claim made upon us, or the value of the good, or the obligatory character of the command. When Paul in Philippians 1:10 tells Christians that they must "approve what is excellent," he certainly does not mean that they must first test what is divinely commanded and recognize it as such. In the New Testament sense to "approve" here means to set aside all irresponsible possibilities and to resolve on responsible action—action responsible to a court which must be acknowledged without test—whose goodness cannot be decided by man. Where there is room for testing the command, where an ethics of being can be pursued in some sense, the good, the command, the claim is undoubtedly present already but it is not recognized as such, its unconditioned nature is not perceived, nor is it realized that Romans 9:20 is applicable here: "But who are you, a man, to answer back to God?" In face of the good that is told to us [cf. Mic. 6:8] we have no recourse to a higher good that is not told to us but that we tell ourselves and whose superiority is obviously our own. The good that is told to us is the good itself, *his* good, not that of our own choice and not the excellence of a standard at our own disposal, even though finally our own excellence reveals itself in our decision and act. |

For this reason there is no possibility of putting off the decisive decision to the next but one moment, of interposing a neutral moment in which we can busy ourselves appealing from the given command to one that is not given, using the standard that is ready to hand, and thus acting as our own judges of good and evil and masters of our own eternal destiny. This will not do. There is no point in such activity. It can only show that we do not yet know that the good has no lord over it—least of all ourselves—but is its own lord; that we do not yet know that the very next moment will bring to us the claim that judges us and should find us, not dreaming as Hercules at the crossroads dreams, but watchful. The content of the present moment should be that we prepare ourselves to come before our judge with our actions. Prepared or not, dreaming or watchful, we *will* come before our judge with our actions. The one thing that we can meaningfully do on our own is to come before him *watchful*. This is the light or shadow which the revelation of the command always casts in advance on the present moment: the cry: "Watch—that the evil times do not suddenly come upon you"[1]—the time when as those we are—with what we do we fall into the hands of the living God [cf. Heb. 10:31]. In its own way the present moment is itself decision, action, and therefore the revelation of the good. But we may add at once that it is so

---

[1]From the hymn of J.B. Freystein, "Mache dich, mein Geist, bereit" (1695) ("Make ready, my soul"). The hymn has "thee," not "you" in the line quoted by Barth.

as a prophecy of the one who comes, who is even at the doors, and hence the cry: "*Watch*. Watch and *pray*" [Mark 14:38, cf. Eph. 6:18]. The judge comes ineluctably, and then our whole pose of being Hercules with a free choice has been just a pose. What will be revealed will not be our own but God's predestination.

2

Thus the truth of the good is the truth by which we are measured as we act, the verdict toward which we go. The point of ethical reflection is that we become aware of our responsibility to this superior court so that the very next moment we act in awareness of this responsibility, not having chosen and grasped the good—how could we, that would be foolish effrontery—but in awareness that we are making a response with our act; in awareness of the absolute *givenness* of the command, over or behind which there stands no higher general truth to which we can look apart from the command, or appeal beyond the given command, but the command which is itself the truth, the truth of the good. |

All this—we are simply analyzing—implies also that the truth of the good is always a *concrete individual command*, just as concrete as our existence will be the very next moment, or as our action—there is no resisting this—will be concretely and individually *this* action. *So* concrete and individual is also the command in which our action will find its judge. If we take seriously the positive givenness of the command against which there is no appeal, then it cannot be just a *rule*, an empty form, to which we must give content by our action, so that the form of the action stands under the command and its content under our caprice. This idea seems to be unavoidable wherever the court which we obey or disobey in our moral decision, whether it be the moral law, or the idea of the good, or the more or less categorical imperative understood in Kant's or some other sense, or the will of God, or our own conscience— wherever this court is thought of as something that is indefinite in content, wherever it is made into a purely formal concept whose truth has first to be investigated. On this view the idea of a necessary and obligatory form of the will is what is described as the revelation of the command and its definition and content—which are moral decision— arise on the basis of free choice controlled by the concept. On this view we mysteriously acquire from somewhere the knowledge that the doing of the good stands under an unconditionally valid rule and must always have the form corresponding to this rule, but assuming this rule to determine what the good is, *what* we should do is our own affair, and no matter how we act we can count on doing *what* is good so long as we conform to this rule. This view, too, is thinly disguised paganism and it is one that is quite impossible. On it our *action* would be free as such and would not be set under the command. It would be a doing of what we *want* and in relation to the claim that is made upon us, our concrete decision would be a decision for ourselves. We should have our own say about what we regard concretely as good, about what we pour into the empty vessel of one of those formal concepts, about what we happily (only too happily) give the form of a claim which we supposedly obey, although in reality we are our own lawgivers. If we take this path, how can even those generalities, those formal concepts, be really understood as command?

Is not the good again robbed of its originality, is it not thought of as placed in the lower order of being, if it is possible to *regard* it as a form which has still to be filled, if it is possible to differentiate it as an intrinsically general and abstract good from the definition that arises only with our own decision, if we can have knowledge of it without what we will and do being automatically determined by it in advance?

A general, formal, and abstract command is obviously *no* command but an object of theory like any other. If the good is indeed unconditioned and therefore not general and theoretical truth; if it is command, claim, a claim made upon us and not just a statement of our own thought that is given the rank of claim; then it is concrete, individual, definite command [a command] whose content is not under our control, but which *is* controlled with the same unconditionality as is proper to its form, a command which comes to us already filled and definite in content. It is then for the first time clear to us that the good is a question which is directed to us and which we must answer with our *act*, with an act which for its part is always concrete and *individual*. Nor will this answer be one that we have given ourselves, so that with our act we shall simply confirm and repeat it, thus remaining faithful to the choice and preference that follows our knowledge (and therefore to ourselves), or at worst being again unfaithful to them (and therefore to ourselves). This agreement or nonagreement with ourselves, which is confirmed by our act, may be an interesting matter but it has nothing whatever to do with obedience or disobedience to the good; if by the good we do not uncritically mean our own goodness but are clear that the good means the challenging of our own goodness.

We clearly misunderstand the meaning and scope of those general concepts, the moral law, the idea of the good, the categorical imperative, the will of God, etc., if we try to find in them the good or the command that is given to us. The *moral law* or the *idea of the good* is, as the name says, conceptualized being, the concept of the good, of morality or the command. It is the good projected on to the plane of being and the knowledge of being in a way that cannot be avoided in *thinking* about the good. It is the good as the ⌈real⌉ *thought* of a norm that unconditionally claims our will and conduct. Even ethical reflection is thinking and as such theory. To limit that plane concretely by the very different plane of practice, to push on to the thought of *the* norm which is not one of being but is original, which is not conceptualized but real—to do this it must first *enter* that place unafraid. How else can it leave it with the ostentation that is needed? But as ethical reflection arrives at the thought of the original and real norm, it negates its reality as simply a thought norm, maintaining that only the command which is issued to us and not a *concept* of it, not an idea, ⌜not a real conceptualized being⌝ of the good, is the court which we must obey or disobey in moral decision.|

The same is true of the *categorical imperative*. It may be understood in the purity in which Kant understood it as a formula for the unconditionally binding character of the idea of the good.[2] Or to the purely formal content of the Kantian imperative there may be preferred the post-Kantian one which includes some general content. Either way, and even in the ethics that is proudest of its content, we can have only a *formula* for the concept of command which is abstracted from the reality of the given command, not the command itself. Command, a truly categorical imperative, can arise only on the far side of ethical reflection, when the course is over and the ethicist concerned, setting aside a *general* formula, has the courage and perhaps the right to come to this or that man and tell him in God's name, as a prophet, what he should do in this or that specific situation or question of life. What he can say before when he is generally formulating the concept of the imperative is not the imperative itself but at best an insight *about* it. This is something quite different. Precisely with his strict formalism Kant is perhaps further away than his followers or critics or supposed improvers from the idea that his imperative or one of his formulae for it is the imperative itself, *the* real command which comes to man and claims him. When the command comes to man, it does not say: "Act in such a way that your action can be the principle of general legislation,"[3] or something similarly abstract and general. It says: "Do *this* and do not do *that* in this unique situation which will not be repeated." In this wholly concrete: "Do *this* and do not do *that*," and not in its formal distinctiveness as an imperative or as an attempt to grasp in general the fulness of concretions, the possibilities of the this and that, it is a *real* imperative. Conversely, to the extent that what encounters man is only the formal phenomenon of an imperative, no matter how categorical, or only what is ultimately the equally formal phenomenon of a formula for what might perhaps be regarded as concretions, to that extent it is certainly not the command that encounters him. The good point about general definitions abstracted from the real command, whether they be formal or material, is that they can be reminders of and pointers to the command which really has been and is issued. They are not even that, however, but "morals" in the worst sense, leading to the illusion in which man himself wills to be good instead of letting the good be good, if they pretend to be the real command, as has happened often enough under the dominion of a rather naive understanding of Kant.|

[2]*Grundlegung zur Metaphysik der Sitten*, 1785 (vol. IV, pp. 413–38); *Kritik der praktischen Vernunft*, 1788 (vol. V, pp. 19–41).
[3]*Kritik der praktischen Vernunft*, p. 30.

The same misunderstanding obtains where *conscience* is made the court which man must obey or not obey in moral decision. Conscience is the totality of our self-consciousness inasmuch as it can be the recipient and publisher of the command that comes to us. It has the promise that it *can*. But this "can" falls in the category of eschatological concepts. Only in the light of coming perfection, the hope of redemption, can conscience be addressed as the organ of the crisis that overtakes our willing and doing and therefore of our participation in the good. It is not a given factor. But the command that conscience can hear and validate to us by binding our existence to it is an absolute given factor. It does not first become this through our conscience, nor does it first acquire concreteness through our conscience, but it either has this in itself or it is not the real command, and our conscience can only witness to *its* givenness and concreteness. Hence our conscience is not the command.

Least of all is the concept of the *will of God* adapted to be played off against the concreteness and particularity of the given command as the real command behind and above it, or to be explained as the empty form that needs to be filled out as we see best. The concept of the will of God brings fully to light the impossibility of the abstraction of the good *in general* from the good *in particular* as revealed in the specific acts of specific people. In the third subsection of the present section we shall have to draw the line more precisely between the concepts "command" and "God." It ought to be clear already, however, that if one would and could and perhaps should equate the good and therefore the command with God, then the good cannot be understood as a schema at whose filling out by ourselves God is present as a spectator to exhort, console, and finally reward. Even less can the concept of God as the concept of a real imperative be united with the distance presupposed there between form and content, with the division of roles between the good and ourselves. In the same way we must be on guard when, in place of the concept of God's will, A. Ritschl, for example, extols that of the kingdom of God[4] or when without express reference to the idea of God the concept of righteousness or of love is exalted as *the* good.

Against all such constructions which relate to a general formula for the good we object that the unconditionality of the truth of the good is very seriously damaged by the idea that the good is simply a divided foolscap page whose columns have to be filled by our application of the general rules, by our deliberations on the special cases that occur. If this synergism in ethics is right, then one must admit that in ethics, too, there can be only conditioned truth. Obviously because people either will not or cannot abandon this synergism which makes man a rival of the one who commands, which makes him one who also commands and who secretly commands alone, almost every ethics, even though it pretends

[4]See *Die christliche Lehre von der Rechtfertigung und Versöhnung*, III, pp. 12, 30f., 275f., 308, 428, etc.

to be ever so idealistic, is obviously an ethics of *being*, an ethics of conditioned truth, and therefore an ethics of empty concepts. It is so because it is an ethics of free choice. For what fills the empty concepts, the source of concreteness, and consequently the criterion of good and evil, is the freedom of human choice, or, in other words, man himself. Those who want to continue in this direction should at least be clear about this connection. We maintain, then, that the very unconditionality of the command does not, as a shortsighted understanding of Kant believes, exclude the concrete and specific determination of the content of the command. On the contrary, it includes it. In moral decision it is a question of obeying or disobeying this or that command which *apart* from our acceptance of it as such is precisely this and this and runs thus and thus. Decision does not lie in deciding the question whether this or that is the good, whether the command wants this or that of me, whether I should do this or that. An ethics which asks questions like this makes no more sense than a dogmatics which asks whether there is a God. The question to be decided in moral decision is whether I will be found obedient or disobedient in my action when confronted with the command at its most concrete and specific. It is not a matter of my freedom of choice but of the divine predestination in moral decision.

To conclude our discussion of this side of the issue, we now have good reason precisely in a theological ethics to make a very special demarcation on this side. It is in keeping with all that has been said that the command addressed to man, as it is present in the message of the *Bible* which the Christian church accepts and proclaims, almost always occurs as a *concrete* command and therefore as a plenitude of commands. Jesus does not merely say to the rich young ruler: "You know what you should do," but: "You know the *commandments*" [Mark 10:19; Luke 18:20]. You know, then, that in this concrete way you stand in decision.|

It will be well to establish as unequivocally as possible the relation between the concreteness of the unconditioned command and the concreteness of the biblical commands. Obviously neither the totality nor a selection of the biblical imperatives, nor any one of them, *is* in itself the unconditioned concrete command that comes to you and me today. This neither can nor should be said either of the Ten Commandments of the Old Testament, Jesus' Sermon on the Mount, or the imperatives of the admonitory chapters in the epistles. Precisely for the sake of a proper understanding of the authority of the Bible we must not confuse the issue by an overhasty biblicism. All the biblical imperatives—and we do not say this to impugn the authority of the Bible but to define it—are addressed to others and not to us, and they are addressed to others who differ greatly among themselves, to the people of Israel in different situations, to the disciples of Jesus, to the first Christian churches of Jews and Gentiles. Their concreteness is that of a specific then and there. Again, as we now have them, they are not ⌐for the most part¬ *wholly* and *absolutely* concrete commands addressed to these and these specific people. Their concreteness is *relative*. ⌐Even⌐ formally they are at least in part—we have only to think of the familiar saying in Matthew 7:12[5]—not wholly unlike the general principles that we discussed earlier. They are in the main general *summaries* of the commands issued then and there to specific people. They are—and I am expressly including the Sermon on the Mount—*witness* to the absolutely concrete command received by Israel, the disciples, and the primitive church. It is in this specific form of *witness* to the absolutely concrete real command that they come to us and can and should apply to us as the absolutely concrete real command. This means, however, that no biblical command or prohibition is a rule, a general moral truth, precisely *because* it comes to us as witness to the absolutely concrete real command. How can it be a general moral truth if it is witness to the command that God has really issued and issues? As such it would conceal and deny what it is supposed to attest. If it were a general moral truth, if, e.g., the command not to kill [Exod. 20:3] or the command to love one's enemies [Matt. 5:44] were seen as a rule that we have only to apply, then obviously in relation to the biblical imperatives, too, we should have to distinguish between their general validity and their validity for us, again filling them out concretely for ourselves—for which of them is so clear and concrete that this is not necessary?—exactly as we do with the principles discussed earlier. The commands not to kill and to love one's enemies are *oriented* to the absolutely concrete command but are themselves only *relatively* concrete. Concretely *different* things may be commanded in line with this orientation, although it would be hazardous to say of the differences that they are irrelevant for the qualifying of our action and that selection among them is left to us. Yet even if the selection is not a matter of indifference, but decision takes place in it, nevertheless, assuming that the command is really meant and treated as a general truth, the good is our good *choice* among the possibilities it offers and not the command itself. A biblicism which thinks it sees the direct command to us in the relatively concrete biblical imperatives, whether individually or collectively, is ineluctably compelled to make use of the same method of the secret autonomy of those who are apparently subject to the law as an ill-advised philosophical ethics usually does with the help of its freely constructed principles.

To be sure, a secret lawlessness rather than "legalism" is the proper charge to bring against a biblicist ethics such as that of the Anabaptists of the age of the Reformation. This has become perfectly clear in the continuation of this approach in Tolstoy.[6] Over against the arrogance which for a change uses the Bible to place man's free choice on the

---

[5]The reference is to the so-called Golden Rule which may be traced back to Tobit 4:16 and is also found in contemporary Greek and Roman philosophers.
[6]Cf. K. Holl, "Tolstoi nach seinen Tagebüchern" (1922), *Gesammelte Aufsätze* II, *Der Osten*, Tübingen 1928, pp. 433–49.

judgment-seat concerning good and evil. ⌐and which makes man and his so-called "best judgment and conscience" the arbiter between two or three different and competing divine commands,⌐ we have to remember that throughout the Bible the biblical commandments are not simple and direct revelation, but like the whole Bible they are *witness* to revelation, and it is in this specific sense which excludes their use as general moral truths that they are God's Word to us. This means, however, that they are not themselves the direct, definite, individual command to us which is alone the real command. Then and there, as specific people heard it, the real command was very different from the recollection of it which, in the form of the Ten Commandments or the Sermon on the Mount, bears witness to us today of the way in which the ⌐divine⌐ Logos, the good, claimed people then and there. In their relative concreteness, however, they point us, as the whole Bible does, to the event of that claiming of men by the ⌐divine⌐ Logos which will be unavoidably the meaning of our own action.

This indication is made with imperious force. Through this witness to God's command the command itself is heard by us, by God's church. This is why the church proclaims it as it receives the biblical witness to it. This is why it gives instruction in the good by means of the Ten Commandments and the Sermon on the Mount. It does this on the presupposition—and with this presupposition the church stands or falls—that here and not elsewhere the command of God is to be heard. But to be *heard* as the command of *God*—which means hearing for ourselves what *we* are commanded by this command as we ourselves are concretely claimed by the command attested in the Bible. And if too much attention cannot be paid to the fact that the biblical witness to God's command almost never speaks abstractly in real proximity to those general principles but almost always speaks with at least a relative concreteness, we shall note not only *that* the finger we see pointing there points us toward the wholly concrete command of God but also in what *direction* it points us. For awareness of the responsibility that we must accept with our acts it is not a matter of indifference but one of urgent importance that ⌐at the decisive point⌐ the command is not that we should kill but that we should not kill, that the Sermon on the Mount does not invite us to take up the attitude of the rich but of the poor in spirit [cf. Matt. 5:3], and that Pauline exhortation does not focus on the concept of the superman but on that of sacrifice and humility. We shall agree that even if the great Old and New Testament command to love God and our neighbor is not the real command, nevertheless it tells us *very* clearly about it. And beyond that we shall always take into account that this and this definite biblical imperative itself becomes directly the most concrete command—why should it not, would it not be a bad thing if it did not?—so that in and with the wording of the biblical witness to God's command the command itself is given that judges our action. When this takes place, however, there is *no* transforming of the biblical

imperatives into general moral truths. How could we be taking seriously
the Word of God that is heard there if by the detour of ethical biblicism
we were again to set ourselves on a judgment seat of the knowledge of
good and evil?

To sum up, when people reached by God's command stand in
decision, it is a particular and definite command that has reached them.
Moral generalities of any kind, ⌐even though they be biblical and in the
exact words of the Bible,¬ are not the command, for over against them
we ourselves secretly are and remain judges and masters. The good is
this or that command that is given to *me* without choice or determination
on my part. It is given to *me*, and I cannot first ask whether it might be
given to others also either with reference to them or to my own action.
We stand alone[7] knowing that we do not stand on ourselves and cannot
be our own judges and masters. Primarily and fundamentally moral
fellowship can mean only that we know—and this is the knowledge of the
Christian church—that we are together and in the same situation to the
extent that we know that we are mutually under the real command that
is concrete and specific. Moral understanding means at root a common
respect for the command which is a special and definite command for
each individual. We should not think and say too hastily that this
involves the negation of moral fellowship. It is tempting to say this, but
if we do we speak superficially. General moral truths, from which we
usually expect moral fellowship, do *not* have, as shown, and no matter
what their derivation, the force of the true command, for in them the
decisive choice between concrete possibilities is still according to what
seems best to us. With this secret centrifugal effect, how can they have
the power to build fellowship? Precisely under the lordship of general
moral truths we cannot be united but can only become constantly
disunited. But we find ourselves together and enter truly common
ground when in the will and act of others we respect the revelation of the
command, the good, which may, of course, be imparted only to them. It
may perhaps be given only to us and not to any others. It may perhaps
judge us as it does not judge anyone else. But in the very particularity as
the command that is given to us it is the one command that judges all.
We can and will ask ourselves whether others have heard aright what is
said to them—having first put the same question to ourselves—but we
trust, and this trust is the act that establishes moral fellowship, that *in fact*
there is also said to them what they have heard either well or badly. We
do not reckon them good—how can we, we do not, it is hoped, reckon
ourselves good—but we reckon that the same participation in the good is
granted to them as we reckon to be granted to us. We enter the ground
of moral fellowship, then, when instead of proclaiming moral
generalities and thereby introducing the seed of disruption into what
may be an existing moral fellowship, we mutually agree that no one is in

[7]There is an allusion here to the song in F. Schiller's *Wallensteins Lager,* Scene 11.

a position to judge the servant of another, for "it is before his own master that he stands or falls" on the confident presupposition with which each of us must approach his own judgment: "And he will stand, for God is mighty to make him stand," [Rom. 14:4]. But again it cannot be ruled out—though we cannot begin here, it must first be discovered, and it will be when it is to be, though only and precisely on this ground—that several or many may see that they are placed simultaneously under the command and claimed by it in the same specific way, so that in the same definite and specific way they are called to reflection, to common ethical reflection.

The actualizing and sustaining of a narrower moral fellowship in this sense will depend, however, on our leaving not to ourselves but to our commonly acknowledged Lord the freedom to encounter each of us with a specific and definite command without being tied to the fellowship that has been set up between us in this extraordinary way. It will depend on our recognizing and acknowledging that we are not so much bound to *one another* as to the *Lord* who commands us. If another can comfort and encourage me by telling me that he stands with me under the same command—and there is no greater comfort or stronger encouragement on earth than awareness of this common bond—nevertheless no other can be *responsible* for my proper hearing of what is commanded of me. Nor can any other bind my conscience. The other is set there to arouse my conscience and I must always be ready to pay heed to him. But he cannot bind me. He neither can nor should judge me by appealing to what he has heard. And although on the basis of what is said to me I can and should be my brother's keeper [cf. Gen. 4:9] and not a spectator, I neither can nor should take from him his own responsibility for hearing properly what is commanded of him. It means liberation from a nightmare that with the best intentions we have made for ourselves when we see that we are neither called nor in any position to alter or improve one another or to set one another on the right path. With such good intentions we persistently judge one another. The wisdom which as an inalienable axiom must underlie all *common* ethical reflection (in the broadest sense) runs as follows: "*Judge not*" [Matt. 7]. All narrower moral fellowship that may arise from time to time, all common ethical reflection, can only be a summons that each should hear aright what is and will be said to *him*. There is no mutual recognition apart from the presupposition of a further and deeper recognition of the mutual agreement with which each *believes* of the other that something more will be said to him and that he will hear it in his own way. Anything else would not only violate the freedom of the other—this good is not the supreme sanctuary of the good that must be respected here—but it would also quench the Spirit [cf. 1 Thess. 5:19], drive oneself and others away from the Lord who commands, and in this way most assuredly destroy the fellowship. It is in this freedom and responsibility of the individual that the Christian church, if it knows what it is doing, accepts and understands and proclaims the real, divine, and biblical command. The command *hits home* to the individual; he himself is unable to hit upon the right. It comes to him as a definite command; he himself does not have to define it. It is *one* command and for each person it is always a concrete command.

3

Thus far we have more or less taken it for granted that the command with which we have to do in the reality of moral decision is *God's* command. We are in fact only adding precision and confirmation to what we have said already when, having equated the good with the command, we further equate it with the divine commanding, i.e., with *God himself*. We may question whether we have heard properly what is commanded of us, whether the revelation of the command finds us open, ready, and willing, whether we are clear about the meaning of the decision that we must always take, whether we submit to the judgment that is passed on us in it, whether it is for us a summons to go watchfully toward our Lord and Judge, who will meet us again in the decision of the very next moment. But we *cannot* question the fact that the command under which our decision stands and by which it is measured as obedience or disobedience is God's command, the command of the absolutely sovereign Lord who reveals himself to us and acts with us through his address and claim, through his Word. Thus far we have believed that we should understand the real command as commission, direction, order, i.e., as an *act* of command. If we had understood it as general moral truth we should have had to equate it now with the content of an absolute body of law. Somewhere and in some way it would have to be true in itself. But according to our previous deliberations it cannot be equated with this kind of corpus—even the Bible with its commands, as we have seen, can never be viewed as such. What makes this view impossible is that it ascribes to man the dignity of judge. The good, the command, *is* not true but *becomes* true as it is *spoken* to us as the truth, as it meets us speaking as truth. We thus stand directly before the concept of God; indeed, strictly speaking we have already achieved the concept. We may thus dismiss as childish the question how we have come to make the equation between the command and the command of God, i.e., God himself. The answer is that it is not at all the case that we *come* to this. If we know what the revelation of the good is in moral decision, if we know the strictly concrete character of the good which reveals itself to us there, then we know therewith and therein that God has come *to us*. We know that we have not first to begin to speak about him but that from the very first we have already been spoken to by him. Where the real command is, there is *absolute, personal, living will distinct from ours*. If this can be shown in analysis, then reserving all further definitions—this whole course of lectures can only be one big attempt to make these further definitions—we have the right to understand this will as the divine will and therefore the command that meets us as God's command, i.e., as God himself.

a. Where there is real command, there is an *absolutely* imperious will. We have seen how with the seriously put question of the good we have recognized the presence of an absolute "ought." I would not advise that this recognition be described as an "absolute position"[8] or the like. Its significance is rather that we, for our part, renounce all absolute positions and simply see that we are claimed, i.e., claimed, if the claim be valid, in our relativity. The positive content of this knowledge of ourselves, which as such can be described only negatively, the thought of the one who so confronts us in this relativity of ours that we can no longer detect any desire to name any absolute beyond for ourselves, this thought is the thought of God. If the true imperious command encounters us, therewith and therein God encounters us.

b. Where there is real command, there is a will *distinct from our own*. Everything depends on whether the command is understood not to be in any way secretly present in us, but always to imply disruption and questioning for us. And this in turn depends on our having to understand it as act and not as being. We are so in control of an object which we can contemplate that even its absoluteness will finally attest and reflect only our own absoluteness. But if the command, the good, is act, this means that we are not in control of it. It is not a criterion at our own disposal but a criterion under which we stand, which we cannot apply but which is applied to us. This is to think the thought of God's command. The step from Kant to Fichte, the true fall of German Idealism, is then impossible. We can only see ⌜with Kant and⌝ better than Kant that moral knowledge is unattainable without transition to worship.

c. Where there is real command, there is a *personal* will. Command is claim. In all cases it is speech, word, logos; not influence, effect, impression. A thunderstorm or earthquake may shake and startle a man and become part of his experience. To be addressed is something different, and it is with this something different that we have to do in the real command. But there is more to it than this. At a pinch a flower or waterfall or work of art might be a form of address. The command, however, claims us. It addresses our conscience. It makes our conscience, the totality of our self-consciousness, an instrument to bind our existence, to put it under obligation. This obligation again is not just a general one. The real command, as shown, always wills something specific from us. All this characterizes our encounter with the command as a personal encounter comparable to the encounter with a man, except that the claim at issue here is inescapable. By this distinction the person with whom we have dealings in the command that reaches us here is

[8]Allusion to the title of K. Stavenhagen's book *Absolute Stellungnahmen*, Erlangen 1925.

shown to be the incomparable divine person. When we think through the thought of the personal nature of the real command, we have again arrived at the thought of God, [the thought of] the eternal Logos.

d. Where there is real command, there is a *living* will. The concreteness of the command is not grounded in the concreteness of our own life. It is not as though man were first alive and then the command of God followed him into the richness of his existence. No, God, the one unchangeable God, is the rich and living God, and the command is at every moment this and this specific command because he has dealings with us, because it is not that a body of law is set up by whose sections we are to be guided, but a ruling Lord is present who never lets the initiative out of his own hands. It may be asked whether Psalm 119, which is so often blamed for its monotony, does not, with its 176 verses in praise of the law, see more clearly than many an apparently more perspicacious thinker the living nature of the law which is finally coincident with the living nature of him who gave it. The inexhaustibility with which our deciding constantly becomes the theater of revelation characterizes this revelation as the revelation of God.

We draw to a close. The absolute, personal, and living will of God which is distinct from our own is the will of *God*. The decision in which we live every moment is a decision for or against *God*. Responsibility to *him* is its point. His judgment is passed on us in it. As we seriously ask about the good, we recognize that we are not on our own but have a *Lord, this* Lord, *the* Lord. We "have" him, as we "have" a master, to the extent that we have his command, that here and now we, you and I, hear his command, that in virtue of this Word of his he "has" *us*. It might be added that we cannot have the Lord, we cannot have God, in any other way. Talk of God apart from the question of the good, apart from the command that is given here and now to you and me, is *not* talk of God even though it pretends to be confession of God or denial of God. God is he in virtue of whose Word my decision is decision for or against the good. He is this God and no other. He is the Judge toward whom we go or he is not God at all.

§6

THE COMMAND OF GOD AS THE JUDGMENT OF GOD

As God reveals his command to man, he judges him. But God's judgment and therefore man's sanctification by God is that God has loved, elected, and declared to be his possession the one whom he has taken up by his command, that God shows his whole decision and conduct to be a transgression of the command, that God for the sake of his own goodness accepts the sinner as a doer of his Word, and that in so doing God orients his sinful conduct to the work of obedience.

1

In this section we come to the true substance of the first chapter and of theological ethics in general. All that has been said thus far has been just a preparation for what has to be said now. And all that will have to be said later can be only a descent from the peak that has now to be won. "Has to," I say, for it would be vanity and even presumption to promise that the decisive word will actually be said and the peak won. The task before us is to give a recapitulatory presentation of the whole doctrine of the appropriation of God's grace to man on the special assumption that this appropriation consists of the placing of man under God's command. This task, if any in theology, is in many respects a venture for both teacher and students. The honorable titles "doctor of theology" *and* "theological student" sound somewhat dubious when we see what kind of a noetic task confronts us here. In addition, however, we stand directly at the point—it has long since given intimation of itself but can no longer remain invisible—where every theological discipline both begins and ends as such, but which it has neither the strength nor the permission to *posit*, prove, deduce, or even maintain, which it can only recognize to be *posited* as it continually starts with it and returns to it. We stand at the point where theology must fight for knowledge in such a way that it lays down all its weapons and unreservedly accepts and acknowledges how threatened is its claim to want to know. This claim is threatened by the fact that knowledge occurs here only in so far as its object gives itself to be known, that it is thus an event over whose occurrence we have no control. This is a situation which threatens theology alone among the sciences and we are now at the point in theological ethics where this situation—which determines the whole and not just this part of the whole—is now acute, where it is no longer possible not to think about it explicitly. In §4 we fixed the point where God's command is to be known as *command*. In §5 we tried to show further how the command is to be understood as *God's* command. If we seriously intend to describe the reality of the command of God we must now go on and try to reach some understanding of the event of the divine *commanding* as such, of the act of the divine claiming or sanctification, without which all talk of command and God's command is left up in the air. It is clear, however, that we now really seem to be left up in the air, since obviously all understanding of this event presupposes that it really occurs; yet its occurrence does not seem to be a factor on which we can count, but we can bring it into our discussion only as a factor in the most literal sense, i.e., as doers. If the decisive word is truly said here as a conclusion to what has preceded, and if the peak has really been won as the presupposition of all that follows, i.e., if we really understand the event of sanctification as such, then by way of introduction we must say that this cannot be the result of a dialectical achievement. No matter how it approaches *this* factor, no theological dialectic can at root achieve more than is achieved if we are content to make a simple reference to the name of Jesus Christ and to leave it at that. If we choose the more involved way of theological dialectic, this is not in order to do something more effective; but in order to summon us to awareness that we stand before the factor which must speak for itself if all that we can do is not to be done in vain. Because this insight is clearer when we make the reference in the harder rather than the easier way, because this insight not only threatens theology but also offers a basis for it, at this point where we must choose between a very simple and a more difficult way, without pretending that we are doing anything better, we opt for the latter.

2

I have entitled the section "the command as the *judgment* of God." It thus corresponds to our deliberations thus far. The event to which all theological ethics refers, God's claiming of man, sanctification, the act of establishing, revealing, and validating the divine command, implies the judgment of God. The point of all ethical reflection is that at every moment of life, including the very next moment to which our reflection relates, we have to respond by our action, i.e., by our existence in that moment no matter what its concrete content might be; that our action, as it occurs, is measured and judged and set under an eternal determination. At every moment our action means crisis, not a crisis we *bring on* but a crisis in which we *stand,* which is brought upon us by the good, the command, God the Lord. We are put on the scales. By the fact that we are put on the scales *now* we are called upon to consider that we will immediately be so *again*, that life is an unbroken transition from being weighed to being weighed again. To the extent that the Word of God heard today is this call, the saying is true: "Thy word is a lamp to my feet and a light to my path" [Psalm 119:105]. Being unable to anticipate the result of our being weighed, we have no choice between good and evil. But we may be awake or asleep. We may live responsibly or irresponsibly. To be mature is to act with awareness of the responsibility of our acts. This is not less but more than that choice. As we come to reflect on the fact that we *are* weighed and that our acts in some way mean responsibility, we recognize that we *will be* weighed and therefore that we *will be* responsible the very next moment, so that it is high time to awake out of sleep [cf. Rom. 13:11], because the meaning of the very next moment will again be the judgment of God. It is at this event of the very next moment that all theological ethics, starting out from the event of the present moment and its call, is aiming.

The first and basic statement that we have to make in relation to this event is obviously that God *accepts us* in it. Even though we weigh too lightly on his scales, nevertheless he puts us there. We may not stand according to his measure, but we are still measured by it. It may be that his judgment means our conviction and condemnation but something worthy of a different judgment might at least have been expected of us. Summoned to give an account to him we are basically and primarily summoned (no matter what the account may be) to recognize that in some sense he counts us his, shares with us, and holds *fellowship* with us. Unable to avoid the insight that we have him as Lord, we confirm thereby the further and materially superior insight that in some sense he regards and treats us as his own, as his possession. As his command becomes the crisis of our conduct, he tells us, as Calvin says (Inst. III,6,1), that he does at least ask concerning the symmetry and harmony of our decision with his own will. Under the influence of the polemic in Romans and Galatians against a dialectically understood concept of the law, and even more so under that of *Luther's* use of this polemic and his to-some-extent-objectionable absolutizing of it,[1] it may easily be overlooked that the origin of the establishment and revelation of the law is undoubtedly *God* himself and the *love* of God. The law should not be so unequivocally grouped with the *devil, sin,* and *reason,* as it sometimes is in Luther, nor should it be understood in a relation to God's *wrath* that is so clearly taken for granted.[2] While one may emphasize the distance and even the antithesis between God and man which the revelation of the command and the occurrence of the crisis manifest, one must still remember above all that this event does at least mean encounter with *God.* And while one may with horror take note of the element of God's holy wrath that characterizes this encounter, nevertheless it must be perceived above all that the fact of this encounter is in itself a proof of the love of God, a love which is perhaps displayed as wrathful love, yet still God's *love.* As God as Commander meets us along the way, he tells us that he does not want to be God without us but that no matter who we are he wants to be "God with us," Immanuel. This is love, and as God's love it must not be furnished with a restrictive "only," just because the event also means more than this. This must be regarded as the thing which dominates everything else. We have a poor view of the crisis in which we now stand, and our reflection on it lacks seriousness, if we will not understand that we move toward, and with our acts have to give account to, the one who counts us his, who does not treat us as strangers but as members of his household [cf. Eph. 2:19], as his possession, who has loved us and will love us no matter how our encounter with him may go. As he gives us the command, indeed through the command itself, he tells us that he will be our God and we shall be his people [cf. Lev.

---

[1] Karl Barth and much of his audience in Münster were still directly confronted by Luther's doctrine of law and gospel. In the summer semester of 1927 and the winter semester of 1927/8 Barth held a seminar on Luther's two commentaries on Galatians (1519: WA 2, 436−618; 1535: WA 40 I, II: LW).
[2] Cf. WA 18, 677,7; 766,25; 39 I, 347,27.35; 477,1; 40 I, 395,20f.; 400,16ff.; 519,35−520,12; 525, 22−25, etc.

26:12, etc.]. That we let ourselves be told this absolutely positive thing is the presupposition of all true maturing. Hear the command, we are told. But even as this "hear" sounds forth, it tells us already that God has accepted us. The saying is not: "Hear, O Moab, Midian, or Amalek," but: "Hear, O Israel [cf. Deut. 6:4, etc.]. "Hear" is not said to Moab, Midian, or Amalek. Where it is said, there is Israel, i.e., there is love, election, calling, the covenant, grace, faithfulness, above all God. When Israel forgot and rejected the *love* of Yahweh and the fact of its election from among the nations, when as a lost virgin it played the harlot with the Baals of the Gentiles as though Yahweh were not the husband who had eternally affianced her to himself [Hos. 2:21], then it forgot and rejected the *commands* too. Hearing the commands, without which there is no obedience, means hearing the love in the command, the election which reveals the givenness of the command, the absolutely primary Yes which God says to us through the command. If we do not hear this gracious Yes in the command, we do not hear the command at all. It is a theological hardness of heart that sees a lower stage of religion in the Old Testament because it does *not* know the abstract differentiation of law and gospel which, even in face of the jubilation with which again Psalm 119 and other passages sing about the gift of the law, dares to operate with the catchword of legalism, or which, according to the same schema, would find in Calvin's joy in the law a relapse into Judaism. How can one really refute the statement of Calvin that the law is from the very outset "graced with the covenant of free adoption" (Inst. II,7,2)? Is not the final point of the law, of the command of God that judges us, God's *promise*, the promise of his *covenant* with us? Can one hear it as command or place oneself under its judgment without recognizing this final point which is also the first one? Are we really mature, do we really know our accountability, so long as we do not know our election?

That God *judges* us means above all that he *loves* us. We have to think two thoughts together here: judgment and love, law and gospel. But in these two thoughts, if we think them aright, we think the one ineffable truth of God. Love is before judgment and above it. Law is simply the concrete form and voice of gospel. As such, however, it, too, has force and worth. The law has "come between" (Rom. 5:20) and is a "taskmaster" (Gal. 3:24), according to Paul's polemic, only as the abstraction of a "Thou shalt" which is something different from the form and voice of an original "Thou mayest," in which lies hidden the fact that first and foremost God has bound himself to man and man to him. In this sense it is the "law of sin and death" (Rom. 8:2). In this sense it is the law that is not really heard as *God's* law. Yet the law is not as such overthrown but upheld (Rom. 3:31). It is "holy, just, and good" (Rom. 7:12). It is "the law of the spirit of life" (Rom. 8:2). Given law means fulfilled promise: the promise that God *has* bound himself to me, that I *am* loved by him. Prior to my decision, *before* it has become true in my act (as measured by his will) that I am his servant, *before* it has also become true that I have been found an unprofitable, unfaithful, and treacherous servant, before all this, God's decision about me has been made, and even though the mountains depart and the hills be removed his grace will never depart nor will the covenant of his peace be removed [cf. Isaiah 54:10]. The love of God manifested in the givenness of the command means a decision of *God* which stands substitute for mine to the extent that, as it is the final point of command that comes to me and judges me, so it also anticipates the final point of my decision, or of the judgment in which I stand with it. In it—and the same is to be said of my decision—*satisfaction*, and indeed full satisfaction, is already done in advance to the command under which I am placed and by which I am judged. If God is for us, then no command, even when and as it judges us, can be against us. In virtue of the decision of his love manifested in the givenness of the command, I cannot be one who is condemned by this command. In the decision of his love, the symmetry and harmony of my decision with his command is presupposed and promised, no matter what else may have to be said about it.

In the decision of his love I have the righteousness which his command requires of me and which avails before him. This revelation of God's love in the givenness of the command is the *gospel*. It must not be separated from the command. Only through it does the law acquire truth and weight. Without it I have not heard the law as God's Word, as the Word that truly binds me. I see the law as the Word that binds me only as I know it to be God's law. But I know it as God's law only as I see God's *love* and my own *election* in it. And I see God's love in it only as I let myself be told—the gospel tells me—that God's love is unconditioned love, that it is not conditioned by my decision but is a love that precedes it, the love of eternal election. It is as one who is unconditionally loved, as one about whom a decision *has been* made, that I am summoned to move on to decision the very next moment, i.e., to be the one I am, not to elect but to be elected and to confirm my election, to fulfill in my decision the decision that has been *made* about me, to be the one whom God loves in *my own* decision in virtue of *God's* decision. What this means will have to be the subject of further discussion.

This, however, is the fundamental and all-controlling and conditioning thing that God's judgment by his command always implies. This is the circle within which there takes place man's sanctification, his claiming by God's Word. In all else that we have to say we must remember that it can be said aright only in the light of God's love, faithfulness, grace, and election. Everything would be abstraction and confusion which meant stepping even for a moment outside this circle.

I think it has already become clear in making this first and basic point that it was not superfluous to issue an express reminder in the first subsection about the uncertainty of the path on which we find ourselves when it is a matter of laying the decisive foundations of theological ethics. To find God's love in his judgment prior to all its other determinations, to see the gospel in the law, is either a nonsensical paradox or it is an appeal to the reality of God himself in his revelation in Christ by the Holy Spirit. Clearly it cannot be the *achieving* of a synthesis but only the recognition of a synthesis already *achieved* if we have recourse to the decision of God's love which in principle precedes our decision and stands substitute for it. This is not a truth on which we have a handle or which we can deduce from some other truth. It is the truth of revelation, i.e., a truth which strictly is true only as it reveals itself, as it itself speaks to us. This is God's eternal counsel and its execution in the incarnation of his Word and the outpouring of his Spirit. We have to reckon with no less than this if we are to speak correctly about sanctification. But how can we reckon with it? Like dogmatics and theology in general, theological ethics can never give a theoretical answer to this question. It can answer only by *doing*, by doing as basically and carefully as possible, yet aware also that it has no guarantee but the reality of Jesus Christ and the Holy Spirit. It can answer, then, only with the counterquestion whether the one who asks should not know this reality.

3

The command that is given to us becomes our judge by showing us totally and irrefutably that our decision is as such *transgression*. By the law—this is the first concrete element in sanctification—is the knowledge of sin (Rom. 3:20). We shall try to clarify this in three complementary discussions.

a. We begin with the fact that we have found the reality of the command in the *concrete and specific command*. As such the command is that which necessarily and unconditionally condemns us as we act and decide. If instead the command were to be understood as a general idea of what is commanded, which we have to fill out concretely for ourselves, then it would be easy, and fundamentally it would always be possible, to view our decision as in conformity with the command and to regard ourselves as justified. For if the filling out and the fulfilling of the command were in our own hands, would it not be simply unavoidable that we should fill it out from the very first in such a way that we would and could later fulfill it, or that having fulfilled [it] as we would and could we should later correct the filling out in accordance with the fulfillment? The imperative falsely substituted for the command, general moral truths taken from the Bible, formal and material general truths of morality, always constitute a focal point for the righteous who need no repentance [cf. Luke 15:7] because they are at peace with the law. They are at peace with the law because they mean by it a general truth that one can accept as one accepts the truth that two and two make four, and when the point is reached where there must be concrete action instead of theoretical acceptance, they are their own lawgivers who do not act according to the law, but like the scribes and Pharisees act according to their exposition of the law, which at its most concrete means according to their own caprice. Is it any surprise that with this identifying of the legislative and the executive they did not see themselves as transgressors? One can here be at peace with oneself and it can even be an unnecessary whimsicality not to try to do so. They correctly appeal to their good conscience. A good conscience is possible so long as it is not concerned about the self, so long as it is not smitten by the real command that is not set up by ourselves but established over against us. This real command, as we have seen, is not a general framework of demand but the most concrete and specific command. The concreteness of the real command spoils our little game of filling out and fulfilling in which we are on our own. It also pitilessly ruins our good conscience. Obviously, in face of it our acts are always deviation, addition, or subtraction. They are always different from the acts that are commanded us. They are thus a nondoing of what is commanded us. We may in good faith regard what we do as commanded, for we may perhaps do it in truly well-intentioned exposition of a general moral truth. We may perhaps think that it was commanded once before or might be later on. We may believe that even now it is commanded of others, perhaps of all others. These possibilities, however, do not alter the fact that we certainly do not act as those who are *really commanded now*. In this connection, in relation to the question how we stand before the command that is issued to us now, it makes no difference whether in our acts we are far or less far from what is commanded. If sometimes we are *far* from it, this should make it clear to us *that* we do deviate from it, which is not perhaps so clear when without being any the better for it we are not so far. It is a dreadful thing to wake up with the discovery that we have wandered *far* from the command, but what we then realize is truer than what we may perhaps dream to be our harmony with the command when we are *less* far from it. If we measure our decision by the real command that is given to us, then we see that it is not imperfect obedience but real disobedience. For our acts are really decision when placed under the command. Decision, however, is a matter of either/or, all or nothing, not more or less. Björnson's mountain parson rightly saw and said this.[3] We constantly find ourselves to be those who, in greater or smaller distance from what is commanded, do not do what they should, so that even though they are at great peace with themselves and their conscience is ever so good, they are in conflict with the law, i.e., with God. Our decision always means that we are disobedient.

b. We begin also with the fact that the command that is given to us is *God's command*. As such it condemns us. This would not be so if we

---

[3]Pastor Bratt in Björnson's play *Über die Kraft*, pt. I, 1883 (B. Björnson, *Gesammelte Werke*, 5 vols., ed. J. Elias, Berlin 1921, vol. 5, pp. 3–57).

could think of it as a law of the natural or spiritual world, as the power of our destiny, written perhaps in our stars, or as the power of the historical situation or process in which we have a part. We might clash with these powers too. We could suffer under them. We could be broken on them. They might crush us. But they could not put us in the wrong. They could not condemn us. For in the last resort we owe them no obedience. Even in the event of the severest collision with them we could still be deeply at peace with ourselves and with them too, even confronting them as superior forces. None of them can indeed demand of us that we recognize it as lord over us, that we cease to be our own, that we really place ourselves under its direction. They want to be respected, but only as powerful, even overwhelmingly powerful partners in the game of life. We ourselves can always be the other partner. No matter how badly we have played, why should we not be finally peaceful, secure, and cheerful? The strange thing about human creatureliness is that according to Psalm 8:5 man is made so "little less than God" that, even though he is the weaker partner who yields and falls and submits in the game of life, he can still defy the gods and assert himself, so that come what may he does not have to fear anything in the whole world, not even fate or death itself. "If the vault of heaven broke and fell on him, the ruins would smite him undismayed."[4] He can stand erect against all things and everything, even though he has become guilty before all in everything. The tragic hero finally triumphs, defying the world, or even blessing it in spite of everything, even in his downfall. He is a type, a respectable type, of man's own upstanding righteousness. The Zarathustra of Nietzsche and the Prometheus of Goethe and Spitteler,[5] like the Prometheus of the ancient Greek story, are figures that have the fear of death and fate behind them, figures that obviously do not stand under accusation, and we must be clear that real life stands behind them. Why are they not accused even though they are so assaulted? Because there is for them no command, no command of *God* that cannot be escaped, as one can escape even the sharpest accusation of the world of nature and spirit or as even on the ruins one can escape the attack of the whole cosmos. There is no true assault where there is no sin. But there is no sin where there is no command of *God* beyond the command of powers and forces and the law of gods and demons. God's command *reveals* sin. God's command *condemns* man. It does so because it smites man at the very point where the tragic hero is strong and good, because it constantly surprises man in his act with the demand that instead of asserting himself he must surrender himself. The command of God wills that we regard God as an unconditioned Lord. We do not want to do this. We do not do it. Whatever our decision may be, finally it is always

[4]Horace, *Odes* III, 3.7.
[5]C. Spitteler, *Prometheus und Epimetheus, Ein Gleichnis*, Aarau 1881–2; also *Prometheus der Dulder*, Jena 1924 (*Gesammelte Werke*, 9 vols., ed. G. Bohnenblust, W. Altweg, R. Faesi, Zurich 1945–1958, vol. 1).

self-assertion. Our sensuality and spirituality, our love and hate, our prayer and cursing—they are all self-assertion. We want to live. We want to be ourselves. Always, perhaps even with God's help, we want to thrust ourselves forward. It is with this true and deepest program of ours that in each of our decisions we stand even against God and precisely against God, as though God were one of the gods whom it is a laudable thing for the tragic hero to encounter. We always deal with God on the basis of a supposed credit. Even when we decide for the ostensible good we always decide as our own masters. We never act as those that are truly bound. This is transgression, sin. The Pharisee in the temple, who unlike the publican has put everything straight and thanks God that he is *himself* and not like these others [cf. Luke 18:11], is the true sinner. Again there are distinctions. It is one thing to assert oneself so wildly and defiantly, to play the superman, the god-man, as directly as Nietzsche did.[6] It is another to rebel in so moderate and perhaps so highly Christian a form as did that good-natured model child, the elder brother in the parable of the prodigal son [cf. Luke 15:25−32]. Yet we must not deceive ourselves. The distinction is irrelevant in this context, namely, in the question how we stand before God. We must see that whether crude or refined it is the same revolt: disobedience. The one is not disobedience and the other imperfect obedience. Both are disobedience. Our action is decision and decision is either/or. Our decision as such undoubtedly means that even at best what ought to be done is *not* done.

c. We begin finally with the fact that the command is not given to us without the promise that we are God's elected covenant-partners whom he loves. It is as such that it condemns us. This is the obviously contradictory description of the even more contradictory fact that precisely the revelation of God's love, as which we must finally understand the command, unmasks us as those who love neither God nor the neighbor in relation to whom our love for God must show itself in concrete decision. Again it would not be too difficult to regard our decision as good and ourselves as justified if we had not to remember this final point of the command, the revelation of God's love. God comes so uncannily close to us that he loves us; that he wants not just our work or our obedience or ourselves, but ourselves in our own freedom, ourselves not merely in our creaturely dependence but also in our creaturely independence; that he does not will to be without us. If he did not love us, the command would not be the question of our response of love. We should be merely effects of a superior cause or slaves of a powerful lord instead of children of an eternal Father. God's lordship would not be most glorious in the fact that he is this Father. In face of the command it would be just a matter of factual observance, of

---

[6]Cf. *Also sprach Zarathustra. Ein Buch für Alle und Keinen*, 1883−85 (*Werke, Kritische Gesamtausgabe*, VI, 1, Berlin 1968).

the fulfillment of this or that outer or inner act or attitude, not of God's heart and our own heart. Why, then, should we not be able to satisfy his command? Along such lines there is so much that we can do and that people have actually done. There have been those who in observance of God's command have offered high things, perhaps the highest, perhaps the final thing of all, their lives. But it is a question of *love* for God (demonstrated in love for neighbor). And loving means freely wanting to be in all things, not without but with the one whom one loves in the same self-evident way as one cannot be without oneself. It is thus that God loves us and calls us to love him in return. In our decision however, in every moment of action, we find that we are those who do not love him in return. Remember that here again it cannot be a matter of more or less. Love is not a quantity. It is a quality that is either there or not. And when do we see ourselves to be those who have this quality? When do we not see ourselves instead as those who realize with shame that in the last resort they would rather be without both God and neighbor, if we are not to say even more clearly, with Question 5 of the Heidelberg Catechism, that we are prone by nature to hate God and our neighbor?[7] We cannot escape the judgment of this question by pointing to the attitude and acts of individuals whose unselfishness, dedication, and readiness for sacrifice seem to rule out the assumption that they do not really love God and their neighbor but actually hate them. It must be remembered that we have to do here with the question which we must put and answer, not for others or with reference to others, but strictly with reference to ourselves. Even if we were among those saintly people, even if we gave an impression of perfect love for others, could we and would we say to ourselves that we have even partially fulfilled the command of love and are justified before God in virtue of this love? This is the question. True saints have not done so, we should have to say. Knowledge of the judgment passed on us by the command always means, even and precisely for saints, knowledge that we are not loving people, that God deals with us in a way that is qualitatively and not just quantitatively different from the way we deal with him, that something meets us in his love for which we are absolute debtors to him, not just partially but totally, not just in our worst moments but in our best as well. Certainly there may be important differences between the different debtors to God's love and between our levels of indebtedness at different times. But there are never any final or decisive differences and we are never nondebtors. Of no one can it be said that he has rendered imperfect obedience, but still obedience. There are no favorable moments in which an individual can appeal at least to a minimum of obedience. From this standpoint our decision is again a faulty and

---

[7]Heidelberg Catechism 1563, pt. 1: Of Man's Misery, qu. 5: "Canst thou keep all this perfectly?" Answer: "No; for I am prone by nature to hate God and my neighbor" (P. Schaff, *Creeds of Christendom*, vol. III, p. 309, Harper, 1919).

corrupt decision. Our sanctification is precisely that, *precisely* as those who are loved by God, we find ourselves to be those who are unworthy to be loved, who have deserved *wrath* instead of love, and what meets us in this discovery, this unveiling of our hearts *is* in fact wrath, the *wrathful* love of God.

We must pause for a moment, however, to consider the great epistemological caveat with which we opened this section. Here, too, it cannot escape us that the way of thought that we are pursuing is not a secure one except in the reality of Jesus Christ and the Holy Spirit. Can we not conceive of very serious and even passionate objections to all that has been said here? Is it true that our acts, so far as may be seen, are deviations from the concrete command that is given us? What are we to say if someone steps up to assure us that he himself, perhaps as one who knows and possesses spiritual realities and gifts, believes he has in fact fulfilled, and does so continually, the concrete command that is given him, and that he thus regards himself as justified? Again, is it true that we can stand upright against the world, death, and destiny, but are always unrighteous before God? How can we reply if someone says that in the best part of him he does not finally know that irresponsibility and rebellion of man against God but does know a deepest basis of his nature in which he is always at peace with God, gives God the honor that is his due, and is therefore justified before God? Again, is it true, is it not a misanthropic exaggeration, to say that we never attain to the deepest meaning of the command of love for God and neighbor, and that placed under the command we recognize that we do not love at all and are thus condemned by the command? What are we to answer if someone tells us with the friendly but triumphant laugh of the worldling or even the Christian that he is not as bad as all that but does love God and neighbor and is sorry we cannot say this about him? And beyond this general contradiction, what are we to say if someone rejects the established either/or, the alternative of obedience or disobedience, and tries to tell us that in the gentle middle between the two there is such a thing as imperfect obedience, and that the relative differences of deviation, which we have not denied, imply from the opposite standpoint relative stages of perfection whose higher half is no longer covered by the statement that "through the law comes knowledge of sin" [Rom. 3:20]? |

It is tempting to answer rather angrily these objectors, who in fact are to be found not only among Roman Catholics, with Anselm's dictum: "You have not yet considered what a heavy weight sin is."[8] Does it not seem obvious that we have here the sleep of the overrighteous? Will not such objectors finally be driven to wake up and see and admit their real situation, so that at least in the hour of death they will no longer be able to find comfort in their supposed fulfillment of the law? Perhaps even now we can really awake these sleepers with a powerful summons,

---

[8]*Cur deus homo*, XXI (Library of Christian Classics, vol. X, p. 136, Philadelphia 1956).

though only if our summons does not represent a perverted Pharisaism, that of the publican, of villainy, but is a witness to the majesty of the divine command to which God himself says Amen. If we realize this, then we will be just as restrained with our charge of a deficient sense of the seriousness of sin in other people as we are with all charges. The statement that we are always sinners [cf. Rom. 3:23] cannot be victoriously asserted and demonstrated by emotional or rational means. Like the statement that the command declares God's love to us, it cannot be forced on anybody, but can only be an appeal to the reality of the divine Word itself and to the internal testimony of the Holy Spirit, to the reality which *itself* bears witness to itself where it is known. Calvin expressed this in the almost intolerably strict formula that "there never existed any work of a godly man which, if examined by God's stern judgment, would not deserve condemnation" (*Inst.* III,14,11). In this formula, however, there should be noted not only the cautious "if examined" but also the fact that the judgment is God's judgment. The statement speaks truth, but highly particular truth, not general truth: truth that may be discerned only in this special case. This case, however, obviously cannot be created by speaking either to or about people, nor can anyone put himself in this case in which his work is really measured by God's stern judgment. This case arises when the judgment takes place. Then man, even and precisely the godly man, does recognize, of course, that his work deserves condemnation. Then, having seen his face in a glass (James 1:23f.), he can no longer go away and forget what he has seen. Then he knows that he is done for. But he has as little accepted or attained this knowledge on his own as he has the knowledge of the love of God and his election. As little as the latter does it rest on his profound experience and great earnestness, and as little as the latter can it become an object of possession or a matter of a habit. He knows because and to the extent that he stands under the fatherly *discipline* of God. Discipline, however, is revelation. And revelation is the act of God. What we can know by revelation, however, is not suitable for use by us to silence others, even though they be the most stupid and unperceptive of objectors. It obstinately refuses to be used in this way. If we really understand the statement that all have gone astray, that all are wicked [Rom. 3:12], that God's people is always the people of the lost, then we will pay almost more careful attention to that perverted Pharisaism than to the usual variety, knowing that this is not our own insight and that we cannot ourselves triumph with it. How can we indeed utter such a statement except with an awareness of the great risk with which every true theological statement is made? It might be that the insight, hidden from human eyes and ears, is much more genuinely present when the fatal objection is made than when the statement about man's plight is perhaps affirmed too readily to be really affirmed under the discipline of the Holy Spirit, just as knowledge of the love of God can be much more genuinely present when the statement at issue is perhaps questioned and contested than when it is uttered as though we had its content in our pocket and the suspicion is aroused that perhaps we have said it to ourselves *more* than we should. As the command itself is grace, so it is grace when, through the command, God shows all our deciding and doing to be transgression of the command. As knowledge of sin by the command is God's work of sanctification, so it escapes our grasp and is an act of our life that is *hidden* with Christ in God [cf. Col. 3:3]. We evade the truth if we try to evade the caveat with which alone we can speak in this regard.

4

As my decision comes into God's judgment, it is—as my decision— condemned. It is, as my decision, measured by God's command, apostasy, treason, and revolt. I do not do the good before God but—there is no third possibility—I do the bad. Yet as *my* decision comes into *God's* judgment, as what *I* do is done before *God*, the "my" and "I" are radically called in question. Certainly it is *my* decision and *I* do what is done, but that my decision and deed are a last word, that they create a definitive situation, that *I* can make an *eternal* choice, is challenged by the fact that I come into *God's* judgment and my deed is done before *God*. Certainly the command of God reveals to me what I have to think of my decision, how I am to understand myself, and as *self*-knowledge the revelation that I am a transgressor is *the* truth behind or above which there is no higher or deeper truth, no self-knowledge in which I find myself to be anything better than a transgressor. But that my *self*-knowledge or self-discovery exhausts the truth about my exis- tence is denied by the same command because it is *God's* command. To stay with my self-knowledge even though final clarity may have been given to it by the command, to refuse to be told more about myself than I can and must tell myself when instructed by God's command, is something I am forbidden to do by the same command because it is God's command. According to the revelation of the command I stand in *God's* judgment and I do what I do before *him*. This means, however, that he speaks the last word by his decision and act, that he creates the definitive situation, that I am fundamentally known by *him* beyond my knowledge of myself, that I am known in a fundamentally *different* way from that in which I know myself, the fundamental difference being that, even in my apostasy, treason, and revolt, he who for his own reasons has bound himself to me from eternity sees me in the quality in which I am elected, loved, and blessed by him. His decision and act is the free good-pleasure which he has found in me by seeing me in Christ the second and obedient Adam, by imputing Christ's righteousness to me as my own righteousness. In this decision of his, in virtue of this free divine good-pleasure, I have the quality in which I am worthy for all my unworthiness, of being the one he has elected, loved, and blessed.

Before I chose what is corrupt, supra lapsum (*before* the fall), I was elected in Christ. *Before* I did not love, I was loved in Christ. *Before* my unsatisfactoriness came to light, satisfaction was perfectly done for me by Christ. God's faithfulness was not overthrown by my unfaithfulness [cf. Rom. 3:3]. If God's command reveals my unfaithfulness, the same command, if I hear it as God's command, reveals God's faithfulness. The thing which, beyond my self-knowledge, even beyond all the self-knowledge illumined by the command, I must let myself be told by the command, by the law that is "graced with the covenant of free adoption," or by the gospel that is not to be separated from the command that is really given us, is that God was and is and will be faithful to me, that God has reconciled the cosmos to himself [cf. 2 Cor. 5:19]. It is still true, of course, that God knows me—and I have to let myself be told that he does—as I myself never know myself in any continuation, extension, or deepening of my self-knowledge. In my self-knowledge as such I must stay with the truth which in the area of *self*-knowledge is *the* truth, God's truth. In this area I look in vain for any quality in which I am worthy to be elected, loved, and blessed by God. According to *my* knowledge, my decision, my existence will never be pleasing to God. If I may and should know that God has elected me, in face of what I know about myself through his command, I can regard the basis for this act of his only as a miracle, as sheer mercy.

It is not true, then, that I *know* myself *as* God knows me—in 1 Corinthians 13:12 this is expressly called an eschatological reality—but what is true is that I have to let myself *hear* this and be *told* it. God knows me without my being able to invoke the corresponding findings of my self-knowledge as witness thereto. This knowledge of myself, which is exclusively *God's* knowledge, which cannot in any sense be translated or dissolved into self-knowledge, by which the truth of my self-knowledge under the illumination of the command is not abrogated, in which this self-knowledge of mine is rather comprehended and empowered—this knowledge is my *justification* in the judgment of his command. It is *God's* knowledge of myself in which my self-knowledge under the illumination of his command, unaffected, unbroken, and unchanged, holy, just, and good, is confirmed in its judging and condemning force, so that out of it no possibility of self-justification arises but all such possibility is now definitively shattered. For in face of the fact that *God* justifies us we stand as those who are not justified by themselves and cannot justify themselves. Divine justification means as such an alien or forensic righteousness and not in any circumstances a native righteousness of our own. My justification in the judgment is that *God* knows me better than I know myself. It is not, of course, as though I know myself better than I find myself to be when placed in the light of his command. It is not as though, beyond this finding, I can say more consoling and pacifying and encouraging things about myself than that I am a transgressor. It is not as though somehow, at some time, I come into a position where I can turn the verdict which is passed on my decision and my existence by God's command into a verdict that absolves me. The truth is always that *God* knows me better than I know myself. If my justification is real justification, it neither can nor should have anything whatever to do with even the sublimest form of self-justification. Even the most refined self-justification means evasion of the sentence imposed on my decision by the command. It means evasion of the command itself and therefore of the voice of God. I am justified when I listen to God's voice, not when I maintain it with my own voice. All that I maintain with my own voice is either the asseveration of an illusory and supposedly better and more favorable self-knowledge or—"we are now justified by faith," [Rom. 5:1]—a witness to the knowledge of myself which is exclusively heard through God's voice and which is exclusively God's. Paul's assertion is not that we are just but that we are justified, and the continuation runs: "by faith," which means that the reality as well as the knowledge is, with the same exclusiveness, ascribed to *God,* man's role being to acknowledge by faith this reality and knowledge that are exclusively God's.

No logical difficulty should lead us astray on the point that this acknowledgment of the knowledge of God involves no self-knowledge and cannot mean either any reference to myself as the subject that knows in faith or any change in the result of my self-knowledge. *Faith* is the apperception in which human receptivity consists absolutely of hearing and obeying in the face of the divine spontaneity, of a hearing and obeying which certainly claims human spontaneity for itself but not a spontaneity correlative to the divine spontaneity. The gospel without which the law does not really reach us as God's law, the theme and content of faith without which there is no obedience, is that my sin, my decision that is shown to be corrupt by the law, is *forgiven* sin. What is meant by forgiven sin? Not sin that is overlooked, forgotten, no longer accused by the command, and therefore not sin which in my self-knowledge is no longer sin for which I must repent before God in dust and ashes; but sin, the corrupt decision, in which God does not drop me but accepts me just as I am, just as I am in my self-knowledge, sin for whose corruption his decision intervenes, making good what I have done amiss. Sin is thus a wicked thing which I myself, illumined by his command, must always recognize to be wicked, which I must guard against changing into a good thing, but which, in face of his superior and not arbitrary, but righteous and free good-pleasure, is good before him, which, in his eyes, because he sees me in Christ and not in Adam, is in the symmetry and harmony with his will which I myself could only deny and for which I can only *pray*: "Forgive our debts" [Matt. 6:12]. Sin that is forgiven for Christ's sake is sin which stands under the judgment, the judgment of the wrath of God, but which, even as such, as the corrupt decision which it still is in my own eyes, is accepted for God's sake, not mine, as obedience and righteousness. This is justification.

I myself never can or should see myself and my work in this new predication. I can and may see the justification of my wicked deeds only in Christ, as an alien righteousness and not my own. This means that I can and may only *believe* it as *my* justification. Believing means seeing oneself as one can do only when looking away from self to Christ, to God's revealed Word in the totality in which it is law *and* gospel, and, of course, without looking back again as Lot's wife did [cf. Gen. 19:26], without looking back again to self. To look back is to see only a city that is burning, that is burning down; it is thus to be turned into a pillar of salt. I do not have my justification as I have myself, but as I have God, or concretely, as I have Christ through his Word and Spirit, i.e., as God has me, as he gives himself to me, as he reveals himself to me, as in free and majestic disclosure and condescension he is my God. I have my justification as *grace*, invisible, hidden, grounded only in God's good-pleasure, always coming to me and coming into force for me by his resolve. If I had it visibly as I have myself, then I could lay my hand on my work as a good work which I have done and whose goodness is my goodness, and the honor of my justification would be at least God's honor *and* mine. The honor of *the* justification which I have only by faith as invisible grace in spite of my wicked work, the honor of forensic justification, is obviously God's honor alone. The command comes to me as a revelation of him who alone will have the honor. Thus faith in the forgiveness of sins, in justification, is my Yes to God's goodness as I completely look away from any past, present, or future goodness of my own, including that of my act of faith. I will not see in the human spontaneity of this act of faith a correlate of what God's does for me, a merit. Faith is subjection to the sentence imposed on my work, which is the last word of my self-knowledge and which embraces the act of faith too. It is not as though faith were the missing good work, the pure act of obedience that finally comes on the scene. I know of my faith nothing other or better than what I know of the rest of my deeds. Our faith as an act of our own spontaneity is notoriously enmeshed in the corruption of our decision. That my faith is accepted as true faith is something that again I can only believe—believe as I believe in the miracle of the divine mercy. How can it be anything other than a miracle that it is true that through the weak, childish, insincere, and partial faith that we find in ourselves we have the forgiveness of sins and justification? I am justified by faith to the degree that in the darkness of my heart, as which I have also to understand my faith, Christ dwells and is enthroned; to the extent that in him the work of God, the act of the Holy Spirit, takes place. To that extent I am really justified, so that being justified has to mean that against all my knowledge of myself, and as I can know myself only as one who is accused and condemned, I am a doer of the Word. For I do God's Word to me in the decision of my act when I allow that God is right in face of myself and my deeds, when I cling to the fact that this God who opposes me in his command does not let me fall in my unrighteousness any more than a father does his child, but counts me his even in my unrighteousness, so that both in allowing that God is right and also in clinging to him I affirm his goodness and not my own. In this way my action, my decision, is the doing of his will.

It is perhaps not superfluous to back up this summary of the doctrine of justification with some widely scattered voices of the Christian church from very different historical backgrounds. We begin with two Russian Orthodox theologians: Constantine Aksakov (d. 1860): "Every Christian is sinful as man but his way as that of a Christian is right," and Alexei Chomiakov (d. 1860): As the church "is conscious of its inner union with the Holy Spirit, it gives thanks for all the good of God who is the only good, ascribing to itself and man nothing but the evil which in him opposes the divine work, for man must be weak in order that God may be strong in his soul" (*Östl.Chrt. I*, 93 and 168).[9] We then turn to Luther

> Thus are works forgiven, are without guilt, and are good, not by their own nature, but by the mercy and grace of God because of the faith which trusts on the mercy of God. Therefore we must fear because of the works, but comfort ourselves because of the grace of God.

(EA, 20, 211).[10]

It is no accident that precisely at this point on our way I need to quote, i.e., to confess that not alone but only in the consensus of the Christian church do I adopt the position I do. Here if anywhere it is appropriate to note again the great caveat with which alone one can present and hear the doctrine of sanctification, i.e., the recollection that in this doctrine we appeal absolutely to the only valid authority, to that which in the thesis at the head of the first chapter we called "the reality of the divine command." This must speak for itself if we are to speak aright here. If it did not, our most zealous concern to speak aright could achieve only a construct that is weaker than the weakest house of cards. Even more boldly than [when] we spoke of the original electing love of God and the divine uncovering of human transgression, we must here presuppose the mercy of God which does not remove but brackets our human condemnation. We must presuppose the vicarious satisfaction of Christ and his righteousness that is imputed to us. We must take into account the faith which takes with full seriousness that condemnation and accepts the alien righteousness of Christ that is promised to it. We must take into account our own faith in which we can never believe in ourselves but only against ourselves. To take into account the Word and Spirit of God is to take grace into account, as we here do in a particularly pregnant way. As far as we are concerned in relation to grace, it is thus to *pray*.

[9]*Ostliches Christentum, Dokumente I, Politik*, ed. H. Ehrenberg with N. v. Bubnoff, Munich, pp. 93, 168. Aksakov (1817–1860) and Chomiakov (1804–1860) were Slavophile leaders, the former as politician, the latter as theologian (p. 373).
[10]WA, 6,216 (*Of Good Works*, 1520); *Works of Martin Luther*, Philadelphia Edition, 1943, 2, p. 203.

The Word is God's Word, the Logos eternally made flesh, yet not on that account given up into our power. And the Spirit is God's Spirit, blowing where he wills [cf. John 3:8] and not where we will. And the faith which, when it is a matter of hearing the gospel in the command, seems to offer the key to the whole, is not for everybody [cf. 2 Thess. 3:2], not only because even as our own weak and feeble act it is the greatest and most difficult work of all, nor because, seen from outside, it always seems to be an absurd grasping after the impossible, but also and even more so because, as the faith that really justifies, it is no more and no less than the all-decisive event of the love of God which he owes to no one, ⌐and because through it¬ Christ ⌐is¬ in us in the Pauline sense of the phrase.|

We can and must remember that grace is assigned to us, that we need no arts or ruses to participate in it and thus to hear and say as truth all that we have said and heard. It is a matter of *grace,* however, and even though it would make no sense to look about for complicated ways to lay hold of it, this does not imply that we need to use only some simple means but rather that there are no means at all, that it is pure gift, and that as such it comes to us with the full freedom of the giver.

We can and do also remember that we are not alone when we venture to count on the Word and Spirit of God as witnesses to the truth of what has been said and heard. In venturing it we stand with the Christian *church,* which is none other than the community of justified sinners, of sinners justified in Christ, and in which we do not make the venture in our own name but by command and under promise. The Christian church is the place where we must at any rate make the venture—it remains a venture even when made in obedience—to follow the summons: Believe in the Lord Jesus Christ [cf. Acts 16:31]. The Christian church cannot guarantee what obviously has to be guaranteed here, namely, the sanctifying reality of the divine command itself. Even in the Christian church no one can believe for another, no one can safely lead another past the dark abyss of offense, unbelief, disobedience, and the despair that does not hear the gospel but only the law, which without the gospel is certainly not the true and divine law—the despair that might always be a mark of our rejection, since God never owes it to anyone, never owes it to us, to elect us instead of rejecting us. Precisely in the church we know that deep down at the decisive point we can appeal only to the Lord and not to the church.|

We can and do also remember that in counting on the Word and Spirit of God we do no other than take seriously our *baptism* as the sign of promise which is given to each of us personally and truly as a sign of promise for our thinking, and therefore with epistemological significance. In this respect the gift of baptism is that I may and should regard myself as one to whose existence it belongs, no matter what may be his experiences or the results of his self-knowledge, to make a comforted beginning with grace, i.e., with the knowledge of God, and with the same comfort to think from that starting point. The comfort, however, again cannot mean power over the Lord of baptism, as though in baptism we were placed in some kind of "it" and not placed in the hands of a "he." Nor is baptism fulfillment, for in it we are commended to the grace of God. Grace means, however, that we should hear the word of fulfillment through it.

When we hear this word through it, then we must always remember that he who stands there must see to it that he does not fall [cf. 1 Cor. 10:12], or, in other words, that all hearing is a summons to hear again and not simply to be content to have heard. Certainly the evident truth is heard here. But what is evident is a participial and therefore a verbal form. Here the truth *becomes* evident. Like the manna in the wilderness it is a good thing that is given to be received and enjoyed, not conserved and stored away. When some people left part of it until morning, "it bred worms and became foul; and Moses was angry with them. Morning by morning they gathered it, each as much as he could eat; but when the sun grew hot, it melted" (Ex. 16:20f.). So it is with the evident truth of grace. We cannot lay our hands on God's Word and Spirit as they are given to us, but we live by the fact that God does not withdraw his hand from us. This is what I mean when I say that we must reckon here with the Word and Spirit of God in such a way that we can think and reflect only as we pray. That our thinking is not without an object but has an object can only be—if we ask how this can be—a matter of the answering of prayer. Without the answering of prayer we could understand theology at this central point only as a vessel with no content. In prayer alone is our membership of the church, our baptism, so powerful that the freedom of the Spirit to blow where he wills [cf. John 3:8] does not alarm us and we need not be afraid, just as God's people in the wilderness did not have to be afraid when they went forward to each new day with empty hands. It need hardly be said, I hope, that this too, and this precisely, is a direction that we cannot follow unless it is given us to do so from above [cf. John 3:27].

5

God's command *justifies* us as it judges us. For God's command, the sentence that it imposes on us, is included in God's promise that even and precisely as those that are condemned by him we are just before him, we are not repulsed by him because of our sins but upheld by him, we are not let fall in our corruption but carried by him. "Jesus receives sinners"[11] [cf. Luke 15:2] and "as you are, you may come."[12] This is the gospel which comes to us in and with the command. Yet we have not fully described the reality of the divine command if we do not engage in

[11]E. Neumeister (1671–1756), *EKG* 268.
[12]From the first verse of the hymn "Kehre wieder" (1833) of K. J. P. Spitta (1801–1859).

a final act of reflection and state expressly that this gospel comes to us only in the *command* and through the *command*. God's command, as, recognized or not, it meets us at every moment of our action as the judgment under which we are set, says two things about us according to what we have stated thus far. First, it says that we are in the wrong before God, and second, it says that as those who are in the wrong before God we are just before him. Since God by his command primarily claims us as his own, counts us his, sees us as those who belong to him and are loved by him, two things are necessarily included. First, as those who are thus claimed by him we cannot help but see clearly how totally we fail to meet this claim. Second, in spite of this failure we cannot help but see in the same claim God's inconceivable and unmerited good-pleasure in us. The two statements, however, spring from the same root, and for this reason we cannot be content to understand them as mere statements. What God's Word says about us in this twofold sense it says *to* us. It is not just truth but truth spoken and heard. As it meets us, it does not continue standing over against us but grasps at us and determines us. Existence in the decision of our act, whose point is God's decision about us, existence under the twofold statement made concerning us, is a highly *determined* existence, an existence determined not by us but by God's Word. This *determination* of our existence by God's Word is according to our presuppositions the essence of our sanctification. It makes sense to subsume election, the knowledge of sin, and justification under the concept of sanctification, as we have done, only if what we are aiming at in all this is the determination of human existence by God's act as thus described, the grasping at us that takes place in and with all this.│

We could not in fact speak either of the knowledge of sin or of justification, and certainly not of God's love and our election, if we did not think of the faith in and for which all this takes place. And if in so doing we have reached the point where the reality of the divine command can only speak for itself, there can be no doubt, we hope, that, *when* it speaks for itself in its unique sovereignty, it speaks *to* us, that real faith, even though we can understand it only as God's work on and in us, is our *own* faith, our absolutely miraculous *being with* that reality in a way that does not derive from our self-determination, our *obedience*. Election, the knowledge of sins, and the forgiveness of sins, in a word, grace, becomes an event when we say Yes to it. Since this Yes of ours is the last and greatest miracle of grace itself, we do well to see to it that before ourselves and others we ground this Yes of ours at only one point, derive it from only one point, and with it stand only at one point—the point where we do not understand ourselves, where we do something which seems to call in question all our other acts as it itself seems to be called in question when seen from the standpoint of these other acts, and yet which is still undoubtedly our own Yes. And if it were not spoken, if our faith were not obedience, the obedience of *faith*, yet still obedience, it would not be faith at all, and all that we have thought and said about election, the knowledge of sin, and the forgiveness of sin, would be without object. That we obey in faith and say Yes to God's Word is the determination of our existence by the command of God which meets us in the decision of our acts and decides concerning us and judges us. As God's Word determines us in this way, determines us for obedience, it is our sanctification. By this Yes of ours we do not in any way gain control over God. There is no cooperation here, no going to meet God, no merit on our part. It is in our hearts and on our lips [cf. Deut. 30:14], it is a characterization, modification, and orientation of our sinful existence and act by the reality of the divine command itself, which does its work by and of itself alone. It is the act of the Word and Spirit whose honor we cannot even partially, even the least little bit, snatch away for ourselves. But in virtue of this act of the Word and Spirit it *is* our Yes, and this Yes is our sanctification.|

This Yes is to God's *grace*, as it is itself grace. But it is to God's *total* grace, i.e., not just to the gospel, but with the gospel to the law of God too. The grace of God is total in this way. The claim of God goes out with this totality. As we believe that God claims us, we accept the gospel. In all circumstances, even though our sin were as scarlet [cf. Isa. 1:18] and his law condemned us to hell, it is peace, joy, and blessedness to be claimed by God. But how can we believe without obeying, without affirming the law, without affirming that this God of the gospel claims us, that that grasp at us is made, that that hand is laid on us? I formulated this final meaning of sanctification as follows: "God establishes our sinful action as the work of obedience."[13] Two statements are needed to elucidate this. According to what we said in subsections 3 and 4, sanctification means the *knowledge and forgiveness* of sin: knowledge obviously by the law and forgiveness by the gospel of one and the same Word of God. What does it now mean that our sanctification takes place in our own Yes to this whole Word of God, to this total grace? What does this affirmation mean? At root it obviously means that we affirm our forgiven sin as *known* and our known sin as *forgiven*. In this respect the meaning of the concept "affirmation," i.e., "obedience," obviously shows itself to be a two-sided one. As we believe in the concrete unity of the divine judgment, i.e., as we see our life under the divine judgment in this unity; as, seeing it, we live it; as, placed under the divine judgment in this unity we proceed from the decision of this moment to that of the next, we obey, we are sanctified.

a. Our forgiven sin is *known*. Only of my forgiven sin do I know that it is known, that it is sin. As it is forgiven me I know it. To be justified by God is to be awakened from the sleep of the view that my act is or can be justified by itself. To have peace by and in God's grace is to have no peace in self. It is God's goodness that calls us to repentance (Rom. 2:4).

[13]See p. 87.

Far from making the knowledge of sin an outdated or less serious matter, the gospel is the very thing that makes it serious. We have seen that sin takes place when, loved by God, we do not love him in return. The gospel is the confirmation of God's love even in the midst of our corrupt decision. If I hear that in my sin and treason I am the child God loves, I then come to realize what an apostate and traitor I am. How could I know that I sin without knowing against whom I sin? I know this, however, only as God's Word is gospel, as my sin is forgiven me. Then I *do know* it, however, and I do so with the qualified knowledge in which I know my own reality, so that my knowledge of sin is also the confession of my guilt and need; the confession that I see myself accused and mortally imperilled by my transgression of the command; the confession that my sin pains me in the double sense that I repent of it as my guilt and bewail it as my need. And beyond both these things the confession that I cannot myself remove it, that there is in me no Archimedian point from which I can master it, that I have no resources with which to escape the disquiet into which it plunges, not something in me but myself, that I am referred instead—kyrie eleison—to the mercy of God. In other words, that I know that I *need* the forgiveness that is given to me, that in face of the corruptness of my decision I have no option but forgiveness if the corruptness and its consequences are not to take their course. When it is truly heard, the gospel forces me to take my transgression seriously as guilt and need, and also to take myself seriously as a transgressor, i.e., as one who of himself can be only a transgressor. To take sin, and myself as a sinner, seriously, is not something that I achieve of myself but something that is thrust upon me by the gospel. It is one side of the determination of my existence by God's Word, of the characterization of my sinful act by the command that encounters me, of my own movement as this is started by the divine judgment in which I say Yes to the grace of God. This Yes means taking the place that is proper to one who can be helped only by mercy, who has a choice only between condemnation and forgiveness, and who then comes to realize that it is not his own choice if he is forgiven. The peace of God creates, not an idle and futile lack of peace in us, but one that is necessary and salutary, the whole distress that Paul depicted in Romans 7. It sees to it that we are not released from it, that we are plunged into this disquiet, that we move forward to the decision of the very next moment. As it thus sets us in repentance, my sinful action is established as the work of sanctification. A good work is always a work of penitence, a work that is done in that repentance and distress and with that cry for mercy. The work of my very next moment is a sanctified work when it is a work of penitence in this sense, when it is the work of one who, just because he has received forgiveness, has accepted the verdict passed on him.

b. Our known sin is *forgiven*. Only of known sin do I know that it is forgiven me. As it is seen, I know it. Real condemnation by conscience takes place when there is real pardon by God. Real lack of peace in self takes place when there is peace through God's grace. Through God's *total* grace, we must emphasize. Peace through grace cannot mean the abolition, but only the establishment of the law, of the law that judges us by holding out before us what God wills from us. That we are forgiven does not mean that it ceases to hold this out before us, but rather begins to do so. To be set in penitence, as happens precisely through forgiveness, is thus again to be awakened out of the sleep of a false opinion, this time the opinion that the corruption of my decision is a kind of final necessity. Though my self-knowledge knows no word that can lead me beyond the fact that I failed, and fail, and will fail, the gospel tells me of a knowledge beyond the limits of my self-knowledge by which what the law holds out before me has another aim than that of forcing me into repentance. The forgiveness without which there is no penitence is God's denial, his nonacknowledgement, of sin. We accept this divine No when we really accept the judgment passed on us by God's command. God's nonacknowledgment of sin means positively the establishment of his good will. God affirms this will by not imputing our sin to us [cf. 2 Cor. 5:19]. If my sin is forgiven me, this means that I am recognized and acknowledged as one who is free, and summoned to do God's will.

Our acceptance, then, is more than acceptance of God's judgment. It denotes a movement of our existence that is not adequately covered by the word "penitence." The Greek word *metanoia* expresses the missing second aspect. Because only forgiven sin can really be recognized and confessed sin, the recognition and confession, if they are to be serious, are not possible without *conversion*. We have understood the law badly if we have not understood that, as it humbles us, it summons us to change from a corrupt decision to a correct one, to readiness to do better next time. It really humbles us only through the gospel. But the gospel, which in spite of our corruption calls us to fellowship with God, tells us about God's antithesis to our corruption, about the miracle of the holy one who comes down to the unholy. In face of this miracle, if we truly grasp it as such, in face of the mercy shown us if we have understood it as such, in face of the very different place which is obviously that of the God of the gospel who calls us to himself by the gospel, we cannot possibly be content with our known sin but are set in conflict with it, i.e, in conflict with ourselves, since we always find ourselves to be sinners, in conflict for God against ourselves. However it may be with us and whatever may be the limits of our self-knowledge, the law comes into force as a demand that we satisfy God's will, as an order to make a better decision, to deny ourselves as we have been, to put to death—mortification—the old man, ourselves as we know ourselves, in order—vivification—that the new man that I am in Christ, not in myself, may live. Contrition of heart and oral confession would undoubtedly not be real *metanoia*, real obedience, real determination by the divine command, if there were no satisfaction of works, no halt, disruption, or break in my sinful action; or, positively, if there were no intimation of the life of the new man, of my hidden life with Christ; if the same law that convicts me of my corruption did not hold out before me the right which I should do instead of the wrong and for which, no matter what else may be said about me, I am claimed; if I did not know that this right is required of me; if my action did not bear witness to this knowledge. Here again we have that qualified knowledge, ⌐practical (like all theological knowledge) and¬ not intellectualistic, in which I really know my own reality and which as such cannot possibly be an idle knowledge. This is the knowledge that because I am forgiven I can have no part in sin; I am as much sundered from it as is God himself who forgives me. Or, positively, it is the knowledge that I belong to God so that my will is pledged to God's will. "We are not our own, we are God's" (Calvin).[14]

This knowledge of my obligation, or of my freedom for God and against sin, is my conversion, or the satisfaction of works, which is the unavoidable other side of real submission to God's command. It, too, is not an act of self-reflection or self-determination, but, as I am forgiven by the gospel the law comes into force with its demand and puts me in this new position in which I must deny the final necessity of my own corruption and affirm a final freedom for my righteousness before God, not on the basis of a discovery that I have finally made in myself, but on the basis of the order which I am given by the law that has gone forth with the gospel, and which I have to take just as seriously as what the same law tells me, by means of my self-knowledge, about my inability to do anything good. This order does not point me to myself, of course, but to Christ. In him I am no longer the old man who must sin, but I am claimed as the new creature, the free man. Knowing myself in him, I must in fact let myself be told by the law: You can because you should! *Letting* myself be told this is the other side of the determination of my existence by God's Word, of the characterization of my sinful act by the command, of my own movement by grace. Grace does not just discipline me but puts me under discipline. Accepting this discipline, the discipline of the law, is the other side of the Yes to God's grace in which grace comes to completion. It means taking the place which belongs to one who has been shown mercy. It means going on to the decision of the very next moment as one who has accepted the order. Good works, then, are works of conversion, works done on hearing the appeal to the new man that I am, not in myself, but in Christ. When our action is done in this hearing, as sinful action it is established as the work of obedience. And as thus established, even though we cannot deny its sinfulness, it is sanctified work, work by which God will be lauded and praised as it is his will that he be by justified sinners.[15]

---

[14]*Inst.* III, 7, 1.
[15]Barth has here the marginal note: "Election—confession of sins—forgiveness of sins—acceptance of the order."

At this last point in our train of thought we must not omit to note in conclusion that all this has been said on the assumption that the reality of the divine command speaks *for itself*. Neither the knowledge nor the forgiveness of sin is given to us apart from this reality, nor is our faith, our obedience of faith that says Yes to grace, to our penitence, or to our conversion. The determination of our existence by the command, our new life in sanctification in which we move on from the decision of this moment to that of the next, is a being in relation to this reality. We have no control over the reality, nor have we, therefore, over its relation to our existence. Our sanctification, our new life, is, all along the line, hidden with Christ in God [cf. Col. 3:3]. Its manifestations are as such unequivocally manifest only to God, as they are really *its* manifestations only by God's act. The new life cannot be abstracted from the free, giving act of God: "in him we live and move and have our being" [Acts 17:28]. This life cannot be reinterpreted as a being, having, and doing of man distinguished from direct knowability from all his other being, having, and doing. We cannot be too cautious in handling all the concepts that might denote a third sphere between God and man and common to both. The Bible knows no such sphere. It knows only the event of the incarnate Word and the quickening Spirit. In this event God is and remains the one who acts, the one who acts, of course, as the one who is. I have in mind the concept of "pneumatic reality." If this relates to the reality of the Holy Spirit, then it is as well to say that it never appears with direct knowability as a second reality of man alongside his secular reality. It is a qualification of the secular reality of our life but strictly a qualification from above, by God, and therefore one that bears witness to itself as a divine act but cannot be said to be our possession or attribute or position. If it is our position, if it *is* so in this way, i.e., by God's grace, then I speak factually on this basis, and he who has ears to hear, let him hear. But the statement or assertion that I speak out of pneumatic reality is an impossible one. In this connection we have already at an earlier point expressed our doubts about the too direct use of concepts like Christianity, Christians, and Christian.[16] To be Christian is to be *en Christo* and the term can be used to qualify human persons, things, and acts only if it is remembered that it refers to the relation which exists only as the reality established by God. The same applies—the same point is at issue—to the concept of the sanctified and the saints. In the Old and New Testaments holy denotes a divinely established relation in which man stands when he is determined thereto by God. Holy in the Bible does not mean devout or virtuous but separated by God.

It is divine separation when our action is sanctified, not a quality immanent in the action itself. Knowing the divine act of sanctification

---

[16]See above, pp. 33.

we can and should *offer* our action to God as penitence and conversion just as a sacrifice is offered (Rom. 12:2). But this offering, the work of the very next moment, is no less subject to the divine crisis than everyday acts. Cain, too, brought an offering [cf. Gen. 4:3−5]. Pagans also sacrifice on the basis of having heard something, but what they have heard is not God's command. In no case is it our intention that makes our action holy. ⌐Even the highest and purest sacrifice is not holy in itself nor is its offering as such.¬ Sacrifice becomes holy by the fact that God *accepts* it. If we have seen the concept of sanctification come to fulfillment in our own Yes to grace, we must emphasize again that it is grace when we say Yes to grace, grace that we *do* say Yes, and grace that we really say Yes to *grace,* that our action is not without an object or does not relate to some other object. If we want to abstract our penitence from God's acceptance of it, over which we have no control, then we have no means to differentiate its salutary disquiet from the useless disquiet of our own self-knowledge when this is left on its own. With our penitence as such, be it ever so sincere and serious, we cannot force the mercy of God which alone gives it meaning. Similarly, if we wanted to take our conversion alone, apart from God's acceptance of it, as obedience in disobedience, how could it be anything but self-deception to think that we are really converted? It is not at all true that God's mercy comes to us as *we* convert *ourselves.* The Word and Spirit of God guarantee the existence of the relation between the divine Yes and the human Yes. They *are* the guarantee as they themselves are the relation. The existence of the relation is not guaranteed directly but *indirectly—* indirectly inasmuch as we must always go back to God's own gracious will and take refuge in *prayer* to find it guaranteed. On the question whether there might also be a direct guarantee of the relation, the ways of Roman Catholic and Protestant thinking divide, although in the course of centuries the distinction has become suspiciously blurred on the Protestant side. Instead of being content to seek the reality of sanctification in the eternally hidden act of divine election, many have thought, and still think, that they should seek it and can find it in some supposedly real saintliness of man which can be perceived and guaranteed directly apart from prayer and the answering of prayer. We should know what we are doing when we play around with possibilities of this kind, when we think along lines such as these. It is hard to see how we can come to do so except on the ground of Roman Catholic presuppositions about God, man, sin, grace, and, above all, the church. On that ground everything is clear when we do it. For everything is in advance, in a masterly way, posited on the direct guarantee of *hagiōsynē* which supplements if it does not replace the guarantee by God. Among us everything is unclear when we do not dare to follow the reformers any more in radically renouncing any such direct guarantee and thus being all the more certain of the indirect and only true guarantee.

Karl Heim in the introduction to the second edition of his *Glauben und Leben*, pp. 29f.[17] brings against the theology represented here the objection that its system of coordinates is incomplete, since it does not have alongside God and man, eternity and time, the third dimension in which there is put on certain men and actions the note or accent of eternity, the concrete speaking of the Holy Spirit as witness is borne to this in the New Testament. Now I believe that I, too, see this problem of the third dimension. I could have described (§§5 and 6) the problem of certain men and actions more clearly than Heim does as *the* problem of theological ethics and theology in general. But in reply I should have to say that theology has not so much to answer this problem as [rather] to recognize that it is posed—posed by the fact that God himself has given and gives and will give the answer here with unrepeatable truth and uniqueness. Theology itself certainly cannot give this answer since it is not the Holy Spirit and has not been appointed the vicar of the Holy Spirit. Precisely because it is a matter of the speaking of the Holy Spirit in this third dimension, I fail to see how we can come to concern ourselves with this coordinate which is the point of intersection of the other two. It is God's act alone to *draw* this third coordinate and thus to posit the point of intersection of the other two. All philosophy, and all theology too, can only *point* thankfully to this act by bringing to light the first two coordinates, if this action for which it is empowered by revelation is not to be without object. Things can be different only if we think that the concrete speaking of the Holy Spirit, the accent of eternity on certain men and actions, is given directly in the reality of the church or—and this surely cannot be Heim's view—in the secret inspiration of individual believers. If we believe the church and if we believe the communion of saints as the *place* and *means* of revelation but not as revelation itself, then all that theology can do is confess the hiddenness of revelation, the hiddenness of our life with Christ in God [cf. Col. 3:3], by refraining from trying to speak into or out of this hiddenness, by being fully content to *bear witness* in the two-dimensionality in which men can speak of God, by leaving the concrete speaking of the Holy Spirit to the Holy Spirit himself. How can theology, however much it might be a theology of faith, ignore the caveat that all that it says out of that reality is in vain if God does not add his Amen to it, ⌐that it *cannot* establish and certify what it says by claiming that it says it out of that reality? It is established and certified thus when God adds his Amen to it, but not otherwise. We cannot link a claim to this Amen with what we say.⌐ Is the caveat unimportant then? Is not the divine Amen itself revelation? When we observe the caveat—and what Protestant theology will refuse to do so?—do we not admit that only revelation itself speaks out of that reality, that the

[17]Cf. Karl Heim, *Glauben und Leben, Gesammelte Aufsätze und Vorträge*, Berlin 1926, 1928[2], pp. 29ff., esp. p. 32; on this cf. K. Barth, "Brief an Karl Heim," *ZdZ* 9 (1931), 451–53.

concrete speaking of the Holy Spirit cannot be repeated, that we can engage only in a respectful, loving, and relevant speaking around it? If it is true, and we have heard it said often enough in recent years, that the essence of Protestant theology in distinction from Roman Catholic theology is to be a theology of the cross and *not* a theology of glory, not a theology that thinks it can inform itself about the mystery of God and speak the Word of God itself, then precisely in the question of that relation, which becomes a burning one in sanctification as nowhere else, it must not become a theology of *impatience.* ⌐Our counterquestion to the theology of pietism, then, is whether it is not a theology of impatience and we believe that Protestant theology¬ has to recognize[18] that seeing the coincidence of the divine Yes with the human Yes is an *eschatological* reality, Jesus Christ himself, whose action does not finally denote a third coordinate but the end and also the beginning of the first and second coordinates of our thinking about God and divine things.

[18]Text A: "It has to recognize . . ."

CHAPTER TWO

The Command of God the Creator

§7

THE COMMAND OF LIFE

God's command applies to me inasmuch as I exist as a creature. As he speaks to me, he acknowledges me to be alive. And as he wills something from me, he commands me to live. I cannot be told this without understanding that the life of the creature in general is ⌐willed by God⌐[1] and is an object of respect.

1

In the first chapter we spoke about the reality of the divine command as such. We saw how it becomes manifest to us in the concrete decision of our acts. We saw that precisely as God's command it is a very concrete and definite command. We saw to what extent its presence is our sanctification. We now take up the task of analyzing this command from the general standpoint that it meets us in the medium of our own human reality. We worked out in §3 a plan of approach to this task. In doing theological ethics here, we will keep to the same concrete understanding of human reality as emerges naturally from God's Word. This Word is the Word of God as Creator, Reconciler, and Redeemer. We recall that this division is necessary on the one side because it denotes the categories above which there are no higher apart from God's name in general. We also recall that the division can have only logical and not ontic significance. To understand God's command as the command that is given to God's man we have thus entered a definite and integrated path, but at every step on this path we shall have to understand the

[1]Text A: "necessary"

command as one and the same even though it meets us in specific forms at the three different points, for according to our deliberations in the first chapter there is only one real command, namely, that which is given to each of us in our own here and now. Ethics does not have to set up the command of God, this one real command. It has to see it as already set up on the presupposition that it is always set up in the life of a *man*. We do not have to show what is commanded us. In this regard no ethics can intervene between God and men. We have to show rather what the fact that we are commanded means, or, conversely, what it means for the fact that we are commanded that the command is given within our human life.

Man is the creature of God. This is where we start. If we know that we have to do with *God*, when in the decision of our acts we are set under the judgment of a command, then we know also that we have to do with our Creator, with him who is in such a way and so much our Lord that our existence over against him offers us no occasion to have even the least reservation about his lordship, let alone to oppose him as Prometheus opposed his Zeus. He does not meet us on the basis of a great or even perhaps the greatest power confronting a small or even perhaps the smallest power, but on the basis of power confronting absolute impotence. We exist, but only from him. He holds us over the abyss of nothing as truly our Creator out of nothing. It is his free goodness that we have our own reality, the reality of our life, alongside and outside his reality. This neither is nor will be, however, anything but a creaturely and therefore a secondary reality which originally is not ours but his, and which never for a single moment does not need the renewing of his free goodness. We do not know the command as command—and it is then no wonder that we do not know how seriously it judges us—if we do not understand it as the command of the Creator and do not understand ourselves, who are subject to it, as his creatures. The claim of the command is one of *right*, for we belong to him who commands from the very first. The claim of the command is *inescapable*, for we have no place where we might command, or co-command, ourselves, our mere existence being a witness to the majesty of him who commands us. The claim of the command is *emphatic*, for he who commands here is not tied to our existence but we are to his, and he truly exercises penal authority over us.

We should not weaken the significance of the command by forgetting that it is always the command of God the Creator and always applies to us also as creatures. It does not begin to apply to us as transgressors and as those who are reconciled again to God; it applies to us already as those who exist. Our existence as such is not a hiding place where, appealing to our ignorance of good and evil and free from God's command, we think we can be left alone. The command obviously comes already to Adam and Eve in paradise before the fall. This is how it always is. The command already seizes us in our existence ⌜as such.⌝ It is inadvisable,

Theology

EDITORS: THE REV. CANON JOHN DRURY THE REV. CANON DAVID E. JENKINS DR JAMES MARK

SPCK HOLY TRINITY CHURCH
MARYLEBONE ROAD LONDON NW1 4DU

From the Editors

PTO

We send you herewith for review:

    Karl Barth   Ethics

Date by which review is requested: as discussed

Suggested total length: words.

Please put at the head of the review in this order (1) the title of the book (and subtitle if any); (2) the name of the author(s) or editor(s); (3) the publisher and the year of publication; (4) the number of pages, and (5) the price.

E.g.

Canterbury Pilgrim BY MICHAEL RAMSEY SPCK 1974
x + 188 pp. £3.25
New Testament Christianity for Africa and the World *Essays in honour of Harry Sawyerr* Edited by MARK E. GLASSWELL and EDWARD W. FASHOLE-LUKE SPCK 1974 xxii + 221 pp. £5.95

Contributors are asked to submit copy in typescript (double spaced) and send it to the editors at the above address. We assume that you will be content to leave the proof reading to us. unless you inform us to the contrary.

Every contributor of an article or review will receive a copy of the number in which it appears.

Many thanks for taking this on. I shall be
interested to see the comments of a non-Barthian
on Barth. You may be in the same position as I
am in relation to Wagner: that is, you may find
him exciting but have your reservations.

I haven't read much bBarth myself, but what
I have read on the political and social questions
suggests fartoo much of an approach from what
he claims as revealed truth , with insufficient
knowledge of the substance of the problems he
discusses. I shall be interested to see how
concrete you finds his thought on ethics.

124/? 126² 494

29/9/81

then, to construct an antithesis between the command of the Creator and the command of Christ. In Christ we have to do with the Creator and in the Creator we have to do with Christ. What the Creator really commands is not a "natural" but a Christian command, and what is really a Christian command is an order of creation. All abstractions between the "natural" and the Christian command lead to a weakening of either the one or the other and therefore necessarily of both. In the shadow of an order of creation regarded as not Christian and a Christian order regarded as not natural the hubris of man usually flourishes, assuring itself of a sphere where man does not come into judgment. No such sphere exists and the area of creation is least adapted to provide one. The command of God always entails a question to the whole man, an attack on the whole man, a promise for the whole man. It is always to be understood as a defect of our hearing of the command, not a defect or division of the command itself, if the command of creation and the Christian command seem to collide. The goodness of God is one. So, then, is the goodness which causes us to exist and the goodness which opposes forgiveness to our transgression. We thus investigate the command of God the Creator with the expectation of hearing God's total command. We may not hear it totally, but it will still be the total command.

It is the total command from the specific standpoint that we understand ourselves, those whom the command addresses, to be *created by God*. It applies to us even as such and already as such. We have to understand the command, too, to be directed to us as such. We realize that ethics is not called upon to establish *what* is commanded us. What is commanded us is and will be established by him who commands here, and no general moral truth, no matter where it comes from, must intervene between him and us with the claim to be this "what." There are, however, unavoidable and generally valid *components* of this "what" which arise as the command is given to us, to *man*, and we must try to guard against caprice in selecting these components by seeking to grasp and structure the concept of man in terms of the Word of God directed to man. As, then, we start with man as the creature of God, we obviously run up against the concept of *life* as the first of the components of what is commanded. My own life is always included in what is commanded. There are, of course, limitations. There are more precise definitions which remind us that what is commanded comprises more than my life and which thus warn us against advancing this standpoint as *the* standpoint and forgetting that when we speak about the command of life this is not the "*what*" of the command but only a specific, unavoidable, and generally valid *modification* of the "what." This modification is clearly restricted, or needs to be supplemented, for (1) my own life is not what is commanded as such but only a *component* of what is commanded, (2) the reference is to my life as something *commanded* and not as something to which I have a claim, over which I have control, and of which I have an unequivocal concept, and (3) the life at issue belongs only secondarily to me but primarily and originally to God, by whose command I have to let myself be told how far it is in fact my own life. We shall have to speak about what this limitation of the concept means for our understanding of it. Apart from this limitation, however, it has also a positive side, and we must speak about this first. |

At this point we come up against the trends in philosophical ethics which are usually called *hedonistic, utilitarian*, and *naturalistic*, and which are characterized in modern times by the names of the English writers J.S. Mill and Herbert Spencer,[2] the French writers Jean-Marie Guyau and Alfred Fouillée,[3] and, in very different ways, the German writers F. Nietzsche, E. Haeckel, and A. Schweitzer.[4] The feature common to all these thinkers is the orientation of ethics to the concept of *life* no matter whether they are thinking of physical or spiritual life, of individual or social life, of the will for life or reverence for life. I cannot see the relevance of the rigorism with which W. Herrmann[5] would remove the affirmation of the necessity of life from ethics as a purely natural and therefore a premoral thought. On the other hand it is one of the advantages of the ethics of Schlatter that in the fourth part, under the title "power," he can do justice to the concern of the ethical naturalists and accept it with all its implications.[6] The man who is claimed by the moral command as the command of God does not begin only above the line that distinguishes him from a purely natural creature. Nor does his claiming by the command begin only here (and we must let ourselves be told this by the ethical naturalists). The danger of an elegant, a far too elegant distinction between moral and natural will and conduct is that man's life, to the extent that in spite of all elegant ethics it is contantly lived below that line, is abandoned to a naturalistic ethics of chance and circumstance. We have to understand the command in its relation to real human action. But real human action, irrespective of its moral character, is always a life-act too. The fact that it is this must not be suppressed in determining what is ethical. The ethical has to be considered and evaluated in this respect as well. The command is given to us not only as the law that encounters us (we shall have to get to know it in this form in

---

[2]Cf. J.S. Mill, *Principles of Political Economy with Some of Their Applications to Social Philosophy*, London 1948; new impression in two vols., University of Toronto Press, 1965; also *On Liberty*, 1859; also *On Utilitarianism*, London 1961. H. Spencer, *Social Statics. . .*, London 1968; also *A System of Synthetic Philosophy*, 10 vols., London 1860—1896 (*The Principles of Ethics*, vols. I and II, 1879).
[3]J. M. Guyau (1834—1888), *La morale d'Epicure et ses rapports avec les doctrines contemporaines*, Paris 1878; also *La morale anglaise contemporaine*, Paris 1879; also *Esquisse d'une morale sans obligation ni sanction*, Paris 1885. A. Fouillée (1838—1912), *La liberté et le déterminisme*, Paris 1872; also *Critique des systèmes de morale contemporaines*, Paris 1883; also *L'Evolutionisme des idées-forces*, Paris 1890; also *La morale des idées-forces*, Paris 1908.
[4]See §1, n. 2 and 3 and §2, n. 4.
[5]Cf. W. Herrmann, op.cit., pp. 12, 14, 38, etc.; 1913[5] (1921), pp. 9, 11, 37, etc.
[6]A. Schlatter, op.cit., pp. 318—76; 1929[3] (1961), pp. 374—436.

the third chapter) but also and already, as it meets us (and it always does), in the fact that we are, that we live. It meets us originally and inescapably because it comes up against our existence, because it comes home to us, so that we have no chance to deny it. This is the concern of ethical naturalism, which in my view should be fully adopted precisely by a theological ethics.|

We shall not, of course, follow ethical naturalism—nor A. Schweitzer, who has recently taken this direction in a very distinctive and impressive way—to the extent that we cannot set up and accept the necessity of life as *the* standpoint of ethics. No standpoint here must seek to be tyrannically *the* standpoint. We simply have standpoints in the plural, or components of what is commanded. It is in this regard, it seems to me, that a theological ethics must be rigorous and pitiless in relation to naturalism, and not, as in Herrmann, by protecting the concerns of idealism. One of the components is the necessity of life. In this respect we must pay heed to naturalism. But if it tries to press a naturalistic imperative on us as *the* command, we have to reply to it, too, that this is *only* one *component* or modification of the command. Problems arise in naturalistic ethics, such as the relation between egoism and altruism which is discussed a good deal by the English authors. Because of its one-sidedness, instructive naturalistic positions exist, e.g., that of Nietzsche, which make plain the limitation of the naturalistic standpoint, just as there are others which show that the spiritualistic moralism of Herrmann for its part can be only one word and not *the* word, the *last* word. The same will have to be said when beyond naturalism and spiritualism we shall have to speak in the fourth chapter about the eschatological significance of the command, about the command as the command of promise. All these limitations point to the fact that ethics, precisely as theological ethics, does not have to speak an ultimate word but only a series of penultimate words. As we shall now show, the necessity of *life* is one such penultimate word, one unavoidable and generally valid standpoint from which the command, because it is given to *man,* has to be understood.

2

What *life* is we know originally only as we know the fact of our own life. My knowledge of the life of my fellows, and, with different degrees of clarity, the life of animals and plants, not to speak of a real or supposed knowledge of the reality of life in general, is an analogous knowledge going back to my knowledge of my own life. In the strict and primary sense of the term, however, we do not, theologically speaking, know even our own life originally. We know it because God addresses us and acknowledges that we are alive. Four points are to be noted here which, together, give us a full concept of life.

1. As God addresses us, he acknowledges, and we are clearly and

legitimately told, that we *exist* and that we are *distinct from God*. If we were nothing, or if conversely we were God, there would be no Word of God that comes to us, is spoken to us, and is heard by us. God's *Word* as such constitutes our knowledge of the reality and autonomy (however understood) of our existence in distinction from the being of God. As *God's* Word it also constitutes, of course, our knowledge of the absolute dependence in which we are real and autonomous in relation to God, the knowledge of the creatureliness of our existence. The reality and autonomy of our existence, understood with this caveat, is the simplest and most obvious meaning of the concept of life. To that extent the life that God ascribes to us by addressing us has a part in the concept of *being*. When we say that it has a part, we remember that being, and therefore life, belongs properly and originally to God alone, so that they are ours only by his goodness which allows us to take part in his life and being.

2. As God addresses, us, he acknowledges, and we are told, that each of us is somebody, this *specific individual* being. God's Word does not presuppose only a reality distinct from God but also difference, distinctness, and individuality in this reality. God's Word is, of course, a Word to all, but this means that it is a Word to the sum of all individuals and not to a totality, not to the reality that God has created and distinguishes from himself conceived of as a unity. God's *Word* as such constitutes my knowledge of the autonomy of my existence in distinction not only from God but also from all else that seems to exist alongside me with the same autonomy. As *God's* Word, of course, it constitutes also my knowledge of the relativity of the fact that I am this specific person. I am this, not in and by myself, not with a certainty which I can control, but through God and for God within the limits of the creature. The second thing that lies in the concept of life is, then, that life is something individual and specific. To that extent the life that God ascribes to us as he talks with us takes part in the concept of the *individual*. We say that it takes part in this, and remember that individuality, and therefore life, belong properly and originally to God alone, and belong to us only as a loan through his goodness, in virtue of which life outside him is real only through himself.

3. As God addresses us, he acknowledges, and we are told, that we exist in *time*, that we are caught up in the movement from a past through a present to a future. God's Word presupposes that we exist in a succession of different moments. This means two things: first, that our existence is identical with itself in a flow of moments, and second, that our existence, identical with itself, moves in a flow of moments. A word spoken to us, whether it be understood by us as information, question, or command, presupposes the ability to accept, answer, and obey it, and therefore the ability at least to be *the same* in a before and after (e.g., the before of the question and the after of the answer) and to be the same *in a before and after* (e.g., in the before of the command and the after of

obedience). God's *Word* as such constitutes my knowledge of the reality of a movement in which I find myself, but as *God's* Word it again constitutes my knowledge of the secondary creaturely character of time and therefore of my movement too. The third thing in the concept of life, then, is that life means existing in time and to that extent the life that God ascribes to me takes part in the concepts of *continuity* and *change*. In saying that it takes part, we say that immutability *and* actuality are qualities of God in which again his goodness allows us to participate within the limits of our creaturely reality.

4. As God addresses us, he acknowledges, and we are told, that an originality, however limited, is proper to our existence. It is not just that we are *the same* in a movement, the same *in a movement*, but that *we* are the same, *we* are in movement. We are subjects of continuity and change. God's *Word* cannot be directed to an individual being that is simply the channel or functioning organ of a movement that originates elsewhere. God's *Word* acknowledges that, within whatever limits, we are the origin of our movement. God's *Word* as such constitutes my knowledge of my autonomy in respect also of the continuity and change in which I find myself, my knowledge that is *my* continuity and change, although as God's *Word,* of course, it also constitutes my knowledge of the dubiousness, of the secondary creaturely character, of my originality. The fourth thing, then, in the concept of life is that my life exists where the movement of something which exists through God begins in and with itself. To that extent the life that is ascribed to me participates in the concept of *freedom*. It participates, for original freedom that is subject to no reservation, i.e., aseity, belongs to God alone and is loaned to us by his goodness.

Thus far concerning the relevant understanding of life in the present context. That I am alive is certainly not the only thing that I know on the basis of its being ascribed to me by the facts of the Word of God that comes to me. Yet on the basis of this presupposition I do know also that I am alive, that I exist alongside God in unrepeatable distinction and individuality, in movement, in a movement which is a predicate of the subject I which the divine Thou encounters in the divine Word and which is finally compelled by this encounter to recognize itself and to take itself seriously as an I. All this stands in the brackets and under the caveat that the *Word* which ascribes this to us is *God's* Word, so that my life is real only within the limits of the creature. It is a created life, created out of nothing, conditioned absolutely by God's goodness. It is of doubtful reality when see in itself, even of illusory reality when seen in its unavoidable correlation with death. It is real only in relation to the Word. It is "upheld" by the Word (Heb. 1:3) which, being God's Word, is the eternal Word that cannot be given the lie by death. In this bracket and under this caveat it is real life.

This life of mine is obviously *placed* in the command of God that is issued to me, whatever it may be. God's command concerns my conduct, my action, my decision. Necessarily embraced in my decision is the fact that I *live*. As God wills something from me he commands—not only, of course, but also—that I *live*. What this means concretely is the content of the command which he himself determines, but which will always also mean life. Life is not in itself decision. But decision is also life, my life. Decision is not made apart from the substratum of a specific life-act. Because the command relates to *my* decision, I cannot abstract it from this life-act or this life-act from it. I cannot regard and treat the life-act as no more than neutral material for my decision. I must see my life itself as reached and affected by the command, in the sense that I also see my life-act as such set in the crisis of the command and realize that I myself am responsible for my life-act as such.|

Really to live is *necessary* and *good*, and is *obedience* to the Creator. The will to live is a good will. But this cannot be an unequivocal statement because the life that we accept and will is not the divine life but our own creaturely life. The will to live is a good will insofar as I will my life in the way that the Creator to whom it belongs would have it. This means already that my will is not good just because I will my life as such. It is good if I will my life as such in this particular relation, in obedience to the Will of God the Creator. Hence this specific relation relativizes the goodness of my will to live as such. It sets it in brackets and calls it into question. We shall be on guard, then, against thinking ⌜with the ethical naturalists⌝ that those forms of human action in which it is predominantly and blatantly concerned with the activation of the will to live are abstractly good acts and their opposites are bad acts. We can only say that in regard to *such* acts the *question* arises whether they are commanded or forbidden by the command of God the Creator, whether obedience or disobedience to the divine command may be seen in them, for in their way they obviously come under this command. In relation to no acts or modes of action have we any authority to *identify* the reality of the divine command and of obedience to God with them, or to *deny* this reality to them. They impress themselves upon us, however, as a likeness of this divine reality. They are obviously a subject for reflection and, if our action stands in question, they are an occasion for our readiness, for our readiness for the command of God that judges us to the extent that it is also the command of the Creator and therefore the command of life.|

Let us recall some of the forms of human action which may be regarded as a likeness of the reality of the command of the Creator, which force upon us the question of what is commanded precisely to the extent that what is divinely commanded is also our life, and which thus demand of us reflection, watchfulness, and readiness. Naturally it is not with any claim to fullness, but only by way of example, that we shall say what has to be said throughout the rest of the present lectures. Nor will it be with the intention of developing all the problems involved in these forms of human action, but only with that of hearing in relation to them the questions that result from the reality of the divine command as this is seen specifically as the command of the Creator. Nor—an urgent warning once and for all—should our interest focus on the unavoidable concretions or the equally unavoidable personally conditioned light in which they appear here, but solely and exclusively on the light of the command itself, which it is our task to see in the likeness when we have come to the point of trying to understand the command as the command that is directed to man.

My life-act takes place every moment in the factual unity of a double event which we usually call that of the soul and the body. Never in any connection do I live for myself and others except in the totality of my being as soul *and* body, although never also, of course, except in the differentiation of the two as well. Both apply here: there is neither one thing nor a third. That is, I am never in any respect only soul or only body, nor am I ever in the synthesis or unity of the two beyond their duality. Materialism and spiritualism, which try to understand man one-sidedly in terms of physis or psyche, are just as unsatisfactory as interpretations of the phenomenon of man as is the trichotomy of older Lutheran dogmatics, which with its distinction of soul and spirit thought it could dissolve the dualism in which we exist into a higher unity. My creaturely life is *unity* in distinction and *distinction* in unity. Will to live, then, is to be construed as will to live as physis *and* psyche. Never will it be either just the one or just the other. But never will it be dominated by either one side or the other. This consideration makes it right for us and indeed compels us to distinguish between the will to uphold and maintain our physical life and that of our psychical life, but also to keep in view that in each we do have to do with the other. Since corporeality is, in the biblical creation story, not only the end[7] but also the beginning of the ways of God, we shall begin with physis and then, as is proper, gradually mount up to psyche, being instructed in advance, however, that at all stages we have to do with the one whole man.

The simplest form of the will to live as physis and psyche is undoubtedly that whose negation or apparent negation may be seen most strikingly in the possibility of suicide. It is the simple *affirmation of life*, the readiness, indicated by a specific action or nonaction, to continue that movement from the past through the present to the future of which our life-act consists. Quite apart from its creatureliness, and as a sign of this, our life is bordered by death. Beyond this frontier we can seek its reality only in God, who has taken back to himself what belongs to him, and in whom we know that it is not lost as we believe in him. That our willing and doing, our life, is not absolute but relative may be seen palpably in the fact that we can make that simple affirmation of our

---

[7]A loose allusion to the famous saying of Oetinger that "bodily indestructibility is the end of the works of God." F. C. Oetinger, *Predigten. . .*, 5th ed., ed. K. C. E. Ehmann, Stuttgart 1902, p. 27.

life only relatively, for "in the midst of life we are in death."[8] Yet we can do it. We have means, effective only in certain connections and only for a while, not absolutely, but still means to evade death. We have also a number of very effective, and even absolutely effective, means to hasten or bring on death. This demonstrates the relative reality of our life, will, and action. The very simple affirmation of our life, or its real or apparent negation, undoubtedly falls already under the *command* of God. It cannot be said that the affirmation of life is intrinsically good. On the contrary, even this primitive will to live can be *the* sin, the revolt of the creature against the Creator, who has given us life not that we might affirm *it* but that in affirming *it* we might affirm *him*. |

To affirm life in obedience to the Creator can mean sacrificing it, not evading death, but hastening it and even bringing it on by inaction or action. When Jesus went up to Jerusalem, he obviously chose this possibility in opposition to the "this shall never happen to you" [Matt. 16:22] of his disciple. But obedience to God the Creator will always mean *also* affirming one's own life. For only affirmed life can be sacrificed. When we are tired of life (when perhaps whole peoples and cultures grow tired of life), when we think we should consent not to use the provided means of warding off death (there is an apparently purely passive and psychical dying), when we hazard our life (perhaps in sport or a duel or for scientific or technical ends, e.g., oceanic flights), when a whole nation resolves to expose itself to the fire of the cannon of another nation, then, apart from all other questions, there also arises *the* question what becomes of the affirmation of life which is not left to our own caprice but is required of us by the command of the Creator, and we always have to consider that our life does not belong to us but that in all its relativity it is loaned to us, that it stands at God's disposal and not at ours. If this "standing at God's disposal" can mean very concretely that we have to sacrifice it, we cannot sacrifice it unless we have first affirmed it. When men do apparently sacrifice their lives, the question always is whether it is in obedience to the command that they give free rein to death, whether their sacrifice is thus a genuine one, or whether it is not negligence or caprice. Death in an air crash or a mountaineering accident does not fall self-evidently under the concept of sacrifice any more than every simple affirmation of life falls under that of the required sustaining of life. In ethics we do not have to determine whether this or that is the commanded or forbidden affirmation or negation of life. God alone determines that. But we do have to consider the rule that the command of the Creator (even though very concretely it may be: Die!) always includes the command of life, the natural *fear* of death which even Jesus showed (and was, of course, obedient in so doing), and the *avoidance* of death that lies within our power. |

In this light the possibility of *suicide* must not be judged as occurs in

---

[8]Beginning of the antiphon *Media vita in morte*, 11/12th century.

most ethics despite all assurances to the contrary, but, more accurately, the divine command must be considered and its relation to *this* possibility. I do not think it right to say with Schlatter (p. 339) that the destruction of one's own life is always in conflict with the faith that lays hold of God, since it is a rejection of God's help, a seizure of unlimited power of control over ourselves, and a rejection of our allotted destiny.[9] How do we know whether this applies in an individual case? Are there not instances in which one might ask whether the direct opposite is not true? Since a public and representative figure is at issue, we are not violating the rights of a fellowman if we take the example of Kaiser Wilhelm II and ask (as Reichskanzler Michaelis has asked) whether he would not have done well in the Christian sense to demonstrate his concept of monarchy and people in the autumn of 1918, and perhaps give a different aspect to the whole subsequent course of affairs by seeking death in the nearest trench instead of offering Christian reasons for not doing so. But if we can and must ask in this way on both sides, if we have also to consider that it will not always be easy to differentiate true suicide indisputably from other related possibilities, we have to concede at once to Schlatter and all the other ethicists who make short work of this issue that the obvious question in face of the possibility of suicide will always be whether the command of life is not misunderstood in a more shattering way because the wrong decision, if it be such, is the final decision of the person concerned, a wrong decision on the very threshold of eternity. Does there not lie in the background here an absence of fear of death for which we have neither command nor occasion, a totally useless fear and a forbidden cowardice in face of life? Is not the first thing that God has put in our hands rejected here in a revolt that cannot be excused on the plea that continuation of the life concerned might have to be judged as an even worse revolt? It is precisely when we stand by the position that we should not judge people and actions but consider the command of God that, in face of the possibility of suicide, we cannot see too clearly that even a voluntary death, if it is to be right, must not rest merely on permission—for what does permission mean if we ourselves have to decide?—but must be done in conformity with the command. Even if the most concrete command is: Die! it presupposes the command: Live! *Is* this command really considered, *am* I ready to meet what is commanded, if for any reason I must take up my revolver? What does it mean for a nation or for a confession in relation to the ultimate question of its existence if statistics show an increase of this possibility within its ranks? The church's task in this regard cannot be to set up and propagate the doctrine that suicide is reprehensible and forbidden. If it does not do this, it must also decline to advance the opposing doctrine that suicide is permitted. Its task is to proclaim the command of God the Creator.

[9]Cf. A. Schlatter, op.cit., 1929[3] (1961), p. 391.

Genuinely leaving the verdict to him, it has to drive home the point that this command is the command of life, so that people are certainly disobedient to this command if, as obvious suicides or in some other way, they throw life away, if they bring disgrace on what they might, or perhaps should, merely sacrifice, and by doing so evade the sacrifice.

The next and very primitive form of the will to live is that which, according to the familiar formula, arises out of hunger and love. Our life is conditioned by the necessity of *metabolism* and by *sexuality*. In view of the unheard-of fact that we spend at least a third of our brief life asleep, I might mention the need of rest as a third primitive motif of life. The form of the will to live triggered by these conditions of existence is not ethically irrelevant and should not be treated as such, for scientifically considered—and there is no reason why it should not be considered scientifically—this is unquestionably the basic form of this will, and any deeper insight into one's own life, or that of others, or the reality of history, makes it disconcertingly clear how vigorously this form of our will persists and asserts itself in every higher form by means of refined, and even very refined, translations. Not everything, but a great deal in the phenomenon of man both individually and more generally may, in fact, be explained by the fact that we are continually hungry, sexually unsettled, and in need of sleep. Not by this alone, but by this too. And it is, in fact, no indifferent matter whether we understand this form of our will to live as a given factor which is self-grounded and not open to question, or whether we are clear that the will and action at issue here come into the crisis of the divine command because it is not in ourselves but as God's creatures that we have life, the life that even in its most refined expressions is also characterized by hunger and love and tiredness. We need not answer the question in what circumstances it is good to will and act in accordance with these conditions, to care for the satisfaction of the needs of hunger, sex, and sleep. God's command tells us when and how and how far this is good, and no ethics must interrupt at this point. It may be seen, however, that caring for these needs of life does at all events stand under the question how it relates to the command that is given us in and with this life and its relativity in relation to its Creator. To put this question is to say that activating the forces corresponding to these needs is not good in itself. Nor is it bad, of course. The *question* arises, however, whether it is good or bad. This question arises because the command of God always concerns this activation too and does not just claim it later.

One might see the question put in different ways. First, if it is a matter of the activation of needs grounded in our creatureliness, does one obey the command of life when this form of the will is perhaps acknowledged either theoretically or practically to be the dominant and possibly even the only dominant one? Does the possibility of a glutton like Lucullus or of a Don Juan in the erotic field mean the possibility of a man who is really "seeing life," as the phrase goes for such people? Are we really "living life to the full" when that activation is given that role? Again, can the economic outlook of a peasant of the old style, with its exclusive orientation to the satisfaction of needs, really do justice to the will to live when this is properly understood? Again, in individual and social life are there not obvious exaggerations of the will for satisfaction in this most primitive respect—exaggerations which no longer stand in any relation to the need that is to be satisfied, or, therefore, to the life-act to which the needs go back, so that we have a pointless enjoyment which no longer seems to be enjoyment but a stupid animality in which one cannot even admire the animal force? Again, are there not aberrant forms and corruptions of this will for satisfaction which, far from really satisfying the needs of hunger and love, threaten the life-act itself? We have in mind alcoholism and prostitution, and also the puzzling dilemma of so-called homosexuals. Yet the question of too little satisfaction arises as well as that of too much. It might be asked, e.g., whether the modern working class had to act as it did when one day, in distinction to the satisfied proletariat of an earlier age, it could no longer be content with the minimal existence allotted to it by employers but took mass measures to better its situation in the most primitive way. Again, if someone willingly—and this might mean with a weak will— stops taking what is needed by way of food or sleep, then, no matter how he may try to justify himself, this person will have to consider not only whether he can do this but also whether he should. And he who theoretically or practically accepts the great possibility of the voluntary celibacy that has often been practiced in the religious sphere, even though he do it for the kingdom of heaven's sake, cannot evade the question (Luther, as is well known, put it with particular emphasis) how this arbitrary nonsatisfaction of the need of sex really relates to the command of creation regarding human life, in which this need is included. Whether the modern vocation of the hunger-virtuoso, or the skills pursued in India regarding the nonactivation of these primitive forces, are really possibilities and not perverse impossibilities in the light of the command, can hardly be a question any more; they resemble, in this respect, some of the forms of activation. But if ethics is to keep to the point, then even in face of the most striking impossibilities it must keep on putting *questions*, or rather showing that they are already put. It should not hand out either good or bad testimonies. It should not judge. Knowing the radical antithesis of good and bad, it should point to the command of God which alone can really and properly judge, and which will tell each of us what is good and bad.

Another noteworthy form of the will to live may be seen in the will to be *healthy*. Our life does not merely will to be lived, i.e., preserved directly from death. Nor does it will to be lived merely in satisfaction of those primitive needs. It wills to be lived also in the maintaining and achieving of its possibilities, in *power*. To be healthy is to be in possession of one's physical and intellectual powers. It is to will what is necessary to achieve and assert these powers. It lies in the nature of the case that physical powers must constitute the direct object of this aggressive will, and intellectual powers the indirect object. Again it should be clear that in itself this will is neither good nor bad, but that the command is present here, too, with its question. The command enters in first where it is not perhaps considered that we owe our life that higher affirmation, the maintaining and activating of its possibilities. Are not air and light and water and mobility, etc., there to fulfill this higher affirmation, and is not hygiene, therefore, commanded of us? Perhaps concretely this or that diet? Perhaps this or that sporting activity? Perhaps prophylactically or in case of emergency the use of the services of a physician? *May we* leave these possibilities unused? We must ask this no matter what the answer may be. Nor can we answer lightly by boasting about the health of the soul apart from that of the body, as though man were not a unity of body and soul in which, to an uncontrollable extent, the whole is healthy or the whole is sick, and as though the boasting about the spirit might not easily be occasioned more by the indolence of the flesh than the vitality of the spirit. Not to speak of a resignation in principle to the possibility of sickness threatening our vital force and perhaps even our life—a resignation for which it might be hard to assume responsibility in face of the fact that Jesus constantly thought it necessary to set up against sickness the sign of the imminent kingdom of God in the form of his miracles of healing. A serious affirmation of life in this regard seems to be commanded, then, not only by creation but also by the hope of the resurrection. Yet the question of the command will also arise when people are perhaps too deeply concerned about what is good or not good for them, when sun, air, and water, the power of various herbs and fruits, the dynamism of hardened arm and leg muscles, and perhaps the possibilities of the medical art have become, in the consciousness of man, something like benevolent demons to which worship and belief are brought and which are served with a concentration and enthusiasm which make it seem dubious whether it really is a matter of the health of real man, i.e., the total man. May it be that concern for a very healthy body has given rise to a threat to the healthy mind? And should we not also consider whether it is perceived that what is always at issue is the health of *the* life which is not our own but is at the disposal of the Creator, so that health is unequivocally present only when his power of disposal is obeyed, which concretely might mean a strong indifference to the question of what is good for us, an intentional lack of concern about the desires of our dear body *and* our even dearer soul, a readiness to serve the same Creator with a suffering body and a suffering soul, not in strength but in weakness, not in health but in sickness, not living but dying? Resignation in face of sickness and the will to be healthy at all costs seem to be equally impossible in relation to the command. Both bravery in the upholding of health and bravery in surrendering it seem to be commanded in the same way by the command. That we live with force the life that is loaned to us is what it wills from us either one way or the other. We may rely upon the fact that its reality is unequivocal. Ethical reflection has rendered its service, however, when it has described this reality with approximate completeness.

We look higher when we understand the will to live as the affirmation of *pleasure*, as the will to be happy. It would make no sense, and would be a very superficial understanding of Kant, if we were not to apply the ethical question to this determination of the will to live too, but were to allow moral action to begin only where this determination is supposedly excluded. Supposedly, for a will to live in which it really is excluded exists only in books and not in real people. In all that we want we also want at least to be happy. Life wills to be lived intensively as well as extensivly. It wills to be lived as life and wonder, in its glory, in the whole unheard of beauty of its reality as this is grounded in the life of God. This is obviously in view when we are in the happy position of being able to confess with Hutten that it is a "pleasure" to be alive;[10] [this] is in view whenever a person may be happy, knowing that happiness exists and can be his too. In distinction from health, happiness is the *intensive* enhancement of the affirmation of life. In itself the will to be happy, too, is neither good nor bad, but it is a very problematical will. Why should it not be good? If it is true that life, being from God, is beautiful, why should not the living of this life mean that it is enjoyed, that it makes us happy? Why should not the affirmation of life be commanded in the sense of an affirmation of the happiness of life? What would gratitude to the Creator mean if we did not want to be merry when we can? On the other hand, why should not the same will be bad?—that is, when our pleasure in life is not, perhaps, pleasure in our real creaturely life but pleasure in a demonic abstraction, in a life of our own which is lived to its own glory and in whose affirmation and cultivation we take pleasure, but a bad pleasure, a pleasure that has nothing to do with gratitude, a pleasure through which we lose pleasure in our real creaturely life. We ourselves cannot possibly draw the line between good pleasure and bad. But it is in fact drawn. We always have at least a warning in this regard when the will to enjoy life collides with the affirmation of its primitive needs or the will to be healthy. But we have an even clearer warning when the will to be happy, instead of fulfilling itself as the affirmation of happiness already present, as the expression of joy one already *has*, must seek means of stimulation to summon up that joy which precedes the joy that is a mark of real joy in life, experiencing its fulfillment only after first establishing this presupposition. This can mean that our will has nothing whatever to do with our real life nor our pleasure with real pleasure. It is clear that from this

[10]Ulrich von Hutten, at the end of a letter (October 25, 1518) to Willibald Pirkheimer, cf. *Opera*, ed. E. Boecking, vol. I, Leipzig 1859, p. 217.

standpoint all the human possibilities that can be summed up under the concept of *festivity* are in a very serious crisis, for a special *apparatus* of joy is part and parcel of this concept. This apparatus can mean that man *is not* merry but wants to be and needs some spur to be so. His will to enjoy life does not spring from the self-evident gratitude of real creaturely life but from the self-will of that fictional demonic life. If, for example, one needs to be a little or very much drunk to be merry; if music is enough to evoke the mood (Saul and David [cf. 1 Sam. 16:23]); if the average man in the cinema or at the fairground can find joy only by the paradoxical detour of a little thrill at the danger, sin, or need of others; if a number of individuals or married couples who would be bored on their own gather together to overcome this unhappy state, and from 8 o'clock to 1, over a meal, etc., most unnecessarily share most unnecessary things under the title of fellowship; if a society (or even a university) anxiously searches the records for the possibility of a jubilee because it wants a celebration; if . . . . These are not bad things—we must not be too schoolmasterish—but they are things in face of which we have to ask whether they can be justified as an exercise of real joy in life or whether there is not something forced about them which makes real joy in life impossible. It *might* be different. We do not know what these things mean for others. For some they could perhaps be genuinely pleasurable, expressing a joy that is already there and therefore expressing gratitude. We on the Christian side would certainly do well to be very restrained in passing definitive judgments on the final meaning of the pleasures of the world. But whether the things that please the world and Christianity really express gratitude is the question, the question of the divine command, which is raised in face of what the human race does in this regard. Nor can we evade the further consideration that if our life as creaturely life does not belong to us, then we obviously cannot be unequivocal about what constitutes real pleasure in our real life. As the affirmation of life in general can sometimes be meaningful only as a presupposition of readiness for sacrifice, so life's pleasure in particular may perhaps show itself at times only in readiness for life's pain. The intensive enhancement of the affirmation of life may perhaps occur only in the form of openness to unlimited affliction in the same creaturely life. Merry feasts can sometimes make sense only in inseparable correlation to bitter weeks.[11] The test of our obedience in relation to the will to be happy is not laughter nor of course crying, nor again the Stoic "apathy" which can neither laugh nor cry, but this correlation between the capacity for pleasure and the capacity for pain; the readiness to honor the miracle of creaturely life, the beauty of the life loaned to us by God, both in its heights *and* also in its depths, both when we speak of happiness and also when we speak of unhappiness; the maturity which can handle both. Whether and how this test is really imposed on anyone

[11]An allusion to the concluding lines of Goethe's ballad *Der Schatzgräber.*

is another question. It is beyond question, however, that the will to live in this form, too, finds its criterion within itself in the sense that our real life belongs to God, so that our joy in life is according to his good pleasure and not ours.

Another form of the intensive affirmation of life is obviously the will to be distinctive, *individual.* Living, whether it be in strength or weakness, in pleasure or pain, means living one's own life. It means following one's native bent, becoming a definite personality, being a character. Discovery of the concept of individuality by Romanticism was analogous to a scientific insight. This does not count against it—why should nature be bad in this regard either?—but it counts against overestimation of the concept. That I find myself; that my one life as such becomes an experience to me; that I recognize the structural laws of my nature, which is mine alone, and that in so doing I recognize the possibilities that are given to me and also, of course, the limits that are set for me; that I try to realize these possibilities of mine and respect my limits; that I try as little to imitate or put on the intellectual face of another as I can alter what is distinctive about my physical face—all this is to live. In this sense the young especially want to live, battling for their own lives against parents and teachers, only to see later, perhaps, that really being oneself, *having to be* oneself as it was so fiercely desired in youth, is also a very problematic affair. For if, as we can, we want to take Goethe's view that "personality" is "the supreme happiness of the children of earth,"[12] this is not to say that the achieving of personality has in itself anything to do with the good. Even to be full of character is not as such to be good. If, however, willing to act in one's own way is an inalienable part of the life-act as such, and if the life-act as such stands in the crisis of the divine command, then here, too, the question of good and bad can and must obviously arise. What is commanded is obviously not the individuality of life in itself. If this were so, it would mean the worship of all kinds of demons that have nothing whatever to do with our real creaturely life. What is in fact commanded—and this is something very different—is the individuality of this *creaturely* life of ours. As we understand our life as such, renouncing our right to ourselves, our will-to-be-ourselves becomes a relative thing compared to the only true will-to-be-himself of God. It becomes a matter of obedience instead of desire. Lack of character, lack of the courage to confess oneself, the sloth of making less of oneself than one should, the torment of making oneself other than one is—all these are threatened by the question whether there is any will to take seriously the life that one has been loaned. At the same time there is an exaggeration of character, a commitment to character in and for itself, which reminds us that we cannot take ourselves seriously with final seriousness; that the picture we see in the mirror, for all the interest we may have in what it shows,

---

[12]Cf. Goethe's *West-östlicher Divan*, Book of Suleika, Suleika.

primarily and finally deserves only friendly-serious irony and not the fervor that Schleiermacher showed for it in his *Monologues;*[13] that real personalities are usually much less concerned about themselves that they should be according to the rules for the cultivation of personality. Individuality is obedience. This is its necessity and it is also its limit. The same may be said of the individuality of nations and families and voluntary societies. It is wholly right that the positive meaning of the command should be in force in relation to them too. Societies have by creation a certain nature which they must realize and not deny. But the fact that this nature is by creation constitutes also its limit. It denotes the glory of the Creator, not the creature. There is no point in trying to speak final words here, for we cannot do so. In the language of modern advertising a car can be a "thoroughbred." The leaf on a tree is "distinctive"—the favorite word of Romanticism. And if we are inclined to speak solemnly of the special nature of our own nation or federation we have to remember that particularity is not a content but a form which is filled with good and bad, and that we are somewhere in the middle between humility and loyalty or indolence and arrogance, not as owners but as good or bad stewards of our particularity—in a middle which concretely can mean either its assertion or its surrender. For in this regard, too, God as the Lord of life can at any moment, with the same creative power and wisdom, cause us to live or to die. Here, too, to be ready for both is what is always required by his command.

In conclusion we return to the extensive affirmation of life when we understand the will to live as a will for *power*. Asserting our creaturely life takes place under demands and restrictions that are not primarily under our own control. For my creaturely life does not exhaust God's creation. It is lived in the sphere and under the determinations of the general creaturely life around it. In the third subsection we shall have to talk about the way in which this gives a meaning to the command of life that basically transcends the concept of the will to live. It also gives rise to a problem, however, which still falls under this concept. This is the problem of power. To be powerful means to be successful in maintaining one's life by using whatever help the creaturely life around us affords, and overcoming the obstacles it poses. This will for power is the will to succeed in this way. The simple affirmation of life, the will to satisfy natural needs, the will to be healthy, the will to be happy, and the will to be individual all mean that I also have the will for power, the will to be able to do what is necessary in all these matters, the will to achieve lordship over the possibilities that arise in all these areas. Conversely, in all these forms of the will to live I practice also and with its own value and weight the will for power. I will in all these forms because I will power. I live as I *can* live. *To be able* to live is itself life. In

---

[13]F. Schleiermacher, *Monologen.* Critical ed., with introduction by F. M. Schiele, 2nd impression H. Mulert, Leipzig 1914, passim

accordance with its radius of activity my life can concretely mean very little or very much without any difference at all in material significance. The serious grasping of a child for its bread and butter, Napoleon's Russian campaign, the enterprise of teaching and learning in which we are involved here, the flight of a rocket to the stratosphere or the moon, what we hope is the gentle self-assertion which is not wholly dispensable in even the most affectionate marriage or friendship, and the powerful gesture of the dictator bringing a million people to order, are all phenomena which occur on the same plane in this respect. Precisely as we always will pleasure, so we will power. And as we know that our life-act is neither good nor bad in itself but reveals itself to be good or bad in the event of our encounter with God's command, so it is with the will for power which is always implicated in this life-act.

As is well known, F. Nietzsche[14] thought and said that it is good as such, while J. Burckhardt[15] in the same remarkable city of Basel thought and said that it is bad. Both statements must first be understood. Nietzsche's doctrine of the superman, who like a "laughing lion" is simply happy in his power on the far side of all ethical commitments, cannot be dismissed with the charge that it glorifies brutality. If Nietzsche might have given some occasion for this charge with many of his words, he did not do so with his life. On the contrary, his concern was for the realization of man in a spirituality which is content with its inwardness and is not therefore serious. His concern was for the call to take seriously as a requirement of life the possibility of an optimum of human ability and of human vitality as these might be seen in certain great leader personalities. He hated the morality of Christianity as a slave morality because in it he seemed to recognize the epitome of the impotence or indolence of the far too many—something he had first hated in the by no means Christian morality of the German cultural philistine of the seventies. In Nietzsche—who admired the Latin, and especially the French, spirit as opposed to the German—the will for power was the will for form, i.e., for the *aristeia* of form. The *aristos* in relation to formation (power must also be beautiful) is the superman. It was thus one of the most malicious of misunderstandings, especially in French war propaganda, to point to Nietzsche as a typically German prophet of force. On the other hand, Germans needed to be reminded by Nietzsche that a phenomenon which did not arise on German soil—that of Roman imperialism with its reincarnations in certain popes, in Napoleon, and obviously at the present time in Benito Musso-lini[16]—does not necessarily stand outside the light of the moral idea and

---

[14]Cf. *Der Wille zur Macht*, Nietzsche's Werke, 2, vols. XV, XVI, Leipzig 1911, passim.
[15]Cf. J. Burckhardt, *Weltgeschichtliche Betrachtungen*, ed. W. Kägi, Bern 1947, p. 166.
[16]Mussolini (1883–1945) attained power with the march on Rome on Oct. 28, 1922. He abolished the parliamentary system in 1925/26 and by royal commission embodied state sovereignty in himself as Duce of the Fascist Party.

that we should not too easily think we should see in such figures monsters from hell. |

If, however, it cannot be denied that in Nietzsche's naturalism, which reaches a climax in this doctrine, the positive side of the problem of power has been worked out in a creditable and unforgettable way, there is no evading the fact that careful consideration must be given to the relative antithesis of J. Burckhardt that power is intrinsically evil. One should call this only a relative antithesis even though it has the form of a contradiction. It is worth noting that the same historical survey, namely that of the powerful princely and papal figures of the Italian renaissance, led both men to their conclusions. The reality of human life is not so unequivocal that the development of its potential may not also mean and be the manifestation of the proponent of an empty abstraction or *un*reality of life which is grounded and exists only in the negation of real creaturely life and therefore only as a demonization of life. With the same naiveté with which other philosophical ethicists and even theological ethicists believe in their ideal pictures, Nietzsche believed in the possibility of an immanent actualization of that *aristeia* of power. In opposition, one must point out that the will for power, too, is never self-evidently the will for the good, or obedience to *the* life-requirement, and that even though it be understood as God's will for power it can never be adequate as a standard for the transvaluation of all values, the radical crisis, in which all human willing and doing finds itself. If, e.g., it is true that knowledge is power,[17] if, then, there is undoubtedly a power of knowledge and learning, this power cannot evade the question whether it is legitimate power in virtue of its actuality, the worth of its object, and the service it renders to life. Behind the unheard-of ability of modern technology there stands the threat of the question *what* can really be done. The war has opened our eyes to the fact that at every point the answer, so far as technological achievement is concerned, may just as well be murder and the destruction of life as its affirmation and upbuilding. We need not waste words on the ambivalence of the truth that money is power, though it is not perhaps superfluous to note, as George Bernard Shaw has clearly shown,[18] that as Christianity, too, grasps at this power in order to put it in the service of the good, it is seizing an instrument to which tears and blood unavoidably cling, so that it might well ask itself whether in these circumstances ("Where would we be without money?") its supposed building of the kingdom of God might not always ineluctably be the very opposite. The powerful apparatus of social and charitable care is undoubtedly another development of power and under the wheels of this machine many supporters and helpers of the enterprise are dragged along by its impetus, not to

[17]Cf. Francis Bacon, *Meditationes sacrae*, 1597, in *Works*, ed. J. Spedding, R. L. Ellis, D. D. Heath, London 1861.
[18]Cf. G. B. Shaw, *The Intelligent Woman's Guide to Socialism*, London 1928.

speak of its objects who often seem to feel more like its victims. And if we admire personalities like Napoleon, Bismarck, and Mussolini because of their unusual ability to serve the political power of their nations by awakening, uniting, and utilizing their resources, here particularly we are forced to ask whether the instrument that such leaders put in the hands of their peoples corresponds to their real situation, or whether the initial successes which seem to be allotted to them in this direction are not dubious from the very outset because a claim lies behind them which stands in no relation to the resources that are really available. This being so, was not their leadership a false one? Is not Burckhardt right? Can we want power, as we all do, without becoming guilty, guilty in relation to the very life for whose sake we grasp this instrument?[19] Where the will for power is present, as it always is, there it is always questionable, and the likelihood is—this is the tragic mistake—that the *relativity* of creaturely power will be forgotten, and secretly or openly the battle [will be] joined for an *absolute* power—a battle in which man on a small scale or a great can only finally rush into disaster.

It seems to be a truism that God alone is absolutely powerful. This truism, however, is the dividing point of good and evil in the question of the will for power. We can also offer the counterproof here that if God alone is absolutely powerful then the relative power of the creature, its true vitality, will necessarily manifest and demonstrate itself just as much in what we call weakness, in being hampered and restricted by the world around us, as it will in what we call power. *How* our power will glorify his, as must be done by the will for power if it is good; whether it will be in our strength or in our weakness; what the *aristeia* of the form is for which he has determined us—this is according to his good pleasure and not ours. The real power of real life does not have to be bound up with our victory and triumph. The criterion of the true will for power in individuals and nations might be whether man is able to live with the breaking of his will for power, whether the breaking of this will means disaster for his life, whether the lion can just as well be a lamb. This is the possibility of the power of Jesus Christ [cf. Rev. 5:5f.]. Here, in fact, is the crisis of our will for power. The command of the Creator, which is also the command of Jesus Christ, is unequivocal in itself, but it can be a two-sided order for us and obedience to it means openness to all the possibilities that are included in the supremacy of God's power over ours.

3

As I let myself be told that *I* am to live, I understand life *generally* to be necessary and it becomes an object of respect to me. This is the second basic thing that we must say about the problem of the command of

---

[19]J. Burckhardt, loc. cit.

creation. The step in thought to be taken here signifies the crux for every *naturalistic* ethics which thinks it can dispense with the fundamental force of the concept of *God* and for which at most this concept has only a later, formal significance. From the concept of *life in itself*, without what is for us the decisive definition, namely, *creaturely* life, there derives forcefully and centrally only the postulate of an affirmation of my own life, around which, according to Spencer, we have first to consider that of my descendants and then in a broader circle that of all other fellowmen,[20] without any serious questioning even for a moment of the healthy egoism of the starting point, and without its altruistic intersection by commanded regard and care for others acquiring the significance of a second commanded attitude to life which transcends in principle the *will* to live. It is hard to see what other option there is. If my knowledge of the life of others is not established by God's command, in itself it can be only an analogous knowledge. The true thing that we know about life will always be that we ourselves live. This life of ours will necessarily be the true content of our will, that of others being so, as we have seen in our discussion of the will for power, only to the extent that this life may be relevant to our own will to live either by promoting it or restricting it. ⌐For this reason naturalistic ethics has always come under the suspicion that it is a system of radical *egoism* sentimentally decorated with an altruistic margin. In terms of its own presuppositions it is hard to see how it can be anything better.⌐

The situation changes when we understand the command of life as the command of the Creator of life. Thus understood the command implies—and this already makes impossible the ringlike arrangements of Spencer's ethics[21]—a radical *relativizing* of my will to live as the will to live my *own* life. I must see my own life both posited and set aside in the thought of God the Creator. In this thought my will to live must be readiness to maintain my life and also to surrender it. What is unequivocally commanded is that I live for God, not that I just live in general. With this relativizing the concept of the life of others already comes into my field of vision, and first of all the concept of the life of *God* which alone is original and self-grounded. If this is so, if in my attention a space has been created for a life that is not my own, this liberated attention, which we cannot direct to the life of God as such, is necessarily claimed vicariously by the fact of outside life of another kind, the creaturely life *outside and alongside us*. We know this life analogously from its expressions as *life*. But through the command, which has told us about our own life, we have to regard it as creaturely life like our own. We have to see that our own life, in spite of all its mysterious *distance* from it (because it is not our own, but inalienably that of another), stands in *solidarity* with it by reason of its being in the same relation to the

---

[20]Cf. *The Principles of Ethics*, I, pp. 532ff., 544f.
[21]Ibid., pp. 47ff.

Creator as we are. Necessarily if I really see my life as a creaturely life that is set under the command, the creaturely life around me is freed from being pushed into the second or third rank of my attention, from playing the part of a mere means to promote or hinder my own will to live. I know it in the relative autonomy that is no less proper to it than to me. Its factuality has a significance, if a very different one, for my willing which prevents me from simply defining the *will* to live as a *good* will. Naturally I can will to live only my own life. An alien life is the life of another which only the other, not I, can will to live. But more important than *what* we will is *how* we will. As I exercise my will to live, what might be more important for this will than its *object* is the fact that I will to live only with *respect*, with respect, of course, for the Creator, but also with a very different respect for the life of his creatures in which my own creatureliness, the absolute otherness of the life of God from which I also have my life, encounters me relatively, in a likeness.

The concept for respect or reverence for life is borrowed from Albert Schweitzer.[22] As an opponent of Nietzsche among the naturalistic ethicists, Schweitzer had the great merit of one-sidedly, but for the first time comprehensively and forcefully, referring to the point which is at issue here, namely, the necessary determination of a good will by the factuality of the life of others as such. |

I cannot follow Schweitzer, of course, when, under the express title of ethical mysticism, he makes the will to live coincident with reverence for life. His own statement is that, when my life gives itself in some way to life, my finite will to live becomes one with the infinite will in which all life is one (K. und Eth. II, 243).[23] This implies an erasing of the distinction between command and obedience, between God and man, which naturally will not do. That we will to live, but to live primarily with respect, may be one in the command but not in human fulfillment. Nor can I agree with Schweitzer when he allows all ethics to be exhausted in the ethics of reverence for life, bringing everything under this one common denominator. This is impossible for a theological ethics which does not know the God who commands merely as God the Creator. Again, Schweitzer himself robbed his argument of its true and final force when he failed to base the command of reverence on the concept of God, but retreated to his mystical experience and thus gave his whole presentation an element of biographical contingency.

Apart from these objections one must perhaps be more grateful for Schweitzer's achievement than Nietzsche's in view of the greater relevance of the weak point in all previous ethics which he has underlined. His concept of reverence or respect for life expresses very beautifully and carefully what is at issue here. It is not a question of our relation to our fellows or neighbors as such. Our fellows become an

[22]See his *Kultur und Ethik*, 1958[11], pp. 227ff.
[23]Ibid., p. 233.

ethical problem through the command of God the Reconciler, and this
problem cannot be simply subsumed under the concept of the life of
others. That another human being lives alongside and with me is
obviously a fact of a distinctive kind. Naturally, he also *lives* with and
alongside me as the alien lives of other beings are lived alongside men.
The concept of this alien life in general, which includes the life of
animals and plants, cannot be an indifferent matter so far as the
definition of the good will is concerned. In spite of his fatal mysticism,
then, Schweitzer spoke felicitously, not of love, but of *respect* for life.
Respect is in fact what alien life as such demands of us, or rather what is
demanded for it by God the Creator. As we exercise our will to live, this
life of others must be handled with awe and responsibility: with
awe—we might also say *piety*, or, more deeply and basically, *sympathy*—
because we know that the divine command can mean life or death at any
time not only for our own life but also for all other life; and with
responsibility because our attitude to this other life, by what we fail to do
as well as by what we do, can mean its life or death, and thus represents
God's own action toward it, so that, whether we admit it or not, we have
to signify and know in some way the crisis of this alien life. It is not that
we are to stand in awe of the alien will to live as such—just as we cannot
understand our own will to live to be good as such—but we are to stand
in awe of the sword of the Lord under which it, too, stands and because
of which its will and ours must be broken into a will to live *and also* a will
to die, seeing that the command of life as the command of God can
mean both. Nor are we responsible to the alien will to live as such but to
the will of God in virtue of which what we fail to do, or do, means always
the hindrance or the promotion of that alien will to live. This takes place
either in the name and service of the Creator or by our own arrogance
and arbitrariness. To act in that awe in face of the threatened nature of
all creaturely life, and in that responsibility for what our own inaction or
action means for it is to act with respect for life.

Albert Schweitzer complained not unjustly about the "narrowness of
heart" with which previous ethics, including naturalistic ethics, had
limited its attention to self-giving to men and human society. "Just as
the housewife, having scrubbed the step, closes the door so that the dog
will not come in and spoil her work by the marks of its paws, so
European thinkers take good care that no dogs will run around in their
ethics" (225).[24] An ethics which knows God's command seriously as also
the command of God the Creator will in fact have to draw its circle much
more widely at this point than is usually done. Let us listen first to what
Schweitzer himself has to say on the point. According to him a person is
truly ethical only when he follows the compulsion to help all life that he
can, and is hesitant to do harm to anything living. He does not ask how
far this life is valuable and deserves sympathy nor does he ask whether

[24]Op. cit., p. 215.

or how far it is capable of feeling. Life as such is sacred to him. He does not pluck a single leaf from a tree or break a flower and is careful not to crush insects. If he works by a lamp on a summer night he would rather keep the window closed and breathe stuffy air than see insect after insect fall on his table with singed wings. If he goes out on the street after rain and sees an earthworm that has wandered on to it, he remembers that it will dry up in the sun if it does not reach in time the earth in which it can crawl and he carries it back from the deadly pavement to the grass. If he comes across an insect that has fallen into a pond he takes time to hand it a leaf or a stalk to save it (240).[25] It was easy, of course, to criticize this teaching by raising all kinds of questions about the practicability of such rules, and even to poke a little fun at it as Alsatian sentimentality. I regard that as cheap. If we divest the teaching of what is perhaps its too indicative or imperative form and understand it as a question, the simple question how we can justify ourselves if we act otherwise, then precisely with its unusual content it is unquestionably the most authentic ethical reflection because it obviously arises out of direct observation, and those who can only laugh are themselves a little deserving of our tears.

It is clear, of course, that the problem of other creaturely life and our relation to it can probably be really *seen* first only in the encounter of man and man, but it does not first *begin* where other creaturely life as human life can state and represent its claim upon us on an equal footing as it were. The test whether we really hear this claim is whether we hear it when it can address us only in silence, when we must detect it in the "groaning of creation" [cf. Rom. 8:22], when it is enigmatically concealed behind the apparent objectivity of animal and plant life. We cannot be deaf here if we really hear in the encounter of man and man. Or has a man really heard the command of life, which, as we have seen, is always also the command of respect for life, if he knows nothing about the *synōdinein* and *systenazein* of the *ktisis* that is shut up in corruptibility, if it does not matter to him that we continually contribute to it in the most outrageous fashion, if for him the slaughterhouse and vivisection, the chase, and the pitiless locking up of all kinds of forest animals and birds behind the bars of zoological gardens present *no* questions, or no questions applicable to him, since directly or indirectly we all of us have a share in these things? By what right does man do all these things to creation? It may be that we have a commission to do them. At any rate we should not put the question in a milder and more comfortable form—the form whether these things are *allowed*. Do we really have a *commission?* Is it not all due to our thoughtlessness, crudity, and folly? Have we a commission, not from our demonized and brutalized will for power, but from God? And if we have, are we remembering that the respect for life with which we must act cannot be invalidated, but must

[25]Ibid., p. 230

simply take another form, so that, fundamentally conceding the possibility of all those possibilities, the question has to be put afresh with each execution of it? Is it not clear that efforts to protect animals represent a concern that has always to be heard as a serious one? Can we deny even to fanatics, e.g., antivivisectionists or those who are vegetarian on these grounds, the relative right of a necessary reaction?|

Naturally an absolute veto, a condemnation of the honest trade of the butcher or of high-class hunting, can as little be deduced from the command of God as an absolute permission or an absolute command on the other side. For we cannot expect either from direct participants in such things, or from all of us as indirect participants, a solemn rehabilitation and confirmation of our conduct. Here again, then, we cannot count on it that ethics will draw a line for us between what is commanded and what is forbidden. The command of God alone draws this line for the one to whom it speaks, and ethics can only recall what has always to be considered to see this line. One such thing is that respect for life as obedience to God's command is respect for the life *created* by God, and this recollection will keep us from one-sidedly understanding by respect merely the will to preserve this life. Created life is life that in relation to both life and death is placed wholly in God's good pleasure. It *can* be, therefore, that we have not merely permission but a *commission* to perform the sacrifice which all creation, ourselves included, owes to its Creator in all its temporal existence. It can be that our own will to live in one of its components must be the instrument to make this offering, just as the world too, from the Bengal tiger to the race of bacteria, seems to be full of an alien will to live which makes us the sacrifice. While recognizing the serious concern of sentimentalists and fanatics in this area, we must say to all of them that we cannot defame the Creator as a blunderer, as Marcion did, and as the poet C. Spitteler has very impressively done in our own day,[26] and as all consistent apostles of the protection of animals do in fact and practice. We cannot attack the will in virtue of which creaturely life, as we first laid down in relation to ourselves, is always life *and* death, becoming *and* decaying; ⌐in virtue of which the big fish does not greet the little fish but eats it;⌐ in virtue of which the perfection of creation is to be sought in the fact that in order to be the site of his revelation it offers a radiant vision of day *and* a terrible vision of night, so that being is always a *struggle* for being, or better, an offering of being. With the same obedience with which we may not ourselves evade this revelation, with the same obedience with which the will to live must also be the will to suffer and die, with this same obedience we cannot evade the fact that

---

[26]Cf. Marcion's *Antitheses* (A.v. Harnack, *Marcion. Das Evangelium vom unbekannten Gott,* Leipzig 1924 [Darmstadt 1960], pp. 265f., also pp. 99ff.) The basic religious concern of C. Spitteler is the pain of the world and the possibility of redemption or redeeming acts through individuals like Prometheus, Pandora, Apollo, and Heracles. Suffering is not linked to man's sin but blamed on the Creator. Cf. L. Beriger, *RGG³*, VI, 259.

we constantly have an active share in this sacrificing. We have to remember that alien life can be only vicariously the object of our respect. We do not argue for any liberation from this respect. We do not plead for permissible exceptions and the like. We contest man's tyranny over creation: he has no right to lord it over even the tinicst fly or the smallest blade of grass. On the other hand, we cannot help but concede that respect for the Creator in the creature can mean severity against the creature, just as God's own goodness to his creation means both gentleness *and* severity.

Having considered this aspect of the matter, in a certain correction of Schweitzer's complaint we may go on to say that the problem of plant and animal life, which is undoubtedly posed and has to be pondered, can finally have only propaedeutic significance in relation to the problem of human life. It is certainly no accident that Schweitzer himself did not take up service in an animal hospital but did the work of a native doctor in Central Africa. "Thou shalt not kill" [Ex. 20:13] means "Thou shalt not kill men." It protects *man* from man. It makes *man* an object of respect. We are not referring as yet to humanity but simply to living human beings. Why and how far has ethics to pay special regard to the life of man? I reply: Because only as life together with man can our life be genuine life *together*, because only as such can it place us primarily before the command of respect for life. Naturally we are not considering here the scientifically verifiable distinctions between man and his nearest fellow-creatures, about which not too much can be stated that is certain and unequivocal. We are starting instead at the point that for us truly and indissolubly alien life is not the life of animals and plants, which on account of its absolutely concealed intellectuality it is hard for us to sense and acknowledge as life or to treat as more than a mere object, namely, an object of respect. *Life*, absolutely *alien* life, which cannot be just object, which is thus the likeness of the life of the invisible God and its primary vicar and representative, is the life of our fellowmen. This always places us *primarily*, and this alone places us *strictly*, before the factuality of an alien life that is to be respected for the Creator's sake, before an eye-to-eye claim of this alien life which—no matter how close we may be to the rest of creaturely life—is alone made on the same footing, a claim to be the object of my awe, my piety, and my sympathy. And [it places] my own life with my will to live in a context of mutual responsibility for the promotion and restriction of life which in fact we constantly cause one another.

We may suitably begin with the problems posed by the possibility and reality that a man may, by a direct and intentional act, transport another man from life to death. In this regard we have to consider (naturally within the limits staked out by us for this chapter) the three related questions of killing in *self-defense, capital punishment,* and *war*. If we take the first of these concepts rather broadly (including within it such special issues as the duel and tyrannicide), the three together cover all the possibilities of permissible and even commanded killing. We can only put questions here. A feature of the admitted or nonadmitted knowledge of the command of life as the command of respect for life is that all these possibilities, which may actually take very different forms, have, in all the historical periods and areas that have made use of them, the character of final reasons, borderline possibilities, extreme and by no means obvious or self-evident necessities. The form: Thou shalt not kill, seems to be one of the most original and powerful ways in which the command has always reached man and grasped him. The genuinely or supposedly permissible or commanded killing of men has always and everywhere been felt to be a final and dreadful thing, or at least something that is surrounded by all kinds of restraints. At this point, then, our first task is simply to emphasize that in all cases it is true that here no less than in suicide we have an extreme, a most extreme possibility which the command of respect for life surrounds with all kinds of possible question marks. Ethical reflection and instruction has done a great deal when it has simply underlined as heavily as possible the borderline character of this possibility.|

But we must now go on to make a second observation. We are today at a stage in human history where—for reasons that need not detain us here—the borderline character of this possibility—for all the constant interruptions and crying contradictions—is *on the whole* being increasingly felt and established. Ethical reflection on the dubious nature of the permission or command that men may be killed even within these three possibilities is now wide awake, where in the Middle Ages it seems to have been at least asleep. We are not saying that men today have become better even in this one respect—what does better mean?—but that they have on the whole become more scrupulous. This can mean, and to a large extent it does in fact mean, that the mutual killing of men now takes for the most part an indirect form, and in this form has a stronger real or supposed sanctioning by permission or command. But this does not alter the fact that for all the episodic exceptions (the 1914–1918 war is an outstanding one) a growing uneasiness about permitted or commanded direct killing is simply a fact. A storm of indignation such as that which rightly or wrongly shook the whole world on behalf of Sacco and Vanzetti[27] would have been quite impossible fifty years ago. And the greatest of all wars was also the first war which, from the very outset and in all countries, was accompanied by a radical protest against all war, a protest which rose and fell but was never totally

[27]B. Vanzetti (1888–1927) and N. Sacco (1891–1927) were two Italian immigrants who in May 1920 were accused of murder in South Braintree, Mass., at a time when a campaign against left-wing forces, especially Italian workers with anarchist tendencies, was at its height. In spite of their alibi and many eyewitnesses in their favor, the two were condemned to death in July 1921 as members of an anarchist working-class movement. Many political and cultural leaders, heads of state, and thousands of American citizens pleaded for them, but they were executed on August 23, 1927.

suspended. In this respect, then, we can simply sail with the wind—and yet not do anything superfluous—as we take the matter, for which others might find a different basis, and set it in the light of the command of the Creator, emphasizing and affirming that there *is* indeed a place here for the sharpest suspicion, for the most exact testing of what traditional ethics has taken for granted, for asking whether the final reasons can really be supported as final after all. No basis for these reasons which has its source elsewhere—and we do not intend to adopt a closed attitude to these reasons—and certainly no contempt for modern sentimentality and the like should prevent us from saying that the *horror* at the thing which is growing today (even though in many forms it may be self-deception), the horror *also* at all attempts to justify it ethically and theologically, is right, not as a definitive answer, but as a sharper form of the *question* as to the command of the Creator. And it is one of the most incomprehensible absurdities in the history of theology that theology has dared to refer to the divine order of creation in order to beat down and silence the concern largely represented here by the children of the world, indeed, by publicans and sinners of all kinds. Ethics, theology, can as little appropriate pacifism as any other -ism, but what certainly should not have happened is that, at a time when (no matter what view we may take of pacifism) the *question* of the command has arisen, the dominant and most articulate theology should be explicitly a militaristic theology.

It is immediately apparent that both the general estimation of killing as a borderline possibility and also the modern protest against it are directed much more strongly against capital punishment and war than against killing in self-defense and all that goes with it. Anyone who has taken part in a discussion of the moral and Christian question of military service will remember the argument: "What would you do if in a forest you met . . . or if you saw someone assaulting your wife and children . . .?" They will also remember how probably even zealous anti-militarists would have to confess that in such cases they would, of course, make ruthless use of their fists or cudgels or revolvers. Then their position regarding war, whatever else they might allege in its favor, would be shaken somewhat, since it is easy to show that war (and the same is true of capital punishment) can very well be understood as a collective form of self-defense. To the question of self-defense, of course, very different and more consistent answers have been heard, and even if they had not we should have to say that the seriousness of the question has nothing whatever to do with the fact that there may be nobody or only a few who are ready to acknowledge that it is put at every point. Its force is not conditional upon the consistency or inconsistency of those who raise it. At any rate, in dealing with this whole complex of problems it is well to begin in fact with the question of *private self-defense* and in the light of this to see how the questions must be put in the matters of capital punishment and war. Private self-defense is an apt starting point because the permission or command to kill seems to be so obvious here that after a superficial consideration one might feel almost compelled to think, and even after a more radical consideration one might still instinctively think, that they are in fact given self-evidently in this case. And because, on the other hand, it may be instructively shown here how naive it is to think that killing in self-defense is self-evident, since (1) it is hardly possible to give an unequivocal definition of the decisive concept of self-defense, (2) the question of awe and responsibility in relation to the life of one's fellowman has to be put here in an extraordinarily personal and direct way, and (3) the possibility of a command to sacrifice included in the command of the Creator is suggested here in a particularly vivid form. Now it is true that I not only may but should protect my life and the lives of those entrusted to me against assaults upon them, and that the life of the assailant does in fact come into the picture as the final cost that might have to be paid when I do protect them. May it be, then, that on the basis of this truth I act in obedience to the command of the will to live. But I must be clear about the fact that the assailant who threatens me—Dostoievski's analysis of the murderer Raskolnikov shows us this—might also argue in exactly the same way.|

The vexed ethical question—I am on a plank in the ocean with another man, the plank can carry only one of us, we do not both want to drown, and neither will drown voluntarily to save the other, therefore may I push him off the plank or he me?—this familiar problem can help us understand the whole situation that is at issue in killing in self-defense. The person who wants to kill me, and against whom I defend myself, is already fundamentally in the position of defending himself against *me*. For we cannot easily say that the situation of self-defense only begins on the spot or, shall we say, ten seconds before the probable start of the action that threatens me. If man is given the right of self-defense, this obviously begins much earlier, namely, with the desperate position of a person from which he thinks he can free himself only by killing someone else—in the case of Raskolnikov[28] the avaricious old woman. When, therefore, I find myself in a situation in which I have to defend myself, I must remember that my assailant seems to think he is in a similar situation, the only difference being that the situation which my existence implies for him, e.g., the purse which is not his but mine, does not in my view (but only mine) have for him the same urgency as that which he creates for me when he looks as if he is drawing a revolver out of his pocket, and I perhaps already have mine under my coat ready to shoot. In order to continue living—and I must leave it to him to say how serious his position is—is he not grasping at the final reason which I have obviously allowed myself too in such a case? He himself must consider how he can justify his action, the attack

---

[28]Cf. Dostoievski's novel *Crime and Punishment*.

which he obviously plans on me. He himself must consider by what higher commission he can make this attack on me in spite of the awe and responsibility which he is commanded to show in relation to my life. I for my part have no well-founded knowledge that he *cannot* justify himself, and if I defend myself against him, if I do so effectively, if I discharge my carefully released revolver while he is still trying to unsettle me with his "Hands up," if I anticipate his attack on my life with a counterattack on his, what have I done? I have undoubtedly placed myself in the same position as he was in. I, too, felt threatened. I, too, wanted to continue living. I, too, grasped at the final reason. I, too, could not possibly know whether he had ultimately more urgent cause to do so than I. But I decided—by what right?—that I did, and I defended myself, and because I was quicker or stronger or more alert or had better luck, I did so *effectively*, i.e., I attacked, I attacked *his* life, instead of letting him attack mine. And since my defense was successful, and he, not I, had to die, and I murdered the murderer before he murdered me, the problem in the situation has been complicated, for in fact—I do not know unconditionally whether he would have gone to extremes, for I took from him the chance to decide—in fact, then, *I* am the one who first and alone willed and did the decisive thing, the killing of another—he was not yet my murderer when I killed him—and it is I who must see to it (for he now stands before his judge for his preparatory will and act) how *I* can justify myself for shooting and by what commission I did it notwithstanding the awe and responsibility that were commanded of me in relation to his life.

This makes the concept of killing in self-defense so difficult that if I make use of this possibility I have to decide whether my situation is really more urgent than that of the other who because of my situation I am hastening from life to death. If I decide in favor of my own situation and not his, I have then to go ahead and play the judge before the act, as if I already had some knowledge of his will and act at the decisive moment, although in fact I undoubtedly do not have any such knowledge. Whether we can take all this on ourselves is the question which we obviously have to put in regard to the possibility of killing in self-defense. If we make use of the possibility, we *have* taken it all on ourselves. It has to be that in so doing we are obedient to the command, naturally not merely in the sense of the will to live but also in that of respect for life. We cannot make ethical reflection any easier than this. It is not a matter of casting off this burden but of doing God's will under the burden of this whole question. It should already be clear, then, that there can be no question of a general permission or command to kill in self-defense in spite of the naive view that it is self-evident, and in spite of the fact that not one among a thousand would take a different course under the pressure of such a moment, but all would act as described if they had the power to do so. Even though it be granted that, on the assumption that our revolver *could* fire first, we would all act in this way under the pressure of such a moment, we still may not regard the permission or command to do so as self-evident, as a generally given truth. On what ground could we do so? No, in the whole uncertainty of our act as depicted, we *have killed.* If we were sure we could and should do what we did, it was not because killing in self-defense is a permitted or commanded possibility. Those who seriously declare it to be such have forfeited the right, or have only the right of the hypocrite, to sit in judgment on the further possibilities of capital punishment and war.

For the sake of systematic clarity, we have presupposed the simplest and the most extreme case, that of the plank in the ocean, in the sense of assuming that we are dealing with a *direct* threat, the threatening of my *life* by someone else. It might be—and perhaps it is in most cases where we speak of self-defense—that the threat, when seen more closely, is really a distant one, and that what is threatened is something less or at any rate other than my life. The weight of what I take upon myself when I make use of the possibility of killing in self-defense is obviously greater as the threat is less direct and I have the chance to ward off the problem that the other presents to me in some other way than by killing him. The weight is greater the more my situation resembles his, for he is in difficulty too. What seems to distinguish my situation from his is that in my view he could just as well do something else instead of threatening me. But it might also be that I could do something else to meet his attack instead of counterattacking first. If I do not do this, the question I have to answer is just as serious as the question that is put to him. The same increase in the weight of the ethical question obviously takes place the less there is a threat to my life and the more what is at issue is something else which may be closely related to it. This something else might be my purse. I leave it to your own discernment to analyze from this standpoint the possibility of meeting a burglar with a weapon in hand. Difficult questions arise. Here, however, we shall now take up the problems of *dueling* and *tyrannicide.*

The logic of the duel rests, as is well known, on the equation of life and honor. Let us take it for granted for a moment that for the members of certain classes and professions there is a *sense* of honor and a *status* of honor (before society), and that a threat to these can, and even must, be the equivalent of a threat to life, so that I stand in the same relation to the one who makes such a threat as I do to the one who directly threatens my life, and to save it I am under the same summons of the command of the will to live. In such a case, saving my honor, if I do it by way of a duel with the other party, unquestionably complicates the ethical situation, since if I kill him, or even resolve to do so, I have not only decided that he must vacate the plank, I have not only done or prepared myself to do the decisive thing in this regard, but I have also reached a decision on the very specific presupposition of this "I or he," the presupposition that one of the two must fall, and in such a way that I have to will that the other party will fall. Apart from any decision about killing in self-defense on my own part, I have decided that the underlying presupposition, the equation of honor and life in the sense of my status and calling, is right. I must now take on this further burden if I think I must fight. In addition to the extraordinary thing that I have to be commanded if my act of killing is to be done aright, I must also be certain that my sense of honor, or the inferences that I now draw from it, is [or are] also commanded, and commanded in such a way that in and in spite of my respect for the life of another I believe I must shoot. If I do not know this, then I do not know what I am doing as a duelist, and what really counts is that we do know what we are doing. |

Things are much the same in relation to the possibility of tyrannicide. To bring the matter closer to home we shall not take the examples of Brutus and Cassius in the assassination of Julius Caesar or of William Tell in the sunken lane, but the more recent slayings of Erzberger and Rathenau.[29] In this case the people responsible were not concerned about their own honor but about the honor and freedom of the German people and fatherland which they thought Erzberger and Rathenau had betrayed; their task being to avenge the betrayal, whether because of their oath of loyalty to the Kaiser or for some other reason. With the same urgency with which they might have invoked the final reason in defending their own lives they were convinced that they now had to defend the betrayed cause of Germany against Erzberger and Rathenau, that they had to attack them with exactly the same logic as that of killing in self-defense. In this case the increased ethical burden was obviously a double one even as compared with dueling. They were now responsible not only for the decision that Erzberger and Rathenau must vacate the plank, and not only for going ahead on the basis of this decision, but in addition they were responsible (1) for the equation of their own lives and the threat to them with the cause of Germany and the betrayal of this cause; for the decision, then, whether they themselves might be appointed avengers of this crime, and (2) for the correctness of the judgment that a crime had taken place, that Germany really had been betrayed by Erzberger and Rathenau, which obviously had to be the presupposition of all that followed. It can be that someone is a tyrant, a traitor, or a public pest of some kind, and it can be that an individual is summoned to do away with him—the stories of Deborah and Judith [cf. Judg. 4 and 5; Jth. 8−13] are not the only ones in the Bible to reckon with this possibility in spite of the "Thou shalt not kill," and Calvin did

[29]M. Erzberger (1875−1921) was a German politician who signed the Armistice agreement in 1918 and supported the Versailles treaty. He was killed by two army officers on August 26, 1921. W. Rathenau (1867−1922) was a Jew who served in the second cabinet of Chancellor Wirth. He was murdered in Berlin by two fanatics of the radical right on June 24, 1922. For details of the first case see K. Epstein, *Matthias Erzberger und das Dilemma der deutschen Demokratie*, Berlin/Frankfurt 1962; of the second, L. Ebermayer, *Fünfzig Jahre Dienst am Recht*, Leipzig/Zurich 1930.

not absolutely rule out the possibility of tyrannicide[30]—but anyone who thinks that he is called to do this, along with all the other things that he has to consider, must be very sure (1) that he can justify himself factually, and (2) that he can really appeal to a call. Ethics cannot pass either a positive or a negative judgment on the acts of those who avenged the cause of Germany, since it is not its job to pass judgment anyway. But it can do something that is more important and fruitful, namely, point to the ethical criteria which apply to these and to all other human acts, criteria by which these acts are measured and *are* in fact judged, although not by us.

Our discussions thus far have now equipped us to take up the controversial issue of *capital punishment,* which is being rather passionately deliberated in Switzerland at the present moment.[31] This question differs plainly from the other questions in this area because in this case the bearers of the awe and responsibility in, and in spite of, which men are transferred from life to death by other men, are no longer individuals who are incidentally called upon to be judges in their own cause, but primarily and very indirectly society and people organized as the state and granting its judges the right to pass capital sentence, then rather more directly the appointed judges who make use of this right, and finally, and very directly, those who do the actual killing, the executioners. Because of the great indirectness with which most of those who speak to the issue have any share in killing in this form, since the way is so long from the theoretical truths which they debate so comfortably to what actually happens in the execution chamber, the danger is all the greater in this case that there will be no realization *how hard* it is here, too, to assent to what ultimately takes place. |

It is remarkable that in no ethics has the problem of capital punishment been regarded as simply the problem of the *executioner.* The Middle Ages, which made free use of the death penalty, knew this, although its solution to the problem was very primitive and much too simplistic. The medieval state found no difficulty in approving and attending every few weeks or even oftener the spectacle of divine and human justice manifested in the death penalty. It praised judges for imposing it and the council, bishop, or king for appointing such judges. At the same time it declared and treated as infamous the executioner and his whole family. For the sake of completeness we might recall the famous principle that the church does not thirst after blood. The *church*

---

[30]Cf. *Inst.* IV, 20, 30–31.

[31]In Switzerland the death penalty had been abolished for political offenses in 1848 and for all offenses in 1874, but it had been restored (except for political offenses) in 1879, its execution being left to the individual cantons. A move toward uniformity brought stormy debates in 1928, the upshot being the restriction of capital punishment to military law. Cf. F. Clerc, E. Steck, *Grundzüge des Schweizerischen Strafrechts,* General Part, Basel 1943, pp. 3, 100ff.

recognizes the legitimacy of the death penalty but leaves its practical execution to the state—an ideological construction which still plays some part in the discussions of modern theological ethicists. This is how man finds help when he feels a moral problem but wants to be at peace in relation to it. The point, then, is that we should regain, on the one side, the sensitivity of the Middle Ages to the presence of a problem at this point but realize, on the other side, that the delegate relationship of the executioner to the court and the court to society does not alter the fact that in the last resort one person has to take it upon himself to kill another. It is natural, then, to renounce the ideology of the Middle Ages, the artifice that treats the executioner as a villain, and the thinking of the church and Christianity. One has to realize that the executioner is simply a deputy for the judges and the judges for society, but also that, from the moral standpoint, *I myself* am society. If I simply ask in general about the possibility of capital punishment instead of asking very concretely whether I myself would be prepared to carry it out, my question is not to the point.

Perhaps the following consideration will lead us to the nub of the matter. As is well known, punishment in general is based especially on three theories. According to the first, it is designed for the offender himself in the hope that setting the dreadful consequences of his act before his eyes will teach him better. According to the second, punishment is for the sake of pure justice, which cannot let evil go unrequited but, because it is evil, must set it under a visible reaction. According to the third, punishment serves society by protecting it against the criminal and imitators of his crime, the former being made harmless and the latter given a terrifying example. |

Unquestionably the death penalty means abandoning the first of these theories. It involves the exclusion of any improvement or education. More generally, it means that among all of us who daily do evil this one, the so-called criminal, has done *too much* evil for us to be able to have any further fellowship with him. For us who also do evil, but not so much evil, life together with *this* evildoer has become intolerable. Since, fortunately, he does not have the power to despatch *us* from the world, *he* must lose his life. I need hardly say how close we are here to the situation of killing in self-defense. The surrender, the capitulation to the invincibility of a man's wickedness, outwardly safeguarded, of course, by the power of superior power, the bold recognition that he is incorrigible, and on this basis an "I or he," an "off the plank with him," is the first thing that one has to take upon oneself in affirming the death penalty. Nor should one find too easy comfort in the fact that contemplating the imminent end of the delinquent will perhaps have a more serious effect than what may easily be blunting life-imprisonment, or that he is not lost even without the earthly society which casts him out by the death penalty (Haering, p. 245), or that the offer of grace is not withheld from him (Schlatter, p. 131).[32] All this simply means that we are committing the delinquent to God while giving him up ourselves. It might be that God's goodness is not in fact withdrawn from him by what we do with him, but we and our deed are not thereby justified. With the same argument we might regard ourselves as exculpated for any final disloyalty to our neighbor in which to his good fortune, but not to our justification, we cannot cut him off from the goodness of God.

As concerns the second theory, that of retributive justice, we should certainly listen to Schlatter when he writes that the total loss of the criminal's rights takes place when the state puts him to death, and that the state's right to take this action rests on his total wickedness. Well put, but why does Schlatter hide behind the state? "L'état, c'est moi,"[33] is what the Christian will say. That is, he will hold himself responsible when the state makes use of the right that is given it and kills. How sure, then, the state, or, rather, we ourselves must be of our cause not only in relation to the incident which gives actual occasion for killing, but also in relation to the question whether or not the offense merits the death sentence. With what different degrees of depth the facts can be investigated—one has only to think how quickly revolutionary or counterrevolutionary courts usually operate in this regard, or military courts in enemy territory. What different standards can be used, and yet, when the ultimate reason is at issue, how everything depends on the facts being perceived with final clarity and an unequivocal standard being used to judge them. Schlatter would limit the death penalty to cases where wickedness has destroyed the life of another (132).[34] This is good, but what is wickedness and could not the worst cases of destroying the lives of others be those which can never be brought to human justice? Should not those who recommend the death penalty for the few cases of public destruction of life (if proved to be such) regard self-execution as a command and a duty in the many secret instances of the same possibility? And does it not cause us to suspect the purity of the whole theory of retribution when Schlatter immediately goes on to say that a people can hardly maintain the conviction that evil should not be committed and is wholly intolerable if it completely removes the death penalty from among its punishments (131)?[35]

We have obviously reached the third theory that evil is "intolerable" to society, i.e., that it is at war with those who do it, that it cannot put up with their beliefs, and in token of this it will wield the sword in some of the worst cases. In a foreign parliament a motion to abolish capital punishment was once greeted by the interjection: "Let the murderers

[32]Op. cit., 1929[3] (1961), p. 160.
[33]This famous saying of Louis XIV (1643−1715) is not well attested and he certainly did not utter it before Parlement in 1655 as the story goes. Cf. G. Büchmann, Geflügelte Worte, Berlin 1942[29], pp. 490f.
[34]Op. cit., pp. 159f.
[35]Loc. cit.

begin then!" (E. W. Mayer, p. 298). Mayer comments that this is not an ethically tenable argument in favor of the death penalty. That may be but, ethical or not, it is at any rate the only cogent argument on which those who accept capital punishment can soberly stand. Society in the form of the state, with the church cannot properly renounce solidarity, finds itself on the defensive against individuals who threaten the lives of its members, or, as we have seen, it finds itself in the position of having to attack first with which superior force. The only palpable enemies here are "murderers," i.e., those who in a blatant sense, which the public law of man can encompass, have become assailants on the lives of others and might become so again. In putting them to death society offers a *demonstration*—it obviously cannot be more than that since, insofar as it snuffs out anyone, it snuffs out only the big murderers who might in fact be the lesser ones—it offers a demonstration, by proceeding against *these*, against this attack *in general*, that it is opposed to the total wickedness of evil and stands for the respect for life which these people seem to have violated so outrageously. Because such things should not be done, these people must bleed. "It is expedient for us that one man should die for the people, and that the whole nation should not perish" (John 11:50). This is the argument for capital punishment. But in it, apart from accepting the capitulation already referred to, we have to take it upon ourselves (1) to single out for the purpose of this demonstration the known big murderers who might perhaps be the lesser ones, (2) to be as certain of the facts of their offense as is proper when the punishment is irrevocable (it might itself be a wicked destruction of life, judicial murder), and (3) really to do to them as they have done to others, and therefore to occupy the same ground with them, the ground of the "I or he," the ground of killing in self-defense, and on this ground to make use of the right of the stronger.|

An absolute ethical impossibility of capital punishment cannot be deduced from its ethical questionability as thus demonstrated, but in view of this questionability we also cannot maintain its absolute possibility even in relation to specific offenses. If we accept it concretely—and we would have great difficulty *not* to accept it in the case of Haarmann in Hanover two years ago[36]—and if for that reason we cannot in principle remove the death penalty from the statute book, we have to realize that we do not do so on the basis of a perceived absolute possibility of the act but only with the ethical vulnerability and dubiety with which it is always surrounded, only by commission and command, i.e., because we think that that demonstration is sometimes commanded even in and in spite of its hopeless vulnerability, and we do not want to

[36]F. Haarmann (1879–1924) was a habitual criminal and impulsive killer who murdered 24–30 young men in Hanover between 1921 and 1924. He was executed on Dec. 19, 1924. Cf. Dr. Weiss, "Der Fall Haarmann," *Archiv f. Kriminologie,* vol. 76, Leipzig 1924, pp. 161–74.

make it impossible. If the death penalty is carried out concretely with an awareness of this vulnerability—this awareness will provide a wide-ranging guarantee against the dangers of the enterprise—then it may *take place* (presupposing that it *must*). And the same awareness of this total vulnerability could also be the justification of the lawgiver who will not give up the death sentence in principle. To repeat, however, a test of the genuineness of a person's acceptance is that having considered everything that has to be considered here he can raise no objection on ethical grounds to himself being the executioner. He must be ready to venture personally, and, of course as a Christian, to do what the state demands at the peril of his own soul's peace and salvation. Justice will then be done to respect for life whether the death penalty be abolished or upheld, and that alone is the final issue in ethical reflection on this question.

In direct connection with this we may now go on to say that if we want to accept the possibility of *war*, as perhaps we can and must, we must not on any pretext be ashamed of, but must very seriously accept, the close association in which it stands to the work of the executioner. War is the execution which a people organized as a state, on account of its will to live, performs on another people which threatens its will to live. The problem of war is the question whether such an execution is possible in and in spite of respect for life. We are dealing here with execution in the most pregnant sense of the term. If war is simply a "continuation of politics with other means,"[37] these means consist of rendering the enemy forces innocuous, which cannot be done without the intentional killing of countless men. It was either a sophism or a fine example of professorial simplicity when Schleiermacher (*Chr. Sitte*, p. 281) tried to avoid the obvious meaning of war by arguing as follows: war is waged only with the purpose of so weakening the enemy that "his only rational option is to do what is demanded. He should be weakened, however, not by killing his subjects but by occupying what constitutes his strength, namely, land and people. The less war is waged in this way, the more it is barbaric and immoral, for if even one's own subject should not be punished by death (Schleiermacher opposed capital punishment, p. 248), much less should the subject of another. If enemies find death, this is not the result of a specific will to kill them nor the result of putting both oneself and them in a particular position, but simply because they arbitrarily offer resistance. Earlier it was different, but there can be no question for us which way of waging war is the more moral, the earlier or the present. Certainly greater personal bravery developed when people simply fought with sword and spear. But because a battle for life and death arose more easily than with the present use of artillery, which is simply designed to make the enemy withdraw before the deployment of a specific mass of natural forces, the present way of waging war is nobler.

[37]C. von Clausewitz (1780–1831), *Von Kriege*, Berlin 1832 (ed. 1957, pp. 6, 34, 727ff.).

The only unchristian thing is the war of outposts and the use of snipers, which are aimed at individuals but by which [also] the least is accomplished." No, we may and must begin with the fact that the final and decisive aim in war, what makes it war, is the killing of opposing forces, certainly only as the means to an end, yet the means to an end which characterizes war as such is that the individual soldier wants to kill and does kill the individual enemy soldier. |

The Middle Ages again recognized the doubtful nature of this activity more honestly than the modern period by not allowing the clergy to bear weapons. This is, of course, another sophism or ideology similar to that concerning the executioner or the church not thirsting for blood. Historical circumstances and conditions made it possible right up to the Napoleonic period for not only the clergy but also many other circles in society to transfer the dubious activity of war from themselves to a special military estate. They could regard war as a matter for princes and their relatively small armies, a matter which did not concern them except as occasional victims. Luther, in 1526, wrote a well-known work on behalf of soldiers which had the merit of basically setting aside the idea that the military estate is suspect by showing that its actions can take place in faith, in love, and in obedience to God's command.[38] |

The intervening change in the situation is that, in both practice and theory, the people itself has increasingly become the agent of war, as may be seen most impressively in the Prussian uprising of 1513. This means that the ideology contested by Luther has become pointless and the problem of military action has become acute in a way that it could not be for Luther in relation to the soldiers of Electoral Saxony. We no longer have soldiers as we have cobblers and doctors but fundamentally everybody has become a soldier (the recent conscription of the whole male and female population from six years up in France and Italy is simply the logical climax of this development,)[39] and it would obviously be a misuse of Luther to support the new ideology by his dialectic and thereby to evade the new and general problem. The new ideology of war, which is to be distinguished from the old one that Luther contested, is that, in case of war, man as a member of the state unavoidably has an active part, whether directly or indirectly. He has an active part, then, in the mass killing of enemy soldiers. To be able to fulfill the old desire to remove the doubtfulness of the enterprise from

---

[38]WA 19, pp. 623–62: *Ob Kriegsleute auch in seligem Stande sein können*, 1526; LW, 46, pp. 93–143.

[39]The draft was in force at this time in almost all European countries except Germany, Austria, Hungary, and Bulgaria, where it was forbidden by the Treaty of Versailles. France, in 1927, passed a law for the organization of the whole population in case of war, with physical training for all boys and girls from the age of six, and preparation for military training from the age of sixteen. In Italy the Fascist militia took charge of military training, which began generally at eight and more specifically at sixteen. Cf. K. L. von Oertzen, *Abrüstung oder Kriegsvorbereitung?* Berlin 1929, 1931[2], pp. 29f., 34.

himself, and even to have the witness of a good conscience in the matter, he now argues in this way. He himself is not the true and responsible *subject* in war. Although it is he who wages it, a third party acts for him in what precedes, claims him for these military acts, and thus assumes responsibility in his place. "Call, my *fatherland,* and see us all dedicated to thee with heart and hand," is sung in Switzerland.[40] "The *king* called and all came," was said in Germany.[41] "The *people* arises, the storm breaks," applies in both.[42] I am there, but in the strict sense only indirectly. It is not my will but that of the fatherland, king, people, nation, state. *I* do not call but *there* rolls out a call like a clap of thunder,[43] and at this call, and ethically covered by it, I prepare to aim and shoot at unknown men who have done me no wrong. The advantage of this indirect view of the matter is not only that I am ethically covered by it but also that it even enables me to make a positive ethical evaluation of what I do. I do not do it for myself but for my people and at the risk of my life. It is service, even sacrificial service to my people. John 15:13 might be applied to it: "Greater love has no man than this, that a man lay down his life for his friends." Not against these thoughts as such, but against their common use in ethics, one has to say that we treat the matter too lightly if we think that with the help of these thoughts, which are right enough in their place, we can solve the moral problem of war.

The saying "With God for king and fatherland"[44] conceals something essential. Who would not and should not be there if it were simply a matter of this "for"? But this "for" is not what makes warlike action warlike. To denote and distinguish it as such the saying would need to run: "With God against every enemy of the king and fatherland." Obviously that beautiful "for" might just as well adorn the peaceful hat of a civilian subject of king and fatherland, while the less beautiful "against" should be on the helmet of the soldier unless that ideological transfiguration of war is intended. The nerve and core of the new ideology of war in the age of mass conscription is that we should hide from ourselves and from the participant in war the decisive thing that he has to do and look at what he *also* does, though this is not the special thing that he does as such, namely, the killing of members of the enemy forces. The first task of ethical reflection in relation to the possibility of war in the modern situation has to be to remove that abstraction, as

[40]The beginning of the then national hymn of Switzerland (1928) composed by J. R. Wyss (1782–1830).
[41]The beginning of the 1813 song of H. Clauren (=C. Heun, 1771–1854).
[42]The beginning of the 1813 poem "Männer und Buben" written by T. Körner (1791–1813) and published in *Leyer und Schwert*, Berlin 1814, p. 78.
[43]The beginning of the song "Die Wacht am Rhein" written by M. Schneckenburger (1819–1849) in 1840 and sung in the war against France in 1870/71.
[44]On March 17, 1813, King Frederick William III of Prussia (1797–1840) ordered every soldier to carry a white metal cross with this inscription.

though the people waged war in the vacuum of an idea but I, the participant, merely served the people, and to state instead that *I* am the people (as I am the state that kills the criminal), that *I* wage war, and therefore that *I* kill. No other person or thing takes my place here. I stand alone, as Schiller rightly has the soldiers of Wallenstein sing.[45] It may well be that I serve, that I am obedient, that I follow the commandment of love for my neighbors, that I finally lay down my life for my friends, but all that does not cover or justify me if God does not cover me with his command in face of the great question that is posed with all this, namely, that I do it all in such a way that I for my part want to kill and do kill other men, aiming at them and shooting them. It may be that Luther's thesis is still true today—and it is—that even in this action I am justified by faith (by faith and not my good disposition and the like), but how can I understand that if I hide behind the concept of the people instead of resolutely taking my stand with my people and thus unequivocally accepting responsibility for the fact that what I am now doing is—not something indefinite for king and fatherland; "sin boldly" applies here[46]—taking aim and shooting at Englishmen and Frenchmen. Only when I soberly and factually realize that this is the issue and not the fine master concept under which, of course, the matter also stands, but without being changed into something different, can there be any meaningful reference to faith and justification.

When I see through the modern ideology as such, when I no longer seek the ethical subject in a hypostasis which represents and magnifies me, when I realize that I am the subject here too, *then* the element of truth can be expressed which lies hidden in this and every ideology. It is true enough that in war, as in capital punishment, the affair is not mine in a general sense but mine as a member of my people—in the next section we shall see that by creation it is part of my calling by God's command to belong to my people—the only difference from capital punishment being that here I am summoned to take an active part. If I accept membership in my people, then I must accept its war, i.e., the actualizing of its will to live in conflict with the will to live of another people, a conflict in which things have gone so far that either my people or the other expects a solution only by the use of the final reason. War is my people's emergency and therefore it is my emergency too. If my people is in this plight, then whether it is right or wrong I am in it as well. "Right or wrong, my country."[47] The situation is thus the same as when someone rightly or wrongly attacks me, or rightly or wrong I think I must attack someone else. What should have been done to avoid war

---

[45]See n. 7.

[46]Luther WA *Briefwechsel*, vol. 2, p. 372, letter to Melanchthon, Aug. 1, 1521.

[47]This principle was stated by S. Decatur (1779–1820) in a toast (1816): "Our country! In her intercourse with foreign nations, may she always be in the right, but our country, right or wrong!" Cf. Mackenzie, *Life of Stephen Decatur*, Boston 1846, p. 295.

has now been let slip and what I could have done I have now let slip. With my life, I have a part in the movement of the life of my people which has led to this critical point, and now that things have gone so far I would need a special commission to refuse to drink the brew which in peace I also helped to prepare by what I did or failed to do. I *am* involved in my country's war even if previously I worked with all my power to maintain peace. The fact that I did this gives me no right when war breaks out to regard it as the business of the rest. In view of the obvious powerlessness of my personal efforts I have to accept the responsibility which my people as such is about to take upon itself. Ethics can as little condemn conscientious objection to military service as it can any other possibility of human action, but it has to remind the objector that he cannot possibly have clean hands in relation to the coming war of his country and that his own hands might be doubly unclean if he thinks that he does not share the responsibility of his country because he does not bear arms.

But if, with or without arms, I am involved in my country's war, then I have to know—this is why ethical reflection on war should be pursued, while there is still time, in days of peace—I have to know what I am taking upon myself with this involvement and with what radical vulnerability my action will always, even at best, be obedience to God's command. As ethics should be on guard against even secretly pushing the demand for conscientious objection, so it should also—and here the need for restraint is even more urgent—refuse completely to let itself be made an instrument of the warring state by devoting itself to providing spiritual munitions for the forces or giving the general staffs the desired repose of a good conscience concerning those who must actually take aim and shoot. Servility of this kind was what made the war theology of all countries in the last war such an abhorrent phenomenon, a phenomenon incomparably far worse from an ethical standpoint than all the aiming, shooting, and killing, because by this servility the *cause* of ethics, at least of Christian ethics, was publicly betrayed in such scandalous fashion. Ethically, the most dangerous form of participation in war is not, then, that of service in the infantry, the artillery, or even the poison-gas corps, but undoubtedly that of the chaplains' service, because this is the place where it is so uncannily easy to betray the cause of ethics publicly and to promote that evil ideology instead of ethical reflection. Unconcerned about the wishes of general staffs, ethics has to tell man in peace and war alike what he is taking upon himself when he is involved in war. If in war it may perhaps be prevented from doing this by physical force, then it must do it by eloquent silence. In any case it must not promote ideology under the claim of ethics. And in peace it must say loudly and clearly what has to be said in this regard.

I have to affirm my country's will to live in affirming war. Primarily, however, this will to live is not a will for unity on the basis of common race, language, culture, or history, nor is it a will to maintain certain national symbols such as the almost mystical idea of the German Rhine or (for Germans and French alike), possession of Strasbourg Cathedral, or, for Russians, possession of the Dardanelles. The will for unity and the will for certain symbols arise only because and so far as there lies behind them a definite will for power. As the will of a people the will for power means: We will . . . we will because we need and we need because we will: we will coal and potash, iron and petroleum, market outlets, commercial treaties, transportation routes, colonies, and, as security in a future war, frontiers which form natural defensive lines, and, finally, as the crown and sum of all else, we will and need prestige, world status, respect for our colors as the presupposition of future and wider actualization of our will for power. Everything else really belongs primarily only to the politics of academic essays, although it is, of course, indispensable in fact, and is thus industriously cultivated in the schools as a stimulus for this will for power. English policy in war and peace has been the cleverest and most successful since Roman times because, presupposing the will for national unity as self-evident and suppressing all political mysticism, it has been able to concentrate on the one thing necessary, namely, the will for power, and only temporarily when required, as in 1914–1918, to press morality into service, the service, naturally, of this will for power. This circumstance, familiarly known as English "cant," was rightly seen through in Germany and became the enemy that was suddenly fought from the high horse of morality, although perhaps there would have been less outrage at hypocrisy and the like if it had been realized that when a people wills to live, and does not think it can do so without invoking the ultimate reason against another people, morality, ideas, and mysticism cannot play any other role, and in fact did not do so in Germany either, the only difference being that the English, when it came to the point, were able to handle the matter in a much more skillful and uninhibited way.|

To handle morality neither skillfully nor unskillfully, but to realize soberly and realistically that actualization of the will to power is what politics and especially war is all about, is the first concrete task of ethical reflection on war. This does not mean that war is ethically condemned but that it is seen in its true reality. This must be the presupposition of all else. Obviously we will accept the ethical possibility of war less lightheartedly when we tell ourselves—when the nations learn to tell themselves—that it is not so much for the so-called supreme values but for coal and potash and the rest that soldiers have to shoot at one another as "enemies." We may still have to accept the need for this, but probably, as is to be desired, with greatly damped-down enthusiasm. ⌐Military nationalism is less likely to perish, if it ever does, from direct ethical attack than from ethical starvation.¬ The second ethical task is to realize no less relentlessly that the actualizing of the will for power in war—there may be other forms—means that soldiers (certainly at the risk of their own lives, but that is not the point) must diligently and carefully shoot at the enemy soldiers.

On the morning of the battle of Leuthen, the grenadier guards of Frederick the Great are said to have sung a hymn asking that they might do with all their might what they had to do according to God's command for them in their calling,[48] and then in the evening they sang: "Now thank we all our God, With heart and hand and voices . . ."[49] One can only say: Good for them that they could do this, and good for us if we can do it too. Being able to sing thus is what human action is all about in either peace or war. But we have to realize quite unsentimentally what had to be *done* and *suffered* by those involved *between* the hymns. This is the second part of ethical reflection. We can spare ourselves an analysis of the ethical situation on the day of the battle between that morning and evening. It is enough to recall that many circumstances have made it harder for us than for the people of Leuthen to sing hymns before and after what a military action means today, that in the last war the mood of Leuthen was incomparably more appropriate at home than at the front, that the theoretical Yes to war could be pronounced much less enthusiastically by those who had to speak it in their bloody work than by idealists, romantics, and professors of theology who were a long way away from shooting that had to be directed at other living men. If I accept war, I accept the fact that because of the will to live, i.e., because of the will to live of my country, I am ready to take the life of the other men that another country hurls against me because of its will to live. As I accept war, I again accept killing in self-defense, the "I or he," the "off the plank"; the only difference is that I now do it as a member, but a responsible member, of my people. It may be that I *must* do it. Ethics cannot forbid war. But it cannot really command it either. It can only point to the Creator's command of life, of respect for life, and say imperturbably, and say again, that in peace and war we humans are measured by this command. This is God's command whose most concrete content we do not control. It may be, then, that we today may also have to will and make war in obedience to this command. But it may also be that as we listen more closely to what it demands of us reason will be taken out of the ultimate reason and the resultant slogan will be: "*Down* with armaments."[50]

It is obvious that in the questions addressed thus far we have not dealt with everything that might be allowed or forbidden in the taking of human life. Along similar lines we have questions to put to those who

[48]From the hymn "O Gott, Du frommer Gott" (1630) by J. Heermann (1585–1647) (*EKG* 383).
[49]By M. Rinckart (1585–1649).
[50]The title of the chief work by the Austrian writer and pacifist Bertha von Suttner (1843–1914) who was awarded the Nobel Peace Prize in 1903; cf. *Die Waffen nieder*, popular ed., Dresden 1896.

advocate *abortion* or to those who justify *euthanasia* in the case of people who are hopelessly defective either mentally or physically, and, in comparison with the questions already dealt with, the result might be an enhanced questionability of such possibilities almost to the point of manifest impossibility. We ought also to go into more refined and perhaps even worse possibilities of destroying life which are covered by no law and seem on the face of it to be extremely vicious. But we have discussed individual issues only by way of example and not with a view to giving a total picture. We chose the questions treated because they have a general and specific relevance which did not allow us to pass them by without trying to apply general rules of ethical thinking to them. Because of shortness of time, and because we have to understand the command in relation to other categories, we must leave a gap here and press on. But first it is necessary to bring the discussion of the concept of respect for life to some sort of conclusion.

This concept, in which we have recognized the second aspect of the command, obviously involves more than the awe and responsibility by which, as shown, the whole circle of possibilities of supposedly permitted and even commanded killing is so forcefully called in question. The life of others clearly wills not to be taken, but even apart from this ultimate possibility it also wills to be respected in its existing state. My conduct in my life together with others can mean a restriction of their life quite apart from the final possibility of killing. To the extent that that is so it obviously comes no less radically than killing under the questioning of the divine command. In so far as human action means, not killing, but restriction for the life of others, we shall deal with it under the common concept of *competition*. As the word indicates, this implies a contest between the will to live of one person and the will to live of another person. But the metaphor is too innocuous, to the extent that in a sporting contest, if A beats B, B must concede the renown and the prize to A, but his will and ability may be comparatively or relatively called in question by my victorious rival but not absolutely so. Things are different, however, in the real contest of life in which we are all involved. It needs the twofold reflection of faith to understand that the seriousness of life is also, from the external standpoint, a game, as Hermann Kutter, among recent writers, has most impressively taught us to do.[51] Primarily, in the simple reflection that we must not skip over, life is not a game of football for a cup, but a fight for being, and, as such, a serious matter. Off the field of sport, except in the case of a professional player, we are running for our lives, i.e., our life-act takes

---

[51]Cf. H. Kutter, *Das Unmittelbare.* . . ., Berlin 1902 (1921³), pp. 279ff.; *Das Bilderbuch Gottes*, Basel 1917, p. 226; *Im Anfang war die Tat*, Basel 1924, p. 207; *Plato und wir*, Munich 1927, p. 311; *Aus der Werkstatt.* . . ., Zurich 1963², passim. Cf. H. Kutter, *Hermann Kutters Lebenswerk*, Zurich 1965, pp. 116f. H. Kutter (1869–1931), a Zurich pastor, was, with L. Ragaz, the most significant champion of the social gospel in Switzerland.

place as we run toward this or that. If others get ahead of us, then we do not just lose this or that. For if in life we struggle for this or that, we do so only because our life is being lived, because it seeks to actualize itself as life, and this or that offers the occasion or even the symbol for it. This or that, and all the things we need according to Luther's exposition of the fourth petition of the Lord's Prayer (Matt. 6:11),[52] are things we could do without as such, as the contestant in the arena can do without the honor awarded to another . . . if only they were not vital to us (this is the difference between play and earnest), if only our life were not restricted and broken when another snatches them from under our nose. The prizes that we chase in the serious battle of life are not dispensable but are part of our very lives. If I beat a rival in this contest, he is not just beaten comparatively but struck in his very will to live, in his being, his will, his ability. For he lived by reaching out for the thing that I took from him. My taking it away from him meant for him, then, the loss, not of something alien, but of something of his own, a part of his courage and joy in life, of his affirmation of life. It meant unquestionably a diminution of his living force. Something happened which fundamentally is on the same level as if I had killed him. It cannot be ruled out that my victorious competition unintentionally approximates to the killing of my competitor. It cannot be ruled out that in seeking victory in this competition I finally perceive and declare a situation of self-defense and therefore adopt the ultimate reason, which, as we have seen, is always the extreme expression of the same human will to live.

Let us consider an example from the first and apparently harmless stage of the battle for existence where the wild beast shows its claws clearly enough for any who have eyes to see. A big crowd wants to get in a train or streetcar and already, in this not very weighty matter, the fine old principle usually triumphs: "Make way for the strong." Now an example from the second stage of unintentional but unthinking approximation to the possibility of killing: there is a fire in a cinema or theater, some people are trampled to the floor, and others boldly seek a way out by walking over their heads. Next the third stage, that of the struggle to get into the lifeboats when a ship is going down, and now revolvers may be drawn, the hands of swimmers are pushed away from the sides of the overloaded boats, and intentional killing begins. On this sharply inclined plane life itself is at stake—our whole life. Here again the first necessary step of ethical reflection is to realize that this is so, that our struggle for being does not begin with these events but is shown in these events to be the true state in which human life together exists. I cannot live without striving. I cannot strive without in some way competing. I cannot compete in the serious competition of life without restricting the life of another, without impairing it in its movement, without stealing a

---

[52]Cf. *Die Bekenntnisschriften der evangelisch-lutherischen Kirche*, Göttingen 1930, 1959[4], pp. 513f., 679ff.; T. G. Tappert, *The Book of Concord*, Fortress, 1976, pp. 347, 430ff.

march on it, and therefore without entering on that sharply inclined plane at the end of which man is the butcher of man. |

The actualization of the will to live in the full sense of the concept described in subsection 2 is fulfilled in acts of *appropriation*. I live as I grasp after this or that which I need to satisfy my needs or to give me pleasure or simply to test and prove my strength, or which I want to lay by, perhaps, as a reserve for future use. The radius of my sphere of life is determined by the radius of my grasping, taking, and appropriating. If this has some natural limits in relation to what I immediately need— even in cases of great greediness I cannot take directly more than I can handle—this radius of my will to live can obviously be extreme in regard to what I lay aside for future use. It is one thing to live from hand to mouth (though even here it makes a difference what claims I make and what I understand by daily bread) and a very different thing prudently to lay aside extra for tomorrow, for the rest of my life, and even for my children and grandchildren, with an excess, perhaps, in reserve. Since the pure will for power, which is not oriented to need, is also an unquestionable form of the will to live, and since it too (in the form of capitalism, imperialism, etc.) takes the form of appropriation, a natural limit cannot be set for this second possibility of appropriation. And if simple appropriation for immediate consumption is more likely to bring me into very slight, slight, and not so slight collisions with the similar activity of others the less my life is solitary and the more it is lived together with others, this life together becomes increasingly a whole system or chaos of mutually intersecting circles and mutually overlapping, obstructing, and intercepting lines of action the more I and others aim at that prudent and potentially unlimited accumulation of possessions for some future use. In this way my action becomes competition, participation in the serious contest of life. As I live for myself, I necessarily live against others. In this action of mine, however, I am answerable to the command of respect for the life of others. We should have to drain the ocean dry if we were to describe the questioning of our action by the command with anything even approximating to completeness. Some hints must suffice at this point—hints which show that we cannot really hide from the question of command, that we have to wrestle with the posing of this quesion at every step.

1. A first point is that the question is put no less sharply when I *do not consider* that my seeking, taking, and appropriating in accordance with the will to live implies fighting, upsetting, and robbing others than when I expressly find for it some explanation and motivation. In ninety-nine cases out of a hundred our will to live is clever enough to make us act without reflection, so that not knowing what we are doing we may act without shame and merrily do what the moment and the situation suggest. To our astonishment we are then suddenly awakened, perhaps, by soft crying or a loud protest on the part of those around us who obviously seem to feel that they are the victims of our naive vitality.

"How could you?" they ask, and we reply, "Dear God, we meant no wrong," as though the hurt had dropped down from the clouds. "But the other goes and weeps."[53] It may be that we had to act as we did in faith and obedience regardless of all the possible tears and protests around us. But even though our faith and obedience, i.e., the command of God, justifies us, it does not justify our lack of thought, our naive vitality. Ethical reflection has to mean the destruction of the naiveté with which we usually assert and justify our vitality. It necessarily forces us to think about our thoughtlessness. God's command is not concerned about the difference between the intentional and unintentional, the deliberate and the nondeliberate. It directs our *action*, and if this action *has* a militant character, it has it. If it is still done in sanctification, this is certainly not because we have not thought about it but, whether with greater or lesser awareness, because of the faith and obedience with which we have wittingly or unwittingly acted, i.e., because of the Word that is spoken to us [cf. John 15:3] and in virtue of which sinners such as we continually are, perhaps with our naive or less naive vitality, can still be righteous and holy.

2. Assuming that we are acting with less naive vitality, that we now *know* more or less clearly what we are doing, we must still be on guard against a whole series of mystifications, obscurations, and exculpations by which we constantly try to escape responsibility for the militant character of the actualization of our will to live. We must go on to say, then, that the command and its question are no less sharply posed where our appropriating and striving are indirect than where they are direct. If I, as a younger person, use the greater force of my will to live to get ahead of an older person in some field, e.g., the academic, if I push him out—"make way for me"[54]—this may happen without my actually doing anything hostile, but simply by the happy fact that I am young and strong and vital, whereas he is tired and battle-weary. Obviously my turn has now come. Only indirectly have I taken anything from the older person. When members of the white race all enjoy every possible intellectual and material advantage on the basis of the superiority of one race and the subjection of many other races, and of the use that for centuries our race has made of both, I myself may not have harmed a single hair on the heads of Africans or Indians. I may be very friendly toward them. I may be a supporter of missions. Yet I am still a member of the white race which, as a whole, has obviously used very radically the possibility of appropriation in relation to them. My share in the sin against Africa or Asia for the last hundred or fifty years may be very remote or indirect, but would Europe be what it is, and would I be what

[53]From F. Freiligrath's (1810–1876) song, "O lieb, so lang du lieben kannst," *Gesammelte Werke*, ed. J. Schwering, Berlin 1909, vol. 1, p. 184.
[54]Cf. C. H. de Saint-Simon (1760–1825), *Catéchisme des industriels*, *Oeuvres*, vol. IV, Paris 1875, new ed. 1966, p. 53, where, quoting the Italian poet, Filippo Pananti da Mugello, (*Il poeta di teatro*, 1808), he calls this the slogan of the Liberal Party.

I am, if that expansion had never happened? Our economic life clearly needs a whole series of delegated relations which apparently—but only apparently—allow the individual to watch the struggle for life in the harmless role of a spectator, and even, it may be, in the very satisfying role of an actively critical spectator. As the legal heir of part of a family fortune—I might be the descendant of a onetime robber baron—what have I to do with the way this fortune was perhaps amassed time out of mind? Much grass has grown on the graves of those who once suffered in appropriating, but not yet enjoying, this property that is now incontestably mine. I did not really take it from anybody, but simply inherited it by law. Or as a great or little stockholder, what have I to do with the way in which the dividends on which I live are earned, possibly in America? What have I to do with the enterprises in which my capital in the bank is advantageously invested? Thank God, I am neither the employee with his wage policy, his overtime, and his contract; nor the merchant with his methods of competition, nor the housing speculator with his blocks for rent, nor the distillery owner in the east of Germany. I simply draw my interest and take what belongs to me before God and the law. But we cannot get away with the irresponsibility of this indirect grasping and taking. Again the law of God does not ask how close or distant our participation is. It asks about our participation or nonparticipation in the act which is an attack on the life of another and which, to that extent, always stands under the crisis of the command. It makes us responsible for our own action, not apart [from], but in the involvement with that of others in which it actually lies, with the action of others which, by the fact that we share enjoyment of its results, as Adam ate the fruit that Eve had plucked [cf. Gen. 3:6], is also our own action. If it can still be justified and sanctified action, this will not be because of its indirectness, because we are some distance away from the front of the real battle, but again if and because it is faith and obedience, because, in spite of everything, it does not lack in *God's* eyes the character of respect for life that the command requires. This will take place in and not outside the crisis which this command means for our action, for our indirect as well as our direct appropriating, struggling, and disrupting in opposition to others.

3. Responsibility will also be no less if my competing is not perhaps an expression of my individual egoism but of a *collective* egoism. We have already indicated the significance of this thesis for the relation of the individual to his country. A bad action does not become good because a group is its primary subject and I am only a secondary subject in the service and with the commission of this group. I am answerable for what my country does. Authentic patriotism exists, and so too does the presupposition of all meaningful participation in politics, only when I accept this responsibility, only when I think and act politically as one who is ready to shoulder personal ethical responsibility for what my country does, knowing that he cannot charge any guilt to others or

shuffle off his responsibility as a citizen. It is a hopeless theory that the country or state as such has a different responsibility from mine, or even none at all as distinct from me. This involves ethical collapse both for the state and for individuals in their relation to it. No, if I want the state to do something, I must venture to be responsible for it as for my personal will. If I want my country or state to act, or cannot stop it acting (as all countries and states do), like an eagle or a lion or a bear or any other wild animal, then I have to realize that no matter how diligently I cultivate a humane private morality, this will not alter the fact that as a member of the great collective, the state, I myself will be acting like a beast of prey. My grasping and seizing will not then be justified because, perhaps, I am acting unselfishly in my capacity as father and provider for my own family. The family is, of course, the mighty fortress of the middle-class morality which can easily unite a touching loyalty and concern for those in one's own nest with the *laissez-faire* of ruthless capitalism. Here is the suspicious point where the natural altruism of the woman, especially the woman as mother, usually suffers a hairbreadth change into its opposite, the sunlit clarity of concern and partisanship for her own children in opposition to those of all other people. Compare this sour passage from Kierkegaard's *Diaries:* "The relation of humanity to the ideal is as follows. The young girl blushes with enthusiasm when she hears of it. The heart of the young man beats strongly. The bachelor respects it. The married man does not entirely reject it. But at the greatest distance from it stands the mother, the married woman. Real raging against the ideal comes from family life, from the lioness" (*Buch d. Richt.*, p. 159).[55] It is also clear that one of the limits of socialism is that thus far even in its most powerful and fruitful manifestations, I refer to the trades union movement, it has not been able to do more than oppose to one egoism, that of the middle-class, another egoism, that of labor, training the worker to be a fighter in the economic war who is fully conscious of his own strength. This is not a judgment on socialism. It is simply an observation that another world has not dawned with it. The Social Democrat will not enter heaven because of his class loyalty. There is justification for the patriot, the father, the mother, and the fighter in the class war. It is not to be sought, however, in the fact that they all act out of collective rather than individual egoism, as though this were suddenly something different and not simply a special form of the general struggle. Here, too, the justification and santification of human action can be sought only in the faith with which we certainly will not escape the judgment of the command.

4. Another mystification is to try to evade responsibility for the militant character of our actions by appealing to our *good intentions* in performing them. The end does not sanctify the means. The cobbler

---

[55]S. Kierkegaard, *Buch des Richers*, Tagebücher. Selection from the Danish, H. Gottsched, Jena/Leipzig 1905.

who stole leather from the rich man to make shoes for the poor was no less a thief. If his sins are forgiven, it is not because he made shoes for the poor, but because of the faith with which, following in his own way the general law of taking, he did it.[56] This is the thing which in every Christian act we cannot consider too much, whether with half or full publicity, before the venture is made to initiate it in the name of Christianity. This is what has also to be considered in relation to the constant concern for true Christian politics if we start Christian unions or newspapers or, as recently in Berlin, an Evangelical bank.[57] This is what has to be considered at every point in church politics both within the church and also in its relation to the state and to the Roman Catholic church. Wherever there is a struggle between man and man, we are in this arena. This is not in itself forbidden. We cannot leave the arena. But it is fit that we should make only very circumspect use of the Christian flag in this arena, for at every smallest step we take the danger is very great that we shall at least compromise severely the Christian name, and, in any case, Christ will triumph in spite of our Christian flagwaving and not by means of it. The ambivalence in which even the best of earthly intentions is necessarily entangled is that leather must always be stolen in some way to make shoes for the poor, or, to speak plainly, we cannot achieve even the best end without trying to secure a majority, money (especially money!), status, and influence, without having to ask where these are to be found if we really want to reach our goal. Are we then, to let our hands fall? No, but we have to realize that as we raise them we make ourselves like the children of the world, and we have no more claim to call our action Christian than any others, our only claim being to the mercy of God with which we do not set ourselves *against* them but can only set ourselves *alongside* them. What makes the Roman church so incredible, or so barely credible, for us as a real church is that it dares so freely to claim that its secular rule, against which there is nothing to say as such, or no more than against any secular rule, is a spiritual rule. If we ourselves do the same in relation to the state, society, and not finally the Roman church itself, if we make of the church's cause a party cause, no matter whether the party be of the right or left, or whether it be a special Christian party . . . then we stand in serious danger of making ourselves incredible as the church too. The good intention will in no case justify us, but the ways that we have to propose to realize it will necessarily place us at the point where our Christianity again becomes a very serious question.

5. We have also to realize that responsibility for our part in the struggle for existence is not lessened by the fact that as a rule it probably

[56]Marginal note: "Problem of Schiller's *Räuber!*"
[57]This bank was founded by the family of Adolf Runck and Sons in Berlin at the time of runaway inflation and was designed to attract the Evangelical church and people away from Jewish competitors. It went bankrupt at the end of the twenties.

takes place in certain generally recognized forms of tradition, custom, and law. Tradition, custom, and law—we shall have to deal with them later—signify in fact a certain necessary channeling and regulation of the militant will to live, a certain dam against chaos, and, as they have their origin in the command of God, they make it clear how grateful we should be to God's command. For who knows what would become of us were we delivered up to one another without this corrective! Tradition, custom, and law, however, do not alter the fact that we are continually responsible to the command of God. We are so—this is where the threat of a false conclusion must be avoided—even when the actualizing of our will to live keeps ever so strictly within their limits.

The concept we especially have to be on guard against overestimating here is that of *property*. My property consists of the intellectual and material goods which are specifically at my disposal to the exclusion of all others. We say too much if we claim that the commandment: "Thou shalt not steal" [Exod. 20:15] protects and sanctifies property. To argue thus is to forget that the concept of property presupposes the conflict of all against all, and that in its own way it also confirms and accepts this conflict. At the same time it sets certain limits for it. Hence it is, of course, a certain reminder of the command of God and of the question which this interjects into our lives. Yet the command of God itself, precisely in the concrete form "Thou shalt not steal," reaches further. Unlike the concept of property, it does not set up a limit within the conflict but sets up God's right and claim in opposition to the conflict as such. If its question is directed to those who violate the property of others, it is directed no less to those who uphold their own property. If it sets up a limit within the conflict, it establishes no less the limit of the conflict as a whole. Here is the relative truth in the paradox that "property is theft."[58] This makes sense as an expression, not of the negation of the concept of property, but of the crisis in which the concept stands. It does not abolish the commandment "Thou shalt not steal," but turns it against the owner, not to call him a rogue—this would make no sense—but to ask him whether precisely in his security as an owner in which he can survive the struggle for existence, precisely in the security which he owes to the commandment, he is not himself a transgressor of the commandment, a spoiler and perhaps a slayer of the life of others. This reversal is not a devilish or communistic invention. It is the radical meaning of the commandment "Thou shalt not steal," because this commandment is God's, not man's. If, as an owner, I am *not* a rogue, this is on account of God's right to property, not mine. It is because God has been pleased to allot me this or that without my being guilty thereby of violating respect for the life of others. It is thus, and only thus, that, as an owner, I am not a thief. Whether this is how things

[58]"La propriété c'est le vol," P. J. Proudhon (1809–1865) in *Qu'est ce que c'est que la propriété?* ou *Recherches sur le principe du droit et du gouvernement*, Paris 1840, p. 2.

are, however, is the question that the command of God puts to even the most legitimate owner, a question that he cannot evade.

The necessity of the *division of labor* offers no safeguard either against this question. Many at least of the advantages that some have over and at the expense of others rest on the fact that calling in the broadest sense (see the next section) extends the radius of action of one as compared with that of another, e.g., that of the man as compared with that of the woman, of the intellectual as compared with the manual worker, of the king as compared with the carter. Again it must be said of the division of labor that it is really good and necessary as a principle of order in the enduring struggle for existence, as a point of reference for a relatively easy and satisfying ranking and division of goods, a point of reference which is truly respectable as a reminder of the command of God which does in fact direct each of us to his calling. But again the command, seriously and radically understood, does not from this standpoint establish any sure claim for the privileged that they may ignore the encroachment on the claims of others that is the correlate of their privileged position, that they need not worry about the muted grumbling of the underprivileged against them. The command which assigns me my calling gives me no assurance that things will go well with me in it, that I have a right to do better than others. This is human law, not divine law. Just because the command of God can by divine right put me in a privileged place, the question is always acute whether I am in fact privileged by divine right, i.e., in obedience to God's command, or whether I am condemned by the same command as one who violates respect for the life of others, whether my legitimately occupied and defended place of privilege has nothing whatever to do with the grace of God but is an insolent usurpation. If within the civil order (and this cannot be avoided even in a Soviet republic) I occupy a position in which in some way I stand in the sun in relation to many others, I cannot excuse myself before the divine tribunal on the ground that in virtue of my calling I have claim that this should be so. If God himself does not exculpate me, I am not exculpated in this respect.

Similarly I cannot disown responsibility for my grasping and taking on the basis of the idea of *compensatory justice*, i.e., the element of truth in the fine slogan "Make way for the strong." What the ethics of the Puritans in England and America, and the ensuing ethics of the Enlightenment, used to extol and preach in a most unsuitable way as *the* ethical truth, is, of course, true. The climaxes of the struggle for existence, even if only in the long run and not without the need for eschatological counterbalancing and readjustment, do always have the character of reward and punishment: reward for concentration, solidity, industry, daring, honesty, and also love of neighbor, fear of God, and Christianity; and punishment for dissipation, squandering, indolence, pusillanimity, dishonesty, crass selfishness, ungodliness, and unchristian conduct. The validity of this state of affairs again establishes a principle of order and equity within the struggle for existence and this principle is again a reflection of the divine command in virtue of which obedience is life and disobedience death [cf. Deut. 30:15ff], each of us being repaid according to his works [cf. 2 Cor. 5:10]. But again it must be said that a sure right to success is given to no one by God's command and the idea of my not being responsible for my part in the struggle for existence cannot possibly be based on my being better and behaving better than others. What was basically overlooked in the great turn in the history of Christian ethics which took place with the transition from Puritanism to the Enlightenment; what was overlooked by, e.g., Benjamin Franklin with his account books of his daily moral state;[59] what seems still to be overlooked by the great majority of American—and not just American—Christians today, is that a morality which has practical success as its reward could finally be one which also makes this reward its goal. For all its strictness and purity a morality which fits us for life, n.b. for the struggle for life, will seem to be, to those who champion it, a competitive morality which presupposes the struggle for a place in the sun and thus sees to it that this struggle can never cease, a morality which differs from cunning and force, from money and guns, only in so far as in fact, at least with reference to its eschatological sanctions, it is perhaps the most effective weapon, superior to all others, in that conscious struggle. Let us use this superior weapon, then, and no others. As well for us if we use *this* weapon. "Always be faithful and honest." "Do right and fear nobody." "The world belongs to the strong." "Everything rests on God's blessing."[60] These sayings, which solid citizens often repeat to their own edification, are *good* sayings. But they should give the solid citizen no occasion for security. Even with this weapon in our hands we are threatened by the other who cannot lay up this blessing in his barns any more than we can, by the whole vulnerability of our success, by the question whether the obvious triumph of the just over the unjust, the visible blessing on the work of the devout as opposed to the ungodly, might not really be as pleasing to God as it is to us, because, in spite of everything, respect for the life of others has been violated and a brutal jungle scenario has been enacted. We might well have been all the more guilty of cruelty and injustice in putting others under the wheels on which we so merrily rolled, even though we did smear those wheels with the oil of morality and Christianity. God might have all the more against us if we think that our grasping and taking is justified by the fact that our advantage proves the superiority of God's cause and is a victory of the good over the bad. If

[59]Cf. *The Autobiography of Benjamin Franklin*, with introduction, notes, and suggestions by W. N. Otto, The Riverside Press, Cambridge, Mass. 1928, pp. 93ff.
[60]Marginal note of Barth: "Hüssy!" The reference is to the family of textile manufacturers in Safenwil with whom Barth as minister (1911–1921) lived in some tension when he championed the workers' rights and whose business ideology is obviously characterized by proverbs like those quoted by Barth.

this is *not* so, if we are indeed justified in our triumph, this is certainly not because world history is world judgment,[61] but because in world judgment, which is not at all identical with world history, there is mercy also for the bit of world history which we have made either morally or immorally, although in this regard we have to expect that the first will be the last and the last first [cf. Mark 10:31, etc.]. True fear of God and true morality begin when in the light of God's compensating justice I and my righteousness are also on the scales and my righteousness might prove to be filthy rags [cf. Isa. 64:5] in which I have wrapped myself so as not to have to be my brother's keeper [cf. Gen. 4:9].

6. We have to point out finally that there also seems to be in life a series of possibilities that have nothing to do with the struggle for existence, so that the question of the command of respect for the life of others does not apply to them. In reality, however, even in these final hiding places the rule is still valid that we compete, and we are thus asked about our responsibility in this regard.

I have in mind first what might be summed up as technology. Technology is the use, extension, and perfecting of human ability, of human rule over nature. Do we not have here a pure action that does not even touch and cannot therefore threaten the lives of others? Yes, we might reply, if human invention, construction, and enterprise took place in a vacuum and if the subject were man in the abstract, as things are usually presented in praise especially of the modern period. In fact, however, neither head, eyes, nor hands are used merely to advance that ability. The moving force behind this vertical progress is the prospect, however slight, of horizontal progress, i.e., on the level again on which there is struggle, overtaking, and pushing back. Even the finest inventions become really interesting only when industry, and through industry the banks, become interested in them. And now that the Atlantic has just been flown for the first time from east to west, in Germany the fact that a German did it, not an Englishman or a Frenchman, is what has stimulated the enthusiasm with which this advance has been hailed,[62] not to mention the fact that the last war made it clear to us that the wonderful world of human technology can in an instant, if need be, transform itself into a veritable hell of instruments of slaughter and [can] thus find itself with man on the plane where killing can be an event at any time.

We do not really move into any cleaner air when we think of the world of *scholarship*. As the disinterested investigation and teaching of truth, which it is normally said to be in academic orations, scholarship does not

---

[61]Cf. F. Schiller's "Resignation" (1784).

[62]Charles Lindbergh flew west to east on May 20/21, 1927, and, with a following wind, took 33½ hrs. from New York to Paris. On April 12, 1928, the Germans Köhl and von Hünefeld and the Irishman Fitzmaurice flew a Junkers W33 for the first time in the opposite direction, taking 35½ hrs. from Baldonnel in Ireland to Greenly Island. Cf. *Der Grosse Brockhouse*, Leipzig 1930[15], vol. VI, pp. 355f.

exist, just as it has never existed without the human subject of this particular human activity. In his quality as the subject of scholarship, too, the human subject is the subject that wills to live, cost what it may. I will not go into the fact that for many students scholarship is simply the milch cow which is designed to provide them with butter some day, nor will I go into the natural struggle for the best positions whose agitations, worries, triumphs, and sufferings play a bigger role even in the professional sanctuaries of supposedly pure learning than the respectful layman usually suspects. Even apart from these general human conditions of academic life, it is becoming apparent today with an increasing clarity worthy of our thanks that the high estimation of scholarship increases as industry and its underlying capital are in close vicinity, as in the technical fields of chemistry and physics, or the sure prospect of gaining a living, as in medicine. If we are inclined to praise philosophy and theology as harmless disciplines in this regard, we have only to take an unprejudiced look at the battle of schools in these fields (and we cannot ignore the real background of appointments here) to be reminded by even the purely intellectual spectacle of the coming and going of the different schools and trends, by their way of establishing and promoting themselves, by the rise and inevitable decline of the various great figures (not inappropriately called "top dogs" and "big guns"), to be uncannily reminded by them of what goes on in the primitive forest, so that we cannot congratulate ourselves as philosophers or theologians on [account of] any purity in this respect. It need only be noted in passing that the same spectacle with the same question marks and exclamation points may also be found in the life of the church, even in the free Christian life of the spirit and fellowship, as also in the secular fields of literature, art, and sport. It is not at all true that the life-struggle for power and influence with all its accompanying phenomena and consequences—a struggle which necessarily seems to raise the question of the relation to what is commanded—is restricted to the special sphere of economic life and that in our own spheres (apart from our participation in the economic world) we others can wash our hands in innocency. If we are acquitted, it is not in the least because of the more ideal sphere in which we have pitched our tents as compared with the merchant or official.

We will close with a glance in a different direction. We refer to *love* in its different forms, from heavenly love to admitted and unmistakable earthly love, and in all its possibilities of expression, from the love of parents and children to the love in which a man may perhaps venture his life to help others in some way. Is not love as such, apart from the means it may have to use, exempt from the law of the struggle of all against all and therefore from the responsibility which we have to shoulder in this struggle? May there not be seen here in the world of ambiguity, of unbounded questionability, in which we normally live, a world of purity and therefore of innocence that needs no justification? Yes, we may say, if we really dare to claim that our love is real love, if we really know an actualization of love in which there is no grasping, taking, and ruling, in which there is no forcing of the one who is loved by the one who loves, if we really know a love in which no pain is caused, no pressure exerted, no burden imposed, no mastery enforced, in which the other is truly sought and not the self. It is true that love is not judged. But who of us has and practices the love that is not judged? Who of us even with his love is not [set] under the judgment of the question whether he does not by his love violate respect for the life of others, and perhaps violates it more seriously than a robber or murderer, because the last can at least be known by their acts, whereas the violations done in love may perhaps be concealed lifelong, both from ourselves and from those we wound, in the beautiful garment in which they take place. Why does the exercise of *Christian* love so seldom make any different impression on the world, and not just the wicked world, than that of a particular expression of the Christian will for power? We should not forget that the love of which Paul writes in 1 Corinthians 13 is an eschatological possibility and that in 1 John [4:8, 16] *God* is called love. If love is to justify us in the judgment, then it will not be the love that we have produced and demonstrated and proved, but the love which we can understand only as the love ascribed to us by God. In this love it may be that the command of respect for life is really kept and fulfilled by us even though, twist and turn as we like, we can understand ourselves only as its transgressors.

§8

CALLING

God's command always comes to me at a limited point and as a definite work of his creation. In my concrete calling by God the Creator it claims me and I have to listen to it.

1

In §7 we have come to know the ethical problem raised by the command of the Creator. God is the Creator and Lord of life. We live. We are living in company with the life of others. His command, then, implies the question that is put to all our acts, namely, whether or not these acts are our will for our own life that God has created and our respect for the other life that God has created. The answer is the judgment from which we constantly come and to which we constantly go. The answer, then, is God's answer as the question is God's question. We are in no position, therefore, to anticipate the answer just as we ourselves did not put the question. We cannot say unequivocally that this or that act is or is not an actualization of the will to live that God demands of us or of the respect for life that he has commanded. This "is" can have the ring only of a general human truth, no matter how freely the ethicists usually bandy it about. As a human moral judgment it can occur only from case to case and subject to the judgment of the higher court. The concrete divine command alone will and does bring this "is" to light. Ethical reflection, however, obviously involves more than simply asking about the *content* of our acts. We cannot and need not be satisfied with the statement that we are asked by God the Creator what we have done and that God the Creator will tell us what we have done. For the command of God the Creator does not just come to us as those who will to live and as those who have to live in company with the life of others. It also comes to us as those who are *this* or *that* and who live and have to live in *this* or *that* way. It comes to us at a limited point and as a definite work of his creation.[1] To pass knowingly from the decision of the present to the decision of the very next moment in which God will meet us with his question and answer as he has met us before—this implies a knowledge that goes beyond the knowledge of our life, a knowledge of the *what* and *how* of our life by which alone the encounter with God acquires the character of real responsibility which we tacitly presupposed in §7. God is not capricious. His command does not come haphazardly into human life, though this is not perhaps totally ruled out by what we have said thus far. It does not come now in one way and now in another. It does not come by chance into the life of an individual. It does not ever come at random. It strikes me as the lightning does, which when it strikes me in particular has to do so according to the laws of magnetism. Or, better, it strikes me as a well-aimed arrow does when it is aimed at me. |

Between God's command and me, when I listen to it and each moment that I listen to it, there stands a definite *correlation* in which it comes to me in this way and not another. In this correlation it meets me according to the what and how of my being, so that indirectly my what and how become witness to the reality of the divine command, and as in a mirror I can find in them a knowledge of the divine command beyond the material knowledge that it is the law of life, an indirect and relative, yet intrinsically clear, knowledge that the command applies to *me*, and to what extent it does. This correlation is posited by the fact that the one who issues the command is also my Creator. That I stand at this moment in the crisis of the command, and that I am what I am at this moment, are the work of *one* hand, the act of the Creator, both the one and the other. God *claims* what *belongs* to him. His claim is a legitimate claim. We have already seen this at the beginning of §7. Hence the correlation between the command and my what and how is not to be taken to mean that my what and how are self-grounded, that God in claiming me has to orient himself to me, to make a subsequent adjustment to me and my freedom. Even my knowledge of myself, of what I am, is not at this

---

[1]See the thesis at the head of the section (§8)

moment a knowledge which belongs to me, which is self-grounded as *my* knowledge. If I go with knowledge of myself to the decision of the very next moment, it is because the present moment as well stands under God's command, because God's command tells me about myself. Even what I know about myself is thus told me by the command, namely, that my existence is limited and defined in this or that way, that I am not a self-grounded reality but one in which I am simply God's creature, the work of his creation out of nothing, and nothing more. There is no question, then, of our being able to take that correlation to mean that on the basis of our reality we can raise a counterclaim against God, a claim that regard must be had to our what and how. For our what and how are already taken into account in the command that encounters us, this command being the command of our Creator. Our knowledge of ourselves by the way of the divine command is to the effect that we know ourselves as his creatures, not just in our life as such, but in the definiteness of our life in which it is at *this* place *this* work of his creation. This robs us completely of any space or breath to adduce this specificity of our life as a ground for shared control over the meaning and content of the command. The situation is that as God has decided on the definiteness of our life, so he decides on the meaning and content of the command that is issued to us. As God's partners in the correlation, then, we are not on the same level as he is, he being perhaps the greater and we the smaller. No, in this correlation absolutely dependent existence meets absolutely independent existence. There can be no question at all of the reversal of the order, of a reciprocity of the relation that exists here, of a relevance of human freedom for divine freedom.

When it has been said, however, that God is the Lord of the meaning and content of the command as he is of the definiteness of our life at every moment, the other point should not be omitted that God is not capricious, that the correlation really does exist between his command and the definiteness of our life. The formula that God is everything and man nothing is false, for it denies creation. Creation is the positing of the absolutely dependent being which as such, as what is created by God, is being, not nonbeing. We do not exist through ourselves in this specificity of ours and therefore we have no right to control God's command, but we *do exist* in this specificity. We also do not know our existence by ourselves but by God's Word, yet by God's Word we *do know* it. It is necessary to know it. It cannot be an inessential but has to be an essential element in the knowledge of the command that we know that it is told *us*. We are not just creation in general, however, nor do we just live in general. We live at a *definite* place and as a *definite* work of God's creation. If the command does not come to us in this limitation and definiteness of ours it does not come to us at all. We are not an empty page on which something will be written. We are not an empty string on which some note will be struck. It is in absolute dependence on God that we have our what and how, but we do have this *what* and *how.* And God's command comes to us in this what and how. God asks and God answers, but this is not a process which we can watch with folded arms, for God's asking and answering relate to our responsible action. On the knowledge of the specificity of our lives depends our knowledge of our responsibility. God's asking and answering relate not merely to our action but to our *responsible* action and therefore to our being. The seriousness of the fact that not just anything or anybody but we ourselves have to meet God does not permit us not to take ourselves seriously, not because of some view of ourselves that we have won, not in any depth of being in which we belong to ourselves—both these are indeed ruled out by this seriousness—but rather in the existence and the mode of existence which we owe to God and in which God again claims us for himself. God does not just ask us: What are you *doing?* but in and with that: Who *are* you? and the first question remains obscure if the second does not come along with its claim and is not heard and drawn into ethical reflection. When and as the command of God the Creator, which orders us to live and to respect the life of others, really comes to *me,* this does not mean that in everything else I am referred to the obscure chance or compulsion of my soul's life or my situation and that I am thus abandoned to myself, to the whims or the destiny of my subjectivity. Precisely as it orders me it is a definite command, definite for me and therewith more definite also in content. |

It must also be said that although we cannot go on to formulate the concrete command—we know that this command is God's revelation—nevertheless we may achieve a second definition which is at all events proper to the concrete command. If, instead of looking at the content of the command, I now consider that it is given to *me,* this means that no matter what the content may be I have to see that when God speaks his command to me I am found by him in the same reality as that in which I find myself. In listening to his command I may not and must not abstract away from my own reality, for this reality of mine stands in correspondence to God's command. It and no other is the place where God holds judgment over me. The judgment of the command under which I stand means not only that I am measured by God's command but also, because it is spoken to *me* and I am a creature of the same God, that I am measured by myself and my what and how. At every moment I stand in the light of God precisely in the definiteness of my life, and I do not understand the command if I do not understand it also in this definiteness of my life. If I could see and understand myself as God does, if the individual were not ineffable,[2] then in each component of our own reality that is truly seen and understood by us God's command would be as clear to us as it is to God. But we do not see and understand ourselves

---

[2] A reference to the medieval principle that the individual is ineffable, i.e., that the particularity of the individual cannot be expressed in a concept, since in accordance with its logical function a concept is general.

thus. The individual is in fact ineffable. The creature is truly seen and understood neither by any other creature nor by itself. It may only be said, but it must be said, that our creaturely reality as a whole, and more or less clearly each of its components, is an *indication* of God's command (in the particularity in which it is given to *me*) in the same sense as that in which we have understood the fact of our own life and that of others to be an indication of its content. Our creaturely reality (always understood in the special sense of our what and how), and [indeed] each of its components, sets us before the question: Who are you?, namely, Who are you as the one to whom the command of God now comes? In relation to the other question: What are you doing? this question is distinctively sharper and more precise. |

Our own reality understood in its specificity as a pointer of this kind to God's command—this is the general ethical meaning of the concept of *calling*. Here, then, we understand the concept comprehensively as the epitome of the what and how of man. Because we have this what and how from God and not ourselves, it can, without itself being God's command, be a voice that calls us, that calls us *to* God's command. It would be inappropriate and overhasty to try to see God's command itself in our calling in this general sense, as Ritschl did directly with reference to calling in the narrower sense.[3] It is true enough, however, that we cannot hear God's command without hearing the voice of our own distinctive reality calling us, calling us to the command. In other words, we cannot hear it unless we are willing to hear it at our specific and limited place in creation. My calling is the limitation and definiteness in which I live among other men and creatures, to the extent that this is not a matter of chance or fate and is not therefore silent in relation to the command that comes to me; to the extent that the command that comes to me attests and declares itself in it; to the extent, then, that it points to God's command if I will see and understand its sign. To take oneself seriously in the sense just indicated is thus to be ready to see and understand this sign of the definiteness in which we all live, to take one's *calling* seriously, not to see one's what and how as neutral or indifferent, but to see it as the direction to God's command which will not deny them to us. In the deliberations on which we must now embark there can be no question, of course, of developing and analyzing with anything like completeness the specificities in which we live. The truly decisive word on what our calling is will have to remain unspoken, just as we cannot say what life is. In relation to some of the narrower specificities of human reality we can only try to indicate what their definiteness is and what is their correlation with God's command.

The particularity itself is not only the secret of the individual, as already stated, but also the secret of God himself. If we cannot repeat

---

[3]Cf. A. Ritschl, *Unterricht in der christlichen Religion*, Bonn 1875, 1881², 1886³ (with some revision). Cf. the critical ed. (C. Fabricius), Leipzig 1924, pp. 10ff., 56, 81, 92f.

fully and exhaustively the direction that our calling gives us, because we can speak only about its general nature and not about the special thing which makes it a direction in the life of the individual, even less can we show how far we do in fact receive more than direction, namely, God's command itself. This second discussion can only show us, as it can and should show us, that the subjective side of the knowledge of the command, the question: Who are you?, must also remain obscure without the question: What are you doing?, so that it is by no means exempt from ethical reflection nor left to chance. It is no accident that I am what I am. And if we can speak of this only in the form of a general consideration of some of the accessible specificities of human existence, it should be remembered that more is not needed to make it clear that in this respect, too, man is called to be on guard and to deal carefully and seriously with God's command.

2

We shall now deal with some of the narrower and broader circles within which life is lived and which, even if they are not exhaustive, since they cannot reach the unrepeatable individuality of life, do still characterize life as a limited and definite life, as a being with its own what and how. In dealing with these circles we shall have regard to the fact that they can have for us the significance of direction to the command that is given us, direction in the question: What shall *we* do?, so long as we treat them as such, i.e., with the intention of pointing to elements in our own subjective reality which can also become elements in the objective knowledge of the command, with the intention, then of pointing to our *calling*, which is itself the great pointer, the signpost and guide to the command of God.

1. We shall begin with a circle that is so universal that at a first glance one might ask whether we are not uttering an empty word in mentioning it. As we are reached by God's command, we have to seek our calling fundamentally along the lines of the insight that we are *men*. We do not find ourselves, nor are we found by God's Word, as any or as these or those among the incalculably many possibilities of creation, but we are found and find ourselves with this particular *what* and *how*, namely, as *men*. At this point, where we seek to understand ourselves in terms of our creatureliness, we need not say more in defining the being of man than that we understand ourselves as beings that know of themselves and their kind that their life transcends the perceptible processes of physical life in time and space. Even if in a form of consciousness that is physically conditioned in time and space, their life participates in a nonperceptible side of the reality of the world. This is a side of creation which—shall we say precedes? shall we say follows?—is at any rate distinct from the physical world even though it cannot be separated from it or known independently as a metaphysics. It is the side from which

alone the perceptible side, the world of physics, can be seen and explained. In virtue of our participation in it, relatively distinguishing between ourselves and our life-act, we know ourselves as *subjects* of this act. "It" does not live; "I" do. My life is not just an event; always also it is my act. One can and should reverse this too. As I act, as *I* live my life, that participation takes place, I am a member of the intelligible world, I live as body *and* soul, I live as *man*. This statement is no more and no less than a description of the special and specific creatureliness of man. God, of course, stands above the antithesis of the visible and invisible reality of the world in which man exists. In relation to God each reality is *created* and *dependent*. Hence I do not have a share in the life of God by being a member of the intelligible world, by having a life of mind and soul as well as body. This caveat, however, does not prevent man's reality from being this doubly determined reality. It must also be said that we do not know whether there might not be other creatures, known and unknown, that live with the same double determination as we do. Our knowledge does not justify us in denying the possibility that animals and plants might have souls. It does not justify us, of course, in affirming such possibilities either. We simply know that we ourselves and our kind live in this double determination. But this caveat does not prevent us from really *knowing* that we and our kind live in *this* determination. It is in it, then, that we hear the command of the Creator, the command of life. |

The will to live and respect for life, in so far as they are obedience to the command of God, are at any rate characterized as *humanity*. As we actualize them they stand under the criterion of the question whether we can understand them to be human. There can be no question, then, of thinking that we can take the concern intimated in the concept of humanity (or, historically, of humanism) and push it under the rug, as this is usually done in some otherwise friendly schools in modern theology.[4] Humanity is the broad basis of divine calling which we cannot *not* take seriously if we are reached by God's command as the command of God the Creator. The humanity of the will to live means that we do not just want to live as animals do or as plants in their struggle toward light and moisture; we will to live in a human determination. The more our will to live approximates and resembles, either in individual acts or in continuous action, the purely vegetable or animal will to live, the less is it the will of the citizen of two worlds as whom God has created us, and the more pertinent, obviously, is the question of the humanity of this will. We have, of course, no unambiguous measure by which to stake out the limits of humanity. We know no humanity which does not share in animal and even vegetable life, and no animal life to which we

[4]In addition to various Lutheran theologians such as F. Gogarten (see §1, n. 30, 31), P. Schütz, (1891), or even E. Reisner (1890−1966); cf. esp. the disciples of the Reformed theologian H. F. Kohlbrügge (1803−1875): H. Forsthoff (1871−1942) and F. Horn (1875−1957).

can categorically deny humanity. No one can say of another or even of himself that his acts are worthy or unworthy of man. God says this. But God does in fact say it to us in addressing his command to us.

As we understand this criterion relatively and not absolutely, we do not deny, but maintain, that the question of our humanity is *raised*, e.g., the humanity of our instinct of self-preservation, our satisfaction of needs, our pleasure. In the light of this question, greater suspicion is *in place* here and lesser there regarding the relation of our acts to God's command. Ethical reflection is thus possible and necessary inasmuch as its only point can be *preparation* and not actual decision between the good and the bad. And the humanity of respect for life will mean that we encounter all other life with the specific awe and responsibility that we know to be human, not as plants live side by side with plants and animals with animals, but with a knowledge of the invisible side of world reality, with a knowledge of the spirit which, although also created, sets for the natural force of our life another frontier than that which is continually set for it by its collision with other natural forces. The more our relation to the life of others approaches the relations of the jungle, the more acute becomes the question of its humanity. We have seen this question arise with force in face of the possibilities of human action which we have summed up under the concept of competition, even more so in face of all the possibilities of the killing of men by men, and even in face of the many possibilities of our relation to the plant and animal world. We know the inner right of this question. In all these relations our *humanity* is in question, the particularity or distinction of man as such in relation to the life of others, of man as the one who knows, who is invisibly hemmed in by himself as the subject of his acts, whose acts cannot be mere occurrence.

Our humanity is *in question*. This alone can be meant when we call one act human and another inhuman in the narrower sense. To take part in the great contest of life, even at times to the most bitter end which can consist of the killing of one man by another, can always be human and commanded. It can be inhuman and forbidden not to do this. But the closeness to the jungle to which we give ourselves when we compete and kill will always make competing and killing a far more dubious action than one which totally or predominantly can be understood as the sparing, upholding, and cherishing of the life of others. From the standpoint of humanity the scales weigh—we cannot say more, and we cannot say a last word herewith, but this at least we have to say—in favor of peace and against war. We cannot possibly say that peace and war are equally possible possibilities. It is decidely more obvious that we should keep peace than wage war. This applies to the whole content of §7,3. Because our calling is to humanity and not its opposite, the unequivocal biblical witness to God's command, if not the command itself, is to the effect: "Thou shalt *not* kill." Away with the knife! The criterion may be as relative as you wish. It may be that, even bearing the criterion in mind, and in apparent contradiction of the biblical witness to it, the command of God may have to be understood very concretely as a command to take the knife in hand. Yet in the light of the fact that the command of life is given to us as *men*, we cannot possibly say that we have no criterion or no indication of what it is telling us. The fact that we are *men* may seem to be general and empty, but it *is* an indication in the question how *we* are to actualize our will to live and our respect for the life of others. If the final and proper judgment on our action, whether it be good or bad, lies in the hands of God and God alone, we still cannot say that we cannot go toward this judgment watchfully, judging ourselves according to our best knowledge and conscience, responsibly and not irresponsibly.[5]

2. Our sexuality constitutes a second circle, or a unique double circle, of the determination in which we all live. We do not live merely as men but as males or females. We must add at once: We live as males *and* females. Or, as we ought to put it, we live as males *or* females in the indissolubly mutual relation of males *and* females. The command of God must be heard by males as males and females as females, yet not by males in themselves or females in themselves—there are no such things—but by males and females in their mutual *relation* to one another. We can only issue a warning here against any male or female self-consciousness in isolation. On either side this will always mean death in the pot [cf. 2 Kings 4:40]. Our true sex consciousness is never a special male or female self-consciousness based on familiar physical and psychological distinctions. There are perhaps no worse constrictions than those that derive from the worship of false gods, the confusion of illusion and reality, at this point. True sex consciousness is neither male nor female in itself. In the male it is awareness of the relation of one's own existence to that of the female, and in the female it is awareness of the relation of one's own existence to that of the male. The distinctions remain. But the essence of neither male nor female is to be sought in the sum of them. The male has no autonomous life but is male in orientation to the female. The female has no autonomous life but is female in orientation to the male. |

The idea of a male or female being which is self-grounded and self-justified and self-sufficient, fulfilling humanity on its own and in some way surpassing and outdoing the other even if only in the form of this proud self-sufficiency—this idea is a totally ironical one, which, for all the fervor with which it is championed, can only be ironical because, in face of the reality of our sexuality, it is an empty and arbitrary abstraction of the male or female individual. On it the reality, which cannot be deceived, will sooner or later be avenged. But there is no way back from it to this reality. That is, the idea of the relatedness of male

---

[5]Marginal note by Barth: "This passage is too short. It should include a discussion of the concepts of human dignity, human right, and human love."

and female cannot subsequently attach itself to it, nor can the thought of a command under which both male and female stand be logically united with it, because in it we have fundamentally moved away from the place in creation at which we are reached by the command. For this reason all the well-meaning and profound definitions of male and female being—however much they may seem to be needed—stand from the very first under the shadow of the suspicion that they are no more than unprofitable and unrealistic declamations, no matter whether we think we should speak with strong conviction about the place of the male as creator, leader, and protector, or more softly and timidly about the motherliness of the female, her readiness for sacrifice, her receptivity, her willingness to be molded. What do we really know about the male and female except that the male would not be man without the female nor the female without the male, that the male cannot belong to himself without also belonging to the female and *vice versa?* All the attributing of special virtues, advantages, and privileges to the male, as in older ethics, which is mostly the work of males, or to the female, as in the noisy ideology of women's liberation, suffers from the fact—and no historical necessity of the modern situation should prevent us from seeing that it really does *suffer* from this fact—that it calls in question the mutual *relatedness* in which alone the male can be male and the female female. In Genesis 2:25 we find the remarkable saying: "And the man and his wife were both naked, and were not ashamed." Why not? Because the maleness of the male and the femaleness of the female rightly become an object of shame (and then modesty very paradoxically becomes a virtue) only when the male and female in their maleness and femaleness seek to belong to themselves and not to one another. To the degree that they belong to one another they may and should both be naked, i.e., the male may and should be the male and the female the female, and the distinctive sexuality of the two should not be denied, concealed, expunged, or neutralized. If the mutual relation is questioned (and this occurs most unavoidably when we begin to offer definitions and allot all kinds of different and competing attributes to either male or female), then both maleness *and* femaleness become a matter of which decent people can only be ashamed and at which, even if we ourselves do not blush, the sharpsighted remainder will simply laugh, but with the evil laughter with which male and female should not laugh, because in so doing they are primarily calling themselves in question in their humanity and creatureliness.

We can sum up positively all that has been said thus far in that other saying from the creation story in Genesis 2:18: "Then the Lord God said, 'It is not good that man should be alone; I will make him a helper fit for him.' " The serious purpose of what makes the male male is that according to the saying of the Creator it is not good for him to be alone, that in the power of this saying a helper will be given him. And the serious purpose of what makes the female female is that she *is* this helper. Neither has anything whatever to do with what is called authentic maleness or femaleness. Authentic maleness and femaleness are both shameful things, in maintaining which the two can only sin against one another. What may be gathered from Genesis 2:18 is that male and female belong to one another and are to be male and female in this belonging.

We shall have to speak about marriage as the principle of *order* of our sexuality in the next section. At this point we cannot proceed without considering a *presupposition*, indeed, in one respect *the* presupposition of marriage, not the order of marriage, but of *entry* into this order. In other words, there arises the question whether we are to understand our sexuality merely as a general and not also, by creation, as a very *particular* relation of *one* male—this one—and *one* female—*this* one. The question arises whether the issue in marriage is not that, while it does not *have to be* and often is *not*, it *can* be the orderly actualization and confirmation of a mutual relation of two people which is in some sense predestined. Marriage cannot create this relation if it is not already there before and outside marriage by the will of the Creator. On the other hand, of course, the lack of this relation (by creation) does not prevent two people from standing under the order of marriage. In such a case the order necessarily becomes a yoke without on that account ceasing to be an order. It may be seen, however, that when *getting married* and entering under that order we cannot enquire too carefully as to the existence of that presupposition of a marriage that does *not* have the character of a yoke. We must ask whether the individual actualizing of the general relation of male and female is to be thought of as resting on chance or the free will and choice of the parties concerned—or whether there is something like an ordination by creation of just this male for just this female, the discovery of which is the secret of what is called true marriage, while its nondiscovery, its confusion with a normal instance of the relation of male and female, is the guilt and plight of ordinary marriage, no less genuine though this may be, of course, with reference to God's order. One might also formulate the question as follows: Is it correct that true marriages are made in heaven? Is it mere illusion or a real possibility that the male can call the female his elect and *vice versa*, not just in the trivial sense that they *have* chosen one another; but in the sense that they *are* elected for one another by creation and *are* thus destined for marriage with one another? If this is so, then every marriage stands under the *question* whether it is *true* marriage in this sense, whether it is or is not a relation of male and female that rests on calling. |

This thought is not refuted by the fact that at one time it is the supposed certainty of the loving couple, and then later it may become for the same couple an object of uncertainty, doubt, or even denial. Such a development might simply be a confirmation that the determination by creation of these people has been *mistaken* and *missed* as regards their sexuality, with particularly incisive and lasting consequences in this respect, just as we often miss and mistake it in other areas, and in all areas it is the grace of God if we do *not* mistake and miss it. Nor is it a cause to reject the thought that it undeniably became a favorite esoteric concept in German Romanticism. Schleiermacher, in a well-known passage in the fourth of his *Monologen* of 1800 (Schiele, pp. 74f.) (ET *Soliloquies*, 1926), presented it with all the familiar bombast of his youthful writings, yet in a way that materially was not unenlightening, and Goethe expressed it poetically in his *Wahlverwandschaften*, in which we cannot miss the serious reservations with which he surrounded marriage, rightly or wrongly contracted.[6] The real point is that the concept of calling in respect of sexuality simply demands to be given greater emphasis and precision in this thought.|

We have not yet perceived the reality of sexuality as the mutual relation of male and female if we think abstractly of the relation of male and female in general and not concretely of the relation of *this* male and *this* female in which creatureliness and humanity become a reality. If a *threat* to the concept of *marriage* be seen here; if a relation is set up which does *not* coincide with marriage as such, which is above marriage and in which marriage is not necessary, which may not even be realized *once* in a thousand marriages, which even in the best marriage cannot be created or achieved if it was not the presupposition of the contraction of the marriage and if that exchange took place in the contraction of the marriage—if all these things seem to cast doubt on marriage, it must be said that this does not apply at least to marriage as an *order*. We cannot speak about marriage without also speaking about the way that it *comes into being*, not as an *order*, but as the standing of this man and this woman under the order. The concept of an original individual relation of male and female which does not coincide with marriage, which is not affected by it and does not affect it, has a place as the true meaning of *entry* into the order of marriage which in this action of two people is either achieved or, in the majority of cases, missed. The *order* of marriage is better and not worse understood as God's command if on the basis of this concept we do not think of its *coming into being* as outside the command of God, if we accept the thought of a relation by creation of this male to this female, and *vice versa*, in the same way as we do the relation of male and female in general. It should not be overlooked that Genesis 2 is not just a witness, as it is generally taken to be, to the created *order* of the married state. It is also and antecedently a witness to the *calling* by creation of Adam to Eve and Eve to Adam. Hence the *contracting* of marriage, the *entry* of two people into the order of marriage, is set in the very serious light of the question whether the original determination of the two is recognized or whether that confusion takes place, disobedience to the *calling* of God, whose painful consequences

[6]Cf. *Wahlverwandschaften*, I,9.

will have to be borne in the contracted marriage, in obedience to God's *order*. We shall have to deal with this question again in the next section, in which we shall be speaking about man's *calling* by creation, to the extent that in its definite affirmation we have to see the necessary climax and execution of the sexual determination of man, apart from which there can be as little hearing of the command as there can be apart from man's determination in general.

With this second form of our calling we are given *criteria* regarding the relation of our action to God's command. We have to act not merely as men but as male or female, i.e., in the mutual relation of the two as just depicted. Two groups of questions must be differentiated here.

In the actualizing of our will to live and our respect for the life of others we have to ask *first* whether we are faithful in this to our calling as male or female, or whether an exchange takes place here, a secret or open substitution of what is demanded of the male for what is demanded of the female, and *vice versa*. We realize that it is wrong to oppose male and female being to one another abstractly. Nor is it just wrong; it cannot be done. Different ages, nations, and cultures have had different ideas of what is concretely suitable, beneficial, and commanded for males as such and females as such, and here, too, ethics cannot set up any unequivocal commands or prohibitions. But when we realize that the nature of sexuality is to be sought in the mutual relation of the two sexes, we also realize that a difference *exists* and that it raises the question—to which ethics must give a sharper edge—how far our conduct is responsible in face of this *difference* of the sexes by creation. This question is plainly the more urgent the more our conduct takes on the character of that of the opposite sex, instead of taking place—which is another matter—in the relation of our own sex to the other. A male who, in the struggle for existence, acts predominantly with female sensibility, and a female who, in the same arena, acts in characteristically male fashion, the type of the lyric poet on the one side and the industrial secretary on the other, both have to ask themselves whether their action really corresponds to the will of the Creator or whether there might not be a substitution here. For example, a male whose will to live prefers to find actualization in psychological study and corresponding discussions about his fellowmen, or, it may be, in seeking and gathering on every hand stimulations that are, let us say, purely intellectual, could well be on the wrong track as regards his calling by creation. Against Schleiermacher's definition of religion as the feeling of absolute dependence[7] the question might be raised, apart from all else, whether there might not be manifested here a unique perversion of the sex consciousness. Schleiermacher's statement in one of his letters that he often

---

[7]*Der christliche Glaube. . .*, Berlin 1821–1823, revised ed. 1830–1831, §32, pp. 183ff.; ed. Redeker, Berlin 1960, vol. I, pp. 171ff.; ET: *The Christian Faith*,

wished he could have been a woman is in remarkable agreement with this.[8] Conversely, in a female whose will to live works itself out explicitly as will for power, in the form of skill in conflict and the ability to rule, disloyalty to her calling by creation could lurk in a sinister way in the background. *Could*, we cautiously say, for things might well look different in the judgment of God from what they seem to be in our eyes. Our caution, however, does not alter the fact that the question is *raised*, and we should be under no illusions here, for there is hardly a possibility of daily and everyday life, even down to clothes and hairstyles—1 Corinthians 11 is not in the Bible for nothing—that is ethically irrelevant in this regard, or that can evade this question. We have no absolute criterion. But we should not act as though a relative criterion were no criterion at all. We do not have to say what is good or bad. But we must not deceive ourselves. In the judgment of God there are no neutral possibilities. In the judgment of God the decision on good and bad awaits us in this respect too and it has to be borne in mind in application to the criteria that are given to us. |

In the actualizing of our will to live and our respect for the life of others the second question that we have to ask is whether in it we honor or do not honor our sexual determination as the relation of the two sexes to one another. One might formulate this second criterion as follows: Can I as a male answer for my conduct to the female, or can I as a female answer for my conduct to the male? In its final concreteness the question is: Can I answer for my conduct to *the* female or *the* male, to *the* member of the opposite sex who, whether I know him or her personally or not, whether I will ever know him or her at all, whether I am related to him or her in marriage or not, is *the* female or *the* male to whom I belong by creation and election, the person of the opposite sex by whom I am thus *measured* very concretely in this regard? Can I *answer* for my conduct here? In other words, does my conduct have the significance of an actualizing of this relation in the broader and narrower sense? Does it take place in the mutual relatedness of male and female by creation? Or does it imply a break in this respect? Does it take place secretly or openly in that bad isolated masculinity or femininity which must be seen as a revolt against the will of the Creator? Within the great responsibility [that we owe] to God, and apart from the general responsibility which man owes to man, in the light of our sexual determination there is this very special responsibility that the male owes to the female and the female to the male, the responsibility for common humanity and creatureliness that the two can actualize only in their relation to one another. Again this raises a question which is the more urgent the more our action has the character of a withdrawal from this relation, the character, then, of a willfully abstract male or female action. Only then does the need for shame arise, for then the male and female have to be

[8]Cf. *Aus Schleiermachers Leben*. In Letters, vol. 1; Berlin 1860², p. 207, 403.

hidden from one another because of the evil laughter of others. Within the relation there can be no possible need for shame. Again, however, we cannot draw clearcut boundaries between what is done within the relation and what is done outside it. It should simply be remembered that they *are* drawn and that there are again possibilities which can evade the question of inside or outside. It might well be that a good deal, far too much indeed, of what male vitality quietly assumes to be a sacred right, e.g., the typical way in which the male usually relaxes and lets go after work, will be shown to be quite impossible by the criterion that no matter whether visibly or invisibly he is confronted by the female and he might *not* see her, and it is all possible for him only because and so long as he does *not* see her. War is also shown to be a dubious matter from the standpoint that it is a purely male affair in which those who take part will not see the female, whether as mother, wife, or sister, one's own and that of the enemy. It could well be that more than one act of apparently womanly virtue, e.g., that of industriousness or modesty, is in reality not a virtuous act at all because in it the woman forgets that she does not live for herself, but that again she lives visibly or invisibly in relation to the man, that it is for her to *see* the man and to see him continually, and that her virtuous act can be truly virtuous only when it takes place in this seeing. It *could* be, we have again said cautiously. For here again things might be totally different from what they seem to be. It is not for us to place a value on our acts. If it is clear that a man has never willed what is bad, we must also see clearly that he is also unable to will what is good. We can only act. But we can watch and pray as we act. We can act with awareness of standards, not absolute but relative standards. One such standard is responsibility to the other sex, the question whether the female is not a living reproach to the male in his action, or the male to the female. All human society would perhaps look very different if this one standard in all its relativity, perhaps by a miracle, were suddenly observed and applied by everybody, in the same way as we cannot wholly forget or suppress our needs. If we are unwilling to adopt and apply this standard because it is too relative, we are like the scoundrelly servant who took his pound, wrapped it in a cloth, and buried it [cf. Matt. 25:14–30; Luke 19:12–27]. This is what we must not do.

3. Analogous to sexuality, but totally different in structure, is the created determination of man for *friendship*, which we have every reason to discuss in describing the place where man is reached by God's command. We can define this determination as the affinity or proximity or the existence of one person to that of others of the same sex. This affinity is more or less native to man, stands out within our general solidarity with all men, and takes place by free choice. Whether—to anticipate—the same affinity or friendship exists between members of *different* sexes, with no sexual determination, is an ancient and well-known question which, apart from a few borderline cases, is probably answered best by a flat denial. Except perhaps for one case in a hundred

thousand, friendship between members of the opposite sex is certainly friendship, but it is *sexual* friendship, whether as a game or in all seriousness. In neither case is it necessarily reprehensible but it undoubtedly means playing with fire. Even if we do not mean to play with fire, we need to know that we are doing so and to consider what it involves. Not the reaching of this critical point, but a bold refusal to realize that one is at this point, the optimistic way in which it is thought that the miracle can be made a matter of custom and habit, was perhaps one of the worst fads of the youth movement before and after 1920. What we have in view here is the normal case of closeness between people of the *same* sex. If two or more people *discover this affinity*, they find that they are *friends*. But the closeness exists without the discovery (as one often has neighbors without knowing them as such) and it need hardly be said that there is friendship which does not rest on that discovery or the created determination. In these cases there is a lack, a fault perhaps, or at all events a need, whether felt or not. For man was created neither for loneliness nor for general fellowship. He was undoubtedly created in the affinity or not so close affinity of his existence to other existences, in the greater or lesser proximity of his feeling for life to that of other people, in the capacity and necessity for an ultimately inexplicable and purely factual trust in some people as distinct from others.

The concept of *friendship* is no more and no less than the root of the concept of the *neighbor* which is so important in understanding the command of God—a concept which thus far we have refrained from discussing. The neighbor is the person standing next to us. Sexuality, too, means neighborliness. So too—we shall have to speak of this later[9]—does relationship by descent, birth, blood, and history. But friendship is the neighborliness which basically and, as a rule, factually too, is first discovered, not resting on blood relationship but on relationship of *soul* and *spirit*. As the free relation of one person to another friendship is the fundamental type of this relationship as a whole. When a man begins to discover himself in later youth, then, as is well known, he does not first discover the opposite sex, nor his father and mother and brothers and sisters. There takes place instead that strange and either mild or bristly aversion to the opposite sex and to family. What he discovers in discovering himself is a friend. It would be a serious gap in his knowledge of his own existence—a gap which does, of course, occur in the lives of most of us as either fault or fate or both—if he did not then discover his family and sex relationship. In an odd way the normal ending of the age of puberty is often spun out until well on in life. The ending of this age, of the development of self-discovery, means that after a man has discovered his friends or has thought he has discovered them, or has wanted to discover them in this

---

[9]See pp. 191ff.

most intimate relation, after he has reached some maturity in the unavoidable disappointments and sufferings of this development, without, it is hoped, abandoning the friend if he has found him, he will find the neighbor in another way and on another level in his brothers and sisters too, and, when it is the right time, in his parents, and finally in the opposite sex. Fundamentally, however, he has found and sought the friend first. The fact that he must then seek and find his natural relatives as *friends*, and a sexual *friend* also in the beloved of the opposite sex, both after the model of the free spiritual choice of friendship, proves to us that this latter type of relation does not take a primary position genetically or, perhaps, by reason of worth, but only in a purely factual way.

My friend is *the* man who as my *fellow* man is characterized by the fact—who can explain it—that his soul and mine have come together, even though there is no blood relationship or sexual relationship between us. They have come together in the sense that to a certain degree I see myself again in him, that in him my own I encounters me with some measure of concealment, so that to some degree his existence means mine and his nonexistence would also mean mine. He is my *alter ego*, as the old phrase finely and correctly states it. One could say this, too, on the two other levels of kinship and sexuality. The matured relation to parents and brothers and sisters will have the character of friendship, and naturally the sexual relation, when it takes place with the completeness to which we referred, and even perchance in a less complete form, and secretly or openly in the very incomplete form of most marriages, can also acquire this character of friendship. But in such cases friendship is a *special* factor which is added to the family or to the sexual relation and which enriches, fulfills, comforts, and heals it. It must be understood as a special factor of this kind. Its distinctive feature is that it implies the characteristically *human* relation of the one to the other. Sexuality and kinship may be found among animals too. So far as we can see, however, a soul is needed for friendship, the ability to choose that is either free or rests on some totally inexplicable necessity. It is in this quality that friendship is the root of the concept of the *neighbor* whom the command of God not only sets over against us but also presupposes as a determination of our calling by creation. The Thou that meets me in the friend as an *alter ego* is at the same time the gate to other people in general and as such with whom I see myself associated once I discover myself. When we seek and find a friend, our soul awakens and we seek and find, not kinship nor sex, but the other person as such in relation to our own existence. This is why the friend is a model of the *neighbor*. The concept of friendship must not be denied because it has a certain naive and egotistical ring. Nor must we fail to see that *on* the field of naive egotism friendship implies a *corrective*, namely, the calling in virtue of which the naive egotism which we shall continue to practice all our lives is set in advance under the command of God.

Because we are determined not only for sex and family but also, in the primary way indicated, for friendship as well, it is not at all true that God's command encountered us as those who, apart from their relation to others by kin or sexuality, knew only themselves, so that belonging to someone else as such was from the very first something alien thrust upon them from without. God's command encounters us instead as those who are ordained by creation to find themselves only as they find themselves also in friends. In so doing, it ties us to the fact that we are capable of trust in some other people on other grounds than their natural closeness or their sex. It ties us to the fact that to be able truly to live we have to open up ourselves outwards in this trust. Finding us in this determination, it commands us to live and to let live, to *will* to live and to live with *respect* for other life. The neighbor without whom I cannot be myself is the concrete unity of these two aspects of the command of life. Because of the neighbor without whom I cannot be myself, I cannot wish to believe that my own life involves no more than itself and that the life of others either does not affect me or does so only in a secondary sense. The neighbor who is my friend, just because he is my alter *ego*, but my *alter* ego, signifies a principal breaking through the possibility of an egotistical life or one that is determined altruistically only by the voice of blood or sex.

To this extent the created determination of our existence which is here at issue has the significance of a *criterion* of *conduct*. In all that we do the question arises whether we do it with that opening up of our naively egocentric will to our fellowman, who is posited fundamentally by the fact that we are created as *neighbors*, as neighbors in *soul*, so that from the very outset we are on the lookout for the other who is of interest to us only because of his invisible soul. The more we are egocentrically enclosed; the more we act in the unbroken naiveté of that natural egocentrism; the more our will and action, even though it has an altruistic character, has it only within that relation of kin or sexuality that does not characterize man as such, the less are we informed by actualized, or even sought or desired or, indeed, missed, friendship for humanity, and the more urgently must the question be put to us whether our action, because God meets us where he has put us, does not signify disobedience, since we have not allowed the friend, whether we have discovered him or not—be it simply through the empty place that he should have occupied in our life—to place us under the gate where, in virtue of one component of our own existence, a vista opens up fundamentally on our fellowman. For though it be a thousand times true that actualized, and even desired and sought, friendship can in fact mean a strengthening of our naive egotism, this can do no more than signify that we are failing to see the calling by creation wherein we find ourselves to be friends of friends. It cannot signify that we do not actually *find ourselves* in this calling.

Not just this or that man, but in this or that man, our *fellow*man as such, is the one who in the form of the friend that is found, sought, or missed has a firm place in our own existence. We can only deceive ourselves if we do not see his presence and respect his mandate as a representative of the neighbor in general. No unequivocal mandates are given us herewith, no absolute criterion. For what it means concretely to will and act in the presence of the neighbor, to love him as ourselves [cf. Mark 12:31 par.], as it is all summed up in both the Old Testament and the New, is not something that we can or should tell ourselves, but something that is told to us if we are ready to listen. If this seems to mean everything and anything, it does not mean everything and anything but something very specific as and when, at the point where we belong by creation, i.e., in this radical openness to the neighbor, we are commanded by God to let ourselves be found by this neighbor. It is enough that in this respect, too, we are not without direction, without the calling simply to be what we are. With this we are to go on prepared toward the God who commands us.

4. The fourth created determination that calls for discussion consists of a relation to others in the same way as sexuality does or neighborly affinity. I have *kinship* in view. We shall have to speak about the family as well as marriage in §9. The point of interest here is the phenomenon that underlies the family as such, namely, that all of us stand in a special, if much graded, proximity to certain people; that they have the same ancestors and to that extent the same blood, that even if we do not all have a common present we share in part a common past, and that in the history of our ancestors we have, at any rate, a common prehistory. That these people—we might mention parents, children, brothers, and sisters—are our neighbors will be discovered and accepted, as described, by the way of family friendship, for it will at first be pushed into the background and obscured by the awakening of awareness of our own existence. Apart from this, however, we can hardly fail to see that we have here a relation which, discovered and accepted or not, is one of supreme naturalness and even corporeality, and just because of this it has, over both friendship and sexuality, the advantage of a self-evident givenness which cannot be set aside or shaken by any forgetfulness or denial. All the unruliness with which a young son, in the zeal of self-discovery, may think that he must look and move beyond his father does not alter in the least the fact that—perhaps unwittingly in his unruliness most of all—he *is* the son of his own father and the heir to his good and not so good qualities. If he does not see this and cannot draw in a little by coming to terms both inwardly and outwardly with the impulses of puberty, no matter how materially right they may be, then along with other serious consequences he will be undoubtedly be punished with a lively father complex with whose help he will dash painfully against life with the horns that he would not allow to be clipped. And if a mother can act no more sensibly toward her daughter than by taking out on her, in the form of lovelessness and repression, her

own feelings of worthlessness and jealousy and her anger at what she has supposedly or really missed in life, she is simply tearing her own flesh, for she is still the mother of the daughter who is seen and treated in this way, the only problem being that she is stopping the springs and barring the roads to everything that the daughter would and could perhaps be to her in her need. Similarly, if brothers, as can sometimes happen in spite of Joseph's warning: "Do not quarrel on the way" [Gen. 45:24], become involved in especially violent disputes, this is often just because they are brothers, and have a common past, and in this past, which may reach back to the nursery, have perhaps all kinds of mutual grudges, and it will perhaps need only an outside attack on one of the quarreling brothers to bring to light again at once their original solidarity, as in the wise old French saying: "La famille est un bloc, elle se dispute, mais elle se défend."[10] All this is a sign that kinship is a given factor at which we may chafe—and what parents and children and brothers and sisters have never chafed at it?—but which to our weal and woe we cannot break. It is obviously a given factor by creation, so that we can as little jump over our own shadow as alter the fact that as relatives we stand in this or that relation to such and such people. Here in this relation that is determined by God, the command of the same God reaches us—here and not elsewhere. In some way within this framework, and measured by its justifiable claims and rules, we have to obey, and not in some other way. If we remember that this is so, that we have to come before God in the reality of being relatives, we shall have done what we can not to be unprepared in this regard as we act and come into God's judgment.

We must now look a little further afield. We need only extend the concept of kinship to arrive by way of the ancient idea of the tribe or clan at the concept of nation or people. We do not have the state in view here. We shall have to speak of that in the third chapter. It does not belong either to our calling by creation or, like marriage and the family, to the orders of creation which we shall have to deal with in the next section. Nation and state are not coextensive. In the true and narrower sense the nation or people is a historically related group of several families whose own unity is that of a family which exists by reason of common descent and blood, by reason of race as it is usually put, and on this basis by reason of a relatively common history and a similar or related language. It is as well to realize that in modern Europe there are no longer any states, or nations in the political sense, which are also peoples in this true sense, but only more or less strong and pure majorities of such peoples. It is only *a parte potiori* that the state in any land today bears the name of this or that people in the strict sense, and we cannot threaten it more severely than by stirring up one of the peoples united within it against the other or others for the sake of this name. But even if we can only warn against political manipulation of the

---

[10]A French proverb.

concept of nationhood as a dangerous game for the state to play, this does not mean that, especially from the standpoint of language and ethos, the people is not a living reality in which we all stand and which is certainly not ethically irrelevant. We at once move away from this reality, of course, if we think we can be happy about our own people by reason of a comparison with others which naturally turns out in our own favor. For this reality does not consist, for example, of Germany having to help the world to recovery;[11] that kind of thing is a superfluous addition to the true reality that we are, for instance, Germans and not Slavs, Neo-Latins, or Jews. The ethical relevance of nationality is that we must meet God in this reality and not another, that in this respect, too, God will find us where he has put us. It has nothing whatever to do with mutual boasting. Concretely it simply means loyalty to the way of my people, to its speech and thinking, not because these are better than those of others, but solely because they are those of *my* people and are therefore assigned in the first instance to me too. Nationhood, too, is a framework for my action as obedient action.

Both kinship and nationhood have the significance of bonds in which we exist, and hence of criteria of action. The bonds are not unequivocal and ultimate and therefore the criteria are not absolute. Who can unambiguously establish from outside either for others or for himself where and how loyalty to kin and people begins and ends? That there are here no final and unconditional bonds is shown by the fact that marital loyalty must sometimes take precedence of family loyalty, and loyalty to state or church must sometimes take precedence of loyalty to people, not to speak of other less general possibilities and the limiting of these bonds. Nevertheless this caveat does not alter the givenness of these realities, their binding character or their character as a criterion. We do not live in a vacuum. We are not just anybody but *ourselves.* This also means that by blood we belong in the narrower and broader sense more closely to these people than to those. If our action takes on the character of a movement or even an attempted movement out of this relation, the question obviously arises whether we are not leaving the place where God wants to speak to us and where alone we can hear him, whether our action is not disobedience simply because it is disloyalty. The question arises. Yet perhaps our action ought to go even further on this questionable path because in fact, and contrary to appearances, it does *not* have that character before God. The attitude of the twelve-year old Jesus in the temple [cf. Luke 2:41−52] seems not to be loyalty to his relatives and the same is true of more than one thing he did in later life. Nor did the attitude of Jeremiah during the siege of Jerusalem seem to be loyalty to his people [cf. Jer. 27; 37; 38:1−6]. A wider sphere of calling by creation appears to open up here, over against kinship and

---

[11]Barth alludes here to the last verse of E. Geibel's (1815−1884) poem "Deutschlands Beruf" (1861).

nationhood, and what loyalty to the latter means can be understood only in terms of this wider circle. Yet even when transcended in this way, the inner circle is not abolished. Astounding possibilities within our relation to kin and people need not be impossible possibilities. Even the transcending of the inner circle by the outer, even the precedence of other obligations over this one, does not alter the fact that this one *exists* too; that real possibilities in some sense necessarily have a place, though perhaps a very puzzling place, within this circle; that in all our acts we are thus asked whether and how far this is so; that from this side, too, there arises for us a criterion which we must not leap over or overlook.

We have still not drawn a final line that calls for consideration in this context. Apart from the orders of creation to which we shall turn later,[12] does a wider circle of this kind exist as a calling by creation above and outside nationhood? We have viewed the friend as a representative of the fellowman, the neighbor, because friendship rests on a free choice of soul and is thus a corrective of naive and natural egotism and a basic recognition of humanity. Kinship and nationhood do not rest on a choice of this kind. They are given factors. In that sense they do not open up higher and wider vistas. They seem instead to hold us down in the depths of naturalness, to refer us to a closed circle of fellowmen to the exclusion of all the rest. Yet in the last analysis this is only an *appearance*. For as the concept of kinship points and extends beyond itself to become the clan and then the people, so we cannot stop at the people. Are not the peoples themselves in turn the members of one big family? In Germany today, in contrast to the age of the Enlightenment and Idealism, the word "humanity" has taken on such a suspicious sound that one is in fact almost afraid to utter it. Yet if, as we must, we venture to consider our blood relationship in general, it is hard to see how the concept of people can be the final possible concretion that must be taken seriously, or how the concept of humanity can be merely an empty rationalistic phrase as compared with that of kin or people. In face of the aforementioned mixture of peoples in the modern European nations, and also in face of the many contacts and connections that peoples now have with one another beyond state boundaries, the refusal to take the concept of humanity with full seriousness itself proves to be an empty rationalistic reaction which is artificial and has no basis in reality. Russians, Japanese, and Indians are no longer the very distant fellowmen who only theoretically come into consideration as such—the favorite position of a nationalistically controlled ethics. If it was madness to talk about humanity in the 18th century, often in an abstract overleaping of the inner circles which we have just discussed, it is madness not to speak of it in the 20th century; and in many different ways it would be fatal if the church were to insist on setting up for its ethical reflection and proclamation a barrier which, if appearances do not

[12]See pp. 216ff.

deceive, is being increasingly tossed aside by facts, especially the facts of economic life. Here, too, we cannot issue too urgent a warning against the misuse of certain Lutheran thoughts and moods and schemata, as though reality, even as reality by creation, had not acquired for us a different and broader aspect than was reasonably possible in Luther's day.[13] In a way that is fundamentally just as sure and specific as in our own nationhood, we now live inside and progressively outside state boundaries in relation to other nations too.

Even if in fact this were not so, even if someone could be as sure of the national purity of his descent as probably only very few can be, and even if he could seal himself off hermetically from other peoples in his own state, by what basic insight could he ward off the implications of the truism that we are all related to one another in Adam? Is the human bond in which we stand any less a given factor because it is that of a broader circle than that of kin and people? And if the latter is a criterion of our conduct, why should not this, as a longer extension of the same line, but no less urgently on that account, be a criterion too? Who would deny this after considering the remarkable role played by the stranger within thy gates [Exod. 20:10] in the law of the Old Testament? This stranger, whether welcome or not, is there. "And the stranger is never the guest for whom Zeus, too, had a special sphere; but he becomes the representative of man among the peoples" (Cohen, *Ethik*, p. 382). Note that the concept of humanity as little abolishes that of the people as that of the people does that of kinship. But even the deepest loyalty to kin and people cannot close our eyes to the fact that both these inner circles are enclosed by an even wider circle of blood relationship in which we stand by virtue of our calling by creation, which also claims our loyalty, and by which our conduct is also measured. Behind the relative is the fellow countryman and behind the fellow countryman is "the stranger that is within thy gates," and it is precisely the last of these who tells us, if we have not heard it before, that the true concern even in blood relationship is *humanity*. Seen and put in a series with this last, the blood relative and the fellow countryman also represents our fellowman or our neighbor as such. When we understand him, and the stranger with him, as a *given factor*, it is clear that the neighbor as such is also a given factor and not an idea. Even on the natural, physical side he comes into our existence as a reality which cannot be evaded or overlooked, and raises for us the question how our conduct relates to the command of the God whose calling consists of this reality too. I need not go into the questions which this poses in relation to the ancient phenomenon of anti-Semitism on the one side or the modern phenomenon of conscious nationalism on the other. These may be possible or impossible possibilities, but there can be no doubt that as principles of human will and action they come

[13]Cf. T. Pauls, *Luthers Auffassung von Staat und Volk*, Halle 1927; W. Elert, *Morphologie des Luthertums*, vol. 2, Munich 1931, 1953[2], pp. 125ff.

under the crisis of the comprehensively understood concept of relationship as we have here come to know it as one component of the reality in
which we stand before God.|

5. Age is another component of the calling in which we stand before
God. Identical with ourselves, we must constantly discover and maintain
this identity in an incalculable but limited series of moments in time
under gradually changing conditions. All of us are somewhere on the
notable way from the cradle to the grave, which is also notable at each of
its many stations. We are set in a becoming which is already from the
very first a perishing and which will be manifested at the end simply as
an enigmatic perishing. This, too, is by creation one of the conditions to
which we are tied by God's command and which must be taken seriously
by us. But here, too, what has to be taken seriously is something very
concrete. What concerns me, the place where God's command reaches
me, is not my life in general but the present moment as it is determined
in some way by moving time, the present moment from which I pass on
to the next one. Things are the same in the philosophy of individual life
as they are in that of history as a whole. If we understand by this the
considering and comparing of various possibilities, it is a futile enterprise. What do we know about our life as a whole? At no single moment
do we belong to ourselves or really see ourselves and we certainly are not
masters of the whole series of our moments nor can we know or say
anything real about them. We are in no position to shape our lives into a
single work, as A. Ritschl thought he could do in all the splendid naiveté
of the later 19th century.[14] All that we can do, poorly instructed at the
human level by the insights, warnings, and directions that we bring with
us as recollections of our past, and truly instructed only by God's Word
that we have to hear today, is to prepare this moment for the next
moment when again we shall not belong to ourselves and only God will
know and speak the truth about us. Any biography, and especially any
autobiography, attractive and instructive though this literary genre may
be, is a very questionable undertaking because it almost always presupposes that we occupy some seat from which we can see the sequence of
moments which constitutes the life of someone, or even our own life,
whereas in fact we do not occupy any such seat. What we are in the
totality of our moments, God knows. We do not. We do not even know
what we are in the present moment. For what God tells us today is not a
revelation of our being but a claiming of our action, which we cannot
consider, but only do. God's command is always at all events: Move on!
Move on as the one you are and have been in the whole series of your
life's moments, but: Move on! As though you were only now beginning,
and not just "as though," for in fact your moving only begins now at the
point to which you have now come, although you cannot understand this
starting point as in any sense your own work. Existence today is no less

[14]Op. cit., pp. 8, 11, 81, 83f.

fashioned by God than on the day of your birth and again the meaning and significance of the decision from which you come stand in the judgment of God. You have neither produced this truth before God nor can you know it or tell it. You can be truly responsible for all your previous path only as you move on.

Since the Creator is the eternal God, we are by creation what we are *now*. Musing and brooding about the past and future means not taking seriously the reality in which God has made us. It is by him that we live and shall live, and his is the judgment on our life. Our existence, however, is the present as preparation for the most immediate future. We are called to this preparation, to action in the knowledge of what God says to us today. We are called at the stage of development of body and soul at which we now are. This means at once that to take seriously the presupposition by creation of our present age is not to take seriously this age as such but, at this or any other age, it is to take life itself seriously, paying attention to the questions, claims, demands, and promises which arise for us out of real listening to God's command and moving with open and ready will to what it will further reveal to us. The special seriousness of each age does not consist of a special attitude that we should take to life in that age, but of the seriousness with which we try to live and move toward the Lord of life in every age, as though for the very first time and as though there were no other age than the one which is now ours.

That a person is, e.g., *young,* is in itself a most uninteresting fact which is not worth all the fuss that is made about it. "While you bandy compliments, something profitable can take place."[15] While you want to actualize your youth as such, you can *be* young as you actualize yourself as a person should do who has grasped the responsibility of the present moment in relation to the next. We are not young in ourselves but can *be* young only as we are those who are motivated by the responsibility of this hour as though it were the first and last. A true youth movement can exist only in the form of being moved by a cause which has nothing to do with youth and age. It can exist only in the relation to an object in which we continue to live, as young people certainly, but above all in which we continue to live, not thinking that we can or should rejoice in our youth as such according to the motto: "Stay, you are so beautiful."[16] We can rejoice in our youth and take it seriously only with the youthful *realism* with which we prove our readiness, attention, and obedience in some field, and not by chasing the phantom of a supposedly *youthful* realism. What is wonderful is the ability to give oneself to an object without considering that the way in which one does so has to be youthful, but, rather, suppressing the thought that the way of doing it might sometimes be really youthful in a violent comparison with the realism of

15Goethe, *Faust,* Part I, Prologue.
16Goethe, *Faust,* Part I, Study.

maturity. If we will to be children, we are not children but childish. If we *are* children, we do not will to be children but even play our games in bitter earnest. This is to move toward the command of this stage of life in true loyalty to its distinctive determination.|

What has been said by way of illustration about youth applies *mutatis mutandis* to the other ages too. Just as we are not young merely by adopting a youthful manner and mode of action in distinction to the style and activity of older people, so we are not adult by renouncing the ideals and errors of youth with an air of widsom, by becoming solid and established, by not engaging in any more pranks, which, according to a not very reliable report, is the rule from forty years and up. Similarly true age does not mean being able to look back on a long past and take comfort in the fact that the responsible decisions which bring on the future have now become comparatively few, and there is the wisdom of a long past to help in making them. We are not truly living people, whether young, mature, or old, by reason of the distinctive determination of these stages of life as such, but by reason of the openness with which, each time, we are in the determination of this or that stage, affirming, not the determination as such, but the claim of life which we encounter within it. At every stage, then, it is in a very special way a matter of judgment and grace. Hence, the stage at which we are becomes itself, in a very special way, a criterion and direction. Obviously it makes a difference whether the command of life in its two elements meets us in the years which are our apprentice years, our journeyman years, or our years as masters (which Goethe did not describe), whether it meets us in the formation of our life, or its developed form, or finally on the dark threshold beyond which we can only commend to God the being that came to be in our life. The command itself, however, is the same, and in face of it our youth and maturity and age cannot be independent lives with independent laws. The boundaries between the ages and what seems to distinguish them physically and mentally can as little be fixed with precision as can the true nature of male and female humanity. Are we not already journeymen as apprentices and still apprentices as journeymen? And is not the future master already there in both apprentice and journeyman? Can the mature and aging form be anything other than a development of the first and original form? Is it an accident that the features of the old man or woman begin to resemble again those of the infant? Is the sequence of our moments anything but a variation on one and the same theme until it is played out or one day mysteriously broken off "too soon," as we say? And does not, finally, the uncertainty of the hour of death, which can place the youngest alongside and even above the oldest, make clear the ultimate relativity of the ages of which we are now speaking? If this is so, then obviously the determination in which we all exist can be important and significant only as the divine determination by creation of the now in which we are called each time as though it were the first and last time.

And the criterion of our acts resulting from the determination does not lie in the distinctiveness of this or that age compared to the others, but in the mysterious yet very real interrelationship of all the ages even *in* their distinction.

Conduct may be suspected of being *nonyouthful* when it is guided by the only ostensibly youthful notion, totally incompatible with the urgency of the command, that in relation to God we still have a long life before us, that the decision we take now cannot be a serious one because many different decisions will presumably follow in relation to new possibilities, that the dreaming and playing and imitating and independent testing which characterize this stage are not strictly responsible like that which will come later. So "rejoice, O young man, in your youth, and let your heart cheer you in the days of your youth; walk in the ways of your heart and the sight of your eyes. But know that for all these things God will bring you into judgment" (Eccles. 11:9). If this is not remembered, if our action lacks, not the fixity and deliberation of maturity nor the self-possession of old age, but awareness of the judgment, then it is a nonyouthful action just because it is abstractly youthful. To be young can mean only to be human in youth.

The action of a *mature* person, on the other hand, is *suspect* if behind it there is blindness to the fact that all *our* decisions, however serious and responsible they may be, are not the divine decision but are subject to the divine decision, in comparison with whose seriousness they are but a game. To be mature is to realize that all serious human action has this character of a game. If at the height of life a person becomes a philistine or a bourgeois, a schoolmaster or even a Prometheus (for Epimetheus and Prometheus are absolute antitheses only in Spitteler and not in reality),[17] if he loses the humor and melancholy with which alone one can do human justice to the divine seriousness, if he becomes solemn and takes himself seriously instead of God, if he comes under the judgment of the saying about being converted and becoming as little children [cf. Matt. 18:3], this means, not that, unfortunately, he is no longer young, but rather that he has missed the real *maturity* of life. Hence the action of the old man becomes the more doubtful the more it has the character of being a match for the question of the command, the character of a mechanical repetition of a previous decision, and the more it claims the supposed right of old age to rest. If the closing of the door is drawing near, the last decision that man has to make before God, then obviously the question before which man is set by God's command cannot become less urgent but can only become more urgent, and the possibility of replying to it by mere repetitions, by continuing along the same supposedly tested paths, can only become more impossible. We are not being too presumptuous if we state that true and truly venerable old people are those who even in, and in spite of, the frailty and

---

[17]See above n.5 and n.26.

weakness of age not only will to be, but have to be, always young, young in their awareness of the full urgency of precisely their own moment. This is why Abraham, who was already sixty-five years old when he left Haran [cf. Gen. 12:4], was in the best sense a more natural old man than the antistes of Schaffhausen, David Spleiss, who at sixty answered certain claims made on him by saying: "J'ai fait ma fortune, I have feathered my nest."[18] or than the emeritus who settles down to follow his hobbies or write his autobiography. This is why it is not a strange thing but a very significant and honorable symptom of normalcy that people like Schelling and Tolstoy and P. Natorp were still beset by storms in their later days and felt a need to make the bold venture of giving their whole life's work a new form and turn in their final hours.[19] This can at least be obedience to the summons: "Go from your country and your kindred . . . to the land that I will show you" [Gen. 12:1]—a summons that is issued no less to the old than the young. Precisely in old age, where the opposite seems so natural, faithfulness to calling has to mean obedience to this summons. "Thine age be as thy youth," is the fine promise of Deuteronomy 33:25. This promise, too, is a description of the calling in which the old stand as such. And it may be reversed: "Thy youth be as thine age"—we have seen in what sense. Either way it is the criterion of what we have in mind here. We can also sum it up in the last sentence of the Old Testament, which tells us that the hearts of the fathers will be turned to their children and the hearts of the children to their fathers (Mal. 4:6), or in Psalm 148:12f.: "Old men and children, let them praise the name of the Lord, for his name alone is exalted."

6. The sixth determination of the calling in which we all stand consists of everything that is comprised in the two concepts of *guidance* and *endowment*. Every moment, and in every moment, the command finds us in a specific state of bodily and mental development, at a specific outer and inner (moral, intellectual, and aesthetic) cultural stage, or at a specific degree of the development of understanding, will, and emotion paralleled, or in many cases not paralleled, by a specific temper and strength and dexterity of the body. From this additional and fundamentally independent standpoint each of us has a place which is absolutely and unrepeatedly his own in a system which can be denoted by the two coordinates of guidance and endowment.

By *guidance* we understand the *historical* particularity in which the life of all of us is always lived. It is obviously not a matter of indifference whether one is born, bred, and educated as a Fuegian, a Baltic count, or a Berliner, as the child of a Dutch merchant or a Saxon worker, as the child, grandchild, or great-grandchild of a Basel theologian, or as the

---

[18]D. Spleiss (1786–1854) was an evangelical theologian in Schaffhausen who was, at first, professor of mathematics and physics and then become the chief pastor (antistes) in 1841.

[19]On F. W. Schelling, cf. *RGG*³, V, pp. 1396–1400; on L. Tolstoy, *RGG*³, VI, 947–49; on P. Natorp, *RGG*³, IV, 1321–22.

child of a general of the old German army, even though all these will be equally feeble for the first five minutes of life and then again for the last five minutes. Very probably the one situation or the other will open up and also close for the person concerned a whole series of possibilities, both good and bad, both helpful and restrictive, but possibilities, at least, whose presence or absence will mark his life in a certain way that will persist through all later influences and admixtures. None of us can select this shaping by parents and childhood just as none of us can select his parents. But each of us has it and each of us will show it in all that he does and says even if it be only in the form of violent opposition or denial, or the hunting out of all kinds of contrasting possibilities. Each of us is what he is. In effect, we can only in very small part choose even the later influences by which we are molded into what we are. What we do know of the mysterious necessities on the basis of which a person now opens and entrusts himself to this other person, now seeks out this circle of friends, now selects this university, and now embraces this profession? Even the cultural influences to which we willingly and wittingly expose ourselves are always, in reality, very different from what we expected and they usually shape us in other ways than we envisaged. Who of you really knew what you were doing when you began to study theology, and to whom did not totally unexpected powers come when you carried out this plan? We are there, of course, and there responsibly. We know that. But that hardly alters the fact that our life as a whole and in detail simply *takes place* in the stream of *history* which we can understand only to a certain degree. And if we are not ungodly we obviously cannot speak of chance or fate in this regard. To explain it, we cannot take refuge in a program fixed for us by the stars. We can understand this ineluctable occurrence only as leading or *guidance*. The Creator by whose will the world was not merely begun but is sustained every moment in every detail as well as in its totality, this Creator, notwithstanding my freedom and responsibility, has brought me out of nothing and then led me in such a way that I have become what I am today. He has done with me what he wished, like the potter with the clay, and has in any case done it well. It is as one who has been guided in this way, then, that I have to meet him again as the one who issues the command.

But that is only one coordinate of our development. The other is my special *endowment*. By this we understand the *physiological* and *psychological* determination in which human life is always lived. It is obviously not the same as the historical determination, though the two lines intersect at a specific point where they cannot be clearly distinguished. Among all the various historical possibilities of life-development and independent of them, not traceable to any of them, I may from the very first be a healthy person or a sick one. I may be short or tall, short people usually having, surprisingly, a distinctive inferiority complex which causes them sometimes to do the most astonishing things, things they would never do if they were of normal height. Napoleon can be fully explained in this way! I may be adroit or maladroit, intelligent or unintelligent, strong-willed or weak-willed, aesthetically dull or sensitive, solitary or sociable. Not all this, and perhaps, under examination, very little of it, can be explained by heredity. Nature, both physical and psychological, *makes leaps,* here placing an idiot in a house full of ancient culture and there putting a genius in a workman's hut, here causing a pervert to grow up in the most respectable environment and there causing a fine and simple and honest person to grow up in the most dubious surroundings. The historical situation, the geographical, political, and sociological determination of a person, may in many instances negate or hide a person's endowment. In innumerable cases it may happen that a very significant person languishes in obscurity, that humanly speaking he cannot achieve what corresponds to his gifts, while fundamentally a semi-idiot may attain to office and honors and even take on significance for world history, simply because the historical position, the leading, we may say, has worked to hinder on the one side and to prosper on the other. It may be that in our eyes historical guidance often has the appearance of an incomprehensibly dreadful fate. What a different aspect the whole intellectual life of Germany would have today if it had not been for that battle in Flanders in the autumn of 1914 when God and a little clever military strategy brought it about that a whole, or at least half, a student generation, including so many of the intellectual leaders that we have need of today, were exposed in compact masses to the English machine guns.[20] All this simply confirms, however, that there is an *individual* development which can be promoted or hampered by the historical development, but which is fundamentally independent of it; which often enough may victoriously assert itself against it; which has, at any rate, to be taken into account when we consider the stage of a person's development (in the most general sense) as a component of the reality in which the command of God meets us.

Not being ungodly people, we naturally cannot speak of fate or chance here either. We understand man as a creature of God and we thus use a term that is common even in secular speech. This is his *endowment.* God gave or granted much or little to me and to others as and when he lifted us up out of nothing. But what right have we to speak of much or little here? As in the case of what we have called divine guidance, we cannot exercise too much restraint in our evaluations. If

---

[20]When the German advance was halted in 1914, the high command tried to regain the initiative in two battles (Oct. 20–Nov. 3 and Nov. 10–18) by throwing masses of volunteers and young recruits into action. At Langemarck, on November 10, regiments composed mostly of students stormed the first line of the enemy position at terrible cost. This attack later became a symbol of the heroic death of German youth in battle, but militarily it was a failure and brought about the stalemate it had been designed to break. The German cemetery at Langemarck contains some 45,000 graves. Cf. H. Thimmermann, *Der Sturm auf Langemarck,* Munich 1933.

we call what has been created good, we mean that it was created by God in this way and not another, so that if it is our own reality, it is *the* reality in which we are called and which is good enough for God to seek us in it. This component of our reality has something to say in answer to the question: What shall *we* do? For it is an element in our *calling*. Whatever we may do, we do it as those who are guided and endowed in this way. God's judgment, for its part, will be passed on us as those who are guided and endowed by him in this way. Again two groups of questions are posed here in relation to our action. |

The first question is this. Does our action correspond to the fact that God's command claims us and seizes us in the whole state in whicn we are considered from this double standpoint? Or is there perhaps in our action a partial or even very extensive holding back? Is it not a fact that we act as if the entirety of what we have become and are were not at issue when we stand before God, but only a part, and perhaps even a very small part? Our action should obviously be viewed the more critically the less we are wholly committed to it, the more we are divided in it and consciously or unconsciously keep in the background as uninvolved this or that possibility, talent, or ability of ours, the more, perhaps, we act casually, not interposing our whole personality, as it is said, i.e., not interposing the total reality of our historical and physical-psychological existence. We undoubtedly engage continually in dividing and holding back of this kind, and in much that we do we act casually in this sense. Thus, in seeking a place of amusement, we say: Let us leave the theologian at home and simply be a man! or: Let us silence aesthetic feelings in favor of other considerations! Or, in the field of scholarship, we let our understanding go like a good horse that can find its stable on its own. Or, in some social situations, we ignore the true state of our moral or intellectual development and apparently (for we cannot do this in reality) arrive at a higher or lower place than that which is proper to us. Or at the most trivial, but the most common and perhaps the most significant level, we are simply indolent, we are tired of striving, and even though we see that something is demanded of us, we have had enough, we are not ready to do it, and we prefer for a time to be left peacefully to ourselves. All this, including indolence, may be permitted and even commanded. It may be quite in order that one part of our existence should often slumber or sleep, should not be involved in what we are doing. In reality we are probably seldom, or never, involved with the whole of our personality and it is better so, for otherwise we should burn out in a few days like a candle. But the *question* whether we are faithful to our calling when this is understood as guidance and endowment *rises up* against us in regard to this situation, and it does so the more energetically the more pronounced the situation is. We should not conceal this. There may and should and has to be some dividing and holding back of certain possibilities of our existence in relation to others. What there has not to be is an attempt to exempt certain possibilities of our existence from the divine claim. What there has not to be is a dividing and holding back that means an abstraction from reality. My whole existence is claimed even in its slumbering or sleeping components. There can be no real putting off of the theologian's coat in favor of freer movement. Our endowment and guidance imply an indelible character which it cannot be good to deny. I am reached by God's command over the whole range of my existence, including its temporarily exempted, or slumbering and sleeping, components. I am claimed in the totality of what I have become and am. If I seriously tried to keep anything back, if I seriously and totally tried to treat it as not claimed, as not involved, as an adiaphoron, as the free sphere and object of my own caprice, then inevitably I should find the true seat of my life in this part of my being that is supposedly freed and exempted from the command of God, and I should not find it in what may be the greater part that is apparently placed under the control of the command. Divisions which mean a real abstraction, a carving up of my action into a more serious and a less serious sphere, will always involve disobedience.|

The canon, then, is whether in the last resort I am totally involved, no matter how one-sidely or with whatever preference in this or that direction. In other words, is the affair one in which I may and can and must be totally involved as the one I am? This is the primary canon by which our conduct is to be measured in this regard. It makes no difference here whether what I am by divine guidance and direction is great or small, whether I or others regard it as valuable or valueless or even dangerous and harmful. The parable of the talents is relevant at this point with its warning against the burying of the one talent received by the last servant [cf. Matt. 25:14–30; Luke 19:12–27]. Whether much or little is entrusted to us, and no matter what may be entrusted to us (including the abilities and possibilities that we may regard as less good or bad), the point that counts is that this is what I am, that this is entrusted to me, and that as I am, I am under obligation to God's command. In any case, how do we know whether what has become of us in our own place, in that system of coordinates, is much or little, good or bad? Even what may seem to be the most obvious of such evaluations are human and not divine, penultimate and not ultimate. God will pronounce his own judgment, and it may well be completely different from ours or that of the human world around us. The first can be last and the last first [cf. Mark 10:31], as we have already stated earlier. What is required of us is not that we should produce what is great or beautiful or extraordinary, but that we should bring what we have and are, that we should not conceal our true state, since it is our state by creation, that we should not keep back from God's righteous judgment anything of what we are and have, that in all our acts we should be *everything* that we are, not for the sake of the totality of our being and work, but for the sake of the totality of the command. More is not demanded of servants than that they be found faithful [cf. 1 Cor. 4:2]. But this is demanded of them.

Our faithfulness to the command means truth in relation to ourselves. It is always untruth or lying against ourselves to conceal the great or small or good or bad things that lie within the circle of our possibilities, to be unwilling for any reason to stand by what we are and have. And it is unfaithfulness and disobedience to God to think that we can come before his face with this incomplete reality that is a different one and not our own, with this falsification of the determination of the place appropriate to us. The truth against ourselves is that we venture to see ourselves without concealment. And faithfulness and obedience to God is that we find ourselves without concealment before him in the calling in which he has fashioned us.│

The second question is whether our action corresponds to the fact that it is *God's* command that claims the whole state of our being and nature as seen from the standpoint of guidance and endowment. *God's* command—this is the command of him who has made us and led us and endowed us up to the present day, who alone finally knows the place of our reality, and whose command can always stand in a most unexpected relation to what we regard as the reality of our calling. For we do not know this reality as God knows it. Is our conduct open? That is to say, are we always ready in it either to be pushed beyond or pushed back behind the limits of our determination as they are known to us? For our own knowledge of them cannot be final, but can be only a provisional human assessment of them. Or is our conduct that of people who think that they know how they have been guided and endowed, as though they had guided and endowed themselves, as though they were their own masters at least in their knowledge of themselves? Our acts obviously have to be considered the more critically the more they are determined for good or evil by the consideration that this is how I am, and even God with his command has to take account of this being and nature of mine and be directed by the historical and physical-psychological structure of my existence: "No one can demand more than is possible."[21] I cannot do more or other than what I am and have. This may be meant confidently and cheerfully, as in the example used by Ritschl when he talked about calling: He was once going uphill alongside a heavily panting worker pushing a wheelbarrow, and he put to himself the ethical question whether it was not his calling to give the man a little help. But he soon came to the conclusion: No, for it is my calling to be a professor of theology; each must remain in his own calling, and therefore I must not have any part in pushing the wheelbarrow, which falls within the calling of this good man. But it may also be meant plaintively and humbly. I do not know how to help myself except by confessing that this or that state of affairs is the real one for me and saying to God: Dear God, this is how I am, this is how you must have

---

[21]Cf. the dictum of the Roman jurist Publius Juventius Celsus (c. 100 A.D.): "The impossible is not an obligation" (*Digests*, L, 17, 185).

me, for I cannot be had in any other way. The slogan that no one can demand more than is possible, and the conduct based upon it, may be permitted and even commanded. But we cannot hide the problems that it raises. We have to know what we are doing when we defend our limits in this way and claim that what God commands coincides with what we can do. A limitation of the divine command by what we think we can do is out of the question. And might it not be that our cheerful or plaintive defense always means that we are presuming to set limits for God? Do we not have to say that we only *think* we know our own limits? God, who has made us, might know much better than we do what these limits really are; and if his command removes what we think are our limits, if, in giving us his command, he gives us authentic information about our calling too, if he says to us: You are and can do much less or much more than you think and give yourself credit for—do what you are ordered, you can, for you should—but we obstinately dig in behind our own opinion of our calling and ability, then our action is obviously disobedience. The slogan that no one can demand more than is possible cannot mean that we may defy God with our possibility or impossibility. |

It may be, of course, that our opinion is right, that we are set before God at the precise point where we see our own limits, and that his command will not will more or less of us than that we should faithfully remain there. But it may also be that God's command implies abasement or exaltation in relation to the known state of things, because another state of things than that known to us is the real one. Since we never know whether the second possibility might not be the right one, since a facile affirmation of the first possibility might simply be a sophism of our own heart, since our inability might be no more than a cover for our unwillingness, the second canon must be to this effect: In relation to the reality of our calling, our action must always be open action on all sides, action in readiness to act differently than we now think we can and should on the basis of our own knowledge of our possibilities. In this second question too, although in rather a different sense, it is a matter of faithfulness to God and truth about ourselves. Truth about ourselves means an honest admission that we have as little knowledge as we have control of the final reality of our existence and its determination. We are not being true to ourselves if, even with the most blameless openness, we say: Yes, this is how I am and I admit it. We are true to ourselves when we go beyond this statement and dare to say contrapuntally: Yes, this is how I am, but I can admit it at any time only if God's command confirms me in this calling, only if his command tells me to admit it. If it does not do this, then I can no longer admit it but must become different and act differently. I *have* to do this because, if God confesses another being than that which I suppose, then I *can* do it, and it is pitilessly required of me. This truth about myself is then *eo ipso* faithfulness to God's command. Faithfulness or obedience to God means standing before him without protection or security or defenses or barricades. It means readiness to see that our real place is another than the one we dreamed about and thought we could, a little defiantly, maintain even against God himself.

These are the two questions that form the criteria of our action in relation to our guidance and endowment.

7. The seventh and last determination of our existence is as general and apparently platitudinous as the first one that we are men. We shall say only a little about it because otherwise we could only say a great deal. It consists very simply of the fact that "it is appointed for us to die once, and after that comes judgment" (Heb. 9:27). To die in the Bible can mean corruption, *phthora,* and it is then the curse and punishment that falls upon all flesh. ⌐In this sense our dying is the death that came into the world through sin [Rom. 5:12]⌐. To die, however, can also mean the finitude of the creaturely as a mark of its distinction from him who alone has life. We are here concerned with the second[22] of these two senses. Our life, and therefore our conduct too, takes place at every moment within the limits and in the determination that we must die, i.e., that there will be an end of us [cf. Pss. 90:12; 39:4], and that behind this end judgment falls. Behind this end means with the absolute supremacy of a competent and powerful judgment on our life. We live and act as those who, in distinction from God, must die, and the question that arises is whether our action corresponds to the fact that this is how it is with him and us. We act within the limit of death beyond which no action reaches, under the aspect of death and the cemetery which we can in no way transcend. Dying is not the judgment on our action—God is not death—but it is the last criterion of our action that is given to us, the ultimate, and therefore the most urgent, aspect of our preparation for judgment. To act responsibly—perhaps we see here for the first time the true weight of the seemingly vague concept of responsible action—is to act in the light of the fact that the moment toward which we go might be our last moment, that the Lord with his judging command might now meet us for the last time and definitively. When do we know that this might not be so? When are we allowed to take our preparation less seriously than when we set what we will in this light? Indeed, even if we knew that our end was still far off—which we do not—would not dying still be secretly there in our present mortal life that is marked by death; could we understand ourselves as anything but dying people, and could we defend ourselves against the fact that this criterion is in force, and with it the question whether our action is such as befits dying people? It might also be that openly or secretly we think we can live like happy gods, forgetting our creatureliness, as though eternity were at our command. Evil would then be forgetting that we must die, and good would be conduct in which the transitoriness of life and the divine eternity that embraces it are remembered. But how can

---

[22]Text A: "We are here concerned with the first of these two senses."

there be here either a forgetting or a satisfactory remembering so that we can venture to speak of good and evil? We can only say that, at this final stage, being called means being called in the shadow of death. Here and thus the command of God encounters us. It is directed to dying people. Here, and as such, we have to respond to it with our next decision.

§9

ORDER

The command of God always means regulation, i.e., the establishment of constancy in my action. It claims me, and I have to hear it, as it commits me, i.e., as it reminds me that my life, both as my own life and as my life together with other life, belongs and is subject, with all that is made, to the one Creator.

1

What shall we do? we asked in §7, and what shall *we* do in §8. We must now put the accent on the "shall." We are asking in the narrowest sense what it means that God's command reaches us, what it is that it brings to us, what it seeks to import into our thinking, willing, and feeling so that these will be *oriented* to it and *determined* by it. Many other things continually affect us *too*. The forces of nature around us (e.g., the heat of summer) continually strike us in a very vital way. Voices of men, good and bad, encouraging and unsettling, knowledgeable and perplexed, calm and excited, called and uncalled, incessantly come to us. There are also demonic voices in the world—we shall have to speak of these later—which affect us. What is the special way in which the command of God reaches us? What does it want of us? We saw in §7 that its content (understood in the sense of its material) is life, so that at all events our life-act, which is the substratum of the "shall," is involved. But what does the "shall" mean in relation to the life-act as such? What makes this a life-act that is imperatively set under the command of the Creator? In what special characteristics does it correspond to the will of the Lord of life? What is the content of the command, not now in the sense of that to which it relates, but in the sense of the bearing of the command as such, the forming of the material by it? In §8 we then looked at man as the *subject* of *life* according to creation, at man in his calling to God's command. We saw that he who commands is none other than our Creator, that our own most proper reality is a determination for God's command and a mirror of it, that our calling stands in correlation to the call that is issued to us, so that obviously this call is to be heard as such. We must now ask *to what* we are called. Man is thus to be understood as also the *object* of the *command* of life. We shall have to think here of the limits of ethics, of the fact that we are in no position to fulfill this coming to us of the divine command, to decree finally and very concretely that this is the action that is commanded, the life formed by the command, my reality as the object of the command of life. God says this, not ethics. But the reminder that ethics cannot establish God's command, but can only point to it on the presupposition that it is itself constantly established by it, this reminder should not prevent us from actually performing the task of pointing to it. If, in §7, we understood God's command as the command of *life* and if, in §8, we understood it as the command that is given to *us*, we have now to understand it as *command*. We have to realize that the revelation of the command of life is not just any event but a *characteristically* determined one that may be *distinguished* very well from others. We have to understand what the characteristic and distinctive element in it is.

We may begin here most simply and relevantly with the fact that in God's command we have to do with *God himself*, with the Creator, in distinction from all the material or spiritual reality of the created world, and especially and concretely in distinction from ourselves. We have to do with a *will* that *meets our will* with the demand that our will bow before it, be subject to it, be in conformity with it. This demand is justified and meets us imperiously because it is the will of the Creator, and our will is that of the creature which would not even be and could not continue for a moment without the Creator. Hence it does not demand of us anything outrageous, unfitting, or indeed impossible. It simply demands that the creature be what it is, namely, a creature. Our creaturely freedom is the freedom that is given to us by the Creator and that is essentially determined for conformity with his divine freedom. Any other freedom, the self-will of the creature in opposition to the Creator, would mean no more and no less than a denial of its own reality and is to be understood *eo ipso*, not as a use, but as an inconceivable misuse of freedom. If we reckon with a freedom of this kind, then we have to realize that we are confessing as reality that which is intrinsically impossible, the mystery of iniquity.[1] In obedience to the Creator is the creature, such as it is. Materially, then, the demand of the Creator's command cannot be anything other than that of the most proper being of the creature. This is the valid sense of the ancient concept of natural law and the modern concept of the autonomy of moral law. Both concepts proclaim that God demands nothing other than what is demanded by the nature of the creature as God created it.

Yet we cannot infer from this, as many have done, that the event of the revelation of the command consists of the ability of the creature to direct the demand of the Creator to itself. While the law of God is in fact no other than the law of the nature created by him, it does not follow in any sense that we have the power to know and establish it. This could

---

[1]Cf. 2 Thess. 2:7.

obviously be maintained only if the relation between Creator and creature, i.e., the qualitative, infinite, and irreversible distinction between them, were to be limited by the deistic myth of the entry of the creature into reality, if it were thus to be confined to the remote act of creation, and its actuality, i.e., the unrepealed determination of this relation by the conditions of the act of creation, were to be denied. In this case the creature would be understood as not only a distinct reality but as an independent one, and the Creator would be simply the past Creator and, in effect, only a reference point for the independent reality of the creature, the metaphysical master concept under which it understands its own self-grounded reality. Knowledge of the will of God would then be no more than knowledge of the creature's own well-understood will, and the demand for obedience with which the divine will encounters us would be understood only as a symbol of the fact that the creature in its own reality, for its own sake and on the basis of its own authority, tells itself what God wills. |

This deistic myth which denies present actuality to the created order of the relation of God and man, and also to the giving of the will of the Creator to the creature, is simply the theory behind the practice of disobedience and ultimately of the denial of God. The theory runs as follows: "Take up deity into your own will and it will come down from its heavenly throne."[2] This theory is a myth, *the* great anthropological myth, the myth of apostasy and revolt, *the* great lie, because deity that is taken up into our will is no longer deity, no longer the Creator. That "the finite is capable of the infinite"[3] means in this respect, too, that there is no God because we ourselves are God. Even if we shortsightedly try to evade this final conclusion, we have to see that the demand we put to ourselves is not the demand of God, and the obedience that we render to our own demand is not obedience to God. If I see myself as a lawgiver, what I have in mind when referring to myself is either explicitly or implicitly my spiritual ego as distinct from nature, the unity of transcendental apperception or the like in opposition to the visible, spatio-temporal, physical-psychological givenness of my ego. A God who stands in this antithesis of spirit and nature, of the ideal and the real, the invisible and the visible, a God who seems to be a God of heaven but not of earth, may be a correctly perceived anthropological reality, and he may also, of course, be a demon, but he is not *God* if aseity, or lordship over all things, belongs to God. Furthermore, if, even without denying God, I interpose myself as my own lawgiver, as a

---

[2] Cf. F. Schiller's poem *Das Ideal und das Leben* (1795), although Schiller has "worldly throne."

[3] This formula is a feature of Lutheran orthodoxy from the late 16th century. A. Adam (*Lehrbuch der Dogmengeschichte*, vol. II, Gütersloh 1968, pp. 402f.) traces it back to J. Brenz (*Recognitio propheticae et apostolicae doctrinae . . .*, Tübingen 1564), who used it in conscious opposition to the opposite view of the Reformed Musculus: "What is finite cannot comprehend what is infinite" (*Loci communes . . .*, Basel 1563, p. 6).

divinely commissioned lawgiver, between God and myself, i.e., my lower self, then obviously it is only dialectically that I can understand God's demand as *his* demand, and by the same dialectic I can understand it as *mine* too, just as on one side I can think of my obedience as obedience to God but on the other side I must see it as obedience to myself. A God who finds himself in this dialectical relation to me that was adopted by the whole of idealism and the idealistic theology inspired by it; a God by whom I can always, "for a change," as Ritschl used to say, understand myself; a God who shares his dignity with me in this pleasant way, such a God is not *God*. We again have what is perhaps an indispensable auxiliary concept in anthropology, but one that we should refrain[4] from confusing with the concept of God. Furthermore, a God who was once the Creator out of nothing and therefore the sole lawgiver, but who has now become a mere spectator on the one side, and on the other a mere viewpoint or point of reference for self-sufficient creaturely reality, such a God is a *"has been,"* a one-time, emeritus God, and it no longer makes any sense to distinguish him as God from an "as if" that is indispensable to the understanding of our own reality, or to maintain a special relation to him under the title of so-called religion. An idealistic theology will find it hard to show that the concept of God as such is not a fifth wheel without which we should really get along much better. If deity comes down from its heavenly throne when we take it into our will, if the finite is capable of the infinite, is it more than a question of tact or taste whether we are prepared to say that God as such has given up the ghost?

We started, however, with the statement that the demand of the divine command is in fact that of the most proper being of the creature. To be precise, we must emphasize that we are speaking of the demand of the *divine* command, i.e., of that which is given and revealed to us by God. Hence our final argument against the deistic myth and the ethics based upon it is that it abolishes the particle of truth on which it rests. For if God is set aside as the sole lawgiver and man is exalted as his replacement, what has obviously happened is no more and no less than that the demand of the one true God is not heard, and therefore the demand of the most proper nature of man is not heard either, so that the concern of humanity is not upheld but allowed to fall. The very moment that the creature snatches at the dignity of the Creator, not listening to *his* command, it loses its dignity as a creature, denying its own true reality. Creaturely dignity, human dignity, consists precisely in *the* freedom, the only possible creaturely freedom, which does not mean creaturely autonomy in relation to the Creator—not even under the title of "the finite capable of the infinite," least of all under this title, we might say—but which means instead the acknowledgment that our life belongs to God, and therefore the subjection of our own will, which is no

---

[4]Barth here uses the Swiss term "unterwegen lassen" for "unterlassen."

more grounded in its own reality today than it was on the day of creation, to the will of the Creator. |

In the command then, we have to do with the will of the Creator and not with our own will. This will of the Creator wills our subjection. As the will of the Creator we have to understand it as a *good* will. For what measure of the good is there in the circle of created reality apart from the Creator through whom alone all that is real is in fact real? Measured by *his* reality, created reality is good or not good: *good* obviously when it conforms to him, and *not* good obviously in the inconceivable nonconformity to him which is conceivable only as the mystery of iniquity. If, then, this created reality is creaturely freedom and creaturely will, the Creator obviously wills its own good by willing its *subjection*. That he is the Lord and that he be recognized as the Lord in the freedom of our creaturely will is what is good, and our will is good, good in itself, when it *renders* this subjection. This is what the command wants from us. And this is why the Old Testament as a whole does not sigh over the command but extols it—Psalm 119—as grace and blessing. At the deepest level the command wants no more from us than our own best. But it has to be understood as *God's* command if it is understood in this sense. By simply underlining it in this way as *God's* command we are already saying the decisive thing about its character and content. Although the concept of the subjection of our will to God's will may sound very general and formal, in reality it tells us everything that we are asking about in this context.

Obviously a will that is subject to God is, in the first place, a will that stands under a *necessity*. Only God is necessary, self-grounded, subject to no further conditions. Only, then, in subjection to his will is there a creaturely will that does not itself have necessity, of course, but does stand under necessity. All other things to which we may subject ourselves are not necessary, for they are only creatures, even if intellectual creatures. We can defy destiny, as has been said already. If all else fails, we can at least oppose natural forces with a *spirit* that is not afraid. That there is no spiritual power that we are unable to escape hardly needs to be said. Our will obviously competes with human wills even and precisely when it subjects itself to them. Our willing, except as it is subject to God, is *never* necessarily determined, but is always undetermined and subject to no command. The only real command is God's command, which as such destroys the last recess of a nonnecessary, nondetermined, and therefore nonreal determination of our will and orients it to what is necessary even in all its creaturely contingency.

A will subjected to God is secondly a *uniformly* determined will. Among all the things that can determine us, it can again be said only of God that he is *one, the one*, and among all the possible determinations of our will it can be said only of that which comes from him that it is uniform and unequivocal. Wherever else we look, the powers of the created world, which can in their way come to us imperiously, are on the one side composite and on the other self-contradictory. They do not have the marks of either simplicity or singularity that denote real unity. Only God is simple and singular, and therefore one. The powers take part in unity but they are not one. Hence that which they want of us, in their own way, cannot be what we wish the one. Every other will than that which is determined by God is one that wills something in opposition to all kinds of other things. It is broken and multiple in itself, for we can will the one only as we do not constantly will other things as well. The creaturely will that is determined by God is also, of course, directed to this or that thing rather than the other, but it is unique because, even in this creaturely lack of uniformity, it acquires a uniform determination, i.e., an orientation to the one, in the same way as it is necessarily determined.|

We combine necessity and unity when we go on to say that a will subjected to God is one that is determined by order. *The* order, the principle and truth of all order in the world, is simply God himself, its Creator. As we bow to the will of God, we do not bow to the power of caprice, whim, or chance; we bow to the power of order. For God is necessary and one. All other necessity and unity are only granted by him and are necessity and unity only through him. All other power in the world has its order in him. We speak of order where reality is not only posited, but is posited as regular reality in a determined constancy of its reality. To subject oneself is to place onself under an order and rule, in a series. To subject oneself to God is to place oneself under *the* order and *the* rule, and in *the* series, outside which reality has neither necessity nor unity and is therefore no reality. There is real subjection, then, only as subjection to God.|

We stand under many orders. Whether they *are* order or merely apparent order may be asked of all orders that are not directly *the* order, that are not finally God himself or direct witness to him. That in standing under many direct and indirect orders—and we cannot transcend either—we should set ourselves under *the* order, no, recognize that we are set under it (they are orders only inasmuch as they are confirmed by God himself as such); that in the nonoriginal and derivative orders we should stand under the original and proper order of God, this is what God's will wills of our will. He imperiously confronts us with this claim upon our will. As he asserts himself in relation to what we will and do, he regulates what we will and do and establishes constancy for it. He removes us from the caprice and whim and chance that characterize creation as seen by the ungodly. He impresses on what we will and do the stamp of the necessity and uniformity that are his own nature. He gives it the direction corresponding to his own order. He gives it the sign of his overlordship, and therefore of obedience. He gives my action at this moment a *character* that has significance not merely for this moment, but fundamentally for the next and all succeeding moments, a character that distinguishes not only my own obedient action but also fundamentally that of everyone else. He gives it the character of what is *generally valid*. He commits me in relation to my action by reminding me that I do not belong to myself but am his creature. He causes me to understand my action as one that is obligated precisely for the sake of my own freedom and dignity. This commitment is what God's will wills of our will. And the revelation of this will of his is the command.

We understand it as the command of life in this context. Inasmuch as our own life and our life together with that of others, our will for life and our respect for alien life, are not left on their own but are the content of God's command, the order of the *Creator* of life is imposed upon them. Not merely by living, but by living in this *order* of life, I live in obedience to the command of life. My conduct, seen as my life-act, is good to the extent that it bears this mark or stamp, to the extent that it has the character of the universally valid (of what is valid for the next moment as well as this one, for others as well as myself), to the extent that I act as one who is committed and bound. The one who binds me is God, no one and nothing else. The limit of ethics may be seen here again in the fact that we can point with absolute stringency to no orders to which our acts are always good when bound and always bad when not bound. Even if we were in a position, which we are not, to set up a complete table of the orders under which we stand, we still could not speak any final word about what is good or bad, since *the* order is not coincident with the totality of the orders. The orders derive their force as real orders, not from themselves, but from *the* order, from the free word of the Creator. He indeed binds us, but he himself is not bound. He is always bound only to himself. To obey the command always has to mean obeying him. Hence, the great relativism of the statements of precisely a theological ethics may not and will not be denied here. What option have we when it is a matter of knowledge of the absolute command? But the reverse must be stated too. God meets us as the one who always binds our will. The Creator is always the God of order. It is always true that good action is action that is necessarily and uniformly determined. We cannot unequivocally say that this action is bound and good and that action is not bound and bad. But we can and must say most unequivocally that bound action is good and action that is not bound is bad.

We can and must set up a further *criterion* of our knowledge of the command. For this knowledge a glance at the existing orders is as little superfluous or misleading as a glance at the determination of calling was in the preceding section, even though we started there with the fact, and constantly returned to it, that concretely our calling can only be God's own Word. Where we stand under *orders*, where our life-act is claimed for a certain regularity and constancy, where we have to view it as measured by what is universally valid, there the *question* arises whether the creaturely, and therefore the improper, necessity and uniformity which force themselves upon our life-act from some point might not represent the commanding God himself, so that we have to consider whether we must not obey them in order not to be disobedient to God. |

There is *more* to it than that. When we speak of *existing* orders, we mean orders that do not exist accidentally, that exist in certain historical relations, that stand or fall in these relations. There are such orders, and we shall have to engage in a special discussion of their ethical relevance at a later point in Chapter 3. But there are also *orders of creation*, i.e., orders that come directly into question (and more than that) with the fact of our life itself as representatives of *the* order, as a creaturely standard and basis of knowledge of the will of the Creator, as words which we cannot possibly overlook in obedience to *the* Word because they are set on our lips and in our hearts with our life as direct testimonies to *the* Word, as words that could not be any different in any historical situation: primal words to which all historically developed and fashioned orders, and all serious attempts to change or overthrow them, must always refer back and appeal as at least their penultimate basis, primal words which at all events proclaim God's own Word, which cannot be questioned as representatives of God's order, which always *are* representatives of that order, which in all circumstances describe the uniform and necessary binding which makes our conduct good and which cannot, therefore, be *not* respected in obedience to God's command. |

Naturally, as we recognize the givenness of these orders of creation, we also recognize that concretely, in the special, direct, and unequivocal sense in which they are coincident with God's command, they can no more be reiterated or indicated by us than can the command of God itself. On our lips, repeated by us, in our understanding, they cannot have that direct, unconditioned, unequivocal force. Indeed, we are not even in a position to name or enumerate them completely. We can mention only some of them in recollection that there are such, that already, as the Creator of our life, God does not keep silence but speaks, that we cannot live at all without encountering his binding claim. To point to this claim, however, all that we can do is to point again to some of the most important relations in which it becomes an event. We can as little refute the idea of a law of nature by indicating the impossibility of understanding and formulating it strictly as we can refute the idea of the command of God by not being able to demonstrate the unequivocal and absolute stringency with which it is always undoubtedly present. We fully confess, then, the *relativity* of our naming and description of the orders of creation. Very *different* names might be given than those given by us, and a very *different* analysis might be given. In this relativity, however, we do name and describe these orders because, no matter how they are named or described, they *exist*. The divine order does not first encounter us in the divine institutions of the kingdom of grace, but truly meets us already in the kingdom of nature. Our life-act as such is measured not only by its own divinely given purpose (§7) and our divinely willed calling (§8) but also by the divinely given order.

We could not grasp and represent the reality of the divinely commanded life with the few concepts with which we explained the will for life and respect for the life of others, nor could we grasp and represent our divinely willed calling with the few definitions of our being and nature. But we could, and here again we can, state that there are such things as a divinely commanded life and divine calling, and also a divinely willed order, and that these are there from the very first with the reality of our creation. It is to be understood in this sense if we now go on to speak of the orders of creation in detail. The right to name these and to speak of them in this way can be established on various material grounds. But it cannot be claimed without a certain contingency, so that the truth of what is said, the demonstration of the divine order of life, is everywhere to be sought in what is intended rather than in what is said. And the right to view things in this way and not another will always, in the last resort, be able to speak only for itself, presupposing that it has something to say on its own behalf.

2

We shall now proceed in four circles. It is divine order that we must understand and live out our life-act as *work*. It is divine order that our sexual life should have its place and limit and fulfillment in the relation of *marriage*. It is divine order that our life with others should have its basic form in the life of the *family*. And it is divine order that all other fellowship among men should take place under the guidance of the two inseparable principles of *equality* and *leadership*.

1. We shall attempt to understand a first order of creation in terms of the concept of *work*. If the term were not so heavily freighted, I might just as well say *culture*. For it is about the problem of culture that we have to speak here. With our creaturely existence as men a task is set for us, and it is an order, an order of creation, that we should work actively at this task. The task is set by the fact that we exist as *men*, i.e., as we recall, in the puzzling dualism of soul and body, spirit and nature, subject and object, with both inner and outer reality. Humanity is not just a calling but also a call. Calling and call stand directly over against one another. Humanity as a call to us is a summons to unity, to synthesis. It startles us away from a purely somatic existence, a purely natural life, a purely objective being, pure externality. It also startles us away from a pure existence of soul or spirit, pure subjectivity, separate and abstract internality. Obviously neither one nor the other of these *ought* to be our life. To be human life, our life *ought* to be lived in the unity and totality which alone make man man in distinction from angels above and animals below. It *ought* to be. This ought is the *idea* and *task* of

culture. Those who speak about culture as a given and existent reality
know little about it. Where and when can we know anything about it but
when we need it and seek it, when we work at the task of culture and
contemplate the idea of it? Animals do not work. Nor do angels. For
them life does not seem to imply a task nor to hold an idea. But however
things may be with them, it does for us. We cannot carry out our human
life-act except in a positive or negative relation to that task and idea.
Always and everywhere it is measured by that relation. To live as man
means for the pile driver no less than for us the shaping of nature by
spirit and the filling of spirit by nature, the objectifying of the subject
and the subjectifying of the object, the manifestation of the inner in the
outer and the essentializing of the outer by the inner, the ensouling of
the bodily and the embodying of the soul. We live in this reciprocal
movement, from above downwards and below upwards (both being
equally necessary). All this means *work.*

Human work is characterized as life-act—formed, regulated, and
ordered life-act, but still life-act—by the fact that it is never done only
for its own sake, but always serves in some way the simple preservation,
guaranteeing, and continuation of the life of the one who does it. The
concept of culture must be protected against the great confusion of
treating it as a kind of deification of man by not letting it be abstracted in
any great or little act of culture from the honest material without which
human action would not be human at all. It is equally true of the farm
laborer, the teacher, the parson, the factory worker, the film star, the
small shopkeeper, the secretary, and the nursing sister that, irrespective
of the special guidance or endowment in virtue of which they do what
they do, irrespective of the cheerfulness with which they do it, they
really do it also so that they can live and because they want to live. They
have found their life's work in what they do, yet this does not simply
mean that they have found their life suitable for doing it, that they have
given and dedicated and sacrificed their life to it, but it has, too, the
more sober, yet no less true, meaning—the strong interest in remunera-
tion found no less in the journals of teachers and pastors than in workers'
papers bears witness to this—in the fact that by doing what they do their
aim is to gain a living, to win a place at the table of life; life here being
understood in terms of §7 as including not only the primitive impulses
but also the higher ones as well. "If anyone will not work, let him not
eat" [2 Thess. 3:10]. Yes indeed, and if anyone works let him show
thereby that among other things he also wants to eat and not just to eat.
This is in the most profound sense really "in order." Our age is perhaps
more honest than many previous ages in the fact that it speaks out
openly in all areas without unnecessary shame. But perhaps it should be
even more honest in this regard, and should act more rarely as if things
were different, if it is to be more protected than it is against the ideology
of work and culture, against the illusion of divine likeness which easily
arises in work the more energetically it is done, and all the more easily

when it seems to imply, in a higher sense, the interpenetration of spirit and nature and soul and corporeality, when it seems to represent more completely the problem of humanity. Do we really do anything special when we work? Does the statesman, scholar, or artist really do anything special as compared with the best handyman? We want to live, and so we work, and we do so according to a mysterious arrangement over which we have no control, the one doing this and the other that, "you in your corner, I here in mine."[5]

There is no reason to go into raptures because we are working, or working at this or that task. For it is simply in order that we should work. At this specific point we have integrated ourselves into the order of life according to the best possible understanding of our special calling. Work is certainly service to God. But to say this is to say that it is the ordered actualization of our creatureliness, the ordered life-act of man in specific antithesis to the divine life-act. We are guilty of a sentimental misunderstanding of the saying about God's resting on the seventh day [cf. Gen. 2:2] if we say that God also works, and it is one of the ambiguities of the Roman Catholic church that it is now in the process of introducing a new feast in honor of "Christ the Worker."[6] What gives our work its true consecration is not that it involves creating like the divine creating or that it is in continuity with the divine creating, but that it is wholly human creating, that it is the necessary form of our human life-act. That it is an *ordered* life-act, an *ordered* actualization of our creatureliness, is the consecration of work which protects it, which also protects all "honest" work against disparagement. The preservation, guaranteeing, and continuation of life demand that man should work, that he should integrate himself at some point into the great system of ends in which the interpenetration of spirit and nature is always sought under the most varied historical conditions. Man cannot serve his most immediate end, the end of life, without also serving the apparently, but only apparently, remotest of ends, the end of man in general. He cannot just grow like a plant or feed like an animal. His life is claimed for a task which in relation to *the* human task can never be more than a partial task but which is still for him *the* human task in general, which because it is partial leads him to respect the work of all others, but which also gives unique dignity to his own work over against that of all others. All true human work actualizes the specific creatureliness of man, is a struggle to achieve a synthesis of the antitheses, of the two worlds in which man is at one and the same time a citizen, and is thereby a witness to the

[5]Barth is quoting from a song by G. Frei (1851–1901), cf. P. Zauleck, *Deutsches Kindergesangbuch*, Gütersloh, n.d., no. 227. Cf. the hymn "Jesus bids us shine" by S. Warner (1819–1885).

[6]This plan was still in its first stages in 1927/28. It threatened to become serious, to the displeasure of those concerned for genuine liturgical reform, only under Pius XII. But it was never carried out. Instead the pope decided in 1955 to institute the Feast of St. Joseph on May 1.

overlordship of the Creator over the *one* world, over heaven and earth. No one can take this dignity of his own work to himself, but again it cannot be taken from anyone. It is the dignity of the order under which we stand, the dignity of the call that goes out to us as we live as men, the dignity of him who has created man in this duality and in prospect of his own unity.

But is our life-act one that is ordered by work? Will the command of God also find us watching in the sense of finding us at work? This is the ethical question that is posed by the existence of this order. If we are to make it more concrete and specific, as our present task demands, then we must define the concept of *work* rather more precisely.

a. We speak of work, of real work in the sense of the divine order of creation, whenever the action of man is characterized by a specific cultural goal, directed to this cultural goal, and disciplined by the will of this cultural goal. A cultural goal, I say, for there may be other goals which have nothing whatever to do with culture, with the human task. We shall speak of this later. We note first that real work is action determined by its goal. This determination is its distinctive objectivity. The work of the doctor, the manual worker, the politician, the general, and the theologian too, if it is real work, has this distinctive objectivity, which may be very different at different times at different cultural stages and with different individuals, but which always, as the rule of this action, claims the will of the man who works, and demands his dedication and subjection, if he wants to work in reality and not in appearance only. He who violates this rule, even though concretely it be ever so individual, he who refuses to recognize it or exchanges it for that engendered by some other goal, he who works unobjectively, is a dilettante or a dabbler, i.e., he does not work at all even if he is ever so busy. Thus the question whether our life-act is ordered by work may first be given this sharper edge: Do we know what we are doing and are we doing what we know?[7] To work is always to do justice to what one is doing according to its specific goal. As objective work, not as dabbling, it always has a part in the human cause, the general cultural goal, which we are to seek in what we do. We cannot stop here, yet it is true that work that is done objectively, no matter what its object may be, has the advantage of being real work in obedience to God's command, and *vice versa*. One Saturday evening I attended a variety show which in every act was perfect of its kind, and then directly after, on Sunday morning, I heard a miserable sermon, and I could not resist the impression that the divinely willed cause of man was better served at the place of very worldly amusement than at that of worship. A reckoning will come if we think that theological and ecclesiastical work does not also come under

---

[7]Cf. the textual variant at Luke 6:5 in Codex D: "On the same day he saw a man working on the sabbath and said to him: Man, if you know what you are doing, blessed are you; but if you do not know you are cursed and a transgressor of the law."

the rubric of cultural work and does not have its own distinctive determination and relevance, as though, in view of the Holy Spirit, we could and should spare ourselves the trouble of doing justice to what we do in the same modest but definite sense as is self-evident for the children of this world, this being the most promising thing about their worldly doings. If it is clear that the boundary between what is objective and what is dilittante cannot be reduced to a general formula, that in relation to others and to ourselves as well it can never be more than a matter of high probability, it is also clear that this boundary is drawn every moment we act, and with it the question is put, not as a technical question but as a thoroughly ethical question, whether we are profitable or unprofitable servants. We are either doing a good job or we are slacking. There is no other option. God knows which it is.

b. Real work, or "honest" work according to the customary and very fine expression that we used earlier,[8] is performed when serving one's personal goal in life means participating in the common cause of man by serving a real cultural goal. Hence we cannot disguise the fact that there is a good deal of work that is done objectively, competently, and industriously, but concerning which we have to ask whether it is real or honest work in relation to its object, since it has no real meaning as human action. I once heard an escape artist, when he had finished his act and the time came for the collection, appeal to the scriptural saying that the laborer is worthy of his hire [cf. Luke 10:7], and subjectively he had every right to do so, for he had done a good job. Yet one can hardly deny that there are skills which, objectively considered, are very probably to be called unprofitable because nonhuman. Indeed, there are whole vocations in the amusement industry and the work of the middleman, and perhaps in the bureaucratic world, especially in the higher echelons, concerning which one might ask whether, in spite of what may be an obvious subjective competence, what we really have objectively is a busy indolence rather than honest work. And perhaps it may be said of far too much academic work which is devoted to examinations and the preparation of dissertations, and to literary production in general, that while a person might obviously live to achieve something thereby and undertake it to this end, it may well be forgotten that if this undertaking is to be work in the sense of obedience to God it must be an achievement in the cause of culture and an effort for the cause of man. This yields a second specification of the ethical problem of work, namely, the question, which is directed also and precisely to the very objective worker, whether and how far his dedication to this or that object is really dedication to the cause of man, whether his special field is meaningful in this sense, whether it is worth the effort expended in relation to it. The question of the significance of the field of work is not the same as that of its higher or lower intellectual or spiritual level.

[8]See above p. 218.

A. Bebel (*Die Frau und der Sozialismus*, quoted in E. W. Maier, p. 257) once wrote: "Rightly considered, a worker who pumps out sewers to protect humanity from dangerous miasmas is a very useful member of society, whereas a professor who teaches falsified history in the interests of the ruling classes, or a theologian who tries to confuse the mind with supernatural transcendent doctrines, is an extremely harmful individual."[9] In so far as he may here be claimed as an ethicist, Bebel is right when he says that the first might well be last and the last first as regards the real significance of their field of work. He is wrong, however, in his obvious opinion that he has a criterion by which to distinguish between meaningful and meaningless fields of human work. All that ethics can say is that the ethical question of work is also posed in terms of the fact that real work must stand in a positive relation to the final end of man's creaturely existence, its cultural goal. Whether God finds us at work is decided not merely by whether we are working diligently and competently, but also by whether what we are doing may be understood as work at the cause that is given to man with his creation as man, or whether this cause is possibly denied and betrayed by the ever so diligent and competent achievement of our own goal. Those who are questioned and possibly accused here are not merely, and indeed not at all in the first instance, those who must do dishonest work in this sense in order to live. Rather, they are actually society as a whole, that brings its individual members or even whole categories of them into this plight, showing thereby that even though its fingers may be clean in relation to most of its members in this regard, it is obviously only half in earnest about the cause of man, i.e., not in earnest at all.

c. We obviously cannot arbitrarily limit the concept of work to that which in the field, in the home, on the street, in the factory, in the office, and in the study may be regarded as real work in Taylor-like categories.[10] Work which may be seen is only the visible side of the work that is required of us. If there are plainly innumerable possibilities of work in which the inner side of it dwindles to a minimum, we have also to reckon with the fact that there are many others in which the outer side forms the negligible minimum. For most people, only a third or a half or two-thirds of their time is filled up with work in the first sense. Furthermore, up to two decades at the beginning of life and sometimes as much again at the end of life usually pass by for most people without their doing any work in a demonstrable sense. We have also to think of the sick, who, for whole stretches and perhaps all their lives, cannot take part in work in the visible sense. Again, in a remarkable but incontestable way, it is also true that in cultural work in the most refined sense, e.g., in the work of the scholar, the artist, or the poet, the boundary can

---

[9]A. Bebel, *Die Frau und der Sozialismus*, Stuttgart 1891[10], p. 289.
[10]Barth is alluding to the system of the American F. W. Taylor (1856–1915), who tried to use the labor force to the full by a systematic breakdown of labor processes.

be fixed only with difficulty, if at all, between work and what the manual worker would undoubtedly call idleness. All these considerations are warnings against any Americanism in our understanding of the concept of work. We issue these warnings, not to justify the persons concerned, but to show that the order of work extends to much more than what is immediately perceptible as such, and that we do not leave this order when we reach the frontier of perceptible work. Play that is only meant to kill time—this is something that applies to children and adults—is also questionable as play. Furthermore, it is as well to view as work that must be done the mastering of what may seem to be purely personal needs and problems, which may not seem to stand in any relation to our life's task, in the form of solitary reflection or group conversations. The concentration, or in some cases the distraction, which thinkers and artists sometimes find absolutely necessary to begin their work, must also be included on the ground that it can and should have the significance of preliminary work, lest the false appearance be given that hard and continuing work is required only of some and not of all. It is as well, then, not to say to someone who suffers from a hopeless lung ailment that he is excluded from work for the rest of his life but rather that in honest wrestling with his fate, which seems to allow him only patient suffering and not activity, he genuinely participates in the cause of men and has a post to fill. Thus the question: Are you working? reaches beyond the sphere of what is a directly visible contribution to society's attempt to overcome the many problems of its goal. Behind all this there stands what is summed up in the fine saying in Isaiah 53:11: "Because his *soul* worked . . ." If the soul is not ready to work in its invisible sphere, the question is in order whether any work is done, whether work, for all its competence and the goodness of the end concerned, is not to be regarded as busy indolence, a question which has perhaps come home to many only in old age or on the sickbed, but which is always posed.

d. The fourth necessary definition of the concept of real work is that it has a limit. We have already seen under c. that this limit is intimated in certain possibilities and necessities of work which at a first glance seem to signify anything but work, which offer more of an appearance of rest, although they are undoubtedly to be claimed as work. We had in mind the inner work which constantly has to be done too. But we must now take another decisive step. Our life certainly stands under the order of work, but that does not mean that all our life must be passed, outwardly or inwardly, in work in order to be obedient to this order, that there is no time whose content does not have to be work in some sense. On the contrary, we may say that our life ought not to be passed in work alone, but there ought to be time in it when we do not work. It is one of the most striking features of the theology of A. Ritschl that because of its battle against metaphysics and mysticism is has no real place for Sunday, but only for the everyday civil life of a world outlook and morality. This is a typically modern and western view of human affairs, but one that is fatally de-eschatologized. The Bible speaks of a "Lord's day" when life does not mean work, when it does not mean work in any sense, but totally and strictly rest. Significant for the meaning of this concept is the fact that it denotes both the *last day* as the general limit of man's time and the *sabbath* as the limit of his six-day working week, and that in the Christian community it is celebrated, in connection with this double sense, as the day of the *Lord's resurrection*.[11] The limit of work is thus none other than the eschatological limit and, as work done according to the order is an action that fills time, so its limit, the day of the Lord, is a *rest* that fills time. If our work is really done according to the order, the day is to be *celebrated* by this rest. It has been set up as a sign of the eschatological limit within which alone work is really done according to the order. The end of time, and concretely the interruption of the human everyday by the resurrection of Jesus Christ from the dead—this interruption of work by rest distinguishes human work according to the order of creation, distinguishes, then, the true work of culture from an unending process that reaches into the infinite, or rather—for there is really no such thing—from the myth of such a process, which is in many circles thoughtlessly and credulously proclaimed and accepted as the truth and meaning of cultural work. |

This interruption forbids us to give ourselves to cultural work with more than the relative seriousness of children playing before God. It reminds us in salutary fashion that, in fact, the absolute seriousness of life is still ahead of us. Culture as the synthesis of spirit and nature may well be the final goal in the life of man. But this final goal of his life rests in God and is indeed God himself, being achieved by his work and not ours. Achieved culture means a new heaven and a new earth [cf. Isa. 65:17; 2 Pet. 3:13; Rev. 21:1] with no antithesis between them, and therefore without any desire or struggle or work to unite them. It means the fruition of God in the perfection of the *seventh* day. We often hear it said that in these circumstances, without work, eternity will be very boring. The answer is that real work is not done because it is delightful or entertaining, but because it is commanded; that it is most inappropriate to judge eternity by our ideas of what is entertaining; and that the work of real working people is not so entertaining that in this regard, too, it cannot be, and does not need to be, fundamentally transcended by eternity, by a restful eternity. But whether it be boring or entertaining, if one insists on putting such stupid questions, we do in fact affirm, confess, and believe this new world of the antithesis transcended even as we work. We work in orientation to it if we really work. To work is to work toward a restful eternity. We do not, of course, make this new

---

[11]Cf. Rev. 1:10; 1 Thess. 5:22ff., with Heb. 4:10; 2 Thess. 1:7ff.; also Deut. 5:12ff.; Exod. 20:8ff.; Acts 20:7; 1 Cor. 16:2; Did. 14:1; on the problem of the relation between the sabbath and the Lord's day cf. also Mark 2:27f.

world by working, but we work, as we are called to *hope*, that God creates it as he created this world. We work as we hope for the *rest* of the people of God [cf. Heb. 4:1–10]. We work "while it is day" [John 9:4]

This "while it is day" is not, as it is customarily understood, a signal of untiring work, but the saving sign of the *limit* of even the most untiring work. We work as those who will one day die, and this means that we shall and must also cease from work. Melanchthon was no worse a theologian because he once rejoiced explicitly that he would be delivered from the mad frenzy of theologians.[12] To remind us of this hope and the related humility and encouragement, the sabbath is set over against the six days of work, and rest is concretely set over against work as an integral part of the order of work. We would not really work, but would work without hope and without God, if our work were not limited in this way. It is a very dubious compliment, then, if someone is extolled as an indefatigable worker. Those who will not relax cannot really apply themselves. Those who cannot really celebrate the scope of all work any more, because the goals of their own work are more important to them, lose the rhythm and composure without which they cannot possibly affirm, confess, and believe that scope even in work itself. Before we make the usual pronouncements about the legalism of Anglo-Saxon Christianity, it might be as well to consider whether the secret of the economic and political power of the English is not, perhaps, by all kinds of detours, connected to a large extent with the English Sunday. Rest from work will obviously be understood as a more urgent command the less the intellectual content of work is, the less the emphasis lies by nature on its inner invisible side where the transition to real rest is readier and easier than on the level of outer and visible work. In this light it seems evident that the battle for *Sunday*, and also for a *free weekend*, for the *shortening* of the working day, and for *vacations* for working people who do not find spiritual compensation in work itself, constitutes, in view of the increasing mechanization of their work, a demand which fundamentally one can hardly evade. In intellectual callings, the more intellectual they are, the matter is less unequivocal. To the extent that a good deal of time is given up to the inner work that is not seen, the need for rest and its justification are obviously less, the period of work can and should be longer, and even the command to sanctify Sunday should not be understood as a statute but according to its spirit. We may then, it is hoped, plan to spend all our academic vacations not *merely* as three-monthly sabbaths.

This does not mean that the sabbath command does not apply to scholarship as well, to the profit and not to the detriment of scholarly work. Anyone who wants to think and speak only as a scholar would probably be not only an insufferable person, but basically an unscholarly one too. It made sense when student government of the old style

[12]See CR IX, p. 1098.

expressly forbade and punished "talking shop" over a glass of beer. Those who cannot resolutely rest at times as professors or students, those who cannot do anything else but work in some way, should see to it that even their work does not become the idle "ticking-over" toward which it is obviously moving. In opposition to the statement of Harnack that in theology it is work that decides (who is right) F. Overbeck (*Chrt. und Kultur*, p. 204) once wrote that "among the Greek gifts, with which the scholar comes endowed into the world, and without which he cannot exist, industry is not the least suspect or questionable. Ruthless industry frightens away all the other gods from a scholar, whereas to ensure the authenticity of work it is most seriously to be recommended that in a side niche a little altar should be erected to indolence too."[13] It must also be said explicitly that we cannot always be doing inner work either. Calvin, who can hardly be accused of any deficiency in either outer or inner activity, summed up the point of the sabbath command in the remarkable words: "If our mortification consists in mortifying our own will, then a very close correspondence appears between the outward sign and the inward reality. We must be wholly at rest that God may work in us; we must yield our will; we must resign our heart; we must give up all our fleshly desires. In short, we must rest from all activities of our own contriving so that, having God working in us, we may repose in him" (*Inst.* II, pp. 8, 29). The reality corresponding to the outer sign will obviously be fully and purely expressed sometimes as real leisure, which does not mean no activity, but no work, in contrast and antithesis to all the effort with which we might think that we can storm the kingdom of heaven either outwardly or inwardly. Under this sign, then, our life-act is really ordered by work. If not, even though it might be an unceasing round of activity, it would be an unordered life-act, not ordered by God. The order of the sabbath, therefore, is inseparably connected to the order of work, and, if the sabbath is as hard to define generally and unequivocally as work is, one should remember that supposed obedience to the order of work is disobedience if it disregards the limit of work that may be seen concretely here, the limit that points to the limit of death and resurrection.

2. We must now discuss the second order of creation, the order of *marriage*. The same standpoint as we adopted for the order of work will serve as a basis for the discussion of this order too. Marriage is an order because it implies humanity, the humanity primarily of sexual life in the broadest sense of the term. Because we live also as male and female, in the mutual relation in which, as we have seen, we are men as either the one or the other, yet also in the mutual relation of spirit and nature and not just as the one or the other; because humanity in respect of sexual life, too, implies not only a calling but also a task, in this regard as well,

---

[13]F. Overbeck, *Christentum und Kultur*, Basel 1919; A. Harnack, *Das Wesen des Christentums*, Leipzig 1900, p. 121; Stuttgart 1950, p. 118; ET *What is Christianity?*

to live according to creation is to live an ordered life, to live in the achievement of what this task requires of us. If we were purely spiritual beings, marriage would not be needed, and if we were purely natural beings it would not be needed either. Because we are men and not animals, basic caprice in this individual relationship is basically forbidden us on the other side. If nature will not agree to an individual lack of real interest in sexual relations, spirit will not agree to an uncommitted sexuality, to a promiscuity of sexual relations. Marriage takes the middle course and implies, generally and fundamentally, an ordered sexual relationship, one that is ordered by creation, one that is divinely ordered, because the sexual relationship, too, is an aspect of the human life-act for whose fulfillment man is responsible to his Creator.

To this general basis of marriage a second may be added, which has something very special to say about the nature of this order. It is valid, of course, only if, in developing the concept of the calling by creation in which we all stand, we were right to speak not only of a general mutual ordering of male and female to one another but, beyond that, of a special determination of two people of the two sexes for one another. If there is this special ordering, this gives us the rule for the individual realization of the sexual relationship and radically determines the meaning and purpose of marriage. The point of this order is that full sexual fellowship between male and female is the realization of a special mutual relationship which is latently present already with the existence of these two individuals. The order of marriage means that this full fellowship, which rests on mutual calling, is the norm of sexual fellowship in general. Hence marriage as an order of creation means at once and *per se* monogamous marriage. Contemporaneous polygamy cannot be called marriage but only a milder form of promiscuity, and successive polygamy (remarriage after the death of a spouse) is marriage according to the order only on the assumption that the second marriage can be understood with a higher degree of probability than the first as a realization of that individual ordering of the one to the other.

There can be no denying that the principle of monogamy, although not marriage in general, can be properly based only on the presupposition of this individual ordering, and *is* therefore based on this presupposition too. Marriage in general is strengthened by this presupposition but not dependent on it. In saying this we remember that we are not saying that a marriage that does not imply the realization of this individual order, but is a failure in this regard, is on that account meaningless or cannot be very meaningful. It would be a bad misapprehension of the dignity of the created order of marriage as such to say that its validity depends on its coinciding with this relationship by calling, that where there is no mutual calling of this kind there can be no standing under the order. If that were so, who could or should enter into marriage at all? Innumerable marriages would not be marriages. They are marriages, however, because even if there is no mutual calling, even if "You and you alone" can be said by the one to the other only with some hesitation, the order has its own dignity and power and also its own blessing. We have to consider that we can in any case know this mutual calling perhaps with high probability, but indeed only with human probability. The sincere conjecture that it is present does not alter fundamentally the fact that entry into marriage is a great risk which has to be ventured according to our best insight and conscience, and in obedience to God, for it lies in the hand and the knowledge of God whether that conjecture rests on error or not. Similarly, in an established marriage, the rise of the conjecture that there is no mutual calling does not alter fundamentally the fact that the marriage exists, and that obedience to God is present in obedience to the order, no matter how one has come to stand under it. The negative conjecture, too, is only a conjecture, and it lies in the hand and knowledge of God whether it might not be a mistake. One can thus say only three things about the presupposition of marriage by calling: 1) that we derive from it the decision that the orderly form of marriage is monogamous; 2) that it implies in relation to entry into marriage a question that is to be answered very seriously, but not with absolute certainty; and 3) that the unavoidable uncertainty in answering it implies for a marriage that has already been concluded a serious stress in the relationship between the couple according to the degree of uncertainty. Since, however, the existence or nonexistence of the mutual calling can only be conjectured in a given case, it cannot come into account as a factor which either necessarily underlies and sustains the marriage or necessarily hampers and destroys it.

We say, then, that marriage in general is an order because we are men in that twofold sense. And marriage as monogamy is an order because the calling of man in respect of the sexual relation is an unequivocal one even though concretely it may finally be hidden from us and we may not be able to infer the existence of the order from the existence of the calling. This is the order of marriage by which our conduct in our sex life is measured. We shall now try to understand it better in detail. But first we shall put what we have said in a definition: Marriage is the spiritual life-partnership entered into by two people of opposite sexes in free mutual love, but also with a commitment to its continuation unto death, and in responsibility to God and other men.

The complexity of this formula, and the admitted impossibility of stating in a single saying all that marriage is, are indications to us that this order of creation too, once we try to understand it and to reflect on its truth and validity, becomes a *problem* and puts a *question* to our being and conduct. This is inevitable when we have to deal with it, not as a matter of civil or ecclesiastical law, nor from the standpoint of prevailing custom, but from the standpoint of ethics, and indeed of theological ethics. It is inevitable when it comes to us, not just as an order, but as an order of God. From the very first it is clear that we come under the pressure of the real *question:* What is marriage? and that we cannot escape from this pressure. Many people are married, and at a first glance they seem in their being and conduct to meet the individual definitions in our formula, and therefore to actualize the order of marriage, either totally or in part, and perhaps as they think (but only think) in the most important part. And many people are not married and they seem perhaps to be covered by some of the important definitions mentioned, so that they, too, seem in their way to actualize the order of marriage even though all the more clearly they seem to stand outside other and no less important definitions. In the strict sense—and we have to take things strictly in ethics—who is not *questioned* at this point? Here as elsewhere we cannot expect to have to reckon with indisputable cases that do not come under question, i.e., to encounter at once a fulfillment of the divine order of marriage either within marriages that are recognized by civil or ecclesiastical law or prevailing custom, or are outside them. Where will not the question that is put to real men mean judgment, i.e., the discovery of the lack of one or more of the indicated definitions? Nor are these individual definitions to be understood as *parts* so that one can speak comfortably of an imperfect fulfillment. The order of marriage exists as a whole. It is a whole in each of its definitions. It is either unbroken or broken as a whole. When we asked: What is work? no aspect could be omitted as less constitutive. The same emphasis had to be put on the objectivity of work, the worth of its object, the unity of inner and outer work, and the limitation of work. So here we have to say that free mutual love between the two concerned cannot make good the lack of responsibility to God and other men, that the readiness for faithfulness, for continuation of the marriage unto death, cannot make good the nonexistence of a real spiritual partnership, and that the existence of this partnership cannot make up for the lack of lifelong fidelity. If the marriage is questionable at one of these points, this means that the fulfillment of the order is questionable in general. And who of us can stand if this be so?

But this is only one side of the matter. The other side is that we cannot expect to find at once, whether within recognized marriages or outside them, a relationship between two people which may be marriage, or resemble it, or aim at it, or be meant as such, but which we can condemn with apodictic certainty because it has no share whatever in the *blessing* on the divine order of marriage. We would be in a poor state if the blessing of this order were not present even and precisely where we do not fulfill it, where we have to recognize that our being and conduct are judged by it. One might ask in all seriousness whether people have done or will do real work in the sense of the divine order of work as we have defined it, and yet see that wherever real work seems to be done, even if only from one standpoint, e.g., that of objectivity, then, no matter how questionable it may be in other respects, there seems to shine something of the confirming and comforting truth of the general order in which even odd workers of all kinds have a share. This is a reflection of the reality of the order itself under which, willy-nilly, we all stand from the very outset, and while this does not justify us, there may be seen in it the power of the divine commanding and the possibility of our sanctification, whose reality is God himself alone. The same is true of the definitions of *marriage*. If it is true that no one can stand before the divine order of marriage, whether within recognized marriages or outside them, it is also true that we should not be too quick in this regard simply to deny to the relationship of two people in marriage or something like it, in the sense of civil or ecclesiastical law or prevailing custom, a share in the dignity, confirmation, and comfort of the order of God because in some respect, which means in every respect, it represents a nonfulfillment or breach of this order. Even though, strictly speaking, all such relationships are broken marriages in terms of God's order, the order that stands over them is never broken and they themselves, in all the brokenness of their being and conduct, while they are not justified, are a living proof or demonstration of the divine sanctity of the command, and to that extent they stand under the protection of its order, in virtue of everything in their relationship that signifies an analogy to this divine order. In this sense the readiness for faithfulness *can* stand in for the lack of free mutual love or perhaps of real life-partnership, and responsibility to God and free mutual love can stand in for lack of responsibility to other men in a relationship that is not recognized. In neither case does this enable the relationship concerned to escape the judgment of God under which it has fallen, and which it cannot evade, as a subjective breach of the divine order, but even *in* judgment and *under* the whole burden of guilt, accusation, and distress which this entails, it means that it will be secure under the unbroken objective divine order which does not let man fall even though he transgresses it many times. The "part for the whole" applies not only in a negative sense in relation to transgression, but also in a positive sense in relation to nontransgression, to what a relationship between two people in marriage, or in what resembles marriage, always displays in spite of everything as it stands in relation to God's command. So long as we, or, concretely, so long as the two concerned do not have to doubt the dignity of their relationship in this sense, they can and may view it as one that is not outside God's order nor declared to be null by this order. It *is* marriage, not by merit but by grace, by the grace of God the Creator and his order, even if it is unhappy as recognized marriage, or even if it does not have the formal recognition of state, church, or custom.

All this must be presupposed if we are to safeguard the concept of the divine order as such. None of the definitions in the formula is to be taken lightly. The questionable fulfillment of none[14] does not mean the questionable fulfillment of the order in general. Conversely, none is not important enough in itself to be able to guarantee our relation [to] the order, not to our actualization of it, but [to] our sanctification by it. There applies to the order of marriage (and to all the divine orders of creation) the same as applies to God's sunshine and rain according to the gospel. It overarches both the good and the bad, both the just and the unjust [cf. Matt. 5:45]. It is everywhere a question and everywhere an answer. We cannot flee it and find concealment in the haven of a really perfect marriage that is in no way out of joint and against which no objections can be lodged. But it also means support, comfort, confirmation, and direction in what are apparently the most confused relationships. We are thus to hear it as we hear God's Word and not to think in a given situation that we no longer *need* to hear it or no longer *can* hear it. The absolutely possible perfect marriage and the hopeless and absolutely impossible marriage are to be understood and used as frontier concepts whose actualization we should always take into account *once* and *again*.

This presupposed, we shall now attempt an elucidation of the individual definitions of the concept of marriage.

a. Real marriage arises with the common recognition of free mutual *love*. We have in mind the accepting, preferring, and choosing of a specific person of the opposite sex in which the relation to the opposite sex becomes a concrete event—a choosing which, if appearances do not deceive, has as its presupposition an election, a special divine calling to this relationship on both sides. But we shall now put aside this background of the problem. Love between man and woman exists when the one becomes, in human terms, indispensible to the other in both soul and body, when the one cannot think of his own life any more without a definite relation to this other, without physical proximity, without belonging, without accompanying this other in everything. The distinction between love and a sensual, or spiritual, or spiritual-sensual, or sensual-spiritual *attraction* is that love implies a total, complete, and unconditional acceptance of the other. As a human act, of course, it stands under the proviso that we cannot know totally either ourselves or the other, that we can be mistaken about ourselves and the other. Love, then, is total acceptance within the limit of what is humanly, subjectively, and honestly possible. But if it is not *total* acceptance within this limit, if it is not a sense of the *full* indispensability of the other in the totality of existence, then we should not deceive ourselves, it is *not love*.

When we love the other only with the senses, or only with the soul, or only with a bit of both, or only in some aspects of life along with restraint or criticism or indifference toward the other, then we have honest or less honest *flirting*, i.e., erotic play. Schleiermacher declared that this

[14]Barth means "any one of the detailed definitions."

possibility is permissible and normal as a preparatory and experimental search for true love.[15] My own comment would be that it is only when we look back that what is in fact play can have been serious preparation in this sense, and even then only when it was seriously meant.|

The other possibility exists that an actual relation between man and woman may be *accompanied* consciously or unconsciously or semi-consciously by erotic play. But there cannot be an intentional will to engage consciously in this erotic play as such. For even at best, only attraction and not eros will underlie such conscious play. True eros does not joke and will not permit joking. When two people think they love one another they must ask first and foremost whether it is really a matter of love and not just attraction. Whether they are really indispensable to one another, whether they totally affirm one another, whether they are ready to be open to one another and to belong to one another without reservation, that is a question which properly (if they realize in time, or are ready to be told, that this is the issue) they ought to be able to answer one way or the other with some measure of developed subjective honesty. If they *cannot* answer it in the affirmative, then no sacrifice is too great and no consideration too important to prevent them from withdrawing as fast as possible from a relationship that has not yet become marriage, for by human judgment all that can be expected in such cases is a marriage that is "unhappy" in this respect.|

Where other motives are central or play a part in a marriage, the question is urgent whether the two also love one another, i.e., do so totally, and at every point, including, e.g., each other's family oddities, each other's failings and fads, with no substraction and with no use of blinders at critical points. Other motives of this type can be regard for money; parental wishes; social advantages; common material interests; pity for the other; high esteem for the character, way, and individual qualities of the other. These may also have a say, but the more they do the more one may suspect that if the couple are moved by all these matters but do not have love [cf. 1 Cor. 13:1−3], things are not as they should be.|

One of the features of the movement of awakening at the beginning of the last century was that people ventured to take their spouses directly from the Lord without having previously seen them. How this worked may be seen from the beginning and end of a section from the story of the life of the Pomeranian, and later Berlin, preacher Gustav Knak (Wangemann, pp. 87f.). Thus in 1833 "the two friends bound themselves together yet again in a plan they had conceived earlier that they would unite in holy matrimony only with a truly converted young lady who was totally committed to the Lord Jesus in life and death, and who was devout and modest and of a gentle and quiet spirit. They both

---

[15]Cf. F. Schleiermacher, *Vertraute Briefe über Friedrich Schlegels Lucinde*, in *Sämtliche Werke*, pt. 3, vol. 1, Berlin 1846, pp. 421ff., esp. pp. 450ff.

kneeled in prayer to place the matter in the faithful hands of the Lord. When they arose from prayer, Gustav said with indescribable joy and sacred seriousness: 'The Lord has now shown me the girl whom he has provided for you as your life companion. She is Caroline Zwarg, the sister-in-law of our dear Lutze, a girl I have known and observed for a long time. Let us kneel down and commit the matter to the Lord.' The friends prayed again and Karl became sure in his heart that the hand of the Lord was ruling here. . . ." The marriage did in fact take place. But now there arises in the same Gustav, too, a "joyousness" to ask for the hand of another young lady whom he did not know personally. But "I do not need to see dear Mathilde first, there are no doubts about her in my heart." In the same night Mathilde dreams about Gustav, whom she knows only by name. The story ends as follows: "With beating heart he came to the rector's house. A female form met him. 'Is this she?' he thinks and his breathing stops—he had thought of her as different. It was not. But when he came into the room, the two who had never seen each other did not doubt for a moment. They hastened to the quiet place of prayer. Where Mathilde had previously prayed for Gustav, she now gives thanks along with her Gustav."[16] One can only describe this, too, as an impermissible and dangerous experiment. Through a similar devotional betrothal Richard Rothe bore a cross for the rest of his life.[17] What is in view is clearly the responsibility to God without which there is in fact no real marriage. But this question should not eliminate the question of simple earthly love. This has its *own* responsibility *alongside* the other.|

Man and woman must be able, of course, to find themselves in God too, but if everything is to be in order they must also love one another as men and women do, and this not merely for the sake of their Christianity. Loving one another means unequivocally preferring each other with their oddities to all others with their virtues. It does not mean saying to each other openly or secretly: I love your manner, your thoughts, your acts, your character, your outward role; it means saying to each other with unconditional honesty: I love *you*, and because of that I love all that you are and have and do, and in all this I want nothing else but to be with you. Then, and not before, we *love* with the wholly earthly eros that has to be allowed to speak here. Anything else is a dangerous dilettantism of love. We must be careful not to say that lack of this love in this strict sense of the term, or self-deception about its presence, will necessarily make a marriage impossible. The responsibility to God and men with which a couple enters into marriage can make good this lack. So can the faithfulness with which they stay by one

---

[16]Cf. T. Wangemann, *Gustav Knak. Ein Prediger der Gerechtigkeit, die vor Gott gilt*, Berlin 1879, pp. 91, 94ff., new ed. with a foreword by S. Knak, Berlin 1928, pp. 72, 75ff.
[17]Cf. F. Nippold, *Richard Rothe*, Wittenberg 1873/74, vol. 1, pp. 248ff.; A. Hausrath, *Richard Rothe und seine Freunde*, Berlin 1902–1906, vol. 1, pp. 193ff.

another in spite of it. A true life-partnership can also step in and make it good. But when we ask how marriage comes about under God's order we cannot point too insistently to this requisite by creation nor can we take the concept of love too strictly. A defect that is covered by the grace of God is still a defect and it would be wrong to determine to sin on the ground that God can cover sin. |

We would not forget to add expressly that sometimes the presence of real love can and must be recognized only later and circuitously, so that there is no need to despair if marriage has already been contracted and the lack of it is then discovered. But it would again be wrong to make this possibility a reason for entering into marriage without real love that is honestly recognized. |

It must be said on the other hand that where this free mutual love between two people is present (we should not lift the final caveat that we can know it even in relation to ourselves only with human certainty), at this point, whatever else may have to be said about their relationship, they stand under the blessing and protection, though also the discipline and direction, of the divine order of marriage, and an unbreakable, even if slender, thread binds them to the sanctifying power of God. No one is justified, either [by] loveless marriage or perhaps love without marriage. But if the order as such can preserve its dignity and force in other respects, and does preserve it in thousands of cases, covering what is lacking on the human level, it can do so in this respect too, where perhaps only this analogy exists. Whether it does so or not is never in our power. It is in our power, however, to take note that the command in relation to marriage is also that marriage, to be real, stands in need of love, of erotic seriousness.

b. *Life-partnership* is what is intended in the concept of marriage, a full life-partnership of body and soul, a fulfilled life-partnership. What distinguishes marriage from love is that in it, if it is real marriage, precisely that which love seeks and desires takes place. Thus, while there is no real marriage without real love, it is something special, a grace and blessing of the order, if there is real love without real marriage. For that which aims at the meaning of marriage as life-partnership is love. Yet this aiming, acceptance from the heart, is something different. So, too, is the actual fulfillment of the life-partnership. As is well known, love is blind. It cannot itself guarantee that what is sought will really take place as such. What takes place might be very different. Real marriage is the testing of love. It is the test of whether the couple not only *know* they belong to one another but actually *are* together; of whether they not only totally *accept* one another in words but *live out* this acceptance in the sequence of an unknown number of days of twenty-four hours each; of whether they not only *love* one another but are really *happy* in each other's presence, in each other's Sunday and weekday face, in each other's virtues and foibles, in each other's vitality and weariness; of whether through all this they can keep on repeating in the same way the Yes, Yes, Yes of love. Marriage is this testing of love. Its authentication can never be taken for granted. One has to say, of course, that real love *stands* this test, that love which cannot stand it has never been real love. But real love comes under the concept of marriage only when it has in some way *stood* this test, only when one does not merely hope but knows from actual experience that one can live together with the other in love. One does not know this too quickly, however, and as a human experience this experience, too, is not without need of repetition.

In relation to this concept of life-partnership we have to consider whether there are not some relations that are *not adapted for marriage* even though love is present in them according to an honest subjective judgment. Civil law recognizes the distinction between lawful and unlawful degrees of kinship, and the delicate casuistry that deals with this question occupies a bigger space than is usually known in both medieval and older Protestant dogmaticians. Reference is also made to "unnatural" marriages when the difference in age is too great, especially when the woman is much older, and also in many cases when there is a striking difference in social rank, or when one of the two parties is burdened with a severe illness. The difficult problem of denominationally mixed marriages has also to be considered in this context. We are confronted here by matters in which we have to be clear that ethics is not hygiene or eugenics or practical psychology. Concretely we must be guided by these different ways of looking at things, but we must not accept them as final authorities if even in such cases we want to render an ethical account to ourselves or to offer pastoral counsel to others. For the ethical question at issue here cannot be: What is healthy? practical? advisable? Ethical reflection cannot end with general evaluations of possibilities of this kind which make marriage difficult. The ethical question is this: What is commanded in view of the fact that marriage is life-partnership? By means of this question ethics will consider for itself each individual case that falls under one of those general possibilities. It could well be that many, and even most, of these cases will in fact be such that the possibility of real life-partnership seems to be threatened either by too great proximity or too great distance between those concerned, that ethics too (or, rather, concrete ethical reflection) can hardly reach any other conclusion than a very definite negation. It is always important, however, to be clear that the man who renders an ethical account of his own action, or who gives theological counsel to others, has not to think and judge as a hygienist, an eugenicist, or a practical psychologist. It would be bringing strange fire to the altar if we were not to remain open to some possibilities in individual cases even where others might regard these cases as closed. One can regard as ethically excluded only cases that fall under the concept of "incest," for here a very different life-partnership is already present, namely, that of the family in the immediate sense, and this cannot, by definition, be coincident with the partnership of marriage, because in it the relationship of male and female, except when we are dealing with sick people, is from the very outset sexually neutral.

Life in marriage is itself to be measured by the concept of life-partnership to the extent that it falls under this order and is not better understood from other angles. It cannot be the task of ethics to give more than hints about the unfolding of the "book of marriage," which has always to be written afresh. Let us simply state that it is a question of fellowship, of the testing of what love thinks that it has sought and found. This fellowship is not just one of body or soul but of both body and soul, and it is one in which the male is thoroughly male and the female is thoroughly female but each [is] *wholly* devoted to the other on the basis of the choice of love. Any "not wholly," any looking aside or living in isolation signifies a *broken* marriage. So does any changing of the married relationship into a different one, e.g., one of camaraderie or friendship, or any retreat from the married partnership of husband and wife to the family partnership of father and mother. It is clear that a change of this kind, an ordered living in isolation for the sake of faithfulness, may in many cases be the only way of saving a marriage. But it will save it only as a broken marriage, i.e., as a marriage which, on account of the drawing apart, is in obvious conflict with the command, even though it may not conflict with it in some other respect, and to that degree it still maintains an analogy to the divine order. When it is in conflict with the command in some other respect, if the case is *not* closed in this respect, i.e., that of life-partnership, the compromise can be no more than that, and in this respect, too, the same order of God which to our salvation has not completely abandoned us can only be and remain an open question, an open wound.

At this point something must also be said about the question of the supremacy of the male and the subordination of the female in marriage. This question has been confused on both sides by a failure to pay heed to the specific context in which the Bible rightly speaks about it and which must be normative for the meaning and understanding of the familiar passage in marriage services. We do not have here any abstract and general supremacy and subordination, or lordship and subjection, but only a special and specific ordering of *this* relationship. What else can supremacy and subordination mean here but that the male is male and the female female and that each must be wholly oriented to the other? Those who know anything about love will be almost tempted to laugh that a problem has arisen in this area. The simple test is that when two people live together in demonstration of free mutual love this separation of functions will just take place—not necessarily in the mechanical and rigid way which ethicists usually recommend here as the solution to the problem, committing the ministry of external matters to the husband and that of internal matters to the wife—but in all freedom (in which there may be apparent, but only apparent, reversals), so that in fact the husband will precede and the wife follow. We thus have a preceding and following, a lordship and subjection, which, seeing that we are dealing with a husband and wife who love one another, are simply the given form of a going together, of a continually new seeking and finding of walking in step, of true life in love. They are the play of real love in which preceding cannot denote any selfish advantage and following cannot signify any angrily or sadly accepted disadvantage, but each must play his role for the sake of the other and therefore also for his own sake. In sum, real life-partnership means that this question is not ignored or rejected but is constantly given its appropriate answer by the life of love. Where it implies an unanswered question, it implies as such doubt concerning the life-partnership of the marriage.

A final point must now be made. We are dealing with the life-partnership of *husband* and *wife*. It is a dangerous, superethical, and falsely idealistic playing with reality to look for the meaning of marriage, especially on its physical and natural side, in the procreation and upbringing of children. Certainly, as a presupposition of the family, marriage is a means to this end. But as marriage, it is also and first of all an end in itself. It is thus neither human nor divine—we must express our agreement with Schleiermacher on this point[18]—to subordinate it to the goal of the family from the very outset. When a man and woman really seek and find one another, then either they do it for their own sake in love—and love has no further end—or they do not do it at all. Precisely in this way, with its own dignity, love is by creation the natural presupposition of the family. Children are the gift of God by which the fellowship of marriage, without being terminated as such, becomes the wider fellowship of the family. The doctrine that children are the aim of the life-partnership of the parents in marriage is one which destroys marriage. It is much closer than one might suppose to Malthusianism,[19] to artificial birth control. The rules and limits that are indispensable here must have their basis in the life-partnership of husband and wife or they have no basis at all, and with their ostensible goal as a presupposition they can change at any moment into their opposite.

We shall now look more briefly at the two remaining points.

c. Marriage is the fulfillment of this life-partnership *in responsibility to God and other men*. I have mentioned responsibility to God only to complete the definition, for all that we are saying here about human conduct is said only from the standpoint of this responsibility. Yet it is

[18]Cf. Schleiermacher's *Predigten über den christlichen Hausstand,* 1820 and 1826, Berlin 1843, pp. 549ff. in which he deals first with marriage (pp. 553ff.) and then separately with the family (pp. 579ff.).
[19]More exactly Neo-Malthusianism, which takes its name from T. R. Malthus (1766–1834), who did not think that what he called repressive factors, like war and disease, or preventive factors, like celibacy or late marriages or continence, are enough to check the growth of population, but saw a need for the use of contraceptives and some restricted practice of abortion.

neither superfluous nor inappropriate to remind ourselves expressly of this general standpoint precisely at this juncture. As God's creatures, we are possibly nowhere so much on our own as in respect of our sexuality, and nowhere perhaps do we need to be reminded more that as creatures we are responsible to the Creator, that even when things may seem to be in order they are in disorder if this responsibility is lacking, and even when they seem to be in disorder they are really in order if it is present. We add at once that responsibility to God will as a rule coincide with responsibility to *men*. I say "as a rule," for our relation to God does not coincide with that to our fellowmen in such a way that we can exclude the possibility that in this area something might take place in responsibility to God but not to men, that there might be unions resembling marriage whose severe deficiencies do not alter the fact that they are legitimate in so far as they have been undertaken and are being fulfilled before God, even though they cannot claim—this is their most serious weakness—the legitimacy of civil or ecclesiastical law or prevailing custom. The exception, however, proves the rule, and here as elsewhere the rule is that, concretely, responsibility to God must be discharged in responsibility to fellowmen, so that if marriage is to be marriage, then apart from inner criteria it stands in basic need of external recognition.

The authorities concerned are the family especially *parents, state,* and the *church.* Recognition by parents, which may have little or no significance legally, is perhaps the most significant ethically, for it is recognition by the closest authority, and the family is an order of creation, which cannot be said of either state or church. Even apart from progeny, marriage means an extension of the family in the narrowest sense. This is what gives parents the right to have a say in the making of a marriage. "To have a say"—we cannot usually say more than that. For we are dealing with adults, even though they are still children. To have a say does not mean to command or forbid. But responsibility in this regard means letting parents have a say and listening to them. Marriage without the blessing of parents is always a venture, and marriage without an understanding with them is probably a very serious mistake. Nor does marriage take place only within the family. It also takes place within society at large. If society is constituted as state and church, this does not rest on any order of creation, but state and church obviously act in the name of society when they demand public notice and approval of a marriage, when they make recognition of its validity dependent on the man and woman for their part recognizing society by requesting declaration of the validity of their marriage from the state and proclamation of the blessing of God upon it from the church. Neither parents, state, nor church can either give them free mutual love or take it from them. Nor can these authorities guarantee them a real fulfillment of life-partnership in marriage. They can only grant them their competent acknowledgment that the step has taken place not only in responsibility to God (which they cannot vouch for) but also in responsibility to men too. In and by itself this acknowledgment does not make a marriage marriage—the way in which Gogarten usually speaks about the nature of marriage in terms of the registry office and the marriage altar surely leads to exaggeration[20]—and yet this acknowledgment does *also* make a marriage marriage; it, too, is indispensable to its reality, or dispensable only if a serious defect is recognized. For marriage is a specific side of the divinely ordained life-act of man. This life-act, however, is not that of a nomad but takes place together with the lives of other people. As work has this relation to our fellowmen, so, too, does marriage. The blessing of the parents and an official and church wedding make sense as witness that the marriage stands in this relation, and therefore indirectly that there is the concrete relation to God in which alone it can be entered into as real marriage.

d. We must now say something about the *lifelong* nature of marriage. Not much, for all the problems of marriage crowd in upon us when we come to this definition. If marriage were just "short-term," as the fine phrase of modern marriage reformers has it, then, at a stroke, there would be no more problems and no more trouble in marriage, for the very simple reason that there would be no more marriage. Principial and permanent flirting would then replace love, a comfortable experimentation with different partners would replace an achieved life-partnership, and a series of private, nonobligatory, and provisional agreements would replace the publicly and responsibly contracted relation. What else can we say about this but that while it may all be very beautiful or not at all beautiful, it is certainly not marriage. It is possible only if the total and concrete relationship of a man to a woman, no matter how broken it may always be in reality, does not in *all* circumstances imperiously have an orientation to unity, completeness, and permanence, and point thereby to an order which cannot be altered in any way by the passage of time or the changes it brings. The concepts of flirting, trial marriages, and provisional agreements, and therefore the whole idea of a short-term marriage, fail to do justice to the problem of this orientation and pointer. One might also say that we have only to take these evil-intentioned concepts seriously, to work them out consistently, and we shall run up against the fact that behind them, too, there stands the concept of a durable partnership. A person has only to try to play at real *eroticism* and he will convince himself that *this* play is serious, that it claims us totally. A person has only to make an attempt at real *marriage* and he will convince himself that if he is really trying he cannot count on breaking it off. A person has only to try to engage in a provisional agreement in *this* matter and he will convince himself that real agreement is possible here only if it is intended to be lasting. Only dilettantes in love and marriage

[20]Cf. the discussion in F. Gogarten's *Politische Ethik*, Jena 1932, p. 118. (This book came out shortly after Barth delivered this series of lectures.)

could have dreamed up this concept of a short-term marriage. For those who know what they are talking about and do not prattle about things they do not understand, the concept breaks apart of itself, illuminating though it may seem to be at first. Neither church nor state invented lifelong marriage. Both of them found marriage in *this* truth, alongside which there is no other. Seriously considered and properly understood, the first and smallest step that we take into the gigantic cosmos of marriage means closing behind us a door which will not be opened again except on the order of the Lord of life and death, and through which there is, fundamentally, no return. This is the terrible seriousness of marriage. This is why the old marriage order in Basel relates the *comfort* of the *blessing* to the *more patient* bearing of the *yoke* of marriage.[21] It is the blessing of marriage, with which man may comfort himself, and its yoke, which must be borne patiently, that its boundary coincides with the boundary of *time*.

We should not, of course, go further than this. No one can swear eternal love. The saying is relevant here: "They neither marry nor are given in marriage" [Matt. 22:30]. Thus to proclaim the continuation of this most beautiful of relationships into eternity is a sentimental blunder which theologians at least should avoid. The definition that marriage is for life is indeed serious enough. It means that the concept of *divorce* can come into consideration only as a borderline one. "From the beginning it was *not* so" (Matt. 19:8). This cannot be shaken. To understand it we may not stop merely at the legal meaning of divorce. Divorce in the legal sense is a final and perhaps unavoidable point in a long series in which a good deal more is at issue in the earlier points than the last one. Divorce is basically the act by which a marriage is negated, in which fidelity is set aside, in which the unity, totality, and permanence of marriage are broken. We have only to ask here whether divorce is permitted or not and we shall see at once that marriage is, of course, constantly broken; that "because of the hardness of your hearts" (ibid.) there may always be orderly forms of this disorderly matter; that there may be beneficial compromises which ease and defuse the situation; that finally there may in fact be also the compromise which is called divorce in the legal sense; yet that all this does not alter in the slightest the fact that in the *order* of marriage which we are now investigating, the possibility of divorce, of renouncing one's troth, is provided for neither in the true and primary sense nor in the secondary legal sense, definitively significant though this may be; but that seen in terms of the order of marriage it always means in either case that someone "breaks the marriage." To the extent that this may imply *ordered* disorder, it may not be impossible as obedience, but to the extent that it implies ordered *disorder* the same act is disobedience. *Forgiveness* and the *recognition* of human sin are two very

---

[21]Cf. *Kirchenbuch für die evangelisch-reformierten Gemeinden der Kantone Basel-Stadt und Basel-Land*, Basel 1911, p. 315.

different things. To find the latter provided for in the divine order is something we should not expect. The definition of lifelong partnership shows that in thousands of cases this order is not actualized by those who stand under it. Can we be surprised if we find them grasping at compromises and perhaps even at the final compromise? Who of us can say on their behalf that they have any other option? We believe in the forgiveness of thousandfold sin, and even more so in the freedom of God's children, even in all the brokenness of their action in this regard too. Yet the fact that we do not judge others and believe in forgiveness for them and for ourselves cannot mean that we bend the command either in their favor or our own. We do not judge others because we know that we are judged with them. We believe in forgiveness and confess thereby that we have sinned. In so doing, however, we acknowledge, and here the matter rests, that divorce is also, even if not first or alone, *disorder* in the true and legal sense, possible ordered disorder, yet still disorder, so that it lays upon us the burden of the question how we can stand before God therewith, and we have to bear this burden. God's order of grace is in another book. This book is always open too. But if we know what God's order is—and if we stand under grace we shall remember all the more, not less, that we stand under God's order—then we have to see that for our good the order is this and not some other.

3. Along with the reality of our being on the one side, and the fulfillment of the natural aspect of marriage on the other, a third order may be seen, the order of the family. This is a relation which by the nature of the case bears within itself a definite principle of constancy. It is the relation to father and mother on the one hand and to one's own children on the other. This relation confronts us with the dignity of the command, with the question how we think we may stand with our conduct before the command of God which it, too, embodies and represents. If there is such an order, then we have to understand it also as an aspect of the divine command of creation, of the law of nature. For this relation and the associated obligation, no matter how we may understand it, and no matter what historical form it may take, is already given to us with our life as such. It does imply obligation, however, and the order exists again because our life is that of men. Age and youth, and dependence, and care and the like as the content of the relation between them, are present, of course, in the animal world as well. But as a rule it is only jokingly that we speak of parents, of fathers and mothers and children, in relation to a family of apes or cats, just as it is, on the other side, slovenly, to say the least, to refer to one's father as "the old man," and every mother should refuse to tolerate her children being described as her young. The fine German comparative "die Ältern" (elders), which like so much else has unfortunately been lost in modern orthography (which has for parents "die Eltern"), shows in contrast to the "parentes" of the Romans that German had some sense of the super-

and subordination which transcends the instinctive content of this relation. The nature of man as both soul and body means that this relation, which in itself is a purely natural one and does not differentiate man from animals, becomes an object of knowledge. Knowledge, however, brings to light the need for the obligation which is present in the fact that we stand in this relation. Knowledge elevates the order into consciousness and translates the givenness of the factual event into a task for action, into a question that is put to our factual conduct. Paul in Ephesians 6:2 made a double observation on that verse in the Decalogue [cf. Exod. 20:12] which is relevant here. He calls this the *first* ἐντολή, i.e., the most obvious and natural of the requirements or orders which are separate from life itself or our individual life-determination. He then emphasizes that it is given in and with the promise "that it may be well with you and that you may live long on the earth." This obviously underlines once again its inalienable connection with our life according to creation. We cannot live—this is perhaps the most immediate point of these observations by the apostle—without at once coming up against this order, and life itself in its constitution and continuation is bound up with this order.|

But what is the special and characteristic content which distinguishes this order from the relation between old and young in the animal world on the one side and from other relations between human beings on the other? "*Honor* father and mother," is the familiar saying of the Decalogue and it is perhaps not so mistaken or arbitrary as might appear at a first glance if the concept of "respect for children"[22] is set in analogy to this. If the term "respect" is used appropriately here, then in regard to the relation of children to their parents—and this gives double weight to the double observation in Ephesians 6:2—it means in the first instance that fundamentally children have to see their parents in the same way—although naturally with the infinite qualitative distinction between Creator and creature—as they see God. The biblical use of the words "father" and "child" for the relation between God and man also points toward this connection. Not every fellowman (e.g., one's partner in marriage) is to be seen in this way, but father and mother are. The connection arises by the nature of the case and should be an object of the knowledge which is relevant for us men in regard to this relation. Elders in the pregnant sense of the term, who are in fact much older than we are, were there already before us, and they were, in the decisive sense, our progenitors, our parents. In temporal reality their fruitful union was and is the reason for our existence, the creaturely repetition of the Creator's cry: "Let there be," in virtue of which we exist as creatures of God. Certainly there is only an analogy here. But it does exist, and for each person it exists uniquely in *his* parents. *They* represent for him the miracle of creation and the Creator without whom he would not exist.

[22]See Ellen Key, *Das Jahrhundert des Kindes*, Berlin 1902, 1905[10], p. 181 and passim.

There thus accrues to parents the special and characteristic honor that they have as representatives to us of the Creator God—something that no others can be for us. Hence this command is the first, not only because it meets man first, but also because it binds him first and uniquely to the Creator. Hence, also according to the Decalogue, the promise of life cannot be separated from observance of the command of creation that meets us in this way, and in the Old Testament its transgression is surrounded by so many terrible threats.[23]

Concretely this honoring of parents means something different for young children on the one side and grown children on the other. In time, as an expression of the same respect, strict obedience necessarily yields to the no less strict listening which befits an independent person. Again, the honoring of parents will be one thing when we have to do with those who are at the height of their powers and another when they have come to be in need in one form or another. Respect which is subordinate, receptive, and open to direction, without ceasing to be real respect, can in certain circumstances become respect that is superior, that helps and guides. Honoring parents can also be one thing in relation to parents who, as we see it, deserve our confidence and respect, and quite another in relation to those with whom both of these have perhaps been shattered in our dealings with them. If there is honoring in joyful openness and commitment, there can and must be honoring also in mere readiness and with relative restraint. No threatening of our obedience can imply a threatening of the command; this is the rule according to which we should think in this matter. And beyond the direct relations between children and parents we may and must work it out as follows: to honor father and mother is to do them honor, i.e., to act in such a way that the sanctity of the analogy of the divine act of creation to which we owe our existence is upheld by our existence and therefore by our deeds, not only in relation to the Creator himself, but, because of this, in relation also to those who, according to his order, were the instruments by reason of which we exist as creatures.

As, then, in the matter of our concrete relation to the other sex, the question is put whether we are known as those who stand under the order of marriage, so now, in relation to our parents, the question arises whether and how far the order of the family, the "honor father and mother," is acknowledged in our conduct. Yet the question is put on the other side as well. It is put to parents in relation to their children. Here, if we are to keep the same term, a very different, indeed a reverse "respect" is in view. If we may and must understand the procreation of human beings as an analogy to the divine act of creation, then the relation of parents to children is regulated by the fact that while they see

---

[23]Cf. Exod. 21:15, 17; Lev. 20:9, Deut. 21:18–21; 27:16; Prov. 20:20; 30:17; Isa. 45:10.

them as one creature sees another, nevertheless within the creaturely world they see them in unique fashion in the same way as God the Creator sees them. At this point we recall Ephesians 3:15, the remarkable verse which tells us that all "fatherhood" in heaven and on earth derives from God. Children do not participate in the honor of the Creator. This is what distinguishes them indelibly from parents. Their honor, however, is that they do participate in the honor of the creature which God willed and called into being in love, which he wished to have in this or that determination of its existence, to which he has thus given its own reality and its own real freedom, which he preserves, accompanies, and rules in its freedom. All that is made exists in and by the blessing of the Lord—this is the deep meaning of the dogma of providence which expands and elucidates the doctrine of creation and which is relevant in this context. It is because of God's blessing that so much is said in the Bible about the blessing of parents as the truly and finally decisive thing which they can do for their children and which they must not fail to do. If only as creatures, yet still by God's order they can truly bless. The ultimate point of all care for children, of all instruction and guidance by direction and especially by example, of all real loving and tending of children, is that we ourselves bless them as mediators of the divine blessing, for this is what God has appointed us to do for these young people—only for these and finally only in this way—by reason of the fact that we are their father or mother. The ethical question that is put to all parental conduct may thus be formulated as follows: is what we do or fail to do justified when it is measured by the standard that *mutatis mutandis* we show them how the Creator deals with them? As they extend their view of us, do they in fact see the Creator or can they perhaps see only a wicked and capricious tyrant, a strange demiurge? It is the responsibility of parents that their children should see in them, ectypically, something of the goodness and severity of God.

So much, then, for the principles of the order of the Christian household whose application, of course, is not a matter of freedom in the sense of caprice, but a matter of the divine command which, as we reflect with the help of these principles, we shall meet in detail as it comes to *us,* to each of us in a very special way.

4. As those who stand under an order, we have to understand finally our life with other people in general. We are again investigating an order of creation. It might seem natural here to take up the concepts of church and state as we took up that of marriage in relation to the order of sexual life and that of the family in relation to the order of the relationship with those closest to us. But if we do not refuse to regard state and church as also orders of God, they are this in a very different sense from work, marriage, and the family. For they are not orders of creation. They are not orders which are posited already with our existence as men. Church

and state both presuppose sin, and they thus embody God's order as his counteracting of sin and in its reality as grace and law. The fact that we also know the orders of work, marriage, and the family only in the brokenness of their contrast to our transgression of them does not alter the truth that they do not have their validity only in this contrast but they have it already as orders of our existence quite apart from the contrast. The same cannot be said of either church or state. Church and state are intelligible only as God's emergency orders. If in very different ways, they both refer to disobedient man whom God has not left to his own devices, and for this reason we shall have to wait until the next chapter to deal with them. Church and state, however, are not without presuppositions in the order of creation. Positive law is measured by natural law, said the older ethicists. We must now investigate these presuppositions.

Obviously significant for church and state is the *equality* of all men which is embodied in them as forms of society. So, too, is the *leadership* with which, commissioned in both in virtue of the same order, individuals emerge from the rest and, in the name of the order that applies to all, act representatively for them and to them. Equality in the church means common acknowledgment of the revolt against God, of which the whole community knows that it is guilty, and also of the mercy of God by which alone it wills to live in all its members. Leadership in the church means the existence of a special ministry for the proclamation of the law and of grace. Equality in the state means the repression of the struggle of all against all, of the oppression of the weak by the strong, through the instrumentality of the law as this is upheld by force. Leadership in the state means the existence of the office of a watchman to preserve the law by the use of force. The equality of men and the leadership of individuals point by their very nature to a severe disturbance that has already affected the relation of man to God and his neighbor. We obviously do not have here an order of creation. But if there is a real order of God here, it cannot contradict the order of creation. It must have its roots in this, roots which are not to be confused with the order of defense and help that we find in church and state, but which are to be understood simply as an order of life. In fact, as we now consider life as the common life of all, it demands from the very first, as work, marriage, and the family demand, and with the same generality and originality as compared to all historically evolved and changing relations, something that corresponds to what church and state mean in the kingdom of grace as the command of God the Creator,[24] a reality of the law of nature on this side too. Older ethics summed up what is intended here in the concept of *justice* or *equity*. I prefer the terms *equality* and *leadership* in order to say something distinct at the outset. And I do not say equality and inequality, but equality and leadership in order that I may be able to

[24]What is meant is the command of God the Reconciler.

say at once what is at issue in the inequality that does in fact correspond to equality. |

The common life of men is based from the very first on their equality. Where this is called in question, their life together is also called in question, and if life always means life together, so is life itself. It is a matter of equality in the relation to God the Creator and therewith also [of] an equal justification of the claim to life and all that this involves. Our common right in this relation is conditioned and limited, but also posited and established, by the fact that we do not have our life from ourselves but from God, and that in order to have it we must receive it each moment afresh from God. In knowing this dependence of mine I know myself as a man—and it makes me a man that I know this dependence and affirm it by my conduct. And as with this knowledge I meet another person, I know him as a *fellow*man, and it makes him my fellow*man* that he becomes for me the mirror of my own self-knowledge as God's creature and that again I affirm him as such by my conduct. Humanity, then, is, on the one side, awareness of our equality before God which no distinction can erase. The fact that there is a rationalism that knows only of this one side, and certainly does not know it as it should be known, does not by a long way justify a Romanticism that wants to know nothing of this side at all and therefore does not know aright the other side one-sidely maintained by it. Even the finest and most justifiable integration of society does not make sense in itself, but only on the presupposition of the essential continuity of all its members on the basis of this equality. Where this is threatened, one may rightly ask in terms of natural law whether the supposed order is not disorder. For leadership, the leading of one by another, is in itself a raw element in the struggle for existence. There are bellwethers and leading elephants in the animal world as well. Leadership makes sense only against the background of equality in so far as all have the same concern. The right in law, right that is right, is the right which is valid for all, which is respected by all, and which also protects all. The criterion of all action in which I lead in some way, and therefore stand out from the rest with more right than others, lies in the fact that I do only what establishes and protects the right of all. |

Under this order, then, stands the will to live, and also the respect for the life of others, by which the law of life is differentiated from mere instinct. There is no claim to life, whether my own or that of anyone else, which does not have to validate itself before the insight that, basically and by right, the claim of all is one and the same. Where this insight is suppressed, the knowledge of God is suppressed, for before God we must all of us recognize that we are called to life in the same sense. But the life to which we are called is especially determined for each individual. That, at any rate, prevents us from understanding this equality by creation as a mechanical uniformity. Not that the inequality in which we exist forms a basis for the higher claim of one as compared to another—we have already rejected this earlier[25]—but it does imply in the common life of all, all cannot have the same position in relation to others, for on the basis of their special calling it is given to some to lead and to others to follow. In order that justice may be done to the concern of all, not all can lead nor can all follow. At different times our life together must be structured and differentiated in different respects, taking very different forms in the political area, the economic, the academic, and the ecclesiastical. From the very first, however, society carries within itself the possibility of such structuring and differentiation, as well as the equality of its individual subjects. Humanity, then, on the other side, means awareness of this possibility. Where this possibility is ignored or denied, the common life of men, and therefore their life in general, is called in question. Our claim, then, to stand alongside others with an equal obligation will have to validate itself before the claim of the question whether we do not have in this or that respect the extraordinary obligation of leadership, and our claim to equal rights with others will have to validate itself before the claim of the question whether there are not others who have to assert against us the extraordinary rights of leadership. It is not merely by the fact that we are sinners who by God's grace stand under the law, but by the very fact already that we live as men, that this super- and subordination continually come into question, not in the elimination, but in the activation of our equality before God. Because this is equality before God, concretely, it can at any moment mean inequality among men. We again forget God if we want to forget that the question of the significance of our conduct is raised in this respect as well.

§10

FAITH

The command of God is fulfilled by me, i.e., my conduct is good, is obedience to the command of life, is in keeping with my calling and is in order, to the extent that I am told, and let myself be told, that it is in agreement with the will of the Creator of life. That I am told this, and let myself be told it, is the work of the Word and Spirit of God the Father, or the reality of faith.

1

We must now deal briefly with the problem of our conduct as such from the standpoint of the command of the Creator. We know that we are determined for *life* in the indissoluble correlation of the will for life and respect for life. We know that this determination of ours is given

[25]Above, pp. 235ff.

precision on the one hand by the *calling* which is issued to each individual in particular, and on the other hand by the *order* which qualifies our life as human life. A whole number of criteria have emerged by which our conduct is measured, partly in relation to its content, partly in relation to ourselves as those who act, and partly in relation to the form of our action. We have not yet inquired, however, into the nature of our action, into the life-act itself which stands under all these determinations, into the subject of all these predicates, or, as we might also say, into the fulfillment of the command of the Creator.

One might equally well, of course, define the state of our investigation by saying that we have been incessantly inquiring into this fulfillment, and that all that now remains is to show expressly that this question is the point of all questions that we have put. Whenever we touched on an individual point we could not help drawing a line or issuing a direction from it to the central point, to the decision of concrete action which has to be taken, in which we do not lie under *a* criterion but under *the* criterion, the unequivocal criterion, in which we have to encounter God himself and his command, in which we are made responsible, in which God's decision and not our own is taken concerning the goodness or badness of our conduct. It was only for the sake of this reference that we touched on all the individual points. Because as men we cannot achieve any central view but can reflect only as we distinguish, knowing that what is distinguished is in itself one, we have engaged in a relative abstraction of the command of the Creator from what God's command also is, i.e., the command of the Reconciler and the command of the Redeemer; we have also engaged in relative abstractions of the three standpoints, and with only penultimate and not with ultimate right we have allowed ourselves, for the sake of example, to take up and discuss only some of the many individual elements, or possibilities, or groups of possibilities of human conduct even from the three different standpoints. It is not for the sake of the concrete instances, but in order to make that reference concretely, that we have dealt with a whole series of concrete instances and shall have to do so again in the chapters that follow. We have neither intended to write, nor have we succeeded in writing, a statute book of the Christian life, Part I: The Law of Nature. We have not tried to anticipate the evaluation of specific actions as good or bad. We have been content to put the ethical question first to our created being as such, to recognize it from the three angles of the determination of life, calling, and order, and primarily to see the Word of God that claims and sanctifies us as indeed the law of nature, yet for its own sake and not for the sake of the law of nature. Even the third angle, that of order, was not taken to imply that an action or a mode of action may be called good or bad because, e.g., in the field of work or marriage, we believe we must say that it is in keeping with the order or not. Even from the standpoint of order, the same action can have a very different aspect when seen, e.g., as an achievement at work or in its significance in relation to the order of the family. Similarly, the fact that we might unequivocally understand it to be in keeping with the order according to §9 is not decisive as regards its goodness. For the same action has also to be evaluated from the standpoint of its content according to §7 and then again from the standpoint of subjective calling according to §8. Even if as ethicists we were in a position to see a specific action either of our own or someone else from all possible angles and in all the complexity of the intersecting lines in this concept of a specific action, and [even if we could then] give what is with high probability a correct answer concerning the goodness [of the action] from all three·standpoints with all the many questions that each involves when we go into it seriously, we should still have to say that this answer, which is with high probability correct, is not the decisive Word of *God* but even at best only the mature result of our preparation for the moment when we have to encounter this decisive Word. As ethical science it is simply what we hope will be a well-considered word of the professor, resting on his broad experience of life, his careful reflection, his profound knowledge of scripture, and his serious practice of prayer. As such it may be overturned at any moment by God's own Word. It cannot be the task of theological ethics, or of any serious ethics, to lead into a dead end of ethical convictions which has been closed off in a way that is ever so masterly, illuminating, and satisfying both technically and architectonically. On the contrary, the task of ethics is to open up again all beautifully sealed-off ethical convictions, not on the side of human caprice but on that of God's own decisive Word and in the direction of the event of the divine commanding in which we can always experience surprises no matter how sure of ourselves we may have been before.|

This means that when, in conclusion, we come to speak about the action itself as a fulfillment of the command, the decisive Word of God cannot be anticipated, and no determining or determination of human conduct can be shown in which we can grasp its goodness or badness in abstraction from the divine decision, in which we can think of it as put in our own hands, so that just before the door is closed we are given again the dignity of Hercules at the crossroads, of freedom of choice. God forbid! We may not and we shall not evade this question of the action in itself and as such. It would be not merely a gap but a serious defect in our presentation of the divine claiming of our action if the appearance were given that the question of the significance of this event were being put from every possible side except that of the action itself, of the event of our decision, as though the answer of ethics to all the questions raised by it were as follows: "Dear friend, you have now heard in how many directions you have reason to reflect on what you do every day even from the one standpoint of the law of nature. Now go and see how you can handle in life the things that you want to do after mature reflection from every angle. First reflect and then act accordingly. Farewell and God be with you." Yes indeed, "God be with you." This at least is fitting if it is meant and taken seriously. The point of this final discussion cannot be anything other or better than an attempt to take this "God be with you" seriously. It obviously wants to be taken very seriously. It wants to be spoken, emphasized, and underscored again in relation to our deciding and acting. It wants to be distinguished clearly from any: "You are on your own," or "You are at the mercy of fate or chance." The end of the song on *this* side must not suddenly become the free will of man, his own bold, autonomous choice between good and evil. At the point where all the lines and questions intersect, Hercules must not come through the backdoor as a *deus ex machina,* as an Alexander cutting the Gordian knot of the big ethical problems, taking control of everything and coming up to the front to speak the final word. |

Not, then, to honor Hercules, but to take final leave of him, we have to put the question: What is it that makes an action as such a good action? What does it mean to fulfill the command? By what measure is my action itself measured as the subject of all the predicates hitherto discussed? We should not fail to recognize the scope of this concluding discussion. Implicitly we are asking here for an answer to all our previous questions. The measure which tells me whether my act as such is good or bad obviously also decides at once and at a single stroke whether it is obedience to the command of life or not, whether I am true or not to my calling, whether it is in keeping with the order or not. Fulfillment of the command is an absolute event which qualifies our relation to God's command in *all* its aspects or disqualifies it as nonfulfillment. For this reason, if theological ethics is to define the concept of fulfillment and not to give up at the last moment, it can use no other concept than one which (apparently squaring the circle) implies on the one side a clear definition of the action as such, thus reminding us once again of our responsibility at the central point, but then on the other hand presents the action as such as one that is defined by God. It must be a concept, then, in acknowledgment of which the attitude of Hercules is ruled out, but the only remaining possibility is that of praying Jacob wrestling with God who elects him [cf. Gen. 32]. The only definition that can possibly come into consideration here is the definition of our action by the reality of faith.

2

What can it mean, and what does it have to mean, if my action as a creature is at this moment good in relation to the command of the Creator, if it is a fulfillment of this command, if at this moment I live, and live together with all other life, in the way that God the Creator of all life wants life to be lived, precisely in the calling to which he has, as the Creator, called me out of nothing, precisely in the order under which he has put me as such? We must be cautious if we call this event or action the enacting or doing of the will of God. Caution is demanded already by the third petition of the Lord's Prayer: "Thy will be done on earth as it is in heaven" [Matt. 6:10]. This obviously means: Thy will be done in the world of finitude, as an action of the creature, of man and not an angel, within the limits in which we live, *as*, i.e., in correspondence, analogy, and conformity with God's own action in heaven, which as such is always as distinct from our action as heaven is from earth. It is inappropriate, then, to describe the doing of the good as a union of man's will with God's. Even the good that is perfectly done by man, even the good that is done by him in God, is always creaturely. To be good does not mean to be like God. The *as (ὡς)* in the familiar saying of Jesus in Matt. 5:48 self-evidently refers to a perfection that is analogous to that of the Father in heaven, to an imitation of this, but not to repetition or doubling of it. To do the good does not mean to take God's place with our goodness. God claims us for the doing of his will as his *creatures*, not as those who are like him either now or in hope, nor in order that we might be raised up to his likeness in the sense of the fourth hypostasis added to the Trinity of which Florenski likes to talk.[1] If we are not to dissolve the concepts of God and command, the doing of the good by us does not imply any deification of man but rather his humanization in true and authentic human action. Without exception, all the determinations of the divine command that we have encountered in this chapter and all those that we shall still encounter direct us *into* these limits and not beyond them. What we are commanded is that we be men and not gods.|

The concept of *faith* lies ready to hand to describe the fulfillment of the command. Faith bridges the distance between creature and Creator without removing it. Faith bridges the distance even as it overcomes it. Faith is the step, but always the step, of man to God. Faith is in antithesis to every mysticism of head, stomach, *and* heart, to all uncritical mystical idealism. It is, then, an affirmation of God which also resolutely and unreservedly affirms the finitude, creatureliness, and, incommensurability of man over against God. Faith and faith alone already does the good simply because it is also the acknowledgment that only one is originally, eternally, and intrinsically good [cf. Mark 10:18]. When doing good takes place, therefore, it does so unambiguously within the limits of the creature, *on earth*. But it does so on earth *as in heaven*, i.e., in agreement with what is done in heaven by God himself. At this point we again think of Calvin's terms "harmony" and "agreement."[2] Good action, then, is human action which is a pleasure to God because on earth, in the created world, it does not perform God's own action, which he himself does, but it does represent it, it is its reflection

---

[1]P. A. Florenski (1881–?), Russian theologian and religious philosopher, who under the influence of Chomiakov *(above n.9)* and Soloviev taught the organic-mystical nature of the church and the transfiguration of the whole cosmos by the incarnation; cf. his main work *The Pillar and Ground of Truth*, Moscow 1914.
[2]Above, p. 81.

and image. It is human action which brings God joy because in it he can
see his own will again as in a finite, creaturely, and temporal mirror, but
still a real one. In this moment we do the good where God finds us,
engaged in the temporal fulfillment of the eternal thought in virtue of
which we exist and live at this moment as we do, with this calling and
under this order; where our action—not of course, our feeling, disposition, or thought, but including all that—our action and existence in this
moment is in its totality a human affirmation of God. The content of this
fruitful moment is obviously *the* answer to all the questions with which
we saw ourselves surrounded in relation to the command of the Creator.
It is no more, but it is also no less. In this moment we live, not a divine,
but a real human life together with all other life as God intended it as the
Creator of life, and we also stand in our calling and under its order. This
existential affirmation of God is faith. For faith is an acknowledgment of
God, not in the predicate but in the subject, as an act of existence. Faith
is obedience. This is obviously at issue if deification is not. Faith as
obedience is *the* overcoming of the infinite qualitative antithesis of the
creature to the Creator, yet the overcoming in which the antithesis is
also maintained. In faith we trust that *God* is right in relation to the
necessity of our existence, that *he* is the necessity of our life, that *he* is
the law of nature. In faith all other possible ground slips away from
beneath our feet and we live in this trust.

But the decisive point has still to be made. How and whence can we
know that there ever was or is or will be such a moment when we are a
delight to God and we exist in the agreement of the creaturely will with
that of the Creator? For what do we have or know but that we are
questioned on every side about this agreement? Have we not recalled yet
again that, as an answer to this questioning, as an answer at our own
disposal, there can only be at best highly probable answers, highly
experienced, highly thought out, highly pious human answers, the
answers which we usually give according to our best judgment and
conscience as, from case to case, we test and choose between the most
illuminating or the most pressing possibilities, the answers of professors
in the textbooks of philosophical and theological ethics in which we will
be told what is good and bad if we really want to be told this by a
professor. But is an answer of this kind, whether it be our own or that of
someone else, really the answer to the question of the good simply
because we regard it as the best? Should we let ourselves be directed by
it in confidence that we are doing the good that agrees with God's will
and is thus a pleasure to God simply because we believe that it is good,
or because it is illuminating to us, or because at least no other option is
open to us, because we find in it, at any rate, the least of all evils? And is
it really faith perhaps, the faith that does good works, to believe, or
should we not rather say, to think, or to be convinced, or to have won
through to the view that this or that is good and should be done by me?
Obviously if we do this we run up against no less than all the

presuppositions with which we started. In this case the good is not what we are commanded but what we have most excellently selected, and faith is finally and properly faith in ourselves as those who make such an excellent selection. It may be, of course, that we can evaluate our action as good in so far as we find ourselves in agreement with ourselves, with the ultimate presuppositions of our existence as they are known to us. But who are we ourselves? And what is this good of ours that is the measure of the good? This is the question that crops up behind every answer that is given by us, and if we try to meet it with a supposed judgment that validates us for judgment, the third question arises against us: from what standpoint can such a validating judgment be provided? and behind the third there is a fourth and fifth question *ad infinitum* . . . Ethical conviction is a good thing, and no one can stop us from calling it faith, but if we do, we have to realize that no ethical conviction or faith of this kind can give us certainty that our action is also in agreement with the will of God. In distinction from every conviction, opinion, or insight, knowledge of *this* is faith in the biblical and reformed sense of the term.

The nature and essence of faith is as follows. First, a *word* is spoken to man. This is not a word that he speaks to himself. It is spoken as the Word of God the *Father*, i.e., of the revealer of truth behind whom no other stands, who is manifest in it because he himself is the truth, whose Word cannot be measured or verified by any other word because it is itself the Word of truth, the original Logos by which all other words are measured and need verification, and the knowledge of which can be achieved, therefore, only in the form of acknowledgment. That this Word of truth is spoken to man is the nature and essence of faith. Secondly, the nature and essence of faith—we are saying the same thing here yet not the same—is that man lets this Word be spoken to him, not as he lets himself be told what he has come to be convinced about, but spoken to him prior to all conviction, and apart from it, by the *Spirit* of God the Father, i.e., as the revelation of the revealer who is himself the truth, over against whom no counterquestion or control is possible, to deny acknowledgment to whom is in no way conceivable as a possibility, but only as an excluded and absurd impossibility, as the mystery of iniquity. This letting the Word be spoken to us by the power of the Spirit of God, this miracle of human perception of the divine Logos, is faith. |

To be sure, we can define faith anthropologically instead of theologically. Indeed, we need to do this in order to remind ourselves expressly that the man who is here spoken to, who lets himself be spoken to, is man in his temporal existence. With Luther we thus define faith as the trust and venture of the *heart* in relation to God,[3] i.e., a trust and venture

---

[3]Cf. Luther's exposition of the first commandment in the *Large Catechism* of 1529, WA, 30, 1 pp. 132f. (Tappert, *Book of Concord, pp. 365ff.*).

in which the center of our being is put in question and compromised, in which we exist, in which we must release and surrender and hazard no less than ourselves, letting God be in our heart and expecting all good things from him: like a swimmer the moment he lifts his foot from the ground and is ready to let the water carry him *totally*, or like the rider of a bicycle who mounts and expects to regain his balance *only* from his rapid forward movement. Yet these two comparisons show plainly that the anthropological definition gains content only from the theological definition. To leave the ground for the water is not yet to swim, though this certainly has to follow. To give up one's balance and mount a bicycle is not yet to ride, though this certainly has to follow. Everything depends upon the water really keeping me up or the rapid movement really taking place. This means that there is a second side to these acts that is totally independent of the first one. The objective content of leaving the ground might be sinking and the objective content of mounting the bicycle might be falling.[4] Hence the trust and venture of the heart, although it must certainly be there where there is faith, is not yet faith itself and never will be. An opinion or conviction or even perhaps a fancy might be the point in this event which is to be described anthropologically. And "God" might be no more than the objective content of an insight determined only by myself in regard to the question of truth. The reason why the theological definition of faith is so decisively important, and the reason why the decisive thing must be put here in trinitarian formulae, is that everything depends on *God* being present where there is this trust and venture of the heart. This alone will prevent faith from being ontologically an illusion or a leap in the dark, even though phenomenologically it might and must seem to take this form. Faith is not irrational staggering but well-considered walking with unheard-of assurance. Where faith is in God, there, as the trust and venture of the heart in and with the full surrender with which this is linked, and also in the uncertainty which is characteristic of this human action as it is of all others, faith takes place, so far as its object is concerned, with the firmness which it is given by this object, with a certainty as hard as steel. Where there is faith, what is believed is that the Word has been spoken to us and that we have let it be spoken to us by the Spirit.|

The certainty of faith, then, is that of the Word and Spirit of the Father, of God himself. Those who boast of their *own* certainty do, of course, leap into the dark and will have to be content with a dubious object of faith. The twofold nature or essence of faith is that man's trust and venture in all its uncertainty participates here in God's incomparable self-certainty because the Word of God is spoken to man here and is

---

[4]Barth has here the marginal note "L.!"—obviously a reference to Luther which implies criticism of the understanding of faith simply as the faith by which we believe (*fides qua creditur*).

accepted by him through the Holy Spirit. Here, here in the reality of faith, in this divine certainty and all man's uncertainty, here, where there is insight, it is insight into the agreement of our action with the will of God. We cannot know what is good and evil as such. But we can be told it and let ourselves be told it in faith. As the moment of faith, the moment of my decision can be the moment of divine clarity in which—as God himself says—I fulfill the command and also, even as I recognize in all seriousness the questions that crowd in upon me from all sides, I *know* that I fulfill it even in face of my knowledge of the severity of the questions and the relativity of the answers that I can give them; I know it in participation in the self-certainty of God, this participation not being my own work but the work of the Word and Spirit of the Father in me, so that wisely I will not try to give it an epistemological basis, since I for my part can demonstrate it only by being enlightened by it, and actually doing what I do in this moment, as the moment of faith, with head inwardly uplifted before God.|

As I believe, I am told and let myself be told that my Creator is gracious, that he is on my side—I do not really know why, but he tells me so and I believe it—and that I am therefore highly pleasing to him just as I am (in an anticipated reply to all the questions that I see put to me). I undoubtedly perceive my judgment too in faith, but how it runs I could not perceive in faith if I did not also and primarily perceive that there is agreement, peace, and correspondence between my will and his, that no mystery of iniquity (though this, of course, is also disclosed to me by faith) can prevent my existence from meaning Yes before God and not No, that even though the full ambivalence of my conduct is counted and seen, I keep and fulfill the command of God. What I do in faith is not sin but is good, even though in all probability—to take the extreme case for the sake of complete clarity—this runs contrary to my own judgment and that of all others. It would be wrong to say that is is good except on the basis of the reality of faith which consists wholly and utterly of my being told this, and letting myself be told it, by God who knows all things and who knows me better than I know myself. It must be said on the basis of this reality.|

In the reality of faith the Creator of life himself guarantees that my conduct is right. In faith I not only may but must act as I do. To doubt my action would now be to doubt God himself. To ask for the judgment of another court would now be refusing to let God be God. To do what I do glumly instead of briskly would now be to suppose that fate or a demon occupies the place of God. If I were to do this, I would *not* believe, I would fall from faith, and, as a work of unbelief, my work, the same work, even though by my judgment and that of all others it might be the most perfect work, would be sin, transgression, iniquity. No doubt, suspicion, or accusation either from within or without can or should upset me or take from me the clear understanding that my work is good and highly pleasing to God, although undoubtedly the same work, as a work of unbelief, is in its *totality* not a good work at all. The work is good, not because of some quality that I have given it, nor because I believed very inwardly and strongly in doing it, but in virtue of what God says about it by his Word and in his Holy Spirit—God the Father who is "the Father of all goodness,"[5] the first and chief authority who, when I believe, has spoken, and spoken definitively.

In faith I *am* righteous. I am righteous in relation to the command of God the Creator. I have not become righteous. I have been pronounced righteous by the same Word by which I was created; and which is the truth of this moment of mine even though I and the whole world cannot grasp this, and how could we do so? But does not this doctrine produce careless and wicked people? we might ask with Question 64 of the Heidelberg Catechism. This control question might well be put, but we shall answer it in three points by trying to present again the nature of justifying faith in so far as it is possible and necessary to do this in the present context.

1. This last and supreme determination of our conduct, in so far as it is determined by the divine claim that is made upon us, involves, even as we state it, a *question* directed to us. Will the moment of our decision toward which we move really be the moment of our faith? Obviously this future thing, being future, is not placed in our hands in such a way that we can sleep like the foolish virgins with their flaming torches [cf. Matt. 25:1–13], nor perhaps—and this seems to be the point of the parable—that we may *stand* in faith now at the present, in the moment of preparation for the decision of the very next [moment]. In this very next moment faith is again a leap, a trusting and venturing, and indeed a trusting and venturing in which we must totally renounce any ability to understand or justify ourselves, a letting go of all props in committal to what is said to us and what we have to allow to be said to us. Those who know how terrible it is to have to believe and to be able only to believe, to have to seek in faith their only deliverance in God's judgment, will certainly refrain from counting on this reality as a comfortable possibility that they have only to grasp in order to be free from all anxiety in face of the great question: "What shall I, frail man, be pleading?"[6] Yes, indeed: "What shall I, frail man, be pleading?," if in the decisive moment it all depends on faith. Truly careless and wicked people will certainly never find peace in *this* aspect of it. Those who do not know what faith is anthropologically do not know that it involves the hardest and grimmest form of perseverance under assault. Those who do know it will not take their being questioned lightly, by casually undertaking to believe, and therefore by saying to themselves that in spite of everything they are fairly good people. On the contrary, the climax and core of all the

[5]Cf. J. J. Schütz (1640–1690), "Sei Lob und Ehr dem höchsten Gut, dem Vater aller Güte" (1675).
[6]From the hymn "Day of Wrath."

questions that are put to us is that we are asked whether we do what we do in faith and whether we know that what is done without faith is sin [cf. Rom. 14:23] even though it might be similar to what Christ himself did at every other point.

2. The question of faith is not one question among others but the absolute question that points to the absolute answer. It is *the* ethical question, the question of our action as such, of the concrete fulfillment of the command. For this reason all other questions are relative beside it. We must be more precise, however, for relativity implies relation. Thus the relativizing of all other questions by this question cannot mean that it erases the others, that the law is set aside by faith. It is not just that faith is itself law, that we always have to speak finally and supremely about the question of faith. Rather, in faith itself the issue is that our work be found good by God, so that only when this question is put do all the other questions come to life as questions. If the question of faith, which is the question of God, were not put to us first and supremely, then we could treat the ethical ambivalence as a matter of intellectualistic scrupulosity which a healthy person would do best to avoid as much as possible, pushing it aside, acting carelessly and wickedly, leaving it to the good Lord and to ethicists. All these questions are *burning* ones only because the question of faith and the question of God stand behind them as the question which is decisive in all of them and the basis of all of them. People who do not believe under the severest pressure do not believe at all. People who do not reflect at every point do not really reflect on the question of faith. To go toward the moment of decision as the moment of faith does not mean fleeing from the abyss which the command of God opens up at our feet in all our relations. Only on the edge of this abyss, and nowhere else, is there readiness for the faith which the coming day will require of us if it is to be the day of our standing in the judgment.

3. The possibility of thinking carelessly and wickedly of the saving possibility of faith is hermetically excluded by the fact that we have no control over the theological nature of faith, over God's being here with his Word and his Spirit. Neither our disposition to believe nor our courage to believe, neither our denial of our own possibilities nor our affirmation of God's possibilities, offers us even the slightest guarantee that our faith might not at the decisive moment be simply an empty opinion, a mere idea or conviction; nor do such things give us any grasp at all of the work of God in virtue of which it is true that our work is a good work. For it is the fact that faith is God's work, an outward work of the holy Trinity—it is the theological nature of faith that makes our work a good work when done in faith. When we realize that the question of faith is the decisive question, what option have we but to lift up our hand in prayer to this triune God? And what can this attitude, which is ultimately no attitude at all but the deep need of the man who knows

that he is lost without the mercy of God, what can this have to do with careless and wicked frivolity in relation to the future?

Here again then, at what is for the moment the final point on our way, we have not heard an answer which is not as such the most fruitful and comprehensive question—the ethical question. But we have at any rate heard an answer.

ETHICS II

Lectures at Winter Semesters at
Münster (1928/29) and Bonn (1930/31)

CHAPTER THREE

The Command of God the Reconciler

§11

THE COMMAND OF LAW

God's law comes to me inasmuch as I am a Christian, a member of his elect people. Judging and showing grace to me as a sinner, God binds me to his law, i.e., to the claim of others as this comes to me in the name of Jesus Christ.

1

The thesis of the preceding chapter spoke of God's command coming to me inasmuch as I exist as his creature.[1] The ethical problem does not just begin with the sinner standing before God in grace. It is true that theologically we know the man who is addressed by God's Word only as a sinner to whom God is gracious. But this pardoned sinner is still the special being whose existence as God's creature is decisively determined by sin and grace, but not expelled or replaced by them. It is not replaced by sin, for sin has not become its substance, as was maintained by an extreme school in the century of the Reformation, that of M. Flacius Illyricus.[2] Nor is it replaced by grace, for what has become a new creature in Christ is still to be addressed as a creature in the first and simple sense ⌜as God's original good creation.⌝ Not for a moment, of course, can we theologically view ⌜this⌝ ⌜first⌝ creaturely existence of ours, our life-act, in abstraction from the fact that it is the life-act of the human creature that was born and fell from God in Adam and is

---

[1]See p. 117.
[2]Matthias Flacius Illyricus (1520–1575) in the course of the synergistic debate advanced the view that original sin is not an accident but the substantial form of man before God. Cf. his *Disputatio de originali peccato et libero arbitrio* . . ., 1560.

regenerated in Christ and therefore in the effective mercy of God. If we were to do so, we should be missing in both thought and speech the reality of the creature that is addressed by God's Word. Yet the reverse abstraction is also theologically impossible. Even in this twofold determination of which we shall have to speak, the life-act is that of this particular creature with all that characterizes this creatureliness even apart from the twofold determination. If a theological ethics has the task of presenting the sanctification of real man by the Word of God, then it cannot overlook his being as such, the problems already involved in his life-act. It must show how the relation of this life-act to the command of God is not self-evident, how we are questioned already concerning this life-act, how it is caught up in the claim of God which is issued to us. |

We have tried to present in Chapter 2 how our existence is caught up in the crisis of the moment which sets us in the divine decision. 1. We have shown what it means to live as man created by God. 2. We have established at what point everyone is reached by this question and called to a life in obedience. 3. We have recalled under what order each of us is set by this call. 4. We have finally tried to understand faith as obedience to this call. Human thought and speech about God's Word suffers from the severe difficulty that we can never say all at once, as we should, the many things about its reality as this is grounded in the trinitarian ⌐reality of God⌐,[3] but have to find help by saying things alongside and after one another in such a way that each member and word, taken alone, gives not only an incomplete but even a misleading account of the matter. In dogmatics, and therefore in theological ethics too, this difficulty can easily become a temptation openly or secretly to suppress the multiplicity of the matter, to lay great stress on one element and focus on it as the only true and important one, and in this way to press on to a unity and simplicity of view which rightly is more sought in theology than in other sciences, and which we cannot renounce carelessly but only after full consideration, precisely because the matter under discussion here is from the very first a multiple one. Remembering this, we have thus far followed a basic line whose theological character could not be validated merely by the fact that the twofold determination of man as sinner and the recipient of grace was our theme as such. [Remembering this] we have spoken of the sanctifying Word of God as the Word of the Creator. By way of precaution we recall once again that in doing this we did not intend that this basic line, and the two others that we shall follow, should really run concurrently, as though we had achieved a natural ethics on which Christian ethics could then be constructed as the upper floors. In fact the lines intersect. Only as God's command comes to us as Christians does it also come to us as God's creatures. If it really comes to us as God's creatures, it also comes to us as Christians. Remembering

[3]Text A: "movement in God."

this, we now turn to the second theme of our theological ethics, the command of God the Reconciler.

We must show first how it is that the Word or command of God that we have understood first as the Word or command of God the Creator may now be understood as the Word or command of God the Reconciler, and from this new standpoint as the command of law rather than the command of life. What considerations and insights force upon theological ethics this change of outlook and theme?

We have understood the command of the Creator, with which we began, as the command of life, i.e., ⌐materially⌐ as the command by which life itself is commanded of us by God, ⌐formally⌐ as the command which is given with life itself, in and with existence. In so doing we have expressly adopted the old idea of natural law. God's requirement is also and primarily that of the innermost being of the creature. Precisely as such it is the requirement of the Creator. It is always God's requirement. Nature is not the lawgiver, nor is man. When man tries to usurp the dignity of the Creator, he forfeits his own proper dignity. This dignity is that of being under requirement, or in subjection. For man the good is to obey God, and it is good that he do this. But the command belongs to him by nature. As we learn from Romans 2:14f., the Gentiles are a law to themselves, showing that the word of the law is written in their hearts. Creaturely freedom is freed to obey this law. The possibility of human self-will in opposition to the Creator's will is not a possibility of human existence as this was posited by the will of God. When this possibility becomes a reality, we deny our own existence as well as God's will. We can view this realization only with horror as a step into complete impossibility and unreality. Our creaturely freedom is not that of a choice between obeying and disobeying. In disobeying, we do not use our creaturely freedom but deny and lose it, placing ourselves, in relation to ourselves as well as God, in the vacuum of a possibility which, since it is not willed by God, can be for us only an impossibility. The demand of our innermost nature, the reason for our existence, the condition under which alone we are real, is always *God's* requirement. As we exist as human beings—and whatever else may have to be said of us we do exist—we are under obligation to *God's* requirement.|

We start with the fact of this obligation. We cannot deny it. We live. In living we stand under the obligation. We live our own lives and we live in indissoluble correlation with the lives of others. But it is not self-evident that this should be so. It does not occur of itself. It occurs through us in the freedom of our wills. Something of this kind always takes place, yet as it does the question arises whether our own life is really lived and whether it is really lived in that correlation. In living, then, we are in the sphere of a command: Live, and live with respect for the lives of others. As we live, this command is present. Or, more accurately, this command is present as we live. It is in place. It comes to us with the event of our life-act as such. There is no avoiding it as though existence came first and the requirement were then added. No, our existence stands under requirement simply by being existence. As we are asked whether we ourselves [are] in place, whether we fulfill the requirement, whether we really live and live with respect, our existence is also questioned. God's Word is the Word of our Creator. As this Word of God becomes a question directed to us, our own existence is called in question by this prior and superior Word. To be sure God's Word always meets us as a new and unheard of Word, as a Word which we cannot say to ourselves because we cannot find it in ourselves or derive it from ourselves. The new thing that it says, however, is also a recollection, *anamnesis*—not self-recollection but a reminder—of the old thing, the oldest of all, the first thing about our own being. As God calls us to *him*self, he calls us also to *our*selves. He tells us that we cannot be ourselves without him. For if we do not keep his command we fall into the abyss of impossibility and unreality. There is possible and real life only in obedience to the command in whose sphere we live. Our life itself stands under the divine command as the measure of its possibility and reality. What this means is a separate question. Without pursuing it here we have to see that we stand or fall with our obedience or disobedience to the command. This is our obligation to God's require-ment which arises with existence itself. It does not originate in ourselves or our existence but in God's requirement. But it is an obligation of our existence. This is why theological ethics has a right and duty not to drop, but to take up, the problem of natural law, understanding God's command, which claims man, as already the command of his Creator and therefore as the command of life, as the command which is given with his life and which affects his life as such.

Yet even in the course of the deliberations that are behind us, at no point could we avoid noting something which now compels us to see the problem of the divine command in a wholly different light from that of natural law, of the obligation which arises with our creaturely existence. We said that this obligation becomes a question that is put to our whole existence. It is an obligation of free beings that are themselves to accept and confirm their being under obligation. Their act, their concrete decision, must be this acceptance and confirmation, this acknowledg-ment of obligation. We have thus seen the command of God the Creator develop into a whole interrelated group of questions: Do you really live? Do you really live with respect for the lives of others? Do you live at the place where you are set by creation, in the calling in which, without repetition or exchange, you are yourself? Do you live in the order which is from the very first proper to human life and without and outside which there is no human life? Finally and conclusively, do you live in faith in the truth, validity, and goodness of the Word of God the Creator that is spoken to you, in the true act of obedience with which all the other questions are answered? The obligation under which God has set us must be affirmed by us his creatures as our existence answers the questions asked and fulfills what is required. Our act must be the required act if it is not to be a step into impossibility. We must be ourselves, not by asserting our own creaturely will against that of the Creator, but by corresponding to the only possibility that the Creator has given us. We must be that which we are as those who have come forth from his hand. In the creaturely freedom that is given us we must affirm the requirement of God as that of our own nature. At this point where the problem is whether our act will respond to the question put by God's command, our first discussions of the command of the Creator have brought to light an area which we could not for a long time enter or even delineate with any decisive words, a central circle to which we saw all the lines of our thinking about the command of the Creator leading from all sides, but without being able to follow them, i.e., to mention the act which is not just the object of a question or of many questions, but an answer, the true answer, the good act.

⌐Are we ourselves with our act the answer to the question that is put to us by God's command?¬ We are dealing with the *human* answer, but with the human *answer* to the *divine* question that is put to us. We are dealing with the act of which it must be said that it is in conformity to God's will, that in it God's will is done, as in heaven, so, within the limits of creaturely events, on earth too [cf. Matt. 6:10]. This conformity is obviously the point of the obligation under which we stand. Only one answer can be considered as the answer to this question. There is only one possible use of the creaturely freedom that is given to us. This freedom is not freedom of choice. It is freedom to do God's will. Hence we do not have two choices. This is why only *one* answer comes into consideration. This answer, as we saw, is faith. Faith is the good act. The Word that belongs to that area which cannot otherwise be entered from any side is this Word. But it has its own very special relation to faith as the true act of obedience. The concept of faith in which our presentation of the human situation in the light of the command of the Creator necessarily had to culminate leads us no less necessarily beyond the understanding of the divine command as the command of the Creator or the command of life. In faith we do not believe in ourselves, in our existence, in the righteousness of our existence, in the fulfillment of the command of the Creator by our own act, in our really giving the answer, the one possible answer, to the question that is put to us. In faith we believe positively in the truth, validity, and goodness of the *Word* that is spoken to us. That we are bound to God, not because we prove the truth of the obligation, but because God binds us to him by his Word, is what faith believes. This is the comfort that it receives and has. This is the righteousness of the act of faith. And in faith we believe negatively our own total and qualitative, not just partial and quantitative, inadequacy and failure in respect of the demand that is directed to us, our own nondoing of the will of God, and therefore our own lack of freedom to do the good, the lostness of our existence to the extent that it ought to be itself the true answer to God's question.

Let us begin with this second and negative side of the matter as it is brought to light by recollection of the concept of faith. As the good act is done in the sense of the command of the Creator; as man, claimed by this command, renders true obedience, he acknowledges that the place which I am meant to fill with my act, my decision, the achievement of my existence, cannot be entered by me. 1. I do not stand with my act in such a way as to be able to say: Look, I am living the life which has been given me by God and I am therefore living with respect for all else that is called life. No, I see and know that this is a different act and happening, that it is not at all like real life, that it is self-willed, and that it is thus in conflict with the life of others. 2. I do not stand with my act in such a way as to be able to say: Look, I am true to my calling, I place myself where God has put me. No, I have missed and constantly miss what is told me when I am placed by God where I stand; I neglect my calling and grasp at possibilities which are not mine and are thus forbidden me. 3. I do not stand with my act in such a way as to be able to say: Look, I have submitted to the order which my innermost being demands and I thus live in the divine order which is the order of life itself. No, I have broken this order and will break it again; strictly—and we have to be strict here—I stand in disorder so far as the eye can reach. And if finally I say and have to say—I would not be the person addressed by God's Word if I did not have to say it—that I believe, then 4. I have to add at once: Lord, help my unbelief [cf. Mark. 9:4], for I know very well that my little bit of faith, my little Yes to the truth, validity, and goodness of the divine Word, is not in itself the good work which is required of me; I know very well that my faith will not justify me for its own sake, but does so only on account of its object, of the divine Word itself; I know very well that even as a believer I am a sinner. Precisely as a believer I know that the sanctuary in the midst cannot be entered even by my faith as my own work and experience. This is what is said by the faith which is the answer to what man is asked by God the Creator. This, the confession of sin, is what takes place when the good act is done in the sense of the command of the Creator.

Let us now consider what this negative side of the matter means, in respect of faith, for our understanding of the divine command. We must ask first how the believer *knows* that he is a sinner. Is this the judgment of particularly honest self-evaluation? Do we hear sober and true resignation speaking, or pessimistically exaggerated despair, when a person, even in obeying, does not grant to his act the character of obedience and dares take comfort only in faith, i.e., only in faith in God and not in the act itself? If this were so, the verdict would mean nothing for our understanding of the divine command. One might ask whether this self-judgment and self-abandonment is not itself condemned by God's command, which as the command of the Creator obviously addresses us as those who can obey it and as those who by nature, as God's free creatures, ought to do so. One might ask whether this self-judgment is not a typical prejudgment, whether it itself, no matter how honest it might be and what good reasons there might be for it, is not the true act of disobedience by which we evade the command. There can be no denying that the confession of sin and the faith that makes it cannot be unequivocally removed from the shadow of this suspicion. We always have cause to consider the question whether faith on this negative side is not simply an agent of this disobedience which first achieves full actuality in our self-abandonment, whether this self-renunciation is not precisely our sin. We have to realize that as our own act and experience our faith is not really protected any more on this negative side than on any other side. But faith does not believe in itself. It does not believe either in the strength with which it rises up to God or in the resignation or despair (even though it be comforted despair[4]) with which it makes that renunciation. To the extent that confession of sin rests on self-confession it will always be open to question. And it has to be said that an altered version of the divine command will not necessarily result from it. Whether we keep the command or whether we rightly or wrongly say that we cannot keep it, what difference does it make to the command? With this insight, whenever in Chapter 2 there seemed to be only a remote possibility of fulfilling the command, we refused to adulterate for this reason the majesty and purity of the command. Our notorious inability to keep it is *not* the thing that can give the command a different aspect.|

But the confession of sin of those who are addressed by God's Word does not really rest on self-knowledge alone. Indeed, in its decisive content it does not rest on self-knowledge at all. Those who believe God's Word do not tell themselves they are sinners, but let themselves be told it. That we are sinners is a truth of faith, i.e., a truth which is received in faith and which we could not tell ourselves just as well if only we were honest enough. Left to ourselves, we could not press on to this confession of our sin. Perhaps we could do it with the lips but not with the heart. Perhaps we could do it in our own thinking but not in God's presence. Perhaps we could and do despair of ourselves but we would not confess that we are wicked. Perhaps we would abandon ourselves, our courage, energy, will, self, and even life itself, but we would not find ourselves guilty. Perhaps we would condemn ourselves, but we would not admit that we are condemned, and justly condemned. We would not see ourselves as standing under God's wrath. This is what faith believes, what faith seeks to confess with that confession. Here as everywhere where faith believes and confesses, what faith believes and

---

[4]For this concept, cf. Luther's letter to Georg Spenlein, April 8, 1516, WAB 1, 35, 33ff., where he speaks of finding peace only in Christ through confident despair of self and its works. Cf. also WA 39 I, 430, 7 ff., which says that despair alone is evil and death, but when the gospel is added to it, it is evangelical despair, which is good.

confesses is a mystery, something which can be seen only on the basis of God's specific attitude to us and dealings with us, only by God's revelation. To those to whom God's Word gives itself to be heard, to believers, in coming to them as the Word of truth it gives them information—God's information—about themselves. It is not the result of their own self-knowledge, however thorough, which tells them that they do not keep the command of life but break it; that precisely the step into impossibility and unreality which by creation we can only regard as completely excluded, precisely the use of freedom which has so little to do with the freedom that is given, can be understood only as a fall into bondage; that precisely the denial of their existence, which stands or falls with keeping the divine command, is the event of their concrete act. Discovery of this fact that is completely hidden from us apart from God's Word; the ⌐revelation⌐ of the "mystery of iniquity",[5] and therefore of the wrath of the damning sentence of God, who cannot recognize his will or image in our reality; the rejection of the creature that has forfeited its divinely willed reality—this is what we come to be told about ourselves in faith.|

Faith is what gives us this divine information. It is faith in that we let ourselves be told this truth by God. All self-knowledge, self-accusation, and self-condemnation, all acceptance of our own inadequacy in face of God's command, can at best be only an echo, a very human and hence a very problematical echo, of this divine information. There is nothing fundamentally theological about it. Remorse is not an obvious or necessary consequence of hearing and receiving this information. There is a remorse which simply shows that we have not heard and received it. There is also a hearing and receiving in which little or nothing may be seen of what we call remorse, in which we may perhaps lift up our heads no less firmly than before. In short, the echo of the divine information in the life of the soul and in attitude and conduct is another matter. The divine revelation of the mystery of iniquity is itself the theological truth which alone can interest us here, the Word of God which not only says to man: Live! Live in your calling! Live under the order of life! Live by your faith!, but also and at the same time shows him that in unheard-of fashion he is not doing this, but that what he calls life—he has only to consider his life at the present moment—is a betrayal of life in every respect, an enmity against others and therewith against himself. If the God who commands tell us this, and if as the one who tells us this he is the God who commands, this compels us to see ⌐that we must take a turn in the path that we have been following if we are to continue to follow it,⌐ that in understanding God's commanding as that of the Creator and Lord of life we have been understanding it only on one side, and that we must now look about for other concepts in order to do justice to its reality.

[5]Cf. 2 Thess. 2:7.

It is plain that if God's Word is really the revelation of our own wickedness and God's wrath, if faith accepts and lets itself be told this great divine No, if in God's Word a gulf opens up between God's will and ours, then the definition of the divine command as the command of the Creator and the command of life is too narrow and says too little. What is ⌜certainly⌝ not contained in this definition is that we stand under a divine No, under God's judgment. The infinite qualitative distinction[6] between God and man is, of course, contained in the concept of the command of the Creator. How can we regard the distinction between the Creator and the creature, the Lord and Lawgiver of life and us to whom this life is given by him, as anything else but infinite and ⌜qualitative⌝? Rightly understood, the very concept of creation rules out any monistic viewpoint, any attempt to think of God and man in synthesis. And if we are really and seriously commanded, how can we think of any other distinction than an infinite ⌜and qualitative⌝ one between him who commands and those who are commanded?|

But obviously this infinite distinction can be qualified in very *different* ways. We have to say that in the relation between the Creator and the creature it is qualified as a *distinction*—a distinction between the free and almighty Lord who is in and by himself, and the secular being that he has created out of nothing and that is upheld and ruled by him. But we cannot say that it is qualified as an *antithesis* between the two. We cannot say that there is here any divine No or any wrath of God. For all the infinity of the distinction we cannot speak of a dividing abyss of rebellion and condemnation. There is distinction in the relation between the Creator and the creature but we cannot speak of any antithesis, division, separation, or enmity. We may not do so. In its early days in the second century, and for a long time after, the church had to struggle against the strong temptation to give a directly perceptible unity to the thought of God by applying to the Creator-creature relation the qualification of the infinite qualitative distinction as antithesis. It was so tempting to carry back into creation itself the enmity between God and man which is the presupposition of reconciliation, whether by viewing creaturely being as an in-some-way unauthorized and illegitimate emanation, as a defection by origin, as intrinsically secession or sin, or by viewing the Creator as a wicked and malicious enemy of his creation, which he made in wrath. This was the great temptation of Gnosticism on the one side and Marcionitism on the other. The church recognized, resisted, and rejected the temptation. In so doing it did not make its task any easier in relation to the concept of God. For, without surrendering the divine immutability and unity, it had to recognize and take into

[6]The phrase goes back to Kierkegaard; cf. *Sickness unto Death*, ET 1946, p. 209, which says that the unavoidable possibility of offense lies in the existence of the infinite qualitative distinction between God and man. Barth found in the phrase a fine expression of his own earlier theological position: cf. his *Romans Preface*, ET 1923. p. 10.

account that this one immutable God has to be thought of from at least two angles in his relation to us: the angle of his wrath against the sinful creature, but behind that the angle of his good and perfect creation, in virtue of which there is distinction but no separation between him and the creature, in virtue of which the infinite distinction—it is infinite in this way too—is qualified, not as enmity, but as peace and fellowship between God and man.│

Peace and fellowship between God and man is the distinctive presupposition of the command of the Creator as such. This is why we have had to adopt the somewhat dangerous concept of the law of nature. This is why we have had to understand the command of life as the command of God *and* the command of our innermost being. This is why we have not denied in advance, but left open, the possibility of fulfilling the command. This is why we have not begun by defining man as a sinner, pressing though the question of fulfillment has been from the very first. This is why it is only now that we have brought to light the antinomy that lies in the concept of faith to the extent that on the basis of God's Word it confesses and acknowledges that man, not from the very first, not as God's creature, but ⌐in a reality that is radically distorted compared to that of creation,⌐ is really a transgressor of the command, a sinner. The concept of faith is the necessary turning point in outlook. We say first: "I believe in God the Father Almighty, Maker of heaven and earth", but when we continue: "And in Jesus Christ his only Son, our Lord", we have already established the negative presupposition, that of the mystery of iniquity on our side, and on God's side his judgment, his wrathful No, to which our confession of Jesus Christ his Son, our Lord, responds ⌐as an echo of a divine Yes but a Yes of different content from the Yes of the Creator.⌐ The infinite qualitative distinction between God and man is now qualified in a very different way. It is now antithesis, separation, and hostility. We now have to speak of a dividing gulf. This second qualification leaves the first untouched. The Creator has not ceased to be the Creator, nor the creature the creature. Hence the command of the Creator is still valid and it should not be overlooked by the doctrine of sanctification nor omitted from theological ethics. Nevertheless, we cannot stop at this command. We cannot put our understanding of the claiming of man by the command in this one framework. We now have to recognize that the one command of the one God is not just the command of the Creator, the command of life, the law of nature, *anamnesis* of the first and most ancient law written on our hearts. We do not simply know it as we know ourselves. It is not just as near to us as we are to ourselves. While all this must not be overlooked or denied, the point is that it now confronts and opposes us as a master does the will of a lazy and disobedient servant or a superior enemy does his foe. What is known is also unknown and strange. The old is the unheard of new. The near is the inconceivably distant. The affirmation of our life-act is also its denial, its frustrating, impeding, and even destroying. What is said in favor of our own being and in deepest harmony with it is also said against and in defiance of our own being, of even the best part of us. All this is not merely quibbling dialectic—if we wanted to quibble we could make a good deal of it much easier—but one of the antinomies which we come up against if we do not put the problem onesidedly—which might help us to avoid such impasses but which is not advisable in the interests of the problem itself.

Taking up the important concept for the first time in its true sense, we have now to say that God's command is also *law*. The law is the command of the God who has been violated in his holiness, who is wrathful, whom we have offended infinitely, who has become our enemy, and whom we now have to fear. We hasten to say that this is not all that has to be said about the law. But this has also to be said and it has to be said first. We avoided the expression "law" when we spoke about the command of the Creator. We did not speak then about the fear of God. Both terms evoke the idea of a separation and antithesis between God and man which ought not to arise there, unavoidable though the consideration of this reality has proved to be from that standpoint. We understood the command there as the command of life. Here and now it is not a matter of life, either in the sense that the command is given in and with our life, or in the sense that the meaning and content of the command is our life. This is still true and it is still important to ethical reflection. But this reflection must now look further afield. We have to see that our life is apostasy from God and therefore from ourselves. We have become guilty, we are no longer free, we are condemned in our life-act. Indeed, it is not really a life-act. We have entered into the darkness of our own impossibility and unreality. As God holds out his command before us, he tells us about ourselves. He holds it out before us as people who stand outside. A place has to be found for the idea of separation and antithesis because it is already in place as the qualification of the infinite distinction between God and man. The command is not *given* to us sinners with our own life; it is *posed* and *opposed* to us by the distant and alien will of a will which is not our will but a stone of stumbling and offense [cf. Isa. 8:14]. Contradiction replaces correspondence. We are checkmated. We are placed under an order of compulsion and force. Our submission is demanded. Such images and expression would not be suitable to describe the command in the relationship of creation. It would not have been in keeping with the real situation between God and man if we had spoken in this way, and only in this way, from the outset. The relationship of creation in which the command is not the command of law but of life is a true one. Those who might reject what we said in Chapter 2 as sub-Christian, or calmly assign it to philosophical ethics, should be careful lest they surrender what the church of the first centuries so instinctively fought for—the claiming of man in his total reality, to which his existence also belongs.

But now that we recall that the mystery of iniquity has been uncovered, and that the wrath of God is manifest over all human unrighteousness and transgression (Rom. 1:18), we have to speak in this way. In this chapter, then, we shall consider the law as the law which claims man as sinner, rebel, and traitor to God and himself. As such we call it the command of law. In so doing we shall have to bear in mind all that the Bible, and especially Paul, says from this standpoint with the heavy emphasis that especially Luther placed upon it, namely, that the law is not the gospel, that it does not justify us or give us life, that it accuses, condemns and slays us, that its saving significance is the recognition of sin, etc.[7] We shall have to bear these things in mind, not speak of them alone, as Luther often did. Luther surely went too far when he sometimes mentioned the law along with the devil.[8] Law does more than smite, accuse, and punish sinners. This is one side of the law which cannot be overemphasized. We shall never lose sight of it for a moment. God's claim does mean our judgment, condemnation, and death. God knows us well—us whom he claims by his command. He is himself affected by what he sees. We may think that we are basically good, but he sees and knows that we are basically bad, i.e., in the basis laid down by us and not by him. We may excuse ourselves but no excuse can alter the fact that God is offended. He tells us that he is angry. Since he does not accept our excuse, it is no excuse. He thus puts the law on us as a kind of bridle. He goes to law with us as with enemies. We have to see ourselves in confrontation with his command. When believers see themselves transgressing the command, they know they are its foes. In weighing the divine claim, we must always remember that we would rather escape this claim if we could. What would we give if only there were no divine command! This is the voice of what is deepest and innermost in us. How could it not be? We know very well that the command destroys us. It is really law—the command as we have to understand it—and we are really rebels—as we have to see ourselves in the light of this second aspect of the command.

We return to the concept of faith. So far we have developed only its negative content. We have recalled what God's Word tells man about himself in order that we may see that the command which is given us sinners is the command of law and as such God's annihilating contradiction against us, our accusation and death sentence. But theological ethics cannot be content with this negative definition of the command of law. The command of God that claims man is also his sanctification, as we saw when laying the foundation in Chapter 1. But if it is our sanctification it has to have another character than that described. Or

---

[7]Cf. p. 104, n. 10.
[8]Cf. WA 40 II, 417, 3ff., where the law is the enemy of God, or 39 I, 426, 31ff., where both the devil and Christ use the law to terrify us but for different purposes, or 39 I, 440, 11ff., where the devil's use of the law is in order that we may perish and die (in contrast to God and the gospel), or 36, 368, 27ff., where frightened sinners whom the devil seeks to bring to judgment through the law are invited to come to Christ and fear no wrath.

rather, this character of the command and therefore of sanctification—sanctification as mortification—has to be understood as the attitude and action of God in virtue of which our action is the good act. Faith is this good act, we have said. But how far? we ask, having established that in faith we know ourselves to be sinners. Three answers must be rejected. The good in faith, that which justifies faith and therefore the life-act that is done in faith, is not the act of faith itself in virtue of some quality or other. It is not even the negative side of this act in virtue of which it is knowledge and confession of our sin. Nor is it a change in our life-act determined by this act.[9]

1. We cannot even consider the possibility that faith as an intellectual and volitional act or as an emotional act, ⌐as a work and virtue,¬ has or can attain to such perfection that we can find in it the goodness that we seek, so that on this account it is the answer to God's question, the fulfilling and keeping of the command of the Creator. What needs to be said here must be formulated in a double paradox. We cannot believe in our *faith* and we can only *believe* in our faith. That we cannot believe in our *faith* means that in our encounter with God and in face of the question that is put to us we cannot rely on what is in us as our faith or on what is done by ourselves, that we cannot see in our conscious nor[9a] unconscious act the good in which God's will is done on earth as in heaven and which therefore pardons us in God's judgment. Faith itself does not justify or save as a meritorious work (Apol. II, 56).[10] Neither faith nor love is evoked by any quality in us (Luther to Brenz, Enders 9, 20).[11] The idea that faith is a virtue which can give Abraham respectability before God is regarded by Calvin as one of the biggest blasphemies that Satan can spew out (*Op.* 23, 688).[12] For if this were so it is obvious that finally we should have to believe in ourselves and affirm ourselves. This possibility is cut off in two ways. First, the judgment under which the believer knows he is placed affects him in all possibilities, in his existence and not just in individual acts. Always as believers we can only doubt, and *must* doubt, the goodness of our faith. We have every reason not to seek its goodness in itself. Faith ceases to be faith if it is not faith in God without side glances at ourselves, if it is not acknowledgment of the goodness alongside which the goodness of the acknowledgment itself is as empty as is the light of the eye compared to the light which lightens it, so that it not only can see but does. The other side of the matter is that we can only *believe* in our faith. That is to say, the goodness

---

[9]Barth has here the marginal note: "Reformers!"

[9a]Original: "or."

[10]Apol. IV, 56 (T.G. Tappert, *The Book of Concord*, p. 114). Barth probably took the figure II from the *Apologia altera* of 1531, cf. CR XXVII, 419ff.

[11]Luther's postscript to Melanchthon's letter to J. Brenz, May 1531 (*Dr. Martin Luthers Briefwechsel*, ed. E.L. Enders, vol. 9 (1903, p. 20.)

[12]*Ioannis Calvini opera quae supersunt omnia*, ed. G. Baum, E. Cunitz, E. Reuss, vol. XXIII (CR LI), Brunswick 1882, col. 688.

of our faith, that which justifies this act and therefore the life-act which takes place in faith, is something that is believed, that is accepted in its outer and inner invisibility, absence, and nongivenness. A thing given, perceived, and at our disposal is not a thing believed. Its acceptance cannot be that of faith. There is no name or species for faith. It is the coming of the mist that swallows up whatever human sense, reason, mind, or intellect can understand. It conjoins the soul with the invisible, ineffable, incommunicable, eternal, and unknowable Word of God and separates it from everything visible (Luther, EA e. 1.14, 81).[13] It is God's work and power (WA, III, 532, 13), God's grace (IV, 127, 18f.). Hence it cannot be accepted for its own sake. When God justifies us by faith this includes the grace whereby he closes our eyes to the weakness of our faith. We are forced to say that faith justifies because of its deficiency. It has no strength of its own but simply receives (Calvin, *Op.* 23, 724f.). Far from leading us astray the infirmity of faith is a good sign (Luther EA e. 1.23, 143).[14] How can true faith be anything but weak faith precisely as real faith, as faith in what makes the believer really good?

2. The goodness of the act of faith is not to be sought in our weakness and humility, in our knowledge as believers that we are sinners, in our sense of the infirmity and impotence even of our faith, in our despair of self, etc. This thought may sometimes be found in the writings of the younger Luther, not without mystical and neoplatonic echoes.[15] It arises out of overemphasis on the thought that God's strength is strong only in the weak [cf. 2 Cor. 12:9]. Calvin speaks for the whole reformation, and along the same lines as the younger Luther, when he points out that this brokenness is not just "some seemly behavior" (*Inst.* III, 12, 6)[16] or putting on a fair show before God (*Op.* 23, 700)[17], i.e., adopting a meritorious and cultivated attitude, but that real contrition is "a wound of the heart" that will not let those who are thrown to the ground get up (*Inst.* III, 12, 6). It is not enough to know that we are poor and sick and indigent; we have to know that we are totally dead (*Op.* 23, 710). If the penitence of faith, the negative content of which we speak, is knowing that we are totally dead, then by the Word of God that is heard in faith we are judged in our existence and therefore in all the possibilities of our existence. Hence the attitude of the humble, of those who know and

---

[13]WA 5, 69, 24ff.

[14]WA 25, 331, 29.

[15]Cf. WA 3 and 4 and 56, e.g., 3, 345, 29f.: We are not justified by faith without humbly confessing our unrighteousness; 4, 111, 29f.: Light arises only to those who are in darkness; those who see this confess that they are in darkness and that light is God's; God gives grace to the humble, so that we cannot separate humility and grace, the former coming first as John the Baptist comes before Christ. Cf. also 3, 172, 35f.; 3, 246, 27f.; 3, 429, 9f.; 56, 403, 1ff.

[16]"This humility is not some seemly behavior whereby you yield a hair of your right to the Lord . . ."

[17]Cf. CR LI, 700: "Humility is not, as many think, making a fair show before God."

confess their weakness, of humility and brokenness and the knowledge of our own questionability, cannot be a justifying work. As stated earlier, we cannot believe in our own remorse. We cannot see in it an assured datum whose goodness may be perceived and in virtue of which we obviously do not need to believe any more. That our weakness is the weakness in which God's strength is strong [cf. 2 Cor. 12:9] is something that can only be believed. The goodness even of our weakness stands only in the goodness of faith with its very *different* basis.

3. Finally, the goodness of the act of faith, its righteousness before God, does not lie—and we shall have to be very precise here—in the change in the totality of the life-act which takes place in the fact that it is the life-act of faith. Now it is true that as believers we stand in a different relation to the command of the Creator from that of nonbelievers. Faith undoubtedly sets us in a definite movement in our attitude to our own life and that of others, to our calling, and to the divine orders of life. This faith justifies and gives life (Apol. II, 62)[18]. "Christ justifies no one whom he does not at the same time sanctify" (*Inst.* III, 16, 1). Nevertheless our act is not good on account of this movement, which we shall have to deal with especially in this chapter. If it is good as it takes place in this movement, its goodness is humanly uncertain and again it can only be believed. Even as believers are caught up in this movement, they are under God's judgment. This movement proceeds in such a way that they are always liable to condemnation before God's tribunal.[19] Of this real righteousness Paul can only say: "Wretched man that I am, who will . . ." [Rom. 7:24]. We have no work proceeding from the saints that, if judged in itself, does not merit shame as its just reward (*Inst.* III, 14, 9). There was never any work of the godly which, if examined by God's severe judgment, did not merit condemnation (*Inst.* III, 14, 11).|

The reformers had to defend this third negation against the Roman Catholic doctrine of faith formed by love [cf. Gal. 5:6], against the doctrine that faith is good and makes us righteous because of the love that is produced by it and united with it. The reformers did not contest that faith works by love. They held this teaching along with their opponents. They said that faith would not be faith were it not this effective faith. They confessed with Paul that no faith justifies but faith working through love, although faith does not derive its justifying power from this working of love (*Inst.* III, 11, 20). For love is imperfect in the saints and therefore does not of itself merit any reward (*Inst.* III, 11, 17). If we had to trust in our love as that which makes faith the good act, how could we be certain of our faith? We should have to say that we do not love as we ought and therefore do *not* love (Apol. II, 110)[20] if the goodness of faith were not certain in some very different way, if we

---

[18]Apol. IV, 62; Tappert, p. 115.
[19]Cf. *Inst.* III, 11, 11,
[20]Barth made a mistake here giving the reference as II, 36 (cf. IV, 110; Tappert, p. 123).

could not believe and then love in faith and in the goodness of faith which has a very different basis.|

This Roman Catholic view came back in the teaching of Andreas Osiander that justification is a real imparting of the divine righteousness of Christ in faith and that the presence of this righteousness may be seen in us at least at certain high points in the life of faith. As he saw it, it would be unworthy of God to speak of justification, of the goodness of the human life-act, if this were not present as essential righteousness in us, but we were just as wicked afterwards as before.[21] Along the same lines, J. T. Beck later understood justification as our real making righteous by God[22] and in our own century K. Holl has taken the view that God accepts us in justification in order to make us truly righteous (*Die Rechtfertigungslehre*, 2nd ed. 13).[23] God, he says, cannot be in fellowship with the sinner. He does not tolerate anything unholy in his presence. If in spite of this he still enters into relation with man, this is inconceivable unless he has the further purpose of transforming man (Luther, p. 119).[24] If God declares man righteous the moment he is only a sinner, he is anticipating the end to which he will lead man. His sentence of justification is analytic; he is pronouncing righteous him who is already righteous in his eyes because he knows the power of his own will. In God's sentence the decisive thing is the final result, the real sanctification of man. If this seems uncertain to man (*Rechtfertigungslehre*, p. 13),[25] if it is completed only with death on the threshold of the world to come (Luther, p. 122),[26] a fellowship of will with God begins in justification (Luther, p. 151)[27] and in relation to this there is a new sense of life and self, created by God (*Was hat . . .?* p. 23)[28] which has the possibility of endless deepening (Luther, p. 136).[29] In the act of faith the new will which will transform the whole being of man is already present in germ (Luther, p. 120).[30] In showing his goodness (in the

---

[21]Cf. Andreas Osiander (1498–1552): *An Filius Dei fuerit incarnandus si peccatum non introivisset in mundum*, 1550; *De unico mediatore Jesu Christo et justificatione fidei*, 1551; also FC III, Tappert, pp. 548f.

[22]Cf. J.T. Beck (1804–1878): *Einleitung in das System der Christlichen Lehre . . .*, Stuttgart 1838, esp. pp. 152f.

[23]K. Holl, *Die Rechtfertigungslehre im Licht der Geschichte des Protestantismus*, Tübingen 1906, 2nd ed. 1922, p. 13.

[24]Cf. K. Holl, *Die Rechtfertigungslehre in Luthers Vorlesung über den Römerbrief mit besonderer Rücksicht auf die Frage der Heilsgewissheit*, in *Gesammelte Aufsätze zur Kirchengeschichte*, I, Luther, Tübingen, 1923[2], p. 119. Barth erroneously has "weitergehende" when Holl refers to the "weitergreifende Absicht Gottes . . ."

[25]Cf. n. 23. Note: Because he knows the power of his own will, not because he foresees what man will do in his own strength.

[26]Cf. n. 24. Note: But it will be completed. Man will in fact be righteous before God.

[27]Cf. n. 24. Note: Holl regards this as the supreme gift and calls it true blessedness.

[28]K. Holl, *Was hat die Rechtfertigungslehre dem modernen Menschen zu sagen?* Tübingen 1907, p. 24.

[29]Cf. n. 24. Note: This enhances the joy of new life.

[30]Cf, n. 24.

forgiveness of sins), God brings man to himself and puts him irresistibly on his course. Out of the shame that results from this goodness there arises a lofty passion, a hatred of self, and a yearning love for God. This love no longer needs any command but knows impulsively what it has to do (Luther, p. 121).[31]|

One may differ as to whether Luther, to whom Holl appeals for all this, really did sometimes express himself along these lines. I myself would doubt it, and I believe that Holl does particular violence to Luther in his interpretation of the Romans lectures.[32] Certainly if this was Luther's real doctrine of justification he kept it remarkably secret and said strangely little about it. Indeed, he often contradicted it directly. Furthermore, Melanchthon, whom Luther highly valued but who comes off badly in Holl,[33] must have oddly misunderstood him at a central point. ⌐The truth is that⌐ Holl has taken an element in Luther's teaching, that of the renewal of life, which Luther does not emphasize, and put it at the center, relating it to the question of justification, of the good in the life-act of believers, in a way which Luther, when he spoke of it, rejected, just as he did with the good works of the unregenerate or faith formed by love. In relation to Luther, one might speak of a certain technical uncertainty in distinguishing between justification and sanctification, or one might speak of some linguistic ambiguity especially in his earlier writings, but one can never say that he put justification and sanctification on the same level in a relation of continuity, as Holl does. Moreover the technical uncertainty is overcome in Melanchthon and even more in Calvin, who states the common reformation view when he says that the teaching of Osiander, like that of formed faith, makes us righteous together with God, weakens our assurance, and wafts us above the clouds (*Inst.* III, 11, 11).[34] Certainly one is to say of faith that as that which receives the Holy Spirit (Apol. II, 99)[35] it gets from God an effective medicine for poisoned human nature, that what makes it a good act is daily purification (Luther, EA e. 1.23, 504, 506),[36] that the consolation it receives is itself a new and spiritual life (Apol. II, 62),[37] that faith produces good fruit (64),[38] that the benefits of justification and sanctification are joined by an eternal bond, so that those whom Christ justifies, he sanctifies, and one cannot have the righteousness which counts before God without grasping sanctification as well (*Inst.* III, 16, 1). But sanctification has nothing ⌐whatever⌐ to do with justification before God, with the goodness of the act of faith

[31]Cf. n. 24.
[32]Cf. n. 24
[33]Cf. n. 24.
[34]Calvin describes this as an "utterly intolerable impiety."
[35]Apol. IV, 99; Tappert, p. 121.
[36]WA 40 III, 726, 34ff. and 727, 21ff.
[37]Apol. IV, 62; Tappert, p. 115.
[38]Apol. IV, 64; Tappert, p. 116.

in virtue of which it is the fulfillment of the command. For it is a becoming, not a being good, and between becoming and being there is logically no fleeting transition, only a change into another genus. With all that man does, whether he believes or not, sanctification stands under the shadow of the divine judgment. It is *not* justification; it ⌐follows it⌐ and constantly needs it. Justification does not mean that we are made righteous, that God renews us in such a way that we are angels (Calvin, *Op.* 23, 706). In relation to our being good before God there can be no contemplation of our own works. What moves God to mercy is simply our misery. He sees us as "utterly void and bare of good works" (*Inst.* III, 11, 16).[39] We who are not righteous in ourselves are reckoned righteous (11, 3).[40] Osiander, Beck, and Holl were right when they understood and established eschatologically their thesis concerning the analytical character of the sentence of justification, when they described the fellowship of will between God and man which already exists in God's eyes, the righteous union with God, as the goal of reconciliation that lies beyond all time. It was naturally the view of the reformers, too, that in the consummation the "double grace" that Calvin speaks of (*Op.* 23, 733; *Inst.* III, 11, 6),[41] the two lines of sanctification and justification, of becoming and being one, should meet. "The chief assurance of faith rests in the expectation of the life to come" (*Inst.* III, 3, 28).[42] But this is not what Osiander, Beck, and Holl had in mind. For them progressive justification, equated with sanctification, is attained on the threshold of the world to come, i.e., immediately before it, and already on this side of the threshold, there are moments and circumstances when we can see our righteousness and dispense with the commands in transports of yearning love for God. This convergence of two lines which can meet only in infinity is what Calvin rejected as "wafting above the clouds," as ethical mysticism or mystical ethics. |

The goodness of the human act which faith believes, and which makes faith a good act, is not one which this side of the eschatological frontier is our own even on the assumption that we constantly need forgiveness and have to make further progress. Hence we cannot regard either 1) faith as such, 2) the humility of faith, or 3) the renewal of life that is inseparable from faith, as that which makes the act of faith, and the life-act that takes place in faith, a good act, a fulfillment of the command. We neither can nor should lose sight of the fact that precisely in faith man must perceive and confess that he is a transgressor. In the

---

[39]Cf. the sentence beginning: "Indeed, it presents this order of justification . . ."
[40]Cf. the sentence beginning: "Therefore, since God justifies us by the intercession of Christ . . ."
[41]CR, LI, 733; *Inst.* III, 11, 6: "As Christ cannot be torn into two parts, so these two which we perceive in him together and conjointly are inseparable—namely, justification and sanctification . . . Yet Scripture . . . lists them separately in order that God's manifold grace may better appear to us."
[42]A mistake for III, 2, 28.

time in which faith hears God's Word there will always be this perception and confession if it really hears. Against this background, then,[43] we must understand the goodness in the act of faith or the righteousness of faith in a different way from that suggested by those three possibilities. They all three suffer from the fault that in them man is in some way snatched from the judgment under which he stands precisely as a believer and from which he will not want to be snatched if his faith is good. They all see things from the standpoint of active reflection about faith instead of faith itself. This is why the reformers fought stubbornly against all these possibilities and why modern theology must fight the same fight. On the basis of all these possibilities the goodness of the human act of faith has to be regarded as removing or reducing the sentence that man is bad, as destroying the frightful but fruitful antithesis of Calvin that believers think of God as "at once angry and merciful toward them, or toward their sins" (*Inst.* III, 2, 12). If we do not think along these lines, if we weaken and trivialize the "at once a sinner and righteous" of Luther,[44] we are not thinking *in* faith but somewhere outside faith we are thinking *about* faith. To emphasize God's anger and man as sinner is also to emphasize the mercy of God and man as righteous. For in faith we have a perception of God's grace only in correlation with a perception of his judgment. How could grace be grace if it were not grace in true and serious judgment? This is why it is so important to cling so inflexibly to the Reformation thesis that the righteousness of faith is in no sense to be understood as our own but always and only as one that is granted or promised to us, i.e., included in the *Word* which is spoken to us and which comes to us, but always comes and hence is never our own possession.

We presuppose these definitions of the righteousness of faith ⌐when we say¬ that it is the righteousness that is grounded and consists in the forgiveness of sins or, more positively, the righteousness of Christ as the Word of God that is spoken to us. Here again we shall follow the teaching of the reformers step by step.|

If we acknowledge that we are sinners standing under God's wrath and judgment, the righteousness of faith cannot be understood as our own or as originating with us. For in regard to both natural and spiritual gifts, and even to our gradual progress in sanctification, we have nothing of our own before God (Luther, *Rom. Sch. F.* 2).[45] There is nothing at all that we can bring (Calvin, *Op.* 23, 706).[46] In respect of works those who live by faith and are righteous are indeed sinners (*Inst.* III, 11, 21).[47]

[43] Barth had "however."
[44] Cf. Luther's Romans Lectures, WA 56, 70, 9f (LW, 25, 63, 258 ff., 336, 434); 56, 272, 16ff.; 57, 165, 12f. Also his Galatians Lectures, WA 2, 496, 39f.; 2, 497, 13 (LW 27, 230f.).
[45] Cf. the Romans Lectures, WA 56, 158, 10ff. and 159, 9ff.
[46] CR, LI, 706. Hence God alone is glorified.
[47] The reconciled, if judged by works, "will indeed still be found sinners."

Righteousness is not a quality to be sought in us (*Op.* 23, 692). Such a quality would not alter the fact that we are totally sinners and unrighteous (Luther, *Rom. Sch. F.* 121).[48] In all things Christians must always accuse themselves (EA e. 1.14, 83).[49] Hence, justifying faith is to be compared to an empty vessel, ⌐an empty hand,¬ or a mouth open to drink. It means our exinanition (abasement) (*Inst.* III, 11, 7).[50] Faith is "merely passive, bringing nothing of ours" (*Inst.* III, 13, 5).[51] Justification is receiving (*Inst.* III, 11, 17).[52] Our righteousness is extraneous, external, and alien (Luther, *Rom. Sch. F.* 2).[53] In faith we hang between heaven and earth, for in no sense do we receive and have his righteousness (EA e. 1.23, 137).[54] We have to see that "every particle of our salvation stands outside us" (*Inst.* III, 14, 17).[55] We must all seek it outside ourselves (*Inst.* III, 11, 23).[56] It is like a coat or mantle (*Inst.* III, 11, 2; *Op.* 23, 710) with which we are covered.[57] But what is the alien character of this righteousness but that of the Word that God speaks to us sinners? How can the Word be to us anything other than something alien that comes from without? If it were other than that, we, too, would be totally different. It cannot be other than that, then, in relation to the righteousness of faith which is enclosed in the Word that judges us and which discloses itself in it. If we were to try to define righteousness as an inward righteousness that becomes ours, we should have to forget that it comes to us only in the Word and that the Word judges us even as it discloses grace. Thus God justifies us as we receive his Word (Luther, *Rom. Sch. F.* 60).[58] For this Word that faith believes as it hears it, and that acknowledges and accepts it as a Word of judgment on us, is the Word of *forgiveness.* |

A second and higher reason now makes it clear to us why the righteousness of faith must be understood as an alien righteousness and why Melanchthon was right when he wrote that to speak of faith is to grasp its object, i.e., the promised mercy (Apol. II, 55).[59] The goodness of faith is an alien goodness. It is an object. It is nothing of our own. It is something which we acknowledge to be ascribed to us. It will always stand in God's Word. For it is the divine forgiveness of our sin. If there

---

[48]WA 56, 287, 20.
[49]WA 5, 71, 8ff.
[50]Calvin speaks of "the mouth of the soul open to seek Christ's grace."
[51]Faith receives from Christ what we lack.
[52]"Faith is said to justify because it receives and embraces the righteousness offered in the gospel."
[53]See n. 45.
[54]WA 25, 328, 32ff.
[55]No room is left, then, for trusting or glorying in works.
[56]Cf. the sentence beginning: "And there is no doubt . . ."
[57]*Inst.* III, 11, 2; CR, LI, 710: Christ's obedience serves as a mantle to cover our rebellions and iniquities.
[58]WA 56, 221, 4 and 15f.
[59]Apol. IV, 55; Tappert.

is any true and serious goodness or righteousness or reality beyond the reality of our condemnation, if we have a means to escape or soften the judgment that has been passed on us, this righteousness can consist only of the forgiveness of him against whom we have sinned and who has rightly condemned us. But what does forgiveness mean? Is Holl right when he says that God cannot be in fellowship with the sinner?[60] Can forgiveness be understood only as a step behind which there may be seen for the first time the true meaning of justification, namely, the transforming of the sinner into a righteous person? In an apparent move in Holl's direction Calvin once said that if God loves us he has to approve of us, and if he is to approve of us we have to be righteous. For God cannot change. He is always the same. For this reason we have to be righteous.[61] But Calvin does not continue as Holl does, that if God forgives us and counts us righteous when we are forgiven, then he must have the purpose of transforming us in a process that lasts until death, when we will finally stand in a perfect fellowship of will with him. Instead, Calvin, with no attempt to elucidate God's counsel, goes on to say that God will have to pardon our sins, forget our iniquities, and not impute our offenses to us (*Op.* 23, 707). This is to speak out of the true faith which knows and never loses sight of the holy and judging God, but knows him also as the gracious and merciful God without being able, or even wanting, to put itself at the point where he can be seen to be the same God. What do those who live by faith know but that inconceivably they live by the mercy of God that is fresh each morning? When and where do they live by their own increasingly perfect fellowship of will with God? Presupposing, of course, that theological thinking does not abstract away from the reality of faith and attempt to waft above the clouds![62] Presupposing that in our theological thinking we place ourselves at the exact point where we really stand in faith! That is to say, in the judgment of God, in which no present quality, conscious or unconscious, changes in the least the fact that we are totally sinners and unrighteous.[63] Can justification be understood there as anything but "the acceptance with which God receives us into his favor as righteous men" (*Inst.* III, 11, 2).[64] This acceptance into the fellowship of God's goodness, in view of that which I see to be my own lack of goodness in the light of God's Word, can have no other basis than that God receives us as righteous. God counts us his. We cannot explain his acceptance by what we were and are, nor by what we will become, nor by a purpose that we ascribe to God regarding our education. For if we grant that God is in the right against us, we not only concede that we are in no position to make satisfaction to him on our own, but must also see that we are

[60]Cf. n. 24.
[61]Cf. CR LI, 707.
[62]Cf. n. 34.
[63]Cf. n. 48.
[64]Cf. the final paragraph of the section (III, 11, 2).

condemned and let fall by him, and how then can we ascribe these educational purposes to him? No, this acceptance is self-grounded no less than God and his Word. It is really grace and nothing but grace. It is inconceivably real grace. It cuts right across not only our whole reality but also all that we can think or expect of God. It is royal, majestic, free, and ungrounded goodness, goodness whose righteousness consists simply of the fact that it is *goodness*, free *mercy*. What other goodness can come into consideration than the goodness, the righteousness of our faith?

This leads us to question very strongly the statement of Holl that God cannot be in fellowship with the sinner. Where would it leave the believer if God would not be in fellowship with the sinner, if it did not please him to want to be in fellowship with the sinner, if it did not please him to want to be in fellowship precisely with the sinner? Yes, God does indeed have to approve of us if he loves us. And we have to be righteous if he is to approve of us. But if we are going to continue to talk about God having to do things, we can say only that he has to forgive us. In this saying the "forgive" obviously transcends the "has to." The inference drawn from God's love, namely, that goodness is ascribed and not denied to our life-act, which we see standing under the shadow of his judgment, that God's goodness is in fellowship with our existence and act, to which we could only deny goodness, is recognized to be an inference that only he and not we can draw. From our standpoint everything both on our side and his speaks against this inference. Nevertheless, it is drawn, but only by God himself. God's Word, the same Word that accuses and condemns us, tells us, not that we are not sinners, or will not be, but that God forgives our sin; not that we are not guilty but that our guilt is taken from us, that God declares it to be nonexistent and set aside, and that, in spite of our guilt, for whose forgiveness we have and will have good reason to pray every day—he *pronounces* us righteous.

What did the reformers mean by this term "declares" or "pronounces" or "reputes" which became the shibboleth of their pure and correct doctrine of justification, as we may say with all due reservations? They certainly did not mean that those whom God calls good are so only conditionally, only with the bracket of an "as if," only to the degree that God *calls* them good whereas in reality they are very different. No, when God really calls us good, there is no higher reality behind this, no "only" which may and can restrict the truth of his Word. This truth is certainly a truth of grace and mercy, a truth of miracle, a truth that we know can be believed only in faith and not outside it. But as such it is truth in absolute *superiority* over all the truth that we might think we could establish on the basis of what we see in our lives. Hence the metaphor of the robe in which we are covered must not be taken to mean that alongside our being as sinners there is the second being of our righteousness before God in virtue of the fact that God calls us righteous. The "sinner and righteous at one and the same time" cannot be compared to a scales on which the two are balanced or oscillate. If this were so, then the frequent accusation of old and new enemies of the pure doctrine, both Roman Catholic and Protestant, would be true. The doctrine would not only contain an intolerable logical contradiction, but would bring an open contradiction into God's Word and therefore into God himself, inasmuch as he would be saying to us both No and Yes, both Yes and No. For God's Word tells us that we are lost and condemned sinners. How, then, with no change in the situation, can it call us his dear children and forgive us without any guarantee of our amendment of life? The answer is that God does not say Yes and No to us at one and the same time, for the *one* time in which he says No to us is *time*, our time, the only time we know as sinners, but the *other* time, the time of the divine Yes, is God's time, *eternity*. Time and eternity, however, do not stand over against each other like two times, but like our time and God's, like created and uncreated, creative time, the one being referred to the other and achieving reality through it as its source. We have time only insofar as we have eternity. Hence what is in time, and is true for it, cannot be in competition with eternal truth, for it is true only because and as it has its origin in eternal truth. It cannot possibly contradict eternal truth, not even when it is No and the other Yes.

We should perhaps take another step forward at this point. Only, of course, in faith, in the faith of the sinner who has found grace, can it be said without speculation that it is not to be expected that for us, who are not only in time but according to revelation are rebels against God and contradict him in our thoughts, for us whose thinking can grasp only brokenly the created reference of time to eternity, for us temporal and eternal truth, without being any the less truth or even one truth, are necessarily related as No and Yes, and yet there is no contradiction in God himself. In us who, even though we hear God's Word and try to think in accordance with it, are not gods but men, and sinful men at that; in us whose theology is theology after the fall, the contradiction is there and we have to confess it ("sin boldly").[65] When God speaks to us, when he makes his thoughts accessible to our thinking, and when we try to give a sober and conscientious account of what we have heard, we obviously have to realize that we are dealing with a twofold fact. First and foremost there is what God says about us. This is what is meant by the Reformation's "declares," "pronounces," and "reputes," and its content is an unequivocal Yes, the Yes of mercy and forgiveness. You *are* good and righteous notwithstanding all that you must let yourself be told precisely on the basis of this Yes. You *are* good and righteous because and insofar as I who am the truth [cf. John 14:6] tell you that you are. We have to do, then, with what is told *us* by God *through* this Yes. This Yes is

[65]Cf. Luther's letter to Melanchthon, 8/1/1521; WAB 2,372,84.

the Yes of mercy and forgiveness. Hence it comes to us as a synthetic, not an analytic, statement, as a declaring, pronouncing, and reputing, as the disclosure of something concealed, not as plainly as we should like, not as something disclosed once and for all so that we can forget both the disclosing and the concealing, indirectly and not directly perceptible in its truth, the content of God's thoughts about us and not our own thoughts about ourselves. ⌐The constant message is: *You are.*⌐ But if this is what we are told, then our own thoughts about ourselves, if they are in the obedience of faith to the Word, cannot be other than those that culminate in the truth that we are lost and condemned sinners. For we are forced to admit that we have not merited the good that is ascribed to us. We are forced to renounce our own love and humility, even the love and humility of faith. We are forced to foreswear our own sanctification of life without which we should not believe. We are forced to abandon everything, even a share in that righteousness. We are forced to accept the No which we ourselves pronounce about ourselves, which is dictated to us precisely by the Yes, and which is the necessary converse of the Yes. In contradiction with it? No, but in subjection to it.|

One might compare all this to the impression of a seal in wax or some similar substance. The positive occurrence is the impressing of the image in the substance. The metal makes a distinctive mark. This is the true and obvious point of the procedure. But the metal has not imparted itself to the substance. The two have not been united or mingled. No fellowship of will (Holl) has come about between the metal and the substance, no essential righteousness has been given. What has happened to the substance is a positive thing which is necessarily very negative, an impress, the creation of an empty space. Where the substance itself has yielded we have the mark of the metal. Where man is negated we have righteousness. The place and work of faith is that everything believed should disappear into its opposite (Luther, EA o. 1.7, 154).[66] For this relation between the two sides in justification, judgment, and grace, Luther coined the felicitous formula of God's strange work and his proper work. In doing his proper work of life and salvation God dies and perishes, which is a strange work, and part of his proper work is to kill our will and set up his own will in us (EA e. 1.14,71).[67] The proper work of God cannot be done unless his second strange work is done in us. There can be disclosure only where there is concealment. We cannot be the recipients of grace unless we are judged. The Word of divine forgiveness cannot be heard by us unless we hear the Word of divine wrath.|

Why not? Why cannot we just hear the *one* Word of God? Why this detour? We may simply reply: *Who* is on the detour, God or we?

[66]WA 18, 633, 7ff.
[67]WA 5, 63, 33f. and 39ff.

⌐Concealment a necessary process for God himself?⌐ God's mask, mummery?[68] How can God speak to us except on a detour when we are not merely on a detour but on the wrong road? If we are not to deny sin, we have to understand that the detour is the right road. Hence faith does not hear two words of different content which we have to accept as true either alongside one another or in alternation. It hears *one* Word whose eternal light human thinking can only see to be in contrast with the shadow that is cast by it into time and over all time. In human thinking, then, the knowledge of forgiveness and the knowledge of judgment are related as light and shadow and not as two different lights. They are thus in contrast, and we cannot soften this contrast or get past it to look for a God beyond grace and judgment and more or less to be God ourselves, which is the quiet secret of every impure doctrine of justification. The light casts the shadow. The shadow is always the shadow of the light. Without the light there is no shadow. Thus the eternal light of forgiveness is alone the content of the divine declaring, pronouncing, and reputing. If we cannot deny or remove its correlation with the shadow of judgment, even less can we take the view that we have the possibility of understanding God's judgment and our sin as in and for themselves the truth of our existence, of evading the Word of grace, of alleging that the prior Word of judgment has smitten us too powerfully and penetratingly. We cannot stop even for a moment to contemplate the strange work of God. |

Relevant here is Luther's well-known and much-repeated warning not to dispute about the God who is hidden in majesty,[69] i.e., about him whom we have to think of as God if we think the necessary thoughts about ourselves on the basis of his Word of grace. We must not think these thoughts about God. Because all our thoughts even at best are such thoughts, we must not try to think autonomously about God. Doing so will inevitably lead us past the Word that is spoken to us, past the real God, and finally, by reverting to self-judgment, past the truth about ourselves. God's Word, the revealed God, points us to God's proper work. If it does not do this without in fact pointing to his strange work, to the God who is hidden in his majesty, to the abyss of the endlessly wrathful God; if it is only in terror of hell that we know what we are doing when we affirm his proper work, then it must also be said that the hidden God that we try to think of autonomously on the basis of our sin and judgment, ⌐the abstract hidden God,⌐ is not God at all but an idol, no matter how dreadfully lofty he might seem to be to us in his negativity. The real hidden *God* is the one who says: "For a brief

---

[68]For these concepts in Luther, cf. WA 15, 373, 14ff.; 17 II, 192, 28f.; 17 II, 262, 37ff.
[69]Cf. WA 42, 11, 19ff., where he tells us not to dispute about God and the divine nature apart from the word or some wrapping, since it is in word and work that God shows himself to us; also 39 I, 217, 9ff., where he says that in our corrupt nature, which has no capacity for deity, we cannot grasp him, but God has given himself to us in external phenomena and sacraments in order that we may do so.

moment I forsook you . . . in overflowing wrath for a moment I hid my face from you"—and this brief moment undoubtedly lasts as long as time does—"*but* with everlasting love I will have compassion on you, says the Lord, your Redeemer" (Isa. 54:7f.).

We should have to deny the eternity of God if, from the standpoint of time, of that brief moment, we were to set up the hidden God of whom Isaiah 54 does not speak, the one who is no Redeemer, as the true God, judging ourselves in reversion to this supposed knowledge of God. The strange work does not take place *in itself* ⌐and abstractly,¬ which would mean the abandoning of time by eternity and of man by God. It takes place in transition from the strange work to the proper work. What we might think we can experience and describe as the strange work, a strange work that we might think we can know otherwise than as the husk which is burst open by the ripe fruit of the proper work, is *not* a work of God at all and from it we should look in vain our whole life long and to all eternity for the proper work, the goodness of God. *That* would not be hearing of the divine No which failed to hear the Yes under the No (Luther).[70] That would not be knowledge of human sin in which there were not first of all knowledge of God's goodness. We should have, not merely semiseriousness, but no seriousness at all, not even on the negative side, if the former knowledge—as our necessary and clear knowledge about ourselves—were not swallowed up by the latter. Nowhere but in grace can we truly and seriously know ourselves as sinners. Luther thought it sacrilege to stop at the first knowledge; the devil keeps stock of sin, not God (EA e. 1.23, 141).[71] The devil is not God. We are already ceasing to think in faith if we regard it as God's last and true Word to us when his Word (also) says that nothing but sin dwells in us and we never get beyond the confession of our sin and lostness. The God whom we meet if we start our search with our sin and God's judgment will not be God but the devil—the devil who with his ancient: "Did God say?" [Gen. 3:1], when pride is spoiled for us, seeks to entice us away from faith by the alternative means of humility, tempting us in this new and negative form to deify time and that which is true in time, so that we cling to ourselves and to our misery for a change instead of clinging to God.

"But Christ is to be contemplated," Luther continues in the same passage.[72] This brings us to the turning point in our whole discussion. We do not understand either the great positive factor of forgiveness or the necessity of an equally strong delineation of the opposite factor of

[70]Cf. Luther's exposition of Matt. 15:21–28, WA, 17 II, 203, 29ff., where Luther says that when tested our heart thinks there is only a No there, but it must turn from such feelings and with firm faith in God's Word grasp and hold fast the deep secret Yes under and above the No, as the Syro-Phoenician woman does, and justify him in his sentence on us, thus winning and catching him in his own words.
[71]WA 25, 330, 32ff.
[72]WA 25, 330, 34f.: "In him we are secure from sins, death and hell."

judgment. Above all we do not understand the need to cut off at the root all ideas of human cooperation in justification. We probably see in this exclusion the expression of an affected and even dangerous pessimism, if not of dogmatic obstinacy, if we do not consider that the reformers gave this strict and exclusive form to the doctrine, not out of scepticism about human possibilities, and even less on the basis of a presupposed empty concept of God's Word or of God's majesty in general, but expressly and consistently in the light of the reality of *Jesus Christ.* Because Jesus Christ is meant as the basis of that declaring, pronouncing, and reputing, one may say that its content is no other than the unfathomable goodness of the divine forgiveness. Because forgiveness is forgiveness for Christ's sake, all human cooperation is sharply excluded from that which is given to us by forgiveness. Jesus Christ is the Word of God to which we refer here: not the naked God of arbitrary human speculation in which, as the offspring of persistently sinful human thought, we can objectively see in fact only the devil, but the God involved in flesh who speaks with us, the real God who in faith speaks with us in this and no other way, the incarnate Word which speaks to us as man to us men, which in speaking to us has united us as members to himself as head, taking our sins to himself as the King of his people and making his righteousness ours. |

"But does not Christ also judge?" one might ask. We reply: "Christ judges us, not only 'also,' but 'precisely.' " So long as we are not judged by Christ we are not judged at all. He is the *one and only* revelation of God in whom both judgment and grace come upon us. But they do so in the relation of strange work and proper work, and not otherwise, as we have shown. In Jesus Christ, his incarnate Word, God himself suffers and bears the condemnation which we know to be passed on us. Since not just anybody, but God himself, suffers and bears it, it is borne and borne off and borne away. Threatening us like an imminent thunderstorm, it can no longer break over us because it is carried and held by him who with right has passed it on us, but with equal right, in inconceivable condescension, has put himself ⌐as God⌐ in our place, under the burden of our sin, under the verdict that man is wicked. He alone can carry the burden of the curse and affliction and sorrow which is necessarily ours with the fall from him. It lies on him, not on us. This is Christ's *vicarious suffering of the penalty.* Our human flesh, adopted and assumed by God's eternal Word, has as flesh rendered obedience to God in all its boundless impotence and weakness and frailty. As Jesus of Nazareth has identified himself with man, with his brethren, even to death, the death on the cross [Phil. 3:6ff.]; as he has set himself in the depths and not on the heights of humanity; as he has taken his place with publicans and sinners, and between the thieves, at the point where unholy man belongs before the face of God; as he has not hidden his face from shame and spitting [cf. Isa. 50:6], he has made good the fault of Adam, who did not want to be a creature but to be as God [cf. Gen.

3:5]. The command of creation has been fulfilled. Man has obeyed. Man, this man, is good, God himself in inconceivable condescension is good in our place. This is Christ's *vicarious obedience*. In virtue of his resurrection from the dead, his vicarious suffering and vicarious obedience—the two are one—is God's revelation to us, God's Word. God speaks with us as he has caused this to take place in history, and through his prophets and apostles he testifies to us that he has caused this to take place in history as this Word (he himself, the exalted Christ) seeks and finds our faith (through himself, the Holy Spirit.)|

Reconciliation means that in this man Jesus of Nazareth God becomes our neighbor, our closest neighbor, our suffering and active Lord who intercedes for us in the power of his deity. This is God's proper work. This is justification. This is the content of his declaration concerning the sinner. In this way he forgives us. He calls us good. And so, as the necessary negative and reverse side of forgiveness, of God's eternal grace in Christ, there is real judgment, real mortification of the flesh, in which the believer, reconciled with God but not yet redeemed or perfected, stands in time, still subject to the contradiction between grace and the law in grace, to the twofoldness of justification and sanctification, to the conflict between spirit and flesh [cf. Gal. 5:17]. We do not overthrow the law by faith but establish it (Rom. 3:31). For in the grace in which faith believes the law is really set up—what do they know of God's law who do not stand in grace? But it is set up in *grace*. Hence we do not mount up from Romans 7 to Romans 8, leaving Romans 7, i.e., the law, behind us. Coming down from Romans 8[35]: "Who shall separate us from the love of Christ?" we continually find ourselves back in Romans 7[24]: "Wretched man that I am! Who will deliver me from this body of death?" This is the sighing or crying, ⌜not of the ungodly, but⌝ of the reconciled. They alone know the distinction between God and man in its qualification as antithesis. They know it because for them it is an antithesis that has been overcome. They sigh and cry, not for lack of peace, but in peace with God, in the fear of love for him on the basis of his prior love for them [cf. 1 John 4:19]. If this peace passes all understanding [cf. Phil. 4:7], if it is the peace of faith that is continually given and must be continually received, it is none the less peace. It is real peace in that it is not the peace of our own heart or conscience but the peace of God. The experiences and states of our own heart and conscience are always varied, vacillating, and unsure. Our assurance of faith is always going through crises. Our knowledge of our inner and outer acts, and our thinking about them, never can or should escape the dialectic of the "always sinner and always righteous." If we had to seek peace in ourselves, we should not find it. Christ is our peace [cf. Eph. 2:14]. In him the conflict into which we are plunged has both its beginning and its end. Both beginning and end mean mercy. In him we are both killed and made alive, but the death, too, is *his* death. |

With regard to our special interest, we must now look back on the whole problem from this culminating point. Only from this point can the almost intolerable sharpness with which it must be posed and answered be illuminating. *Why* forensic righteousness? *Why* is the Word always a strange Word through which God tells us, the wicked, that we are good, thus unmasking us for the first time as seriously wicked; yet not in order to nail us to it but to grant to us, the wicked, the fellowship of his goodness? *Why* is it a Word whose content we cannot assimilate, which we cannot grasp for ourselves, which in this time of ours we can always seek only in the Word itself, which so long as we live we can only believe to be valid, to be valid for us? *Why* is this Word so irremovably *God's* Word about us which no love or humility or sanctification can change into our own word about ourselves? *Why* can we never describe the relevance of this Word to us except in sentences which express our looking away from ourselves? It is in Christ and apart from ourselves that we are counted righteous before God (*Inst.* III, 11, 4). Whether we do well or badly, we have Christ who suffered for us (Luther, EA e. 1.23, 139).[73] Why does the apostle say of Christ that he is given to us, not to help us to attain righteousness, but to be our righteousness himself (*Inst.* III, 15, 5)? Because, we may reply, the Word of God comes to us only in the irremovable strangeness and otherness of the man Jesus of Nazareth who was crucified under Pontius Pilate, and precisely in this way it is secured against our arrogance, which would like to snatch it itself and make it our own word about ourselves and thus rob it of its power. |

Here in the question of Christ, Calvin in particular saw a clear break between Osiander and the Reformation. Luther was right when he spoke of the justified as those whose faith apprehends Christ, holding him as a ring does a jewel, so that he is present in the heart (EA Gal. I, 195).[74] He was also right when he very boldly said that Christ is the object of faith, yet not just the object, since he is also present in faith. Faith is an obscure knowledge which sees nothing, and yet Christ sits in the darkness and is apprehended by faith as God sat on Sinai and in the temple in the midst of the clouds (EA Gal. I, 191).[75] Calvin made this thought the basis of his whole doctrine of the mode of receiving Christ[76]—the thought of union or communion with Christ[77] which he can uninhibitedly call a mystical union (*Inst.* III, 11, 10).[78] Christ has to dwell in us (III, 1, 1).[79] We must become members with him, indeed, one with him (III, 2, 24).[80] He must grow into one body with us until he

---

[73]WA 25, 329, 35f.

[74]WA 40 I, 233, 17ff (LW, 26, 132).

[75]WA 40 I, 228, 31ff (LW, 26, 129f.).

[76]The title of Book III of the *Institutes* is: "The Way in which we Receive the Grace of Christ."

[77]Cf. *Inst.* III, 1 passim.

[78]Cf. the sentence: "Therefore, that joining together of Head and members, that indwelling of Christ in our hearts—in short, that mystical union . . ."

[79]Cf. the sentence: "Therefore, to share with us . . ."

[80]Cf. the sentence: "But since Christ has been so imparted to you . . ."

becomes completely one with us (III, 2, 24).[81] The "outside us" does not mean "at a distance": "We put on Christ and are engrafted into his body . . . he deigns to make us one with him. For this reason we glory that we have fellowship of righteousness with him" (III, 11, 10).[82] This thought is in fact unavoidable if the primary and supreme idea of representation, which is decisive for justification, is to have any force. Christ must really take our place, as the New Testament says. The doctrine of union with him states the infinitely simple and, for that reason, most profound and difficult truth that God's Word of forgiveness is not just spoken, but through the Holy Spirit is spoken to *us* and received by *us*. It is present as a fact in our own reality and existence even though it is inconceivable and hidden in the darkness of the knowledge of faith, in the mists of the heart. We do not merely have the gift of Christ; we have Christ himself. |

Nevertheless we should not overlook the fact that when Luther spoke of Christ he always had in view the incarnate Word, God living in the man Jesus of Nazareth. He is the one who is present in faith.[83] Osiander, however, spoke of something quite different; namely, of the eternal divine righteousness of Christ which comes to us and becomes ours. He did not at first exclude the thought of mediatorship, but did so later by presupposing an already completed mediation, an already present effect of mediation. He regarded an essential and substantial union of man with God as the essence of justification and equated the faith which receives justification with Christ.[84] Luther and Calvin refrained from doing this in their bold formulations. Calvin called it "a gross mingling of Christ with believers" (*Inst.* III, 11, 10).[85] If the peace with God which passes all understanding is not drawn back again into the dialectic of the human heart and human life; if the reconciliation of man with God is not sought again in man's own work; if God's grace is always to be grace and therefore free, justification must remain an act and the mediator must not cease to be the mediator as though he had already done his work on us and his work could cease and give place to an effect, as though the distinction of giver and recipient did not remain between the concepts of Christ and faith even and precisely *in* their supreme union in the form of engrafting into Christ.[86] The critical reminder that is in place here is that Christ came in the flesh and made vicarious satisfaction for us, and that he is present in this and no other

---

[81]Cf. the sentence: "Not only does he cleave to you by an invisible bond . . ."

[82]Cf. the sentence: "We do not, therefore, contemplate him outside ourselves from afar . . ."

[83]See n. 75.

[84]Cf. *Inst.* III, 11, 7: "Yet in the meantime, I do not admit the distorted figure of this Sophist when he says that 'faith is Christ.' "

[85]Cf. the sentence: "But Osiander, by spurning this spiritual bond, forces a gross mingling of Christ with believers."

[86]Cf. n. 82.

way, certainly through the Holy Spirit but through the Holy Spirit as this man Jesus of Nazareth. Even with the strongest emphasis on the "in us," this reminder safeguards the objectivity of the "for us" on which the freedom and therefore the power of grace as grace depends. To maintain our union with the Son or Word of God without this reminder is to maintain and commend the deification of man, which can turn at any moment into ungodliness because deep down—notwithstanding the earnestness with which it may be taught—it *is* ungodliness, because it claims what does not belong to us, because it rests on a failure to hear the real Word of God and therefore on disobedience, because it claims that we already *have* and no longer need to *receive*, that we already *are* and no longer, precisely at the most important point, need to *become*. The fall into unbelief from the height of this supposed faith can only be a matter of time and clarity.

For faith even the Christ who dwells within as a divine subject, as Paul says in Galatians 2:20, is always another, a second, someone superior and strange. He is the Head and we are his members,[87] he the King and we his people: there is a lasting distinction here. It is in this distinction from him that faith has Christ[88] and receives his gift. But this distinction hangs on the servant form of the incarnate Word, on the humanity in which Christ suffered and was obedient for us, and in which he stands before the Father in our stead. That Christ has done and does this as man makes the "gross mingling" impossible. Not even in the thoughts of our religious arrogance can we cause this man in his concrete there and then to merge and disappear into ourselves in our here and now, or *vice versa*. If a lack of distinction between God and man is of the essence of mysticism, then this (mystical) union rules out all mysticism. In it Christ remains *another*. He is our neighbor, our closest neighbor, but precisely as such he still stands over against us. His very humanity safeguards his dignity as Head and King and Lord. He has to be revealed constantly to us in his humanity, in the hiddenness in which he is here God's Word to us. He has to give himself to us. He has to exercise toward us his prophetic, priestly, and kingly office. ⌐He has to nourish us with his body and blood.¬ The fellowship into which he receives us and the blessings that flow from it always have to be an event. He is not our Head, King, and Lord because he is man, a particularly good, devout, and distinguished man. He is so because he is the eternal God. But he is true *God* as true *man* and this safeguards his dignity in the atonement and therefore the reality of the atonement. The humanity of Christ blocks the new sin of the reconciled, i.e., a continuation of wanting to be God under the new title of grace. This is why Luther, long before the controversey with Osiander, argued so obstinately that

---

[87]From the first verse of the hymn "Herz und Herz vereint zusammen" (1735) by N. L. Graf von Zinzendorf (1700–1760).

[88]Barth has here the marginal note "annulus—gemma" ("ring—jewel"), see n. 74.

we must focus always on the crib of Bethlehem and the cross of Golgotha. We cannot identify ourselves with what we see there, as the heathenisms of the world have so easily done with abstract deity. From there a Word that comes to us strangely can and must be heard because a man stands there, because God became man there. Between there and us there can only be an event and not a state. What is there stands above the dialectic in which we stand. On this depends no less than the truth of our justification. This is the justification of the sinner who has every reason to be glad that in no sense does he have to seek his righteousness in himself. By keeping the mystery out of his own grasp the very humanity of Christ assures him that he may seek this righteousness in God.

In the restatement of the doctrine of justification that is now behind us we have seen how matters stand with the believer who is a doer of the Word and who fulfills the command of the Creator. The survey has shown us with what right and necessity we must look at the command from a new and second standpoint. The command is not just that of our Creator. It is also that of our Reconciler. We now know how far the believer fulfills the command, how far he is righteous and good when measured by it. He is this solely through grace in Jesus Christ. He is it as a Christian, i.e., as a member of the body of which Jesus Christ is head, as a member of the elect people for whom its king and high priest intercedes. He is it, then, as one who needs grace, whose sin must be covered, who is not good and righteous in himself. Hence reconciliation includes judgment as well as grace. God the Creator does not judge us, but God the Reconciler. Not the human race but the household of God is the place of judgment [cf. I Pet. 4:17]. Not those who are outside, uncalled, are subject to the law, but in and with him in whom they are elect and called, the elect and called. It is they who are contradicted as the Word of God is spoken, not to the others, but to them. We have now to understand the command as the command of God the Reconciler, as the command of law or of the divine contradiction which comes only upon those whom God holds dear. In understanding the command of God the Reconciler as the command of law we recognize that the Christian or believer or justified person suffers also and indeed especially from the divine contradiction, being justified only by grace and not by works, and accepting the contradiction as merited and necessary. And in understanding the command of law as the command of God the Reconciler we remember that this contradiction is only God's "strange work" whose point lies in the "proper work" of the divine goodness, so that it accuses us because God's goodness wants us to be pardoned; it beats us down only to raise us up and set us on our feet, it slays us only to make us alive. The two aspects are inseparably one in the command of Christ of which we have to speak, not with the unity of two parts of the same thing but with the unity of a Whence and a Whither, of a movement, of past and future in each present moment, of time and eternity, or, as we might put it best and most pertinently, in the unity of the crucified Jesus of Nazareth and the eternal Word of God. As the concept of law cannot be interpreted apart from the atonement that has taken place in Christ, so the concept of atonement cannot be interpreted without thinking of the law. As the command of the Creator is formally and materially the command of life—formally because it is given to us in and with the life that God has created, materially because we are ordered to live this life that God has created—so the command of God the Reconciler is the command of law—formally because it is given to us as we are directed by grace and put under law, materially because we are ordered to acknowledge God's contradiction of us by the law, and in this submission to give God the glory. To live by faith is to love God and fear him, to fear God and love him. This is the vivification which is the point of our mortification by the Word. ⌐All that preceded [was] introductory or transitional.⌐

We shall proceed as we did in the chapter on the command of the Creator. In a second and special subsection of this first section we shall have to show first what it means in relation to our concrete life-act that by the grace of God, as those who are bound and held and sustained by God, as members of the body of Christ, we are set under law. We shall have to show how far there is established by God's command the contradiction against us which binds us concretely to God and demands our recognition. *What* shall we do? What is the law? In a second section, corresponding to the earlier one on vocation, we shall then have to locate the place where the contradiction meets us and the confrontation of the command that makes it law takes place. What shall *we* do? How far does the law apply to *us* (authority). Then in a third section, corresponding to that on order, we shall have to develop the real content of the demand of law. Where does it point us? What character will it impress on our acts? What direction does the will take when God directs it? What *shall* we do? This is where the emphasis must now fall (humility). Finally, in a fourth section, corresponding to that on faith, [we must pose] for a new and second time the question of fulfillment, of the completed work, but now from the standpoint that the command is the command of the Reconciler and the work is the work of faith. We cannot be content, then, simply to say again that the completed work is faith itself. This is true, but we have now to indicate how far faith is a work, the good work; what it means to live by faith, what is the answer to the question: What shall we *do?* Not how I acquire, but what is the nature of the goodness that is promised to me by the grace of God? Or conversely: How far is my act really the act of one who has heard this promise of God's grace and directed himself by it? The reformers, as mentioned, did not reject the Roman Catholic question about "formed faith."[89] They did not contest

[89]See n. 34.

the fact that the righteousness of faith must demonstrate itself in a particular form of faith. What they could not accept was that because of this necessary form the righteousness may be claimed as a righteousness before God. They could not accept this because even in this form the righteousness cannot be established. This form, too, must be understood as grace and not as a human work. Nevertheless we must not set aside the question about this form. It will be answered in the final section of the chapter (love).

2

We now turn to our first question, that of the meaning of the law. What does it mean, and how does it take place concretely, that I am contradicted by God's command and that I know through this experienced contradiction that without and in spite of any merit of my own I am upheld and sustained by God? What does it mean, and how does it take place concretely, that God binds me to his law? Where and how does this commitment come? *What* shall we do? In what connection can I understand my act as submission to the command of God the Reconciler and in this sense as a good act?—as an act with which I may stand in God's judgment because I really do it as one who has experienced mercy? As the act of a sinner who has received grace, how far it is lawful and not unlawful?

Its lawfulness—to begin with this possibility—might lie in my doing it under a compulsion, an obligation, a necessity, which in some way, whether by reflection on the nature of man in general and in particular, or as the constant accompaniment of my emotional life, or as the result of an experience that has suddenly or gradually gripped me, and whether I call it my heart or my conscience, I find *within myself* and see to be posited in and with myself. If I am truthful to myself, I have to recognize that this inner imperative under whose constraint I now will to do what I do is a given, or is at any rate given to me. If I am to be faithful to myself, I must obey it. Is this not law? Can there be a higher truth, at any rate for me at this moment? Can I recognize as the command any other truth than that which, with strict truthfulness to myself, I recognize to be given to me? Is there any better faithfulness, at any rate for me at this moment, or is any other faithfulness required of me, than the faithfulness of obedience to this truth which is known by myself and therefore guaranteed by myself? How else can I demonstrate my reconciliation with God than by acting in reconciliation with what is deepest and most proper in myself? The phenomenon of inner necessity which is at issue here is familiar to all of us. Indeed, in all we do and leave undone the question also arises whether it is done or left undone with inner necessity in the sense described, whether it takes place in harmony with our clear or obscure self-consciousness, in which our free decision seems to be an obligation and our obligation seems to be a free

decision. The more this agreement is present, the more we are at peace
with ourselves. The less it is present and the more we have the
impression that we are not quite comfortable or not quite ourselves in
this or that act, the more unsure and threatened and exposed we feel.
Like the cat that always falls on its feet, even the Christian, the
believer, instinctively grasps for this norm. |

But we must now consider *what* we are really grasping for. If
justification is by faith, and if it is apprehended with all its implications,
then happy and self-evident operation with the self-consciousness, with
inner necessity and truthfulness and faithfulness to the self, is no longer
so obvious. Three objections necessarily arise and in the light of them
affirmation of the doctrine of inner necessity seems to be possible only
with very strong reservations and corrections. |

First comes the fundamental recollection that for faith law is God's
contradicting of man. Is it likely, then, that we shall encounter it in our
deepest agreement with ourselves? If our innermost being must be
investigated, shall we not have to ask about that point in our self-
consciousness where we confront ourselves as questioning strangers,
where there opens up between ourselves and ourselves a gap that we
cannot bridge? Is not the norm of peace and harmony with ourselves
shattered when in faith we see ourselves as transgressors? What has this
peace with ourselves to do with the peace that is given to us by God? Is
not the justification of the wicked forgotten already if we can set up such
a norm as self-evident? Is it not historically palpable that this authority
was set up as such when Protestantism began to yearn after the fleshpots
of Egypt which it had left when it thought that it could no longer survive
the thin, cold air of Reformation truth? |

The second point follows on from this: How can I measure valid truth
by my truthfulness to self, or demanded faithfulness by my faithfulness
to self? Even though the voice of my heart or conscience be ever so loud
and credible, who has given to it the authority of a final word, the
authority of God's command? What kind of an equation has preceded
this bold equation? Might it be the equation of God and myself, i.e., the
true and typical equation of sin in which we do not love God but want to
be God? And what will be the broader consequences of this for our
truthfulness and faithfulness to self? Conversely, the voice of the heart
might really proclaim valid truth to us and command from us the
faithfulness that is really demanded. But if so, the voice would simply
be the echo of another voice, would speak only with borrowed force, and
would represent a very different authority. The other voice, then, would
have to be heard in it as the concrete law that is simply mediated by it,
and it would be a fateful error to confuse the two. Are we not simply
continuing in sin [cf. Rom. 6:1] if when the love of God is poured into
our sinful hearts [cf. Rom. 5:5] these sinful hearts want to put
themselves on the throne of God? |

Third, when we call our self-consciousness the final authority that we recognize, so that we have to give its verdicts the character of law, what do we mean by self-consciousness in this context? Consciousness of the self whose voice we have to note and obey with true and final respect? Are we ourselves, then, so present and available in this capacity that we have only to knock at our own door and, perhaps by a trick which modern counsellors can easily help us to perform, we come across this self? Is the child of God within us that has heard the voice of God so simply at hand, so easily to be experienced in the depths of our own lives? Is this child of God who, we trust, knows very well the will of the Father, so present that it can be our lawgiver and its counsel law? Are we not forgetting that this child of God is in us as the grace of God is for us, and as Jesus Christ is present—only as a gift that is indeed present, yet always inconceivable? In faith have we not renounced the direct identity of our own goodness and God's which is presupposed when we emphasize our self-consciousness? Does not faith mean taking seriously the saying: "I am the way, and the truth, and the life" [John 14:6], and therefore not taking the self with this final seriousness? On this renouncing and taking seriously and not taking seriously does not everything depend if we are to share in God's real goodness and if we are to know that the Child of God in us, or rather the child of God that we are, is protected against confusion with one of the many little demons that are also in us? In other words, who are we that we dare so naively to equate our inner necessity with the law and the law with our inner necessity? What have we that we have not *received* [cf. 1 Cor. 4:7]? We ourselves are not the presupposition of the necessity. We ourselves do not live, but Christ lives in us [cf. Gal. 2:20]. We are told that we are liars [cf. Rom. 3:4]. It would be the most superficial misunderstanding of Kant's *a priori*, the doctrine of the legislative power of reason,[90] to try to see in this *a priori* something present in or behind our sensory existence, the law of a true self known to us, or the like. Philosophical idealism opens up before us depths of a different kind when it reminds us of the law of reason. This is a transcendental court which precedes in principle all real or possible experience. Its law has a dignity for which that of no conviction, no enthusiastic commitment, no experience, however profound or true, can ever be a match. It has the dignity of the idea, of the original truth which asserts itself against all derived truths with self-resting force. In demarcation from it theology will find it necessary to shift the accents, as we have done. Yet the error of truthfulness and faithfulness to self as the source of law cannot fittingly appeal merely to idealism. In contrast to many lesser minds Kant knew very well that while the pull of the heart can indeed be the voice of fate,[91] the voice of God, even though it uses the voice of the heart, is for

---

[90]Cf. I. Kant, *Critique of Pure Reason*.
[91]F. Schiller, *Wallenstein. Ein dramatisches Gedicht: Die Piccolomini*, Act III, Scene 8: "The pull of the heart is the voice of fate."

all that a very different voice.[92] Hence our act is not made lawful, nor characterized as that of a pardoned sinner, by its being done with inner necessity or in truthfulness or faithfulness to self. By this definition it might be something very different from the act of a believer.

But its lawfulness—a second possibility—might consist of its being done under the pressure of fate. My fate differs from my inner imperative inasmuch as it is understood as the totality of the outer necessities that are posited with my specific concrete position in space and time, in nature and history. It is the forming of my will that seems to be unavoidably proposed to me by the reality of my existence, which is distinct from my consciousness of it and is therefore external in that sense—a reality in which I really find myself at this point or that point and in this or that modification within reality as a whole. Our own age is familiar with many important technical possibilities, important for theology too, which make clear to us the proposal which is made by our particular position in reality as a whole and which may sometimes be pressed upon us in black and white in the form of scientific estimates based on fairly objective criteria. I have in mind the establishment of the psychological and biographical determination of our existence by psychoanalysis and psychotechnology, its characterological determination by the astonishing art of graphology, or, finally, its cosmic determination by astrology—all unusual sciences which are rather suspect to quiet citizens, which are unavoidably unsure in the use of their methods, but which can appeal to innumerable verifications by experiment, so that, purely scientifically, we can hardly question the presence of a cosmic offer to each of us; and those who feel a desire or need to do so can sometimes keep fairly cleanly and clearly before them the offer that is made to them by their lives, the offer of fate.|

Can we go on to say that in accepting this offer we are accepting God's law? Not my inner imperative as such, but my fate which this imperative answers and indicates—is this the law? Does this not meet the definition of law whereby we are dealing in the law with something that is opposed to us, with an alien will, with a superior counterpart? Recognizing the will of this superior counterpart, taking it up into our own will, is this not obedience, is it not an act in which, submitting to this counterpart, we are reconciled to our fate, so that it is the act of the reconciled and is thus a lawful act, a good act? We reply that once again, for three reasons, this is more than doubtful.|

First, my clearly or obscurely known fate differs from the law because by fate we have to understand the totality of the determination of my will and action as they are proposed by the reality that is distinct from me. Certainly this totality is the world that God created. If, even apart

[92]For Kant's distinction between the voice of God and the voice of the heart, cf. his *Grundlegung zur Metaphysik der Sitten* (1785).

from faith, I could see myself directly and see in myself a doer of the command of the Creator, the command of life; if I were able, at once, without confusion or error, to hear the voice of God in the voice of the world outside me; if I could recognize my determination by God in my determination by space and time and nature and history, then I could accept my fate as it might be known perhaps from my handwriting, or perhaps from a carefully prepared horoscope, or perhaps instinctively without such devices, and in this acceptance I could do good and lawful acts. But this is not the case. Hearing God speaking to me in the totality of the world is negated by the knowledge that I have fallen away from God the Creator. Faith hears God's Word in Jesus Christ. Jesus Christ is not the totality but a specific part of the cosmic reality that is distinct from me. Even in this specific part, what speaks to me is not cosmic reality as such, but the Word of God which has become cosmic reality, human reality, flesh, and whose givenness I cannot establish in the way that I can establish my fate. What the world has to say to me outside this specific part stands under the strict proviso that my ears must be opened by this specific part of the whole for what God the Creator might also be continually saying to me through the totality of the world created by him. My fate can become God's law for me only in Christ. Apart from Christ I know it only in the mirror of my self-knowledge which is not immune from confusion and error because I can reach it with some objectivity by the scientific methods quoted. It is a matter of truth and error in relation to God; of the question in what sense and direction I have to take orders from the multiple and ambivalent proposal of my fate; which of the many relations in which I might find myself is the dominant one by which I may and must see myself to be controlled and to whose pressure I may legitimately adapt and render responsible obedience. My well-known fate may be my temptation. It does not tell me what I need to know in order not to fall into error, i.e., whether it has the authority of an order. My own inner imperative will again have to speak the decisive word which gives preference to the one relation that has to be taken seriously as compared with others, which selects this or that thread out of the network that the psychoanalyist or astrologer or myself presents to me as the network of my life. In the long run my inner necessity will not only accept my fate but *be* my fate. "In thy breast stand the stars of thy destiny"[93] and we have already shown that this authority cannot have the character of law. |

Second, my fate differs from law because, even assuming at best that I know it well in the concrete culmination of all the outer determinations of my life at this moment, and with a clarity that makes the corresponding determination of my will and action seem almost unavoidable, I can still know it only as a proposal. That superior partner has brought a certain decision close, even infinitely close. If I really consult my fate as

[93]Cf. F. Schiller, op. cit., Act II, Scene 6. Barth erroneously has "stand" for "are."

a norm of my action, I can think of it only in correlation with my own freedom of choice. I consult it as I do a doctor, not without the secret proviso that I may still decide whether to follow his advice or not. If I do not, and things turn out badly, I can go back to him next week—he will still be there—and get new advice for the new situation, still receiving this advice with the same freedom. Similarly fate, whose nod I ignore today, will still be there tomorrow. Psychoanalysis, if it is to be therapeutic, cannot avoid appealing to freedom of choice as well, and it is worth noting that modern astrology includes this factor as the great and ultimately decisive X in calculating our determination by the stars. No matter what force or superior force we may assign to fate, we always stand with it on the footing of two partners negotiating and reaching agreement with one another. We may oppose it or complain about it or have occasion to be content with it. We may reconcile ourselves to it, even if sometimes only partially or with some reservations or attempts at evasion. We may embrace it with the enthusiasm of despair. Whatever we do, however, we are always free and ourselves. The cleverest way to master one's fate might well be to embrace it. "To master one's fate"[94] is a bold but not inappropriate expression. One can submit to fate and in so doing become its master. One can recognize and accept its offer as advantageous for all that might be said against it. Fate can finally serve us even as we yield to it. |

God's law, however, is not an offer and one cannot master it even by submitting to it. If we obey it because it serves us, we have perhaps obeyed our well-known fate but not the command of God. The command of God does not come to me as partner but as lord. It does, of course, address my creaturely freedom. It wants to be fulfilled in this freedom. But it does not give us a choice of obeying it or not—what kind of an obedience would that be which might perhaps be disobedience? It does not grant us the privilege of turning aside from it today and perhaps coming back tomorrow. It takes me captive in my freedom so that the only alternative to the freedom of obedience is lack of freedom. In Christ the law is set up in my life, as the life of one who is reconciled to God, in such a way that what the law wants from me has to be done and is done with the necessity compared to which the supposed and so-called necessity of fate, with which I can at any moment play cat and mouse, seems to be a mere game—with the necessity of the truth of the judgment of grace that God has pronounced upon me, with the necessity of Jesus Christ whose vicarious and justifying righteousness cannot be shaken nor called in question by any of my decisions. Here we are mastered, not masters. Here we are ordered in such a way that we obey. Here is a command, not a proposal. We are thinking outside faith if we

---

[94]Cf. W. Shakespeare, *Julius Caesar*, Act I, Scene 2: "Men at some time are masters of their fates" and F. Schiller, *Wilhelm Tell*, Act III, Scene 3: "He cannot complain of hard words who is master of his fate."

try to confuse the command of God with the proposal of fate, if we will not see that we are confronted here by a counterpart which will pursue us into the hiding place where the heavenly and earthly powers that constitute our fate, and on which we are dependent enough, will leave us alone, and from which, if we are clever and wise, we can even become their masters. Where we are not decided as we decide, but can have convenient reservations, there is no law, no law of the atonement made in Christ.

Third, my fate differs from the law that is given to me because it does not judge me but is a neutral entity. And my subjection to my fate, assuming that I agree to it, differs from obedience to the law because in making it I do not see myself to be accused or condemned. If I ask what my fate is and what is the command that it gives me, I simply look at myself in my relation to the reality around me, to my psychological and biographical and historical and possibly cosmic determination. I do not stand in all this but alongside and above it. Typical of the safety and security of our situation in relation to fate is the curiosity with which we inquire into it. Sometimes this curiosity can become morbid like the curiosity with which we read the account of a murder trial in the newspaper. We can even reach the point of looking at ourselves with the eyes of a detective when we consider our fate. But this is natural and by no means fatal. The voice of fate tells us, perhaps, that this is how it is with us. Things are fairly bad. You are in a dangerous corner. These are the possibilities open to you. Choose the best. It cannot say more than this. Even the modern sciences to which we have referred are typical natural sciences. Going to a psychoanalyst or astrologer is like going to a doctor. It may be that what this doctor says to me, or what I must say to myself with reference to my fate, is calculated in not a bad way to startle and frighten me. I may be stimulated to feel some sorrow for past mistakes. But this sorrow does not really touch me. I sit in a safe cave and look on and wait for what will come. If the doctor really smites my conscience, he does not do this as a doctor, and if I really feel smitten in conscience, this is different from merely learning my fate or receiving advice about it. Fate as such is a neutral force in relation to the truth about myself. I can remain unaffected in face of the darkest fate, considering only how best to meet its effects. Knowing my fate, I know fairly clearly how things stand with me but not that I am guilty for how things stand with me. The voice of fate can reveal to me my sickness or trouble or plight or at most my foolishness or incompetence. It can make me wise. As described, it can suggest to me how I might find relief. It can sometimes show me the way out of an impasse in which I find myself. What it does not tell me is that I am bad. However dark or threatening fate might be, it cannot touch me. Watching my lowering fate, I sit in the audience at the theater of life, seeing how helpless I am in relation to that superior power on the stage, yet always able to forget that I am the one who seems to be in such a sorry plight there.

The law, however, does touch us. When it is given to us, we are in the middle of the stage and that powerful other comes to us and becomes truly powerful as the other, so that we cannot break loose from the grip with which it has already gripped us. Reached by it in our act, we no longer have time to be interested in how far this might be conditioned by the location of the stars at our birth or our historical situation or our psychological makeup. Whatever the conditioning might be, here where the law speaks the only thing that counts is that we ourselves, no matter how we are conditioned, do this or that and act in this or that way. As this law is Christ's law, as it comes to us as grace and forgiveness, as the decision is made concerning our act that it is done for Christ's sake as an act of obedience, our act is set aside as our own act, and in being forgiven we are accused and pronounced guilty. The dark and damaging and dangerous thing that, for all its horror, we can hold at bay when we think of fate comes to us when we think of law and reveals itself to be that which is dark and damaging and dangerous in us. Compared to it the threatened dominion of heavenly and earthly powers outside and above us again becomes a mere play of shadows whose course and conclusion is really our least concern. The wicked thief whose pursuit we watched with such interest is caught and imprisoned. The tense detective story is unfortunately finished. But lo, we ourselves are the thief who is finally put away and may reflect on guilt and destiny, but must finally make answer for his acts. The believer need not fear fate, even though it might be the devil himself. The devil may plague and tempt and harass us. But we can always make nice little compromises with the devil; we all do so more often than we think. It is God that we must fear, the God to whose Word the believer is directed and clings. For God judges, and only as a judged act can our act be also a good act before Him. In this regard, the situation is the same as under the first two heads. Fate finally leaves us untouched. We can always be in the right against it. We can escape its blows. Our own inner necessity has the last word on whether we are aware of being punished by it. But when will we ever concede by our own inner necessity that we are not just plagued but punished by it? Always we would rather bid defiance to the enmity of fate and perhaps we are not too wrong in this. But God's law punishes us. We must not confuse conduct determined by fate with lawful conduct.

It is not easy to grasp and name a third possibility of reinterpreting law and lawful action. It is even more difficult to state and establish the necessary objection to it. We have in view what I might call the confusion of law with essential and omnipresent deity, the *Deus nudus* of Luther,[95] and in connection with this deity timeless truths. One might also call it the confusion of law both with the concept of law in the

---

[95] For this phrase cf. WA 40 II, 329, 3ff.; 386, 8ff.; 42, 10, 3f.

singular and with concepts of law, with generalities, abstractions, principles, and ideas in the plural. We have to do here with the most important and widespread and also the more serious and imposing of these fatal possibilities and it would be as well to devote unusually careful attention to it in our exposition.|

Let us assume that we know we cannot give to the question: What shall we do? the good, but too good, answer: "A good man knows the right way by inner compulsion."[96] Let us also assume that we cannot trust the voice of fate in this respect either. Let us assume that these two possibilities with all their variations are behind us. We have become critical. We have learned that what is given, even though it be the most powerful either subjectively or objectively, even though it be my own innermost necessity or well-known fate, cannot be my law because, in the first case, there is no confrontation between me and the supposed law and, in the second, I can escape the confrontation. We have learned, when we hear the term law, to look upward and outward, to think of distance, to reckon with something absolutely transcendent and also with an inescapability with which we are claimed by it. The first of these features of real law does not fit our own inner necessity, and the second does not fit our fate. If we are to know real law, we must exclude them both. We are looking for a law that is both transcendent and actual. There are many ways in which we might reach this alteration of our position and sharpening of our investigation. Perhaps in some school of thought, sitting at the feet of a master of philosophy like Plato or Kant, we might acquire a concept of the law which is superior to every actualization, which mocks at such, but which also underlies every serious actualization. We might learn to find it in the practical reason which precedes all apparently pure reason in the strength of its origin, or in the transcendentally contemplated truth which contemplates us and claims us, or in the idea which as the idea of all ideas is the idea of life. Or, in studying religions and especially the biblical religions, or studying Christian and especially reformation dogmatics, we might come to see that we must accept the divinity of the law, the insuperable distance between it on the one side and ourselves and the whole world on the other, if we are ever to dare to link it with the name of God; that we must also accept the urgency with which it presses upon us if it is really to make itself known to us by God's revelation, and the holiness, the very aggressive holiness, in which Yahweh (and Jesus of Nazareth) is concealed when he really confronts us with demands as a lawgiver. Or—and this is perhaps the easiest and safest path—we may have gone involuntarily in some way through the school of life and experienced the alien character of law. In the extended or sudden disasters which have come upon us as we sought the law either in our own breasts or outside in fate, it has perhaps been shown to us that we are without law so long

---

[96]J. W. Goethe, *Faust*, Part I, Prologue in Heaven.

as we do not know the height of Sinai from which it has truly come down to us, so long as we are not terrified by the "wholly other"[97] which differs from the self and fate and which grips me here and in so doing takes me captive. Let us assume that there has been this sharpening of our investigation of law. Let us assume that the idea of the eternity of law (which includes its absolute urgency) has come to us in some way, with greater or lesser clarity, from afar, as is appropriate, yet unmistakably and unforgettably. Let us assume that we have been unsettled in some way and from some source, that the admonition to the soul not to seek among creatures, but to leave what is earthly behind and launch out beyond nature,[98] is no mere phrase. Let us assume that all this is so. If we do, then we are forced to say that if this note has been given emphasis and the matter has acquired this seriousness, the hour of great temptation has really struck for us. In opposition to the confusion of the law with the first two possibilities some good plants have grown. To those who honor their truthfulness and their faithfulness to themselves and to those who honor fate, Kant can first be given, then the New Testament and especially the Old Testament in this instance, then a couple of volumes of Luther, and they can be invited to live their lives rather soberly and with no great stir. But what plant has grown up against the possibility that now, at the sharp corner where we have finally learned to lift up our eyes to the hills from which our help comes [cf. Ps. 121:1], the concept of eternity will be confused with that of timelessness and the living God with the *Deus nudus*, who is only a reflection of our own knowledge of our own fall?

Eternity is God himself. To think the thought of eternal law we must think of God himself. But here where error and truth are separated only by a hairbreadth, but also by a deep abyss, a decision must be made. Are we going to think of God himself as he is God *for us*, for us who have fallen away from him but who are also held by him, as he has therefore revealed himself? Or, overtaken and seized by the idea of eternity, but bypassing God's Word, are we going to think of God in the otherness and hiddenness which, as we measure them by our own reality and that of the world, we merely imagine to be his true otherness and hiddenness?—namely, the otherness and hiddenness of self-resting deity and timeless truths? The latter option is so infinitely tempting to us. We have seen through our own reality and that of the world as through the veil of Maya. We have seen them in their shattering noneternity. We know that the law will not encounter us in them. Where else should we seek it, then, but in essential and omnipresent deity? Where else should we seek it, as timeless truth, but in the

---

[97]Barth seems to have borrowed this phrase from R. Otto, *Das Heilige* . . . (1917) (ET, *The Idea of the Holy*, 1925). Cf. Kierkegaard's description of God as the "absolute paradox" in his *Philosophical Fragments*.

[98]Cf. the second verse of the hymn of J. H. Schröder (1667–1699): "Eins ist not! Ach Herr, dies Eine."

timeless world of spirit that lies behind temporal reality? Is it really impossible to find it there? Have we not already found it in learning to seek it there? In and with the painful discovery have we not also made the happy one that essential deity and timeless truth exist, that they exist for us? Have we not already come to know them, and acquired a share in them by letting ourselves be shown that distance, by accepting that criticism of reality, that twilight of the gods? Did we not discover our own true relation to the world of the spirit, our own spirituality? Was not our horror at that disaster full of secret rejoicing as we came to understand the saying of the sage that the world of spirits is not closed to us and we may tirelessly bathe our earthly breasts in the sunrise.[99] We have become critical. Epistemologically speaking, we have learned to abstract, to think principially. We have discovered the mystery of the concept, of synthetic *a priori* statements. We have discovered the majesty of what is valid because it is rationally valid and universally valid. Dying to the world of the given we have risen with joy in the world of the nongiven, of what is true in itself. As we came to suspect the law in our breast and the law of the cosmos, we saw—did we not?—the law of freedom. Shining above us and beyond us, infinitely high above both the stars in our breast and the stars in the visible heaven, yet as our real stars, we saw the eternal stars of God, reason, the logos itself, which is totally remote and distant but to which everything real in and around us is oriented, which is thus infinitely near to everything real, which is not absorbed or imprisoned in any of its manifestations but may yet proclaim itself in all its manifestations, which we cannot apprehend but apprehended by which we can apprehend ourselves, before which we lie in the dust but in which we still live and move and have our being [cf. Acts 17:28]. In submitting to this law, do we not act as those who are reconciled to God? Is it not subjection to the judgment of grace when we become open to the eternal in this way?|

We face the question whether we should give this law a name or content. Perhaps we hesitate for a moment. "Who can name him, who confess him?"[100] "Name is sound and smoke, obscuring the glow of heaven."[101] Is it not enough to know and confess that when the husk is peeled off, when we have mounted up from reality to concepts and from concepts to pure concept, [we] have to do directly with God himself and his will? Is not the highest and ultimate and only possible thing said when we speak of God and the soul and the soul and its God?[102] Is not everything that we might add by way of definition or clarification or

---

[99]Barth quotes here from Goethe's *Faust*, Part I, Night.

[100]Cf. J. W. Goethe, *Faust*, Part I: "Who may name him? And who confess: I believe him?"

[101]Loc. cit.

[102]A. Harnack, *Das Wesen des Christentums*, Leipzig 1900, p. 22; ET, *What is Christianity?* New York 1902, p. 61.

interpretation simply a return to the given, a desecration of the mystery, a clouding of the truth of the law under which we see ourselves put? But perhaps we have gone further. Perhaps we know that that can be only a penultimate consideration. If God, by whom we know we are claimed, is the idea of ideas, pure concept, why should not ideas and concepts— even granting that they cannot be final words in definition of the word—still have a share in the truth of the word? Is not the process of abstraction, or the possibility of principial thinking that we have found in ourselves, a witness that we ourselves as rational beings can have a share in divine truth? Would it not be disobedience to bury the pound that we have been given [cf. Matt. 25:18]? Where but in reflection of our own critical reason have we learned to know God as *the* reason or logos? With his properly understood transcendence, have we not also seen and acknowledged his immanence, his spiritual immanence, his immanence in our own reason and its ideas? Can we hear his claim in any other way than by seeing his image in the reflections of our reason even though we know that he is higher than all reason [cf. Phil. 4:7], than by recognizing as his law the laws of our reason even though we admit that he himself must always write them in our hearts? Would not a mere "God and the soul and the soul and its God," an evasion of name and content, perhaps deliver us up again to the demonism of our inner necessity and our fate? |

If we take this line of thought, we come up against principles, names, concepts, generalities, and ideas in which we think we have to do with the concrete law of God. There then takes place what might be called the birth of morals out of the spirit of mysticism.[103] We recognize the mediacy of timeless truth in the timeless truths of our thinking about human action that corresponds to this truth. Like the Greeks, we will perhaps find the law in the idea of the beautiful and the good.[104] Or, as in Kantian ethics, we will perhaps find it in the rule of the good will which will impress upon us as a norm of the good that which has general validity.[105] Or, as in Thomistic ethics, we will perhaps find it in the four philosophical and three theological virtues.[106] Or, taught by the New Testament, we will perhaps find it newly summarized in the idea of love. We listen to Goethe: "Noble is man, helpful and good."[107] Or we let ourselves be told by A. Schweitzer that in short the good is compassion.[108] It need hardly lead us astray that the spiritual world into

[103]Perhaps an illusion to K. Joël's *Der Ursprung der Naturphilosophie aus dem Geiste der Mystik*, Basel 1903, a title which in turn was perhaps influenced by F. Nietzsche's *Die Geburt der Tragödie aus dem Geiste der Musik*, Leipzig 1872.

[104]Cf. Plato's ideal of *kalokagathy* for the ruling classes of his day with its uniting of beauty and virtue.

[105]Cf. Kant's *Grundlegung zur Metaphysik der Sitten*, 1785, and *Kritik der praktischen Vernunft*, 1788.

[106]Cf. St. Thomas Aquinas, STh II, 1 q. 61 a. 2: prudence, justice, temperance, fortitude, and q. 62 a. 3: faith, hope, love.

[107]J. W. Goethe, *Das Göttliche*, 1782.

[108]Cf. A. Schweitzer, *Kultur und Ethik*, 1923.

which we look here is obviously so rich and manifold that the reflections of eternal reason in our finite reason are so many and varied, that its name can be proclaimed in so many languages. What does all that matter so long as we know that we are addressed and claimed by the world of timeless truth, and that in this mediacy we are claimed by God. "Let each emulate his free love uncorrupted by prejudices."[109] We can adapt ourselves to the skeptical background that the genuine ring was probably lost.[110] If we know that we are claimed by that world, we *have* the genuine ring. Goethe saw deeper than Lessing and had a better knowledge of the one essential deity in the apparently many deities in which it is present to our spirit: "Love of life flows out of all things, the smallest star as well as the greatest, and all pushing and striving is eternal peace in God the Lord."[111] If we respond to the claim which comes into our reality from what is beyond all reality, then we obviously submit to the true law and act as those who are reconciled to God. Who can deny that? Who can reject the guidance about law which undoubtedly the best and noblest and most profound and serious of human spirits have unanimously given us in their own ways and different forms of speech? Is not what we have described as mysticism and morals in their mutual and indissoluble correlation the finest legacy of all the more advanced nations on earth? And is not this guidance Christian guidance too? Has not Christian reflection on God's law in all countries and centuries, and under the banner of all confessions, always taken this way, the way of abstractions, the way of idealism in the broadest sense of the term? Has not Christian apologetic against atheism, skepticism, and materialism quite naturally had an intimate part in this discussion? Can Christian mission, whether abroad or at home, get along without it? Are not Christian dogmatics and preaching and edificatory literature and hymns and individual and corporate prayerbooks saturated, as it were, by the thought of the transcending of reality in a truth that lies behind it, of the necessary turning aside from all inner and outer visibility, of the solitariness of the soul with God and of God with the soul, and then, on further reflection, with the thought of the eternal truths in which we have to recognize our concrete law? Where would Christianity really be without mysticism, without the doctrine and practice of entry into timeless fellowship with God, and without morals, the teaching and practice of general concepts of law? We shall indeed be badly placed if we undertake to express our doubts on this point and to call this whole path the most enormous of all temptations. There is every reason to ask whether this is not an iconoclastic undertaking in which we shall attack many people at their most sacred point, arousing the opposition, not of the wicked but the good, not of the world alone, so far as one can see,

---

[109]Cf. G. E. Lessing, *Nathan der Weise* (1778), Act III, Scene 7.
[110]Loc. cit.
[111]J. W. Goethe, *Zahme Xenien* VI.

but also and very specifically of the church. For if we rob the church of mysticism and morals, by what will it live? It is by no means easy to say that the self-resting deity with its transcendence and immanence is not the living God and that timeless truth, whether it hears a Greek or Christian name, is not the truth of God, the law of the Reconciler, the law of grace and judgment. But this is precisely what we have to say.

We have to measure the doctrine of the law of the *Deus nudus* and timeless truths, of mysticism and morals, of idealism, by no other measure than that of faith and its law. But we do have to measure it by this law. We do have to ask whether faith's law is identical with this law, whether we can have knowledge of faith's law by the depicted way to the world of pure spirit and its reflections in finite reason, whether God in himself, as he is supposedly revealed to critical reason, is the lawgiver, and whether the concepts of reason in which we seek to apprehend his claim are the *law* of faith. We accept all the good things that can obviously be said about this view in the fields of intellectual history and scholarship. On this plane it undoubtedly represents a big advance on the two possibilities that occupied us earlier, and that, in comparison with this third possibility, undeniably have a certain naiveté and even triviality. At least in the case of a truly critical idealism, of an idealism that tries to do equal justice to the problems of the loftiness and actuality of the law and the transcendence and immanence of God, that takes equally seriously both the concerns of mysticism and those of morals—here at least the limits of humanity, which are also its foundations, are contemplated, perceived, and brought to light in their negative and positive significance. The dialectic that constitutes humanity, that of spirit and nature, of the conditioned and unconditioned, is developed here. An unheard-of awakening of humanity, its coming to itself and to reason, takes place. May it not be that a last word was spoken in this regard some centuries ago, and that constantly repeating it in new translations and variations is not a superfluous task for the changing philosophies of the ages, because always, awakening the rest and calling upon them to arise, a spiritual and moral elite will confront the much greater majority of the human race, which, regarding demons as gods, and unaware of its foundations and frontiers, has sunk into uncritical sleep?

Our concern here, however, is with theology and the relation of this view to a theological approach. Is it really true that theological ethics should accept and champion this view as its own? Or is it at least true that we should evaluate and recognize it as a view which is very close to that of theological ethics, which is akin to it, which does at any rate prepare the way for it? We can forestall the second question. The reply to it is in the negative. When we rated idealism higher than the other two possibilities and preferred it to them, we were *not* speaking theologically. Idealism has certainly been regarded as a schoolmaster to Christ. But as idealism, as a self-enclosed view of life and the world, it is not this. Paul was thinking of *God's* law when he used that expression in Galatians 3:24. And it is a question whether the law of mysticism and morals is God's law. Even if it seeks to be, it is not. The law in the sense of idealistic theology is not a schoolmaster to Christ but the very opposite. The asserted kinship and closeness seem to lie in the distinctive combination of remoteness and relationship in the concept of God, and of the elements of the call for repentance and the more general summons in the appeal to men, which characterizes true, critical, and serious idealism. Surely the eternity and revelation of God, his judgment and his grace, are really in view. Is not Christ, with the reconciliation with God that has taken place in him, the dot on the "i" which we have only to add and it will be clear that everything was really being said about him, and the logos? It must be said that we have here an imposing if negatively abstract *copy* of Christian theological truth in which, if the artist is able, the whole of Christian dogmatics up to eschatology and sacramental theology can sometimes be seen. The dazzling thing about idealism in this regard is that with some good will it can say almost everything that Christianity can, and say it much more beautifully and impressively than poor ⌐nonidealistic⌐ theologians with their inept and worn-out stock of biblical concepts. It is no wonder that theologians old and new have gone over totally to this school. And we should not be so ungrateful as not to recognize that it makes some sense to go over to this school.

The idealistic view can give to theology, which moves in the same sphere as itself, a most important tool in the presentation of Christian truth. It can be its teacher from a formal conceptual standpoint. When it is a matter of *thinking* the thought of God or the appeal to man dialectically, as theology seeks to do, then wittingly or unwittingly, skillfully or unskillfully, we ⌐constantly⌐ follow the idealistic track. ⌐Theology is a dialectic of abstraction and concretion in the sphere of the human mind. Inasmuch as it cannot dispense with abstraction, it is always idealistic. That there has always been a noteworthy school of ontologically realistic thought does not alter this.⌐ We surely have to learn, and should wish to learn, in the school of a thinking which ⌐in its own way⌐ makes the surveying of that sphere its own task and which ⌐in its own way⌐ can almost completely fulfill the task.

Nevertheless we should not overlook the fact that this type of thinking with its *copy* does not lead at all to theological truth. Even if it could really lead in this direction, it would not be able to do so by first developing a very general human truth and then amiably declaring that this is Christian truth and that Christ is the dot on the "i." Using Christian terms could not change the fact that here the copy obviously makes the original superfluous, pushes it aside, and finally entails its denial. This plainly happens wherever idealism arises as idealism, as a view of life and the world, as religion, or as theology, no matter how friendly it may be to Christianity. Precisely when it is so close to theology that it can easily be confused with it or regarded by it as true theological thinking, idealism can bring the most dreadfully conceivable disruption and destruction to theological thinking. Its proximity can mean that first the decisive utterances of theologians, then all their other statements, are taken out of their mouths and so pronounced, translated, and interpreted, that nothing is lacking except their original relation to specifically Christian and theological truth; that they have become very profound and fruitful expressions and symbols of a generally true human insight which fundamentally does not need that specific truth. We should be alerted at this point by the fact that this insight can be reached basically by a purely philosophical path, as well as by way of the attentive reading of the Bible and Luther, or by way of fundamental and universally accessible experience. Kant and Jeremiah, John and Plato can all lead us equally to this type of general truth. Jesus is the classical leader in this field. Finally, all of us may discover it for ourselves by experience. But this general truth is not Christian truth. And if the concept of law in idealism is described as such, if the law of mysticism and morals is commended to us, in (friendly and indulgent) antithesis to the dark particularity of Christian truth, because it is so universally accessible, then theology must reflect twice before it is prepared to welcome this neighbor as a helper who is particularly dear and valuable because he engages only in peaceful penetration and will say Yes and Amen to all that we say so long as we permit him to understand us better than we understand ourselves. *This* neighbor could in fact be the worst of all. If he claims to be an idealist, he certainly is. If he calls himself a *Christian* idealist, he most certainly is. And if he is an idealistic *theologian,* there is no room for doubt at all. He is brother Jacob [cf. Gen. 25:29−34] offering us the pottage of his beautiful copy in terms of universally accessible truths in order to buy from us the birthright of the connecting point of all theological statements which for various reasons is not universally accessible. |

Clearly the two other neighbors, the one that honors his own immediacy and the one that honors fate, are not so dangerous by a long shot. They are obvious pagans who can be recognized as such from afar. The gospel can be proclaimed in this darkness. Sudden conversion is a possibility here. But if the pagan, on the small condition that we expressly or tacitly accept his own position, is willing to say God instead of the Absolute; if he will, when required, say eternity instead of the timelessness that he really means, or judgment instead of critical negation, or grace instead of relation, or church instead of fellowship, or sacrament instead of symbol; if he will so adapt the concept of revelation that the theologian is struck by the littleness of his own faith, not having realized before that God's revelation takes place always and everywhere and in all things, and that by revelation we are to understand the gigantic scroll that on an etching of the painter Welti we see passing so beautifully over men and animals and baby carriages;[112] if he will even give due recognition to the Lord Jesus as *the* symbol of hidden but omnipresent and self-disclosing deity; if he is ready at any moment to swear on the gospels; in short, if his conversion is superfluous because he says everything that we say and a good deal more; if there is no darkness here but pure light, in the presence of which we feel a little like poor pagans ourselves—what can we say to *this* neighbor? A schoolmaster to Christ? I think that is doubtful. We would say Yes if it were only a matter of an understanding, taught by the gospels, of the knowable nature of man apart from the limits set for this enterprise and apart from openness to the truth which cannot be the subject of man's understanding of himself, ⌐for which idealism always hands us *one* tool, namely, that of abstraction.⌐ If it were only a matter of this, then theology might ⌐also⌐ study under this teacher. But we have to say No when idealism brings the relation of God to man within man's understanding of himself, not realizing that the concepts of remoteness and relation do not lead us to the concept of God but rather put an end to the concept of man, and hence seeking to be total knowledge on the basis of universally accessible and apprehensible truth. We have to say No because idealism never stops trying to grasp Christian truth and to interpret the statements of the Bible and dogma merely as expressions, and because in not stopping this it shows itself to be still secular, still raising the claim to be able to drive out and replace Christian truth. It is inadvisable to grant to the idealistic concept of law anything but a formal affinity to the law of theological ethics—an affinity which even as such is still dangerous.

We must now answer the question how far, then, there is difference here and not identity. Already we have incidentally referred to two distinguishing marks by which we may differentiate the law of God in theological ethics, as the law of faith, from the law of mysticism and morals. The first is that we cannot ascribe to God's law the universal accessibility which is the pride and glory of the idealistic concept of law. To know this law we cannot point to any philosophy or any possible experiencce alongside the Bible. We can point only—the "only" confers unique significance on this source—to the Bible, to holy scripture as *holy* scripture, as witness to the Word of God which he himself spoke once and for all and uniquely, in a way that cannot be repeated, and which can be received only through himself. The revelation of the law of faith, the claiming of the Christian, is an absolutely *single* event which is characteristically distinguished from all other events because God acts

---

[112]Albert Welti (1862–1912) was a Swiss painter. The etching to which Barth refers was done in 1903 and a reproduction may be found in A. Welti, *Gemälde und Radierungen*, Berlin, p. 49.

exclusively in it. His action finds reflection in our finite reason, but our reason does not on this account share or cooperate in the action. Faith knows human reason as the reason of sinful and fallen man. Hence it knows the law not as the law of God *and* man, but exclusively as God's law, and hence it knows its revelation exclusively as God's revelation and not our own. Even holy scripture cannot, of course, be described as human access to it. The reference to scripture is a reference to God's special coming to us, not *vice versa*.

The second distinguishing mark has to do with the purpose of the copying of divine truth in human concepts. Theological ethics, too, can describe divine truth only in human concepts. It could not argue with idealism that it is using these concepts in a different way, and would not have to defend itself against idealistic reinterpretations, if there were agreement on the point that there can be nothing here but a copying of the truth and not a crowding out and replacement of it by the human concepts. The theologian, too, can speak only two-dimensionally in his concepts. This corresponds to the sphere that he shares in common with all other men. There can be only dialectical theology as there can be only white mildew (Gogarten).[113] It is in fact easy to show that all theology that presumes to be more than that is not more, and it would be good if theology would refrain from the pride of wanting to be more. With its dialectic, however, theology *aims* at the third dimension, at the sphere of God's Word and Spirit. While working well or badly, like philosophy, in the two-dimensional world of spirit and nature, of the unconditioned and the conditioned, of the objective and the subjective, of the nongiven and the given, it explicitly does *not* aim at demonstrating God's Word in this world but at something very different, i.e., pointing to it—⌐and even this only as God's Word can use it as a pointer to itself, only as it has the promise.¬ From the standpoint of theology the ambivalence of idealism is that it does not have this explicit aim but, engaged in peaceful penetration, it gives the appearance, and far more than the appearance, of wanting and being able to commit itself to giving a demonstration of God's law in that two-dimensional world, namely, in the upper half of that world, in the world or half-world of spirit, of the nongiven, of the unconditioned, of abstraction, of concept. This spirit is not the Holy Spirit, but the spirit that belongs to the nature of man and to the created world. It is not clear whether it is not the deification of this spirit that gives to that copy its distinctive fervor. Theology itself does not entirely escape this ambivalence nor can it be protected by any technical safeguard. Both philosophy and theology have to consider that this spirit is a reality of this world no matter how heavily its transcendence may be stressed. Its transcendence cannot be stressed unless its immanence, its immanence in reason, is stressed at the same time. This shows that we have here, from a theological

---

[113]An expression probably used in conversation.

standpoint, an impermissible deification. The God whose law theology sees to be established in the inaccessible sphere of God's Word is the Creator and Lord of the world, the Creator and Lord of heaven and earth, of all things visible and invisible (Nic.).[114] This secures its place not only beyond all reality but also beyond pure concept, which can never be more than that of man. It obliges theology to seek the law elsewhere than in the world of spirit no less than in that of nature. Theology aims at another world than that which is given and known in that antithesis. Schleiermacher saw this in his philosophy,[115] although without drawing the necessary theological inferences. This was his great advantage over the popular idealist A. Ritschl, and we should never forget it. Theology is a study of neither spirit nor nature. It is the study of the Word of God to the extent that this is revealed to us. It does not present this but witnesses to it: not in order to reach it by a way that excels the art of philosophy but because it has come to men and has a church, its call having gone out as the event of the divine action. Theology answers this call. It does not repeat or replace it. It does not pretend to be able to speak God's Word itself. It serves it. Woe to it if it wants to do anything else! It simply copies the Word without even the shadow of a claim that its copy is creative or that its abstractions and dialectic are the real content—without even the shadow of a claim that it can itself set up God's law. It knows and bears witness, however, that this law has in fact been set up.

This brings us to a third distinction. The law of faith differs from that of idealism in that it really is set up. This is to be taken in the strict sense that knowledge of it can take only the form of acknowledgment. It is knowledge of what is already set up in itself and primarily. In no way or sense does it have a part of this. One cannot say of it that in knowing that the law is set up it sets it up itself, as one undoubtedly has to do in relation to the law of idealism. A serious idealism, of course, will not say that the law is set up and put in force only by human knowledge. It will not fail to emphasize strongly the objectivity of the law, its self-grounded truth and validity. But in a type of expression beloved of idealistic theologians it will explain that the setting up of the law is "at once a divine and human act." It will also be very careful to guard against the idea that the tension between the two statements is ever removed, for the true vitality of the concept lies in this. Only our freedom can give us law and only law can give us freedom.[115a] The spiritual act of knowledge of the law naturally does not take place unless it does so as the revelation of the law itself. But there is no revelation of the law that is not the spiritual act of knowledge of it. Hence the

[114]Nicene Creed (381)
[115]Cf. F. Schleiermacher, *Sämmtliche Werke*, 3, *Zur Philosophie*, vol. IV, pt. 2 and vol. V.
[115a]Cf. Goethe's concluding lines of the sonnet in "Was wir bringen" (1802): "If we want great things, we must concentrate; the master shows himself in limitation and the law alone can give us freedom."

statement that the law is set up means always that I have set it up.|

We need not engage in immanent criticism of this view. But we cannot refrain from saying that the concept of the law of faith involves the strongest conceivable attack on that tension in the concept of the law, of its establishment and knowledge. That tension has no place in theology. There can be absolutely no question of reversing the concept of the law of faith in that way. This law cannot in any way denote our own freedom and act as well. We have no share at all in setting it up even in the form of knowledge. The presupposition of that tension, of that "both God and man," rests on an antithesis of spontaneity and receptivity which is constitutive for human knowledge of the world. But this antithesis can only be regulative and not constitutive for knowledge of God. This is the theological thesis that we have to develop here. For a theological dialectic which works with human and worldly concepts and images, for a human presentation of the law of God, the antithesis is no less fundamental than it is for a philosophical dialectic that works in the same realm. Theology, however, must remember that even in this realm, which as a human discipline it can as little leave as any other such discipline, even in the form of discursive worldly and human knowledge, it has to fulfill, declare, and mediate the knowledge in which the antithesis has no place. It can make no use, then, of the possibility, based on the antithesis, of reversing as needed the relation of the subject and object of knowledge. In no way can it describe the relation of the "from above" and "from below" as one of tension. It has to describe it honestly and consistently as one of exclusive contradiction which cannot be secretly overcome within itself but which we can acknowledge to be overcome only by a miracle without being able to deduce from this any reciprocity of relation. For if a miracle does in fact take place, ⌐if it is true that a "from above" meets our "from below,"⌐ this means that I do not control it, so that I am unable even for a single moment to maintain that reciprocity.|

In refraining for the moment from a theological presentation of the knowledge of God, we take it to be a theological presupposition that there is no place for that antithesis in the knowledge of God and that this is the first thing that a proper theological presentation of this knowledge has to consider. Knowledge of God occurs above the antithesis. Above! Calvin's definition of faith as "something merely passive" (*Inst.* III, 13, 5)[116] must be taken very strictly. It does not say that the knowledge of God is a knowledge in which the spontaneous but not the receptive activity of reason is excluded—an idea to which one could only attach the foolish label "irrational," since a receptivity of reason without spontaneity would be like wooden iron. The Christian knowledge of God is not a state of trance in which we lose control of our five senses and have to give up ordered thinking. This would be a knowledge of

---

[116]Cf. n. 51.

demons, not God. In the knowledge of God neither the spontaneous nor the receptive activity of reason is excluded. Man is as rationally active here as he ever can be. But this activity receives direction, guidance, and order from something above itself which has no part in its antithesis and cannot be drawn into it. Whether spontaneously or receptively, receptively or spontaneously, the activity of reason is totally passive in relation to this "above," just as reason itself is passive, i.e., obedient. This is the special feature in the knowledge of God which differentiates it from all other knowledge. |

But how does it stand with this something that is above the antithesis of spontaneity and receptivity? How does faith come to reckon with it and thus to refrain completely in its presentation from any open or secret equating and reversing of the "above" and the "below"? This can be shown. Knowledge in that antithesis characterizes our knowledge of the world of created things, of objects, whether empirical or intelligible, natural or spiritual. When we know things, the receptivity of our knowledge must correspond to its spontaneity. That an object is posited and that we posit it are interchangeable concepts. There is a place for "both God and man," although it is obvious that this God is not really God but the immanent object, whether natural or spiritual. Might not knowledge of the object, perhaps, be also given the name of God? Why not? We are here in the sphere of eternal tensions in which Buridan's ass may decide who is truly and finally king.[117] In insisting on the correlation of spontaneity and receptivity even in relation to the knowledge of God; in insisting on the interchangeability of the role of God and man, as taught, if not by Kant, at any rate by the so-called "consistent idealists" who followed him,"[118] idealism shows that its God is the quintessence of created spirit, of objectified human reason, and not the Creator of reason. Nothing is more natural than the sudden plunge of German culture, after Hegel, into the darkness of materialism. (For a similar plunge in the middle of the 12th century cf. Reuter, *Gesch. d. rel. Aufklärung im M.A.* I, 173.).[119] If God is to be sought in the world, why in the long run should spirit be king? Could not the ass decide in favor of nature for a change? From the standpoint of Christian faith in God it is no less mythological to declare that human reason, even at its purest, is God, ⌐and that the kingdom of spirit is the kingdom of God (Ritschl),[120]¬ than to do the same with nature. For where does reason

---

[117]The Franciscan J. Buridan (c. 1300–1358) used the example of the ass that died of hunger because it could not decide between two equally attractive bundles of hay to illustrate Aristotle's thesis that the will lies behind the act.

[118]For the expression "consistent idealists" cf. W. Lütgert, *Die Religion des deutschen Idealismus und ihr Ende*, 1, Gütersloh 1923², p. 41.

[119]H. Reuter, *Geschichte der religiösen Aufklärung im Mittelalter vom Ende des 8. bis zum Anfang des 14. Jahrhunderts*, vol. 1, Berlin 1875, reprinted Aalen 1963.

[120]Cf. A. Ritschl, *Die christliche Lehre von der Rechtfertigung und Versöhnung*, vol. 3, Bonn 1874, p. 240f.; cf. also pp. 279, 284f., 444ff.

know itself except in that correlation of spontaneity and receptivity, i.e., in relation to an object, to something that is set over against it in some way? The question has to be left open whether God, if he is in the world as the last, true, original reality, is not to be sought just as much in what is set over against reason as in reason. Nor can it finally be denied that reason itself, in terms of what is set over against it, is itself something that is set over against, i.e., an object. From the standpoint of Christian faith, then, the equation of God and reason is just as mythological as the equation of God and nature.[121]

In believing in God the Christian faith does not believe in any of these antithetical and obviously mutually limiting things, in any of these things to which unconditionality can be ascribed only in relation to opposing conditioned things, and between which the relation can at any time be reversed and frequently enough has been reversed. Faith believes in the Creator of all things: the Creator and no other object; the Lord of both reason and nature; the origin of their being and their being over against one another. ⌐God has objectivity inasmuch as he has existence not only in our knowledge but also over against it, not in the understanding alone but also in reality (Anselm),[122] inasmuch as he really is, and inasmuch as he is the basis of all objects, of all the things that stand over against our knowledge. But God is no object.⌐ Where the Creator himself is understood as an object, as that which stands over against all cosmic reality, the question unavoidably arises as to the Creator and Lord of the two new antitheses that arise in this way. We might then accept the mythological idea of an infinite regress or the equally mythological idea of an object that we call the last one and therefore God. But what do these ideas amount to but our ignorance or denial of God the Creator? If faith is knowledge of God the Creator, it is not knowledge of an object. Nor is it knowledge in the antithesis of spontaneity and receptivity that characterizes knowledge of objects. Nor is it knowledge with interchangeable roles between knower and known. Nor is it knowledge in which man can see himself more or less as the creator. The law of God has been set up without my doing it or cooperating in doing it. Any law that I set up or cooperate in setting up would not as such be God's law. Christian knowledge of God's law is knowledge of the law that was set up absolutely without me and absolutely *for* me.

How are we to describe this knowledge in contrast to idealistic knowledge of the law? I have called it ac-knowledgment. This, too, is knowledge. Its difference from knowledge that is not acknowledgment is that I know secondarily, and with respect for him who has preceded

---

[121]Cf. B. Spinoza, *Ethica* IV, Praef.: "the infinite being which we call God or nature"; propos. IV: "the power . . . is itself the power of God or nature," etc.

[122]Cf. Anselm's *Proslogion* 2 (Library of Christian Classics, vol. X, ed. E.R. Fairweather, 1956, p. 74): "Without doubt, therefore, there exists, both in the understanding and in reality, something than which a greater cannot be thought."

me, a truth that has been seen and spoken first by another. Pure acknowledgment, as is well known, does not arise among us poor mortals, and we have every reason to treat it with caution. If I acknowledge a truth that is championed and expressed by other people, I do so not merely because they have convinced me about it, but also because I have convinced myself about it. The two sides of the process are in principle and in practice interchangeable. I play a creative role in the process even if I act postcreatively. I tell it to myself as I have been told it, and only as I do so do I acknowledge it. For all the acknowledgment, it might well be—as often happens between students and professors—that I can even know it and say it much better than the one who first told it to me. As I say it to myself, the one who told it to me begins gently to become for me "a man of yesterday."[123] The relation is reversible like all human relations. We must first try to construct a concept of pure acknowledgment if we are to reach a concept of the knowledge of faith which rules out reversal. In pure acknowledgment I will noncreatively recognize that what I am told is self-illumined even as it illumines me, for it is *said* to me and it does not therefore become illumined only when I say it to myself. When the phrases "I myself have perceived it" and "I say it to myself" play no role in knowledge, not in the sense that they do not occur, for this is impossible where there is true knowledge, but in the sense of establishing known truth as truth; when they play no such role because everything has been done in this regard by him who tells us the truth; when any reversal between imparting to me and reception by me is ruled out, then we have real acknowledgment. This pure acknowledgment is the knowledge of faith which we have constructed here. We have constructed it *a posteriori* and not *a priori*. As pure acknowledgment of this kind, the knowledge of faith is that of the law which has been absolutely set up for me. But thus far we have described only the negative side of this knowledge.

How far is it knowledge of the law that is set up for me and that truly confronts me? Whence, from whom, and how far can something be said to us that we simply have to let be said to us in this way? If the law belonged to the world of objects, it would obviously not belong here. It would meet us on human lips and in human concepts and images and even at best could not elicit pure acknowledgment from us. Even if I turned aside from human instruction and made reason itself my guide, I still would not leave the world of the objective. We have seen that reason and nature make mutual demands on one another and by their indissoluble correlation are characterized as objects. In my knowledge of objects, however, I myself am the basis of the truth of my knowledge.

[123]Cf. Barth's Preface to the 6th edition of his *Römerbrief* (1929), in which he alludes to a report that he is gently beginning to become a man of yesterday, and comments that as the dead ride quickly, successful theologians ride even more quickly, and that he could not have written his book if he had not been theoretically and practically prepared for this even before he became "a man of today."

Strictly, then, reason, even pure reason, cannot be my guide. It can be so only as *my* reason. Without this final seal of *my* reason, reason would be Hecuba to me.[124] And with my own reason I continually think that I can know a little better than reason as such, no matter how objective or lofty I allow this to be. Reciprocity is in full play here. Hence the knowledge of faith cannot be reason's knowledge of the law. Reason cannot be the guide that I meet in pure acknowledgment. If reason is God, then my relation to God is the same as to an object. The roles are interchangeable in just the same way as when nature is God. Letting ourselves be told the truth, however, is possible and necessary if God has spoken to us beyond all objects. If the miracle takes place, it is obvious that he wanted to speak to us, to make himself known to us, both possibly and necessarily, in the form which we have been able to describe only as acknowledgment. His Word has to be received by created reason in such a way that all questions and controls, all evaluations of the truth by a standard apart from its own, and all knowledge that seeks to be seeing instead of hearing, are completely excluded. Before it is lifted up to beatific vision, to the seeing of God face to face, reason can approach only objects with sight. God the Creator can only be heard. He can be revealed to us only through his Word. By its very nature knowledge of God the Creator differs from the knowledge of objects.|

To be sure, human reason can render an account of its knowledge of God only in the form of knowledge of objects, in the form of concepts and images. Hence the human knowledge of faith, or what the New Testament calls *gnosis*, or theology, can arise only in the same sphere as philosophical knowledge and it is caught up in the same dialectical movement. In distinction from philosophy, however, what it says does not lie in what we have said to ourselves but in what has been said to us by the unrepeatable, irreplaceable, incomparable, and incomprehensible Word of God. It knows this only as human reason knows, but it knows it as, in Paul's words, it is known by God [cf. 1 Cor. 13:12; Gal. 4:9], without reciprocity, without the open or secret presupposition that this being known may be only an interchangeable concept for which we might just as well substitute knowledge. The difference between the setting up of the law and our knowledge that it is set up is just as ineffaceable as the distinction between heaven and earth, subject and predicate, command and obedience. In this strict sense, the law of faith, as distinct from that of idealism, is the law of God. We have not proved that there is such a law. We shall take care not to try to do so. We have to say rather that "there is" (*es gibt*) no law of God, "there is" indeed no God, in the sense in which "there are objects or nature or reason or world." In this sense "there is" no God unless we have false gods in

---

[124]Hecuba was the wife of Priam of Troy. The allusion is to Shakespeare's *Hamlet*, Act II, Scene 2: "What's Hecuba to him, or he to Hecuba, that he should weep for her?"

mind. Similarly "there is" no law of God. The law that "there is" is not one that is set up and that makes an absolute claim to our acknowledgment. The law of God is the law of faith, i.e., the law that "God gives" (*Gott gibt*) as he gives himself in his revelation. Now, as theology must always do, we have presupposed the reality and occurrence of revelation. Again we have demonstrated *a posteriori* what is meant by law, in contrast to idealistic notions, when theology, on the presupposition of the reality of revelation, speaks about law; what is to be understood here by the establishment and validity of the law; and what is the relation of this establishment and validity to our knowledge. Idealism, which even at best presses on to a "both God and man," undoubtedly has in view something very different from sound theology when it uses the word "God." If it did not, it would no more dare to use "both" than to put an equal sign between God and man. Knowledge of God by faith alone, which theological knowledge wants to be and has to be, demands strictly and unequivocally: To God *alone* be the glory. |

In clarification of the concept of the law of faith in distinction from what idealism calls law we have thus far made the three points: 1) that the law of faith is not a universally accessible law; 2) that it is not interchangeable with the law of the spirit; and 3) that it has been set up by God and not by us.

In all this, however, we have only hinted at the positive statement that we need to make. This statement has stood behind all that we have said. But it must now step forward itself. We might sum up all that has been said in Luther's warning against contemplating the (divine) majesty.[125] We must be on guard against the inevitable abstractness of the concept of God, against confusing the concept of God with a conceptual God. Though it has often been overlooked—and this indicates an illegitimate simplifying of the problem—Luther did not make his warning against contemplating the divine majesty unconditional. He did not question the need for a concept of God. He knew very well that in dispute with Jews, Turks, and heretics, theology, to differentiate itself from them, is forced to say what it means when it utters the word "God." It has to use concepts and abstractions and whatever else is needed for successful debate.[126] Nor did Luther merely say this; he also practiced it in his *Bondage of the Will*.[127] A theologian must be able to say and show to an Erasmus and his like that they do not mean God no matter how often they use the term, and this cannot be done without contemplation of the majesty. Yet Luther saw the danger that lurks in the concept of God as such. Erasmus can be defeated only

---

[125]WA 40 I, 75, 29ff. In asking for diligent observance of the rule not to contemplate the (divine) majesty Luther points out that neither the human body nor the human mind can bear it (LW, 26, 28).

[126]WA 40 I, 78, 27ff. (LW, 26, 29f.).

[127]WA 18, 600–787.

by Erasmus. In being defeated, however, he may return with even greater strength. Theological dialectic can be the Trojan horse by which the enemy enters Ilion. Even the most cautious theological dialectic is not secure against this danger. It necessarily moves in the sphere of antitheses and therefore of objects. As we have said, it can copy the unrepeatable Yes and No of God only in opposites which do not by a long way do justice to his suprasecular reality.|

Theology is always in danger of forgetting this and confusing the majesty or glory of God which it has in view with the majesty and glory of a supranatural and spiritual object concerning which, for good or ill, it has to speak, but which, if it is regarded as God, can only be an ultimate and supreme idol invented and constructed by man. Luther perceived in this seeking and finding of God in a concept, this rational apprehension of the majesty of God (Gal. 1:47),[128] what is at first sight a surprising parallel to the monkish righteousness in which, in an attempt to satisfy God, we interpose ourselves with works and fasts and cowl and tonsure. All this was for him a Luciferian enterprise which could end only with horrible desperation in which we lose God and all things. For God in his divine nature is more than our human nature can bear. Those who behold his majesty are overwhelmed by glory.[129] Treating the God of the human concept of God lightly, we can apparently be exalted and intoxicated in the divine likeness which it entails, but serious seeking and finding here can end only with the "numinous" which Otto has not only described in his book on the holy, but also depicted with a truly devilish grimace (2nd ed., p. 70).[130] All that this "Wholly Other" can finally be for man is judgment without grace, i.e., hell. "There you have *your* Wholly Other, there you have what I am not, there you have what I am so far as you yourself seek and find me," is the reply that God himself, who will not be mocked, gives to us through this grimace [cf. Gal. 6:7]. Theology must do all it can to prevent its concept of God from being confused in this way with God himself. For this reason, although it is a human science, it can be idealistic theology only with considerable reservation. It has to know what it is saying when it says "God." It must know how far it can and may contemplate the majesty. It must also know that in this contemplation and in its concept of God it has not found or posited or set up God himself but only given a human account of the God who, neither sought nor found by us, has revealed himself. God himself is the revealed God, revealed by himself alone. *His* law is the law of faith. Faith is not the Luciferian seeking and finding of God in a concept of God, no matter how deep or pure it may be. Its law is not the norm that corresponds to the God of this Luciferian seeking and finding. In basing itself on faith, theology—because of its unavoidable Erasmian trait—mistrusts no one and nothing more than it does itself. Because of

---

[128]WA 40 I, 76, 22f. (LW, 26, 28).

[129]WA 40 I, 77, 17ff. (LW, 26, 29f.).

[130]R. Otto, *Das Heilige:* Picture of Durja, a Bengal goddess, between p. 70 and p. 71.

its unavoidable contemplation of the majesty and its unavoidable concept of God, which may at any time become an idol, it must never forget for a single moment that faith is not a bold human venture but obedience. Nor is it obedience to a God whom we have secretly or openly found and posited and set up for ourselves. It is obedience to God himself who has revealed himself and sought and found us. If we obey our concept of God or our conceptual God, we merely obey ourselves, i.e., we do not obey. We have apparently moved off and raised ourselves high up above ourselves and met a Wholly Other, but in reality we have never been so hopelessly alone: alone with the grimace of the *Deus nudus* who is simply our own reflection.

Faith, however, believes in the God who has sought and found us before and without any seeking or finding on our part, who has sought and found us with his grace and also with his judgment. We have seen that grace cannot be shown except to the guilty. We recognize ourselves to be guilty as grace is shown to us. The accusation and sentence that we accept in faith makes quite impossible the task of seeking God in our own concept of God. Who are we then that we can think we can seek and find God in even our purest and deepest concept of God? How can we approach God in this way? Is not even our purest and deepest concept of God a sinful human work which needs forgiveness and which we can do only in faith—not in faith in our work but in faith in the Word of grace and therefore in obedience and without any claim? Who are we not to know that *our* contemplation of the majesty has as such nothing whatever to do with the majesty of God and can indeed be no more than contemplation of the majesty of the devil? On the ground of mysticism and morals we do not know what sin is. That enterprise is undertaken in a remarkable absence of any horror at ourselves. We cannot move off in this way or scale the heights or raise ourselves above ourselves or grasp after a Wholly Other if we know that we have merited judgment. But if not, do we know what grace is? Can there be any pardon where no serious sentence has been heard? We are not questioning here the Christian faith of those who stand on this ground. We are not talking about what takes place between them and God, which may be more profound and serious than what takes place in the hearts of those who do not stand on this ground. We are speaking only of good and bad theology. There are often happy inconsistencies between the true and hidden life of men with God and the theology they espouse. And we want to make it clear that even the best and most consistent theology cannot guard us against serious disaster in that hidden personal relationship. God's ways are not our ways [cf. Isa. 55:8] and we must not anticipate his judgment with even the slightest suspicion regarding the personal position of others nor the slightest pride regarding our own. We can only say that those who put themselves on that ground are poor theologians, for to do that does not tally with the fact that in believing they can see in themselves only the pardoned thief [cf. Luke 23:43]. In so doing, in spite of their poor theology, they do not live by the grace and under the judgment of their conceptual God. Their faith is better than their theology. But no matter how it stands with them or us, and even granting that their faith is real and ours hypocritical, we still cannot yield to them. Our task is to engage in good Christian theology. Even if we ourselves are found reprobate in doing it, this does not make bad theology good nor does it justify us in calling good theology bad. The most authentic and best attested personal faith gives no warrant to engage in just any kind of theology. Christian faith, whether those who represent it are true or false, demands distinctively Christian theology. Hence for all our high personal evaluation of those who stand on the ground of mysticism and morals, we ourselves cannot stand there but have to say that it is not a place for good theology. The law of faith is the law of the revelation of God.

Let us now speak more plainly. It is the law of Jesus Christ. He is God's grace to us. He is also God's judgment on us. As he is God's judgment on us, as he puts us where contemplating the majesty as a seeking and finding of God by man is ruled out, he is also the law of God that is truly given to us. We are now near the goal that we have been seeking on the long path that lies behind us. At the climax of the first section we saw that Christian faith is faith in God's mercy in Jesus Christ.[131] In contrast to a universally accessible knowledge, the revelation of God is hereby described as a specific, unique, concrete event. In contrast to the timeless truths of the spiritual world, of which we may say with some elasticity that they are "revealed" to us as truth encountering us in time; in contrast to the God in whose deity, as shown, we participate, it is the revelation of the God who is God before us and without us and who as such can only be acknowledged by us. All this is meant when we say that faith is faith in the mercy of God in Jesus Christ.

At this point, however, we must be careful not to move to the other ground that can do nothing for theology. When, in the first section, we established faith's relation to Jesus Christ, we were instructed by the warnings of the reformers to emphasize that by Jesus Christ we do not understand a mere symbol or transparency of the real Word which lies behind Jesus of Nazareth, which is in some way made visible by him, and for the knowledge of which he is no more than the means, the key, or perhaps the practically necessary transition. [We saw] that we must take with bitter earnestness not just the deity of Jesus Christ but his deity in his humanity. If we were to regard his deity as a something that lies behind his humanity, we should show thereby that we think we are in a position to distinguish between deity and humanity, as though we already knew in a general sense what deity is. What would this mean but that outside Christ we were already contemplating the majesty, having

---

[131]See above pp. 281ff., 286ff.

sought and found God in our concept of God? Although God wills to meet us as this man, although this man was crucified among and by men, although sentence was thereby passed upon us, we seem to have enough self-confidence to try to find a symbol or to see through a transparency here, continually dreaming about a knowledge of revelation to which we have general access in principle and which we have found to be confirmed in the knowledge of Jesus Christ. Its content would then be again a timeless truth of the spiritual world and its fulfillment would at least be our own act as well as God's. Christocentric though we might pretend to be, we should stand on the ground of mysticism and morals where fellowship with God may be realized apart from the concrete event of divine revelation. |

This is why Luther uttered his famous warning against contemplating the majesty, not just in a general way, but in the particular context of his doctrine of justification. He attacked it as a foolhardy human work, typical of Turks, Jews, and all legalists, which should not be imitated in Christian theology as he found it imitated in the mysticism and morals of monasticism.[132] He realized and saw that it could, in fact, be imitated even in a Christian garb and with a solemn and fervent invocation of the name of Christ. Hence the positive content of his warning is a reference to Christ the Mediator, i.e., to the humanity of Christ, the incarnate Word. We are to begin where Christ did, in the virgin's womb, in the stable, at his mother's breast, etc. He himself came down, was born, went among us, suffered, was crucified and buried. He sets himself before us thus. He fixes the eyes of our hearts upon himself in this form. He thus forbids any ascent to heaven or contemplation of the majesty.[133] There is no need for any new ascent to heaven. It is prohibited by the revelation of God in Christ. The Word of God does not just come to us through the man Jesus of Nazareth, as though we could later have heard it and know it in itself and apart from him. The Word of God is this man as man, and always and inescapably it has spoken to us as the reality of this man and not otherwise. This is God's mercy, that precisely in the reality, no, as the reality of this man, God is Immanuel, God with us, God among us. This is also our judgment, for we have crucified this man who is God himself. And God's law that is given to us is that this man is set over against us. This man, in all the uniqueness and concreteness with which he is man, we cannot dissolve into the conceptual God of theology, into a universally accessible truth, into a part of the life of the spirit, into something posited by reason. Here is special, concrete law, God's law, law which has come to us as such and can only be acknowledged by us. What is not acknowledgment in the pure sense, the acknowledgment which is the obedience of faith, is a failure to know, i.e., nonknowledge. There is no other alternative. The idealistic

---

[132]Cf. WA 40 I, 76, 13ff. (LW, 26, 28).
[133]WA 40 I, 77, 28ff. (LW, 26, 29).

possibility is ruled out no less than the law of inner necessity or the law of fate. As Christ's law the law is incarnate law. |

We must now clarify the backward and forward range of this statement. When God the Reconciler claims us, we are claimed by a man, no, by this man. When the existence of this man becomes a command for us, God's command encounters us. In this man's existence, God's command is real to us. As it encounters us thus, as it is real to us in this man's existence, it is the true law of God and is secure against all confusion or exchange. It could not be more divine than it is in human form in this man. We always evade God's command and fail to meet God, simply seeing ourselves in a mirror, if we try to hear God apart from this man or change this man into a mere symbol or instrument of God. Christian faith does not believe in God in himself, not even as the Father in himself or the Word in himself, but in God as the Father of the incarnate Son and the incarnate Son of the Father [cf. John 1:14]. Christian faith trusts in God by trusting in his revealed Word, i.e., in this man. God is present to man, according to Christian faith, as this man is present to us, our Lord in the power of his deity and one with us as our Lord. |

Undoubtedly this is a very serious relapse from an idealistic standpoint. Does it not surrender the loftiness of God and the incomprehensibility of his nearness? Does it not mean that the fate and inner necessity under which we stand are again exalted as law? The infinite made finite, the unconditioned conditioned, eternity time? ⌐Is not this the demonizing of revelation (Tillich).[134]¬ What basis is there for it? Why this man? This is the question of idealistic theology and we shall understand neither the question nor ourselves if we pause even for a moment to explain "why this man." We shall not understand the question, for behind it stands the idealistic axiom that there cannot be a "this man," a becoming concrete, an actualizing of the law which mocks at concepts, a uniqueness of its claim. And behind the axiom stands the idealistic will to seek and set up for oneself the law that is true law. In face of this axiom and in conflict with this will, all apologetics, all attempts to answer the question: "Why this man?", are from the very outset an artificial, feeble, inadequate, and hopeless venture. Armed with this axiom and supported by the armor of this will, idealistic theology has denied at the very beginning of the discussion the very thing that it asks us to explain, and we can only make ourselves ridiculous if even for a moment we try to offer reasons. We cannot debate principles with those who negate them.[135] No answer can be given except to make it plain that we, too, begin with a presupposition

---

[134]Cf. P. Tillich, "Die Idee der Offenbarung," *ZThK*, NF 8 (1927), 403–12. In fact, Tillich argues here that making the conditioned unconditioned is demonism, religious demonism being the worst (p. 38).

[135]Cf. Aristotle, *Analytica posteriora*, II, 19, and Thomas Aquinas, *In Librum Beati Dionysii De Divinis Nominibus Expositio*, ed. C. Pera, Turin and Rome 1950, p. 40, n. 124.

which is given prior to the discussion and which lies outside it. Explanation can be given only in the form of steadfast assertion of this presupposition of ours. |

If we embark even for a moment on any other explanation we do not understand ourselves either. For when Christian faith recognizes this man as God's law it does not, in fact, do this because it has attained to this insight by general considerations apart from faith, because we ourselves have sought and finally found without faith, because we ultimately have adequate reasons to accept this man as the true law of God. That would not be acknowledgment. We should again have said the decisive thing ourselves. We should incontestably have followed an idealistic path in refuting and convincing the idealists. This man would not really be himself the law of God but a manifestation, perhaps the supreme manifestation, of the law of God which is obviously already known to us in itself, and which by diligent and not unsuccessful seeking we have finally found incarnate in this man, so that we have found him to be confirmed, if not as the giver, at any rate as the leading preacher of the law of God. With any attempt at explanation we should show that we ourselves really doubt and question what we are trying to prove, namely, that this man is the giver of the law, that he is himself the law. For if he is himself the law, there is no higher vantage point on which we can set ourselves to assure ourselves and others that he really is. If even with the best of intentions we set ourselves on such a point, we deny the very thing that we are trying to defend: that he *is* the law. If he *is,* then we can only place ourselves under this law as those who *are* placed there and who in what they think and say about it, in their theology, argue as those who *are* placed there and who cannot even hypothetically place themselves anywhere else. The confession that we make by arguing thus can be meant by us only as witness. This is true of our demonstration that the idealistic God is not God and that the idealistic law is not law. It is also true of our positive demonstration that the law consists of our being committed by this man. |

That the God who is mere spirit and not the Lord of both nature and spirit is not God; that the God who can exchange roles with us is not God; that the law that we have sought and with commendable perspicacity have also found is not law; that commitment to the law is not serious so long as it is not commitment by this man and to this man—these are all good arguments against idealism, but they are also good arguments of *faith,* so that we understand ourselves very badly if we think that we can make them impressive by persuasion to those who, in what they think and say, place themselves alongside faith and especially alongside the insight that we are all wrongdoers. Placing themselves alongside faith and alongside this decisive insight of faith, they still retain their wonderful freedom, in spite of our argument, to regard their conceptual God as God, to regard the interchangeability of roles as a devout and delightful thing, to regard their own law as law, and to regard commitment to this man as an irksome and even an unworthy heteronomism whose overthrow is the breakthrough of real Christian faith. When theology discharges its office strictly and properly, it knows very well that in speaking to those who have placed themselves on this other ground it is referred to, and lives by, the truth that its witness becomes the witness of the Holy Spirit. If it does not—and it has no way of making it do so—then in the eyes of idealists, at least, it moves on the lower and vanquished plane of the law of inner necessity and fate. Its confession: "I believe in Jesus Christ . . . my Lord,"[136] is a highly contingent internal conviction about a highly contingent external fact. We have in our hands no means to make our witness, be it ever so clever, into the witness of the Holy Spirit. We can tell our opponents very distinctly and definitely what is wrong with their idealistic theology as such. We can suggest that they might at least stop pretending that their teaching is really theology or their God is really God or their law really the law. But the distinctness, definiteness, and force of this polemic are those of faith. We invite the idealist to get down from his high horse and confess with us that he is a sinner who lives by mercy. But we cannot issue this invitation with such force that he will really get down and see himself as a sinner. We cannot lay upon him the commitment out of which we say all this. ⌜We cannot even be certain in principle or once and for all, but only at given moments, that we ourselves are speaking in this commitment. We can be certain of it only with reference to the forgiveness of sins and in the obedience which refuses to say later: "I *have been* obedient."⌝ Nor can we prevent the other from reversing things and pitying us from the lofty perch of his knowledge as poor psychics or authoritarian bigots or even romantics. For good or ill we have to come to terms with the sorry appearance that we cut in his eyes. |

That does not mean, however, that we really are and do what he accuses us of being and doing. Even if we cannot escape his suspicions, we may have a good conscience in relation to him. We can answer: No, you have things wrong; it is an optical illusion that we seem to be bringing back the categories of inner necessity and fate. If Christian theology does this, ⌜if, in order not to be idealistic, it becomes realistic and ontological,⌝ this is a weak and illegitimate action that justifies suspicions.[137] Hence we must not, in avoiding the Charybdis of idealism, fall victim to Scylla. The relation of theology to idealism and romanticism is not a symmetrical one. The former is a big and dangerous opponent, the other a little and relatively harmless one. But this should not cause us to fall into the arms of the latter when threatened by the former. As we have seen, inner necessity and fate are authorities which we can set up ourselves and with which we can exchange roles so that we

---

[136]An allusion to Luther's exposition of the second article of the Creed in his Short Catechism of 1529.
[137]Text A: "and qualifies itself as romantic theology."

become authorities in their place. They are mirrors of ourselves which we cannot recognize as our law when we know that we are judged by God. In accepting them we do not acknowledge them; we accept ourselves as spectators of ourselves. They do not bind us; we may be other things in relation to them. We are finally their masters as we are masters of the general truth of idealism. Idealism's criticism that in them we have to do with demons and not deity is justified, even though it may be finally turned against idealism itself.

Christian faith is no inner necessity nor is Jesus Christ fate. If they seem to be this from the standpoint of idealism, it is an unavoidable illusion caused by a shortening of perspective. Theology betrays itself if it accepts this illusion and tries to retreat to naturalistic categories in opposition to idealism. It cannot be too much on guard against psychological and historical arguments. If it is not, it becomes demonology instead of theology. If, with a view to speaking about faith, we talk about states and experiences of the soul, and if, with a view to speaking about Jesus Christ, we talk about the events and turning points and effects of history, we come under the legitimate criticism of idealism and then of the criticism that may be brought against idealism. There undoubtedly takes place not only a relapse into the romantic-natural sphere that idealism has overcome but also, secretly, into idealism itself, into its autonomous spirituality. Thus, when Jesus Christ encounters us as the law of God, this is not, and it must not be described as, a special instance of our general fateful historical involvement in the world around us. A wise person will not try to establish the objective truth of Christ in this way. And if we believe in Jesus Christ as our Lord, this again is not a special instance of our individual inward life of the soul, it must not be described as such, and a wise person will not establish it in this way. In both cases we are speaking about a divine, *the* divine, work and occurrence which constitute a category of their own—so much so that as a category it stands absolutely opposed to every other category.

This man who finds this faith, this faith in this man, is the action and occurrence that falls under no order known to us, whether spiritual or natural. It is God's own action and occurrence in his revelation. Because God is the one Creator of both kingdoms, he gives both kingdoms a share in his revelation, though this cannot be perceived or demonstrated in either. There is, of course, a possibility of confusing his kingdom with either one of these kingdoms or both. In his *truth*, in the inexpressible distance and proximity, proximity and distance, in which he encounters us precisely in the man Jesus Christ, God seems to be what we call spirit. If we do not remember that he is the Lord, and if we do not remember our own limits, we see and have in him the God of idealism. In his *reality*, in all the concreteness and particularity and directness in which again he meets us precisely in the man Jesus Christ, God seems to be what we call nature. If we do not remember that he is the Lord, and if we do not remember our own limits, we see and have in him the God of realism,[138] the God of experience and history. Christian faith, however, keeps a middle course between these false gods. In faith we remember that God is our Lord and we remember our own limits. In faith we pray: "Thy kingdom come" [Matt. 6:10; Luke 11:2]. God's kingdom, however, is a third kingdom. No, we do better to say that it is the one kingdom above all worldly kingdoms. Not the kingdom of nature or spirit in whose context and contradiction we live, but the kingdom of God himself, the kingdom of heaven, has drawn near [cf. Mark 1:15 par.] as and when God meets us in Jesus Christ, no, *as* Jesus Christ.

When the Word became flesh [cf. John 1:14], the third word, no, the one word was said which was meant but could never be said in the two words which we can and must say and which, plunging either to right or left, we easily and frequently confuse with the one real Word of God. This one Word of God binds us: in *truth*, because it is *God's* Word, in *reality* because it was made *flesh*. The law of realism[139] does not *truly* bind us, for it is not heard as *God's* Word. The law of idealism does not *really* bind us, for it is not heard as the *incarnate* Word. The Word of God that was made flesh binds us truly and really. But this Word is Jesus Christ, true God and real man, in the unity of both that is present *only* to faith, but really is *present* to faith. When God assumed humanity, not just in general, but in the special act and manner of the manifestation of Jesus Christ, divine law was set up in our life. This is what needs to be said in elucidation of the statement that the law became man with a backward glance at the two other possibilities of understanding the law which we looked at earlier. We shall now finally turn away from these possibilities and take a forward look.

Jesus of Nazareth is the law of faith. He is also, of course, the promise of divine mercy which is given to faith and grasped in faith. But it is about him as the law of faith, as the divine claim on us that goes forth concretely with the promise, that we have to speak in ethics. ⌜Promise and claim, gospel and law, are two different things, but⌝ the Word of God is not just gospel. It not only justifies us; it sanctifies us too. It is command. If it finds faith, this faith is also obedience. This is all concrete and full of content because the Word of God became flesh, because Jesus of Nazareth is the Word of God. The obedience of faith is obedience to Jesus. Jesus is the revealer of the imminent kingdom of God. He reveals it by the messianic proclamation of the forgiveness of sins, by mighty helping acts in which the end of all things and the redemption of creation seem to be anticipated and made visible as if by lightning ("signs and wonders" [Acts 2:22] they are rightly called), by his resurrection from the dead, which gives his manifestation power in, against, and over the world. But he does not reveal anything strange,

---

[138]Text A: "romanticism."
[139]Text A: "romanticism."

different, or behind himself. He reveals what he himself is and what is done by him. His person and work do not merely display but *are* the imminent kingdom of God, the reconciliation of man with God. He *is* these things because in his manifestation as such, in the way from Bethlehem to Golgotha, in the special action which constitutes his manifestation, he is something specific, namely a sacrifice for his brethren to the extent that in his vicarious suffering and obedience God's mercy to us is real. He thus reveals reconciliation by being himself the Reconciler. This reconciling, this way of his to the cross for us, characterizes his command to us, to his people, to all those whom he calls to repentance in the light of the enacted atonement and the imminent kingdom of God. Hence his reconciling, his way to the cross for others, characterizes the claim to obedience that is heard in faith. It characterizes sanctifying grace as it is also the basis of justifying grace. |

The synoptic "Follow me" [Mark 1:17 par.], in which the imperatives of Jesus reach their climax, says something very specific. If it first and very simply describes how certain people were told to take Jesus as their teacher, we should recall at once that the twelve disciples to whom it is directed are also the twelve apostles, the representatives of the church (*ecclesia*), of the new people of God that is gathered in the midst of the old. "Follow me" is the summons of the king of this people. It is the demand that they should do what befits this people. But inasmuch as it demands action that conforms to that of the king, of Jesus himself; inasmuch as it demands imitation of Christ, we have to take note of the explanatory statements which accompany it in the gospels. Following Jesus means not looking behind [cf. Luke 9:62], letting the dead bury their dead [cf. Matt. 8:22 par.], not having anywhere to lay one's head [cf. Matt. 8:20 par.], selling everything [cf. Mark 10:21 par.], leaving everything [cf. Mark 1:18 par.], and taking up one's cross [cf. Mark 8:34 par.]. The last express statement is hardly needed to make clear to us that the way of Jesus to the cross is what we have to keep before us as the concrete point of the conformity which he demands of his people. We must not substitute abstract moral concepts for this wholly concrete direction: neither trust in God nor love for men, neither moral earnestness nor moral freedom, nor even the purity of heart of Jesus. It is not a question of Jesus' character, but unequivocally of his work and way. To follow Jesus is not to become like him. It is not to acquire his outstanding virtues. It is to be with him on the way, on his way. But his way is the way of suffering and death. It is not the way of sacrifice for sacrifice's sake. In his sacrifice there is no trace of denial of life, of asceticism, of mystical self-negation. His sacrifice is sacrifice for the brethren. The human life of the Son of God is offered up for the brethren as a life that is bound and pledged and given to men and given up for them. He did not come to be served but to serve and to give his life—not in general and not in the void—but as a ransom for many [cf. Mark 10:45 par.]. He does not suffer for himself, to bear his share of the universal curse that lies on the human race. None of this curse lies on him. He suffers as and because he binds himself to others, to us. Nor does he obey for his own sake. He needs no sanctification, just as he needs no justification. He is righteous and holy as he is who he is. But he obeys in solidarity with us, "to fulfill all righteousness" [cf. Matt. 3:15]. To follow Jesus, then, is not only to be sacrificed with him but to be sacrificed with him for the brethren, to be bound to men, to be bound in life to our neighbors as those to whom we owe our life. Thus the command of God is summed up in the one and twofold saying: "You shall love the Lord your God with all your heart, and with all your soul, and with all your mind, and with all your strength"—this is the sacrifice—and: "You shall love your neighbor as yourself"—this is the distinctively Christian relation in which the sacrifice is made [Mark 12:30f. par.]. "I will make you fishers of men," is the immediate positive explanation of "Follow me" in the chief passage in Mark 1:17, and in Matthew 25:31ff. the possibility of being pledged by and to Jesus without being pledged by and to our neighbors is unambiguously ruled out: "As you did it to one of the least of these my brethren, you did it to me," and: "As you did it not to one of the least of these, you did it not to me." Judgment follows on this basis. This is the concrete meaning of his command. |

Paul did not misunderstand the "Follow me," but understood it very well when, in particular, he brought to light the indicative behind the imperative and traced back the need for obedience to that union with Christ in virtue of which he is our Lord and we are not our own. As children and heirs of God and therefore as joint heirs with Christ we *have* to suffer with him (Rom. 8:17; Phil. 3:10). As an apostle Paul *is* offered up (2 Tim. 4:6) and bears the wounds of the Lord in his own body (Gal. 6:17; 2 Cor. 4:10). The crucifixion of the flesh *is* the lot of Christians as such (Gal. 5:24; Rom. 6:6). For, baptized into Christ, they are baptized into his death, planted into the likeness of his death (Rom. 6:3,5), and buried with him (Rom. 6:4; Col. 2:12). Paul deduces imperatives from these indicatives but the presupposition is that the imperatives lie in the indicatives. We do not choose to be sacrificed. It happens. It is a claim under which we stand. We cannot escape it. We do not place ourselves in the discipleship of Jesus. We are called to it. The imperatives remind us of the decision and choice that has already been made concerning us. We *are* put to death in the reconciling death of this man. On this basis and only on this basis we can be told and can tell ourselves: "Mortify your members" [cf. Col. 3:5]. It should be noted that in Paul, too, the Christian's dying and being dead and buried with Christ has nothing whatever to do with an unrelated self-negation and asceticism that is of value only in itself. When Paul describes himself as exhausted and wasted and spent like capital, he adds: "For your souls" (2 Cor. 12:15). He is offered up "upon the sacrificial offering of your faith" (Phil. 2:17). He fills up what is lacking in the suffering of Christ in his own body "for the sake of his body, that is, the church" (Col. 1:24). It is thus said expressly by Paul that the necessary sacrifice of the Christian is as little unrelated as is Christ's own sacrifice. The humiliation which Christians undergo in fellowship with Christ as those who are baptized and reconciled to God through Christ, like the humiliation of Christ himself as described in Phil. 2:1–11, is not an end in itself. Not humility as such, not the virtue of humility, is commended in the exhortation to have the same mind among ourselves as is in Christ Jesus. What is commended is the humiliation or humility in which we all look to the interests of others and not just our own. Similarly, in Romans 12, when he begins by exhorting us to offer our bodies as a living, holy, and acceptable sacrifice to God, Paul has directly in view the understanding of life in the Christian community as the life of many members in one body.|

The third main voice in the New Testament, that of John, should also be at least remembered: "We know that we have passed out of death into life, because we love the brethren" (1 John 3:14). "By this we know love, that he laid down his life for us; and we ought to lay down our lives for the brethren" (3:16). "If God so loved us, we also ought to love one another" (4:11). "God is love, and he who abides in love abides in God, and God in him" (4:16). "He who does not love his brother whom he has seen, cannot love God whom he has not seen. And this commandment we have from him, that he who loves God should love his brother also" (4:20f.). We have this commandment from him. There can be no doubt that it is the command of Jesus, who directs us away from ourselves to God—this is the sacrifice—and to our neighbors or fellows—this is the point or relation of the sacrifice. In passing we recall that the same point and relation of sacrifice may sometimes be seen in the Old Testament witness as well, as in Amos 5:21ff., which calls for the replacement of sacrifice by the justice and righteousness shown to neighbors or fellow Israelites.

Let us now try to elucidate what we have as yet only stated by means of the biblical witness, namely, that the claim of God the Reconciler is concretely the claim of our neighbor or fellow. We have seen that the command of God the Creator, the apparently simple command: "Live the life that God has given," must ultimately and primarily be interpreted to mean that we are commanded to have faith, i.e., to seek the demanded goodness in the goodness of the demanding God himself.[140] In so doing we have understood God as not only the Creator but also the Reconciler. In seeking to understand ourselves as believers we have had to see that we confront God not merely with some imperfection, as those who do not fully keep his command, but rather as rebels and opponents; that our action is not just insufficient but sinful. And we could

[140]See pp. 246.

understand the goodness of the demanding God, which faith grasps and clings to as if it were its own, only as inconceivable grace and mercy. What constitutes the goodness of our own life-act is the righteousness of Christ to which nothing on our side corresponds or comes near. Has the command been canceled? Or has it changed? No, it is still in force and it is still the same, just as God himself is still the same. But for us who have now to understand the Lawgiver (God) as our Reconciler it has acquired a new origin and a new content. The new origin and content of the command are stated in the name of Jesus Christ. The same God who has given us life also gives us Christ. And if we had first to listen to what he commanded in giving us life, we have now to listen to what he commands in giving us Christ. These are not two different things. But they are different in our ears and for our concepts, which are not God. We have thus to consider them separately. What God has given us with our life is our I, our own human existence. We are commanded by the command of the Creator to exist, to be ourselves in our own act, to live the life that we are given in free decision as the life that we are given by God. This gift and this command are in force and the course of ethical reflection can never evade this starting point. But Christ is also given to us as the goodness of God which graciously and mercifully stands in for our own totally deficient goodness and which, in faith, but only in faith, we grasp as our own goodness. This interceding goodness of God, however, is quite different from our own existence. It is so different that we have to recognize that our own existence is questioned and judged by it.

We confront this goodness as sinners, and if it sets us up instead of destroying us, if it stands in for us, this means that it stays over against us, that as it is spoken to us it must be heard by us as God's Word and not viewed by us as a quality of our existence. This hearing is faith. As we are here given something different from our own life, something totally different is commanded of us. Faith is act, and therefore, we have said, it is obedience or subjection to the understood command of the Creator. But if it is obedience to God in Christ, to the God who in his grace and mercy himself intervenes for us, it is clear that being oneself, living one's own life, etc., can no longer be regarded as the content of the command. If we were to insist on fulfilling only the command of the Creator and thus seeking goodness only in the richest, deepest, and strongest living of our own life, we should only show thereby that we have not really paid attention to the command of our Creator. We cannot think through this command without being led to the conclusion that this command is also that of the Reconciler. It reaches its climax as the command of faith. In faith, however, we see that we are judged and that our righteousness lies only in the alien righteousness of Christ which comes to us from outside, and which cannot be seen but can only be heard as the Word that is spoken to us. Thus the command is not now given to us with life itself. It is not just the command to live. The command is now given to us as law. God speaks with us now from that alien place which lies outside us and confronts us. As law the command is now an alien determination of our existence from outside. Our existence as such is not now the revelation of the command nor is it its content. We have now to seek both outside us, as the concept of law tells us. The command is not in us; it comes to us. And the affirmation by act which the command requires of us is not now in any sense the affirmation of ourselves, but the affirmation of a claim which comes to us and which differs from that which is posited with our existence. The law of faith is Christ. In and by Christ, God himself now commands us and Christ himself is now the command of God. In Christ, God's goodness stands in for our totally deficient goodness. Christ takes our place. Christ is the goodness of God which confronts us and which is promised by grace. As Christ comes, the command comes to us. It is no longer in ourselves. And Christ's claim differs from our own claim. The command requires of us its affirmation by act.|

Christ! But we have always said emphatically: *Jesus* Christ, the man Jesus of Nazareth who is the Word of God. In the power of his deity, but as true man, he interceded for us and is the Word of God's free goodness toward us. Again in the power of his deity but as true man he is also the command of God. Our obligation to God has been concretely fulfilled by this man and is in force. This assures to the command the character of law, the character of otherness, strangeness, and supremacy. Hence the command of the Creator can be understood only when it is understood as the command of faith. That the command is man in Christ determines first that its Whence, the place from which we receive it, stands irremovably over against us. A Thou speaks here in unavoidable distinction from our I. Any inversion, any exchange of roles, any understanding of the law as self-posited, is ruled out when this *man* is the law. If in a naked God (*Deus nudus*) we can and must finally and supremely see our own reflection, and if in the order (*sic jubeo*) of his command we can and must finally and supremely see the will (*sic volo*) of our own decision,[141] the incarnate God (*Deus incarnatus*) is as such the other who, as he draws near, as he is present with us, as he may even become one with us, is always the other, so that his command is always an alien command that comes to us from outside. This humanity of God's command also determines its content. This man Jesus of Nazareth, like every other person, does something definite and unique. As he does this, God speaks through him to whom he wills to speak and to whom he gives ears to hear this Word. His specific act is thus the content of the law of God, of the claim that is made on us. But this act, ambivalent at first for a general scrutiny which is neutral regarding the question of faith or unbelief, is his way to the cross, which for faith is

---

[141]Cf. Juvenal, *Satire* 6, 223: *Hoc volo, sic jubeo: sit pro ratione voluntas.*

unequivocally the divine goodness of a sacrifice, of a suffering and obedience, whose necessity is grounded, not in the existence of Jesus himself, but in his full turning to the others, the many, whose existence is sinful. In this determination, on the way to the cross, or rather on the way to this sacrifice of his for the salvation of many, Jesus of Nazareth is this man. If in this determination he is the law of God, this being the point of his "Follow me," as the New Testament has reminded us, then this means three things for our understanding of the content of this law, of the claim that is made on us in Christ.

1. The bearer of the goodness of God to me, and, since I myself am not good, the bearer of goodness in general, is *another man*, a man who is definitely distinct from me. This involves a unique concretion of the knowledge of our sin and of God's grace. It also involves, as we are forced to say, a decisive test of whether our corresponding confession of sin is genuine. That God is good, that we are bad, and that we have to expect all that is good from God, is not too difficult to admit in a general and abstract way. But things are different when this relation is concrete in a relation between man and man, as it undoubtedly is between Christ and us. This man stands in my place as one who is good, as I am not. If his goodness becomes mine, it is because and to the extent that he grants it to me. If he does grant it to me, this means that I myself do not have it, that I need it, that I have to seek it with him who himself is only a man. In relation to Christ it is not at all self-evident that we should not reject this situation, that we should not refuse to give to a man this position in relation to ourselves, even though in general we do not dispute our sinfulness and need before God. But if we take this course we obviously show that we do not know what sin or grace is, that in reality, on both counts, we have not yet noted the decisive thing in our relation to God as well, and precisely to God. |

Let us be more specific. Granted that we are willing to come to terms with this situation in relation to the man Jesus, we are still inclined to tell ourselves, and to find comfort in the fact, that this concretion is an exception. We are obviously very different in relation to all other people, and especially to those with whom we are directly confronted in our lives. I see, of course, that some others are more or less kindly disposed to me. But which of them has in my place a goodness that I do not have? Which of them has to give me what I lack and what I can seek only with him? Though I owe many things to others, am I not, in relation to all of them, one who also has and gives? I believe I see them, too, suffering and trying to obey, but how can that be a sacrifice for me like the sacrifice of Christ? Are not their suffering and obeying a need of their own existence, as mine are? Do they not suffer and obey as sinners, as I do, so that, like me, they are finally concerned about their own need and not mine? Is it not true that many of them are not the bearers of any goodness at all for me, but bearers of the common curse that lies upon everyone, so that I will be able to see in them nothing but human sin and folly and weakness? Have not most of them turned away from me in indifference, so that they are revelations of the dreadful or uplifting truth that I am left to my own devices? Is not the saying: "God helps those who help themselves,"[142] the conclusion that I have to draw finally from my encounter and life together with all others? We are justified in putting these questions, but only as those who have not yet heard the law of Christ. If we let these questions and the statements that lie behind them be our final word, we simply show that even and precisely in relation to Christ our knowledge of sin and grace, while it may be felt and stated very strongly, is basically defective and has not yet become real knowledge. If we really see this one man Christ standing in our place, then over against this man we are really needy, and inevitably the concretion extends further and becomes even more serious. For inevitably we know that others are different, and our own relation to them is different, from what we first stated and believed to be true.

It should be remembered that the full turning to us which may be seen in Christ is not in fact a manifest truth but a very hidden one. All of us might see the way of Jesus of Nazareth to the cross without seeing anything of this turning. Who tells us that a sacrifice for us takes place here? Who tells us that someone is not suffering for his own sin here? Has he not lived and died "in the likeness of sinful flesh" (Rom. 8:3)? Who can force me, in the light of his appearing, to seek God's goodness only in him and not in myself? Who can guarantee that even in relation to this crucified man I am not finally and permanently left to my own devices? Does he really say to me: "I did this for you,"[143] or does he say: "God helps those who help themselves"? No one, is the answer, no one can convince us but the eternal God himself who here in act, in concealment, became flesh. How else can it be since he really did become flesh? It is revelation, faith, when our relation to Christ differs from our relation to all others. But when it does, when the hiddenness in which this man is in fact the bearer of God's goodness is his disclosure as such, when our relation to him is such that we no longer seek all goodness in ourselves but in him, then undoubtedly this involves an alteration in the way in which we see all other people and our relation to them. It is not as though, at a stroke, all others become Christ to us (it is

---

[142]A proverb.

[143]Zinzendorf wrote the words: "I suffered this for you, what have you done for me?" below a picture of Christ by the Italian painter Domenico Feti; cf. E. Beyreuther, *Der junge Zinzendorf*, Marburg 1957, p. 169; also A.G. Spangenberg, "Leben Zinzendorfs" in *N.L. von Zinzendorf, Materialien und Dokumente*, ed. E. Beyreuther et al., 2 vols., Hildesheim/New York 1971, p. 99.

better to be sparing in our use of this occasional formula of Luther's).[144] It is not as though we are in a position with Novalis[145] suddenly to find long-lost brethren at least in his disciples, i.e., in others who believe with us. The noted concealment of the neighbor as a bearer of the divine goodness is in fact very deep. Surprisingly, it might be that not infrequently it is deepest of all in the so-called disciples of Jesus, who can pose the most difficult of all riddles for us. We do not know very well the concealment in which Christ himself is the other who takes my place if we think that anything is self-evident in this regard between ourselves and others, no matter who they are or how strong their faith is.

Nevertheless, it is truly not for nothing that God bears *human* features in his revelation. These are ineffaceably specific, nonrecurrent, and absolutely unique features. But they are human features. For all the particularity which marks off the way of Jesus from all other human ways, for all the mystery of deity by which it is surrounded, his way is a human way. If this way is the truth, if the face of God may be seen in these features, then it is not impossible, but fundamentally necessary, that the features and ways of others, of our own fellows, who certainly cannot be mistaken for Christ, should become for us an obscure reflection of his features and ways. He who was God's eternal Word, but was a fellowman and not an angel or a star, having assumed our humanity, our human nature, fundamentally reveals—whether we see and hear it or not is another question—each of our fellows to be a question, a promise, a supremely living reminder of *his* humanity. One cannot say that the revelation of Christ is the revelation of the fellowman in general. But one has to say that by this revelation the fellowman—not each person in general but the one that stands over against me—can and must and will become for me a witness, a messenger, a reminder and confirmation of revelation, of Christ himself. We cannot reinterpret God's incarnation in Christ as a general incarnation of God, but we have to take it seriously as an illumination by Christ's incarnation of those who confront us. As they confront me, so also the man Jesus Christ confronts me: in the same concealment in which at first and on its own the eye sees only sin, as in all others. The unheard-of process to which we must agree if the needy fellow who stands over against me is really to be the bearer of God's goodness is the same as that which in faith takes place between me and Christ. Just as it would be staggering if this person were to be in a position to say to me today: "Your sins are forgiven you," so it is staggering that Christ does in fact say this to me [cf. Mark 2:5 par.]. What actually takes place between Christ and me is

---

[144]Cf. WA 7, 35, 32ff.; 7, 66, 25ff.
[145]F. von Hardenberg (1772–1801), *Geistliche Lieder* (1799), no. 5, v. 5: "My country is where I have him, and every gift falls like a legacy into my hand, and I find long-lost brethren in his disciples."

not, as we think, less surprising, but much more surprising than all that might take place between a fellowman and me in this regard. We do not exaggerate if we say with Isaiah 53:3 that he was the most despised and least esteemed of men. The original light of God in Christ is not less but more hidden than the reflection of it in the life of the one who confronts me, so that if we neither can nor will see the latter, how can it be true that we have seen the former?

Whether or not we see and understand the image of Christ in our neighbors—as Matthew 25 states unequivocally—is what decides whether our seeing and understanding of Christ is authentic or whether it is perhaps that of a naked God (*Deus nudus*). Seeing the image of Christ in neighbors, of course, is by no means easy. All that might be argued against it is true. Neighbors are only partly the image of Christ, or not at all. Indeed, they may even be bearers of the common curse for us. I have, perhaps, good reason to assume that I may be more, and give more, to them than they to me. I have no reason to regard them as bearers of a good thing that I really lack. It may be that they cannot finally help me. Yet for all the hiddenness with which they confront me, there can be no denying the image of Christ, the enlightenment that comes where Christ is, the possibililty of Christ, which, since and with the way of Jesus from Bethlehem to Golgotha, has found a place on this dark earth. Their hiddenness cannot make it impossible that they should be Christ's messengers to me.

They may be preoccupied with themselves. They may not have anything to do with me. They may come under consideration only as recipients of my own possible goodness. They may be great sinners compared with whom I am a saint. If I still have to see in them the least of the Lord's brethren and find in their dubious humanity a reminder of Christ's humanity, what can and should this mean for me? With or without any pleasure or conviction on my part, my judgment on them must be reversed and I must believe without seeing that, not in my own good heart and clever head but out there in these others, my good is to be sought. I stand like a beggar in front of these poor people who are perhaps a thousandfold poorer than I am. I must seek my good among them. I am referred to them—not on account of themselves (I may think of them what I must and may) but on account of the image of Christ, and to that extent on account of themselves too. The first thing that has to be said about the law of Christ is obviously that, in this matter of the good, it points us away from ourselves and it points us specifically to others whom we may see to be caught in the bondage of sin as we are, and perhaps worse than we are, but in whom, as those who bear a human face that differs from ours, we have to see, for all their great sinfulness, the image of Christ.

It is surely plain that this implies something other and more than the respect for life of which we spoke in the chapter on the command of creation. A. Schweitzer rendered a great and significant service to theological ethics when he discovered this principle and stressed it so emphatically.[146] But it would be an error to make it the common denominator of all theological ethics. Respect for the life of others is demanded because I *myself* live. In the deepest sense I accept and prove myself when I honor, protect, cherish, and care for the life of others. Respect for life is not the respect for a true transcendent which is appropriate when we are judged and need grace. Respect for life does not yet know the difficult truth that the real other, the real transcendent, the alien Thou, is man. The command of the Reconciler, which puts our own life under judgment and grace, orders us to look away from our own life and, in commitment rather than respect, not to look at the life of others—for what shall we see there that we do not know only too well from our own life—but to turn from the human I to the divine *Thou*, i.e., to *Christ*, who in our place has the good that we lack, who alone can give it to us, and to whom we are simply directed. Yet looking at Christ, in whom the divine Thou meets us as man, I can see nothing but those in encounter and fellowship with whom my life is lived, ⌐in whom⌐ the Thou, if not the divine Thou, truly meets me.

Not the divine Thou? No, but how do I know that I am open to the divine Thou in the man Jesus Christ if I am closed to the human, the only too human Thou that meets me out there? How do I know that this *human* Thou will not remind me of the *divine* Thou of the man Jesus Christ? Do I not have to realize and assume and expect that the human Thou is set before me for this purpose? If I do not live by what I am in myself, but by what I am in relation to this man Jesus Christ, this primary relationship of life—this is now the issue and not my life—has to become concrete in the secondary relationship of life in which I stand to the other, to my neighbor who is not to be equated with Christ. If it does not become concrete here, how can it be true? In Christ we are commanded to take the secondary relationship very seriously for the sake of the primary relationship, so seriously that while we receive our justification, the forgiveness of sins, and the goodness that we lack and have to receive, only in that primary relationship to Christ, we are still not to seek it outside but inside the secondary relationship, so that we know that we are bound, not now to the life of the other, but rather—and this is much more—to the alien human Thou as the messenger of the divine Thou of the man Jesus Christ. This turning away from and away to is the content of the command.

2. The definition of the law of God as the law of Christ, as the law of following Christ's humanity, means that God's goodness is shown to us, and is made a norm, as a human goodness which is unrestrictedly and

---

[146]Cf. pp. 139ff.

unhesitatingly opened up and addressed and offered to others. This man, Jesus of Nazareth, is good in such a way that he intends and affirms and wills others and not himself. The revelation of God in Christ, the sacrifice of Jesus of Nazareth, is, of course, an act; indeed it is *the* great act of the self-assertion of God, of the establishment of his sovereignty over human sin. As we may calmly say in spite of Ritschl,[147] it is the act of the outpouring of his wrath on all human unrighteousness and insubordination [cf. Rom. 1:18]. In Christ, specifically, we are placed under the judgment of God, for Christ is in all seriousness our Judge, and faith in *him* includes in all seriousness an awareness of our fallenness and lostness. Yet even and precisely in his self-assertion in the revelation of his sovereignty and wrath, God is totally different from us. For he does not simply assert himself by willing to be good in and for himself, by separating himself in his goodness from us who are not good, by willing to be good alone and to let us who are not good fall, by willing to be the light which triumphantly differentiates itself from our darkness and sets itself in contrast to it. That would be the naked God of our sinful imagination but it is not the incarnate God who encounters us in faith as the real God. That would be human, all too human goodness, and not real goodness but its opposite. |

It is thus that *we* think we can lay hold of goodness and roll it up and represent it in ourselves. In so doing we make goodness an instrument of our pride and a weapon of our mercilessness. We use it in the fight for existence, so that if all else fails we can at least be in the right against others, even if only in our own eyes. We are good, and the inner characteristic of our goodness in relation to others is that we are better than they are. What would human goodness be without the motivating power of the comparative? Human goodness always lives a little, and often totally, by the greater lack of human goodness, i.e., the lack of it among others, in contrast to which our own smaller lack of it can pretend to be good and feel calm and comfortable and secure. This is true even and perhaps most of all when we seem to be totally and perhaps very seriously and passionately devoted to others. Our goodness has need of their lack of it. Where would we be if this were suddenly to disappear and with it the substance and foil of our goodness? This is the secret of the failure which at the last usually accompanies all human goodness. We may not see it but others do. The unsaved, over against whom we regard ourselves as the saved, note that finally we are not concerned about them but that we ourselves, in our goodness, are the object of our concern and affirmation and will. This is why our anger at the wickedness in the world and our pathetic fight against it are powerless. This is why no one takes them seriously in the long run. The revelation of God in Christ is designed to tell us that there are reasons for the

---

[147]Cf. A. Ritschl, *Die christliche Lehre von der Rechtfertigung und Versöhnung,* vol. 2, Bonn 1874, p. 154.

frequently lamented failure of the good in its battle with the bad. In this sign the good cannot conquer. This all-too-human goodness of ours is our sin, and it is worse and more dangerous than what we label as wicked in ourselves and others. This so-called wickedness is only the visible and less harmful exterior of the real evil. The revelation of God in Christ is designed to tell us that the God who sided with the good as we do, whose goodness would be, like ours, a goodness that triumphs by being self-enclosed, self-separated, and self-differentiated, would not be God at all but the devil. The devil is not as abhorrent and wicked as we like to think for our own comfort and security. His "you shall be as gods" [Gen. 3:5] does not suggest a depraved figure but one who is very respectable and eminent and religious and moral, ⌐who is deficient only at the one point that he wills to be good (and is good) in and for himself,¬ whose one lack is a lack of love, who, because he lacks this one thing, is, as Paul says, nothing [cf. 1 Cor. 13:2], and who in this very nothingness is the devil.|

But God, God in Christ, God revealed and incarnate, is not good *for himself*. This is the divinity and the reality of his goodness. While he maintains his goodness against sin, rebellion, and the fall, [his goodness] is not the goodness that triumphs by being self-enclosed, self-separated, and self-differentiated. God is really good *for us*. He is good wholly and utterly in his turning to us who are not good. He is thus the light that shines in the darkness. He shines by illuminating, for he is real light. He differentiates himself by elevating. He is strong in carrying. He says No in saying Yes. He judges by pardoning.|

In this turning and relationship to us he reveals himself in Jesus of Nazareth. And in it he is our law, the claim that is made on us. For there is no passage in the New Testament in which we find Jesus out at the front with an outwardly active and aggressive human goodness fighting to put things right. Jesus does not stand on that pretended frontier where a smaller lack of goodness can regard itself as good in the face of a larger lack of goodness. He removes this frontier. He also removes the frontier that separates God's goodness from the lack of it which characterizes us all. He proclaims the forgiveness of sins. He opens the closed door of righteousness from within instead of rejoicing at being within and hiding himself behind the door. He brings the unrighteous in instead of talking to them through the closed door and taking pleasure in their being outside. No one is told that he is a sinner, neither the Pharisee, who is recognized to be at least a better sinner, nor the publican, who is notoriously a worse sinner [cf. Luke 18:9–14]. Sin is the serious presupposition of all of us, and of all of us equally seriously, when he calls us to repentance, but for Jesus himself it is not for a single moment the presupposition with which he charges us. It is instead the question to which he gives the answer, the simple answer, namely, that he is present for these better-or-worse sinners, that he seats himself at the table of both the Pharisee and the publican, that he does not regard his being like God as booty, as a treasure that he must guard and handle frugally [cf. Phil. 2:6], but that with the Word of forgiveness, let the seed of this Word fall where it may, on the path, on stones, among thorns, or on good ground [cf. Matt. 13:3−23 par.], he lavishes it on the unworthy, on those who do not have any of the presuppositions for sharing in God's goodness. He thus spends his life, pours it out, and finally pours out his very blood for the hardened, the dejected and the hostile: not asking who they really are; not asking what they are doing; not asking what he will get out of it; not asking anything, but simply acting for those who do not deserve it, turning to them as the Lamb of God which really takes away the *sin* of the world, which really *takes* it *away* [cf. John 1:29]. This, then, is the divine goodness in the human goodness of Jesus of Nazareth: goodness which this man does not for a moment possess without giving it away. We do not see him rich; we see him richly sharing. We do not see him on a height; we see him descending to us from a height, from the highest height of all, he who is from above coming down to us who are below. We do not see him differentiating himself from the wicked except as he is in process of removing the differentiation. This attitude of Jesus to sinners is decisive.|

The sin of our fellows always gives us plausible grounds for separating from them and withdrawing into ourselves and our own uprightness. Again we *need* the sin of our fellows. We live by it. Even when we bewail it or them, even when we turn to them with our own efforts to improve and teach and train them, we accuse them. Sin interests us, not because we take joy in evil but very naively for our own sake. We need it as a foil. We are never more intensely concerned about ourselves than when we are concerned about the sin of our neighbors. In fact there is no stronger revelation of our own lack of goodness, of our own sin, than this far-from-good attitude to the sin of others. *Moral* sin, the sin of our closed goodness which is no goodness, is the real sin, and again the *moral* devil is the *true* and *proper* devil.|

About the worst that can happen is when we go further and see in Jesus a moral sinner like ourselves. Naturally we do this to evade the command that we ourselves should also be completely different. We will not see that his goodness is not one that is confined to him, that justifies him, and that distinguishes him from the wicked world around as noble, helpful, and good,[148] but one that streams forth continually, imparting and giving itself. Here we have a fellowship with God that has nothing whatever to do with the lonely greatness of the religious genius, but is present as a Word to the many who are neither religious nor geniuses. Here we have a purity of heart that does not consist of differentiation from others, from the weak and impure, by a specially keen conscience or powerful will, but of a lack of any reservations in his heart against

[148]See n. 107.

even the weakest and the most impure. Here we have an obedience of suffering which we cannot for a moment equate with the most noble martyrdom, since the conflict is not for a bloody crown for his own head—the supreme goal of ethical direction in the early church[149]—but he offers himself for others as a priest and thus brings a pure offering [cf. Heb. 9:14, 26ff]. The true deity in Christ's humanity, his sinlessness, is not that he lived an angelic life, even as a Thomas Aquinas very definitely maintained,[150] but that he was free from the moral sin in which original sin, the sin of Adam, is constantly renewed in all of us, to which we unavoidably fall victim even in our best moments, and in which precisely the best part of us has the greatest share. |

Thus the worst and true denial of the deity of Christ—every revolt in dogmatics rests on a revolt in ethics—is when we deny that Christ has come to seek and to save the lost [cf. Luke 19:10], when we change the divine goodness that is at issue here into a human goodness, when we change the seeking and savings of the lost into the image of our own supposed improving, or arrogant and impotent desire to improve others, in which we do not affirm them but in the strongest and most refined and incorrigible manner affirm ourselves. It is no wonder—when the cloak falls the duke must follow[151]—that we then want to know nothing more about the true deity of Christ. ⌐When justification by faith was no longer understood, christology could not be understood either. For the moral distinction that was still ascribed to Jesus, the predicate of true deity was in fact no longer needed. Christ is true God only when he is the Savior from sin.¬ We should not forget that with the totality described in Luke 15 he went after the lost coin and the lost sheep and became the brother (but not the awkward elder brother) of the lost son. We should not forget that any moralistic reinterpretation of Jesus is no less than a denial of his crucifixion, for concretely the scandal and offense that Israel took at his messianic claim was that this not only *speaks* about the sin of men and the forgiveness of sin, but that sin was actually *forgiven* here, that the barriers between the good and the bad fell, that a Savior of sinners was seen instead of the expected moral pharisaic Savior; that from him the best found only forgiveness, and the publicans and harlots found forgiveness too, and the command is that all reckoning with God to one's own advantage, and the disadvantage of one's neighbor, must cease. We should not forget that we ourselves are lost if we will not have him as the Savior of sinners, if, in the words of

---

[149]Cf. Cyprian, *Ad Fortunatum; De Opera et Eleemosynis; Epistolae* X, 5; LXXIII, 21; Tertullian, *De corona militis; Scorpiace;* also Clement of Alexandria, *Stromata* IV, 9; Origen, *Exhortatio ad Martyrium.*

[150]Cf. *Acta Sanctorum, Martii,* e Joanne Bollando S.I. Colligi feliciter coepta, Antwerp MDCLXVIII (Brussels 1966): *De S. Thomae Aquinate Doctore Angelico, ordinis praedicatorum,* MCCLXXIV, 7 Martii, pp. 655–745.

[151]Cf. F. Schiller, *Die Verschwörung des Fiesco zu Genua* (1783), Act V, Scene 16: "When the purple falls, the duke must follow."

James 1:5, we will not have God in him as the God who gives to all of us generously and without reproaching us. If we were to fall into the hands of the absolute God of our pious or impious imagination, we could only perish and go to hell, for this God is really the God of *this* world [cf. 2 Cor. 4:4].

If we are ready to leave Jesus as he is, if we are ready to have him as the Savior of sinners, and if we know that we really live by forgiveness, then we must also have him as our law. On this second side, then, the other, the neighbor, the fellow human, comes before us as the authority that we cannot bypass if we are to know what we are commanded: not the *ideal* fellow human, not the one in whom we see ourselves again, who is there in virtue or in vice to confirm that we are right, but the *real* fellow human who will not serve this kind of end, who lives his own life, and who displays himself rather as one who needs us: the real fellow human who is also undoubtedly, as we detect, a great sinner, and who is thus a great annoyance to us every day. What am I to do about the claim of this annoying person who thus confronts me? Shall I use the fact that he is annoying, the fact of his sin, as an excuse to break free from him? Shall I use it in a crude or refined way to give myself the right not to be used by him, but triumphantly to rejoice against him in my own goodness? This is the option that we usually choose. Or shall I see that he needs me because of that in which he is so annoying, that I have to be there precisely for him in his sinfulness, that he claims me as a sinner? This is the option of Jesus. This is how he heard the claim of his neighbor and was obedient to it.

We are not Christ. We never shall be. Hence it is only with great caution and reserve that we can say that we are commanded to be Christ to our neighbor.[152] We must not deceive ourselves even when we see very clearly what is commanded. We live our own lives, bad and good. We are concerned about ourselves and our own justification. We are at best good only in that shuttered and reserved manner. Even fellowship with God is for us a supreme and secret image of our self-love. Even purity of heart, to the extent that we have such, is for us, above all, a differentiation from the impure. When we suffer and obey, we sacrifice only to save ourselves and to make satisfaction for ourselves. We use the sin of our neighbors as a pretext and means to free ourselves with good reason and in the best way from their pressing claim. Our goodness is human goodness. In it we are sinners—at best moral and devout sinners—but still sinful sinners. Again, then, we cannot turn and be pledged to our fellows in the true and primary way in which Christ is. We will as little reveal the Savior of sinners to others as we can reveal him to ourselves unless he *himself* does it. In what we are commanded by the Savior of sinners—let us be under no illusions—there can be no repetition or replacement of his action, of his merciful condescension to

---

[152]Cf. n. 144.

⌐the lost⌐ and his presence here below among the lost. We cannot ignore our neighbors worse than when we forget that. We cannot do anything to provoke more aversion and hardness than we do when we secretly plan—the gestures, posture, and tone of voice are familiar—to play the Lord Jesus to them. We cannot remember enough that we can meet our neighbors truly and honestly only as lost ourselves, i.e., exactly as we are, and not in the role of saviors. Only one comes down to all of us to save, and only one can meet us as Savior. |

In accordance with our limitations, however, there is demanded of us a secondary turning and commitment to our neighbors, a human analogy of the inimitable divine original, a witness to the Savior of sinners. What is now meant is the general witness of deed and life of which the special witness of the Word, the church's witness, can only be a particular instance: "So we are ambassadors for Christ, God making his appeal through us. We beseech you on behalf of Christ, be reconciled to God" (2 Cor. 5:19). Reconciling is the work of God's goodness. But we are commanded to be witnesses of the divine goodness to our neighbors, as we have previously heard that we must welcome and accept them as witnesses of it. The power of this witness cannot have its source in us. Witnessing needs a commission and authority which is not at our disposal and which we cannot acquire. The preacher does not control the Word of God to which he testifies. God himself must speak if man is to speak aright. Yet the witness of the preacher is required and commanded, and so, too, is that of the Christian life in general. God alone can give force to what is still the witness of sinners, at best of moral and devout sinners. God alone can cause that we who are Pharisees to the core of our being—and mostly so, perhaps, when we feel closest to the publican—can declare his unconditional goodness through our acts, the goodness which simply gives itself, undeserved and with no reproaching [James 1:5], to our wicked fellow humans as to ourselves. But how can it give itself to us if, in the movement of what is at best our pharisaic life there is not manifested this countermovement, the witness to the better righteousness [cf. Matt. 5:20] that has come to us? Forgiveness is a summons to forgive. The person who is forgiven has heard this summons and, no matter how great a Pharisee he may still be, he is the city that is set on the hill and cannot be hidden [cf. Matt. 5:14]. His action cannot take place without a recollection of that by which he lives. If this recollection is not present, he only shows that he does not yet live by it. He will see his neighbors, no matter how things may be with them, as people who like himself still wait for the same unconditional goodness with which alone there can be help for us evildoers. If he saw them otherwise, he would necessarily be waiting for some other goodness, perhaps a goodness manufactured or merited by himself. He will remember that his moral sin is his true sin for which he must show penitence in his acts, no matter how imperfect this penitence may be or how corrupted by the same poison. If there is no penitence, if there is not the slightest break in our Pharisaism, the break in which for the first time, willingly or not, we really stand alongside our neighbors, how can this true sin of ours be forgiven? I have no control over whether my action on the basis of forgiveness is confirmed by my Lord and thus becomes a true reminder of him to my neighbors. But this result is in God's hands and I have not to worry about it. What I have to do is to obey, to do what I am commanded to do, to be what I am, one who is reconciled to God, to be always ready to be told that my action seriously compromises this being of mine, but always to be ready again to obey. This means forgiving, living by forgiveness. |

My life in all its most unsaviorlike orientation to itself is now set under the Savior's command that it be fundamentally open to others in and with their sin. By what right may I seal myself off against them in my own goodness? By what right may I confirm and strengthen myself by comparison with them? By what right may I think of them, or talk with and about them, or act toward them, or live with them, except on the basis of forgiveness? By what right may I encounter them in all my impurity except as Christ encountered me in his purity? This right is taken from me. This ground has been removed from under my feet. If I place myself on it I place myself on empty air and fall. We fall every day and every hour but we have to realize that this is really falling, that we cannot stand there. We can stand only as we go, namely, as we go on the way of Jesus. The thing in my action that stands in God's eyes—I myself can only *believe* that I stand, since what I *see* is falling—is my going on this way. But this way leads directly away from myself to where what is puzzling and hidden and inconceivable stands, the neighbor who is my brother or sister: not a foil against which I am happily shown to be different, not an object of missionary and educational activity, not a pupil under instruction who is just what I need to display my mastery, but my brother or sister whose claim I must hear, not although, but just because, he or she is so annoying to me, because it is the claim of such a great sinner into whose power I have fallen in my own virtue or vice and to whom I am under obligation. If this is not so, I have not heard the superabundant Word that is spoken to myself.

3. We have said that in Jesus Christ the goodness of God meets us as a human goodness that is open to others and turns toward them. It shows me these neighbors for the first time to be neighbors, brothers and sisters, from whose existence I can as little abstract myself as from my own. It shows them to be the authority in relation to which alone I really exist. What I may think and know about others is certainly that Jesus regards them as worthy objects of God's goodness, that he sees good reason, and knows himself to be called, to turn to them. To them! I do not see him first turning to me but to others: to the Syro-Phoenician woman [cf. Mark 7:24–30 par.], to the centurion of Capernaum [cf. Matt. 8:5–13 par.], to the paralytic [cf. Mark 2:1–12 par.], and to all

the rest, and I can only put myself, or thrust myself, among these if I am to see that he turns to me too. This takes place in the act of faith that I can let what was said to others be said to *me* too, to me *too*. It is impossible to forget that I am only added, that I am invited to the feast to which others were first invited [cf. Luke 14:15−24 par.]. From what was said earlier it might have seemed that we were more than this, that we were not just added to others as recipients of the grace of God, that our being added was the first and true and final concern. Is not our obligation to our neighbor perhaps imposed and commanded solely in our own best interest, because we cannot have God if we are not ready to have our brothers and sisters too, because we must become necessary to them and they to us as reminders of our primary life-relationship to Christ?

It would be a gross misunderstanding of these ideas to construe them in such a way that we are bound to our neighbors because and insofar as we need them for ourselves in the best and deepest sense. This would be tantamount to saying that ultimately we do not need them; that for us they and our commitment to them are finally no more than a means to the end, a stage on the way, a means that can be dropped once the goal is attained; that they are only transitorily our brethren; and that there is a final hidden place where we can again live our own life as such when our brotherly duty to them has been discharged. There can be no doubt that so far as the eye can see our commitment to our neighbors does in fact have this character. But there can also be no doubt that to this extent it is not real commitment. For if neighbors have become for us real messengers of Christ they cannot have ceased to be this nor can we have ceased to be the same for them if we have once been it. If we really have to fulfill the mutual function referred to, then, no matter how secondary it may be, it confers upon us—this is an important element of truth in the Roman Catholic concept of the priesthood—an indelible character and, in an original and ultimate way, which can neither be ignored earlier nor set aside later, we are set in an order. From the points of view discussed thus far it cannot seriously be said that we are pledged and committed to our neighbors only insofar as we need them for our own sake. We ourselves are not ourselves without them. We shall have to speak about this in more detail. |

The neighbor is really the first to whom God's goodness comes, and through him I am then added as a second. I do not just need him if God's goodness is also to come to me. He is there from the very outset. We cannot forget that we do not ever stand in a direct relationship to Jesus Christ if we take his humanity seriously. His presence, even in that mystical union, in that life of Christ in us, is indirect presence, presence in the witness of scripture and the church. We hear his Word in and through that of the prophets and apostles. As this original witness awakens faith and is passed on in faith, it constitutes the church. We believe within the church, i.e., at second hand, not at first hand. We do not hear Jesus Christ speak with us directly. When we *really* hear him and really hear *him*, we hear him through the word of others, which by his Holy Spirit acquires the power of truth of his own Word. This is how his Word has come to us and must always come to us. We thus receive God's gift by indirect impartation—by doubly indirect impartation, we even have to say, to the extent that Christ's humanity entails its concealment and this carries with it a second concealment when it comes to us by way of others. This twofold concealment is for us its appropriate disclosure. It is the way by which the gift of the eternal God can come to us who live in time. Hence it is not an obstacle that we want to be removed. It is a means, a necessary mediation. Only in this indirectness are we directly related to Christ and in him to God. |

This indirectness of our reconciliation to God has to be taken seriously. There is mystical *union* with Christ only in his mystical *body*. Christ lives in us insofar as we live in his church. We are thus brought up against the concept of the church and we shall have to come back to it more expressly in the next section.[153] This concept does not mean that the subject of faith has now suddenly become a plural, a collective "we." In our use of the word "community," which has become so fashionable today because it reminds us of the civil community, the Russian "Mir," etc., we have to exercise some care. "The church believes" cannot be simply translated: "We believe." It was for good reason that all the great confessions of the early church began with the singular "Credo" and not the plural "Credimus," even though they were meant to be confessions of the united church. Only Christ himself could say "Credimus" in the name of all of us, for as the Head of the body he alone is its unity and he alone can speak as such for the collective plurality of his members [cf. Col. 1:18; Eph. 4:15f.]. The collective "we" as the subject of faith is to be rejected just as definitely and for just the same reason as the collective "I," as which the Roman pope claims to be speaking when he makes an *ex cathedra* announcement. Faith is never a collective act. It is the decision that is required of *me* and God's decision in relation to *me*. If this decision is to have a symbol it will be that I *fold* my hands and not—all honor to the summer-solstice bonfire, but it has nothing whatever to do with faith—that I join them with the hands of others in a chain.[154] Faith is not contact with an electrical current and the church is not such a current. In strict personal solitude faith is my being called and my answering. No one can act here on my behalf. No one can either create the call for me or even partially take away the hearing and obeying from me. To the extent that I think that another can take my place, or that by contact

---

[153]Cf. below pp. 349ff.

[154]Barth is alluding to the way in which youth groups sang songs and made a circle around the midsummer night bonfire to link their own experience of fellowship with the high point of the year.

with flesh and blood I can receive something which I would not receive otherwise, or do something which I would not otherwise do, I am a spectator in relation both to Christ and myself, and I do not really believe at all.

I believe inasmuch as I myself am claimed. But I believe within the church. That is, my primary relationship to Christ becomes concrete in the secondary relationship to my neighbor. The personal pronoun which denotes the concept of the church is not I nor We but Thou. Thou differs from We because it definitely does not mean I. It means a real other who encounters and confronts me, who neither openly nor secretly can be interpreted as I, as may happen in the case of We, in which we are next to one another but there is no confrontation, so that the I remains free and can imagine that it is at least the middle point in the circle, and perhaps very soon the connecting point of the whole. Thou assures to the claim made upon me its strangeness, strictness, and supremacy. It characterizes it as a real claim that cannot by any device be changed into a pronouncement. Naturally we are also not dealing here with a diffuse You, with confrontation by a plurality of claims. In its courtly form the You (*Ihr*) can very easily become an impersonal third person (*Sie*) that bears no reference to myself and that I can thus ignore. We and You imply that people are alongside one another without really being together. For them to be together there has to be honest confrontation. To say Thou is to bear witness that I have heard, that the other affects me. When he does, he always does so in the singular and hence in the second person singular. In the church, then, I believe that it is always the one, this one, the Thou, who becomes Christ's claim for me. "I believe within the church" means that I believe as the member of a body whose other members are all members of Christ. I thus believe concretely. My action at this moment is that of faith to the extent that it takes place in commitment to one or another member of this body and to that extent in relationship to Christ as the Head of the whole body and in unity with him. I believe concretely to the extent that my specific action at this moment, being related to Christ, takes place in this specific relationship to the Thou, in the hearing of this specific claim that is made upon me. That there is such a body with such members; that there is such a people of the Lord in which the personal pronoun Thou is so decisively important and in which a brother or sister is constantly there for me, ready and commissioned to claim me in a specific way, to speak God's Word to me—this is the miracle of the church that I believe and confess if my faith is obedience. The church is really present where this claim is made upon me and heard by me and obeyed in my action.

Let us also remember here that our fellow creatures are sinners as we are, and perhaps much greater sinners than we are. I need only charge them with their sin and I would be rid of their claim. But I would also be rid of my faith, of the forgiveness of my sins, and of Christ himself. I would have denied the miracle of the church instead of believing it. I would then be outside the church. I would be without God in the world. It is no accident that in the third article the ancient confessions linked confession of the Holy Spirit with that of the church and that of the church with that of the remission of sins. In fact, we do not have the one without the other, but the one is declared to be true only by the other. The church is the communion of saints only as a church of sinners. If we do not want to see any sinners, but to wait for saints who have the right to claim us, we simply show thereby that we have not yet resolved to let ourselves be claimed and we certainly shall not see any saints. For sinners *are* the saints, the very wonderful saints of Christ. Hence my neighbor who is a sinner, and from whom I would rather break free for this reason, has the right to claim me. His sin does not affect me, and should not do so, except to tell me that I have to be on hand for him, if, that is, I let myself be told, and am prepared to hear, that God will not let my sin affect him except in having mercy on me because of it. If my neighbor's sin does not affect me then I have no reason for breaking free from him. His claim is in force inasmuch as I am in the church and Christ died for me. This neighbor of mine is also there first. I cannot rejoice comfortably about my relationship to Christ and only then look around to see if something, and if so what, might take place in my relationship to the neighbor. The neighbor was there before me. The least brother or sister, the hungry, the thirsty, the stranger, the sick, the prisoner, the sinner from tip to toe that he is, wills that I be there for him and if I am not, then infallibly—*hic Rhodus, hic salta*[155]—I will be put with the goats on the left hand and eternally lost [cf. Matt. 25:31–46].

For if my secondary relationship to the wonderful saints of the church is not authentic, neither is my primary relationship to Christ, since he comes to me in the form of these wonderful saints of his church and not otherwise. Why should not wonderful things happen here when the church itself is a miracle, a wonder? And why should not the church be a wonder when it means my participation in reconciliation?—I know myself and yet I also know how inconceivable it is that I should be reconciled! No, I cannot evade these wonderful saints if I am not to evade Christ. And as my faith, my faith within the church, will be a new decision each new moment, as the primary relationship of my life to Christ will constantly have to take place concretely in the relationship to my neighbor, so he can never be for me a means that becomes dispensable or a station on my way that will be left behind. I stand or fall with him in my existence as one who is reconciled to God. God is always my Reconciler, the God who loves his people [cf. Deut. 33:3], as is shown in the event of the church. Always, then, I must take seriously

---

[155]From Aesop's Fable no. 203 or 203b: Someone claimed to have made a big jump in Rhodes and appealed to witnesses who had seen it. A bystander replied: "Friend, if it is true you need no witnesses. Here is Rhodes, jump here!"

the one who confronts me if it is true that God the Reconciler has taken me seriously. He has taken me so seriously that he first took my neighbor seriously and set him over against me as a proclaimer of his Word, even though wrapped in the garment of a very human claim. It is thus that I myself am taken seriously. How, then, can I slip away and not take my neighbor seriously both before and after?

Let us look back on our path thus far. In the first subsection of this section we have shown, in the form of a lengthy recapitulation of the reformed doctrine of justification, that there is a command of God from the standpoint of reconciliation, and that this command has the specific character of law. Then in the second subsection we have answered the question as to the meaning of the law. We had to clear a space for ourselves here by discussing the two romantic answers and the idealistic answer to this question, namely, the law of the God of inner and outer givens and the particularly tempting law of the God of the nongiven. In contrast to these ostensible laws we have understood the real law as the law of Christ, but this as the law of his humanity, his discipleship, as the law of self-sacrifice, as the law of the neighbor. Thus the saving command of God contradicts us by placing a Thou over against the I and in opposition to it. God binds me by binding me through and to the neighbor. The character of my act as submission to God's command is that it takes place in listening to the claim of this other. As one to whom mercy has been shown, as a sinner who has received grace, I act lawfully and not unlawfully when I act in this secondary relationship which, from my standpoint, is always the primary one. We do have a criterion when we ask: "*What* shall we do?" We are to do that which at all events means responsibility to those who confront us. We are to do that which at all events means a testimony of deed that we have heard those in whose closer or more distant spheres of life our own life is lived and who, with their own lives, from a lesser or greater distance, impinge upon the sphere of our life. We have to be answerable to them with what we do. "There is no other way to Küssnacht."[156] To say Christ is to say Thou. To say Christ is to say orientation to this Thou. To say Christ is to say commitment to this Thou. For to say Christ is to say church—in faith, but still *church*.

§12

AUTHORITY

God's command comes to me as superior direction by a specific fellowman commissioned by him. In this concrete subordination, controlled by God the Reconciler, it claims me and I have to hear it.

[156]F. Schiller, *Wilhelm Tell* (1804), Act IV, Scene 3.

1

In §11 we have pinpointed the ethical problem posed by the command of God the Reconciler. *What* shall we do? God the Reconciler binds us to our fellow humans. Hence his command entails a question that is put each moment to our action: Does it take place within this binding or not? Does it show adequate or inadequate responsibility to the claim of our neighbors? Though hidden from both their eyes and ours, God's verdict is present with our neighbors and their claim. Neither we nor our neighbors can anticipate this. God *alone* judges. But he does *judge*. Our action towards our neighbors entails responsibility, and God knows whether or not we respond, whether our action takes place within that binding or not, i.e., whether we have acted within the church as members of Christ's body, in faith, as sinners to whom grace has been shown. Even theological ethics cannot foresee God's knowledge and verdict. It cannot try to give any universal or ultimately valid description of adequate or inadequate responsibility, of action that is really bound or nonbound, good or bad, in the sense of the command of the Reconciler. As we act, God and God *alone* is our witness and God and God *alone* is our judge. Theological ethics can only state, as we have done in the preceding section, that our action will be judged by God as action in relation to our fellows, our neighbors.

But this statement can and must be made concrete. "Who is my neighbor?", the famous question runs [Luke 10:29]. How do I really stand each moment of my life in relation to my neighbor? Among the many, near and far, whom I see around me, who is the Thou to whom my I is now bound and must do what God wills within this bondage? And what precisely shall *I* do? What is *my* place within the system of human relationships that can and does change each moment? What is the place where *one* relationship is *the* relationship in which I am responsible, in which, as a Christian, I must fulfill my responsibility to the other, sacrificing my I to the claim of the Thou? The more urgently we ask this, or realize that we are asked it, the better.

If we are asking it in earnest, we presuppose two things. First, the command of Christ, if it is really his, has to be a very concrete mandate that comes home to me very directly and specifically. When God's command goes forth, it is simply but strictly a matter of *my* being summoned. The concept of the neighbor, of which we spoke earlier, was not the concept of the neighbor in general but the singular concept, with a unique and unrepeatable content, of *my* neighbor. If I have heard only of commitment to neighbors in general, then silently, as usually happens, I have changed the Thou on whom so much stress was laid into a He. I have missed the point that the reference was to *my* being bound to *my* neighbor. I have heard something very different from God's command, namely, a general and very dubious moral truth. Second, and in the same connection, the question obviously presupposes that the neighbor has to be a specific individual, that one person confronts me as the neighbor according to the divine command. This is true even though my action, as may often and even regularly happen, has consequences not only for one person but for many. This simply means that I am responsible to each one of the many as such. There is no responsibility to a group. If we see people en masse we usually act irresponsibly. Nor is there any responsibility to an idea or cause that may unite the group. We have seen that to serve ideas, if this is really possible, leads off into irresponsibility. We do not confront a cause, but people, if we really confront the command of Christ. Hence we have every reason to ask: *Who* is my neighbor? Who is *my* neighbor?

We must also remember that earlier we understood the neighbor to be the counterpart who is set over against us by Christ, representing Christ, in and with the reality of the church. We have to realize that when we ask: *Who* is *our* neighbor? God controls and decides this as he controls and decides concerning us, so that in the knowledge at issue here we have to establish how far we owe acknowledgment to the neighbor and his claim. The neighbor would not be our neighbor in the sense of the command if we wanted to know about him from any other source or in any other way than through God's Word, as whose messenger and bearer he comes to us. Through the Word of God that he speaks to us with his claim, this near or distant person becomes the neighbor to whom we are under obligation. Because God's Word has and is authority, when it causes itself to be heard, this person, without whom God will not speak it to me, becomes an authority for me. This means four things.

1. That this person is my neighbor is something that I have to accept as a necessary, unchangeable, and specific reality, with all that this implies for what I owe him. God is not capricious. It could not be just as well that this person should not be my neighbor. God could not just as well have willed that things be different. As this particular person *is* my neighbor, I have to recognize that God planned this from eternity. In this regard God's command comes to me like a well-aimed arrow aimed specifically at me. When I hear it, and each moment that I hear it, there is a specific correlation between it and me in which alone it comes to me. This is what we said in the corresponding section (§8) of the chapter on the command of God the Creator.[1] It was said then with reference to the particularity of being and nature in which I am I, in which I am myself. This particularity, the particularity of calling, is no longer at issue here. Our present concern is with the particularity of the command as law, and therefore the divine particularity, not of the self, but of the neighbor. From the standpoint of reconciliation my neighbor, and not I, is now a witness to me of the reality of the divine command. It does not now encounter me in my own being and nature, but in the authority and

[1]See p. 173.

commission with which this person meets me. A fellow human can have this authority and this commissioning power. If I were to deny this I should also be denying the law itself, and therefore Christ and my reconciliation. My reconciliation and my being put under the law are the work of one hand, as are my creaturely existence and the divine command of life. In God we have in both cases one and the same thing. God is the Lord of the church in which I am called to faith and also to obedience, to freedom in Christ and also to commitment to this least of all his brethren. The neighbor, then, is not an empty page which has still to be written upon. If I am to obey God's command, I serve this neighbor determined by God, *my* neighbor. If I do not obey God, I do not serve this particular neighbor determined by God, *my* neighbor. My obedience and disobedience to the alien law of the Reconciler are individually characterized like faithfulness or unfaithfulness to my calling in relation to the command of life. The only difference is that the individual factor is not now to be sought in myself, in my special existence as God created it, but outside me in the *other* who is *my* neighbor.

2. Since we are again dealing with the command of God, it is not for me to say who my neighbor is. I do not have to choose my neighbor, whether by illumination or deliberation. As with the knowledge of God, insight comes here without any prior insight. It consists of seeing that, prior to any illumination or deliberation on my part, the neighbor is already there, that I am already committed, adequately or inadequately, to responsibility to him, that, with him, judgment on my action is already an event. Hence I can only look ahead to the next moment, realizing that, whether I know him or not, the neighbor, the authority to which I must submit, is already present, that the court which will evaluate me is not set up by me but is already awaiting me. When we engage in ethical reflection, then, it can only be a matter of reflecting on the neighbor already determined by God, never of autonomously determining who the neighbor is. I accept this specific person as my neighbor. A neighbor chosen by us instead of recognized to be chosen by God would not be the neighbor in the sense of the command. In such a case the neighbor would go unrecognized, to the detriment of our obedience. Hence the question: Who is my neighbor? can be meaningful only if it is asked with a readiness to obey and not as a purely theoretical question. I can never see this neighbor if I try to consider him and decide on him in advance. I can see him only as he comes to me and I hear or do not hear his claim. For, faithful or unfaithful, I am always found and discovered by God before I find him. But God finds me in his church. He thus finds me through other people. This moment he undoubtedly finds me through the person whom I myself do not first distinguish as the concrete form of the law but who is distinguished by God as such.

3. It need hardly be said expressly that the determination of my neighbor is not left to chance or fate nor to the natural or historical conditions of my situation. Naturally God's command comes to me in certain natural and historical circumstances. But if we were to pursue this, we should come back again to the concept of our calling, of our own being and nature, which in its own place, along with all that belongs to humanity up to and including our mortality, we have already honored as an important element in the concept of the command of the Creator, but which we have now to leave behind us as we try to see man, not in the light of creation, but in the light of his sin and God's grace. The neighbor, as the law under which we are set, is not part of our ⌐own⌐ calling. He is the authority that confronts us in all our calling. Hence we must set aside any recollection of the natural and historical conditions in which we stand, and in which we are also led along with these specific persons, if we understand by them intermediate powers that are relatively independent of the will of God, hypostases and necessities that differ from the necessity of God. Through all the powers that apparently stand and rule between it and us, the command of God comes to us, often with them, often in opposition to them, i.e., to the image that we have of them. A neighbor determined by fate—we recall how often we are the masters of fate as well as its servants—would undoubtedly be a neighbor openly or secretly chosen by ourselves. And as such he certainly would not be my law.

4. Again no person as such has the right or competence to come before me and say: *I* am thy neighbor! *My* claim is the law that is imposed upon thee! This would be very questionable. I am not bound to man in general or as such. Even though I am in fact bound to man, man as such is not God. He can be for me only witness to the reality of God's command. He can impart to me only indirect, relative, and provisional knowledge. He can be for me only a human authority, i.e., one that is not grounded in itself but that mediates and points beyond itself. He can be for me only a messenger of Christ. He has to be marked off to be this. He has to have a commission. And I have to hear this commission if I am to hear God's command through him. Hence, as we said at the start, no man can judge the other. Here again we stand afresh at the limit and frontier of theological ethics. It is on the one side a frontier that separates teaching as such from life, even though the teaching expressly devotes itself to life and wants to be only teaching about life, as is especially true in ethics. It is also on the other side the limit that is simply set for human thought and speech as such and that thus corresponds to life only too well.

Ethics—and this is its first specific frontier as teaching—can try to describe in general how far God's command claims us and is to be heard in divinely controlled subjection to superior direction by a specific person whom God has commissioned. It can thus state that there is authority, human authority, and that submission to this authority is the formal criterion that is to be consulted in the question whether we are obedient or not. We shall have to deal with this thesis in the present section. But it cannot produce this authority, this specific person, or cause him to speak, or validate or establish his commission. This does not belong to teaching but to life. It is not ethics but an ethical event that takes place between two persons. There may be seen here in ethics a peculiar difficulty which is present in life itself, and which ethics must respect if it is in contact with real life. In life, in the ethical event itself, we are in no position to see and understand the neighbor in his mission as he is sent to us by God, i.e., fully to understand him only in his mission, and fully to understand his mission, and thus to hear God's Word directly in his claim. "The individual is ineffable," we had to say when it was a matter of our own divine determination by creation, of our own calling.[2] As God sees and understands us we do not see and understand ourselves. The Word of God that is spoken in and with our divine determination is the Word of God which is hidden in an indication and which we can hear as such but cannot repeat when it is truly spoken to us. What we can repeat, what we could thus say about our calling, was an indication of the Word of God that is spoken to us. By way of analogy we now have to say: "The neighbor is ineffable." As we never have our own calling, so we never have the call of the neighbor, human authority, in such a way that its character as divine authority may be seen directly, that we can repeat the call that we have heard exactly as we heard it, that we can indicate to others specific human claims which are also divine as such. If we could do this in life there could be, and would have to be, a corresponding teaching about life. But as there is a plain limit in life at this point, the same may necessarily be seen in teaching too.

What we really have in the call of the neighbor, what may be repeated and presented as teaching, is again an indication, witness. Hidden in the human indication of God's Word the Word itself reaches us in this respect too. We can only obey the hidden Word of God in virtue of which the indication is, of course, more than indication. We can also speak about it if we must, telling others that this or that indication is for me the Word of God itself. This is why I must obey it. Consider whether it seems not to be this for you, so that you can act differently. To speak thus is always possible, actual, and necessary. Albert Schweitzer is an example. As he would say, the medical needs of uncivilized peoples are for me the command to go to Africa as a doctor. Another might say that the injustice of the situation of the proletariat is for me a summons to confess communism. Another might say that the ravages of alcohol which I have witnessed force abstinence upon me.

[2]See p. 176.

Speech of this kind is necessarily and essentially witness which has to be articulated and has to seek open ears and find obedience. It obviously has to *become* God's Word for anyone else. As human speech it can never be more than an urgent question addressed to others. Though it may be an established law for the speaker, he can never make it that for others. This is especially true of ethics as a general, didactic, and nonsituational attempt to consider the range of the divine command. We can act here only with reference to the indication given in real life and therefore only in this twofold reflection on the Word and command of God. But with this reference we can and must act, for real life is full of such indications and it is no little thing if these are fundamentally present.

We have said all this in elucidation of the statement that who my neighbor is falls always under God's control, or, negatively, that we cannot seek and find our neighbor apart from God's Word. We have thus established 1) that at this moment he is related to me as my neighbor by divine necessity; 2) that I do not have to determine who he is but to recognize that he is determined for me; 3) that he is determined for me neither by fate or chance, nature or history, but directly by God; and 4) that he is my neighbor because and to the extent that he bears and delivers God's commission to me. We have to place the question: Who is my neighbor? under these four regulative considerations. In relation to them we can formulate the question as follows: Where does authority encounter me? It is not unintentionally that I have chosen the word "authority" as the heading of the section. The fact that *Autorität* is a loan word in the German language, which has no exact equivalent for the Latin *auctoritas*, makes it all the more impressive and instructive here. We are in fact dealing with something which fundamentally and supremely is alien, which cannot be translated or appropriated but only acknowledged. An author is one who is the initiator, founder, creator, establisher, and inventor of a matter, and to that extent its representative, controller, guarantor, witness, and model, and to that extent its pacesetter, spokesman, promoter, forerunner, leader, director, and teacher. The act, significance, effect, and power of an author is his authority. Authority in a matter belongs essentially to the one who originally has it, i.e., the author. The author cannot cease to be this and no other can be it in his place. Authority can be loaned, conferred, and delegated. But it cannot become anything other than that of the one who originally has it. The authority of a state official is always that of the state, not his own. Yet because it is conferred it is not a lesser authority. The whole authority of the state is in this case and at this point contained in that of the official. The only thing is that as a conferred authority it finds its limits, measure, and criterion in the original conferring authority. The authority of the official has to be that of the state if it is to be authority.

This is what makes my neighbor who he is in the sense of the command. My neighbor is there where there is authority and therefore an author. He is there where another person precedes me with the law of action, where this law is first in him and not in me, where I must see in him the representative, witness, and controller in matters of my conduct, where I must bend to his instruction and guidance and superior direction if what I do is to be lawful. This outside person who commands me is my neighbor. Naturally he has only a loaned authority. The one outside who originally and properly commands me is God, and the superior direction is originally and properly God's direction. The authority of the neighbor finds its limit, measure, and criterion in its origin. Again, we cannot seek and find our neighbor outside God's Word. The neighbor is only a substitute and representative author. But he is that. In God's Word we always find the neighbor too. In the church of Christ there is this vicarious representation. As a sinner to whom grace has been shown, as a citizen of Christ's kingdom, I am bound to the precedent, witness, and direction of the neighbor. And it is from this standpoint, from the standpoint: Where does authority encounter me? that we have to test our life's relationships if we want to see how Christian they are, how much in conformity with the command of the Reconciler. If, then, we want an answer to the question what it means to be claimed by God as a pardoned sinner, the answer is that my action is bound by the representative authority of the neighbor.

When we look at things from this standpoint, we may be surprised how embarrassed we are. For not merely at a first glance, but even after honest and profound consideration, we are forced to say that among all the people among whom we live none is even remotely an author for us, a substitute and representative for God. Instead, after honest and profound examination, we find ourselves completely isolated with some kind of law of our own within ourselves. We move on to thousands and thousands of moments of action, many of them, perhaps, not unimportant, and, at least in our own eyes, seen through our own spectacles, the place is completely empty where the neighbor ought to stand. There seems to be nobody there with superior direction for us, just a lot of people to whom for various reasons we cannot or may not grant authority. Without counsel in this regard, or with only the counsel that we must give ourselves, we move on to the moment, and without counsel (in the deep sense, i.e., in the Christian sense of without direction) we act without any counterpart of Thou, centered on the I as though we were Adam before the fall. I-centeredness need not exclude morality and piety. It need not exclude a serious searching of conscience. It need not exclude prayer. On the contrary, it reaches its peak in prayer. It comes to full bloom in conscientiousness and prayer. Nor is this uncommon. What we think are our best moments are when I-centeredness comes to bloom in this way. Yet it is still I-centeredness. What are we to say concerning it? Not, at least, that it is unavoidable. If we do not see the neighbor, this does not mean that he is not there. Our lack of direction does not mean that no direction is given. We would not really believe if we were to deny that we are in the church of Christ or that the neighbor is there with an established authority, waiting for our openness and subjection. We should then have to say: How frail is our sanctification! How meager the Christian element in our conduct! My fault,[3] in many areas I am an unmistakable pagan! There can be no doubt that in many areas we do in fact act without the neighbor, without authority, without law, without the commitment in which we are placed. It will be like this until the hour of death. Our last moment may perhaps be a moment that is without authority and unsanctified because it is solitary, and therefore not Christian but pagan. And we may well be glad that our justification is not to be sought in our sanctification and is not dependent on it as on its completion by us. Yet this does not alter the fact that our sanctification is demanded by our justification, that the I-centeredness of our action is most sharply called in question and judged by God's mercy, and that the question concerning our brother Abel is put to us [Gen. 4:9].[4]

There is thus good reason for embarrassment and more than embarrassment when in this way we so often know no neighbor or authority but only our isolation. Let us assume that in many instances we are not totally without counsel. We think we know people who are surely authors and have been such to us. At certain moments we act under authority. Yet when we consider this honestly and profoundly we can say it only with reservations. For even when there is this acknowledgment of authority it is made only with certain reservations and deductions. At least partially and inwardly, in thought and feeling, we ignore to some extent the Thou of the neighbor even though we do not evade his authority completely. Even outwardly our submission is probably only partial. There is in our conduct only a broken commitment to his authority. Even as we are directed we are always concerned to escape from this direction as quickly as possible. We let ourselves be bound but we are glad that there are gaps in the meshes of the net through which at least the smaller fish may sometimes slip away, and we sometimes see to it ourselves that there will be such gaps. We must look especially at the relation between inner and outer authority and inner and outer obedience if we are to realize how weak our commitment to authority really is (there being no such distinction for authority itself). It is a naive error to think that the child is really more bound to authority than the adult, the medieval than the modern, or the Roman Catholic than the Protestant. The distinction offers to the child, did so to the medieval, and does so today to the Roman Catholic, the greater opportunity to escape real

[3]*Mea culpa*—from the prayer in the mass: *Mea culpa, mea culpa, mea maxima culpa.*
[4]Marginal note by Barth: "Who is my neighbor? Where does authority encounter me? Namely, representative superiority to our I-centeredness that proclaims God's authority? Embarrassment! No neighbor! No authority! Hence pagan moment."

commitment the more there is external fulfillment and acknowledgment of it. "Thoughts are free, who will guess them?"[5]

Real commitment is easy to avoid. At any rate it is rare among people of all ages and times and confessions. Even when it does occur it is probably never to be found in a pure form. On a strict and unsentimental analysis the visible reality of human conduct will always have to be described as a more or less solid paganism devoid of authority and not at all Christian. Like everything Christian it has to be believed to be Christian. Only in faith can we regard ourselves as obedient. We cannot point to certain acts or attitudes and say: That is committed conduct, that is true responsibility to the neighbor and therefore to God, that is obedience to the superior direction received in Christ's church. We can only say, and we must say, that human action is good in the Christian sense to the extent that it is recognized by God to have been performed within this commitment, by the God who searches the heart [cf. Rom. 8:27] and judges righteously. What, to the best of our knowledge and conscience, we must regard as action within this commitment, we may venture to do—leaving a clear space for God's verdict. Indeed, we *must* venture to do it. The fact that we must say in advance that our conduct is good only to the extent that it really takes place within that commitment, and God decides as to the reality of the "to the extent," should not prevent us from seeing that the "to the extent" (which may be very lacking in our conduct and about whose reality God decides) is in any case required of us and cannot be completely lacking inasmuch as we exist as those who are reconciled to God. We are referred to the mercy of our Judge, but this merciful Judge pardons us only as he himself determines the "to the extent" in our action according to *his* eyes, judgment, and righteousness. We can and must realize that the decisive mark which will make our action the very next moment into Christian action, or action in the church, will be its commitment to authority, i.e., to the neighbor as the precursor, witness, and teacher of the lawfulness of our action. *My* place at which I have to live as a Christian, and do what *I* should do, lies in this commitment and not in the absence of it.

Insofar as my action occurs without counsel or with reservations, I still act as a pagan, as one who is not called, who is outside the church, and who thus moves into a vacuum where I cannot stand as a called Christian and a member of Christ's body, but can only fall. Thus consideration of the question: "*Who* is my neighbor?" causes me embarrassment. It shows me that Christ has his kingdom among sinners, I being the chief [cf. 1 Tim. 1:15]. Nevertheless, we *cannot* maintain that we are unable

---

[5] "Thoughts are free,/Who can guess them?/They fly past/like shadows of the night./No man can know them,/No prison hold them. The matter rests:/Thoughts are free." The beginning of a popular song that arose shortly before 1800 in South Germany, cf. L. Erk/F.M. Böhme, *Deutscher Liederhort*, III, Leipzig 1894, pp. 575f.

to know and say what it means, with all due modesty, to be embarrassed, unable to know and say what is the way of obedience in this embarrassment.

2

We shall now consider what it means to encounter an authority or to receive superior direction. We must ask first how far our action needs the alien direction and instruction that comes to us from outside. In this regard we have to remember that our action is understood here as human action which is poisoned and disrupted by sin, which is in rebellion against God, and which is thus in contradiction with ourselves. Adam in paradise before the fall needed no authority. He too, of course, stood under the command and became its transgressor. But this command had no other authority for him than the direct authority of God himself. It was not law. No Moses had to come between him and God as a human guarantor of the covenant. The command under which he stood was the command of the Creator, the command of life. It was given to him in and with his existence and calling. In and with these, God's order was manifest as the order of the Creator which it was natural for him to affirm, as natural as to affirm himself. Only in such statements about Adam, which rightly sound mythological in our ears, can we speak about a natural obedience, with no authority or direction, that corresponds to the command of the Creator. To speak of this is to speak of something that we know nothing about and that is contrary to all our experience, so that we hear only empty words (Luther, EA e. 1.1, 79).[6] We do not render that natural obedience. At every point we lie outside our calling by creation and we are thus at odds with ourselves as we are at odds with God. Our calling by creation remains, and we have still to think about it. But we cannot do so on the assumption that we are obedient to it. Because we know nothing about obedience to it, we have also to consider that the command, the same command that was meant to be nothing but the command of our own life, must now encounter us as something alien that comes from outside, as law, authority, and direction. Hence we cannot be obedient now without the intervention of Moses. Moses is not the mediator of peace between God and man. But Moses is Christ's witness over against man who has fallen but whom, nevertheless, God will not let fall. Moses testifies to what this divine refusal to let us fall means for us who have fallen. Moses represents Christ's kingdom of grace among sinners. And in Christ's church Moses is the neighbor: hence the neighbor's authority and direction. Our position is radically different from that of Adam and Even in paradise. To be sure, we live together as they did, but unless we let ourselves be

[6]WA 42, 47, 31ff.

intoxicated by empty words we cannot say this without adding that we do so as sinners and that between us a function must come which is very different from this living together as such. Because we are in the church, because we are reconciled sinners, we must accept the divine claim in the form of human authority. This will not be the last word about our situation. In a third chapter we shall have to understand the command of redemption, the command as promise. There we shall have to speak about the freedom of conscience over against authority. But we cannot jump across the stage of law and authority. The word "conscience" should not be uttered until in full seriousness we have uttered the word "authority." If we are impressed by the fact that we are really in Christ's church as sinners, and that we know nothing about obedience to the command of the Creator, then this constantly leads us to the command of the Reconciler and keeps us at the point where we stand under the grace of God as those who are judged by him. At this place we cannot in any sense appeal to the freedom of our conscience—this would entail the romantic confusion that we are still Adam before the fall—but we recognize instead our need of direction. What does direction mean?

It might be useful by way of explanation intentionally to choose again a word that is a loan word in German and say that what is generally and comprehensively meant by the authority of the neighbor which claims us, and to which we have to listen, is "correction." This says more clearly than the German *Verbesserung*—we think of the way that a teacher corrects student exercises or an author corrects proofs—that the emendation is not yet made, but only that the fault is noted, not without some displeasure and censure, and that instructions are given for the emendation that must be made by the student or printer. This is precisely the way it is. The divine claim which in the church of Christ comes to me through the neighbor does not change me as such. Our sanctification is not our justification. Our sanctification is really that the exercise is first corrected. The exercise is still ours with all its faults. But when we are obedient to the divine claim it becomes a corrected exercise. The issuing of the divine claim means that an objection is made against me and an exhortation is imparted to me. Written by another hand, these stand in red ink in my exercise and, no matter what else this may suggest, it means that I have encountered an authority. We may regard this authority as small but we cannot regard it as nothing. It makes a difference whether it is there or not, whether we go about with a corrected or an uncorrected exercise. At all events, the direction received—this is why we call it a superior direction—means that something has taken place against us even though it is in our own truest interests. It is against us as the Thou is against the I among sinful people. We should not remove from the concept of direction the idea of rebuke, blame, censure, punishment, and, to that extent, pain, which all lie in the term correction. Positively, of course, correction is a setting right. But where this is necessary and really occurs, it is inevitably related to a certain unpleasantness. If the direction received is not painful, it is not direction. If we have sought it ourselves, it is not direction. If we could just as well have given it to ourselves, or have in fact done so, it is not direction. Real correction is not very acceptable. We do not seek it; it comes on us unexpectedly when we think we have done a good job. To the degree that we can do it ourselves, we do so, and this makes correction pointless. If we need real direction, this means that our monologue breaks off, and as we receive direction dialogue begins. We now have a partner. There is always something to be said and done in opposition to what we might go on to say and do. We can try to kick against the pricks [cf. Acts 9:5] but we will not succeed. No matter what we do, opposition and exhortation will result. We are not in the kingdom of nature but in that of grace. God's grace is that we are not left alone with our acts, but there is now this determination from outside and a determinative factor outside us confronts what is within us.

As we make room for it and acknowledge this determination, we act in the grace of God as those that we *are* in Jesus Christ. But we must analyze further the concept of direction in the sense of correction. We shall not now expand upon the fault that is noted. Materially it is always the same. Self-evident obedience to the command of the Creator has become self-evident disobedience. We do not live our lives as gifts of God; we live them as ourselves the lords of our own lives. This is the sin which is forgiven in Christ. This is also the Christian sin, for we handle God's grace with the same thieving autonomy. This is also the Christian sin which is forgiven us in Christ. This is our faulty exercise. But how are we to understand the objection and exhortation which necessarily follow if the forgiveness of sins is proclaimed and believed? What does God want from us and with us when he sets us under the claim of the neighbor?

Before we give the material answer we must first give a second general and apparently, but only apparently, formal answer. God wills that we be *his* people, i.e., the people among whom his honor dwells as this can dwell among sinners, the people among whom his faithfulness is proclaimed and received, received and proclaimed, in face of all human unfaithfulness. In giving us direction, God wills to be present and to be recognized as great and holy in his community. We have to value the establishment of his law as also, if not exclusively, an end in itself to which we owe respect as such. From the eternal standpoint everything has really happened that has to happen with the fact that Christ's kingdom *is* present among us sinners, that the sinful I *cannot escape* his Thou but is subject to it, that our exercise *is* corrected. God's grace is totally and sufficiently triumphant in the fact that we are not just sinners but are assembled in the church, are unsettled by the church, and mutually unsettle one another as the church. We are put in check and will continually be put in check in the game in which we are engaged, and mate will not fail to follow. What may or will speak for us apart from the one thing that we share in the unsettlement of sinners by the church, namely, that after a fashion, and perhaps as the last in line, we belong to the people among whom this unsettlement in relation to sin cannot be stopped, which constantly has to see a line drawn across every human calculation?

We must emphasize that if God's will is to be done with us we have to share in this unsettlement. God wills that we also be willing to have this direction or correction as he wills it. He waits for us to accept his ways with us even if we can do it only with the shock and pain and, let us quietly and openly admit, the resistance with which one accepts correction. At issue here is a will that is contrary to our will. At issue is an obedience, the obedience of faith, in which each step is a surrender, not being a surrender only as the obedience of faith. But what would faith be if it were not obedience, and what would obedience be if it were not acknowledgment of the righteousness of the judgment that is passed on us? To belong to God's people is to accept the direction that is imparted to us, to recognize its objective validity and necessity, no matter how painful this may be. But this participation in the unsettlement prepared for us cannot possibly be merely passive. We acknowledge that it has to happen. This acknowledgement that it has to happen would not be genuine but would be the idle statement of a spectator if we were not really unsettled. But we cannot be really unsettled unless we ourselves become unsettling. The direction that we have received belongs to us now. We are a corrected exercise. Hence the direction passes on through us and—whether we intend it or not, this simply happens through what we are—it becomes a direction to others. Or, as we might say more cautiously, it can at least do so. In the church we give as well as receive. The church is a fellowship and not just an institution. It is not just the community in which each of its members lives but also the community that proclaims revelation. It is not just the place where we find authority but also the place where authority must be found in us. Acknowledgment of the direction that is imparted to us is both passive and active. What is in some way required of us is simply that we obey, that we find authority and accept it. But the more serious this acceptance is, the more we *are* found as those who *have* found. Because we have become subject to the Thou, we are qualified to be the Thou ourselves to God's glory and that of Christ's kingdom among sinners. No matter who or what else we may be, the accepted claim of God wills to be passed on and the righteousness of the divine judgment wills to be proclaimed and to shine in God's church in its objectivity, validity, and necessity. Hence, as the claim of the neighbor is heard by us as an authority, God's people arises in which it is heard again and again, this time through us. The church constitutes itself, or, rather, is constituted, as the recipient and bearer of the divine light. Direction is thus a two-sided concept. All that we have to say about its content, if it is truly understood as the content of the divine direction, has not merely to be viewed as an experience that we undergo, but, because it is a real existential experience, it has also to be viewed as our own act and task. This does not alter in the least the presupposition that it is always sinners who confront one another in the church of Christ. We have not based the authority of the neighbor over us on his perhaps being a lesser sinner than we are. On the contrary, it is because there takes place in the church of Christ this mutual confrontation of sinners with a divine task and mandate, and because, painful though it may be, we have to accept this confrontation with all its distressing significance, that we must desire—or we do not really accept it—to let this direction be passed on through us in the way described, and to give God the glory thereby. God does not just will something *from* us; he always wills something *with* us too.

On the basis of the formal presuppositions indicated, we can now try to give a more precise material definition of the direction which the neighbor gives us and in which we have to recognize the reality of the divine command. There are three standpoints which are decisive here, three possible ways in which the neighbor can become an authority for us. I shall describe them by the three words education, right, and custom. We shall try to see the differences between them but we shall also consider that in the reality of life, and especially in its quality as an expression of the divine command, none can arise or be fully estimated without the other two, so that even if we deal with them one by one we shall always have to understand the one authority of the neighbor according to the three different emphases and characteristics.

a. The Thou becomes an authority for us from the standpoint of the education that it imparts to us. We sum up under the one word education the concepts of both instruction and formation, and by formation we mean that of the will and character and heart as well as the understanding. Theologically the concept of education belongs to the order of reconciliation, the law, and the kingdom of Christ among sinners, and not anywhere else. It does not belong to creation. Education by others is a different phenomenon from the fact of sexuality or that of belonging by blood to a particular people. The latter facts are among the things that make up our being as humans, as this or that person. Education is something we undergo, with all the painful associations this term might have. People and epochs that are enthusiastic about education usually veil from themselves and the objects of their craft the small but not insignificant circumstance that by nature people as they are, seen without illusions, do not go willingly to school or let themselves be educated. It is a very different matter that those who are not wholly stupid or lazy are ready to learn. Learning as such, the extension of knowledge, strengthening of the will, formation of character, etc., may be described as a life-activity. People undoubtedly want this, and the more vital they are the more energetically they will want it.

But the more energetically they will also view it as their own affair, the more energetically they will take in hand their own education, seeing and treating parents, teachers, books, and all more permanent or temporary instructors as merely the means to a goal in life, and the more energetically, wherever they can, choosing their own instructors, who will not try to shape them too much or make them innocuous in some other way, and even those whom they choose—test everything; hold fast what is good [cf. 1 Thess. 5:21]—they will approve of only selectively, and having received from them what they want will say farewell to them with differing degrees of gratitude. Insofar as education is in this sense self-education with the friendly assistance of some others, it does come under the order of creation, though not, of course, apart from the great question mark and exclamation point of the fall under which this order now stands. One might say: Happy are those who are in a position to transform all their education so cheerfully and naturally into their own life-activity and self-education, and happy are all of us to the extent that the matter has something of this aspect for us too. To the extent that it has this aspect, however, we have not yet perceived the true problem of education. Remarkably enough, the model children of all ages, who learn easily and are ready for all that is good, do not know as such what education is. Openly or secretly—this is why they are so much liked by parents and teachers—they have taken in hand their own education, openly or secretly they are really in charge of the game, and the pleased parents, teachers, professors, etc., have every reason to consider that it is not they who are winning in this game but the good little people in front of them, who are only waiting until they no longer need them (as deep down they do not need them even now). One might also say, of course, that these clever and well-behaved youngsters are still *waiting* for their real teachers, since those who are now so pleased with them do not really seem to be this. |

The problem of education begins on the far side of open or secret self-education. The child that struggles and twists in its mother's arm because it does not want to go to bed, the youngster that does not want to go to school and do sums and write sentences with accusative objects, the high school student that puts his pencil behind his ears, the freshman[7] that finds his assignments boring, the student that wanders from university to university and professor to professor and always hears or presumably sees things that rebelliously he is not prepared to be told, the person who finds it bitter to contemplate leaving his own style of life and being instructed in that of another station, profession, union, or even perhaps marriage—these are all ⌜examples of⌝ the real objects of real education. The real educator, whether good or bad, the very image of the educator in whom the problem of education becomes acute, is as such the other, the stranger, and education is something that we do not

[7]German "Verbindungsfux"

really like by nature. Education means that our natural development and activity are intersected. It means a refined or crude intermingling in private matters. It means interference on the assumption that this is in our best interests and with the immediate accusation and threat that I am an impossible creature, that no one likes me, that I ought to be ashamed of myself, that I shall never amount to anything unless I permit this interference. Education means that someone wants more or less skillfully to take from me one of the many horns that I invisibly carry on my forehead, and of which I am as proud as a stag, and to put some kind of strange hat in its place. I am supposed to adapt myself to an attitude whose value I should never have come to see on my own. I am supposed to think about things, and pehaps even to learn things by heart, that have little or nothing to say to me, no matter whether this be my childish illusion or my mature conclusion. I am supposed to do this even though my mind is wandering in very different regions, which, even if they are only dreams, are at least my own. I am supposed to obey to the letter, as they finely put it, even before I know what purpose the required action will serve or what its point might be. I am supposed to wrestle with truths that did not grow in my own garden and for which I do not think I can find any place there. And I should do all this gladly and gratefully, recognizing that everything is well-intentioned and for my own good, though the threat of punishments and other forms of unpleasantness, e.g., approaching examinations, always sees to it that I cannot reflect too long on what is good for me, but must do provisionally what is desired. I *must*. The vile Thou of the educator is always there to tell me very simply from a loathsome position of superior strength that I must. It is in this "I must" that there lies—for human beings as the objects of education, as we all are and always will be—the problem of education. |

Perhaps, in the main, I have had teachers who understand how to make this sting of the matter almost imperceptible, convincing me that fundamentally I myself want all the things, or most of the things, that they want from me. Perhaps I have been dealt with according to the happy modern pedagogy in which at first it all seems to be an entertaining game, then it becomes a vigorous common enterprise of teacher and student,[8] and finally it seems at least to merge into self-education in which the teacher is no more than a kind and clever adviser. Perhaps the Thou of the educator with his harsh claim succeeds to some extent in making itself bearable and gives me the feeling that I am standing and going on my own feet, or almost on my own feet, as we all wish to do, for this is man's natural concern as an object of education. Why should not this approach on the part of the teacher be permitted?

[8]Barth uses for this term "Arbeitsschulunterricht," which was first used for technical education but then came to denote an alternative to book-learning in which the student's own activity was recognized and fostered as an essential element in education; cf. G. Kerchensteiner, *Begriff der Arbeitsschule*, 1912, 1959[13] and H. Gaudig, *Freie geistige Schularbeit in Theorie und Praxis*, 1921, 1928[6].

We shall have to speak of this side of the matter later. We shall have to say that it is fundamentally commanded if the teacher has heard and taken seriously the claim of the one who is to be taught. But this type of pedagogy fails badly, and the older style of teaching is to be unconditionally preferred, if the result is that the Thou of the teacher is set aside, his harsh claim is conjured away, the "I must" is eliminated, and the problem of education is thus robbed of its point. An education that is not training is no education at all. But training means painful opposition. If I cannot live with this, then either I shall be an Adam before the fall living in paradisial innocence and needing no education—this dogmatic presupposition is the secret of more than one educational reform—or else I shall be an Adam after the fall who, for all his supposed self-education, is sadly in need of real education and is still[9] waiting for it. There is no other option.|

A sinner—and it is in the education of sinners that theology is interested—a sinner to whom education is given, or upon whom it comes, must be prepared, whether as child or adult, to accept something which from the very outset is not at all acceptable, namely, training, opposition in all its undesirable and alien character. To the degree that he is really educated he cannot stand and go on his own feet. He must pay heed to the word and obey it. Luther, in his Genesis Commentary, did not regard it as mere fantasy to depict man before the fall as a being of pure intellect and complete memory and the sincerest will, living in beautiful security (EA, e. l.1, 77).[10] The difference between man and beast was much greater then than it is today (84).[11] Man had sharper eyes than the lynx or eagle and could handle lions and bears as we do kittens (78).[12] He did not have to fear either fire or water (79),[13] enjoyed perfect knowledge of nature, animals, herbs, fruits, trees, and all other creatures (80),[14] and worked with the greatest pleasure (81).[15] He was the finest philosopher that can be conceived and had accurate understanding of the stars and all astronomy (83).[16] If he had not fallen, his children would have sprung to their feet immediately at birth like the chicks of a hen and would have found their own food without troubling their parents (128).[17] Morality, of course, would have been a wholly self-evident matter. In short, Adam did not really need to go to school, nor should his children have needed to. If one branch of learning was *not* present in paradise, it was undoubtedly pedagogy. Adam and Eve lived

[9]Barth uses here the older term *annoch* for *noch immer*.
[10]WA 42, 46, 19f. (LW, 1, 62).
[11]WA 42, 50, 16ff. (LW, 1, 66).
[12]WA 42, 46, 23ff. (LW, 1, 62).
[13]WA 42, 47, 22ff. (LW, 1, 63).
[14]WA 42, 47, 35ff. (LW, 1, 63).
[15]WA 42, 49, 4ff. (LW, 1, 65).
[16]WA 42, 49, 39ff. (LW, 1, 66).
[17]WA 42, 78, 5ff. (LW, 1, 102).

with full right and authority in self-education. But we are *not* like that. We *have* to go to school. We cannot handle ⌐fire and water naturally, nor can we handle botany, zoology, astronomy,¬ logic, or morality naturally. With the fall, our intellect, memory, and will have come to be in need of instruction. Natural science, philosophy, astronomy, and other useful things have ceased to be present in us by nature. The education of the sinner cannot be self-education. At every point, for good or ill, it has to be correction. To learn, we now have to be taught. Our best must come to us from outside. Education means being educated. I cannot be myself without acknowledging the contradiction of myself. This contradiction becomes concrete in the burdensome form of the teacher. To the extent that he is a real teacher he cannot basically spare me the experience of this contradiction. And to the extent that I am ready to be really educated, I must accept this contradiction.

Whenever, then, we are confronted by a fellowman and his claim, the question first arises whether we might not have here an appointed teacher. And wherever, well or badly, voluntarily or accidentally, permanently or transitorily, the characteristic element in the attitude and position of a fellowman regarding me is that his acts or intentions toward me consist of education, the question arises for me whether, things being as they are, because and insofar as I am sinful Adam after the fall, I can really evade his claim. He might have been appointed for me by God. And the more, perhaps, the painful element in all education predominates in his attitude toward me; the more I sense the schoolmaster in him, the more urgent the question becomes whether he really is this. It may be that he is not, that he has not been appointed to this office. Our fellows have not been appointed teachers in general and as such—thanks be to God, we say with a sigh of relief—but they may have been, and even the most unexpected and apparently least qualified person may suddenly become and be my teacher. We need education, and at no moment in our lives can we be sure that we are not somewhere being offered education that we have to accept. The worth of the teacher—no matter how unworthy he or she may be in other respects—is that of meeting us in God's name at a specific time and place and in a specific matter. "In our own best interests," we must also add, although not without the caveat that we shall have to be more precise about this later. We have already considered the offense that we have to be confronted "in our own best interests" if we are to be educated. This is what characterizes the authority of the teacher as such. The teacher corrects. The teacher is in general the Thou of the neighbor that reminds us of our limits and therefore of God as the one by whom we were made, from whom we have fallen, but by whom we are not allowed to fall but are upheld. With the claim with which he meets us, the teacher points us to the place where God in his grace wants to have us in the midst of this dark world. But the special aspect of the neighbor as the agent of education (and not of right, of which we shall have to speak next) lies in the very intimate and intensive way in which he wants us here. He seeks my agreement with the correction of my exercise. He seeks my acceptance of it. He seeks to put me, in relation to myself, in the place of the one who has made the correction. Hence the neighbor as teacher touches a very special nerve.

To the degree that education is more than self-education we have characterized its problem by the two pregnant words "I must." The special feature in the demand of the teacher—that which makes it such—lies in our having to put the emphasis on the "I": "*I* must." When we come to the question of right we shall have to stress the "must": "I *must*."[18] The "must" is present in education too, and we shall see that the "I" will have to be so in right, but what makes my education education in distinction from the right under which I am set is that *I* must. When I acknowledge the direction of the neighbor as my teacher the accent does not fall, as in the question of right, on the acknowledgment ("*An*erkenntnis")—although this is essential—but on the knowledge ("*Erkenntnis*") within it. The teacher as such wants to teach me, and obedience to the teacher as such means learning. The appeal for learning is in a very special way an appeal to *me*, to *my* insight as my own and *my* will as my own. That the teacher confronts me as the representative of various truths, values, and valid judgments does not in itself make him a teacher. Nor does the fact that he is in the right in his confrontation with me. Even if he makes me acquainted with various truths, values, and valid judgments—no matter whether we are dealing with the materials of some science or the rules of this or that life-style— this is simply the prelude to the true act of education, the means to the end of earnestly inviting me to become the subject of this science or the bearer and representative of this life-style. All pedagogical method deals with the mode of this invitation. As I am educated, or, rather, when the attempt is made to educate me, something genuinely or supposedly better than what I already know or want is brought to me from outside and set before me, not with the intention of showing me a play but of summoning me to the stage myself. It is brought to me and set before me to the end and goal that I should grasp and seize this real or supposed better as really better for me, that I should accept it as really better for me. One of the ceremonies at the graduation of a Roman Catholic doctor of theology is especially significant in this respect. An open book is first handed to the graduand with the reminder that as a doctor of the wisdom of the past he should always accept knowledge that comes to him through the open book, i.e., from outside. The same book is then closed and handed to him with the admonition that as a doctor he should now have this wisdom apart from the book, i.e., inside, and he must be able to teach it himself. To learn is to learn both outwardly and inwardly. As regards the difference between the doctor and the student, the emphasis

[18]See below pp. 376ff.

obviously falls on the second part of the act. Outward learning—this is its real bitterness—aims from the very outset at inward learning. The painfulness of all study is that in its decisive act it consists of appropriation.

If the teacher really deals with us in the name and by the commission of God, the heart of the matter is that he comes at us with something "better" in the expectation and with the demand that I see it and want it as such, as better than what I previously knew and wanted. If he really acts in the name and with the commission of *God*, what he teaches is not just supposedly better but authentically so. This does not mean that he possesses some panacea[19] which, if I let myself be educated by him, will make me holy and righteous instead of sinful. Only God can do this and it is his very hidden work upon me. This is why we must use a modest term. No teacher can educate me in what is "best" for me, only in what is "better." No human teacher can bear or represent *the* truth and *the* good. We see plainly here the difference between the one who commissions and the one who is commissioned. If it is not to cease to be education, education does not mean and should not try to mean the changing of man, his elevation to a divine or godlike status. This is why the teaching of model students is not education. Education can mean only the *correction* of people. But it *can* mean this. Christ does not stay at a distance from us. He comes to us in the church. The hidden work of God upon us is not without visible tokens in our life. My sin can at least be corrected or amended sin. I can accept this correction, see its necessity, and receive my exercise back in its emended form, no matter how painful this may be for me. This visible sign of the invisible work of God upon me is my education. And this education comes to me through my fellowman if it comes to me at all.

If it is not the whole essence of my being in the church, it is also part of it that I am educated by my fellowman. God has entrusted to those around me the task of presenting to me a reminder of my limits, and therefore of himself and the place where he would have me in his grace. They become my teachers by reminding me of all this and arousing the recollection in me. As this takes place, as I am taught something that is truly better in this sense—better than what I already knew and wanted—Christ comes to me in his church as he wills to come on this side of the eschatological border, on this side of the consummation when I will no longer be a sinner and no longer need any law. To this extent God, as he reveals himself to us in Christ, and deals with us as those who are reconciled, places himself with *his* authority behind the human teacher. To this extent all real education is not just Christian education but church education. That every subject and every life-style must be taught, brought to us from outside, and offered to us for our appropria-

---

[19]A general remedy, from Latin Panacea, daughter of Aesculapius and goddess of healing.

tion, is the necessary expression and established sign that we stand under the law. Or, as we should say more cautiously, no subject or life-style that can be suggested for our appropriation cannot become this sign, a summons, the knowledge of God. The other thing that is brought to us from outside can really become better for us, and can be recognized by us as such, because only in acknowledgment of it are we sinners who are corrected by God and who thus stand in his peace. The neighbor as teacher, with his claim that I should learn something from him— whatever it may be—can be for me, outwardly and inwardly, with open book and closed, the finger of God which makes a correction in my exercise, and does so in such a way that I see that it is justified and that I want it in my exercise, saying Yes and Amen to it. I should fail to realize that I am under the law, and should deny not only the church but also faith, grace, and Christ, if I were fundamentally to refuse education in this strict sense in which it differs from all self-education. I need ⌐refuse,⌐ and should refuse, only the education that is really non-Christian, nonchurch, and profane. Profane education is that in which an effort is made to make me holy and righteous instead of sinful, to make me forget my limits instead of seeing them more sharply, to deify me instead of putting me in my place on earth, on this dark and sinful earth. All education is profane which is enthusiastic, which is idealistic in the sense described, which aims at mysticism and morals instead of obedience, which tries to teach me not only something better, but openly or secretly a best. Such education, the education of antichrist, we not only may but must avoid.

We need not respect the education which aims at leaving me to my own self-education and involves no training. Indeed, we should reject it. For it is not really education at all. To the extent that we are in fact constantly exposed to this education of antichrist, as the objects of human education we constantly stand in decision: May and must I learn what is required of me? Or may and must I reject this learning? The answer is that real learning is commanded. But learning from the teachers of antichrist is not real learning just as they are not real teachers, for their supposed teaching seeks to thrust me back into self-education. Real learning means learning obedience, the obedience that we owe to God. Christ and antichrist undoubtedly meet us in teachers, the one in real teachers and the other in ostensible teachers. Often, indeed, Christ and antichrist may meet us in one and the same teacher. Antichrist also has a church, an apparent church, and often what we know as the church may be the church of Christ in one regard and the church of antichrist in another. Here is the decision in which we stand. No ethics can anticipate it. For the one who makes it is not active man in his acceptance of this education or his rejection of that which is no real education; in the one action or the other it is the divine Judge of man. We are responsible to him as we do the one thing or the other. And he knows and says whether we respond validly or invalidly. Ethics can only say what is at issue when the response is valid. A valid response means that we accept the better that a fellow human has to say to us, that we let ourselves be reminded of that which, as sinners, we had forgotten and continually forget, that in some regard we wittingly and willingly let ourselves be put back in our place. This involves learning both outwardly and inwardly. And knowing that learning means going on to the next moment entails readiness. This is the criterion with which we can go on to the next moment. Whether we learn, really learn, i.e., learn in the church of Christ, will be decided by him who commands us and whom we shall then encounter as our Judge.

The authority of the teacher has also the very different aspect that we should not only accept it as it comes to us in other people, but we should also exercise it toward other people. As we take the divine authority seriously in the neighbor, we cannot avoid the truth that, as it is made valid against us, so it is to be made valid, not *for* us, but *through* us. We speak of born teachers. But it is best not to do this for fear that we might be referring to the same individuals whom we have learned to know as model children that make a mock of all education because they steadfastly educate themselves. We cannot be born teachers but, as we are called to be Christians and baptized as such, so we need to be called to be teachers and baptized as such. But calling and baptism always mean that we are first taught and must let ourselves be taught. Those who know no authority can have no authority. Those who do not really learn—in the present tense and not just the past—cannot teach. The converse may also be said to our consolation. Those who know authority have it and may and must claim it. Those who really learn not only may but must and can in some way teach. To know authority and to be a learner is the real "gift of teaching" in face of which all other things are secondary, in which we may have the full assurance of comfort, no matter how much else may be missing, and which, like all the other pounds entrusted to us, we must not in any circumstances bury in a napkin [cf. Matt. 25:18]. Essentially and intrinsically this gift cannot be nature. It is grace—which is a very different thing.|

We have seen that the teacher's dignity in relation to us consists of his meeting us in God's name in order to teach us something better in some respect, i.e., to remind us of our limits and in so doing to remind us of God. My own dignity as a teacher in relation to others can consist only of the same thing. This has the following implications:|

First, I have to recognize that I can meet others only *in God's name.* Certainly my I must be the Thou that binds them. But it must bind them, not to me, but through me to Christ. Whether I be a pastor or doctor or teacher or father or mother, and whether they be children or adults, if I bind them to myself, or make myself a model for them, or let them make me their model on which they fix their gaze; if I do not serve instead as a window through which they can see; if by kindness (however profound) or force (be it ever so spiritual) I establish my own authority; if I proclaim my teaching as my own and seek to make them my own students—I have certainly not been called to be a teacher no matter how great my pedagogical skills may be. I am a teacher precisely to the extent that my authority is present, but not as my own authority, precisely to the extent that it is not ascribed to me, but that those who are taught meet God's authority through it, beyond which the question of my own authority can only be a matter of indifference. To teach is not to rule. It is to obey in the name and with the commission of the rule of God. It is to obey by teaching, advising, commanding, and forcing. But above all else it is to obey. To the extent that I obey, I teach, and I then have authority—although that is no concern of mine. Everything depends on the first point that the place of God's name must remain free and open for the teacher and must not be replaced by his own name. For from this source he does not have, but constantly has to acquire, that which makes him a teacher. |

Second, the teacher must take it quite seriously that he has the painful task of *confronting* others in the name of God. To be sure, he has to teach them what is better and to confront them on their own path with this something better. But with this task he does have to confront them for good or ill. We have already touched on the concern of modern pedagogy to make this encounter as peaceful as possible by means of the greatest possible accommodation of the teacher to the independence of the students.[20] This is simply a new turn in the understanding of what was already the problem of education in the days of Socrates, namely, that the pupil must want what he has to have, that he must grasp and take as better for himself the better thing that is imparted to him through the teacher. He has to be involved. If not, no matter what is brought to him, he will remain uneducated. Modern pedagogy is right to remind us more sharply of the Thou of the student. Relevant pedagogy is always characterized by humanity. The Thou of the student claims the I of the teacher just as fully as the Thou of the teacher claims the I of the student. I have to realize that I really *teach* only when the pupil *learns*. My greatest activity is inactivity if the pupil is not also active himself. I have to involve him if I am really to be a teacher. Teaching is an uninterrupted wooing of this involvement. But because his independence is at issue, there can be no escaping an attack upon this. Theological ethics, at any rate, cannot presuppose that the student is already fundamentally involved, that he already knows and wills what he is about. Hence it cannot agree that the role of the teacher is accurately described when, after the manner of Socrates, we call it that of a midwife,[21] as though the better that he must be taught were already latent in him and had simply to be born and brought to light with the assistance of the neighbor. No, if the pupil is really involved, this is not

---

[20]See above pp. 365f.
[21]Cf. Plato Theaet. 184b, 210b; W. Jaeger, *Paideia* II, 1944, pp.74ff., 103ff.

nature, not even hidden nature, nor natural grace, but grace in the strict sense, the grace of reconciliation, something wholly new that befalls him, not analysis but synthesis. Precisely when the teacher is convinced that he has to say to the other something that is not just good but really better, we have to count upon it very seriously that this better is something fabulously new, that it makes a true and unheard of demand for hearing and obedience, and that the immediate and expected reaction to this attempt at education will be an energetic protest on the part of the old Adam. Truly to see the Thou of a child is to see its protest. To miss seeing the protest is to miss seeing the real child. The real child, including the grown child, is childishly inclined by nature to hate God and his neighbor, to be incapable of any good, and to be inclined to everything evil (Heidelberg Catechism, Qu. 5 and 8).[22] We must love the child as such if we want to teach it. We must not imagine that knowledge and will are already present in it as though it were a little angel. Only then can we take pains in wooing pupils. Only then can we believe in the seriousness of the task of education. A faith in children which, forgetting the doctrine of original sin, is faith in their natural goodness instead of faith in the grace that is available for them, can easily go hand in hand with indifference to the task. Hence pedagogical skill should not aim at sparing the children the attack, the offense that their education means a calling forth, an invasion of the immanence of their being and nature, that in every single act it signifies a wholly new beginning. If education avoids this offence, then it ceases to be itself and becomes a much more pleasant occupation. As education itself is obedience, it must teach obedience. Knowing, of course, how hard it is to obey, that it is indeed a miracle to obey themselves, teachers might be discouraged by taking seriously the childish element in the child. The seriousness to which we refer must begin with a sense that education is a commission and that God himself is the true and primary teacher who does, in fact, perform the miracle of bringing us to obedience, and whom we can only serve with our action. Only with this commission can we venture to confront others and, in spite of their protest, teach them something better, as the teacher has to do.

Third, we have to teach people *something better*. Theological reflection, too, can quietly begin at the point that the goal of education is to fit man for his position in the world and, the older he is, the more specifically for his particular position in it. To be fit is to be able to do what is required, with a stress upon the word *required*. For the sinner, to have a calling cannot mean living one's own life, developing one's own talents and interests, engaging in one's own pursuits (as it might have

[22]Heidelberg Catechism, 1563: First Part: Of Man's Misery, Qu. 5: "Canst thou keep all this perfectly?" Answer: "No, for I am by nature prone to hate God and my neighbor." Qu. 8: "But are we so far depraved that we are wholly unapt to any good and prone *to all evil*?" Answer: "Yes: unless we are born again by the Spirit of God," P. Schaff, *Creeds of Christendom* III, pp. 309f.

meant for Adam before the fall). It means being claimed for, and required to be at, a particular place in human society and history with one's own particular abilities. On this side of the eschatological frontier, obligation to God means being commandeered in this way. All the real education that comes to us consists of being directed by men, in God's service, to this place and to these limits, our abilities being oriented to what is required, i.e., to a goal, not that we set, but that is set for us. This fact that our abilities and powers are commandeered is the better that we have to be taught. Thus all education, upbringing, and instruction that comes to us is designed to invite us either with gentleness or severity to see that our abilities are set in the light of this commandeering and to understand ourselves as those who are bound to God within these specific limits. The act of education, of any kind, is a real education when this is taught and learned in it. Behind every subject there always stands in some form—and this is what makes it a real subject, in distinction from an intellectual game—life itself with its claim on us. The claim that I put before my pupil is not my personal claim, but the awaiting claim of life which is to be proclaimed through me—the claim of God under whose patience the life of men takes its course and who determines for each the place where he will be patient with him. This is the new thing which comes into their lives through education. Their life is a life that is required by God, the Lord of life. But they are sinners and so they do not understand of themselves that their life belongs to God. Hence the demand has to be brought to them. Hence this demand is really an invasion of their life, which they would rather live without this obligation. Hence they protest against it and defend themselves as best they can. Hence I have to confront them as a teacher, as already said. But to do this is to teach them something better that is really better for them. Education is a blessing. Salvation comes to sinners as they are put in their place. They could live their own lives only to their destruction. If I really teach a person, i.e., if that person learns, then, humanly and ministerially speaking, I am the savior of his soul from chaos and the instrument of his sanctification. This is the beautiful and rewarding and hopeful aspect of all the work of education. But like everything beautiful we should not expect to see and grasp it. What we always see is the attempt of pupils to escape the demand that I seek to lay upon them. To our teachers, if they entertain no illusions about us, we small and great children and sinners resemble a crowd of fugitives who do not seek their salvation in commitment but in flight from it. Teachers who would like to see themselves surrounded by a bountiful harvest necessarily cut sorry figures, and those who do see themselves to be surrounded by such a harvest cut comic figures. The fine saying that teachers "shall shine like the brightness of the firmament, and those who turn many to righteousness, like the stars for ever and ever" (Dan. 12:3), is an eschatological promise with which we have little to do directly in obituaries and on gravestones. Temporal reality, precisely when one sees its eschatological margin, has a more sober look. True teachers, being truly taught, will realize that they, too, are always among the fugitives and they will thus believe in the others without desiring to see. But to believe is to believe in one's task, in God. Here again the concept of commission is pertinent. We do not have to create in our pupils the better that is committed to us. We have to trust that it is better both for us and for them. We have to obey. We have to hope, and in hope we have the bit of joy which we need every day in order to press on with ourselves and others.

Fourth, we again return to this beginning when we add that, while the teacher has to teach something better, he has to leave the *best* to *God*. In the better a best has to be hidden, and in the requirement and obedience the freedom of the children of God has to be hidden, if they are really genuine. But as the children of God are born only of God himself, so their freedom, the hidden best in the better, without which it would not be what it is, is exclusively the gift of God. No one can give it to another that the other should dedicate his heart to God and thus that his soul should really be saved from chaos. God alone does this and knows it when it happens. Education that wants to do it and know it can only be antichristian education. This exists. There can be education in mysticism and in the morals of divine likeness. We can only warn teachers against this possibility, for it is tempting to take it, to seek something visible. We recall the temptation in which the serious and well-meaning pastor finds himself in relation to his core community, the little church within the church (*ecclesiola in ecclesia*), or [in relation to] his confirmation class, especially in the final weeks of instruction. But we must also recall that this temptation means not only a small crossing of the border but also the self-destruction of education. In relation to pupils it means nominating them for self-education and thus leaving them uneducated. On the part of the teacher it means the rebellion of the one who is commissioned against the one who commissions. The true teacher will know his place. At the last moment, when only a step seems to be needed to reach the final goal, at least in appearance, he will remember what the real issue is, and that, while he can stir up a little breeze, he cannot make the Holy Spirit blow. At the decisive moment, then, he will always step back, not in resignation but in hope, leaving the Word to him who alone can speak this Word. From this angle, too, he will not want to reap, but untiringly to go on sowing as though nothing had happened and he had done nothing at all. Education has a sabbath like all real work: "You shall not do any work" [Exod. 20:10]. Without this sabbath, work cannot be done well. Thus education, from the standpoint of the teacher too, means decision. With that power and commission do we confront those who are to be educated? Do we dare confront them? To what will we point them if we do? Are we aware of the limits beyond which education will necessarily turn into its opposite? We can arm ourselves with these questions so as to be ready when the moment of action comes. We can know with what measure we shall be measured when we do act.

b. The Thou of the neighbor becomes an authority to us from the standpoint of the right (or law) which protects him and which is represented by him. He claims me as the bearer of the right. He demands my obedience in acknowledgment of right. By right we understand the order of human life in society that is publicly known and recognized and protected by public force, made known and recognized by the decree of society and protected by its power. All of us all the time find ourselves in the sphere of this order to the extent that we live with others, and this common life is placed under the *sine qua non* of this order. Theologically the concept of right (or law), like that of education, falls under the concept of reconciliation, of the kingdom of Christ among sinners. It does not fall under the concept of creation. In that connection we naturally had to speak about the conditioning of life by its being lived with others. But there is obviously a big difference between right order and living a common life with others, even though we may be conscious that this life as such stands under the order of God. In relation to the command of life, even though I see the concept of order operative in it, it is a new thing that there is an abstract order of human life together which embraces and determines my life from outside and concretely confronts me in the orders of society around me; that through this order a fundamental and factual supremacy is given to society, and that my own life, to the extent that right is at issue, has to be regarded as life in society, that society has legislative and penal power in relation to me. We cannot possibly regard all this as an order of creation. It is law. If God is present in it, it is as Christ among *sinners*. |

That we *have* right and are bearers of it—not the right of society but that of our own lives—might be made understandable as an order of creation. In living with others we more or less dictate to them the order of our own lives. We know no other. We are convinced that this order is the right one, and if we had been Adam before the fall we would have been right in this conviction. Life would be power, the power to practice our own order of life. If we were obedient to God this could only mean that we would be setting up God's right. And we are in fact slow to see that the right of society means anything other than the setting up and confirming and protecting of our own right, and therefore of God's right. We submit to it as the best means to further our own activity. We can not only acquiesce in it without collision, but even rejoice in it, whether because[23] we are such gentle creatures by nature that our will for life does not easily tempt us to oppose society, but at all points sees itself happily supported and advanced by it, or whether because we are clever and skillful enough to present the harmony between the order of society

[23]The Swiss editor put "sei es, dass" here for Barth's "teils weil."

and our own activity in such a way that we can thumb our nose at it, i.e., give the impression that we are content with it, while in reality we can escape through its loopholes into the free and undisturbed action of our own will—a procedure which does not have to make us wrongdoers, and in which we all probably engage much more than we know or think. One can only say that, insofar as we are in some way successful in either naturally or artificially harmonizing our own will with that which encounters us as right, we have not yet encountered the real problem of right. The problem of right does not arise, or no longer arises, where by nature or art we have right and are in the right in what we will. Very different questions from that of its own right are to be put to our activity. The problem of right begins where the collision of my own activity with the social order begins; where this collision cannot be eliminated; where the neighbor and not I has right; where he claims publicly acknowledged and protected right for himself and against me; where I am thus confronted by the question whether he does not really have right for himself and against me; where I have to decide whether by my act I shall allow that the social order that is represented by him and that protects him is in the right over against the order of my own life, or whether I must uphold this order against it; where obedience, then, is not doing what I want to do but concrete obedience to the law that concretely encounters me in this person. |

Like education, right is not in us but comes to us. Nor is real right set up without pain. Pain in our experience of the neighbor as a bearer of right differs, of course, from pain in our experience of the neighbor as a bearer of education. No comparison is possible, and which pain is greater or less cannot be determined. The teacher seeks our agreement, we said. He troubles us with his urgency. The pain of right, however, is that agreement is not sought here. We are confronted by a *fait accompli*. *This* is right and we must either submit or transgress. The bearer of right does not have dealings with us. He has not the slightest interest in whether we are glad or not about what he wills, whether we understand it or not, whether we do it on our own initiative or with trembling protest. He simply wants our agreement as agreement to live with others—an agreement from outside and on the outside. He wills only that my action should be formally right in the sense of being an external fulfillment, in relation to the lives of others, of the order that prevails around me. Unlike the teacher, the neighbor as a bearer of right touches a raw nerve by his indifference. In his own way he confronts me, but he does so in cool superiority and remoteness. He lets me feel and even will what I want so long as I finally do what is expected, what society has determined to be the law. If that happens he has won the game and withdraws. And if it does not he has really won the game, for if he is really in the right, if he really represents right and is protected by it, I am open to punishment. I run the risk that the society whose right I have reduced by my resistance will repay me by reducing my own right, by demoting me, or by an extraordinary claim, supported by force, on my well-earned property, or by a restriction of my freedom of movement to the painfully small and uncomfortable space of a prison cell, or, finally, and most painfully of all, by a complete withdrawal of right by summary execution. In punishing me, society confirms by force, insofar as this is possible, the fact that its law is valid and that it is binding on me too.

In the painfulness of right (or law) we come up against something whose presupposition again is obviously fallen Adam expelled from paradise. What distinguishes the concept of right, namely, its establishment in the form of public legislation and its upholding in the form of public punishment, makes sense only if man is a sinner against whom others have to be protected, who has no competence to make his own order of life a law in his common life with others, from whom the right of unlimited development of his own activity has been fundamentally taken away, or upon whom at least a number of very burdensome and encroaching restrictions must be imposed. Man is under the serious suspicion—each and all of us are—that without these restrictions the exercise of his own specific right in life will be unpleasant for his fellows. It is well known that in the eyes of the law everybody is always a suspicious person, an unreliable citizen, until there is proof to the contrary, which needs to be produced every moment. Although they may be friendly and polite, the police are latently prepared in some small way for the worst in any of us. It is intrinsic to law that society plans and prepares for the worst in all of us, plans and prepares to confront and confine us if need be. Wittingly or unwittingly it accepts thereby a very theological presupposition. We are forced to say that the dogma of original sin is much better preserved by the police than by teachers and even by modern pastors. Society, as the bearer of right, no matter how optimistic its voice and mind may be in other matters, does not count on the natural goodness of humanity. In all who bear a human face it sees necessary objects of innumerable regulations and ordinances, and possible objects of civil or penal proceedings. The neighbor as the bearer of right, beginning with the traffic police at street crossings, with the legally binding claim that I must not ride by bicycle at night without lights, is a living witness to the truth that "the imagination of man's heart is evil from his youth" [cf. Gen. 6:5; 8:21]. There is a particular kind of persecution mania in which the victim cannot see a policeman without the greatest distress. The presence of the law does in fact remind us painfully that we are in the wrong, and that any moment this can become as manifest to men as it has long since been manifest to God. In accepting the order of society we accept the fact that people rightly believe us capable of anything, and therefore try to protect themselves against us in every possible way. Anarchism, which does not want any society, is simply the culmination of a liberalism which, among all dogmas, no longer wants to know anything about the dogma of original sin. "People" protect themselves against us, we have said.

"People" do not do some things and have to do others. Why some and not others? Obviously because they have to live together, and this common life has to be protected in some sort by rules that apply to all. In some sort: law cannot bring *absolute* protection. It wants to. It aims at it. But it cannot do it. There are loopholes in every law. Even when I have a light on my bicycle, I can carelessly run over someone. All our rules and regulations can protect our life together only partially from the follies and faults of which I am capable. Yet they can do it partially. And this is what "people" want. This is what society wants with its law and order. As much as possible, anticipating as many possibilities as it can, it wants to give protection against what I am seen to be capable of. It proposes for my urges, whatever they may be, a not wholly satisfactory but bearable compromise: certain limits within which I can move, but without proving to be disruptive or troublesome so far as it can provisionally judge. But how does society come to play itself off against me in this way?

To understand this matter we must consider the debate about the origin of right or law. The question arises whether, originally, law was meant in the sense in which we have thus far understood it with its content in view, i.e., as *ius*, as the epitome of the norms that society has adopted to protect its interests, or whether *fas* (divine law) is earlier than *ius*, i.e., whether what was intended in the establishment of law was acknowledgment of an order given by a deity that was interested in the welfare of society. Ihering takes the former view,[24] Kohler the latter.[25] Looking at the content of law, one cannot escape the rightness of Ihering's view. The aim of society is to prevent, so far as possible, the possibility of collisions of interests that run on more or less converging tracks, and, where such collisions are unavoidable, to make them as harmless as possible on both sides and for all the three parties concerned. Life together is to be ruled by an arrangement which partly prevents or restricts convergence, or at least heads off its foreseeable consequences. To this extent law is *ius*. There is no law which, from the standpoint of content, cannot be understood also as a security measure on the part of society against the constant threat of individual caprice. But Kohler is right too. Every measure takes on the force of *law*—and only thus does it become the right. The safeguarding of the possibility of common life on the part of mutually suspicious people takes on the character of necessity, of permanent and universal obligation, without asking the individual concerned whether he or she agrees to the arrangement, but presupposing that it will be in force for the individual with or without his or her consent. Society underlines the necessity of its

[24]Rudolf von Ihering (1818–1892). Cf. his *Geist des Römischen Rechts* . . . 4 vols., Leipzig 1852–65 (Aalen 1968), and *Der Zweck im Recht*, 2 vols., Leipzig 1877–1883 (1923[8]).
[25]Josef Kohler (1849–1919). Cf. his *Das Recht*, Frankfurt/Main 1909, pp.66ff., and, with L. Wenger, "Allgemeine Rechtsgeschichte," in *Die Kultur der Gegenwart*, ed. P. Hinnenberg, II, VII, 1, Berlin and Leipzig 1914, pp.3f.

measures. It shows this at once by promulgating them as law, by imposing punishments on their infraction, by claiming the right to answer reduction of right by reduction of right. In fact, it obviously means to act in the name of a higher authority superior both to itself and to me. In fact, it presupposes that it is the will of the deity which is proclaimed by its arrangement and is to be acknowledged in it. Right becomes divine law through that which distinguishes it from a private argument. I have to obey, not because this is right for a vast majority of other people, but because this vast majority is the mouth which expresses, and means to express, what is right in itself. By being given the status of law, and by the thesis that transgression is punishable—both acts which, strictly speaking, only deity and those that represent deity can perform—the sociological requirement takes on religious significance.

The ambiguity in the origin of right characterizes its nature. Theological ethics must be careful not simply to take the side of Kohler in this debate. All right is essentially human right. Where it confronts me, I am confronted by the agreement of a preponderance of others, and I can live with them only on conditions which they prudently dictate to me in their own interests and because of their mistrust of me. This is not just an irksome, but a dubious claim even though I have reason to submit to it and even though I see clearly and convincingly that a fairly imposing power lies behind it. No law is so venerable, no penal force so strong, that it can stifle my own life-will or free me from the suspicion that, when the right is set up against me, the situation is such that there might not be some suppressed right, or even the greater and fuller right, on my side as opposed to the power of the monarch or the majority. We neither can nor should conceal this reservation when the neighbor confronts us as the bearer of right. We can acknowledge him to be such only in spite of and with this reservation. Right seeks our acknowledgment, not as the right which has fallen from heaven, but truly and honestly as human right, as what it undoubtedly is in its whole content, namely, the codified prudence of all others in opposition to me, and the organized defense of all others against my possible encroachments, a defense and prudence in face of which I cannot possibly forget that I, for my part, have to rely on them too in relation to all these others.|

That the others are sinners too, against whom one must be on guard, is not contested in legal thinking. On the contrary, as I acknowledge right, confirming it as public right, I confirm that the prudence and defense are set up against others too, and thus share in the attitude of society toward others which I myself find so painful. Confronted by the question of right, in relation to other sinners, to people who might be just as much in the wrong as I am, who are just as much in the wrong, who in some respects, known or unknown, may be more in the wrong than I am, I grant even and precisely to them the competence to make rules for me, to threaten me with punishment, and to raise against me the qualified claim of bearers of right. Kohler is right, not Ihering, when he says that this acknowledgment is not possible or actual on a eudemonistic, but ultimately only on a religious basis. In the conflict between my well-being and that of society the concept of right will always be sold short. With good grounds, not without, there will always be something to be said for our own right against that of society, for inevitably the rules and judgments and punishments of society, which is made up of sinners like myself, will be wrong even when we call them right, and perhaps most wrong precisely when they are thought to be most right. The monarch or the majority (even when this is the whole minus one) is not intrinsically protected against error, folly, or wickedness, but in every decision is an unjust judge before God. If we are to acknowledge the right, we must seek some other ground than that of the conflict between my interests and those of the many others represented by the state and the police. But the religious ground on which the right can be acknowledged will have to be Christian. The deity of people or police which might be invoked as the giver and patron of the law will arouse in any reasonably bright Athenian the same suspicion as the monarch or the majority. He will not believe at root that this is a real deity. He will not be able to set aside the politically dangerous question whether the monarch or majority with their interests, the well-being of society with its very dubious claim over against my happiness, do not really come first, and Pallas Athene with her spear is simply a second thing that is deduced or added—a salutary fiction designed to emphasize and support the dubious right of society, a bourgeois ideology, to use the language of class warfare, good enough to uphold religion for me and the people, i.e., to keep me in divinely willed dependence on the laws of the monarch or the majority, but deserving no more, if no less respect than any other human, only too human concept. |

The Christian ground on which alone we can fruitfully proceed here differs from that of religion in general because on it the only too human aspect of right is taken seriously as such, with no ideological elucidation or reinterpretation. On the Christian ground we know that society's supreme law not only can sometimes be its supreme injustice,[26] but before God it always is. But just because this insight is so radical, it cannot lead me into a continuation of the battle for my own right against that of society. For on this ground I know of myself first, not of others, that I am in the wrong with my right, even my supreme right, that right is necessarily set up against me and I must submit to it. By whom? By an angel from heaven? By a righteous man? By a righteous society? Waiting for right from these sources I could only put myself more and more in the wrong, becoming, as Michael Kohlhaas says,[27] a highway robber.

---

[26]*Summum ius, summum iniuria,* Cicero, *De Officiis,* 1, 1, 33; Terence, *Heautontimorumenos* IV, 5, 48 *(ius summum saepe summa est malitia).*
[27]Cf. the story of this name by H. von Kleist, 1810.

No, he through whom I must be brought to submit to the right is my very unrighteous neighbor, human society without Pallas Athene, the society that protects its interests in a very dubious way, society as it is with all that can rightly be said against it a thousand times. An authority (*exousia*) which, not merely before God's eyes but according to my well-founded suspicion, is not solomonic but very neronic, like that of Romans 13, is still "God's servant for your good" (Rom. 13:4). The Christian view of the neighbor is that he is ordained by God for me, not as a saint or a righteous person, not as one who has a better standing before God than I do, but as one who is on exactly the same footing before God as I am and who, precisely in this concealment, acts as God's servant toward me. He can do this as a bearer of education; he can also do it as a bearer of right. The law in whose name and in protection of which he crosses my path, even in all its human questionability and with all that may rightly be alleged against it, can be the correction which must be brought to my life-will, because this is evil from youth up [cf. Gen. 8:21], not merely in the form of the instruction that is imparted by the teacher, but also in the form of a contradiction which cannot fail to be heard, which unexpectedly avenges itself sharply on deaf ears, and which is set over against me by him who is able to make the social order valid for me. And it may be that the punishment with which he threatens me or which he inflicts on me is the hand of God reminding me that if I do not accept God's grace I will fall victim to a very different reduction of right than even the worst that men can impose. To the extent, then, that I who have forgotten what divine law is, choosing always that which is against it, can at least be called to order by right, even in the great transgression of this law in my decisions, right can be divine law. |

Again, but this time from outside, from the standpoint that my life is a life with others, I am put in my place and set within my limits at the point where God wants me to be and will have patience with me in this temporal order. When the goal of right is reached in me, then the "I *must*" will become an "*I* must." *I* will then submit, not to my neighbor, nor to society, but to God, yet to God in submitting to my neighbor and society, in acknowledging that I have deserved and need that intrinsically very irksome and dubious claim of the monarch or the majority. My sanctification takes place in this acknowledgment. The neighbor, as a bearer of right, cannot reconcile me to God or free me from the discord in which, hopeful but sighing, I must pass my days even as one who is reconciled to God. Nor can the teacher do this, as we have seen. But he can and should proclaim the law to me as a sinner that is reconciled to God in Christ, the salutary law of the gracious God. He can and should remind me of my commitment as a member of the people of God. This commitment can be concealed in even the most perverted and unrighteous commitment to the right of society. Right as it now is and is in force can open my eyes to the neighbor whom I constantly overlook in the pride of my own impulses and from whom I would rather be free. With the special impress that is proper to right as such, he can tell me what I need to hear for God's sake and in order not to fall from God's grace: that I cannot break free from my neighbor, that Christ is present for me as my fellowman, no matter how questionable or disreputable he may be, is really present for me. When the bearer of right, whether he confronts me in its name or merely to protect it, discharges this function in relation to me, he practices toward me the true right which will be sought in vain on the ground of the conflict between individual and social welfare, even though a deity be invoked to guarantee the latter. The right that he has for himself and against me, even though he be the worst of pagans, is that of the church, i.e., the domestic order of the community of Christ which is fulfilled by him in relation to me and which I have to acknowledge as a member of the community. For this reason and to this extent I have to submit to the right. For this reason and to this extent the church does not simply have the state somewhere alongside it, but essentially it has it in itself, acknowledging its function as necessary within the earthly and temporal city of God, which can only be one. We shall have to speak specifically about this relation later.[28]

What we see at this point is that the church, as the fellowship of the justifying and sanctifying Word of God, can neither refuse acknowledgment to the state nor attribute to it a different dignity from its own as the final goal, that it must acknowledge the state's authority as the bearer of the true right that represents the domestic order of the community of Christ, but that in so doing it must claim this function as one of its own functions. The decision which I must make when I am confronted by the neighbor as the bearer of right is whether I have to *obey* him as the bearer of the true right of the church, of whether I may and *must* evade him as the bearer of a purely profane and secular right. There is profane right as there is profane education. There is a state that is the beast from the abyss [cf. Rev. 13]. We not only do not owe this state obedience; we owe it disobedience. We have to speak of profane right when the neighbor with the law on which he relies and the punishment with which he threatens me wants me to act and live in accordance with my evil life-will which would be interrupted by the right if it were true right; when his supposed right, in distinction from what right should be as social order, is an invitation to initiate or perpetuate social disorder and to engage in personal aggrandizement; when he himself is the God with whom it is my peace to be reconciled. This profane right is wrong, not merely human wrong but the devilish and antichristian wrong to which we should not submit.|

It is clear that we can never decide definitively and unambiguously in advance as to the presence of true or false right, of the state that is in the church or the other state that is the beast from the abyss. It may be that

[28]See below pp. 440ff.

true bearers of right in one situation may be bearers of wrong in another, in face of whom we must obey God rather than man (Acts 5:29). It may be that obvious bearers of wrong in one regard may have to be respected as bearers of right in another, as is plainly provided for in Romans 13. Ethics is not a philosophy of history which can undertake to test whether right is true or false, whether it is in the church or outside it. If we can know and affirm even the church itself only in the moment of the decision of faith, how much more is this true of the state that is comprised within the true church. We can only say that we have to know and consider that there *is* a distinction between true and false right, that in all that we do a distinction is made by God as our Judge, that we must therefore *put* to ourselves the question of true right because our action will in any case be a refusal or nonrefusal in face of this question too. In no respect must we let ourselves get confused about this question of right. There is true right, and the neighbor can be the bearer of it. He can have the task of being the instrument of our sanctification in this way too. There can be no more basic and serious acknowledgment of the truth and dignity of right than that which takes place in the act of Christian obedience, no fuller legitimacy than that of Christian obedi- ence. But there is also wrong in the solemn mask of right, the highly diabolical wrong of opposition to grace which often likes to appear precisely in this mask. The neighbor can also be for me simply a messenger of the tempter. There is in this case no more basic or radical a revolution than that which takes place in the act of Christian faith itself. There is in this case a collapse of the same Christian obedience that submits to right—and woe to this false obedience if it does not, for it then ceases to be obedience. Both these things can be possible and necessary, for the neighbor lives with us in this temporal order, i.e., in the world and in the church, in the spirit and in the flesh. We are summoned to acknowledge the right of the church. Let us make no mistake. Without exception the children of God who have to present this to us—even in the church in the narrower sense—come to us in the garb of children of the world. But let us also make no mistake: it is not self-evident that those who come to us are indeed the children of God whose right is the true right to which we must submit, just as it is not self-evident that we ourselves are such. As worldly right that is set up in face of us in God's name can at any moment be church right, so at any moment church right can be the right of Satan over against which legitimacy on our part means revolution and revolution legitimacy. Necessarily, the believer walks here on a ridge on which he cannot stand but can only walk. Necessarily in this respect, too, we can and should act only in faith, since the judgment concerning our obedience has not been put in our own hands.

But the concept of right has another side. We are summoned not only to let right be declared to us, but also to be bearers of right who establish it for others. We have thus to think through this aspect of the problem too. We can begin with similar statements to those[29] which we formulated at the corresponding point in our discussion of education.[30] No one has right. No one is born with it. But one can have it by calling and baptism. We can acquire right. We acquire it by acknowledging it, by submitting to it. From an ethical standpoint we thereby become subjects, *active* subjects of right. In ethics we must regard submission to right as man's free act. Where this act takes place, where we give free rein to right, we establish it. We do not simply adjust to the order of society. We adopt it and validate it. Rightly understood, the much berated "L'état c'est moi" of Louis XIV can be the well-considered consequence of the much applauded "The king is the servant of the state" of Frederick the Great. The concept of service can in a very significant way suggest both duty and commission on the one side and authority on the other. The point here is that those who know authority have it. The right acknowledged by them courses through them to become right for others. Fundamentally they cannot and should not try to evade this. In the people of God, there can no more be mere objects of right than there can be mere objects of education. God's honor wills to dwell among his people. For each individual this means submission *and* orientation to the neighbor, the orientation being no less a command than the submission. I cannot will only that right come to me. A purely passive relation to right is a sure sign that I have not yet thought of the concept of right as that of necessary conflict between the public order of life and my private order. There may be people who for laudable or less laudable reasons can do this. But if in this as in all other fields there are people who do not know what they are doing, this does not alter the fact that there is a truth to be known in this action. In truth, the right that is a mere experience, that in experiencing we do not have to adopt, cherish, and validate, is no right at all. As the true object of right, one will necessarily becomes its bearer, the bearer of the social order with all that is to be said for and against this. In detail the following points must be considered: |

First, I act in God's name when I really represent right to others. True right is that which is made over and loaned to me, loaned directly from the source of all right. Neither by its having become my right—as it has—nor by its having been addressed to me by society—as it has—but simply by my administering it in God's name is it right. The formal "by the grace of God" in the title of kings and emperors, dubious though it may often sound and has sounded in specific cases, makes good sense, as does the opening phrase of the Swiss Constitution: "In the name of Almighty God,"[31] and as did similar formulae in the past in the ledgers of big and small commercial and industrial firms. It cannot be just a

---

[29]German "denen," originally "die."
[30]See above pp. 371ff.
[31]The Constitution of May 29, 1874.

matter of formulae. Their use may give rise to well-founded objections. But it is unequivocally clear that the venture to establish right is impossible except on the presupposition indicated by such formulae. This presupposition has to give the venture its character. Neither as an official nor as a private person protected by right can I have and promote right in relation to others without remembering that before God I am just as much in the wrong as they are and that essentially my momentary right in relation to them cannot be my own but can only be the right with which I am commissioned. I am not covered even by actually having the social order on my side. At any moment, my confidence in the existing social order might be confidence in the order of antichrist and my action in this confidence might be the action of an unreconciled sinner. Whether I have on my side the social order that God will use in all its lack of sanctity for the sanctification of my neighbor is a question which I am asked every moment and to which I must give a responsible answer if I am to administer the right. That my right is one with which God has commissioned me does, of course, vindicate me. If I act in God's name, then neither my personal sin and guilt, nor my insight into the human lack of sanctity of right as such need hamper the resolution of my act. They ought not to do so, for I cannot refuse obedience to my neighbor, who has right against me, on the ground that he also is a sinner and his right is only human right. The name of God is the limit *and* the basis, the basis *and* the limit, of all right in the human world that is not forsaken by God's grace and patience. For this reason, the name of God must denote in the bearer of right who is really the bearer of right a free spot which must not be filled by his own name, or that of the social authority that he represents, if he is not, with the final question that is put to him, to lose the authority that finally validates him.|

Second, it must be taken very seriously, of course, that we cannot spare the neighbor the *requirement of submission* to the right. We cannot remove the sting of the fact that the divine Thou must also encounter him in the form of the neighbor who is validated by his right, nor can we refuse to be this neighbor to him. Anarchism in all its forms, even in its Christian forms and variations, means not only rebellion against the task that society, in all its lack of sanctity, can have in relation to the individual but also a weakness toward the other which finally results in non-Christian hardness. For truly, we do no good to the other, and spare him no ill, by granting him exemption from an encounter with the right, much though he would like this in his folly. "Count, be hard"[32]—not for your own sake, nor for the sake of the right or the order of society, but for the sake of God and therefore of the neighbor, who vitally needs your hard resistance, whom I treat as one that God has abandoned if I set no limit for him, painful though this process might be. This is true no

[32]From the ballad "Der Edelacker" (1817), W. Gerhard, *Gedichte* (Leipzig 1826, p. 2), based on a story about Ludwig the Iron, Second Count of Thuringia (1140–1172).

matter whether I am an official, i.e., a public functionary under the public order, or a purely private citizen, i.e., a private functionary under the same public order. Thus, I can be commanded as an official or judge or responsible politician to give free rein to the right, to proceed against the other, or a majority of others, with the law, or with threats of punishment, or with actual punishments, in the full rigor of the letter which is on my side when I think I see that they will not submit to the right unless I become hard. But I can also be commanded to take a private action seriously, e.g., a complaint against someone, and to fight it to the bitter end with every legal means. In this connection Michael Kohlhaas must be mentioned again and this time with all due honor.[33] I *can* be, I said. The right of right, even of my highest right, has a natural limit in the meaning and purpose of right. If I think I have these on my side, then I believe that that procedure is demanded of me. And to the extent that I do not just believe this, to the extent—and I am asked this—that it really is demanded, abandoning the position of right in relation to the other is just as permissible as is disobedience to him when he is in the right. It is clear that those who know how hard it is really to submit to the right, and those who also know that it is hard because the right to which we have to submit is unholy human right, and those who also know themselves and feel it to be presumption to have to approach others as possessors of the right, those who see to some extent the whole abhorrent impossibility of possessing the right against others, even against the worst of criminals, will feel that they are severely hampered at this point and will not act without realizing what they hereby ascribe to others and arrogate to themselves, and, realizing this, will act differently from those who do not realize it. Yet if we are commanded to be in the right, we must not let ourselves be hampered. The greater and true purity of ethical feeling is to take that abhorrent impossibility upon oneself and for all the personal and universal wrong in which one is undoubtedly more deeply implicated, to establish and uphold the right, to let right be right. "A nasty song, fie! A political song."[34] This is true of all the action that is in view here, and only in full acknowledgment of its nastiness, not under some ideological cloak, can it be regarded as commanded. Yes, we have to say that politics in the broadest sense of the term *is* nasty. Those who do not or will not recognize this, but wrap it up in an ideological cloak in order to be able to boast of supposedly clean hands, had better keep their hands out of it. They will not establish right but wrong. They are certainly not called. But those who know radically that we can act in this matter only by divine commission may not keep their hands out of it but have to act, and should know that their hardness is the demanded mildness, that their neighbor to whom they must do what undoubtedly he does not like is fundamentally

[33]See above pp. 381.
[34]J. W. Goethe, *Faust*, Part 1: Auerbach's Cellar in Leipzig.

grateful on an understanding that is superior to his self-understanding. |

Third, and in consequence, right is a *favor*. For all the pain that it means concretely for those whom it smites, for all the pain that it necessarily means for them on account of original sin, it is still a blessing. The aim of right, like that of education, is that those who in their folly and wickedness are always inclined and ready to forget this should be reminded of God and put in their place. Right has to promote this beyond the possibilities of education. It is good for man when it is done. For this is his sanctification, and his sanctification is a visible sign of invisible grace.[35] Least of all should the bearer of right forget that right is a favor. The determination that I do not have to represent and uphold my own right as such, or the right of society as such, but both in the name of God, is relevant here too. Because right has a purpose that does not lie in itself, but to which it points beyond itself, all practice of it is an interpretation of it. The claim that I address my neighbor in the name of right must correspond to the purpose as well as the letter of right if it is to be a true claim. If its only order is bureaucratic, it is not in order. Its being in order can at any time break through bureaucratic order, for in the conflict between letter and purpose it is always purpose and not letter that prevails. The claim of the Jew in *The Merchant of Venice*, if appearances do not deceive, is not a true claim, for while it has the letter of the law in its favor, it does not have the purpose of the law on its side and therefore it does not have true law or right.[36] In this regard, too, we are asked about the right of our right. That it corresponds to the letter of public law and is really ours offers no protection. It is true right only if it is a benefit or favor. This sets a limit for our practice of it, an inner limit, a limit in defining which we cannot rely on the right as such, which is always the letter, a real limit, because right is a task and it is to be administered according to the understanding of him who gave the task. We are asked how far we may and can and will go in practicing the right (or law) that is ours. We think here of the problems of the death penalty, the duel, tyrannicide, and war. We have expressly dealt with these in the chapter on the command of creation[37] and will not do so again, because they can be put more sharply there. But we do have to ask at least whether the last resort of the social order, the putting to death of those who oppose law, can have for us the appearance of true right. Can I understand the killing of others as a benefit, as an act that serves their sanctification, as a visible sign of invisible grace, and to that extent as an honoring of God? Can a sinner who is reconciled to God say this final word to another: "You are guilty of death"—even though he has supreme right on his side? May and must this last verse of the nasty

---

[35]Apparently a free rendering of the saying of Augustine: "The sacrament is a visible form of invisible grace," *Quaestiones in Pentateuchum* III, q. 84 (MPL 34, 712); for the interchangeability of "sign" and "form" cf. *De civitate Dei* X, 5.
[36]Cf. especially Act IV, Scene 1.
[37]See above pp. 143ff.

political song be sung too? Or do we have here an illegitimate transgression of the inner limit of the administration of right? Does intrinsically wrong human right become here *diabolical* wrong before which we must halt with fear and trembling? The limit can, of course, be set much earlier. It could well be that the first verse of that song would be better left unsung because it is intrinsically lacking in purpose and therefore in right. The modern tendency to soften penal laws and verdicts and punishments, the movement of pacifism, the instinctive distaste of many who are not the worst of people for all that has to do with law and politics, the indifference, even of Christians, which no theological teachings or exorcisms can banish, toward the life of the state which is so permeated by the poison of the mere letter, the thesis of Sohm that the establishment of church law was the apostasy of the church from its true being[38]—all this can make sense as an assertion of a true position on right, of the meaning and purpose of right. It must be understood as at least a necessary, if perhaps materially defective reaction to a right of the letter which is diabolically wrong. The question to the bearer of right rightly has to be put, and recognized as a question, from this side too.

We close by recalling that the bearer of right, too, must know and consider that God alone can do right. The concept of the "city of God" is a good one.[39] But it is also a dangerous one. Any city of God that we seek and in which we can be at work—as we are called to be—can never be more than an earthly city of God. No monarchy or democracy can ever be theocracy except very indirectly. Not everywhere will people be imprudent enough openly to make the indirect relation a direct one as in imperial Rome, in Münster in 1535,[40] atheistically in the Soviet Union, and sometimes at least, it would seem, in modern America. Nevertheless recognition of the indirectness of the relation, which we find in Calvin,[41] which we cannot deny to at least the official theory of the papacy,[42] and which even the clever Mussolini does not seem wholly to reject,[43] does not protect us against a danger which threatens us in spite of all our establishing and upholding of the right, namely, that of the deifying or idolizing of man and his right, by which the latter destroys itself. This recognition has to be put into practice and it is by no means self-evident that this will occur. In the practice of true right man must

[38]Cf. R. Sohm (1841-n1917), *Kirchenrecht I* (Munich and Leipzig 1892), p. 700: "Church law is in contradiction with the nature of the church."
[39]The title of Augustine's famous work composed between 413 and 426/27.
[40]In 1535 Dutch and Friesian radicals tried by force to set up "the kingdom of Zion" in the city of Münster, but were ousted by the bishop and neighboring princes—a victory for conservative forces which would have fateful consequences for the further history of Anabaptism in Europe.
[41]Cf. *Inst.* IV, 20, 1–3.
[42]Cf. the two encyclicals of Leo XIII, *Diuturnum illud* (6/29/81) and *Immortale Dei* (11/1/1885), Denzinger (1858 and 1866).
[43]Cf. above p. 135, n. 16: Mussolini's 1929 pact with the Vatican.

indispensably give place to the one who commissions him. There is a sabbath of law too, as was significantly perceived in the law of Israel with its institution of the so-called year of jubilee [cf. Lev. 25:8ff.]. We must always remember that the giver of the commission and its bearer are not the same. Recollection of this will prevent the church from merging into the state and the Christian from merging into the executive of law. Even as executives of law we can only be people, and as such we ought especially to be this—not gods, either in judgment or in blessing. Crossing this limit on either side sets up diabolical wrong in the right. In the question whether we are aware that we are human and not divine, one can see summed up all the questions with which we are encircled and about which we have to speak here.

c. The Thou of the neighbor becomes an authority to us from the standpoint of the *custom* which he represents. The concept of custom has in common with that of right that it, too, denotes the order of human life in concert. There do not necessarily have to be special contents of custom as distinct from those of law. Any custom can become law, and what is law can also be custom at the same time. The difference is that the order of common human life that is denoted by custom is not based on public acknowledgment or protected by public power, but only on the free consent and practice of a majority of people at a given time and place. The obligatory element in custom lies in the quiet, but all the more intensive force of a consent and practice of the majority which is not expressly stated in any letter and does not visibly rule by any external power. In the element of freedom with which this authority comes before us, the concept of custom resembles that of education. We can understand all education as an introduction to free integration into what is customary around us, and we can understand all custom as the free product of a particular education. Yet the authority of custom differs from that of education by reason of that which links it to right or law. Its starting point and goal are not the individual, but human life in concert. Its appeal for my voluntary obedience still means, finally, a specific renunciation of my freedom in favor of the agreement and practice of the majority.

Here again, theologically, we are not on the ground of creation but on that of Christ's kingdom among sinners. The mystical entity "they," which was often mentioned in our discussion of the concept of right, and which is decisive for that of custom, is understandable only when men stand in disobedience. In paradise there were no schools and no police. Similarly, and in view of its intensity we must say especially, there was no gentle, unseen, and all the more penetrating "they" of custom. Nothing is more distinctive of Romanticism, which will not take the loss of paradise into account, than its repudiation of custom, its emancipation from ruling practice which, linked perhaps with an external but scornful acknowledgment of law and a tacit but superior acceptance of education, hides among or behind these concessions. If it is not the caprice of the individual, this will, of course, in its last stage, self-ironically, crystallize without fail into a new habit, into a custom that crosses out custom. This is the unavoidable outcome of every sectarian and freelance movement. But these are meant to be a return to Adam and Eve, who do not need to listen to "they" but only to their own inner voices in order to act morally. Let us make no mistake! There is always a bit of the Romantic, the sectarian, and the freelance in all of us. Man is ingenious. He sees that the education that he is given has its limits and that the right that encounters him has its gaps. Even if he submits to the authority of both, he is still left with an almost infinitely broad area in which he is beyond the reach of those authorities. Who of us can deny that we feel at home in this area—"Here I am, and may be, man"?[44] The solemn demonstration of this "Here" is, of course, the carnival with its freedoms, at which teachers silently shake their heads, which the police benevolently and tactfully ignore, and in relation to which one can forget for a while that even the carnival is possible only as a custom, a breach of custom only within custom, a breach of custom regulated by definite customs.

The problem of custom becomes acute when it is obvious that our ingenuity deceives no one, that the "Here" is an illusion, that where education and right or law fail they are pitilessly replaced by unwritten tradition and practice, that we are pursued by "they" even into the breach of custom. Let us grant that there really is for us an infinitely broad area with no teachers and no police. If I cannot boast of being Robinson Crusoe, the neighbor or fellow human is still in this area, and even before he wills to teach or correct me, even as he does so and even beyond these possibilities, he expects from me my willing assent to a specific line of conduct which makes it possible for him to live with me, judging and dealing with me according to the standard of the question whether my conduct is that which is expected of me in this sense. The willing assent and line of conduct that are expected of me will in content be different in times of carnival and times of fasting, in rural and urban areas, in social circles that esteem ancient traditions and freer groups of discontented people, in London and Patagonia, ⌐in middle-class society and proletarian society.⌐ Its content can encounter me in a fixed and unequivocal form—or as something that is engaged in development or decay, unclear, equivocal, and self-contradictory, as "they" that do not yet know, or no longer know, what they really want. Nevertheless, embodied in my neighbor, it always encounters me as education and right encounter me. It claims me. It sets me before decision. It tells me that free area is not really free to the extent that in it, too, I am questioned and I have to answer either by submitting to custom or breaking it.

Where education and right end, custom takes over as a third authority,

[44]J. W. Goethe, *Faust*, Part I: Before the Gate.

as a third source, not grounded in ourselves, of the demand that is directed to us, as a third thing that comes upon us. Custom, too, is undoubtedly a painful experience, and, as such, an authentic one. It is painful because it searches me out in my last robber fastness. It is painful because of the self-evident way in which it usually attacks again at once when it has hardly been repulsed. It is painful because of the almost mystical way in which that which allegedly holds good seeks to maintain and establish itself against my own individuality without any external letter or force, and yet with all the otherness of what is proper to my fellowmen. It is painful because the demand of the customary, unlike that of the right, applies to the whole of life, because it allows no private life in which, when the eye of the guardian of custom exposes me, I can act contrary to custom without penalty. It is painful because of the way in which society takes revenge on me when I break custom, rendering me innocuous by no longer treating me as an individual with whom one can have dealings on the ground of free tradition and practice, but taking me seriously only as an object of its education and law. Where no fellowship of custom is possible between individuals, an impersonal and objective sense of superiority usually comes into play on the part of those who feel that they are the advocates of violated custom. Behind all custom stands the warning: If you do not give your willing assent to what is customary here, once we know it, you will be an impossible person for us until we have taught or corrected you, until we have shown you in some way who is master. We shall no longer talk *to* you; we shall only talk *about* you as we talk with astonishment about what is impossible. We are possible as persons among persons only if we do what "they" do. The paradox, the harshness of custom is that in our freedom (the freedom that is provisionally left to us by education and right) we are not free. We have to follow the unwritten law of those around us. If not, we risk the loss of all the spontaneity of those around us in relation to us. |

It is clear that we have a new thing here, and perhaps the most incisively new thing of all compared to paradise. Where custom is set up and upheld and silently or explicitly applied to the individual, his person is questioned in a way that does not happen through education or law. "They" claim his private life. "They" replace him and his true being. "They" judge him. "They" take him seriously only to the degree that he submits. The question is: How? And here again we must candidly admit above all the ambivalence of the authority that claims us. In fact, it is only men that stand behind custom: people with the great selfishness with which they do not want to be disturbed by my occasional extravagances either in their rest or in their own greater or lesser extravagances, with the great anxiety on the other hand with which they mistrustfully expect such extravagances from me, and finally[45] with the great self-righteousness with which they have set themselves up as my

---

[45]The original repeated "on the other hand."

watchers and judges so that perhaps, probably, indeed certainly, as they watch and judge me, they may grope their way to some free area where at last, at last, they will find no authority over *them*. The great entity called "they" is, on the one side, our personfiied fear of ourselves, of the desires by which we are driven and know that we are driven, and, on the other side, the personified resentment of prisoners against those who, in contrast to themselves, can break through to freedom.|

This is one side of the matter. But this matter, too, has another side. It would be and is romanticism to proclaim obedience to custom on the ground of this true insight. There is cause for that fear and resentment. "They" are not just a demon. They cannot just be dismissed with a grand gesture on the basis of a Christian view of life: "Begone, we are enlightened!" On a Christian basis, I must start with the insight that nothing good is to be expected of me, of my free person, of the being that would like to follow its own inclinations on the far side of education and right. I have to understand the neighbor when, in his dealings with me, he tries to safeguard himself as much as possible even beyond the spheres of education and right. I myself really need the neighbor in that free area. I need him as he is in all his questionability, in all the slimness of his claim, in all the demonic distortion which I find gaping at me in the "they" of his custom. It may be that I see through it all. It may be that I have no illusions about it. Indeed, I have to be without illusions if, in this form, too, I am to perceive a superior authority in my neighbor. What is in question is not that I esteem and value *him* but that I honor in him (in him as the representative of the custom of those around me) the wonderful messenger of God. For my sanctification takes place in this acknowledgment: the sanctification which I need also, and especially in the sanctuary of my private life into which custom peers so penetratingly. The neighbor who searches me out in such an unpleasant way as a guardian and judge of custom, the neighbor who tacitly or explicitly, occasionally or constantly, controls me with the question whether my conduct is tolerable or annoying to those around me, whether people will continue to speak to me or will have to begin speaking *about* me—this neighbor on his watchtower cannot, of course, reconcile me to God, just as the teacher and policeman cannot do this, but he can and should remind me of the law of God to which I am under obligation as a member of the people of God.

Why should not this law and obligation be hidden in the best custom, even though its content may seem to be unimportant, even though it may be simply a matter of questions of decorum and politeness, and even though these questions may not seem to be properly answered by the custom concerned? We have no chance of escaping the claims that custom might mean for us. In so doing we might be evading God himself whose human instruments are always in truth poor instruments. Not only did Paul direct Christians, in Romans 13, to the right of the pagan *state*. More surprisingly, in Philippians 4:8, he obviously directed them also to the validity of pagan *custom*: "Whatever is true, whatever is honorable, whatever is just, whatever is pure, whatever is lovely, whatever is gracious, if there is any excellence, if there is anything worthy of praise (acknowledgment), think about these things." Precisely as the guardian and judge of custom encroaches upon us in this way, as the representatives of education and right cannot do, he is in a special way the neighbor from whom we will not want to be free if we do not want to be free from Christ. When and as he makes us think and understand—and this cannot take place in an externally nonexistent matter—that we stand under obligation as those who are reconciled to God, then no matter who he is or how things may be with him and what may be the motive of his reproach, he is for us the bearer of Christian or church custom. There is no little decision about our adjusting or not adjusting to custom that might not carry within it the great and final decision about our obedience or disobedience to God. Custom can always seem to be profane and non-Christian or antichristian. If it expressly calls itself Christian, more rather than less caution is needed in this regard. If the point of custom is not truly to put me under obligation, if it protects my pride instead of attacking and pruning it, if it exalts me above my neighbor instead of humbling me before him, if it has become either unlawful or pharisaic custom—and the two are closer together than might appear at a first glance—then it must be repudiated and broken. Paul tells us to *think* about these things [Phil.4:8], not to *do* them, as he says about the gospel's command of faith which is heard through them [4:9]. It may be that we are summoned to upset or destroy an ancient custom, knowing what the results will be for us, ready to accept them, knowing also that upsetting and destroying an ancient custom can only mean setting up a new one for which we then accept responsibility. The question arises, and we are asked, as to our relation to custom, but again in such a way that given custom as it meets us in the claim of the neighbor has a relative advantage, since we have to consider it and what may be its positive bearing. We can never sell out to it. It can never be impossible for us to have to break it. But we always have to take seriously the fact that it is there, that it is there in constantly new forms, and that in its own very intimate way it has a voice as a criterion by which we are *also* measured.

It is very hard to speak of the extent to which we are also summoned to represent the authority of custom to others. It is hard because custom as the free order of sociey and the private life of its members is a much finer, sharper, and more dangerous weapon than right or education, a weapon which one hesitates to put explicitly in human hands because of the immeasurable mischief that can be and is done by it. Would it not be better to say nothing at all about the active side of this matter? If promoting education and right is a task which we will not seek if we know what is at issue, the office of a guardian and judge of custom seems to be from the very first an impossible one. Nowhere more than in the concept of custom do we see the relative, fleeting, changeable, and transitory nature of all human authority. Nowhere does human authority prove so oppressive and restrictive to others. Nowhere do its retaliatory measures in the case of resistance affect so incisively the lives of others than when it is exercised in the name of custom. Nowhere more than when we ourselves undertake to exercise authority in this sphere do we stand more sharply before the question whether we are not hypocrites laying on others burdens that we know we cannot bear ourselves, though perhaps in some other respect. When we know all this, when we have perhaps been already the object of the guarding and enforcing of custom by others, when we know what it would mean for us if custom were enforced on us in all its stringency, or when, conversely, we have already had experience of the role in which we experience the grim necessity of having to accuse ourselves of being hypocrites, we shall be inclined to shrink back more from the active side of the problem than from the passive side, and to keep away in horror from the office in question. Would it not be better to leave the enforcement of custom to all kinds of pedants, pharisees, reactionaries, and sticklers for principle who feel called to do this to their own hurt—for how can those be good people and who will not steer well clear of them?|

"Do unto others as you would that they should do unto you."[46] Where does this apply more than here? How can we not seriously wish that others would not do this to us? But this wish is romanticism, secret lawlessness. We have to count on it that the custom of those around us, with all the burdens it means for us, with all its human, only too human determination alongside and in the fact that it is the result and product of human sin, no better and no worse than that which opposes it, contains within itself, like education and right, an inescapable divine claim, proclaimed through our fellowmen, upon the sphere of private life which education and right cannot touch, a final correction of the arrogance of individual life. If we see that this claim is indeed inescapable, if we see the necessity of custom, then let us be honest and confess by our own act that it has to be protected and upheld and enforced. We must not leave this task to those unpleasant people and watch them make themselves more and more unpleasant. Here, too, we must not try to keep our own fingers clean. The worst hypocrisy could well be that of anxiously avoiding the company of hypocrites, of not accepting the danger and need of having to accuse ourselves of being hypocrites, of simply letting ourselves, as it were, come to this conclusion about others. The most profound indifference, coldness, and harshness in relation to others could well be that of refusing to do to them what we know has to be done simply in order not to expose ourselves. Our clean fingers regarding pharisaism could well be the worst pharisaism. If we do not just fall in with custom as an external

[46]Cf. p. 81, n.5.

necessity, so that we can feel superior to it in our hearts, if we affirm it as a necessity of life to which we as sinners must submit, as we do to education and right, then we must obviously accept it, and here, too, we obviously have to become active subjects and not just objects.|

This very difficult question is a particularly decisive question regarding our attitude to human authority in general, and therefore to the law of God under which we stand as Christians, and therefore to Christ, and therefore to the truth of our reconciliation. "Hic Rhodus, hic salta,"[47] one might say again at this point. If we hold back here, if we accept custom with gnashing of teeth or a grin as something that comes upon us but refuse to be its bearer to others, to let them see that we accept it seriously and gladly, then do we really accept it at all? Are we not still secretly romantics? Not seriously accepting custom, obviously trying to keep a free area for ourselves, do we really accept human authority in general? But then do we really accept the law of God which is infinitely superior to it but whose acknowledgment stands or falls with acknowledgment of it? But then do we really accept Christ and our reconciliation? Do we not stand outside the circle in which we are put as Christians if we want to stay clean here? Is not our staying clean, then, an infallible sign of our hidden uncleanness? If we submit to custom, knowing what we are doing, submitting to it as the bearer and expression of the divine claim that is made upon us, then we *have to* stand up before others in its name and represent it to them. And we *are able* to do this: not by birth, but by calling and baptism.

Let us be more detailed. I must and can represent custom to the extent that I can do it *in God's name*. Both positively and negatively we have to stress this here all the more strongly—more strongly than in the case of education and right—because the demand that I make on others is stronger. The mere presence of custom as such certainly does not justify me in seriously demanding that others should submit to it. In itself it is a phenomenon that has no motivating power either for them or for me, i.e., no power to motivate obedience. It may be ancient or beautiful or useful, but, no matter how true these evaluations are, their truth does not enable me to present custom as having the authority of God's law in the Christian sense. Least of all can I appeal to the fact that society, i.e., the majority in society, stands behind it with its mysterious, unexpressed, and yet expressed decision, with all the weight of habitual practice. All this may explain to others what custom is, but not that it is a command for them. To say that I need a commission. I have to be directly responsible to God if I say it. Whether I can say it in relation to a specific custom is no less a question for me than it is a question for them whether they will let themselves be told it in relation to a specific question. God must have given an answer both to them and to me. On the basis of having heard and grasped God's answer in faith, I

[47]See above p. 348, n.155.

may venture to demand and they may venture to obey. God's relation to custom, like his relation to education and right, is not a static or permanent or fixed one, but one that he fixes, one that always means a breakthrough and a decision. Hence custom becomes a command. If I abstract from this I can never be certain that I do not represent the custom of antichrist even though the custom may be the best and ostensibly the most Christian. In representing it to others I must know in detail and not just in general that I have a commission. I can represent it to them only in faith. In faith, however, I not only can but must; no matter whether its content be illuminating or less illuminating, important or incidental, old or new; no matter whether I myself in some respect need to be reminded of it and possibly more so than the others do; no matter whether I cut a sympathetic or less sympathetic figure to the others. As, if I have no commission, it is no help to me to represent the most illuminating, important, or ancient custom, or to be a most moral or eminent person, or to make by my action a most striking and winning impression; so, if I have a commission, the implausibility of the content of the custom at issue, my own moral vulnerability, and the appearance of the Pharisee that I have for others, will be no hindrance to the execution of the commission. In order that we may tread with sure steps here, here again we need above all the free spot which can be occupied by no other name than the name of God in which alone we may speak and must speak—or else keep silence.

On this presupposition, then, I cannot fundamentally refuse to cause my neighbor the unsettlement that custom must mean so very intensively for him as it does for me. We would do him no service if we left him alone, as he wishes, in the area beyond education and right, if his paths were not constantly crossed by others even in the ultimate preserve of his private life. To be for him the neighbor who with the uplifted finger of custom reminds him that here, too, there are things that are fitting and things that are not fitting, and that there is therefore a standard by which human conduct is measured, is something to which I may be called. Contrary to his own view, I must agree to make him unsettled here. Hence I may be commanded to point out to him that custom exists and that it is valid and binding for him as one who lives here among such and such people. I must do this with all the means available when it is a matter of making clear to others that they can do this but not that. I must do it by a silent proclamation of custom as I myself keep it, and thus give an active demonstration of it before their very eyes, and I must do it by openly resisting their transgression of custom. I must do it by trying to come to a friendly agreement with them, and I must do it by withdrawal from them, by transition to purely objective dealings with them, when I have to resolve on this because agreement is impossible. All these things *can* be commanded. *Whether* I am commanded in the name of custom to adopt an unsettling attitude to others, and *what* I may be commanded to do in detail along these lines, must result from reflection on the fact that the divine worth of custom in relation to them is at all events their sanctification, and that they are to be under obligation, not to a thing, but to God. This will lay some restraint upon me. It will forbid me in advance to use many means which unthinking guardians of custom usually adopt. But in some circumstances it can command me to engage in ruthless offensives and to adopt most astonishing means. I have to realize that in it I am in a strange role, that I have to play this part, as I do that of the bearer of education and right, as though I were better, or at least not so great a sinner as the other, and that I cannot think this, or at any rate cannot encounter the other with an appearance of thinking it. Yet realizing this should make me capable rather than incapable of discharging my commission. Without it I should certainly not be called to be a guardian of custom and there is always good cause to ask whether I really am called to be this. If I do realize it and am obedient to the task, then I may not refuse to place myself in relation to the other at the point where intrinsically a Pharisee might also stand. I have to show my confidence, not in my humility or the like (which might be very weak), but rather that the truth and power of a real commission will take care of themselves, that at this moment I am not just a Pharisee, and that the other will be grateful that I have adopted and not declined this thankless role in relation to him.

Still, there has to be a *purpose*. Custom, too, is *benefit* or favor to the degree that it is not just human custom but the bearer of the divine claim. Those who are summoned to represent custom have good reason to consider that it too, and it precisely, should be for the benefit in relation to which they now represent it. Representing custom to others usually stands under the severe threat that those who represent it, for all their good intentions, want to benefit themselves in the first instance. Guarding custom, like practicing education and right, means a strange enhancement of vitality for those who do it. To that extent it is pharisaical and has nothing whatever to do with the divine commission. It may be that a feeling of heightened vitality is unavoidable when we represent order to others, but this feeling must at least be strongly suppressed and fettered by the sense of hopeless jeopardy in which we put ourselves with this attitude. This sense in turn must open us to the fact that in representing order our real concern is with the others and not ourselves. A very critical circumstance here is the fact that society finds itself compelled especially to speak and to reach an understanding about those who violate its custom. Such an attempt at understanding others can have the good intention of seeking clarity as to the way in which the benefit of custom can best be imparted to them. But it often has the fatal intention of benefiting ourselves by means of the confirmation and strengthening that comes through an illuminating contrast with others: "We are not at all as they are! We stand on the ground of order on which we can live together." This consoling cry should not last more than a moment, and all related discussions of others should be as brief as possible, if we are not to run the risk of talking ourselves out of the calling which we ourselves need later in relation to what is at fault in us. People are needed who are resolved to do good to others in God's name and not to benefit themselves at the expense of others. Then none of the means that are used against others will have the character of revenge against them or triumph over them. To the extent that custom is simply used and asserted against others as an instrument of personal anxiety or joy it cannot possibly be an instrument that brings honor to God. Thus the urgent question arises in this regard: What do I want when I remind the other or others of custom? It is not enough simply to do it. There is a real need that in doing it I should will what is right so that what is right will be done.

A fourth point that has to be stated and considered, then, is that God *alone* can establish true custom and true morality. We have said that society with its custom can have a task, beyond that of education and right, in the service of the sanctification of men. But it can have this task only if it is aware of the limits of its activity, i.e., if it realizes that it can only serve their sanctification. This will keep custom from ossifying, and its use of custom from ossification. It will neither establish nor use its custom without exercising modesty in face of him who is the source and Lord of all custom and morality. This means concretely that it will do neither without counting constantly on the possibility of forgiveness. In the sphere of the concepts of education and right, forgiveness has no place, but it does have a place in the free sphere of custom. As we make use of custom, as we can always forgive those who transgress it instead of proceeding against them, as we can forgive those who transgress it even as we proceed against them, we do not abolish custom but proclaim its ultimate and most proper basis, saying the last and strongest thing that can be said about all human authority, namely, that it is itself only service to him who alone can have authority.

§13

HUMILITY

God's command means that my action as repentance before God becomes service to my neighbor. It claims me, and I have to hear it by letting myself be told that my works as those of a sinner who has been reconciled to God in Christ can only be a sacrifice of my life.

1

We must now speak about the *content* of the command of God the Reconciler. What is willed of us by this God and what should we do as the children of this God? What does it mean for us that the command of this God comes to us? What norm does it bring to direct and determine what we think and will and feel? We know from §11 that as sinners reconciled to God we have to understand our deeds as done under the *law*, i.e., as bound to the claim of our neighbor. But what is meant by "done under the law" and by being "bound" to our neighbor? In §12 we have found that it is characterized formally by the authority of the neighbor, by which we are shown that God's command comes to us concretely as law and that our neighbor is really set in relation to us as the bearer of the divine claim. We must now go on to ask what is said to us in this claim, what is the conduct that is formed by it. We realize that we cannot issue definitive decrees here, that we have not to take God's Word out of his mouth. We can only point to the reality of God's Word as it comes to each of us concretely. We can only set up criteria relating to the recognition of its content. But this can and must be done. That God's command, demanding obedience, comes to us in Jesus Christ is a characteristically distinct event that differs from all others. If it is not in our power to demonstrate it as such—for then we should have to cause it to happen—it is in our power to show in what direction it will be visible when it does happen.

This direction has already been generally established by our exposition in §11. We know that the command of God as it is now the object of our discussion does not, like the command of the Creator, coincide with the command of our own being, but is unequivocally law. We no longer need, then, to discuss the fact that what God wills of us, what ought to be done by us, encounters and confronts as something other, as a second thing, what we will of ourselves and what ought to be done in accordance with our own nature. The command is really God's command and not ours. This "not" denotes not merely the difference between Creator and creature but also the antithesis between the Holy One and sinners. Here, too, we can understand the essence of a good human will as subjection. But the subjection at issue here is characterized as that of repentance.[1] The courage (*Mut*) that we can have here to satisfy the divine claim can only be that of humility (*Demut*). We know the divine order of creation, to which our life is bound and of which we spoke at the corresponding point in the previous chapter,[2] only as a disrupted, violated, and broken order. With our disobedience, with our snapping of the bond in which we live, we have corrupted this life of ours. We live our own life as such and as a life together with others as though it belonged to us and not to God, as though we were left to ourselves and were our own lords. This means that we do not live for the right. If we see our disobedience, we can know ourselves only as those who are given up to death. Unbound willing and doing are evil. Evil

---

[1] Barth struck out here the original continuation "and as service, and indeed, as service to the neighbor, the obedience to the order of God that is at issue here."
[2] Cf. pp. 212ff.

willing and doing means leaving the only reality of life, in which we were created by God, for the absolute nothingness of that which God did not foreknow or will. When these inferences are drawn our situation is such that, although we live in the shadow of death [cf. Luke 1:79], all is not yet up with us [cf. Lam. 3:22]. On the edge of eternity, from which we can expect only our merited judgment, we again and again have time (and with it hope in relation to impending eternity). A space (for repentence) is still left for our life, for our willing and doing, even though we have to say that there really is no space for it before God, that with its goodness it has lost its freedom and dignity, and with its freedom and dignity it has lost its possibility of being. Being lost, we stand under a patience which will not let us be lost even in our lostness. For this is the reality of our reconciliation to God, a reconciliation which we have not achieved but which *has been* achieved for us by Jesus Christ and which we have *in him*. |

Our reconciliation to God means that, in spite of our fall from him, God does not take away from us fellowship with himself, but remains faithful. The primitive but vivid expression of this reality is the simple fact that we still exist, that the abyss of nothing into which we have fallen does not swallow us up, that we are held up over this abyss by the Creator who is also our Reconciler, a miracle to ourselves; that we still have life even though it is this life that is threatened by death. This already is more than is due, or beyond nature, as Roman Catholic theology would say. It can not be understood in terms of creation. It is the grace of God and it takes place for Christ's sake. As, by grace, fellowship with the life of God is not taken from us, so by the same grace, fellowship with his good will is not taken from us. In other words, his claim persists. It is not simply his claim on us as his creatures, just as God is not simply our Lord as Creator. It persists as his claim on us as those who, in spite of their guilt, are held and carried by him in the shadow of death, as the new creatures of his grace in Jesus Christ. It has as such another form, as we have seen. It is not just presented to us with life itself; it confronts this corrupted life as law. Obviously it also has a new content. Subjection to the will of God must now mean our conformity, the conformity of the sinful and lost, with him who will not let us be lost as such but who, in spite of all expectation and in defiance of all logic, loves us as such and keeps us in fellowship with himself. Subjection to the order of creation is still demanded of us, for even as sinners we are always God's creatures. But now it is also demanded of us that our willing and doing should be that of the objects of a blessing that is inconceivable even to themselves, of the recipients of the divine mercy. We sum up all that is lawful and good in this willing and doing under the concept of *humility*. One might, of course, speak of the humility of the creature in face of the Creator. To that extent we could understand the good act, even in the sense of submission to the order of creation, as an act of humility. It is more appropriate in this case, however, to speak of respect and to use the term humility in the New Testament sense of *tapeinophrosune*, specifically and expressly for the attitude of the sinner who is upheld by the grace of God.

That we are lowly does not belong necessarily to the concept of our creaturehood. Strictly speaking it contradicts it. But it does belong necessarily to our being as sinners whom God has graciously blessed. Again, that our act has to be a confession of our lowliness if it is to be good does not belong necessarily to our submission to God. There might be an appropriate submission to God which has about it nothing of lowliness but is an actualization of our own freedom and dignity. But such lowliness does belong necessarily to the submission of those who are rescued like brands from the burning [cf. Amos 4:11] to him who has rescued them in this way. There can be no question here of the legitimate self-consciousness with which man might subject himself to the order of creation (because in this obedience he would be living perfectly his own divinely given life and thereby obeying God). For from the very outset there stands in the background the recollection that he does not in fact do this, that the basis of his life is taken away from him by his own guilt, that he has not deserved to continue in life, but that God has continued to turn to him. Self-consciousness is possible here only in the negation of all self-consciousness, as God-consciousness. The mark of our fellowship with God is a strict "from above" which we cannot reverse and cannot even conceive of as a "from below." It is the coordinate that we can grasp only as the limit of our own life's system. It is the reality by which we are constantly judged even as we are blessed. Here, then, we are lowly in a twofold sense. First, it has been brought to light that we have humbled ourselves by our guilt, that by our own fault we have fallen from the height of creaturely freedom and dignity on which we ought to stand before God, that we have deserved our fall and can advance nothing at all in our favor. Second, it has been shown that God loves us and seeks us out even in this sinfulness of ours, that he has spoken to us afresh and drawn us to himself, that in our lowliness, in the lack of any majesty, greatness, wisdom, righteousness, and divine likeness of our own, he stands in for us and may be had by us. To let this God-consciousness be our self-consciousness, and therefore to act always in this lowliness, is humility. Humility is courage. It is the attitude of those who are held up in their fall and saved in their lostness. It is not despair but trust in despair. The act of humility is a good act. God gives grace to the humble [cf. 1 Pet. 5:5; James 4:6]. But the courage, goodness, and grace of humility are new and different. The content of the demand that we should walk humbly before God [cf. Mic. 6:8] is quite distinct from that of the demand that we should respect the order of creation which is the order of our own life. In both cases there must be acknowledgment of the overlordship and honor of God. In both cases it must be shown that he is our Lord and we belong to him. But God's rule in his creation differs from his rule among his enemies [cf.Ps. 110:2]. His honor shines in one way in the establishment of his original and inviolable order, and in another way in his mercy to those who have broken it. There is a difference between our belonging to him by birth and our belonging to him by the new birth of grace.

Obviously, too, there is a great difference when, as submission to God's will is required of us, we have to contemplate the miracle of our creation and existence in the light of the miracle of our reconciliation. The demand now is plainly that we should stay in this life, that we should not for a moment leave it, that all our acts should be done in this light. Its decisive content now is plainly that we should not forsake, but confess the lowliness with which we stand before God, not because the sin in which this lowliness has its basis is now good, but because for us all goodness lies in the fact that God has sought us out in our sin and accepted us in and with our sin. Negatively, the humility that is required of us now consists of taking heed that we do not aspire to a purity in which we will no longer see ourselves as sinners, since Christ dwells only in sinners, having come down from heaven, where he dwells in the righteous, in order to dwell in sinners, so that in him we may have peace through confident despair of self and its works (cf. Luther to Spenlein, 1516, Enders 1, 29).[3] The only good act now is the act in which we confess our sin, reach out to God as sinners, and yield to him where he has sought and found us, because that is where we really are. It cannot be the act in which we claim to stand and act in the direct fellowship with God, which we all lost in Adam's fall and which among all men belongs only to Jesus Christ who reconciles all the rest of us to God. The arrogance of trying to be unfallen Adam, or even Christ, is now the real mark of a bad act, good though it may seem to be in content. Our fellowship with God has been restored in Christ, but, as we have seen, it is now an indirect and mediated fellowship, and our obedience to God cannot now mean that we are not sinners, but that we act as sinners, yet as sinners that have been sought out and accepted by God in Christ. At every step, then, the true Christian life will be the Christian life to the extent that it is penitence before God and therefore service to the neighbor, or, in sum, to the extent that it is offered as a sacrifice. In this section we shall speak first about the connection between sacrifice and repentance, then about the connection between sacrifice and service, and finally about the divine institutions of church and state which constitute the orders of repentance and service.

2

The Christian life whose characteristic determination we are now investigating is constituted by the miracle of the mercy of God. When

---

[3]Letter to Georg Spenlein, April 8, 1516 (WAB 1, 35, 28ff.).

we reflect on our existence, and on the claim of God under which we stand, in the light of the fact that we exist as those who are disobedient to God but to whom God does not impute this disobedience but imputes instead the obedience of Christ, and that we are claimed as people of this kind, then we must understand our existence as one of being inconceivably upheld over the abyss of the death to which we have fallen victim and which we have merited. But then, obviously, we must understand the claim that is laid upon us as a requirement to establish and demonstrate the fact that we are inconceivably upheld over the abyss in this way. "What shall we do?" "Be what we are," is the answer that must be given. But seen in the light of our reconciliation in Christ we are no more than brands plucked from the burning [cf. Amos 4:11]. That our deeds should bear witness to this is what is required of us. We have already pointed out that the content of the command of reconciliation has in common with the command of the Creator that in both cases we belong not to ourselves but are under obligation to God. Strictly, however, it is obviously only in the second formulation of the divine command, where the application is to favored sinners, that the obligation is one of guilt as well as debt (the two senses of the German *schuldig*). That we are under obligation to God means, here, not only that our right to ourselves is essentially subordinate to God's right to us, that our claim to life can be legitimate only in the framework of the claim that he by whom our life is given has upon us, but also that we have to offer our life to God as those who have corrupted it and who have to bring with this offering an equivalent of their having fallen victim to death. We now have to understand our existence not merely in the simplest and most natural sense as a gift, the gift of being created, but also as a gift of the divine goodness and patience which cover and bear our sin. We are now in debt to God as those who have put themselves in debt, although God has not drawn the consequences from this which result by right, and which necessarily affect, therefore, the meaning of the claim of God under which we stand. The consequences that could and should be drawn are not drawn for Christ's sake. The fully justified wrath of God, which ought to take its course, is arrested in Christ. But in Christ the divine claim is still made upon us and it is now obviously a claim on people who in the double sense belong to God and are sanctified to him. Primarily, then, we have to say that, by adding the second sense, the understanding of the command as the command of God the Reconciler, far from weakening its character as divine control over us, very strongly underlines, so that we cannot possibly miss it, the categorical "We are not our own but God's"[4] which already forms the content of the command of the Creator. The action required of us is obviously not only action in the reverence that is proper to the creature which has no reality without God, but action in the humility of the creature whose reality has

---

[4]J. Calvin, *Inst.* III, 7, 1.

fallen through its guilt and which has received again the time that it has, not now as an attribute of its creaturely reality, but as a pure gift of grace, a gift to which it has no right in the framework of creaturely claims. Relevant here is the biblical description of man as a servant of God in the sharp sense of a slave, of one who no longer owns himself but is owned by another. Human action is now good when it takes place within this bondage. We shall speak first of what this means inwardly in relation to God, of the claim that is made upon us to repent. In the next subdivision we shall then speak of what it means outwardly in the concrete relation to other people, of the claim that is made upon us to live a life of service.

If, first, we ask from this new standpoint, what we are to do in relation to God, the Bible in both Old Testament and New offers us at the decisive point the concept of sacrifice. We shall try in what follows to answer the question with the help of an analysis of this concept and in so doing find out how appropriate it really is.

a. To sacrifice is to take something vitally important that belongs to us and freely to offer it in recognition of the higher right of the one to whom it is offered. Sacrifice by man to God is possible only as the act of the man who has come under obligation to God in that twofold sense. In the Bible, sacrifice begins only after expulsion from paradise [cf. Gen. 4:3f.]. In paradise, God's higher right to what belongs to man is acknowledged, not by offering it to God, but by possessing it to God's honor. There, in the limits of his creatureliness, in the bounds of his obedience, man is instituted lord above all not only of his life but even of all creation [cf. Gen. 1:28]. But sinful man, who does not make that acknowledgment, who as the possessor of his own life violates God's honor, stands under another order. In virtue of God's mercy, life is not taken from him but his right to it stands now in open collision and friction with God's higher right, and only God's goodness and patience prevent it from simply being taken from him. He does not exercise his right as it ought to be exercised in virtue of its essential subjection to God's right. He is now wrong in his right. He has a right to his life only insofar as God puts grace before right. He can exercise it at root only as a loaned and undeserved right. The expression of this is sacrifice to God as it is found not only in biblical religion but in almost every religion. As man has a distinct or less distinct awareness of his disobedience; as he realizes that he has ruined his life by it; as, nevertheless, he still has life; as he acknowledges God's higher right to this life; as he also knows, however, that by his continual disobedience he violates this higher right of God in its true and original sense; as he constantly does what Adam did—he tries to make good in detail what is missing as a whole, and sacrifice results. A part of life, an important part of what is his, is dedicated to God in order to show in part, by way of indication, symbolically and demonstratively, the truth of something that unfortunately is not true in the real sense, namely, that we stand under the control of him who has created us. Because this does not take place in the proper sense, it has now to take place in the improper sense. God's right cannot triumph now in our possessing our own life as a whole and in detail and in living it to him in the consecration of real obedience. Consecration is now a specific and extraordinary thing, and it takes place in the form of forfeiting possession. What God requires of us in the kingdom of his grace and in the light of the truth that we are sinners from whom, however, he has not withdrawn his hand [cf. 1 Kings 8:57], is rightly perceived wherever sacrifice is made, namely that there has to be an offering. Wherever the good is done in this order of human existence before God, there has to be sacrifice in this sense. Man has to accept an intrusion into his own right to life, fully aware that this is not the real thing, that it is not adequate because it can be only this act and not much more, not a very different act. The order of self-denial is not the original one. In submitting to it—as we have every reason to do—we acknowledge that we are not doing the original will of God. Denying ourselves, we are not doing at all what really ought to be done in relation to God—which would be done in peace with him and with no renunciation or denial of our own will which God created good and free. Our action, then, can have no praise or greatness. It can only show that it is in some way the obedience that is proper to sinners who cannot be obedient in the exercise of their right to life but only in a demonstrative reduction of it. Yet this is in fact demanded of them to the extent that their act may and should be a true confession. If we want to obey as sinners, and hence improperly, then we must at least sacrifice. It is required that our act have the character of a voluntary diminution of our right to life, whereby we at least proclaim, and show at least in detail and symbolically, the truth of something that as a whole and properly is unfortunately not true, whereby in the collision between God's right and ours we show what should be true in peace between them, namely, that we are God's. To the degree that our action has this character, it stands under the promise that it can be obedience, the obedience of sinners to whom grace has been shown. To the degree that it does not have this character, to the degree that we succeed in not giving it the significance of a self-emptying, its character as obedience will have to be called doubtful. One cannot say that all self-denial is intrinsically good, for even from the standpoint of sacrifice its goodness still depends on some very different factors. But one can say that, in the kingdom of grace, goodness does at least always have also the character of self-denial, so that an action which lacks this character, in which we constantly affirm ourselves instead of having to deny ourselves in some regard, a supposedly paradisial action in which we think we can act as the friends of God without being forced into sacrifice, certainly cannot be a good one.

b. Sacrifice also rests on the revelation of divine reconciliation, on the recognition that mercy has come to us sinners. This is the crisis in which we stand as those who do sacrifice. This is the basic distinction between biblical, Christian sacrifice on the one side and pagan sacrifice on the other. The presence of real sacrifice or self-denial presupposes that God has given himself to be known by man even outside paradise. A sacrifice that rested merely on my own confused assertion that all might not be well with me if I am left to myself, that my corrupt relation to some higher powers might not be without guilt, and that this relation might perhaps be improved by various achievements of my own—this would be a typical sacrifice to idols such as that which the priests of Baal offered on Mt. Carmel [cf. 1 Kings 18]. If a sacrifice offered to God is to be a meaningful act, we must ask whether God has really revealed himself to us, and in his revelation demanded that we should do what we are doing. If not, then even the most zealous and sacrificial offering, even the purest and most perfect self-denial, is an act which without any distinction or significance takes place within the framework of humanity's great universal disobedience, which does not deserve to be called obedience even in the improper and symbolical sense, but which, like all the acts of what is called religion, represents the culmination of rebellion against what God truly wills. Engaged in this rebellion, haunted by unavoidable unsettlement by our own action, we venture the last and supreme act of serving ourselves with the forgiveness of sins, of using a self-invented achievement, which stands in no relation to our fault, to secure ourselves with the unknown God, or with the known God made in our own image, of making a small part payment whose mode and measure we ourselves have appointed. The Christian has to ask continually whether this is not *ethelothreskia* [cf. Col. 2:23] which makes the situation worse instead of better. Yet when we say that we need an order from God's revelation, this revelation cannot be understood in a general sense but has to be understood as the revelation of the reconciliation made by God. We have to realize that before God we are only guilty and always guilty. Without this, our sacrifice may seem to be serious but it lacks the real seriousness of an obligation. We will do what might be left undone, or do this when we might just as well have done that. We do not know in what jeopardy we stand. We do not realize that those who do not render true obedience at least *have to* sacrifice, and that they cannot offer any sacrifice but must sacrifice under specific direction. The *ethelothreskia* in which we flee from God rather than being truly obedient, the human pride which never runs to seed more than as religious pride—even and precisely under the guise of sacrifice—this, too, can be cut off only by the self-knowledge that is grounded in the knowledge of God in Jesus Christ. Similarly, real sacrifice can be made only on the ground of the knowledge of God the Reconciler. For the presupposition of all sacrifice must be that God has turned to man in and in spite of his transgression, that even outside paradise there really is not only a divine patience but also a divine faithfulness, a perseverance of God in his purpose to draw man to himself. Human sacrifice presup-

poses the divine mercy which has descended and come to us even before
we come to him and in order that we might come to him; which always
wants something from us, even and precisely from us sinners. With this
demand made also on sinners, God says and affirms that he does not let
us fall. He does not despise even what sinners can do and give. He
accepts as real obedience the improper and symbolical obedience which
we can at best render. He dwells in heaven, but also with those who are
of a humble and contrite heart [cf. Isa. 57:15] and who fear his Word [cf.
Isa. 66:2, 5]. We do not control this dwelling of God among sinners
without which all sacrifice would be pointless. It has always to take place
by God's goodness. We can sacrifice only in faith, hearing and obeying
his Word. This is the second criterion that has to be considered here.
Only in faith does man really sacrifice, really deny himself, really accept
that diminution, really bow before the God against whom he has sinned.
The Word of God and hearing the Word of God is *the* great and
fundamental breakthrough into our right. We have to accept it because
we need it. Without faith, supposed sacrifice is full of secret self-
assertion. It acquiesces in the disobedience in which we live, no matter
how big or how many sacrifices we bring. In what we do, we are asked at
the first and decisive point whether we do it in faith and whether we are
ordered to do it by the merciful God.

c. I have called the sacrifice that is required of us improper and
symbolical obedience. It is improper measured by what ought to be done
if we did not know in advance that in all that we do we are necessarily
accused as those who have gone astray. The idea is not that this
improper obedience is not as strictly required of us as the proper
obedience that we never render. Nor is it that we are less existentially
claimed by the requirement of it. Our existence as we know it is that of
sinners. The requirement being from God, it extends to the full depth
and totality of our being. But, plainly, what we do when we sacrifice,
when we deny ourselves, even though it be done in faith, can have the
significance only of a substitute achievement. God himself does the true
and decisive thing in Jesus Christ. Our action even as Christians, even as
disciples of Jesus, even in union with Christ, makes no contribution to
our reconciliation and cannot compete with the reconciliation that is
made in Christ. It cannot in any sense have the significance of merit. It
is debit, not merit. The Roman Catholic concept of grace, which sees it
as possible and even necessary that those to whom God is gracious
should be put in a position to acquire merit, i.e., to cooperate in their
salvation, rendering satisfaction to God intrinsically—this concept of
grace as a divine likeness[5] infused into our thinking, willing, and doing,
differs as a concept from grace itself. If grace triumphed by putting us in
a position to render true obedience to God, like Adam before the fall or

---

[5]Cf. Council of Trent (1545–1563), Sess. VI: *On Justification* (1547), Denz. no. 797
(814), 798, 800, 803, 804 (828) (834) (836), cf. also 809 (842).

like Christ, it would obviously triumph by ceasing to be grace for us, by being no longer needed as grace, and all the fresh grace that we seek and find could only cease afresh to be grace or to be needed as grace. But this is unacceptable, for there is no human act of obedience in which we do not necessarily find ourselves accused and guilty of going astray, no act of obedience in which we do and do not deny the real thing that we are created to do, none, therefore, in which we do not need grace afresh as grace, as the divine forgiveness, as the mercy of God. To speak differently is not to speak of what takes place between God and us even in our best moments, even at the peak of our Christian reality. Precisely our existential obedience is that of sinners, the doing of God's will not merely on earth but on this *dark* earth where even in the good and the best we are hopelessly entangled in endless error and confusion, and that not merely outwardly or occasionally, not merely because of the assaults of this wicked world which we can none of us escape, not merely because in concupiscence the tinder of sin is fatefully at work in us as an accidental remnant of original sin,[6] and not merely because there is nothing perfect on earth, nor in such a way that we are unassailed, good, and innocent in our best and innermost part. No, it is in our very best part that we find the source from which error and confusion constantly spring afresh, we ourselves being the ones who make the earth so dark. It is also true, and especially true, of Christians, and especially of serious Christians, that they must judge themselves in this way.|

I know that I render obedience, not in relation to what I do, but in relation to Christ, as I cling to the Word that is spoken to me. This is itself, when it happens, the grace that my act has found before God, and nothing more. Never do I not need the divine mercy, never does the goodness of my own action enable me to make a claim upon God. In the obedience that I render I can see no other than a substitute achievement about whose improper and symbolical character I can entertain no illusions. I can intend to be obedient—and this intention is what is usually called a good will—but I cannot appeal to this intention before God, nor seriously seek in it the goodness of my action, if I realize what it means that even my best will is *my* will. Granted that we sacrifice some of our time and energy and love of self and joy in life and will for life and power and life's potential. But when and where does not the self which is supposedly denied remain victoriously present in some greater or lesser concealment? When and where, when we have perhaps penitentially bowed our heads, do we not succeed in taking them under our arms like the three saints in the arms of the city of Zurich[7] and go merrily and confidently on our way? When do we so bury ourselves, even in dreams, that in our graves we are not already thinking of

[6]On concupiscence as the "combustible material" of sin cf. Peter Lombard, *Sent. lib II* d. 30, 7 (MPL 192, 722); Thomas Aquinas, *Quaest. disp. de malo*, qu. 3 a., 4, *S. Th. III* qu. 15a, 2, qu. 27a, 3, and Council of Trent, Sess. V: *On Original Sin* (1547), Denz. no. 792.
[7]Cf. *Schweizer Lexikon*, vol. 7, Zurich 1948, p. 1108.

resurrection? No, everyone who knows man, and especially himself, knows that man cannot really be destroyed until he dies. The virtuosos of eastern and western ascetic mysticism have sincerely attempted this in their own way. But one can hardly be persuaded that the complicated technique of self-elimination commended and described by them has anything more than the name and the appearance in common with the self-denial that God would have from us. If we really deny ourselves, either with or without mysticism, then we can never say that we have done it, but only that God in sheer grace has found it in our action. Yes, if we really hazard and give our lives, perhaps as martyrs, or as soldiers on the battlefield, or as mothers in the service of their children, does not even this stand under the proviso and limitation that we cannot give more than we have, that the self which is offered there, perhaps finally and truly, is our sinful and disobedient self, a gift that is no less unclean than anything else that we can give and that really needs the cleansing and grace and mercy of God no less than all the little things that we formerly saw ourselves constrained to offer? As we sacrifice we bear witness to our good will. But that it really is a good will testifying to our having heard and obeyed what is commanded, that by it we really do bear witness that we live by the goodness of God and nothing else, is always concealed in a mist and surrounded by a thousand question marks, and if, faced by an either-or, we have to say whether we regard it as obedience or disobedience, we can only say that even with the best intentions of which we might be conscious we can regard it only as disobedience to the extent that even here our Adamic nature finally shows through and characterizes it, and we can regard it as obedience only in the sense of the improper obedience whose acceptance by God as real obedience does not stand under our control. |

All this is more than a pessimistic recollection of the presupposition under which all goodness, even that of Christians, stands. It is a third necessary criterion of the goodness of our action, of the answer to the question: "What shall we do?"—a criterion which we certainly cannot leave out of account in the interests of the brave and resolute act of faith because, as fools think, it might have a "crippling" effect.[8] To be good, our acts must be done under the proviso that they are only a substitute achievement, that they do not measure up to what should be done, that they do not stand in any real relation to it. They have to be done in the submission which is understandable when we realize that we are unprofitable servants even when we have done all that we are commanded to do [cf. Luke 17:10]. They have to be done in need, not in a need that can be quenched, but in a constant need of the grace of God.

---

[8]Barth seems to be alluding here to a discussion that he had with his brothers Heinrich and Peter early in 1928 on the question whether there is progress in sanctification. Peter advocated this, Karl denied it. But when he uses the word "fools" he does not seem to have his brothers in mind but "humanists" and "pietists" in general; cf. K. Barth/E. Thurneysen, *Briefwechsel, Vol. 2: 1921–1930*, Zurich 1974, pp. 570–78.

It is by no means true that this proviso cripples the resolution and bravery of Christian action. The reformers, who unanimously and strictly saw all our good works set under this proviso, were obviously less hindered from brave and resolute Christian action than we are when with our familiar whimpering we first want to be sure that what is required of us is possible. There is no resolution or bravery except on the ground of truth and within the limits staked out for us. To want to ignore these limits shows poor moral enthusiasm or force; this kind of courage will be wrested from us. Protestants who find something to whine about here should simply ask themselves why, if they cannot agree to this, they do not move to the point where, on the basis of the Tridentine doctrine of justification,[9] they can be rid of all their anxieties and of all need to raise objections. The Christian action which can be crippled, which is crippled from the very outset, is surely that which cannot stand by this criterion. Those who think that by their action they can do more than simply and without claim set up a sign that they have heard, undoubtedly do less. Those who think that they have taken up God's will into their own will and therefore do not need to feel shocked, shocked to death, at their own acts, but have every reason for satisfaction with their achievement; those who believe that their sacrifice is an achievement that meets the requirement, that they are acting in continuity with Christ or with Adam before the fall; those who are not prepared to be the sinners to whom the divine claim is issued and who alone can satisfy it, undoubtedly stand in disobedience, and for all the good will of which they boast, precisely in its goodness and because of the resultant boasting, they repeat and renew the great presumption which is the secret of our Adamic existence, rather than giving the demonstration which is required as a minimum from us children of Adam to the extent that in Christ we are not just children of Adam but also and much more—even if as such—the children of God. Once again, Christ dwells only in sinners,[10] i.e., in the moral disarray in which we stand and in which we can regard moral victory only as the miracle of God and not as our own achievement. The connection between sacrifice and repentance is what may be seen here. That the whole of the Christian life ought to be penitence was Luther's charge against medieval Christianity at a decisive hour.[11] The Christian life, the life of self-denial in faith which is required of us, can have only the character of repentance. Repentance is a substitute achievement, not a proper one; it is an improper making-good of our infinite fault before God that cannot be made good by us. In no sense can repentance continue or support our reconciliation with God or compete with it. It is possible only because there is reconciliation apart from it. Only because God has

[9]Cf. Council of Trent, Sess. VI: *On Justification* (1547), Denz. no. 792a−843.
[10]Cf. above p. 403, n. 3.
[11]The first of the 95 Theses of Oct. 31, 1517: "Our Lord and Master Jesus Christ, in saying 'Repent ye, etc.' meant the whole life of the faithful to be an act of repentance."

said to us: "I absolve you,"[12] are penitence and sorrow, the confession of sin, the work of contrition, the work of self-denial and faith, the work of sacrifice, demanded of us. They are not demanded in order that the absolution may become true thereby, but as our human, very human answer, as the required answer, to what is proclaimed to us and accepted by us, as a work in the shadow of death, which is not here taken from us but into which the light of God's mercy has shone. If our work takes place in the submission appropriate to those who know that they must sacrifice, but that they can offer only unclean sacrifices, that only one clean sacrifice has been and will be offered in time and eternity, and that our sacrifices stand or fall by being accepted for the sake of that one sacrifice, then, from this standpoint at least, it is a good work. We have to realize that we are questioned from this standpoint too.

d. We must now look more specifically and closely at the positive aspect of sacrifice. We have called it a sign, witness, symbol, and demonstration. We should not say too quickly that this is not enough. What is more might be not only an impossibility but disobedience too. To witness that we have reconciliation in Christ is precisely what we can be summoned to do as sinners. It is what we *are* summoned to do. It is precisely what we *can* do, by God's grace, as sinners. We *ought* to do it. We start by being in debt to God, by seeing our existence as sinners as forfeit to him. This fundamentally entails our end; it means death. God's Word slays us by addressing us as those who are guilty of death and to the degree that our place in relation to it can only be that of those who are given over to death. In this light we can understand all that is required of us as those who are put to death but are to live. This background is plain in the Old Testament concept of sanctification in the inalienable sense of the life of many sacrificial animals pouring forth in blood. This aspect is not left behind as a preliminary stage in religious history but comes to fulfillment in the vicarious obedience and suffering of Christ as an obedience and suffering even to death. Christ is an "expiation *(hilasterion)* by his blood" (Rom. 3:25). In Christ we have really fallen victim to God. Materially, and not just symbolically, his is a wholly adequate sacrifice. In it God himself lifts the burden of our fall, of our having fallen victim, and in Christ's resurrection he shows himself to be the one who does not desire the death of the sinner but rather that he should be converted and live [cf. Ezek. 33:11]. As God himself—this is his mercy—intervenes for sinners, offering up himself in their place to the death that they have deserved by his unbreakable order, there takes place once and for all the true and proper thing which establishes and constitutes peace between God and man in spite of the latter's sin. As the bloody sacrifices of an earlier age could only foreshadow this event,

---

[12]On this formula cf. Thomas Aquinas, *S. Th. III*, qu. 84 a., 3; Council of Florence (1438–1445), *Decr. pro Armenis* (1439), Denz. no. 699, and Council of Trent, Sess. XIV: *On the Sacrament of Penance* (1551), Denz. no. 895 and 902 (919f).

so the obedience of Christians can only reflect it. We can only "be planted together in the likeness of his death" (Rom. 6:5). *This* is all that is required of us. But it *is* required of us.

A real and direct and more than symbolical likeness of our sacrifice to Christ's would not be the obedience that is required of us. It would be disobedience. We cannot fulfill our forfeiture to God by destroying ourselves, by giving up ourselves to the death that we have deserved. If we try to make good our indebtedness to God by giving away our lives, we rebel against him. We miss the point that the death of Christ that we seek to emulate was not self-destruction but obedience and suffering. We also forget that we can no more do the true and proper thing that Christ did than we can jump over our own shadows. Above all—and this is where we rebel against God—we neglect the fact that God has given us life in Christ. We neglect what has taken place once and for all in Christ. We neglect his resurrection. We are trying to do better what God has already done. We are refusing to accept God's grace. We are trying to reconcile ourselves again to God, with means that are not only inadequate but forbidden, instead of accepting the reconciliation that has taken place. Everything that has the character of self-destruction lies along this line of disobedience. The question that has to be put to all our ascetic endeavours is whether they are not oriented to this forbidden self-destruction which has nothing whatever to do with the commanded Christian self-denial, but is its exact opposite. Thus we neither can nor should fulfill our own forfeiture to God. For us obedience is precisely that, living on the basis of God's goodness and patience, we should respond with our lives, our sinful lives, to the reconciling death of Christ. We are certainly slain by God's Word insofar as it pronounces that we are forfeit to God. But as those who are put to death by God's Word we neither can nor should seek to put ourselves to death. We can and should *live* as those who are put to death by the Word. This is what is required of us. But what does it imply?

We have rejected the Roman Catholic doctrine of grace according to which we no longer need grace as grace inasmuch as we receive it, but begin to be no longer sinners, a righteousness of our own being imparted to us in our justification, a possibility of earning merits, even if on the basis of Christ's merit, and therefore of having a part in the accomplishment of our reconciliation. But the fact that we are still sinners, even though sinners saved by grace, does not rule out the fact that the life of sinners is totally different if God is gracious to them from what it would be if he were not. It is "totally different," we say, to the extent that in human differentiation and within our relative distinctions we can say that anything is "totally different." It is not totally different in the way that the holy God is totally different from us fallible humans. It is not totally different in the way that we are totally different as God in his grace sees us in Jesus Christ from what we are as we have to see ourselves under his judgment. It is not totally different in the way that

God's thoughts are higher than our thoughts and his ways are higher than our ways [cf. Isa. 55:9]. To think so would be to take the Roman Catholic view of the new life of the Christian, before which, if we are not completely out of contact with the insight of the Reformation, we can only start back with horror as before the expression of unheard-of religious arrogance. But if God speaks with us sinners as such, if he wants something from us, if we are to *live* as those who have been slain by his Word, if penitence is required of us as sinners, this obviously means that there are differences in what we can do, distinctions of more and less, of nearer and more distant, in relation to the standard by which we are measured, changes in conduct between the mere confirmation that we are sinners and the confirmation that we are sinners saved by grace, possibilities of giving a sign that we have heard and understood that God is gracious to us as distinct from other possibilities in which it is simply shown that we stand in need of mercy but not that we have received it.

We realize that these differences stand under two provisos. The first is that when we think of the judgment under which we stand, of our having been put to death by the Word, they undoubtedly stand on the same plane like different levels on the surface of the earth when seen from the sun. The better possibilities cannot entail any deification of man, or even any participation in his reconciliation, any merit. The second proviso (and this qualifies the comparison that we have just used) is that the differences are not as solid as different levels on the earth's surface, small though these may be when seen from the sun. It does not lie in our power to make these distinctions, i.e., to see in our conduct something different, and in and with this something better. The possibilities that we reach after do not have intrinsically this or that symbolic force which we have only to use correctly in order to be obedient. That even relative distinctions *really do exist* between this and that human action in relation to the grace of God, that the signs and testimonies that we can give are not empty but significant, that our demonstrations are meaningful, depends in each individual case, no matter what signs we reach after, neither on us nor on the signs, but on God's acceptance of what we do, on his good-pleasure in it according to the free and righteous judgment which he alone exercises. Cain, too, brought an offering and God did not take pleasure in it [cf. Gen. 4:3ff.]. Hence we can only obey and we have to realize that it lies with God whether he finds in our action the obedience that he requires of us. But we *must* obey. This means that we must take seriously the possibility of differences for all their relativity. Our life that is forfeit to God is now lived in the sphere of these relative differences. It is God's grace that we can be obedient in this sphere, that we should not be so shut up in disobedience [cf. Rom. 11:32] that there is not constantly put to us, as those who are disobedient, the question of obedience, the question of unassuming obedience that raises no claim and is referred to God's specific pleasure, yet very truly and very seriously the question of obedience. We do not stand before God like those who have looked at the sun and can no longer see, but in his light we see light [cf. Ps. 36:9]. To be sure, it is only a small earthly light, no more and no less, and we see even this only in his light. But in his light we do see light, and we must want to see it, and may not act like the lazy servant who, because he had received only one pound, and argued that his master was a hard one, went and buried it instead of at least putting it to work [cf. Matt. 25:14–30 par.]. In the life of those who are slain by the Word there is always something totally different to which they must do justice and orient themselves, and for which they must strive, namely, the possibility of a holy and living sacrifice that is pleasing to God [cf. Rom. 12:1]. This lies always under the provisos mentioned, yet because of them one must not say that it does not exist. Three things, it seems to me, need to be said about this relative but serious "wholly other" in the life of the Christian.

1. The sinner saved by grace is at least called to *metanoia*—we come back to the concept of repentance. "Be transformed by the renewal of your mind, your thinking," is the way that Paul puts this in Romans 12:2. In an antiintellectualistically inclined age like our own we need to contend a little for the basic significance, not to be ignored because of all the outcry against reason, of new and correct thinking. Paul does not speak about thoughts but about thinking itself, to which he allots a decisive significance for life. Thinking, as he says later, is the true instrument of the decisions that we constantly have to take in our relation to the will of God. Everything depends, not on what we think, but on how we think. We are summoned, as the term *metanoia* implies, to think correctly. Repentance is fundamentally a return to correct thinking. It involves a renewal of reason and understanding. In and with the new thing that reason acquires through the Word it must itself become new, i.e., open to the miracle of mercy which is, of course, higher than all reason [cf. Phil. 4:7], open to this thing that is higher than itself. The unheard-of thought: You and not I! I only through You!, the transvaluation of all values by the Word of forgiveness, the inconceivable thought of the freedom and lordship of God, must now take it captive as a first and necessary thing which all else can only follow and to which all else must be subject. We must strongly underline the relativity of this new and open thinking which, knowing about God, is moved and determined by the miracle of God. We must insist that it depends on God himself whether it will become the theme of our thinking, whether the miracle which takes our thinking captive will really be God's miracle and not a lying miracle of Satan. What is certain is that if it is so, if this relative thing that is wholly determined by God's grace really happens, if this new thinking takes place in us, if our thinking is done from this new center, then something significant is present. A sign is set up, a sign among other human and demonic signs,

yet a sign. Obedience is rendered and a sacrifice is offered: Obedience because God undoubtedly wills it, a sacrifice because over against what we usually think in and of ourselves a new thinking of this kind is undoubtedly a surrender, a *sacrificium intellectus*. This takes place in the midst of our lives and yet as something "totally different." In it we have not for a moment ceased to be sinners but we have done something to bear witness that we are not just sinners. Nor can we deny that we are summoned to do it.

2. The sinner saved by grace is at any rate summoned as such to make a protest against his sin, i.e., against himself. As God is gracious to him, he also judges him, and he must confess that this judgment is just, i.e., that God is in the right against him. This participation in the attack of the Word upon us must be seen as something no less decisive in the act of repentance than the commencement of new thinking. Or rather, we must say that the new thinking would not commence and would be merely a new thought—possible for unrenewed thinking and therefore a work of our refusal to repent—if it were achieved by our own will and did not signify the breaking of this will of ours. The sinner saved by grace is a special sinner who differs from others in that his will is a broken one, that even as a sinful will it is also a will for God who, in the sinful self-will of the sinner, has regenerated him as his own child by his Word of power. This cannot be said about man as such. It can be said only about the man who is sought and found by God in Christ, who is in the church. This entails for man, of course, the situation of Romans 7. It means that man is entangled in the most unheard-of self-contradiction. This self-contradiction is not to be equated with the contradiction between soul and body, between the spiritual and material nature, in which the sinner as such is entangled, and which is described in Goethe's saying about the two souls that dwell, alas, in my breast.[13] It is a far cry from this to Paul's saying: "Wretched man that I am! Who will deliver me from this body of death?" [Rom. 7:24]. In all its hopelessness, Paul's "Wretched man that I am!" characterizes the Christian situation. This is the contradiction between spirit and flesh, between the beloved child of God that I am and the Adamic man, the child of wrath by nature [cf. Eph. 2:3], that I also am. To be sure, redemption in Jesus Christ removes the contradiction. But we have only the expectancy of this redemption, the Holy Spirit as its pledge [cf. 2 Cor. 5:5, etc.]. This expectancy of the redemption of the body [Rom. 8:23]—and this is the grace in which we stand [cf. Rom. 5:2]—is the ground of the contradiction in which we also stand. Not every sinner, but the sinner to whom God is gracious, stands in this contradiction. How can those who have not received the Spirit stand in the conflict between the Spirit and the flesh [cf. Gal. 5:17]? How can they know how dreadful it is? Only those who are God's dear children really know this. Hence we must

[13]Cf. J. W. Goethe, *Faust*, Part I: Before the Gate.

confess the grace that has come to us by confessing the contradiction: not that we contradict God, but that we are contradicted by God. Let us not be under any illusion that we can succeed in demonstrating unequivocally even to ourselves our standing in this protest against ourselves. The whole tumult of the battle into which we are plunged as reconciled people will outwardly be similar, even to the point of confusion with the din of the strife in which unreconciled people also find themselves. A distinction can never be made with true and final clarity by any ears but God's alone. We are in no position, then, to differentiate with ultimate and compelling clarity between ourselves as the reconciled and others as the unreconciled. Only God knows how many whom we regard as complete children of the world might not have stood for a long time, and more fundamentally than we ourselves, in the same great and saving contradiction and therefore in the peace of obedience. Nevertheless, no matter how it may be with others, whose judges we are not in any case called to be, and no matter how dependent we may be on God's good pleasure for all the ultimate seriousness of our obedience, we are in fact summoned to this obedience and therefore to this protest. The reaching of the goal to which we are summoned is not in our power. The authenticity of our protest rests always with the judgment of God. Nevertheless it is at each moment a "totally different" thing whether or not we let ourselves be summoned, whether or not we aim at the goal. Aiming at the goal will not make us righteous. But as those who are made righteous we have to aim at the goal. With our being made righteous, this is demanded of us by him who makes us righteous. The brokenness of our will is a symbol that cannot *not* be visible. We can and should set up this symbol, this sign which can at least signify. We are asked every moment whether we do this. If we are—and those who are reconciled to God are—then there is no time to ask the counterquestion what we achieve thereby, what it might mean for us.

3. The sinner saved by grace is at least as such opened up and ready for the will of God. This can be the better sense of the protest, of the brokenness of his will. The latter can have a worse sense. It can mean that man is opened up and ready in a downward direction to do his own wicked will. It always makes his situation like that of the rider on the Bodensee.[14] It always means that he is held over the abyss of perdition. But it can also mean positively that man is for God, that out of the depths of his need he cries to him: "I will not let you go, except you bless me" [cf. Gen. 32:27]. The sighing of man in Romans 7 is not that of one who is forsaken by God but of one who is bound to him and therefore plunged into that self-contradiction. He neither would nor could sigh like that if he could not later rejoice (which secretly precedes

[14]Cf. G. Schwab's ballad "Der Reiter und der Bodensee" (1826), *Gedichte*, vol. 1, Stuttgart (1828), p. 364.

the sighing): "Thanks be to God through Jesus Christ our Lord!" [Rom. 7:25]. The strength of his need is not that of the devil nor of his own sin but the strength of God who has visited him in his sin. As man, set under the judgment of God, justifies God against himself, there necessarily arises the free place to which we have often referred already, the place where the name of the Lord can count in his life, and where God has a grip on him. His voice cannot possibly be no more than one of protest against himself. If it is really that, it is more than that; before it is that, it is the voice of praise of God, out of the depths, yet *praise* of God. There is no shaking without final certainty and security. There is no sadness without the most secret joy. There is no falling and lying without standing up again. There is no Romans 7 without Romans 8, we might also say. We could think here of some of the characters in Dostoyevsky, e.g., of the murderer and harlot in *Crime and Punishment* who read John's Gospel together in the attic.[15] They seem to be totally impossible people, but that is an impossibility which this author more or less plainly displays on the margin of almost all his characters. We must try to grasp this impossibility if we are to protect ourselves against the idea that fundamentally it can be other than in the greatest improbability of outward appearances that a real openness to God can come into consideration in our own case too, even though we are not murderers or harlots. We should be glad that it can at least come into consideration. The extreme that is denoted by the concept of penitence can have this double aspect. Even when considered as a human act, not only can it denote the divine No, but it can also be a demonstration for the Yes without which the real divine No is not spoken to us. Our will would not be truly broken if it were not open upward too. To be sure, man cannot in his own strength rise above the ambivalence of all human reality. Those who would find in Romans 7 only the self-despairing Pharisee, and in Dostoyevsky only man in the last convulsions of his bestiality, and in themselves only sick pig-headed people; those who would take the human denial of God, which extends over the whole surface of human action, more seriously than God himself, who has patience with those who deny him—who can persuade them to the contrary? Psychological analysis cannot serve as a means to reveal in man not only his sin and not only his protest against himself but beyond that his saving openness to the will of God. In ourselves and others we can see this only in faith, as it can be a real event only in faith. But let us assume that in faith it is a real event. With it, is not something "totally different" made visible in human life? Is not a sacrifice made that is pleasing to God [Rom. 12:1]? Without man's deification, without his acquiring any merit, improperly and against all appearances, do we not have here a sign of the true saving reality of Jesus Christ, in the humility which alone can stand before God, yet as the act of obedience that is required of us?

[15]Pt. IV, chap. 4.

If there is nothing here of which we can boast, because we can boast only in God, because this penitence really takes place only when seen in God's light; if we can venture to obey only with the greatest uncertainty, can we deny that we are summoned to this, to the inglorious and uncertain venture of becoming open to the will of God?

Living as those who are slain by God's Word means, then, a new thinking, and a brokenness and openness of our will. It means responding with our life to the reconciling death of Christ as those who are "planted together in the likeness of his death" [Rom. 6:5]. It means sacrifice as repentance toward God. If the sacrifice is accepted, it is God's mercy. For it is God's mercy if the repentance is real, if something which, relatively, is "totally different" is seen in it in our lives. The goodness of our action is always in the strictest sense God's own goodness, and the power of the witness that we give in it is his power. But when we ask: What shall we do? we cannot evade the fact that this witness and sacrifice are demanded of us. If we do, we ask dishonestly.

3

The concept of repentance would be an abstraction if the required sacrifice were understood only in its relation to God and not at once and at the same time as service to our fellowmen as well. As we do not have Christ to the extent that we do not want our fellowmen, and as there can be no divine authority whose acknowledgment does not imply and enclose the acknowledgment of human authority, so there is no Christian humility which exhausts itself in repentance before God and will not become ministry to the neighbor as well. The two things are not identical. We can equate them only to the detriment of either one or the other, i.e., by damaging and dissolving the totality, which is the one totality only in the unity of the two. We can neither lose repentance before God in service to the neighbor nor service to the neighbor in repentance before God. In the former case no real service would be rendered to the neighbor and in the latter case there would be no real repentance before God. Neither of the two can be genuine without the other. Again, the two are not equal in order. Undoubtedly repentance before God comes first and service to the neighbor must follow. One must say of the former that it acquires its concreteness and seriousness only through the latter. But one must say of the latter something even more far-reaching, namely, that it has meaning and is possible only against the background of the former. Yet it must not be deduced from this order that there can be genuine repentance even for a moment if this does not become concrete in service. God's law, and God's law alone, demands my daily penitence. Against God alone I have sinned [cf. Ps. 51:4] and he alone has reconciled me to himself. To no man do I owe repentance, no matter how grievously I have sinned against him. My new thinking and my brokenness and openness of will can relate to

God alone. But, concretely, God's law is my neighbor who is given to me in the church as a member of the people of God. If my repentance can be only before God, and can be declared valid only by God, I, of whom it is required, can validate [it] only to my neighbor as the one whom God has commissioned and set over against me—validate it in faith that God will accept its validity, yet validate it only to my neighbor. This validation to my neighbor of my repentance before God means serving my neighbor. Before taking up this point in detail, we must first look back again at the concept of sacrifice which overarches the concepts of repentance[16] and service and in the light of which we can see the connection between them.

Old Testament sacrifice is not only improper, like all human sacrifice apart from that of Christ. It is also incomplete, being only prophecy and as such ambiguous, to the extent that in it the connection between repentance and service, as the intrabiblical conflict between priests and prophets shows, is still at least a question to which various answers can be given. On the one side sacrifice is obviously required of the people as an act of repentance for the forgiveness of sins. On the other side, which is really another side, the divinely expected demonstration of a good will that is ready to sacrifice is obviously righteousness and love in relation to fellow members of the people. In the Old Testament the one truth of sacrifice has the appearance of two truths which seem to be in tension and even in mutually exclusive opposition at some high points in the Old Testament history of revelation. That God and the neighbor belong together; that a cultus which is abstracted from action in social commitment, as often seems to be the case in the official religion of the temple in Israel, is no real cultus, no matter how strongly it expresses human humility before God; that action in social commitment cannot on the other hand simply suppress and replace the cultus, or direct sacrifice to God, as seems to be possible if the thought of an Amos is carried to extremes; the whole concept of "spiritual worship" (*logikē latreia*) as Paul developed it in Romans 12—all this as the perfection of what is intended and prophesied in the antithesis of the Old Testament witness to revelation can be seen only and for the first time in the light of the fulfillment, of Christ.

Christ is not only the proper sacrifice but also the complete and perfect sacrifice because the sacrifice of his life is at one and the same time offered *to God,* an act of repentance that makes good our human disobedience, and also offered *for men,* an act of service to the neighbor whose whole plight Christ carries and whose need he meets with his obedience. Christ is the true High Priest and Mediator inasmuch as he represents men to God and God to men, the former first, then the latter, but not the one without the other. To this perfect atonement our humility, our own totally improper sacrifice, has to respond. The

---

[16]In the original Barth mistakenly had "sacrifice" here.

difficult problem of a Christian doctrine of humility is that it must be thought out in relation to Christ, that it must see and present the two lines of the twofold commandment of love [Mark 12:29ff. par.], which intersect so obscurely in the Old Testament, as two parallel lines which are infinitely close but still will never meet. The danger of the two forbidden extremes always arises. The one is acute when repentance before God acquires such independent weight in the form of a solitary or even a corporate cultus that one forgets that the living law of God is our neighbor to whose service all worship and all the ordering of our relation to God in the practice of penitence can only be the necessary prelude. This is, generally speaking, the extreme which can be a constant danger in the Roman Catholic doctrine of humility,[17] though we concede at once, of course, that it has cast a broad shadow in the Protestant church and theology too. The other danger occurs when service to the neighbor in the form of the social commitment in which we stand acquires such independent weight that the need to repent before God as the presupposition of real service to the neighbor threatens to be smothered in the heat of the claim of the neighbor, which we seek to meet with all our force and attention and in comparison with which the claim of God might seem to be only a cultic and mystic chimaera. In this case service to the neighbor might be evading the necessary Why? Whence? and Whither? which make it obedience. We have to see here the specifically Protestant danger as it threatens at least in two such totally different phenomena as the Social Gospel of North America on the one side[18] and the Thou-and-I theology of Bultmann and Gogarten on the other.[19] It is perhaps like trying to square a circle to steer a middle course between the two extremes. Who of us does not tend to veer off either to the one side or the other? We can only say that a Christian doctrine of humility must at least attempt the middle course.

But let us now turn to the task of understanding the sacrifice demanded of us as service to the neighbor.

a. The difference between the neighbor as an authority for me and the neighbor as one who claims my service is that *in spite of* and even *in* his own human questionability and need he is the brother whom God has set there for me. The sin of the fellowman, with all that it includes and entails, is the obstacle which we must leap over with a Nevertheless in order to understand him as what he is, namely, the bearer of the divine command. If we are to understand that service to the neighbor is required of us, we must understand that his sin is precisely what should

---

[17]Cf. Thomas Aquinas, *S. Th. II*, 2 qu. 161 a.1 ad 5; for a general view, cf. V. Cathrein, *Die christliche Demut*, Freiburg i. Br. 1920. 2,3.

[18]Cf. W. Rauschenbusch (1861–1918), *Christianity and the Social Crisis* (1907).

[19] E. Brunner rather than R. Bultmann should perhaps be mentioned with Gogarten as the representative of this view, but for Barth's coupling of Bultmann and Gogarten, cf. his letter to E. Thurneysen of Jan. 16, 1927 in *Briefwechsel, Vol. 2: 1921–1930*, ed. E. Thurneysen, Zurich 1974, pp. 453f.

motivate us. If we will not see him in his deepest plight, we shall never see how far we are in fact under obligation to serve him. So long as we expect him to be totally different from what he is; so long as we demand that he correspond to the idea of man, that he be a greater or lesser saint, or at least be "noble, helpful, and good;"[20] so long as we do not grasp that he is in revolt against God and therefore caught in the split which affects his whole being and nature; so long as we do not realize that a bad tree can produce only bad fruit [cf. Matt. 7:17], we shall not be able to serve because we shall not want to do so. We shall not believe that he needs our service, i.e., our help, our assistance, our aid. We shall not even know what he needs, what he should receive from us. We shall start instead with the presupposition that he might be different if he would only be genuine and serious. We shall wonder why his better part does not assert itself, or, when we think it does, why it is so weak and hopelessly unsuccessful. We shall shake our head at him. We shall exhort him. We shall do this or that for him. But what we perhaps very kindly say to him, and perhaps very energetically do for him, will always be said and done against the background of "God helps those who help themselves,"[21] i.e., not in such a way that we give up our opposition to him, nor otherwise than from our lofty superiority, nor without turning aside even as we approach, nor without accusation or at least a question, nor without leaving open a line of retreat for ourselves to a point from which he is immediately the other again, different from us, not concerning us fundamentally in any way. This corresponds only too well to the problem of our life together with one who has transgressed and still transgresses the command. A common life with him has in fact become impossible. In transgressing the command of the Creator he also violates necessarily and continually the rules which make it possible for us to live intimately with him as we should. Always, and more or less clearly in all others, we see against the background of his nature and conduct a very alien face, one might almost say the face of an idol, something curious, unapproachable, and constantly disturbing. This is obviously himself. I have to reckon with who he really is, the more so the better I know him. This fatal something that is himself leavens the whole lump of his existence in all its expressions, and in fact gives me reason enough to look and wonder and hold back. To the extent that I may or must continue a common life with him, I have also reason enough to look aside when I approach, to adopt an accusatory attitude, to engage in that quiet or abrupt retreat into myself by which I show him that fundamentally he does not concern me. I have reason enough for all these things. The neighbor, in fact, is Adam after the fall, not before it. Does not that justify me in adopting such an approach and attitude toward him? The only point is, of course, that there can be no question

---

[20]From the opening lines of J. W. Goethe's poem "Das Göttliche" (1782).
[21]Proverbial saying.

of serving him. I see the reality of his great sinfulness, but the conclusion that I draw is that because of it I can have nothing to do with him. He ought to be different, totally different. He disappoints me in my expectations of him, and I am guided by this. I want to live with him as if we were in paradise. There was no service there. Life together was simply a higher and more extensive living of life as the life that is common to man with everything around him and especially with his fellowmen. I see myself to be disappointed in the expectation of this possibility and I give more or less restrained expression to this disappointment. Perhaps I still expect more of him, but I expect him to help himself. If he does not, and if God does not seem to help him either, then I cannot help him, but may pass by on the other side as the priest and Levite did with the man who had fallen among thieves between Jerusalem and Jericho [cf. Luke 10:31f.]. I cannot help him because it has not been shown me that I should, that his great sinfulness implies a summons to me to serve him. Hence we stand and sit in confrontation, each on the battlements of his own castle,[22] looking at one another with telescopes and acutely noting what impossible things are constantly taking place, constantly disturbed and disillusioned, and constantly resolved not to leave our own skins in any event, but to protect them all the more vigorously. And the idol over there continues to look at us and we shake our head all the more and learn to know people better and become older and all the more certain of our own cause and—well the whole life of men in friendship, marriage, family, society, nation, and humanity is indeed poor in quality. |

Is there any way out of this difficulty that is posed by the great sinfulness of the neighbor—any other way than that of getting to know him better and arming and safeguarding ourselves with ever greater superiority, force, and refinement against him as he is? For us there is no other way. Perhaps, however, everything is already won, and the way out is already visible, once we see that there really is no other way out for us. When I see this, when I see the complete inadequacy of what I regard as my well-meant approach to my neighbor, the inadequacy of my good example, my friendly speech, my stern injunctions, and what I can do for others, then I will acknowledge what I have not thus far considered, namely, that, at least by my incapability, I too, am guilty of the disruption of our common life. I have reason to be disappointed not only with the other but also a little with myself, disappointed that I cannot succeed in restoring life together with him as it ought to be, in removing or at least notably improving that alien feature on his face, that oddness of his behavior, by my influence on him. If I see that I really cannot do this, perhaps I will let my telescope drop and for a moment look at myself in the mirror with the question how it is that the owner of

[22]Cf. F. Schiller's ballad "Der Ring des Polykrates" (1797): "He stood on the pinnacles of his roof . . ."

the face that looks at me there cannot do something decisive for the other, notwithstanding all his good intentions. The difficulty in relation to the other might then become the occasion for repentance on my part. I might realize that a kind of idol is set up here which certainly does not look at the other in a friendly way that awakens confidence, but in relation to the expectation of a paradisial life together is perhaps just as disappointing to him as what he shows me of himself is disappointing to me. It might be that we slowly cease to wonder so naively that our good intensions evoke so little response. It might be that the expectation that the other will be a saint, or noble, helpful, and good, so that I can begin a genuine common life with him, will slowly become a utopian dream in which I can no longer truly believe. It might be that in virtue of my own plight I will slowly begin to notice that the other is in need too, and perhaps in the same plight as I am. It might be that I shall start to consider what it means for me if, in my plight, the other regards me as I regarded him, speaking to me, doing this or that for me, but all in such a way that in it I can perceive only his superiority, his remoteness, his disappointment, his plain line of retreat into himself. How lonely I should then feel, the more lonely and helpless, perhaps, the closer the other comes with his good intentions! How, to his doubled disappointment, I shall not be able to be grateful but shall always be looking for something different and better that he still owes me—still owes me because he has first looked away from me, he has wanted me to be a saint, he has quietly told me that "God helps those who help themselves," he will not believe how bad things are, that I cannot really help myself, that I simply am what I am, and that telling me what I ought to be, treating me from the standpoint of the good that slumbers in me, or appealing to my conscience or will can only make my plight worse. It might be that on this detour it will strike me what is required of me by the great sinfulness of the other, what I owe to *him*. And this would be the possibility of serving him. It might be that I will make the great discovery that not just the other stands under another order than that of paradisial life together but that I really stand with him under this other order. I am imprisoned with him. It is in this prison, not somewhere else, that I must live with him, and all expectation of another life together can only be imagination and a loss of time in relation to what is really demanded as things now are. It might be that I see my solidarity with the other not just as a human being but as a sinner, and that on this basis I perceive that the position and attitude of an observer and judge, good reason though there may be for it, is simply disobedience— disobedience because in it I want to break out of the order in which we now are and find a community of saints where God himself has made me a member of a church of sinners.|

It might be, we say. And we have said that the difficulty in relation to the neighbor might become an occasion for repentance, and by way of repentance open up the path to service. We must now be more precise.

The difficulty in relation to the neighbor, the knowledge that we have no way out of it, really becomes clear to us when and insofar as we already stand in repentance, when and insofar as there has come into our own relation to God new thinking and a breaking and opening up of our will. We shall never see ourselves to be also guilty in relation to the neighbor, but continually find excuses for ourselves in this regard, if we have not seen that we are guilty in relation to God. Only God can pronounce us guilty. Only God really does this. If we will not be guilty before God, we certainly will not share guilt before our neighbor. The secret of our observing and judging the other, of our offended and disillusioned attitude and position, of our turning aside as we approach, of our not thinking that we should serve the other even in his corruption—the secret of this whole possibility is very simply the fact that we are still[23] or again refusing penitence before God, that we are still or again sitting on the throne of sinners who do not know or will not have it that they are such, but believe that they are in the fold with the 99 good sheep that need no repentance [cf. Luke 15:4−7].

It should be obvious by now why we may not proclaim service to the neighbor at the cost of repentance before God. To serve man is not just to want to live together with man as such, but to want to live together with the sinner, not ignoring his plight, his deepest plight, as though with a little good will it might not exist, but taking it into account that this is how he is, that he stands before us in all his ambivalence, or rather in all his lack of it, and accepting him as such. The sinner who does not himself stand in repentance never thinks of trying to live together with sinners. He is the very one whose mind is always full of the saints that others should and could be if only they would. He is the very one who is always dreaming of paradise, of the paradise of his own goodness, and therefore of the goodness of others, and therefore of a common life with no service, a life which we have only to live in order to fulfill the command of God. He is the very one who lives it, or plays at living it, for the reality is completely different from his dreams; and since he sees this at least in the other, in the offended and the disillusioned, he necessarily cannot really serve, his approach to the other is always full of aversion. The real beginning of service is when we see ourselves completely linked to the other with no remnant of superiority. Already service is sacrifice in this regard. We have to surrender, not in relation to God but in relation to the neighbor, whatever small advantage we may have over him, our being different and better, concerning which something might be said in all seriousness, the claim which on the basis of this might be put to the other on behalf of our own right and intactness. When we surrender, when we draw alongside others without reservations, when we plainly and honestly recognize our own plight in theirs, we begin concretely to serve. This sacrifice has to be brought. It is no other

[23]Barth uses here the older term "annoch" for "noch immer."

sacrifice than that which we owe to God in penitence, the demonstration of our awareness that we are forfeit to him. He demands this sacrifice concretely with the fact that our penitence can take place only in the church, as there is faith only in the church. The adverse neighbor, the bearer of the divine claim, stands before us as a member of the church. We are asked whether we will meet this claim.

b. The neighbor's claim to our service is no more and no less than a claim to our person. If all the human relations in which we stand are secretly or openly so inadequate and unsatisfying in spite of all the goodwill and efforts and actual achievements that are perhaps to be found in them, one may say very definitely that we have not understood, and in its depth and reality will never understand, the fact that the neighbor in his need lays personal claim to us. And where there is in the relation to which we stand some distant success in living together, at least as a promise, as the light of a friendly greeting from another world, one can again say very definitely that we have heard that claim, at least a little, at least for a moment, perhaps without properly knowing or desiring it, yet genuinely heard it as the claim that the neighbor makes to our person. My relation to my neighbor, then, stands under the blessing of the fact that I myself was there for him a little. It stands under this blessing to the extent that I was there for him, not according to my own judgment and perhaps even against it, but according to God's judgment and therefore in reality. Being there for another is the Christian sacrifice, highly pleasing to God, which we have to bring to God in penitence [cf. Rom. 12:1f.], and for the bringing of which he has concretely set us over against our neighbor. The French have the phrase "payer de sa personne" for what we have in view. In relation to God, and therefore to our neighbor, too, we can pay only with our person: not in relation to God alone, but in relation to our neighbor too. If I receive a visit or a letter and someone obviously wants something from me, then in respect of the question whether I am really at the service of this person everything depends, not on how much time or attention I give, nor on how clever my counsel or information is, nor on how impressive is the inner or outer help that I provide, but on whether, even if only for a moment, even if only in an unassuming and incidental turning to him, silently perhaps or vocally, enthusiastically or with restraint, whether I am really there for this person, seeing him personally in his concern and standing by him in my own person.

I do not serve him if I "deal with him" as at post office counters or in other government offices. To "deal with someone" is to get rid of him by adopting various measures to that end. The same procedure, painful on both sides, is what usually takes place between us and beggars who come to our door. A whole ocean of official and private charity, both Christian and secular, for this reason is no real serving of the neighbor, the true point of the relevant measures and institutions being to rid society, government, pastor, and individual of needy fellowmen. The neighbor, however, does not have this in mind nor seek it when seeking help. He does not want us to get rid of him. He wants us to be there for him. If this does not happen, he is not served, even though the true meaning of his concern may not have been at all clear to him, even though he may seem for the time being to be fully satisfied with the way, with what we hope will be the polite way, in which we have been able to get rid of him. His claim has not been heard and in some way it rumbles on and will reemerge and take revenge for not having been heard. The wound with which the neighbor comes to me or lies before me shows that I should serve him. All that I do for him is done in vain if its real point is my denial of service. He needs *me*, not my deeds, though he needs these too, but before and in all my deeds he needs *me*. If I deny him *myself*, then I deny him my service even though I do everything else for him. It is clear that all intensifying of the art of healing the neighbor's wound, all narrowing and multiplying of the net of mutual assistance, all refining and humanizing of this help as this is expressively symbolized in the modern change of name from poor relief to social security, and also all political and economic socialization of society—all these things are simply like pouring water into the vessels of the Danaides[24] if they are only new forms of getting rid of the neighbor, of secretly or explicitly denying him help, and so long as the supposed helpers—new forms of the people concerned are not created—will not let themselves be told that they themselves are required, not their money, their cleverness, their urbanity, or their work—or perhaps all or some of these too, but in them all and before them all themselves. At all levels of social culture, from the lowest to the highest, needy people are looking for helpful people, and primarily and decisively for the *people* in and with the help. Thus it always was and thus it always will be. Ultimately human society will always be sick because ultimately we will not help by paying with the person, with ourselves.

I also do not serve the neighbor when I use the encounter with him to display myself. Naturally every claim upon my help is a greater or lesser incitement to my vanity, an occasion for self-importance, a spur to the exercise of my own will for life and power. If someone visits me or writes me a letter with some concern, whether I can help this person or not, this is certainly a temptation for me to put on a little performance in which I show him radically and advantageously what kind of a person I am, in which I attempt above all to enhance and extend, if possible, the respect and expectation with which he has turned to me. It is now possible for me rightly to enjoy the solo part I play in what I have to say and do in such a situation. Incidentally, this is what makes the social life of the so-called upper classes the impossible thing that we cannot

---

[24]As a punishment for murdering their husbands, the daughters of Danaos were condemned, in the underworld, to bale out water endlessly in vessels with no bottoms; Lucian, *Timon* 18; *Hermotimos* 61.

possibly deny it to be 99 percent of the time. (I have already expressed on an earlier occasion the righteous indignation without which one cannot speak of this.)[25] It all seems to be so beautiful and meaningful and humane—mutual introductions and visits and whole evenings and meals together. But in reality it has no meaning—it is indeed nonsensical, for what happens when these fine folk solemnly proceed to church on Sunday, what happens on those evenings together, 99 percent of the time is pure theater, not an attempt to be there *for* one another, but a constant and strained attempt to be *before* one another as heroes and prima donnas. That is why their occasions of supposed fellowship are so boring. That is why, fundamentally, people are so obviously glad to escape them. We do not really *seek* this when we are together, and if we find no more than *this* and in time come to seek no more than *this*, then we might as well give up seeking it. Again, in the case of very many supposed works of care and charity, we have to ask seriously whether ultimately the individuals concerned, or the relevant society or church or community, or the state and society in general, are not simply putting on an act to show and prove their worth and their right to exist, without considering that real help cannot be a goal that is secondary to some other goal, that we cannot help others merely in order to find pleasure or comfort in so doing, or to display to the world the social insight of the church or the power of Christian love, or to commend the state to certain strata of the population, or to maintain one's convictions about the humanity of modern culture, or to give a voice to any other subsidiary purpose, praiseworthy though it might be in its own right. Why was it, in view of the model system of social security set up at the beginning of the last Kaiser's reign, that Social Democracy flourished so catastrophically and revolution was finally possible? Why did the social manifesto of the Kirchentag at Bethel make almost no impression at all?[26] We cannot search the heart, but there are signs which give us good reason to ask whether the people there were really *for* other people and, if not, why there should be surprise and censure when those who first of all were apparently—but only apparently—being sought refused to be found either by good words or good deeds. In the long run, however, neither the Soviet state nor that of Mussolini will succeed if it turns out that behind their good intentions and acts on behalf of other people there is finally sought only the self-centered achievement of the excellence of a specific political and economic system, ⌐the triumph of a heartless objectivity.¬ Ingratitude is the reward that the world has always given the world, and always will. Nor can one demand that people be grateful for putting on a show for them and failing to take note of the people themselves.

[25]Cf. pp. 132.
[26]The first German Evangelical Kirchentag took place at Bethel near Bielefeld on June 14–17, 1924. Its final resolution was entitled "An das deutsche evangelische Volk!" Text in *Beth-El, Blicke aus Gottes Haus in Gottes Welt* (1924), no. 8/9, pp. 196–99.

Again, however, I do not serve my neighbor if when he wants something from me, or, rather, when he wants me, I seek to win him to me. To put it plainly, help cannot be a business transaction. A business transaction is a matter of reciprocity. This is not forbidden, just as it is not forbidden to dismiss another and act alone. But this has nothing whatever to do with repentance and service. We have not heard the claim of the neighbor in need if we link our hearing to the condition that he hear our claim too. This is not yet or no longer the Christian situation between us. I may legitimately seek the regard, friendship, or gratitude of my neighbor, or try to win him over to myself and my convictions. But I should not call this service no matter how strenuous my efforts may be, how great my sacrifice, how great my achievements on his behalf. In the background of all such "transactional" relationships to the neighbor there lurks always the possibility that my whole turning to him might change into aversion if he does not correspond by turning equally to me. For all my turning to him in such a relationship, I myself remain aloof, ready to leap away, ready to withdraw if he does not keep his side of the bargain. In this kind of help I do not give myself. On the contrary, I try to safeguard myself, to safeguard myself in the being which I always keep back no matter how available I make myself in my relation to the other. Hence I have not really helped the other with what I can be for him and give to him. He has waited for the self which would be opened up to him without reserve. I could help him only by giving myself. What disturbs or interrupts the service that he wants of me is not that I seek something from him, but rather that, having time and inclination to make counterdemands upon him, I obviously keep back my real self and am not totally or truly available to him at all. I need not illustrate the limit that is posed here for all that I might regard as service to the neighbor. One need only think of all the reciprocity, or of some of the reciprocity, that is undoubtedly present in every human relationship and ask whether there would, in the long run, be any readiness to serve at all if this were not present, or whether by this standard anyone would ever hear or answer the claim that we should be available to others.

Why is it that whenever the other can claim my service he does not basically want this or that but simply myself? It is because the other, like myself, finds his greatest need in himself, is in the worst possible isolation and darkness, and cannot deal with himself. He is sick of life. It is probably only a small symptom of this sickness that he brings to me, a superficial wound in relation to which he asks for advice or aid. But behind this small thing there stands, concealed or unconcealed, the big thing that he is totally without counsel or help. What he needs is someone else to bear his burden. What he really needs is to be represented in the task of living his life, someone else to live decisively and totally for him. Wherever and however the cry for inner or outer help reaches our ears, we can be sure that at root it is the man himself wanting someone else to take his place, to be there for him, because he himself knows that he is impotent, or perhaps he does not know it, and certainly he does not know how impotent he really is, but he is at any rate impotent, and yet he must still live, and therefore he calls upon the other to represent him. Again, we have to say: This claim in the full radicalism with which it is put to us would be impossible in paradise. If we want to appeal romantically to the possibilities of paradise, if we abstract away from the fact that the fall stands between us and man as God created him, then we shall reject the claim of the fellowman that I myself should be totally available to him as a completely unfounded and unreasonable demand. Who but a sinner should be in such a position that he cannot bear the burden of his own life, that he should simply lay it on me, that he should simply ask me to be available to him? If there is no sin, there is no such need. I thus have a full right to try to break free from the neighbor, to see to myself, to have dealings with him on a *do, ut des*[27] basis. If man is good, all this is normal. It is a proper fulfillment of my will to live. When the other makes obviously exaggerated claims on me I may rightly point out to him in a friendly but forcible way that "God helps those who help themselves." If service means that I should be available to those who want me, then, presupposing that man is good, the whole idea of service, as a gross exaggeration of the correct notion that human life should be lived in fellowship, ought to be rejected. Again, everything obviously depends on whether I know from my own experience that we do not live in paradise; on whether I know myself, too, as a sinner; on whether I also know that we cannot live properly on our own; on whether it is clear to me that the small or great wounds with which I also am tormented go back to such a severe and incurable sickness that I, too, must capitulate and look around for some other who can be there for me and carry my burden. If this is so, then no matter whether I can meet it or not I must see and concede the justice of the claim that is put to me. I might still say: Who are you that you come to me? How can I help you when I myself am helpless? But we cannot fail to hear what is demanded of us when in what the other demands we have to hear plainly the echo of what is our own demand. We have to accept the other—and perhaps the decisive thing already happens with this—as a brother, and his demand as intrinsically justifiable. And we shall understand that what is demanded of us is really sacrifice, the giving of what is most vitally necessary, namely, of the self that we would rather withhold.

c. In what is required of us as service to the neighbor, it is a question of what, according to our exposition, amounts to no more and no less than being, in Luther's words, "a Christ to the other."[28] Let us set aside

---

[27]The formula derives from Roman law, cf. H. Grotius, *De iure belli ac pacis*, Paris 1625, II, 12, 3, 1. Bismarck gave currency to it with his *do, ut des* politics; cf. his *Politische Reden, Hist. krit. Gesamtausgabe*, ed. H. Kohl, Stuttgart 1892–1905, vol. VII, p. 257; X, pp. 292, 413.

[28]WA 7, 66, 25ff. Cf. above, p. 335, n. 144.

for a moment the question whether and how far we are able to meet this demand and show first what the requirement implies. We have not been able to avoid the concept of vicarious representation, which strictly applies only to Christ, in our attempt to bring out what it really means that if we are truly to serve another we have to be available to him, to be there for him. We sense at once that the use of this concept is improper in this context. After what has been said about repentance we are not unprepared to explain that we can understand our service, too, only as an improper service, and we shall come back to this shortly. But this caveat or explanation should not prevent us from taking seriously the demand that is made on us, or seeing that the concept of vicarious representation is indispensable here. If the neighbor comes to me in his need, this means, as we have seen, that I face at once the question whether I realize that I am in solidarity with him, in the same need, his fellow prisoner. Without this I cannot see that his claim is well-founded. I can still think that he can help himself as I think that I can help myself. I will be hard toward him. All the hardness with which we encounter one another has its root in our failure to realize that we are all involved, that we are like the wicked servant who, faced with his fellow servant, forgets that he should be imprisoned because of his incomparably greater debt to his master [cf. Matt. 18:23–35], thinking we can forgive our own sins and not knowing what sin is or what it means that we are sinners.

When the neighbor comes to me in need, this means that I have to ask whether I am penitent. But the concept of repentance implies more than knowing what sin is and what it means that we are sinners. We would not know that we stand under God's judgment if we did not know first and fundamentally that God is merciful to us and that our sin is forgiven. Hence the question that is put to me is whether I realize that I stand in grace and whether I will confess this. Now we know that first and fundamentally grace means our union with Christ, that Christ took our place before God, the place of sinners, and that clothed with his righteousness we may stand in his place before God, God seeing us in Christ and viewing us favorably for his sake. The divine favor that rests upon me for Christ's sake is the reality of my standing in grace. But then the claim of the neighbor that I should be there for him in the strict sense is not only grounded in itself but grounded also as a claim that is directed by *him* to *me*. |

To the extent that I stand in grace I have every reason, first, to open my eyes wide and see who it really is that comes to me burdened with need. Might it not be Christ in the servant form which he has assumed for my sake, Christ breaking under the burden of the sin of the world that is my sin laid upon him, Christ in the form of the lost and rejected in which he is God for us? Is there a question, a care, a sigh, a complaint, a burden, a plea that comes into our ears through the voice of our neighbor which does not have its deepest root in the fact that the world, the human world, lies in the power of the evil one [cf. 1 John 5:19], that we are a corrupt generation [cf. Phil. 2:15], that we have to suffer unceasingly from our corruption? Is not the crying or cursing of each individual on account of his own pain an expression of that from which we all suffer, and finally an appeal for the removal of the corruption in which we all stand? But if this is so, and if the incarnation of the Word is as serious as I know it to be as one to whom God has been gracious; if God himself in Christ has taken to himself our corruption; if, borne by Christ, it has become his robe, the robe in which he has come to us and will be with us to the world's end [cf. Matt. 28:20], then whenever and however we encounter this robe of human corruption in the form of this person or that, can we really turn aside and refuse to be there for such a person in hostile self-affirmation and self-defense? Against whom, perhaps, am I defending myself? Should I not be available for Christ? Do I not live by the fact that he is always ready to accept me? Is this not grace upon grace? Is not a readiness for him the necessary act of faith in which I affirm my own reconciliation? Or is it not Christ who there, in the humble form of my neighbor, in all the weakness of the flesh, demands my humility? Certainly it might not be Christ. Christ lives in his members, in the church, not in people in general and as such. I am thus asked whether I want to be in the church with him who comes to me there. There is no prior agreement as to where Christ demands my humility in the form of my neighbor and where he does not. I can answer only with the act of being available or not. He, and not I, decides when and where and how he wills to meet me in the neighbor. I can know only that he does so in the church. I can only obey when he does so. Only with each encounter with the neighbor can I perceive that Christ has now done so, so that I shall perhaps be resisting him if I refuse to be available for the other, and if I am not to bring into question my own being in the church, I have every reason, perhaps, to be available at once for the other. For Christ's vicarious suffering, which I myself need, is there for me in all the weakness of the other even before I am summoned to achieve it in all my weakness for the other, summoned for my own sake to give myself totally, to be wholly at the disposal of the other in his need. Without appropriating this suffering of his, I should myself lose my only comfort both in life and in death.[29] But this is only one side of the matter. |

Secondly, to the degree that I myself stand in grace, the other has in

[29]Heidelberg Catechism, 1563, Question 1: "What is thy only comfort in life and in death?" Answer: "That I, with body and soul, both in life and in death, am not my own, but belong to my faithful Savior Jesus Christ, who with his precious blood has fully satisfied for all my sins, and redeemed me from all the power of the devil; and so preserves me that without the will of my Father in heaven not a hair can fall from my head; yea, that all things must work together for my salvation. Wherefore, by his Holy Spirit, he also assures me of eternal life, and makes me heartily willing and ready henceforth to live unto him."

fact the right to seek Christ in me. It would be an idle excuse to point him and his great or little concern away from myself to God or Christ or the Bible: "Go in peace, be warmed and filled" [James 2:16]. Naturally I could do this. I would not finally have served him if my service were not to him a revelation of the great service of Christ. Yet this does not release me from the claim that this revelation of the service of Christ is sought in me and my service. Or am I not clothed with his righteousness? Am I not pleasing to God in him? Have I not received his Holy Spirit? As a hearer and therefore a doer of his Word, have I not been born again by this Word as God's dear child? How can I deny all this if I believe? Faith is a Yes to all this. And how can I stand in grace if I do not believe? I must confess, then, that, as one to whom God is gracious, I am rich in God [cf. Luke 12:21] and that my neighbor in his poverty has the right to rely on me and that he is not demanding anything inappropriate or impossible if he wants me to be there for him. Christ does not dwell in me so that I should become poor again but so that I should be really rich, yet not rich in and for myself but rich to the honor of God and to service in his community, a light in the dark house and a city that is set on a hill [cf. Matt. 5:14]. How could I say: "Not I, but Christ lives in me" [Gal. 2:20], if I refused to be available for the other in Christ's church? Christ *is* for the other in his church. He *is* the other whom all who know their lostness seek and who may be found by all who know their lostness, as do those who are in his church, in the fellowship of those who are called by him to repentance before God. He *is* the other whom man seeks that he might live for him because of his own inability to live for himself, and he would not seek him if he had not already found him,[30] nor can he have found him without continually having to seek him afresh. He *is* the one to whom the other really comes when he comes to me with his concerns. He is the one who bears the sin of the world, the human world, this individual [cf. John 1:29]. If I am in Christ and Christ in me, then no matter what may become of me I have no option but to admit that what is expected of me is what Christ does, that I should not keep myself to myself but surrender myself. Again I am asked whether I know that I am in the church and a member of Christ's body. And on this side again there can be no question but that I am in the church with the other. The church—we must remember—is not a closed circle but one that is constantly opening, widening, and then closing again. God's honor seeks magnification with God's community. Since God's honor is its basis the community cannot simply seek to edify itself; if alive, it is always a missionary community. With its message it addresses equally both those who are inside and those who are outside.

---

[30]Cf. Fr. 553 in Pascal's *Pensées*: "Le Mystère de Jésus." "Console-toi, tu ne me chercherais pas, si tu ne m'avais trouvé," which echoes the thought of Augustine in *Confessions* X, 18, 20 that the search for God has its origin in the recollection of blessedness.

Hence the question whether the neighbor who has come to me is himself a member of Christ can have no meaning for me. So far as I know he may become a member tomorrow even if he is not one today. So far as I know I may be the one who is summoned to show him Christ, and the Father through Christ [cf. John 14:8f.]. Perhaps I do not recognize the hidden Christ in him, but we should not abandon even the most ungodly neighbor too quickly, since Christ, for all we know, has perhaps been pleased to call this ungodly neighbor his brother, so that I necessarily deny the Christ living in me if I refuse to meet this neighbor in Christ's stead, being convinced that he is unworthy of Christ. Again it is Christ and not I who must decide. And I must obey.

But what does it mean to obey here, to represent Christ to the other? What does it mean to be available to the other in this pregnant sense which is defined by our being in the church? We can only answer: Exactly the same as what service means in the case of Jesus Christ. Certainly, between the being and action of Jesus Christ as that of the Head and ours as that of the members there stands the full and unfathomable abyss of the distinction between the proper and the improper. We can be and do only in human weakness what he is and does in divine power. The strength with which we are and do this in his name is only a loaned and transferred strength. Without him we can do nothing [cf. John 15:5]. Nevertheless, all this does not alter the fact that when we are confronted by the question of obedience we do not have to ask what our being and doing are or what is the substance of our obedience. The point of it all is that sin is not imputed but *forgiven*. All else that we might do in being there for others is enclosed in the fact, as the whole gospel is enclosed in it, that Christ forgives us our sins. We can sum up all criticism of what we might regard as our service to our neighbors in the one thing—that what is lacking in our service is forgiveness. If this is lacking, then in all the things that we do for others the decisive thing is not done. If, perhaps, it is not wholly lacking, the decisive thing is in fact done even though we may seem to have done nothing. We know what the neighbor lacks when we know at least what we lack: simply that he, too, is in some way a rebel, that both in general and in detail he is in total conflict with his creaturely destiny, that he does not know himself except under this sign. He waits for us to say to him, not: "You must be different"—he has often said this to himself already, and, if he has not, then many zealous fellowmen certainly have; nor: "You could be different"—his problem is precisely that he cannot; but rather: "You *are* different. You are not the one you know yourself to be and as whom all others address you. In spite of your rebellion and in it, in spite of the whole undeniable truth that you are a rebel, and the living reality in which this constantly stamps itself, you are not a rebel, you still belong to the God against whom you revolt, past whom you rush, against whom you rail, whom you blaspheme with words and works. You have been saved in your lostness. Truly, I tell you this."

Being told this is what the neighbor lacks. No one does tell him. It is the last thing he can tell himself. What he can tell himself, if he is honest, will necessarily be the opposite. This is why he seeks another who can tell him this as the truth and therefore speak for him as the truth, lifting the burden of life from his shoulders and living for him by telling him. |

It is obvious that something unheard of is at issue here. How can we tell people this? How can we tell them a truth that is contrary to the irrefutable truth that they are what they are? How can we contest the very manifest reality of their lostness? Only on the basis of the miracle of God and the grace of Jesus Christ can we tell them this. The pronouncement: "Your sins are forgiven you" [Mark 2:5 par.], must not be secretly identical to the statement: "Man is good." If it is, then undoubtedly I am secretly proclaiming the law to them again instead of the gospel. But the riches of the grace of Jesus Christ are there where his church is, where a person lives, not to himself, but to Christ; they are there with me when I myself am in the church, in grace. This unheard of Nevertheless, this far side of the most manifest truth, is something that I cannot deny if I am not to deny that mercy has been shown to me [cf. 1 Tim. 1:13, 16]. Is the miracle less than what happened to me when what is at issue is the truth for others that they are not what they are, that, even as those they are, they are God's dear children? If I believe that God counts me his own in spite of everything that speaks to the contrary, can I do any other than count my neighbor as God's in spite of everything that speaks to the contrary, and depending, of course, on what can take place only between himself and God? Do I really believe in the mercy that is mine if I can neglect to proclaim it to others, and is not the neighbor, who is now in the plight in which obviously only the grace of God can help him, sent to me as an occasion and order to engage in this proclamation? To forgive sin, very simply, is not to call evil good, nor to keep on calling it evil, but to move beyond the question of good and evil and to regard people as God's, just as God himself has taken me myself beyond the question of good and evil. Christ did this. Face to face with the manifest sin of men and women, he proclaimed, not blame or punishment or the necessary amendment of life, but the kingdom of God that has come to sinners and not the righteous. Unconditionally, truly unconditionally, he counted sinners to be God's and precisely in so doing summoned them to repentance [cf. Mark 2:17 par.]. He bore the sin of the world and therewith fought against it. |

There is no other way of following Christ than that of telling our neighbor that whereby we ourselves live. In most cases, however, our encounters with neighbors do not take, or take only occasionally, the form of telling them this in words. Only in the rarest instances do they come to us openly and directly with this issue. Yet always, even when we use words too, we are to encounter them with our whole attitude as people whom God truly counts to be his just as he counts us to be his. What good will all our fine words about forgiveness be if we meet people in such a way that our attitude does not show that we *believe* in the truth of these words and take them seriously as children of God rather than sinners? We are for them when we *do* this. Then Christ speaks through us. Then we serve him. I do not need to point out that this places a burden on us: the whole burden of the Nevertheless which we are always inclined to regard as more difficult in relation to others than ourselves. I do not need to point out that we have to bring a sacrifice, the real sacrifice of ourselves. We always see sin and not forgiven sin much more clearly in others than ourselves. We have every reason to balk at the task that service ought to be: the forgiving of sins. But we can hardly deny that this is the Christian task in relation to our neighbor.

d. We have now to put the concept of service expressly under the caveat which is set for it, as for that of repentance, by the master concept of sacrifice under which both of them stand. This caveat does not concern what is required and has to be done. It does not imply any diminution, any quantitative limitation. But the question of obedience does involve an either/or. The demanded sacrifice, understood as repentance or service, is a whole, and we ourselves are this whole. But since we can bring only ourselves in repentance before God or service to our neighbor, the caveat is pronounced. It concerns the inner worth of what we can do, the level on which it is done, the assessment which it is accorded. If I serve my neighbor, this means, if I understand my action according to its deepest and finest content, that in spite of his sin I count him to be God's as I am, treating him as one for whom I believe in God's grace as for myself. This is to forgive sin insofar as one person can forgive the sin of another. I do not believe in either the good in him or the evil, but in God in whom there is mercy for him. In this way I am available for him. All else that I can do for him, as for one who is imprisoned with me but also shares with me the hope of deliverance, all else that I can do to alleviate his plight that is also mine, must and will be a consequence of the one thing—that I do this for him. All else depends on the possibility and the reality that I can do this one thing for him, and do it. If I devoted all my time and effort to him, if I sacrificed my health and fortune for him, if I finally gave up my life for him, but did not do this one thing, I should not have served him and would stand before him with empty hands. This is the one thing that he lacks and seeks from me, and if I cannot give it he comes to me in vain, for the value of all else wherewith I might serve him depends upon it.

In this light we can understand why in human relations, no matter in what close relationship countless people may live together, and for all the goodwill that exists in the world for those who are distant and even very distant, which is far more than moral pessimism will often concede, and no matter how much advice and assistance of all kinds we may in fact give to one another—why in spite of all this the presence of real service in human relationships is so doubtful, broken, and ambivalent in its manifestation and so hard to establish. Behind everything that we can and will do for others, and actually do, there stands the question whether we can and will do, and actually do, the one true Christian thing with which alone we can serve others. This stands behind the primitive relations in which people hardly begin to awaken out of the sleep of a brutal egotism to some sense of responsibility. But it also stands behind the greatly multiplied and activated attention, readiness, and actual vitality with which people are available to one another both in finely developed and nurtured personal relations and, if rather more crudely and externally, in a highly civilized society such as the modern West has undoubtedly become. What is it that really happens when there are in the best sense sensitive, tender, and caring dealings between people and when a social sense and social action have come to be almost taken for granted in the life of society in the broader sense? Why is it that we cannot escape the suspicion that with all this nothing essential is perhaps done, and why do the facts teach us—not always, but to a large extent, that nothing essential is actually done, that for all the good that is intended and done no real comfort, counsel, help, or liberation is given to the other? We see how the other can be served, and we want to serve him and have done so, and yet he *is not* served and therefore we *have not* served him. This is not always so, but it often is. And we have no final assurance that it is not always so.

If, however, all else that we can do depends on the one thing, then this puzzle and the uncertainty in which we find ourselves are understandable. But how about the willing and doing of the one thing? If we could will and do it as we do all the others; if we could will and do it in and with all the others, like putting a nail in the wall on which everything else must hang if it is really to be something; if we could render this service in virtue of which people are truly served by our service, why should not this supreme willing and doing be found and visible and actual at least in some of the finest and most developed of human relations and on the highest stages of general social culture? We note, however, that the doing of this one thing by no means parallels the development of social culture or the refining and practicing of all the rest that we can will and do, as though wherever the rest is rightly willed and done there would also spring forth as the last and finest bloom of human willing and doing the one necessary thing that we are available to one another in the true Christian sense, that we reckon ourselves to be God's, and that we forgive one another our sins. The willing and doing of this one thing may, of course, be linked to the refined and practiced willing and doing of all the rest. But it does not have to be. It may, unfortunately, be completely absent from it. All the development and practice may finally be laughable in face of the fact that there is withheld from the other what he needs and truly seeks even though we wrap him up in cotton wool and put him in a little paradise. Conversely, it may also be absent when the willing and doing of all the rest do not get beyond their primitive origins and there will probably be a concern to try to increase human effort and achievement in relation to all these other things. Effort of this kind is good and necessary, but it does not advance the one thing. The one thing will not necessarily be done when advance takes place. Nor will it necessarily be absent when, individually and socially, people do not get beyond those origins. It can be linked, too, with the very primitive willing and doing of the rest. We need to remember what the one thing involves so as not to find this unintelligible. That in and with all the other things that I can will and do in the service of another, I can be available to him as the other from whom he receives forgiveness of his sin and who tells him that in and in spite of his rebellion against God he belongs to God, who relates him to God again and thus makes possible again his own life—this cannot be willed and done by me even though it takes place through my act (which is the issue), nor can it be the culminating achievement of individual and social culture. If it really takes place, it is a reality which is free in relation to any plus or minus in the calculating of all the rest, which may be present at every possible stage, and which we do not adopt into our plan but which at best can have adopted us into its own. If it is to take place through our action, then we can never confront it except as a miracle. We cannot be surprised that it largely does not seem to happen, but have to be surprised when we believe we may suppose that something like it has in fact happened and that here or there we may have really served someone. And inevitably the statement that this is so will always be surrounded by supreme uncertainty. How can we ever boast of such a thing? How can our service ever seem to be a merit of ours?|

Let us assume that I have the clearest and most honest sense of having been truly and fully available to someone. I was not merely helpful to this person in this or that but turned to him and was all ears and all heart for him. I entered into his need and tried to lift him and hold him up from the only possible place. I also did everything in my power to give him comfort and help. Only rarely can we say this with complete honesty. But perhaps once in a while we can, in fact, say this about ourselves. And holier people might be able to say it more often, for at least in part such an attitude can become habitual. Let us assume that we are among those holier people. Even then we should have to consider that it is not normal but a true miracle if one person is really served by what another does for him. How does this come about even if we are holier people of that kind? Are we not also human? Do we give anything greater or purer to others when we give ourselves? Is it not the normal and expected thing that when I open myself and give myself wholly to others they will turn away in bitter disappointment because in me—in me!—they find only another man who has enough, and more than enough, to do to look after himself, who is fully—and perhaps much worse than they—in the same plight as they are, and who in giving himself really gives nothing? Who is not acquainted with this disappointment of seeing an honored and beloved person, who has not turned aside but openly turned to us, suddenly lit up as if by lightning and becoming aware of the all too human element in himself, of the rebel who is hidden in the saint, and of experiencing a loss of all confidence that we can be truly served by him? Nor does it perhaps take very much to bring us down to earth in this way, and we know what and who resides on the earth. Can we be surprised if we receive no service? Must we not be surprised if it happens that a sinner, a great sinner, can forgive other sinners their sin? But this is the issue. Obviously I can only *believe* that I forgive sin and really serve others thereby. And what I can only believe is not nature nor merit nor achievement but grace. We have seen that no more and no less is required of us than that the one should be a Christ to the other. But what we will and can do stands to the willing and doing of Christ in a totally incommensurable relationship inasmuch as we might at best be there for our neighbors as saints but not as Christ, for precisely in faith in Christ, in faith in his indwelling in us, we can know only that in ourselves and as such, on the ground of our nature that can hardly remain hidden from the eyes of our neighbors, we are rebels. |

If it is still true that our service may be real service, if it is still true that something essential takes place for others through what we will and do in our turning to them, then we have to say that this is done in and through God himself, that our willing and doing, as we [saw] when speaking about repentance, is *accepted* by God as a holy sacrifice that is pleasing to him [cf. Rom. 12:1], and is thus made effective in the service of others, whereas of ourselves we know only that it cannot possibly be pleasing as real repentance before God, and therefore it cannot possibly be acceptable as real service to our neighbors. Hence we can only give praise and thanks to God that he in his mercy is greater than our heart [cf. 1 John 3:20] and we can never forget for a moment that even with our most perfect service, as with our most perfect repentance, we will still be debtors to both God and our neighbors. This is the caveat that we have to remember here. In this regard we can view our obedience only as inauthentic obedience. In this regard we can use for our achievement only the term symbol or demonstration. It can be authentic only by grace. Its relationship to what is required cannot be calculated. It is authentically fulfilled in *Christ* and Christ alone. We can perceive it to be authentically fulfilled by *us* only as we believe in Christ. But again, this caveat does not affect the content or extent of the requirement. Nor does it alter the force with which the requirement is put to us. The sacrifice has to be brought. It lies with God to accept it, to give strength to our service. We cannot be surprised in the least if this does not happen. But we are left no time and given no chance to pronounce on this. Precisely when we know that our action is placed under this caveat we are claimed for service. Precisely when we believe in Christ as him who fulfills the law we are set under his law, i.e., in encounter with the neighbor who claims our service. Our awareness that we can only set up symbols with our own willing and doing does not justify us in acting like the lazy servant with his napkin [cf. Luke 19:20f.]. These symbols *will* to be set up. The same divine grace that alone can give them reality sets us at the place where it is not beneath us to be obedient with no guarantee of success, where the "only" can be no reason for flight or slackness. The same God who alone is good [cf. Mark 10:18 par.] makes us responsible, even as those who are not good, to be available to him and therefore to our neighbors.

Precisely in the light of the caveat of which we had to speak in relation to our service, it makes sense if I sum up what we can do to serve our neighbors as Christians in the statement that we have to pray for them. In praying for them we recognize the caveat under which even our best and purest service to them stands. In praying for them we commend them to God, and what can be the nerve and content of all that we do for others but to commend them to God? In praying for them, we intercede with God for them, and how can we do this honestly and in truth but by realizing and declaring that we are responsible before God for them? How could we pray for them if we were not ready to work for them to the full extent of our power, different though this is from the power of God? We have always to be pointed again to that lacuna which there is in all human service and which, in its impotence in spite of all our good will and works, always seems to be so shattering. We cannot fill this gap even with our prayers. But we can pray in face of it, and if our prayer is sincere we can render obedience thereby, bringing the sacrifice that is required of us. The impotence of our service, as of our repentance, should finally be related always to the divine answer that we have not sought the grace of God sincerely. "He *gives* grace to the humble" (1 Pet. 5:5; James 4:6). This is the secret of both our sickness and our cure.

4

CHURCH AND STATE[31]

Humility is the disposition of the creature that says Yes to the fact that its existence is spoiled by its guilt and lives by the divine patience, that confesses the mercy of God which meets it in its lostness, that understands and wants fellowship with God as a fellowship which is

---

[31]This section of §13 is not found in the 1929 text. Except in subsection III it follows the new version prepared for the repetition of the lectures in 1930/31. Up to the end of II, then, it is all Text B and the additions denoted by ⌐ ¬ do not here (as elsewhere) indicate materials found in B as against A but marginal insertions by Barth with hints perhaps of the 1933 revision. The 1928/29 original is preserved in a copy by an unknown hand and is reproduced in the Appendix.

mediated by the divine incarnation. This creature is sinful man to whom God has been gracious in Christ. In being what he is called to be in the new covenant between God and man, in believing therefore, man obeys the commandment of humility. He obeys in mediated fellowship with God. He obeys the incarnate God. He obeys the order set up by the incarnate God. We have understood this obedience as sacrifice, as the vicarious achievement, corresponding to our guiltiness before God, of a life that signifies and represents our forfeiture to God as our Judge. We have tried to understand the two fundamental determinations of this life: toward God, repentance, and toward men, service. If our reconciliation is to be understood as reconciliation by the God-man, our life in reconciliation, insofar as it is obedience and therefore humility and therefore sacrifice, is obviously to be understood as repentance and service. This is what God wants of us in Christ. The concrete and visible divine order in which man is obedient in this new covenant, and thus brings sacrifice and repents and serves, is, however, the double order of church and state. That Christian service is linked here to this concrete and visible order rests on the fact that the fellowship with God is a mediated fellowship, mediated through the incarnation of God. The concrete and visible orders as such are a sign of Christ's humanity, and in their claim for acknowledgment and acceptance they are a sign of his deity. They are thus to be recognized in faith and affirmed in obedience. That Christian obedience is referred to those two orders of church and state rests again on the fact that it is obedience to the God-man Christ, first to the fact that the obedience of faith calls man on the one side to repentance before God and on the other to service to the neighbor, and second to the fact that it is one thing to be obedient as a sinner to the *grace of God* and another to be obedient to the grace of God as a *sinner*. As repentance before God includes service to the neighbor, but as the acknowledgment of the grace of God is also more than this, there is as a comprehensive outer circle the order of the church and obedience as action within it. As service to the neighbor is included in repentance before God and acknowledgment of the grace of God, but as the acknowledgment of human sin is less than this, there is as a narrower inner circle the order of the state and Christian obedience as action within it. The relation of the one divine order of life in the kingdom of grace is as follows: The church always has the state in it but it is not the state. Alongside the state, which it has in it, it is in a distinctive way *only* the church. The state is wholly church, too, but it is so in *its own* way and it is not the whole church. The relative dualism of the two orders expresses the provisional character of the kingdom of grace as the kingdom of faith and antithesis, of decision and hope in relation to the kingdom of God in which the relative distinction of the functions of church and state is removed.

I

THE CHURCH

1. The church is the sign, set up by God's revelation, of the concrete and visible order of life by and in which people are summoned to repentance before God on the basis of accomplished reconciliation. This calling takes place, the order of the church is effective, and the sign comes into force "where and when it pleases God" (CA V), i.e., in the promised free act of grace in which God makes his revelation and saving action present. On the presupposition of this divine action, the church is both the divine institution and establishment of a constantly new affirmation of the reconciliation that God has accomplished in Christ, and at the same time human fellowship in this constantly affirmed reconciliation. In accordance with the character of the church as a divine institution those united in it achieve repentance before God by the proclamation and hearing of the Word of God in preaching and sacrament. In accordance with its character as a gathering of sinners saved by grace, it achieves repentance by common worship. As those who are called by this institution and in this fellowship to render service to the neighbor along with repentance before God, its members finally give the witness of free acts of love in the church. In relation to the decisive presupposition they know that this can be done in a right and holy way only by faith and therefore only to the honor of God who has accomplished reconciliation, who has willed this sign, and who has promised its fulfillment, i.e., the confirmation of accomplished reconciliation.

2. The church is not the kingdom of God. This means a. that the church is not an order of creation. According to Luther a "most bare and pure and simple" nonchurchly religion accords with creaturely life in obedience (EA 1, 133).[32] b. The church, however, is also not an order of eternal life. In the heavenly Jerusalem there will be no more temple according to Revelation 21:22. The contrast between promise and fulfillment, as between proclamation and worship or repentance and service, but also the "where and when it pleases God" as these are essential characteristics of the church, presuppose the antithesis between sin and grace which is not yet present in creation and will no longer be so in the redemption. At the beginning and the end there is no church. As a sign of the mediated fellowship between God and man the church belongs to the middle, to the time between the times, to history.

3. As an order of reconciliation the church, affirmed and willed in faith and to the honor of God, is one, legitimate, free from error, and binding on everyone. The norm by which it is measured and must direct itself is ⌐the promise that is given to it, i.e.,¬ the prophetic-apostolic witness to the completed atonement whose recipient and bearer it will be continu-

---

[32]WA 42, 80, 41—81, 1 (LW, 1, 106).

ally. The confessions of the church document its earlier recognition of the necessity and nature of this continuity. But for all its concern to be right and holy in obedience to scripture and respect for its own confessions, the church can understand the divine verdict, in virtue of which it really is this, only as grace, and therefore it can count upon the validity of this verdict only in faith, i.e., only in the fulfillment of repentance.

4. The humility of the sinner saved by grace, which is required of the individual, implies concretely, therefore, that his acts be done in this order of reconciliation and be a confirmation of this order. Reconciliation rests upon the enacted incarnation of God. Participation in it is conditioned by its promised constant confirmation, i.e., by faith in this promise, and therefore by the divine institution and human fellowship in which this faith is exercised. Here in the elements of proclamation, worship, and loving action the sign is set up which humility can never in any circumstances ignore. To take human reality seriously as a state of sin *and* grace is to accept and want the church; ⌐fundamental¬ denial of the church, on the other hand, presupposes a Romantic or sectarian view of humanity which no longer corresponds to the reality, or does not yet do so. The possibility of a practical break with the existing concrete form of the church, as at the Reformation, is a special case for which those who venture it must not only claim but also prove an insight resting on extraordinary divine authority and commission.

5. As a human work, the church's activity shares in the folly and wickedness of those whose sin is forgiven, yet has not for this reason ceased to be sin, but rather demonstrated itself therein. The church will not let itself be diverted from its promise or its task ⌐by its loneliness and impotence,¬ by the indifference and opposition that is shown it by the rest of the world. All this will constantly remind it of its own worldliness, but also of its call to continual return to its starting point in the free grace of God. The same humility in which it constitutes itself will prevent it both from flight into inwardness or invisibility, i.e., from abandoning itself as a concrete and visible order, and equally from claiming or seeking any abstract fullness of the truth and power of the community or its offices, i.e., from abandoning its foundation in the free divine act of grace. As the bride of Christ it is also his handmaiden, and therefore it must do its work aright, yet it must do it within its limits as service, not with any confusion or presumption. As the earthly body of its heavenly Lord, it will take its *earthly* existence quite seriously, fully affirming, willing, and practicing it as such.

6. The human work of the church is divine service as the setting up of the sign of proclamation, worship, and acts of love. Generally understood, it is fundamentally the work of the whole life of all its members done with regard to all human reality. To this extent, repentance before God embraces service to the neighbor, and the

church embraces the state. But as, in fact, not all the life of those gathered in the church is identical with the doing of this work, so our fellowship with God does not coincide in fact with our fellowship with our neighbor, the sinfulness of both being manifested in this. ⌐Similarly the church is not visible as Christ's church in the state, but concealed,¬ and the church needs a special and distinctive function, a specific existence as the church, in distinction from that of the state. In this distinctive existence, it is uniquely ⌐visible as¬ a sign of God's free grace that establishes fellowship between God and man, forgiving all sin and covering it. This distinctive function and existence consists of divine service in the narrower and proper sense of the term, i.e., of worship.

7. The decisive elements in the divine service of the church in the narrower sense are a) preaching as the personal ⌐repetition and¬ transmission of the biblical testimony to Christ, and the administration of the sacraments as a necessary confirmation of the existence of this testimony prior to all human speech; b) congregational prayer and praise as the church's attestation of its responsibility to this testimony; and c) the voluntary work of aid to all kinds of threatened and disadvantaged people as a witness to the unity of repentance and service and also to the hope of the kingdom of God by which the church lives.

8. A series of subsidiary tasks flows from this task of divine service: a) the Christian education of young people as a mediation of the ⌐intelligible re¬cognition of the elements in the divine service of the church in the narrower and broader sense; b) individual pastoral care, both physical and spiritual, understood as concrete personal proclamation supplementing public proclamation, as a demonstration of the directness of the divine address which proclamation must serve; c) evangelization and overseas mission as a necessary expression of the life of the church and its responsible communication to the rest of the world for which Christ also died and which, even though it may seem strange to it at first, it must humbly reckon to be God's; and d) theology, i.e., the never-and nowhere-superfluous reflection of the church on its divine origin, on the consolations and warnings of its human history, and on its task, which is the same in every age but which must be taken up afresh in every age.

9. The promise and task of divine service in the narrower sense is given fundamentally to the church as such, i.e., to all its members. The special offices of pastor, deacon, superintendent, and theological teacher are ⌐certainly gifts of the Holy Spirit but also¬ commissions of the community in its discharge of the office of Christ entrusted to it, although the office of a bishop construed as a pastor set over other officers in the church, when seen in the light of Christ's position as alone the chief shepherd, is not a possibility in the church but mistakenly copies the monarchical form of state government. In the community of Christ all can serve only the sovereign Lord and therefore each must render equal service to the other.

II
THE STATE

1. The state, too, is an "external means of grace" (Calvin, *Inst.* IV).[33] It is the sign, set up by God's revelation, of the concrete and visible order of life by which and in which, on the basis of accomplished reconciliation, we are summoned to serve our neighbor. This order, too, is effective in the free act of God's grace and, under the presupposition of this act, but *only* under it, is both a divine institution and a divinely willed human society. The state fulfills its aim and purpose by making all responsible for each and each for all through the establishment and maintaining of public law and the control and support of public education. Because truly mutual service in this sphere is conditioned by the existence of repentance before God, the true and ultimate aim and goal of the order of the state has to coincide with that of the church; people should be not only with others but for them in the state, too, on the basis of mutual forgiveness. Each specific state has to ask therefore, whether, in order to be a real state, it not only has law and culture but is also a Christian state in the church's sense.

2. The state, then, is not the city of the devil deriving from the fall of the wicked angels, resting on human self-love, and standing over against the church as Cain stood over against Abel (Augustine, *De civitate Dei* XI, 34; XIV, 28; XV, 1.17; XXI, 1). Yet it is no more identical than the church is with the incarnation (Hegel)[34] or the kingdom of God (Rothe).[35] It is not an order of creation, for it did not exist before the fall and is a necessary remedy against corrupt nature (Luther, EA 1, 130).[36] Nor is it an order of eternal life. It is an order of the sustaining patience of God which is necessary and good because even those who have been blessed in Christ are wholly and utterly sinners. It, too, presupposes that repentance before God and service to the neighbor are in an antithesis that has not yet been overcome. It, too, rests on the "where and when it pleases God." It, too, is a sign of the mediated fellowship between God and man. It, too, once was not and one day will not be, so that it belongs with the church to the time between the times, to the kingdom of grace.

3. As an order of reconciliation the state in all possible forms can serve in God's stead (Rom. 13; the authorities, according to Calvin, are God's

---

[33]Book IV, in which the discussion of the state forms chap. 20, bears the general heading "The external Means or Aims by which God Invites us into the Society of Christ and Holds us therein," or, in brief, "Means of Grace."

[34]G. W. F. Hegel, *Sämtliche Werke*, Jubilee ed., in 20 vols, ed. H. Glockner, vol. 11, Stuttgart 1949, pp. 85f. Hegel refers here to the principles of the state as determinations of the divine nature.

[35]Cf. R. Rothe, *Theologische Ethik*, 3 vols., Wittenberg 1845–1848; 5 vols., Wittenberg 1867–1871[2], vol, 2, §§449–458. Rothe refers here to the general organism of the state as essentially the absolutely completed kingdom of God, absolute theocracy (quoting J. G. Fichte, *Politische Fragmente* (*Werke* VII), p. 613.

[36]Cf. WA 42, 79, 7ff.

"vicars" [Op. 20, 320][37] or "lieutenants" [Op. 49, 637f.]).[38] To the extent that it is the free act of divine grace which alone can make, but can really *make*, Nero's Rome or Calvin's Geneva into what the state ought to be as an order of reconciliation, its divine dignity and its character as a divine institution and a divinely willed human society are, as in the case of the church, a subject of revelation and faith, so that in the historical situation of the Reformation period the recognition rather than the contesting of temporal authority is rightly made a subject of the church's confession.[39] This means that God acknowledges the requirement of obedience to specific forms of state although he is not bound to any one in particular and may at any time call any of them in question, either in part or as a whole.

4. Concretely, then, the humility demanded of the sinner saved by grace consists in detail of action within this order and of a confirmation of it. Here again we must think indeed of the incarnation of God, in which we have a share only within the divine institution and divinely willed human society, in which faith in the promise is confirmed. The state is an institution and society of this kind, and a given state can be so. True humility, truly taking seriously the reality of the human condition as one of both grace and sin, cannot ignore this sign, in contrast to all romanticism and sectarianism. It is Christian obedience, then, to give the state what belongs to it [cf. Mark 12:17 par.], i.e., to affirm and desire it as a sign of obligatory service to the neighbor and to be a sincere and consistent citizen of it. Concrete affirmation of the state in a specific form is limited, of course, by God's freedom over against any form. We must obey man, i.e., the existing form, for God's sake. But we must obey God rather than man [cf. Acts 5:29]. We can obey man only in obedience to God. We cannot obey man in disobedience to God. It may be, then, that in obedience to God we cannot obey. Concrete affirmation of the state must sometimes take the form, then, of working with a party which seeks to improve or alter the form of the state. A revolutionary alteration of the form of the state, because of the use of force that seems to be unavoidable in such a case, and especially because of the temporary overthrow of the state in general which it undoubtedly entails, because of the danger of its total jeopardizing, is a last resort to which (as to the reformation of the church) one may have recourse only in extreme and very rare circumstances. As Christian obedience, the

[37]This reference is wrong, but cf. *Inst.* IV, 20, 4, 6: "acting as his viceregents"; "if they remember that they are vicars of God."
[38]Cf. CR LXXVII, 637f. "God ordains that there should be justice and those who are elected and authorized to govern are like his lieutenants."
[39]Cf. CA XVI, 1 (Apol. XVI, 53); XXVIII, 18; Small Catechism; Large Catechism; Geneva Catechism, 1542, 194f.: Ecclesiastical Discipline, 1559, 39; Confession, 1560, chap. 24; Belgic Confession, 1561, art. XXXVI; Heidelberg Catechism, 1563; Second Helvetic Confession, 1566, art. XXX (cf. P. Schaff, *Creeds of Christendom, Evangelical Creeds*).

desire for this or that form of the state is not inviolable but in contrast to anarchy, which forgets the reality of man, the desire for the state may be described as such. This desire for the state in general is the decisive and by no means time-bound content of the Reformation confession of the state.

5. As a human work, the state shares in the corruption with which man, far from forgiving sin, pursues his own ends with cunning and force in the struggle for existence, something which is no different or better because it is here done collectively. The existence of a specific state is questionable at every point as service to the neighbor. For a. each state ⌐even a liberal one,⌐ will finally be self-willing and self-seeking in its sponsoring of education and culture, not teaching each to serve the other but all to serve itself. b. Each state, ⌐even the conservative one,⌐ will order the common life on the untenable presuppositions that the right of the individual to order his own life, apart from the state's own claim upon him, is an ultimately inviolable good which must be protected by every available means, and conversely that each must be brought to account for his own offenses. c. The final weapon whereby each state defends itself against its members is the coercion with which it dares to forestall God's own claim to men. d. Each state is simply one among many others over against which it relies upon the usurped right of force, and appeals to it, to maintain its own existence. ⌐e. Almost every state is a nation-state, i.e., the state of a particular people that rules in it but is confronted by national minorities whose nationhood is more or less suppressed in this state.⌐ Thus each state contradicts its very nature as an order of service to the neighbor. This participation of the individual state in sin can sometimes mean that as it is before God it will not be tolerated but rejected, that it will thus have to be altered or renewed by its members, although we have to realize that even a new and better form will in its own way still participate in sin. Yet the participation of an individual state in sin can also take place under the divine patience and forgiveness as a necessary fulfillment of the divine will of the Creator, although we have to realize that it is not thereby justified. Hence the dignity of any given state can be regarded only as inauthentic, and the respect that must be shown it only as provisional. The individual state can be willed and affirmed as service to the neighbor only in repentance before God, i.e., under the proviso of God's grace and in faith that God will make good what we cannot help but do badly.

6. The human work of the state is generally understood as the building up of society among men by establishing the sign of ⌐commonly discovered and accepted⌐ right or law, ⌐protected if necessary by force,⌐ and ⌐commonly sought⌐ education. This is fundamentally the work of the total life of all its members and it relates fundamentally to this total reality of human life. It thus embraces the work of the church as well, inasmuch as this, too, is service to the neighbor. The distinctive function of the state in comparison with that of the church may be seen

first in the concrete state, which is primarily oriented to sin and not to grace, and which on the one side, as a nation-state, desires and seeks to build up society only within geographical and ethnographical boundaries, and on the other side, as a mere state of law and culture, does not press on to the perfecting of human society by mutual forgiveness, needing in both areas to be supplemented by the church, which is different from it.

7. The decisive elements in the upbuilding of society by the nation-state with its law and culture are a) the constitution, i.e., the basic regulation of the relation among the legislative, executive, and judicial powers which needs, if not the express will and cooperation of the citizens, at least (even in the case of the dictatorship of a minority or majority) their freely given confidence; b) legislation, i.e., the regulation of common life for the ends of state, the best possible safeguarding of its unity, law, and freedom;[40] c) proper government, i.e., concern for the full, equal, and appropriate execution of the existing laws; d) the administration of justice to give definitive and independent rulings (independent even of the ⌐current¬ government) in cases of dispute.

8. ⌐Concrete¬ tasks of the legislative and executive branches of a nation-state, with its law and culture, include at all events a) the ⌐making possible,¬ supervision, consolidation, and protection of national labor; b) the counteracting of the temporary or permanent favoring of individual groups of citizens which might arise through faults in economic organizations when this is left in private hands; this might take the form of the partial or total taking over the economy by the state itself; c) the ⌐external¬ protection both of the social structures of marriage, family, and people, which rest on the order of creation, and of the formation of freer societies of particular interests or concerns insofar as these new groups can be understood as an affirmation of the state, i.e., of the common social structure which is superior to all of them; d) the ⌐external¬ protection of the existence of free scientific research and the supervision and appropriate organization of education and culture for its members; e) the external protection of the free activity of the church as the specific society in which there is recollection of the ultimate and sustaining purpose of the state outside its own sphere.

9. The task and promise of the work of the state derive from God. It is correct, then, that the validity and goodness of this work depends on God's grace. But because its task and promise are from God, it demands fundamentally, if in different ways, the will and deed of all. Not just the male sex, or one of the constituent peoples, or a single family or group of families to the exclusion of all others, is called by God's grace to do the

---

[40]Cf. the beginning of the last strophe of A. H. Hoffman von Fallersleben's (1798–1874) "Song of Germany" (1841), the later national anthem: "Unity and law and freedom, for the German fatherland . . ."

work of the state. ⌐In this sense all the power of the state comes from the people.⌐ To lead the work one individual may be called in a smaller or larger circle, who in virtue of the confidence reposed in him does in fact more or less lead the many. The question of leadership is thus one of an event which is the mutual venture of the leader and the led. ⌐The leader may also be a usurper with a great power of suggestion, and confidence in his leadership may be a matter of hypnosis.⌐ A specific decision about the sacred place from which the leadership comes cannot precede this venture. ⌐Before, as, and after it is ventured it stands under the question whether it is to be regarded as obedience to God or service to the neighbor.⌐

III

CHURCH AND STATE

1. As Boniface VIII rightly presupposed (Bull *Unam Sanctam*, 1302), church and state, expressing one and the same temporally, though not eternally, valid divine order, are two swords of the one power of Jesus Christ.[41] The dualism of the orders is conditioned and demanded by the dualism of man as the saved sinner who is reconciled to God. Christian humility will acknowledge equally the *relativity* of their distinctness and the *necessity* of their relative distinctness. It can thus accept neither an absolutizing (metaphysical separation of religious and secular spheres) nor a one-sided eliminating (caesaropapism or theocracy) of this distinctness.

2. Between church and state there is no equality, but superiority in the church's favor. The temporal authority must be subject to the spiritual, as Boniface says.[42] The temple comes before the home (Luther, EA 1, 130).[43] State and church coinhere. Yet the church is not first in the state but the state in the church, just as repentance before God establishes but does not presuppose service to the neighbor, and conversely service to the neighbor presupposes but does not establish repentance before God. The Christian is always a member of the church first, and only then, and as such, a citizen.

3. The church, if its responsible representatives are not to cease to be humble, can assert its basic superiority over the state only to God's glory as Lord of both church and state and not to its own glory, and only with its given weapons of proclamation of the Word and repentance, and not, like Boniface, with the direct or indirect uniting of both swords in its

---

[41]Nov. 18, 1302. The bull argues that the two swords produced at the last supper are both in the hands of the disciples and represent the spiritual and temporal powers, both in the hands of the church, the former to be used by it, the latter for it, and the former superior to the latter; Denz. no. 468, 469.

[42]See above, n.41.

[43]WA 42, 79, 7 (LW, 1, 104).

hand, with the exercise of a quasi-temporal authority in competition with that of the state.[44]

4. Insofar as the church acts as such, it will renounce not only any appeal to the individual instinct of self-preservation or any assertion of the distinction between good and evil, not only the use of external compulsion within and force without, but fundamentally, too, the establishment and enforcement of any fixed law ⌐corresponding to the laws of the state.⌐ Canon and dogma are not legal but spiritual norms and may be used only as such. Church law in the strict sense can only be the church-recognized law of the state itself existing in the church. The formation of a special church law, as an unavoidable change into another genus, can be regarded only as an incidental and doubly inauthentic function of the church. It comes under the rule: The less, the better.

5. The church will in practice be subject to the state, the guardian of law, as one society among others. Things being as they are, it will have to accept the concrete national individuality of the state and its own necessary national separation and distinction from other parts of the church.[45] The freedom and superiority which it reserves for itself precisely in this way is not linked to the measure of independence of its leadership and organization in relation to those of the state, nor to the presence of a visible international unity of the church, but to the measure of confidence with which it maintains itself as a fellowship of proclamation of the Word and repentance over against the justified and unjustified claims of the state, with a much larger task which is in fact a uniform one and therefore international. A state church which knows and is loyal to its own cause, and to the unity of this cause, is to be preferred to even the most vital of free churches as a symbol of the final unity of church and state.

6. The church recognizes and helps the state inasmuch as service to the neighbor, which is the purpose of the state, is necessarily included in its own message of reconciliation and is thus its own concern. It will take up a reserved attitude toward the state to the extent that this diverges from its purpose, being unable as the church to accept co-responsibility in this regard. Finally, with its own given weapons, it will move on to protest against the state if the latter's actions mean a denial of its purpose, if it is no longer manifest and credible as the order of God. In one way or the other, it will positively confess the purpose of the state and the individual state with it.

7. The state, if its responsible representatives do not cease to be humble, can assert its practical superiority over the church only to the glory of God as Lord of both church and state and not to its own glory—and only in its own field as the guardian of law, not as the

---

[44]See above, n. 41.

[45]An allusion to the lively debate in Germany after 1918 as to whether state boundaries should also be church boundaries; cf. O. Dibelius, *Das Jahrhundert der Kirche*, Berlin 1926, 1927², pp. 98f.

preacher of a world-view that fits in with the state's own *raison d'être,* nor with the desire to set up a special civil Christianity. It gives freedom to the church to set up its own worship, dogma, ⌜and constitution,⌝ and to promote its own preaching and theology.

8. The state for its part cannot in principle be tied to a specific form of the church. It recognizes and supports the church insofar as its own purpose is grounded and included in that of the church. To that extent it is neither nonreligious nor nonconfessional. But it is supraconfessional to the extent that it is tolerant in face of the confessional division of the church, i.e., to the extent that within the limits of the law it fundamentally assures all church fellowships of the same freedom.

9. Yet in practice, without intolerance to other churches, and as an expression of the distinctness with which it is aware of its own purpose, it can claim that one form of the church is in a particular way the form of the church and treat it as such, just as the church does not shrink from recognizing the concrete nation-state. A qualified recognition and support of one church as a symbol of the unity of church and state is, even from the state's own standpoint, more appropriate than the system of a real ⌜organizational⌝ separation of church and state.

§14

LOVE

God's command is fulfilled by me, i.e., my acts are good, are obedience to the command of the law, and take place in acknowledgment of the authority set over me and as a work of humility, to the extent that I am told, and let myself be told, that I myself am bound to God and through him to my neighbor. That this is told me, and that I let it be told me, is the work of the Word of God and as such the reality of love.

1

In relation to the command of God the Reconciler, too, we have now to consider briefly the problem of our conduct, of our keeping of the command. We have learned to know this command, i.e., the one command of God, in a particular perspective, as the command of the law of God as this is concretely given to us in our encounter with our fellows. We have found the requirement of the command, as it is issued to us in this specific form, in the concept of humility or sacrifice expounded in the concepts of repentance before God and service to the neighbor. Again a number of criteria of conduct have become visible, questions by which it is decided, or partly decided, whether it takes place in obedience and therefore in sanctification. Yet we have not so far investigated our conduct as such, the subject of all these definitions. In other words, the question has still to be asked explicitly who or what we must *be* to stand in humility under the law, under authority, and therefore to be Christians—this question[1] which is the point behind all the other questions. Again all the points that we have touched upon on our path refer us to a center, the decision of specific action that has to be taken, of action in which we are placed under *the* criterion before God himself. Only in further elucidation of this central event did we allow ourselves the abstraction, which underlies this chapter, of a law of grace along with the further abstractions that we have made in developing these concepts. We realize that from none of these standpoints, nor from all of them put together, are we in a position to press on beyond what are at best only highly probable as correct answers to the question of the goodness of our acts. God himself, and God alone, gives the decisive answer to this question as he finds us, or does not find us, in the decision that has to be taken by us in obedience. If theological ethics seeks to be more than a compendium of highly probable correct answers, i.e., of ethical convictions, then even its answers can have no other character than that of the *questions* specified. These must always be open, not on the side of human caprice, but on that of the Word of God that alone decides. Except with this fundamental openness, we should not ask or answer the question of our conduct as such or our own being in it. Yet we must not evade this question, for it has to be made plain that we too, and we specifically, in the decisive question of our own decision as such, [of] our decision in relation to the law of grace, stand before the decision of God. We have to do here, I have said, with the decisive question. All answers to the question: How do I act as one who is reconciled with God? must obviously be and remain open answers, answers which in the last resort can only seek to ask because in some sense they are themselves only preliminary or eventual questions pointing us to the decisive question whether I act as a reconciled person. Whether I *am* set under the law, whether I *stand* under authority and in humility, all these things depend on the first and great Whether. Is there any possibility of bringing this great Whether under a concept which will characterize itself as an ethical concept, as the representation of a claiming of our conduct, by expressing not merely the fact that the answer to the great Whether is in God's hands—it must obviously do this too—but also that what is really in God's hands is our own responsible action to which we must, of course, have been *chosen*, about which we can only *pray*, but to the doing of which, as we pray about it and are chosen to do it, we are also *summoned* with ultimate urgency, being made fully responsible for it in the process? According to the direction of the Bible in both the Old Testament and New, as well as that of theological tradition, which is more or less unanimous in this area, and also of the approach which we

[1]The text eliminated the original "eben diese Frage als" as redundant in the German.

have followed up to this final question of ours, the definition of our conduct of which we have to think here is the reality of *love*.

2

What can it and ought it to mean that my conduct as a Christian, in relation to the command of him who makes me a Christian, is at this moment good, is a fulfillment or keeping of this command, is Christian, that I at this moment stand under the law, bow to authority, and offer to God the sacrifice that is a pleasure to him? In such a case the will of God is obviously done. But in another way than at the corresponding point in our chapter on the command of creation[2] we now clearly have reason to consider that what is at issue is the doing of the will of God *on earth*, from which the same doing of the will of God in heaven is to be distinguished [cf. Matt. 6:10]. On earth does not now mean simply within the limits of creatureliness or with the essential imperfection of all created and finite perfection. On earth now means more, i.e., within the limits of the fallen and corrupt existence which by God's inconceivable mercy has not been allowed to fall but upheld in its fall. How, then can we ever think of describing our doing of the good as a uniting of our human will with the divine will, of trying to take God's place with our action? We are told that we are to be sinners saved by grace, not that we are to be as gods [cf. Gen. 3:5]. It is for this reason that *love* is the fulfilling of the law [Rom. 13:10]. Love bridges the gap between the sinner saved by grace and the God of all mercy and comfort [2 Cor. 1:3], while not removing it. Love affirms it even in overcoming it. Love seeks and finds its object, as faith does. So long as it is love, love does not [become] a mystical sense of identity with its object nor set aside its object. Love is already in a true sense the doing of the good because it seeks and finds and has the good in God. It not only [seeks and finds and has the good], like faith, in God as the one, original, eternal, and self-grounded good—it naturally does this too, loving God also as Creator, and thus far being simply faith—but it also [seeks and finds and has] God as the one who inconceivably as the Creator, as he who alone is good in himself, turns to the creature that has fallen from his goodness, inclines toward him, and shows him his goodness as well as his being the good. This inconceivable following and preceding goodness of God is what love seeks and finds. It seeks and finds and has God in the miracle of counterlove. In love, as distinct from faith, it is not just a matter of the agreement of our will with God but of our *commitment* to him. As and because we love him, we comprehend him as the one who holds us up over the abyss *against* all our comprehension and expectation. How, then, should not our love, in a deeper sense than faith, be an action within the limit that is set for us, a

---

[2]Cf. pp. 249ff.

limit that is qualified not merely as that of the creature but also as that of the sinner?|

Again, in this regard it is already the good, the action that is required of us. But we must go further. If love is the fulfilling of the law, then we must already say about it that in it the will of God is done "on earth as it is in heaven" [Matt. 6:10]. Within that limit our action, to be called good, must be, not an actualizing, which God reserves for himself, but a representation, copy, and mirror of the divine action. Our action is a doing of the good the moment it meets with God's good-pleasure because he sees in it the fulfillment of his thoughts of peace concerning us and to that extent the affirmation of his merciful will. The content of this moment, then, is obviously the answer to all the questions by which we see ourselves beset through his command. This moment we live under the law, standing under authority and in humility. This existential affirmation of God is now, in relation to the law of grace, love. Love is the epitome of the obedience of the sinner saved by grace. Deification is not the issue, but this is. More is not demanded of him, but this is demanded as the basis and epitome of all else. The act of love is the act of the committed person. We affirm God the Reconciler as we act as those who are bound, bound by the fact that the ground of our existence is the miracle of his mercy. We forfeit ourselves if our action is not the answer to the counterlove that follows and precedes us in the mercy of God, if we will not love in return. Love means affirming the commitment in which we are not lost but saved.|

Yet we have every reason to ask whether there ever was or is or will be any such moment of good pleasure, of the commitment of our will to God's will. What do we have or know except that we are asked concerning it? In the act of love, then, we cannot seize upon this or that answer to the questions that are put to us and say that it is the most convincing one, the one that is necessary for us. We continually do this and, if one will, this might be called the grasping of the most probable possibility of love. But we should not call this love in the sense of commitment. For are we ourselves not the ones who here commit us? Who has enabled or authorized us so to bind ourselves by seizing upon this or that answer to what we are asked that in binding ourselves thus we also bind ourselves to God? There can obviously be talk of love in the real sense only where we have not bound ourselves but *are bound*. Love grounds itself in the counterlove that is sought and found and sought again, in the object that awakens and evokes it because it itself loves. We do not resolve upon love; the beloved object resolves upon it for us. Love is no accompaniment to our seizing upon this or that possibility. It is itself a grasping only insofar as it is first a *being grasped* and all grasping of possibilities can only seek to be an expression of this being grasped. If it is a matter of our being bound to God and therefore of love, of the pure love that is free of all self-binding (and to which all our love of creaturely objects can relate only as a likeness), then we can in some way suitably express our being bound, the conditioning of our love by its object, only by seeking its basis, what makes it love and therefore the doing of the good, in the fact that we are *told* about our being bound, and let ourselves be *told* about it, told about it by the *Word* of reconciliation that has come to us.|

As we speak about telling and the Word at this unexpected place, we maintain, first, that we are speaking about the fulfilling of the law, about love of the God who stands over against us as the Reconciler in the antithesis that has been bridged but not removed. We do not know about him, nor can we love him, on the basis of any prior knowledge that we have of him. He has to speak to us and we have to hear him. In speaking about telling and being told, we emphasize, second, that love really is the content of the law that has been issued to us, and is thus real commitment through its object and love of its object. Love is pure love in that it does not rest on its own inner necessity nor consist of its own grasping, but is an event totally in the totality of the Word that comes to us from outside and "from on high" [Luke 1:78] in a way that is not true of any love that is directed to any human or creaturely objects, seeking us who could never have expected or known it of ourselves. And, third, we speak about the Word here, about telling and being told, because pure love, which is the doing of the good, is not played out in a sphere of the immediate and ineffable but in the *mediacy* of real life where God certainly confronts man, but does so as the God who conceals himself in the unassuming form of the fellowman, and therefore in the sphere of typically human relations. It is here and thus that the Reconciler has come to us. It is here and thus, in the claim of the fellowman, that the command of love is an event, and it is in the hearing of this claim that love itself becomes an event.|

If we are not *told*, and will not be *told*, that we are bound, then we certainly are not, and our love could only be an arrogant grasping of our own whose character as a fulfilling of the law is up in the air. If we *are* reconciled with God, then we also love. The love of God is shed abroad in our hearts by the Holy Spirit [Rom. 5:5], i.e., we act as those who are committed to God, and through him to our neighbor, not because we have resolved upon it, but because God, and through him our neighbor, has resolved upon it for us, thereby deciding whether we stand under the law, under the authority, in humility, or whether all this is mere appearance and imagination. Our action thus corresponds to our love, i.e., we do not want to be without God and therefore without our neighbor in what we will and do. This not being without God, and therefore without our neighbor, is the being which means being good from the standpoint of God the Reconciler. In this commitment we are doers of the Word. But how else can this take place except as we *are* reconciled, and how else are we reconciled with God except by the miracle by which God himself has reconciled us with himself? On this miracle depends the reality of love, and therefore our keeping of the command, the answer to the question of the goodness of our conduct. Hence the reality of love cannot be understood except as the reality of faith. "In this is love, not that we loved God but that he loved us" [1 John 4:10]. Love is grace.|

We cannot take to ourselves the decisive thing that has to take place; it has to be given to us. This is the leading theological determination of the concept of love. But it must show itself to be authentic by translating itself into the anthropological realm, though always in the light of the basic text. It must present itself as responsible human action. The possibility and necessity of this are given by the fact that we do not understand the gift, i.e., grace, the love that is shed abroad in our hearts, as a kind of physical infusion (as many have done in an undoubted misunderstanding of Paul's saying), but as a Word that is spoken to us, and that we allow to be spoken to us.|

Thus love is in the most literal sense *responsibility*. In loving we do not obey an impulse that comes upon us like magic; hence, if we do not love, we cannot make the excuse that the magic has not come upon us. In loving—this is something very different—we are asked whether we have really heard the Word of eternal love and whether, if we have, we can do anything else but love. For loving is an action, the action which takes place in the commitment that we have described by the terms law, authority, and humility and which is the underlying meaning of these concepts. One might call love, like faith, a "trust and venture of the heart."[3] One might also say of it that the issue is to see that the center of our being is called in question, and that we have to let go and surrender and hazard it in order to let God be our Lord in the definite form of openness to the law which is given to us in the givenness of our neighbor. One might use here the illustration of the swimmer or cyclist who must give up his balance in order to move ahead. But beyond what love has in common with faith, the decisive thing for it is the character of the *necessity* of its venture. The work of love is necessary work to the degree that it relates to a need. Grace does not simply denote God in general as him who is high above our need as the Creator. It denotes God as the Lord of our necessity. When it is a matter of the Word of eternal love we are asked whether we should not really see our need in Christ and therefore in the least of his brethren [cf. Matt. 25:40]; whether we are not bound to him and therefore to them because the need means no more and no less than our lostness; whether we have any other choice than to love if we are not to be lost. To venture the heart with this necessity is to love. What is ventured outside it in relation to God or neighbor is not love—not love in the sense of the command. We might bind ourselves, perhaps very strongly, but we could not claim that what we do is obedience to the command of the Reconciler. Perhaps we

[3]Cf. Luther's exposition of the first commandment in his *Large Catechism* of 1529, WA 30, 1, 132f.

might claim that it is obedience to God the Creator. But in relation to God the Creator in his totality, we are transgressors, and this is the need in which his grace encounters us, and in and with grace the command of the Reconciler, which always claims us as those who are in need and whose love, therefore, cannot consist of their binding themselves but of their being bound. Love stands in this being bound to God and the neighbor. It thus stands in the venture undertaken in this being bound. What distinguishes it from every other source is that this is a venture of *submission,* and if we call it the venture of the heart, it is the venture of a submission of our heart to a foreign claim in all the foreignness which contradicts our own heart. Our heart cannot love in this sense. It is our sinful heart just because it would rather venture anything else, it would rather bind itself very strongly than be bound. It is our consistently sinful heart inasmuch as it has not perceived its being bound by the divine necessity, and therefore it has not perceived its own need but persists in being unbound. We love in the sense of the command when we hear the claim that is issued to us also and precisely as the contradiction that is spoken against us, when God and the neighbor are real entities for us which are to be distinguished from ourselves, as their desires are from ours, so that we cannot find them in ourselves nor can we translate their desires into ours nor reconcile them with ours: entities which persistently and definitively resist all our attempts to identify them with our own entity and to which we are bound in such a way that we *must* submit to them.|

We *must.* This is the word that, explicitly or not, has accompanied us through this whole chapter. It is the word that denotes the love that is required of us by the command, the doing of the command as such. We do the good when we *must;* this "must" is Christian love. Adapting to it in opposition to ourselves is the venture of Christian love. Paradoxically, but necessarily, we have to say that Christian love comes from the heart when it is against our heart and therefore cuts us to the heart. "Thus the sailor finally clings to the rock on which he was perishing".[4] This has to be so if we keep in view the theological as well as the anthropological nature of the concept and find here its true and decisive content. But we must look back again from the one to the other.|

Phenomenologically, Christian love, like Christian faith, offers the alien aspect of a leap in the void. How can we be bound if there is nothing correlative in us to bind us? How can there be any resolve which does not consist of our being resolved? What kind of an act is that which I have to do, which I do wholly out of necessity? If we are to achieve clarity and truth here rather than illusion, if we are to tread with sure steps, then God has to be here, not just our idea of him or intention regarding him, but God himself in the reality of his love. When all is said: love as responsibility, as venture, as submission, as necessity, and

---

[4] J. W. Goethe, *Torquato Tasso* (1787–1789), Act V, Scene 5.

therefore as the true and decisive thing in the question whether we stand under the law, under authority, and in humility—it all depends on God being there, on his giving himself as an object to us, and his doing this through the neighbor. If we had no object, we would not and could not love, and all the rest, responsibility, venture, submission, and necessity, would collapse upon us. Ontologically, too, they could be regarded only as illusory. That we have an object, however, it is not enough merely that God is God and that we do not seem to lack for people around us. If it were, we should be able to love in the same self-evident way. We realize, however, how seldom we love. Indeed, to be quite accurate, we have to say that even though God is God and there is no lack of people around us, we do not love of ourselves, and therefore we have to choose whether we shall torture ourselves trying to do so or decide to give up the whole thing as obvious madness. Hence we cannot give an anthropological definition of love without closing the circle and defining love theologically again as the love with which we *are loved*, as God's own love in which—miracle of miracles, we may now say—he is not just God but God *for us*, confessing that he is called in question by our plight, which is our guilt against him, but also answering the question, taking, as it were, his own steps into the void, the step into the nothingness to which we have given up ourselves, bowing to a claim which he not only gave us in creating us but which can be only the compulsion of his mercy. Thus God becomes an object for us, and thus the neighbor becomes an object too. Thus love becomes possible and real. We cannot lose sight for a moment of this being of God for us if in speaking of love we are not to speak of a mere schema. But have we really understood this element if we try to include it in our definition otherwise than as the element for whose presence we can only pray, since never for a moment is this presence grounded in anything but itself?

Thus, remembering that the clarity and truth of our love stand in the divine love, in our being loved, and that we have no control at all over this decisive element, we can go on to say that in loving we are bound to the will of God, and our action, as that of the sinners saved by grace that we are, is good. As the moment of love, the moment of my decision can be that of the divine good-pleasure in which I keep the command. My whole knowledge of my sin, including my nonloving, is not set aside but is refuted by what God holds concerning me in seeking and finding me, in loving me, and thus in awakening and summoning me to love in contradiction of my sin and nonlove. Love is undoubtedly the discovery of my nonlove but I would not love if it were not my refuted nonlove that is discovered. Every other "whether"—whether I see my neighbor as God's law, whether I stand under authority and in humility, whether I meet the whole claim made on me—arises in all its greatness as a living issue only when I love. When I love, my answers to such questions are right answers that are pleasing to God even though—for every single moment apart from my love—everything with perhaps the highest degree of probability tells against this. In love, I act as God wants his people to act, as brands whom he has plucked out of the fire [cf. Amos 4:11]. In love, everything comes together that otherwise does not come together. The proviso of the inauthentic, which we have always to make otherwise, is removed. This is a proviso that we ourselves certainly cannot remove but which is removed in love—namely, that God must give his participation and acceptance to our conduct if it is to be good. There *is* this participation when we love.|

In a famous passage Paul said unreservedly of love: "Love is patient. Love is kind. It is not jealous. Love does not boast. It does not puff up itself. It does not offend against what is fitting. It does not seek its own. It does not become resentful. It does not take evil into account. It does not rejoice in unrighteousness. It rejoices in the truth. It is all bearing, all believing, all hoping, all enduring" [I Cor. 13:4–7]. Paul put all other things under provisos: speaking in tongues, prophesying, knowledge, believing, sharing goods, martyrdom. One can have and do all these things and still be empty brass and a tinkling cymbal [I Cor. 13:1]. All these things will "pass away", as he says [ICor. 13:8,10]. But he speaks differently about love. From all that he says about it, we can see that he has in mind the human act, love as it is practiced in relation to one's neighbor. We can also see from the many negative things that he says in describing it that it does in fact mean a contradiction of us, a departure from what we would really do in and of ourselves. It is instructive, too, that precisely at this point Paul does not speak of the loving person as the one who does all these things, but almost impersonally of love itself. The unconditional way in which he describes its work is obviously related to this, cf. its "all bearing, all believing, all hoping, all enduring." Who can overlook here what we have called the theological element in the concept of love? But this did not prevent Paul from speaking of love as a *way* [I Cor. 12:31] to which he thinks he can point, a way for us where another love is really present for us in our total lack of love, totally present for our half-presence, yet there for *us*—a way of human participation in the divine love. And it was certainly of this human love which participates in the divine love that he made the unheard of statement: "Love never ends" [I Cor. 13:8]. Our love, of course, does end. But participating in God's love it, too, does not end. There is good reason why, precisely at this point, Paul speaks of the limitation of our human knowledge. When we consider the mystery of love and therefore the fulfillment of the command in and in spite of our sinful humanity, we stand before what is perfect, so that we can understand it only as coming and future. We know it only "brokenly" (ἐκ μέρους, I Cor. 13:12). We are set on an inconceivable way. The impossibility of thinking or speaking of love except by describing it as the action in which we ourselves are loved reminds us of the limitation with which we partake of the perfect here and now. Yet within this limitation there is a full and real participation in the perfect. There is a doing of the good. God gives it. "Love never ends." "He who abides in love abies in God, and God abides in him" [I John 4:16]. This is why Paul finally puts faith and hope alongside love as their center [I Cor. 13:13]. In love they acquire and have, or we who believe and hope acquire and have, the object that we need. Faith justifies because it believes that we are loved. This is why, in faith, we cleave to God himself and will live even though we die [cf. John 11:25]. Hope will not be ashamed because it grasps what is to come as the present [cf. Rom. 5:5]. This is why in hope we cleave to God himself and will live even though we die. But love is the greatest of the three. One can say of neither faith nor hope that it is God. But we can and must say that God is love [cf. John 4:8,16].

CHAPTER FOUR

The Command of God the Redeemer

§15

THE COMMAND OF PROMISE

God's command applies to me inasmuch as, being his child, I am an heir of eternal life. In speaking with me, he promises me his presence as my redeemer from the provisional state in which I am here and now his creature, and from the contradiction in which I am here and now a Christian, and he thus bids me wait for this future of his and hasten toward it.

1

If theological ethics speaks about man, it does not have in view man as he understands himself but man as he knows that he is understood, as he finds himself addressed by the Word of God that has come to him. The man in view is none other than the reflection of the presuppositions about man which we have found to be made in the claim that is made upon us. About this man, it may be said that his reality includes more than that he was created by God and that, in the state of sin which contradicts his divine creation, the inconceivable grace of the same God reconciled him to God. In and with these two elements, in relation to which we have tried to understand God's command thus far, there is a third element: the eschatological reality of man. It is fitting that we should speak about this third element of human reality at the end of theological ethics, for here we are really dealing with the end—not of man, for on a true understanding it must be said that we have here his true and proper beginning—but the end (as just indicated in our

461

reference to 1 Corinthians 13)[1] of what there is to be *said* about man, the point where description of the claiming of man by God's command has to come to a halt with a recognition of the broken nature of our knowledge. "When the perfect comes, the imperfect will pass away" [1 Cor. 13:10]. To the extent that, in this chapter, we shall have to speak about the goal of man, about his reality as it is oriented to this goal, it might well be said that the proper course here, face to face with the reality of the divine command as it aims at this goal, is formally to lay down our arms and openly to accept the inadequacy of even the most eloquent theological endeavor in relation to this theme, to the eschatological character of this theme, which we cannot truly ignore in ethics either. Hence it will not just be an embarrassment, not just an unavoidable recognition of the fact that theological ethics, too, is an enterprise that is undertaken in time that moves on ineluctably to its close,[2] if this final chapter turns out to be quantitatively the smallest of them all. Inevitably our breath runs out when we venture to speak about the last things. If we try to say a lot, we do not know what ought to be said. Yet the little that has to be said cannot just as well be left unsaid. Far too many works of theological ethics suffer clearly because their authors seem not to have remembered that there is in dogmatics an independent eschatological standpoint which inalienably has a place with all the others, even through differing from them. How can we seriously present what God wants *of* us without recalling what God finally wants *with* us? Is what he wants of us not really affected and co-determined by this? In relation to many parts and passages of scripture and innumerable problems in the history of ethics which cannot be evaluated except from this angle, to overlook this third aspect involves a suspicious narrowness and poverty; indeed, it is a simple failure to face up to the ethical reality in which we stand.

If we have tried to sum up our understanding of the command of God thus far in the formula: Be what you are, namely, my creature; do this, and do it in such a way as corresponds to your being as my creature—also one who is reconciled to me; do this, and do it in such a way as is appropriate to one who is reconciled to me—we are still forced to admit that something is left out, something future: a being of mine to the extent that it is claimed by the God who not merely wanted something with me in creating me, and not merely wanted something with me in the presence of the conflict between his grace and my sin, but also wants something with me as the goal and purpose of what he wants as Creator and Reconciler. This missing element, this goal, reached neither in creation nor reconciliation, of the way which God walks with me as my Lord, this being of mine which has not yet appeared [cf. 1 John 3:2] but

---

[1]Cf. above, p. 459.
[2]There is a double reference here. Barth has only a short time left before the semester ends.

which, from God's standpoint, is no less my real being, which is indeed my most real being as the divine goal of my being, this future man whom I cannot be in and of myself but whom I truly am through God, this future man cannot possibly be overlooked in any attempt to understand what God's command means for man in his total reality, in his total divinely willed reality, for real man. This future man is here. The command of God applies to us as those who are this future man. From the standpoint of eternity how can we fail to be, not just creatures, not just sinners saved by grace, but this third thing which presses into our present from ahead as our creatureliness does from behind? It is true that as we do not stand or speak in the future, but in the present, we can speak of this future being of ours only brokenly and in the mirror of our present knowledge. Hence we can say only very little about it. Yet we cannot say nothing at all, for the mirror of our present knowledge—insofar as we have in view our present as hearers of God's Word—shows us this picture too, the picture of the future man who is also our own reality.

That we are God's children, and that the obedience required of us (is) that of children, is something that we could not say from the standpoint of the command of the Creator. That we are created by God does not mean that we are his children, for conception and creation are two different things, and with good sense the church has always resisted the temptation to construe creation as conception. Creation is creation out of nothing, and the relation of the creature to the Creator is not that of sharing the divine nature but of having an individual being that is determined by the strictly different being of the Creator. Hence the obedience of the creature might be compared to that of the slave or serf, except that this comparison is much too weak to express the determination on which obedience rests from this standpoint. That we are God's children can be said, not in the light of creation, but only in the light of the *goal* of creation, of completed creation, to which the present creation only points. Even the kingdom of the grace of Christ is not the true locus for the term. What is man here? A member of the people of God, elect, called, justified, one who has received mercy, whose sins are forgiven. And what is obedience here? Submission, we have seen. Submission to the law, sacrifice, repentance, humility. Authority and discipline apply here. Man is here in conflict with himself. Even his conflict with God is not yet over. God's conflict with him has to continue. We have thus to speak here about education, law, and custom, about church and state. Obviously none of this has anything to do with the obedience of children. The term takes on meaning again only when we think about the *goal* of reconciliation. We came into its sphere only at the climax of the discussion of the first two standpoints, i.e., when speaking about faith in relation to the command of creation, and love in relation to the command of reconciliation. When the command of life is in fact fulfilled in faith, then not merely the serf obeys but the child of God in the serf;

then man is more than mere creature, and his future reality is present. And when the command of law is fulfilled in love, then not merely the elect obeys in response to his election, but the child of God in the elect, and such terms as church and state are in themselves too narrow to serve as frameworks to denote his conduct, for man is now more than reconciled, and the future of his reality, i.e., redemption, is present.|

That we are children of God, and that the obedience required of us is that of children, is something that we have prudently refrained from saying thus far. It has its special place in the economy of God (if one can speak of such), in the inner logic of our being claimed by God. But precisely because it is such a big word in Christian ethics—the decisive word in view of its link with the fulfillment of the command—we ought to use it more sparingly than is customary in the language of edification and theology. The great presupposition of the invocation in the Lord's Prayer, namely, that we may and should really address "Our Father" [cf. Matt. 6:9], the Pauline statement: "For all who are led by the Spirit of God are children of God" [Rom. 8:14], and John's saying: "See what love the Father has given us, that we should be called children of God" [1 John 3:1]—these are all too often treated as small change by those who ought to know better, and then, naturally, by those who know no better. We must pay attention to the specific imprint of this coinage if we are not to cast pearls before swine at this point [cf. Matt. 7:6]. Its specific imprint is eschatological. Eschatological does not denote a truth that has still to become the truth or that has to come home to us as such. It does not denote what is only hereafter and not of the world, not yet valid and significant for us, remote from the reality of our existence, held in God and reserved for us for some later eon. Eschatology is positive, not negative. It is positive in a very distinctive way. Or, rather, it is, within God's Word and its truth, a highly distinctive element of truth that differs clearly from others and that characterizes this truth in a particular way as act and path and guidance, so that our relation to it is also characterized as obedience in a very special way.|

Eschatological means above all *final*, i.e., conclusive, definitive, and unsurpassable. Hence we do not truly or properly, i.e., eschatologically, call a person a child of God if we simply have in view a state in relation to which we cannot avoid the dialectical recollection of very different states. One cannot assume, e.g., that Paul in Romans 8 considered the possibility of calling the children of God at one and the same time "rascals," clever and true though this might be, if we could finally call people the children of God from the standpoint of the creature.[3] When the term is used in its true sense, as at those high points of the New Testament witness to revelation, it denotes something that must not be

[3] An allusion to the statement of Erich Przywara (1889–1972) who, visiting and taking part in Barth's seminar in Münster in February 1929, in a discussion of sin, accepted "the fine credo that all we men are rascals"; cf. Barth's letter to Thurneysen of February 9, 1929, *Briefwechsel 2: 1921–1930*, ed. E. Thurneysen, Zurich 1974, pp 652f.

shaken or weakened, even though finally it depends in some way on the concept of the child. The child of God does not sin. The child of God believes, loves, and hopes, but does not sin. There applies to the child of God not only *posse non peccare* (like Adam before the fall)[4] instead of *posse peccare*, but *non posse peccare* (and here we stand at the end of the ways of God). *Per se* and on the far side of all dialectic, the child of God is the obedient child of God. If God's Word tells us, and we let ourselves be told, that we are God's children, then—if this is really so, and we do not let ourselves be told something different and less significant elsewhere—this is a final, unassailable, and indisputable truth. The Reformation assurance of faith and salvation—a concept which is very closely related to that of divine sonship—is characterized as an eschatological truth by its being a final certainty in the sense described. Certainty which can revert to uncertainty may be a fine certainty and it must not be despised but it has nothing whatever to do with the assurance of the children of God in Romans 8. It is thus fitting to be more careful in our handling [of this] in the marketplace and the church.

"Final," however, is only one aspect of "eschatological." The other is that eschatological truth is truth as the future in the present, as the truth which does not merely encounter us, as has to be said of God's Word as the Word of reconciliation, but which comes to us. If we have described God's Word generally as a Word that comes to us, this is necessary and right, for God's Word as a whole is an eschatological entity. We have it as it comes to us, not otherwise. We have it as one has eschatological truth. The distinctive feature of eschatological truth as such, however, is its presence not *in* the future but *as* the future, as coming to us. What is meant, then, is coming being, our own coming being, when we are told the final thing that we are the children of God. The reference is to an inclusive and not an exclusive present: "The Kingdom of God is at hand" [Mark 1:15; Matt. 4:17]; hence: "Thy kingdom come" [Matt. 6:10; Luke 11:2]; or: "Behold, I stand at the door and knock" [Rev. 3:20] or: "We are saved in hope" [Rom. 8:24]; or "The Lord is at hand" [Phil. 4:5]; or, with express reference to sonship: "We ourselves, who have the first fruits of the Spirit, groan inwardly and await our sonship" [Rom. 8:23]; or: "We are God's children now; it does not yet appear what we shall be" [1 John 3:2]. What does it mean that Christ bids his people wait like servants for their master [cf. Matt. 24: 45−51] or the ten virgins for the bridegroom [cf. Matt. 25: 1−13]? Does it not all denote distance, remoteness, transcendence, nonpresence? Yes indeed, and yet we should not forget the other aspect, namely, the direct nearness of what is distant, the coming to us of what is not yet present. The future as such is not absent, and therefore we cannot say that what it brings, our own future reality, is absent. It would not be adequately described if we were to say simply that it lies in the future. For our future is not just the

[4]Cf. Augustine, *De correptione et gratia* XII, 33; *De civitate Dei* XIV, 27.

future. It is the future in the *present*. We *have* the content. We *are* what we shall be. The necessary prayer: "Amen, come, Lord Jesus" [Rev. 22:20], does not prevent us from hearing the promise: "Lo, I am with you always, to the close of the age" [Matt. 28:20]. Pauline faith without sight [cf. 2 Cor. 5:7] does not rule out Johannine faith as the having of eternal life [cf. John 3:36]. We have this in promise. Having in promise is the having which characterizes this object, our future reality. We are heirs. Being an heir is distinctive inasmuch as it refers to future being. This having and being are highly indirect, but one cannot deny that they really are having and being. On the contrary, we have to maintain this according to this understanding. |

In the twofold sense of being "final" and of "coming," then, it is an eschatological truth that we are the children of God. With reference to the second or coming aspect we cannot be too much on the alert when we take this precious coinage in our hands. The being and having of God's children cannot be described or affirmed except as those to which we are—in the present, yet in the present with reference to our own future—*directed*. If, when I call myself a child of God, I thought I could be other than what I *shall* be, than my coming I, if I thought I could ascribe the *none posse peccare* to myself otherwise than in faith, love, and hope, if I were to claim assurance of faith and salvation otherwise than in the act of seeking what is above [cf. Col. 3:1f.], of pressing on to the goal that is set for me [cf. Phil. 3:14]—then everything would again have become a mirage and not the unassailably last thing that is at issue here.

I say, then, that finally and ultimately the Word of God requires of us the obedience of children. We are not addressed and claimed by God merely in our creatureliness nor merely as sinners saved by grace. If I hear God's Word, then I hear it not merely as the Word of him to whom I belong because without him I would not be, nor as the Word of him to whom I owe myself because without him I would be lost. I hear it also—and for the first time truly—as the Word of my Father. To be sure, it is not that through the Word an original and intrinsic Father-child relation between God and me[5] is brought to light. It is not God's nature to be my Father or man's to be God's child. But as this must be told me by the Word, so it is true only in the Word. In the Word, in the Son of God, in his relation to God the Father, or, concretely, in Jesus Christ, I am myself God's child, a partaker, according to 2 Peter 1:4, not merely of the undeserved good-pleasure of God the Creator, nor merely of the unmerited good-pleasure of God the Reconciler, but a partaker of the divine nature, i.e., as truly dear and pleasing to God—for this is what the image of father and child denotes—as he is dear and pleasing to himself, or, from our standpoint, as much a part of God as we are of ourselves, as parent and child, without being one person, and with all the distance that the relationship also denotes, are of one blood. Not in

---

[5]In the original Barth had "between me and God."

himself, but as the eternal Father of his eternal Word, as the eternal Speaker of his eternal Word, or, concretely again, in Jesus Christ, God is the Father of men. And not in themselves, but as those whom God has loved from all eternity in his Son, as the hearers of his Word, or, concretely, in the revelation of Jesus Christ, men are the children of God. In this way and for this reason this is final truth. The metaphor of father and child denotes an indissoluble and irreversible relation. Beyond the antithesis of being and nonbeing, beyond all dialectic, it is true in Jesus Christ that God is our Father and we are his children. In this way and for this reason it is also *future* truth that comes to us. We are not in ourselves the eternal children of God; we *become* so as the Son of God comes to us, as the Word of God is spoken to us. We have to be conceived and born by the Word as God's children [cf. 1. Pet. 1:23], and this new conception and birth, this reality of ours as God's children, is our awaiting, future, and, only to that extent, present reality, seeing that we have the Word and are hearers of it only as it constantly comes to us. In this way and for this reason it is eschatological truth that we are God's children. But in this way and for this reason it is truth. Hence the claim that is made upon us by the Word extends also and precisely to this final coming being of ours. In and with this true and proper thing that God wills *with* us as he speaks to us, we are told what is the true and proper thing that he wants *from* us: The incontestable readiness and willingness of the child for the Father, for obedience not just in secondary but in primary and personal agreement with his will, and this as the coming of our own being to which we must therefore orient ourselves. Because the command of God is one total command, it cannot contradict the "Be what you are," as which we have understood it here. We cannot evade the command of life and law in favor of a different and higher obedience. As in the innermost of three concentric circles, it shows us what obedience is in the two outer circles. From this standpoint it thus denotes an action which, as it is performed in the sphere of the creature, and of the sinner saved by grace, also points beyond these. Beyond these spheres it has its own sphere. We can and must test and question human conduct especially by the fact that,[6] if it is really sanctified conduct, it will also undoubtedly have in some way this character too, the character of childlike obedience.|

2

Because obedience, considered in this light, has the character of an orientation—within the great "Be what you are"—we cannot go further without considering at least briefly the goal of this orientation.|

At this point we must come back to two concepts that hitherto we

[6]In the German construction the editor substituted a "dass" here for Barth's original "als."

have only touched on very lightly: "Being heirs" and "having the promise." That God speaks his Word to us means that we are made his heirs and given his promise inasmuch as true and full fellowship is established between him and us. By his Word God confesses us across the great distance between Creator and creature and also across the abyss that separates the Holy One from sinners. By his Word God gives us that participation in his own nature and makes us new creatures as children who belong to him, to whom he will be faithful as a father is to his children. This truth of his Word holds good even in face of the limits in which we exist on the basis of our creatureliness and in the conflict of grace and sin. This twofold limit is indicated to us by the reality of death. But the Word is spoken to us as those who must die and who cannot fail to see in death the wages of their sin [cf. Rom. 6:23]. Its truth holds good also and precisely for us as such. What God gives us in giving us his Word is not just anything. God does not give us things. By his Word he does not grant us participation in a created nature, even a higher created nature. He does not exalt us to be higher beings, even angels, in granting us fellowship with himself. If he did, what he gives us would have its limit in death. It would mean only that we are given to know him within the limit of death, to know him as him who, as he was in the beginning, so he will also be at the end, who stands above the contradiction, but who finally—and this is what death would mean if God gave us no more than things that can be ours only on this side of the frontier of death—who finally would let [us] fall into the nothingness out of which he called us into being. God, however, gives us himself in his Word. For this reason his truth holds good for us also and precisely as those who must die.|

As God is not only our Creator but also speaks to us as such, giving us his Word and in his Word himself, by reason of creation he makes himself known as our Redeemer, i.e., as the God who, as he stands above the provisional state of this world, as he is himself the God who is not subject to death, wills to give us a share in this freedom from death, a share through his Word, the share of promise. And as he speaks to us as our Reconciler, causing his grace to reign where we deserved wrath, and death should have been our merited sentence, he confirms himself as the Redeemer, not leaving it an open question whether our standing in contradiction might not also mean our remaining under the judgment of death—the dark shadow under which we still stand even in faith and love and the kingdom of Christ—but declaring himself truly as the one who has taken all power from the death that we deserved, not merely the death that is necessary as an order of nature, but the death that we merited as a punishment [cf. 2 Tim. 1:10].

Again, in his Word, in Jesus Christ, he does not stand among us as the living among the dead but as the ζωοποιων [cf. John 5:21], the life-giver among the dead, giving life as by his Word he gives us a share in himself, in his own superiority to death, and thereby giving us eternal life.

Precisely where my future as a creature means death, and my future as a sinner saved by grace could basically still mean only death, my future is that of a child of God whom death cannot accuse because in its Father, in him who is its Father by the Word, it has its Redeemer, the one who perfects its creaturely existence and frees it from bondage as a being that exists in the contradiction of sin and grace—and from this Redeemer it has eternal life. God's Word would not be his Word, i.e., would not be himself, if this were not so, if in and with his Word we were not given the promise and made his heirs. What is promised, the inheritance, is that God is not only in himself the A and O, the first and the last [cf. Rev. 1:8; 22:13], but that there is for us a last as well as a first, that our temporal life does not begin with God and end with death, but ends also with God, that it thus has eternity for all its temporality. This is what is meant by the promise, the inheritance. This is what is told us here and now in the midst of the temporality and provisionalness in which we exist here and now as creatures, in the midst of the contradiction in which we exist here and now as Christians. This is the future in the mirror of the present and also—necessarily—in the mirror of our present *knowledge*, which cannot actualize the concept of *this* future as it could if what God gave us were something less, a created thing, and not God himself and therefore our definitive, absolute, and *unconditional* future.

Because the Redeemer himself, his *parousia* and presence, not now as the Word which is the beginning of all things, nor as the Word by which we are upheld above the abyss of our own lostness, but as the Word by which God draws us to himself in the fellowship of his perfect and blessed being—because the Redeemer himself is what is promised, the inheritance, and in him and by him that fellowship, and because he is the Redeemer from death, from death as the epitome of all the provisional state of our existence here and now, we have here our absolute future, which cannot be compared to any future within time or within the boundary of death, our true and genuine future which is actual at every moment. For this reason we are claimed here with no less strictness than from the other standpoints previously mentioned. Indeed, we have to say that all the strictness of the claim that we could not escape earlier has its basis in the existence of this last eschatological standpoint. We are the children of God. Our citizenship is in heaven [cf. Phil. 3:20], in the Jerusalem that is above [cf. Gal. 4:26]. This is no less true than that we must die. It replaces that truth. Where we see death coming, the Lord comes, the kingdom of God, that which is perfect [cf. 1 Cor. 13:10]. We are responsible to this future of ours. Whether our conduct can stand when measured by the standard that we are God's children and on the way to this goal is the ethical question from this final standpoint. It is required of us that we should walk and act as those who have the promise, who are heirs of God and joint heirs with Christ [cf. Rom. 8:17]. We are asked whether we are true to our calling, not now our creaturely calling alone, nor our calling to be members of the people of God, but, as the point of these callings, our heavenly and eternal calling. What this means we must now consider.

3

We overlook a whole sphere of ethical problems if, in understanding the claim under which we stand, we do not take into account as supremely relevant man's eschatological determination, his nature as we have just tried to outline it. An ethics that thinks only in terms of creation or of the status of sin and grace usually cannot do justice to the fact that, beyond our being as God's creatures and as sinners saved by grace, we are claimed in a way that cannot be deduced from those formulae, and that, precisely in the Christian life as it manifests itself in history, apart from phenomena that can be explained in terms of those two aspects, we always find others that very obviously cannot be reduced to those categories, phenomena which seem to indicate that in addition to having to live in the great context of created life and to having to stand under law, the law of the neighbor, man continually stands under another compulsion, being in a movement whose strange inner dialectic shows it to be a very unusual one, reaching beyond those spheres, or within them extending to their very limits, so that in it he seems to have to reckon with a final relativity of those orders, or with a third order which is ordered to them and which he thinks he must in some way respect if in the orders he is to see *order, absolute* order. |

Ethicists who find a place only for a command of life or law, or one or other of the two, when they come to speak of this not wholly concealed tendency in human life, and especially in the Christian life, usually reject it with an unkindly glance. Theologians among them, with whom I would number Gogarten,[7] tend to speak about mysticism, illusionism, enthusiasm, and the like. Ethics should speak only about the order of creation and the law of the neighbor, usually trying to reduce the two to one and the same thing. Anything beyond that is to be suspected as a humanistic-idealistic failure to take seriously the true human situation. In such ethicists—and again I am particularly interested in Gogarten— there is a good understanding of all solutions and possibilities lying in a natural-civic-ecclesiastical milieu, but a total lack of understanding for all those lying in a radical milieu, e.g., to take only two illustrations, the Roman Catholic ideal of monasticism on the one side and something like Bolshevism on the other (and there are many others in between). Protestantism in particular seems here to be very definitely and un- equivocally a matter of a moderation that seeks to be free of all illusions,

---

[7]Cf. F. Gogarten, *Die religiöse Entscheidung*, Jena 1921, 1924²; also *Illusionen, Eine Auseinandersetzung mit dem Kulturidealismus*, Jena 1926; also *Glaube und Wirklichkeit, Ges. Aufsätze*, Jena 1928.

and in practice of a muffled conservatism that boasts at all costs of its tidiness. Gogarten's ethics[8] (and the same could be said especially of the ethics of Ritschl[9] and his followers) always remind me of a tariff law whose rigorous provisions condemn some to hunger while aiming to feed others. Some conservative tariffs have notoriously had this effect in all countries. Now it is true that there can be no ethics that does not have to pass through the narrow gate of a fundamental consideration of the standpoints denoted by the terms creation and reconciliation. An ethics that sought to begin and end with the fact that we are God's children would in fact do justice neither to the reality of the divine command nor to that of the human situation. I do not think that anyone can accuse us of jumping ahead in this way. But the warning to which we gladly pay heed, even if it is unnecessary, ought not to be confused with the narrow gate of which the gospel speaks [Matt. 7:13f.]. *This* narrow gate is God's own command. We must all be on guard against missing it. Because of it all ethical reflection stands under the warning never to forget that we are primarily creatures and sinners saved by grace. But because of it we also stand under the warning not to stop at these standpoints and definitions. That we are God's children, and that the command is the command of promise, should also not be disregarded, and the less so if it is contested. God's command is richer and broader than all definitions of it, and going through the narrow gate, at least in relation to ethical reflection, might consist in avoiding overhasty rigidity and being as open as possible to being led in circles from one definition to the other.

We have, then, a *heavenly* calling that cannot be reduced to what we said about calling in the second and third chapters. We have more than life and more than law.[10] We also have promise, the promise of redemption, of the perfect which is coming. We are in fact asked—this is no mere matter of human caprice—whether, subject as we are to the command of life and the command of law, we are also reaching after this promise, whether our conduct is that of the children of God. An enthusiasm which was not subject to that twofold command would not be obedience, and a preliminary question that has to be considered in everything that we say here is whether we do really stand in that twofold subjection or whether what we have here is an enthusiasm that may rightly be suspected of mysticism and fanaticism because it evades the command of life and the command of law. On the other hand, the

---

[8]Cf. F. Gogarten, *Ich glaube an den dreieinigen Gott*, Jena 1926; also *Glaube u. Wirklichkeit, Ges. Aufsätze*, Jena 1928. Cf. also the later works *Wider die Ächtung der Autorität*, Jena 1930; "Das Problem der Ethik und die Erziehung," *Schule u. Evangelium* 6 (1931/32), 225ff.; *Politische Ethik. Versuch einer Grundlegung*, Jena 1932.
[9]Cf. A. Rischl, *Die christliche Lehre von der Rechtfertigung und Versöhnung*, 3 vols., Bonn 1870–1874, vol. III, pp. 537ff., 588ff.; also *Unterricht in der christlichen Religion*, 1875, 1886[3] (Gütersloh 1966, §§26–33, 55–77).
[10]Cf. pp. 117ff., 173ff.

question also arises whether there is real subjection where our creaturely life and the neighbor as the corrective of our sinful existence form our only points of orientation. Do we really obey if we do not obey as children? In addition to life and the neighbor, does not our being as God's children form a third point of orientation without which we do not really perhaps see the other two even though this is itself a will-o'-the-wisp if we have not first sought the other two? If we cannot obey the heavenly voice while obeying the command of our Creator and Reconciler, in relation to obedience in this specific sense are we not asked about our obedience in the other sense, whether it might not be an intolerable compulsion, and, in relation to scripture, a kind of rationalism, if we were to reinterpret the heavenly voice, the eschatological determination of the command that is issued to us, and reduce it to our claiming by God the Creator and God the Reconciler? If God is also this third thing in his revelation, our Redeemer, who has regenerated us as his children [cf. I Pet. 1:3], then are we not asked about this third thing, our obedience to the command of his promise as a specific determination of our obedience?|

We have touched on the concept of enthusiasm. This is a loaded term. Originally ἐνθουσιάζειν or ἔνθεος εἶναι simply means "to be in God," or it denotes the extraordinary activity corresponding to this being in God. The idea of all kinds of irrational states of rapture which has become associated with the term because of certain well-known phenomena in religious history should not mislead us into finding in a contrasting state of sobriety as such the one state that is always and in all circumstances appropriate for a Christian, unless we wish to exalt ourselves as schoolmasters of the first Christians and even their apostles, not least of all the apostle Paul himself [cf. 1 Cor. 14:18; 2 Cor. 12:1ff.], who did not always show that much concern for the sobriety which, according to A. Ritschl, is alone worthy of a Christian.[11] Even less should we turn aside from what seems finally to be meant by enthusiasm (apart from the psychological question), namely, the anthropological, if not ontological, possibility of a directness of human action on the basis of the fellowship between man and God.|

Above all we will be forced to challenge the possibility of prayer, to which we have had to refer at more than one high point in our previous deliberations,[12] if we want to reject altogether what is meant by enthusiasm, the activity of the child of God, of the person who is a partaker of the divine nature in the promise. Prayer, as talking with God, in which we can count on an answer as well as a hearing, can be understood only if we humans are more than God's creatures and more than sinners saved by grace. Prayer is the actualization of our eschatolog-

---

[11]Cf. A. Ritschl, *Unterricht in der christlichen Religion*, 1875, 1886³ (Gütersloh 1966, §§ 63, 65, 67, 70f.).
[12]Cf. pp. 104, 106, 504ff.

ical reality that is possible here and now. Because we actualize our eschatological reality in prayer, because we understand ourselves in it to be the coming I, to be living in Christ, Christian prayer must say finally: "Not my will but thy will be done" [Luke 22:42] and there applies to it what Paul said in Romans 8:26f. about the intercession of the Holy Spirit for us, since we do not know how to pray as we ought. This justifies the apparent extravagance with which the Roman Catholic church calls the choral prayer of the liturgy the *opus Dei*. [13] Yet none of this can alter the fact that the purpose in prayer is to talk with God and to be heard and answered by him. Where this purpose is not present, where we talk to ourselves and or talk about God to our own edification and strengthening, we do not pray and do not even continue for long the exercise in edification. That we ought to pray is obviously part of the content of the divine claim that is made upon us. The divine claim seems even in some sense to exhaust itself in the fact that we should pray. But what has prayer to do with our life or with the claim of the Thou of our human neighbor? Certainly we do not pray aright unless, in doing it, we are set before the claim of life and the neighbor. It should not be overlooked, however, that, as one who prays, I do something different from what I do as a creature or as a sinner saved by grace, that in prayer I stand in a relation to God which cannot be understood as a mere manifestation of these other relations, but that I stand in the overarching relation of a child to God as its Father.|

Perhaps all that needs to be said about our claiming by God from this third standpoint may best be understood if it is seen in the light of prayer. From this ethical standpoint our conduct must conform to the measure of our being truly related to God as we are when we truly pray. Prayer is the primal and basic form of human action in which man looks and reaches beyond his reality as a creature and as a sinner saved by grace, in which he acts as ἔνθεος, i.e., as one who belongs to God, who has his home, his father's house, with God. Outwardly, everyone who really prays will look as Hannah, the mother of Samuel, did in 1 Samuel 1 when Eli thought that she was drunk [1 Sam. 1:13f.]. The person who for the sake of decorum will not become guilty of this drunkenness does not pray. Does he obey then? Are we not summoned specifically to call upon God? Can faith and love at their high point as human action be anything other than invocation, adoration? Can we respond except as we answer, i.e., speak with God as he, in inconceivable condescension, willed to speak with us? Can all the steps that could be taken in the first two spheres be really taken meaningfully except as, in and with them,

[13]The original has *agnus Dei*, but this is obviously incorrect and destroys the point of the sentence. It is probably due to a mistake in deciphering Barth's handwriting. For the usage, cf. I. Hausherr, "Opus Dei," *Orientalia christiana periodica* 13 (1947), pp. 195–218; K. Hallinger, "Papst Gregor der Grosse und der heilige Benedickt," B. Steidle (ed.) *Commentationes in Regula s. Benedicti*, Rome 1957 (Studia Anselmiana 42), pp. 231–313, esp. 288–92.

this notable step is taken beyond those spheres? We have to ask in all earnest whether the action required of us must not proceed on a much broader plane than that of prayer in the narrower sense if it is to be obedience, whether it must not have also that character of looking and reaching ahead, whether it must not participate as a whole in this special character of prayer if it is to be real obedience.

If we do not simply reject the term enthusiasm for what we have in mind here, this does not mean that we must regard as essential to human action an emotional agitation that may be described psychologically. Enthusiasm is, in fact, a good word for nonsobriety. As we have to say in relation to the ultimate possibility of prayer, the good Lord does not take pleasure only in human possibilities that are from a psychological standpoint subdued and controlled. For all we know, the beautiful control or moderation that may rightly be a directive for Christian life in the mainline churches can also conceal indifference and skepticism, and it is thus as well to look beyond this to more lively Christian possibilities such as we find in the Salvation Army or other eccentric groups, or even to what are supposedly, or in fact, more secular forms of excitement, and to realize that in our own times, as in biblical times, God might be better pleased to be worshipped in less sober ways than our philosophy dreams of.[14]

Yet it is not a matter of emotional excitement but of excitement in general, which is neither ensured nor excluded by either emotional excitement or sobriety. When we ask concerning the relation of our action to the possibility of prayer, we ask whether it has the openness which it ought to have as obedience to God, as real walking before him. What counts is openness to the goal, to the perfect that is coming. An action that is oriented only to the concepts of life and law and is not set under promise will obviously be closed to what is ahead and therefore resigned. We have seen that we are then inescapably set before the twofold limit of our conduct—that of being only creatures and that of being no more than sinners saved by grace. It is good and necessary that we should stand before this twofold limit but obviously we ought not to find a final word in our standing thus. We have honored as strongly as we could what Luther said about comforted despair,[15] but this ought not to be a final word. As God's Word demands an answer from us, and we can finally give this answer only by praying to God, there is impressed upon our conduct what I now call the character of openness: openness to what is ahead, to the fact that God's ways do not end with the fact that he created us and that in our sinfulness he reconciled us to himself. The final word has to be *hope*, or concretely, waiting for and hastening toward

---

[14]Cf. W. Shakespeare, *Hamlet*, Act I, Scene 5: "There are more things in heaven and earth, Horatio, Than are dreamt of in your philosophy."
[15]Cf. above, p. 403, n. 3.

the future of the Lord [cf. 2 Pet. 3:12].[16] We shall have to discuss what this means in our final sections.

§16

CONSCIENCE

God's command strikes me as my own strictly moment-by-moment co-knowledge of the necessity of what I should do or not do in its relation to his coming eternal kingdom. In this concrete fellowship of mine with God the Redeemer it claims me and I have to listen to it.

1

It might be a matter of surprise that here, right at the end, we propose to speak about conscience, which has been such an important concept in the whole history of ethics. But perhaps surprise is at least as justified in relation to the procedure of most other ethicists, who have thought they could begin with this concept in one of the first sections as though it were, if not self-evident in ethical reflection, at least based on the first and most obvious fact that man does have what may be called a conscience. Whence do we drive this important datum? Conscience means *syn-eidēsis, con-scientia,* our human knowing of what, not merely according to our own presuppositions, God alone can know as he who is good, as the giver of the command and the judge of its fulfillment, namely, of the goodness or badness of the act which I am about to commit or upon which I look back as already committed.|

How does this knowledge—this very astonishing knowledge—arise? It is overhasty to call it part of man's constitution by creation. Althaus, whose ethics I have in mind as an example, understands conscience, over against all that we described in §8 as man's individual creaturely calling,[1] as a new and essentially underived and autonomous thing. He does not detach it from history and revelation, but he grounds its reality, not in the phenomenological terms of nature and sociology, but with an

[16]In the formula "waiting for and hastening toward," which goes back to 2 Peter 3:12, Barth found a summary of the witness of the person and work of Christoph Blumhardt (1842–1919), which had such an influence on the early development of his own theology. What is meant is the mixture of patient waiting for the decisive action of God himself and man's active hastening toward the coming kingdom of God. "The unique or, as we say advisedly, the prophetic thing in Blumhardt's message and mission lies in the way that in his words and works hastening and waiting, the secular and the divine, the present and the future met and joined and supplemented and constantly sought and found one another," K. Barth, "Vergangenheit und Zukunft," *Neuer Freier Aargauer,* 14, No. 204/205 (Sept. 3/4; 1919).
[1]Cf. pp. 173ff.

appeal to the moral prophets, with a differentiation between the proper norms of higher morality and the experience of utilitarian biological values, between moral values and biological desires.[2] If all this is correct, then conscience cannot have its locus in the life that God has given us. Adam and Eve before the fall had no conscience to the extent that the ethical question was very simply posed by the command of life itself, not by a judicial voice in themselves which is in fact to be distinguished from this command and which we call conscience. We have to think more of faith than of the fulfillment of the command of creation if we are to understand obedience as obedience to conscience. But this means that we have to remember the eschatological determination of the one total command of God. Again, we cannot count so easily on the presence of conscience from the standpoint of reconciliation as is usually done. That in Christ we are God's sinners saved by grace does not really involve our having co-knowledge with no less a being than God himself. We have to do here with the command of law, and we have to put all the emphasis on the fact that in this relation law is not a voice within us but an alien voice that speaks to us from outside. We have found it in the Thou of the neighbor, and at the appropriate point in the preceding chapter[3] we have had to speak strictly and exclusively of the authority in face of which we have nothing whatever to say but by which we have to let ourselves be told what is necessary. From this standpoint, then, what is conscience but the ever erring and fallible voice of our own heart which is constantly resisted and refuted? What can be said about conscience except that it must learn obedience? How can we understand it even for a moment as a sanctified and obedient conscience except in all its immanent wickedness? *Con-scientia?* Yes, but co-knowledge of the goodness of our conduct only with reference to the goodness of God, and co-knowledge of our wickedness, of its own wickedness, with reference to our own conduct as such. Again we have to think of love as the fulfillment of the law [cf. Rom. 13:10] if we are to understand our obedience to the law as obedience to conscience. Again we must remember the eschatological determination of the one total command of God.|

Only on this basis, in the light of the command of promise, can one see any possibility of conscience being the authority that theological ethicists call it. There are good reasons for dissatisfaction with what naturalistic and idealistic ethicists say about conscience. A new, unheard-of, underived, and autonomous claim is in fact made when conscience is ascribed to man. It cannot be done without the help of the concepts of faith and love. But to the extent that the reality of conscience is found to

---

[2]P. Althaus, *Leitsätze zur Ethik*, Erlangen 1928, pp. 4ff.
[3]See pp. 353ff.

be posited in that of faith and love, we are again construing these two essentially as hope. We are also positing in faith and love the fact that, as those who have true faith and love, we are the children of God and partakers of the divine nature [cf. 2 Pet. 1:4]. The final thing is being presupposed that can be said about man from a Christian standpoint. And it is fitting that this final thing should be stated and discussed really as the final thing if in spite of our controversy with naturalists and idealists we are not to run the risk that what we say will be confused with what they say and pearls will thus be cast again before swine [cf. Matt. 7:6]. How can we have co-knowledge of that which essentially only God can know except on the presupposition that the "co-" is not just logically possible but—even perhaps as a logical impossibility—is indeed a fact? This factual reality, however, is our divine sonship, the reality of our eternal future reaching into our present, i.e., the future of the Lord who, in bringing himself to us, brings our own future. |

If there is concrete fellowship with God the Redeemer,[4] then and only then there is such a thing as conscience. *This* has always been maintained when the reality of conscience has been maintained. But in matters of ethics as well as ethos we have to know what we are doing and keep clearly before us the very specific determination with which alone we can speak about conscience. To have a conscience is no more and no less than to have the Holy Spirit. For "no one knows what is in God except the Spirit of God" (I Cor. 2:11). To have a conscience is to know what is in God, to know his judgment on our conduct. To have a conscience is to look and reach beyond the limits of our creatureliness and our reconciliation, as we do in prayer. When we have a conscience we are not on our own but are at least also ἔνθεοι, our own judges. [If we were on our own,] our judgment on ourselves would necessarily be an arrogant and unauthoritative affair. It would be the mutual self-accusing and self-excusing which according to Romans 2:15 takes place among the Gentiles. It could never be more than a witness to and prototype of the judgment of the true conscience that is captive to the Word of God. A conscience that tells us the truth has to be this conscience that is captive to the Word of God, and this captivity has to signify no more and no less than its elevation to participation in the truth itself. Our self-accusing and self-excusing thoughts cannot remain on their own. This self-dialogue has to have a share in the dignity and truth of the Word of God. Something has to be possible and necessary which thus far, from the standpoints of creation and reconciliation, we have almost anxiously set aside: namely, that we can tell ourselves, not other than what we are told, but that we can tell ourselves what we are told. If we could not do this, then we ought not to speak about conscience, and if I

[4]See the thesis on p. 475.

am correct, it would be in line with the thinking of Gogarten not to speak any longer about conscience but only about authority.[5] But how can we think through the thought of authority, how can we think of a real acknowledgment of authority, without going beyond the concept of humility to that of love? How can we really think of telling ourselves if we do not also think of letting ourselves be told, and how can we let ourselves be told unless we also tell ourselves? The other level, with its own distinctive center, the level where conscience is a reality and *its* voice is that of the divine command, where we really tell ourselves the Word of God, this other level comes ineluctably into sight when we really traverse the two other levels to the very limit. We have to see, however, that we have here something really new and really final. We understand man here from the final aspect of his reality, according to the illumination and declaration of the Spirit, as his own counterpart, so to speak, for which we can only reach in prayer as we reach after God himself. We have a conscience, we have our own voice as the voice that proclaims God's Word to us, as we have the coming Christ, namely, in the Holy Spirit, who according to the New Testament view is the vicar of the coming Christ, the pledge and deposit of the promise that has been given us [cf. Rom. 8:23; 2 Cor. 1:22; 5:5; Eph. 1:14], in the here and now of our existence in which the future can be the present only as still the future.

As we carry through the primal and basic eschatological act of prayer, we have a conscience that tells us the truth. In prayer—and not for nothing is "Come, Creator Spirit" the prayer that includes within itself all prayer—we ask God not only that he would view us in a very different reality from merely that of his creatures and his sinners saved by grace, but also that he would give us this reality, the reality of people of the Spirit, that he would let us be our own counterpart which comes to us in Christ, that he would conceive and bear us as his own children. In the superabundance of *this* action we have concrete fellowship with God our Redeemer, we have a conscience, the command of promise claims us in the form of our own co-knowledge and our own speaking with ourselves, and in order to hear we must listen to what we tell ourselves. Theological ethics will have to reject all more primitive ideas of conscience, the idea of a voice of truth immanent in man by nature, or that of a voice of humanity which sums up supposedly individual voices of conscience, i.e., it will have to show that faith and love are what is meant in all these ideas, and that what is meant is a reality only as these are more closely defined in the concept of divine sonship, the Holy Spirit, the *parousia* of Christ, prayer, i.e., as they are defined eschatolog-

---

[5]Cf. F. Gogarten, "Die Frage nach der Autorität," *ZdZ* III (1923), 6–27; later *Wider die Ächtung der Autorität*, Jena 1930.

ically. Thus defined, the concept of conscience is not to be rejected. It is not to be left unnoticed or undiscussed because of its dangerous proximity, possible only on that primitive preunderstanding, to the ethics of naturalistic or idealistic subjectivism. On the contrary, all honor must be quietly paid to it.

2

What can it imply that from an eternal standpoint we do really and literally have a conscience? Certainly not that we have in our hands a subjective principle by means of which we can measure the possibilities of life in general and once and for all, playing the role of Hercules at the crossroads with the norm of God in our hands. Certainly not that before the closing of the gate we have found an authority by which to develop an ethics of answers instead of questions. If this were so, we should be wrong to have looked around so late for this saving authority. Against this understanding of conscience as a principle that we can control, as a general principle that we can seize and use at any time, we are protected by regard for the eschatological character of the concept. If it is true that the voice of conscience is our own voice only inasmuch as in Christ our own future is present; if it is true that only by the illumination and declaration of the Holy Spirit, only in the prayer "Come Creator Spirit," we have conscience seriously as God's voice, as the voice of truth about us, then we have to abandon any desire to control it. It is clear, too, that all the mischief associated with conscience when it is exalted above the superior concept of the Word and command of God both has been and can be possible only when we will not see its eschatological character, but ascribe to man as such and to the Christian as such a capacity which makes the enterprise of ethics very easy, but also in the true sense superfluous. For ethical reflection would be simple, so simple that we could dispense with it, if conscience were an available authority which we had only to use to have information about the good, perhaps in the form of a well-constructed table of values and the reverse. For good reason, the simple projection of an ethics of answers from the supposed presence of conscience has hardly ever been attempted. Instead we find that ethicists who have discussed conscience in the rather overhasty fashion mentioned still recognize with some concern the significant twofold fact that conscience 1) is really a voice, i.e., a word, which is not simply there in general and once and for all, but in order to be there has to be spoken about; and 2) is a word which, if we let people tell us what their conscience is saying to them, can have almost any concrete content, so that if the ethicist is not merely to present the ethics of his own conscience, it is as little adapted to establish an ethics of answers as any other principle that might come into question for such a purpose.

This twofold fact ceases to be a disruptive and disturbing phenomenon, and can be understood in terms of the nature of conscience, if the situation relating to it is as we have presented it.

We shall now try to consider what can be known and said about conscience from three angles.

a. In conscience, our own voice is undoubtedly *God's voice*. Our own voice: naturally only from the very remarkable standpoint, which cannot be understood except eschatologically, that we find ourselves divided and confronting ourselves, as it were, in the process. When my conscience speaks to me, I am *addressed*. Someone *encounters* me, coming from outside into my present reality. But this someone is not another person, a fellow human. He may encounter me as a fellow human does. This will often happen. But it does not have to be so. Often things are very different. At any rate, the other person is not the someone. The someone is myself. *I* judge myself. *I* command this and forbid that. *I* warn myself. *I* give myself this or that permission. *I* console myself. In relation to an approaching or past moment of action *I* set myself under a final truth by which my action is measured. When conscience speaks, I find that I am on both sides, both listening and speaking. When conscience speaks, I find that I am in a dialogue. The two partners are very dissimilar—on the one side I am in my present state, which recapitulates all my past, while on the other I am in a state of pure futurity which is a fact even though I can neither perceive nor grasp it—yet *I* am both the partners. In this light we can see why the term conscience, *syn-eidēsis, con-scientia*, has not been understood as we understand it, i.e., as co-knowledge with God, but purely anthropologically (R. Seeberg) as man's spiritual self-synopsis,[6] or, more briefly, as human self-consciousness. This is undoubtedly a correct designation of one side of the matter, for the speaking and hearing of conscience do in fact take place withim my human self-consciousness. But if we take this side of the matter seriously, how can we think it through to the end without unavoidably coming across another and very different side on the basis of which alone this first side is possible?|

Let us suppose that conscience does not tell me something of no account, but with a forward or backward look tells me the decisive truth about myself. Let us assume that the ideal case of an absolutely unambiguous and enlightened judgment of conscience is the concept in terms of which all other judgments of conscience are to be understood. If this is so, we cannot avoid ascribing God-consciousness to our self-consciousness to the extent that this reality is included in some measure, although only in that unheard-of division of the self, in the whole antithesis of my constitutionally given I and my objectively nongiven I. To the degree that there is granted to the act of conscience

[6]Cf. R. Seeberg, art. "Gewissen," *RGG*[2] II (1928), 1164–69.

even a very small and mixed and opaque share in the judgment of truth itself, to that degree how can our self-consciousness (in its division into that encounter and antithesis) fail to be God-consciousness? Schleiermacher and his whole school would have been right to assume that there is a God-consciousness immanent in human self-consciousness[7] if only they had not overlooked its nongivenness, its pure futurity, and if only they had described it as conscience, i.e., as the Word of God which does not belong to the human self-consciousness but is *entrusted* to it. We have conscience as a judicial authority within us to the extent that God has us in his Word. To this extent one cannot deny that God speaks to us through ourselves. If I cannot fail to see that the someone that encounters me in the voice of conscience is myself, I can as little fail to see, when he really encounters me in the voice of conscience, that now, to the extent that I am like God, my own voice (is) God's voice. The proviso with which alone all this can be said lies in the thing itself and cannot be missed if this is correctly perceived. That we are God's children, partakers of the divine nature [cf. 2 Pet. 1:4], and therefore co-knowers with God, is present only as our own future. We shall come back to this later. With this proviso, however, the statement has to be ventured. |

When conscience speaks we have an unconditional command or prohibition or an unconditional judgment. Whether I hear and receive it as such, whether I let the voice of truth, which in this instance is my own voice, really strike home where it comes to me, is another question. One should not forget that conscience is not an executive but a judicial power,[7a] that it, too, sets me in a decision between obedience and disobedience. What I say to myself as a child of God I hear as a sinner saved by grace, and in the whole dialectic of my existence as such. I say it out of my future into my present. What else can one expect but that I should hear it very differently from the way in which I say it to myself? *I* say it to myself, but as I do the beam of light breaks at once in the prism of this "myself" so that the unconditional judgment is the ideal case which never happens, or does so only in the brokenness of all the other real instances of statements of conscience. Yet this does not alter the fact that what is pronouned is in fact an *unconditional* judgment. It is meant to be unconditional, indeed, it is known to be so. This is the point of the whole process when I encounter myself in the voice of conscience. No matter how things really are, we know that in the voice of conscience we can receive the truth about ourselves (if only we can *hear*) and that we *have to* obey it. If we obey conscience we grant to it *authority* over us, a *last* and decisive authority. We intend to act or not act according to the

---

[7]Cf. F. E. D. Schleiermacher, *Der christliche Glaube*, Berlin 1821–1823, 2nd rev. ed., 2 vols., Berlin 1830–1831, vol. 1. §4.

[7a]Cf. Luther, *De votis monasticis* (1521), WA 8. 606, 32ff.

judgement of a supreme court; either way [by acting or not acting] we have to act. We act under a necessity that we ourselves definitely distinguish from the necessities of vital impulse, even though to our joy and satisfaction its command may coincide in content with that of vital impulse. And when we really regard ourselves as condemned by our conscience, we know very well that this condemnation, providing we have heard it aright, is not just any condemnation but a *final* judgment on us, not just any restraint that might be placed upon us but the restraint that is placed upon us when we are condemned to death.|

We ourselves have authority in relation to ourselves in the declaration of conscience, namely, that of the voice of God. But the matter is complicated or elucidated by the fact that in God authority and freedom are one and the same. Unconditional authority, such as that of God, is obviously freedom too. It is not conditioned by anything else. It is self-grounded. If the voice of conscience has a share in divine authority, and if it is we who speak to ourselves in conscience, then the thought is unavoidable that in conscience we confront ourselves in freedom, not conditioned by anything else, but grounded solely in our being the children of God. It is inconceivable to me how anyone can try to speak of conscience in any other way in this connection, for the important concept of freedom of conscience cannot be made intelligible except as the freedom of the children of God [cf. Rom. 8:21]. How can theological ethicists at least come to speak about any other freedom than this? Freedom in its full sense as sovereign divine freedom can be ascribed to man neither as God's creature nor as a sinner saved by grace, but only as a child of God who is a partaker of the divine nature precisely at the point where we see man, as God's creature, standing in a certain calling[8] and precisely at the point where we see him, as a sinner saved by grace, placed under authority.[9] Conscience is *the* freedom of man to the extent that in its pronouncement he makes an unconditional decision about himself. He does this in virtue of his being as a child of God, as which alone he has a conscience that establishes his freedom and does not destroy it. As a captive to the Word of God, he *is* free. As authority and freedom do not compete in God but are one and the same, so the freedom of conscience finds no competitor in the authority of God but is freedom in virtue of this authority. As the freedom of the *children* of God, it is no other than God's *own* freedom which is in itself authority too. When we call man free, we have in mind his pure future in his present. His pure future is his redemption. Redemption means liberation, liberation from the limits within which we belong to God here and now as his creatures and as sinners saved by grace. The decisive limit in this here and now of ours is the character of the divine command as law, as we have learned to see it in a previous chapter.[10] In this light,

[8]Cf. pp. 173ff.
[9]Cf. pp. 349ff.
[10]Cf. pp. 261ff.

obedience means submission to authority. It means accepting the fact that the fellowman comes between us and God with his claim. It means that repentance and humility are the final words to describe obedience. But if what we are to be and will be belongs also to the reality in which we are addressed by God, then we are not just reconciled but also redeemed people who, from the standpoint of our future I, are already beyond the sphere where the command of God is only an alien command that comes to us from outside and can be to us only law and authority.

The obedience of the redeemed person, of the future child of God, but the future child within the present, is freedom; not because God is no longer authority, but because this is God's authority. The voice of this redeemed person is the voice of conscience; this is why we have to speak about freedom of conscience. What does this imply? It implies that no purely external disposition can be made concerning us as God's children; that for us as God's children there can be no command of God which is not also our own command, no authority which we do not exercise over ourselves; that we can subject ourselves to all other authority only in and of ourselves, in freedom; that all our positive or negative attitude to all other authority is conditioned by ourselves and not by that authority. Over against all the authority of church and state, i.e., over against the whole claim of others, the question and criterion is freedom of conscience, i.e., the authority of God from which that relative authority has its commission. Especially in §12 we have often enough come up against the question of the authenticity of the authority that confronts us, of the legitimacy of the claim that the neighbor makes upon us. We can now give to this question the twofold answer: Conscience decides whether we have to do with genuine authority, and genuine authority attests itself as such to conscience. We can also say that the child of God recognizes in the voice of genuine authority the voice of his father which he obeys spontaneously and in freedom. "My sheep hear my voice" [John 10:27]—because they are my sheep. To the extent that one cannot be obedient unless one has been born again as a child of God by the Word, and to the extent that the child of God necessarily obeys in freedom, we have to say that conscience is in fact the final court and ultimate criterion in the question of obedience. This is why there can be no compulsion by conscience. There cannot be such because it would eliminate the last and decisive court in the question of obedience. Again, there cannot be such, fortunately, because conscience will not let itself be coerced, because by nature it is one's own. To talk of appealing to someone's conscience or laying a matter on one's conscience for someone else is to use totally impossible expressions. Nor can one seriously speak about educating the conscience or about a public conscience (that of the nation or humanity), for where, then, is the unconditionality of its judgment that depends on our being the children of God, a being into which we cannot be educated but which we must have directly from God, and which we can have, not in relation to other people, but truly only in our own relation to God?|

All this is not just the Protestant doctrine of conscience but the Roman Catholic doctrine too. But there, because of the dreadfully pervasive deeschatalogizing of the whole of Christianity, it is present so modestly, as such a half-suppressed secondary statement, that at first glance one might think that Roman Catholicism knows only authority as God's Word and only subjection to it as obedience. At least theoretically, however, it also teaches that "the majesty of conscience finally decides in all questions of faith and morality, in the whole matter of spiritual attitude. It finally decides even in the question whether the Roman Catholic can be justified in proclaiming obedience to the church." Even if a person may err and the judgment of conscience may be objectively wrong and "not free from ethical objection," one is still bound to conscience alone if it has really spoken thus, i.e., even against the judgment of the church (Adam, *Wesen d. Kath.* pp. 213, 215).[11] Or, according to an older Roman Catholic theologican: Conscience is above all other human courts, and if we are of good conscience we ought not to fear and will not be condemned by God even though all men, who do not see the heart, judge what is done very differently (Bellarmini, *De Rom. Pont.*, I, 4, 20).[12] If Roman Catholicism can also speak in this way, there is every reason why we should very definitely do so; especially today, when we particularly need to learn again what authority is, we should not let ourselves be driven by antiidealistic and antihumanistic reactions into a corner where we are more papist than the pope. The Reformation was a reawakening of an awareness of the eschatological character of Christianity, and it was thus a rediscovery of the Pauline liberty of the children of God, and very logically it was thus a rediscovery also of freedom of conscience, not in the much too simple and direct sense in which this concept was later used and was then fatefully confused with the Reformation view, but freedom of the conscience that is captive to the Word of God, yet still—and this is in no way to be undermined or retracted—*freedom* of conscience. From an eternal standpoint, the claim of the neighbor is not the last word, or it is so only in correlation with the Word that we have to say to ourselves. Even in relation to the neighbor, we are truly obedient only when his claim is also the claim of our own conscience. So truly is love the fulfilling of the law [Rom. 13:10]. For the concept of love includes that of one's own conscience and its perfect freedom.|

The necessary caveat in respect of all that has been said here is provided by the fact that I can never forget that as a hearer of conscience I differ greatly from myself as its spokesman, so that I have every reason

[11]Cf. K. Adam, *Das Wesen des Katholizismus*, Düsseldorf 1927, pp. 213, 215.
[12]R. Bellarmine (1542–1621), *Controversiarum de Summo Pontifice Liber Quartus: De Potestate spirituali*, chap. XX in *Opera omnia*, 12 vols., ed. J. Fèvre, Paris 1870–1874, t. II, p. 136.

to take a very critical stance in relation to what at any given time I may regard as[13] the conviction of my conscience. When everything is taken into account it is better not to speak of an erring conscience. Conscience does not err. But we err in our hearing of it. Even as the children of God we tell ourselves something very different from what we learn from it. Our self-dialogue is undoubtedly a constant self-misunderstanding. We hear the voice of our future I with the ears of this present I. Only cautiously and with restraint, then, do we use what we regard as the voice of our conscience as a criterion to establish genuine authority in relation to the voice of the neighbor. We do not arrogate freedom of conscience to ourselves in the form of the mad autonomism which has come to characterize the deeschatologized consciousness in both its modern and its Roman Catholic version. We use human authority to correct our very human sense of conscience and vice versa. Even as the children of God who have freedom of conscience we constantly seek ourselves in God, realizing that what we shall be has not yet appeared [cf. 1 John 3:2]. This is the caveat. But with this caveat the truth holds good that in conscience our own voice is God's voice.

b. We have to speak about the *content* of what conscience declares. We have stated that one must accept the definition of conscience as co-knowledge with God. But what do we co-know with God in conscience? The answer is that if conscience is really the voice of our future I in the present, then its command has to do specifically with the relation of our acts to the coming eternal kingdom of God. The measure by which we are measured by conscience is not the epitome of our creaturely life. We have said already that the necessity under which conscience sets us differs characteristically from that of vital impulse, not merely in its mistaken form, but in itself and as such. The goal to which conscience points lies on the far side of our creaturely existence as such. Nor is the measure by which we are measured by conscience that which is fitting for us as sinners saved by grace. Conscience does not acquiesce in the submission or brokenness or humility which from that standpoint are the final thing required of us. Conscience is such an uncannily restless thing precisely because it points beyond the pain of sin as this is comforted by divine forgiveness, beyond repentance before God and service to one's neighbor. What always causes a live and watchful conscience to be suspected of excessive enthusiasm is that it cannot be put off with a reference to supposed or real orders of nature and creation nor with a reference to the dialectic of the Christian's position in Christ's kingdom "in the midst of enemies" [Ps. 110:2 Vulg.], to the "always righteous and always sinner." To be sure, conscience speaks to us about what we do in these spheres. Without it we would hear neither the command of God the Creator nor the command of God the Reconciler. As life and law must speak to us, so

---

[13]The Swiss editor substitutes "für" here for an original "als" ("halten für").

the voice of both must be taken up by that of conscience if they are really to come home to us. We have said already that we must be the children of God if we are to live in faith and fulfill the law in love. "Be what you are" is truly said neither to man as a creature nor to man as a sinner saved by grace, unless man also says it to himself in his conscience. The inner circle of the ethical problem in which we now find ourselves is the center which governs and controls the totality around it. But the conduct that conscience requires of us does not lie only in those spheres. In a very distinctive way it also transcends them. This is why, where conscience speaks most vitally, it is so easily suspected of excessive enthusiasm. This is why it is such an unsettling and incalculable element both for individuals and society. This is why average leaders in church and state usually do not want to know too much about it. It poses questions and makes demands that make no sense from their standpoint. It seems to designate a third sphere of human action beyond all that does make sense from their standpoint. We do not understand conscience if, like A. Ritschl, e.g., in his discerning essay on the subject,[14] we merely consider how it also speaks when the command of the Creator and the command of the Reconciler are really spoken to us. The distinctive thing that conscience declares to us is the command of God the Redeemer, the command of promise. |

In conscience we co-know with God that we belong unconditionally to him. We co-know his absolute rule over all people and things, the rule that we do not yet see actualized here and now in God's creation or even in Christ's kingdom. Our belonging to God is, on the basis of our creaturely life, a great question to which we ought to give an answer but do not. Our belonging to God on the basis of the law that is given to us entails the dialectic of sin and grace, of the concealment as well as the disclosure of truth. The conditional nature of our belonging to God means the conditional nature of his rule, at least to our eyes. Our creaturely calling and the authority set over us in the economy of grace do not tear away this veil. The voice of conscience does. The voice of conscience has its origin in our unconditional belonging to God, in the absolute kingdom of God. In conscience I hear my own voice as that of the redeemed child of God. It is thus the characteristic call to me to reach out for what is ahead [cf. Phil. 3:13], for my approaching eternal home. The measure by which my conduct is measured by the command of conscience is not that it should be faithful to my calling (Ritschl),[15] nor that I should submit to the claim of my neighbor upon me— conscience can and does require these things but they are not the distinctive thing in its own particular message—but whether and how far my conduct, my conduct at this moment, is a forward step, i.e., a step

[14]A. Ritschl, *Über das Gewissen. Ein Vortrag*, Bonn 1876.
[15]Cf. A. Ritschl, op. cit., pp. 22f.

toward the future which is promised me by God's Word, the future of the Lord and his lordship over all people and things.|

We now take up again the formulations of the previous section. We are asked whether our conduct lies along the lines of the prayer in which we have found the primal and basic act of human conduct as it is eschatologically determined. We are asked about our openness to the perfect that is coming. We are asked about our waiting and hastening [cf. 2 Pet. 3:12]. Ultimately we may simply say that we are asked whether we have a hope, not just any hope, but fundamentally and radically *the* hope, i.e., the orientation of what we are and do to what we are to become according to the Word of God, in keeping with his will, and in his strength. Conscience is the living and present message of the coming kingdom of God. Hence the unconditionality of its requirement, hence also its freedom in which it dares to speak in God's place, hence also its infallibility in spite of all the fallibility with which we hear its voice, and hence the disquietude which it brings into the present, into our natural existence, but truly also into our Christianity, into church and state. "When the perfect comes, the imperfect will pass away" [1 Cor. 13:10]. This does not apply only to Christian knowledge. Proclaiming the absolute future, conscience proclaims the relativity of everything present. Directing us to the former, it detaches us unavoidably from the latter. In its true and final point, where it is totally itself, it is a revolutionary principle. We best see that this is so when we consider what that waiting and hastening[16] might imply, what it has in fact implied for all kinds of people who have said that they followed their conscience, and what finally it could and *must* imply for us—why not?—if we would listen to conscience. When conscience speaks to people, it involves a categorical command to wait. Why? Because it proclaims their future *in God* and demands that they seek it wholly and utterly in God and expect it from God. What they do and do not do is measured by whether they really expect their future from God: not from the natural course of events, not from the state and not from the church, though these might be the best, and not from themselves, even though they might be capable of the most strenuous and successful of efforts; but solely and totally from God, who will validate his Word to those who believe it. When conscience speaks to people, it also involves a categorical command to hasten. Why? Because conscience proclaims to them *their future* in God and demands that they seek it in God, not just expecting everything from God but really expecting *everything* from him. Thus they cannot be content with things as they are. They cannot build huts in either the kingdom of nature or that of grace as though they were to stay there [cf. Mark 9:5 par]. They have to march out, become pilgrims and strangers, and in these kingdoms move boldly toward the

---

[16]Cf. pp. 475, n. 16.

coming kingdom of glory. Are not these commands contradictory? Since they are both given by conscience, they are certainly not. How can there be any contradiction in expecting one's future *from God* and expecting from God *one's future*? Waiting *and* hastening, says scripture [2 Pet. 3:12]. Even the fact that scripture uses two words here indicates already that for our ears the one command splits into two, which only a few really hear at the same time and to the same degree. All the more important is it for all of us, then, to realize that it is the one revolutionary voice of conscience, the voice of hope, which on two sides points and pushes those who hear it beyond things as they are in the kingdoms of nature and grace. |

The command to wait can plainly mean for some a requirement that within the limits of the here and now they should above all become open and free and transparent for the God who will make all things new [cf. Rev. 21:5]. Conscience directs such people to rest in face of all overhasty impatience, in face of all attacks of longing for the absolute which will be in the present but which by nature cannot become the present because it is the eternal future. This rest, however, will be restless and the waiting active. It cannot mean passivity[17] truly to wait for the Lord, truly to set one's hope in him, truly to be someone who in the present awaits the eternal future. This has to entail a summons to supreme inner tension and activity. Ripeness, readiness is all:[18] The commands of God are living commands. Life, earthly life, confronts us as a question and what we live becomes that anxious waiting of creation, the στενάζειν and ὠδίνειν against corruption, against our own insufficiency which is the secret of that corruption [cf. Rom. 8:22f.]. In the dialectic of sin and grace the soul flees to him who supports and holds it in this antithesis, who is the Lord over the rift, whose grace is greater than our sin, and who will not leave the righteous eternally in disquiet [cf. Ps. 55:22]. The balance of "always righteous and always sinner" is upset for them. I am commanded—and this is an action too—to be still, to learn obedience to God who is more than my Creator and Reconciler, to learn to taste the powers of the world to come [cf. Heb. 6:5], to accustom myself to the atmosphere of the redemption that is hidden in the future, to become at home in advance in my eternal home. Demolition is required of me, for finally all this is inner work, work on myself, which makes the waiting into hastening. We have said more than once that the vacuum in which only the name of the Lord should dwell is the presupposition of all real obedience. It is a matter of exercising ourselves in *experience*—we have to use this word here—of the coming Redeemer. But in what should experience consist but the formation of that vacuum? He is still the coming Redeemer for whom we

---

[17]The editor changes the original order here ("*nicht etwa Passivität*" instead of "*nicht Passivität etwa*").
[18]Cf. W. Shakespeare, *King Lear*, Act V, Scene 2: "Ripeness is all," and *Hamlet*, Act V, Scene 2: "The readiness is all."

can only prepare the way. This is not only done to us but should also be done by us. We are summoned thereto. We shall gain the experience by watching and praying. Our conscience, the conscience of the children of God, wants us for this work. It wants the whole pressure of our creaturely existence, the whole bondage in which we exist as sinners who live only by mercy, to serve this end and not another, the doing of this work. |

This is the great concern of what one might sum up as the exertions of Christian inwardness, of what we can see to be, at core, the concern of conscience in the specific sense. This busy waiting for the Lord is what has obviously been the point of the mysticism of all ages and types with its drive to cultivate the life that is hid with Christ in God [cf. Col. 3:3], of the monasticism of the Roman Catholic Middle Ages to the extent— and it had other interests as well—that the development of the contemplative life is one of its characteristics, of the older Lutheranism of a Paul Gerhardt with what Troeltsch called his inner-worldly asceti- cism,[19] and of the Eastern Church with its humility—a humility which calls in question the present form of the world—before the absolute miracle of the future-present risen Christ. At its core this was also the concern of Pietism. Historically A. Ritschl was surely right to see the relationship of Pietism to the Anabaptist opposition of the Reformation period and also to medieval reforming movements within Roman Catholicism.[20] But this does not prove that Pietism is in substance a betrayal of the Reformation. It is true that the original eschatological impulse of the Reformation was very quickly muzzled in the churches of the Reformation and that the voice of the free children of God, the voice of conscience, was very quickly silenced again. But Pietism, in the very features that are censured by Ritschl, in its concern for a holy commu-

[19]Cf. E. Troeltsch, *Die Soziallehren der christlichen Kirchen und Gruppen, Ges. Schriften*, 1, Tübingen 1912, 1919, pp. 444f., 506f., n. 230, and 645ff., n. 336; cf. also M. Weber, *Die protestantische Ethik und der Geist des Kapitalismus* (1904/5), *Ges. Aufsätze zur Reli- gionssoziologie*, Tübingen 1922, pp. 118ff. Cf. Gerhardt's Christmas hymn "Ich steh an deiner Krippen hier" (1653), his Passion hymns "Ein Lämmlein geht und trägt die Schuld" (1647) and "O Welt, sieh hier dein Leben" (1647), or his hymn of trust, "Warum sollt ich mich denn grämen" (1653).
[20]In debate with church historians of his age, Ritschl developed this thesis in two steps (cf. *Geschichte des Pietismus*, 3 vols., Bonn 1880–1888: vol. I: *Geschichte des Pietismus in der reformierten Kirche*, Bonn 1880, "Prolegomena"). On the one hand he followed the view of M. Goebel (*Geschichte des christlichen Lebens in der rheinisch-westfälischen Kirche*, Coblenz 1849) that Pietism was a more moderate or weakened form of the same movement as 16th-century Anabaptism (p. 5) while on the other he rejected Goebel's theory that both Pietism and Anabaptism are a more basic, resolute, and complete fulfillment of the reformation of Luther and Zwingli (p. 6). As a Protestant theologian he stood by the judgment of the reformers and found in Anabaptism something very different in both means and ends, namely, a renewal of monasticism (pp. 22f.). This is how Anabaptism and Pietism come to be related to medieval attempts at reform and how Ritschl, appealing to J. J. Herzog (*Die romanischen Waldenser*, Halle 1853) can advance the thesis that like medieval reforming movements they stand on Roman Catholic soil and are rooted in it (p. 19).

nity, for ascetic sanctification of life, for inner surrender, in its legalism, its indifference to church and state, its emphasis on the eschatological aspect of the biblical message, can be regarded, for all our recognition of its dangerous and more than dangerous character, as a reaction against that silenced voice and muzzled impulse. The Pietist, in antithesis not to the original Protestant but to Ritschl's view of him, could be the one who can never forget that as a real hearer of the Word, beyond his standing in creatureliness and beyond his standing in the justification of the sinner, in comforted despair, he must also wait for God, and live his life in this waiting, this supremely active waiting, if he is to be a doer of the Word or its existential hearer. Pietism has the possibility of being obedience to the command in the specific form of obedience to the command of promise. Those who merely disapprove of it should see to it that they do justice to its underlying concern and that their disapproval does not have its source in a lack of awareness of this concern, even though it is of relevance to them too. We do not have to become mystics or monks or Russian Orthodox or Pietists or Christians who say: "Command thy ways."[21] We may have good reasons for not wanting to do so. But we cannot conceal the fact that we are responsibly drawn by our conscience in the direction of all these possibilities or impossibilities.

The revolutionary summons of conscience, however, may have a very different meaning and content. Waiting and *hastening* are commanded. Those who have heard the "waiting," if they have heard aright, will in some measure have had to hear the "hastening" too. Failure at this point is undoubtedly the source of the sickness of all those movements in which the "hastening" has been missed or not heard properly. "Hastening" means that *we* are summoned. It means that we are summoned in the present but for our future: to surrender, but to surrender to the *living* God; to rest, but to rest in the unrest of the *act* of life. The surrender and rest have to be taken seriously if our hastening is really to be obedience to the command of conscience. The same conscience does indeed say with great urgency: "Wait." But it also says: "Hasten." We have time, but we have it for eternity. We cannot be content with merely inward exertion and activity. A purely preparatory and inactive readiness and openness cannot be what is required of us, but an open and ready action. Sighing for redemption, dissatisfaction with self, questioning our present in the light of our future, loss of the balance between "always righteous" and "always sinner," has to take on form. We have to *breathe* in the atmosphere of the redemption hidden in the future. We have to *act* in the experience of the coming Redeemer. We are ordered to fight, to build, to work, to organize, to fashion things. The same conscience which drove us inside relentlessly drives us outside. Responsibility is responsibility that something should happen. We cannot build up the

[21]Cf. Gerhardt's hymn: "Befiehl du deine Wege" (1653).

kingdom of God or bring it in by force. But when it comes we cannot be idle. We are summoned to go to meet it. Our waiting can take place only in our acting, our hastening. |

The whole complex of phenomena which might be summed up under the concept of Christian activism must obviously be considered at this point both in its legitimacy and its illegitimacy. The ideal of the manifestation of Christ's kingdom in the Roman Papacy has a place here, as has also the old sectarian dream of a millennium (the third kingdom of the Spirit), the mad phantom which was pursued 400 years ago in this city,[22] *mutatis mutandis* the more original form of Zwinglianism and Calvinism, the activism of the Jesuit order, the activism which also came to characterize 19th-century Pietism, i.e., its application of private edification to outer and inner mission, and all that is usually understood by Christian or religious socialism. In this context it is again unnecessary to point out the dangerous nature and the obvious failure of all these phenomena, the innumerable short circuits which always can and do accompany this active Christianity, the evil confusion of the kingdom of God toward which one was supposedly moving with more or less imposing secular kingdoms of one's own invention. How can there fail to be danger and failure when the divine Word of conscience is heard by human ears and accepted by human wills? It issues its call to "hasten" in the present, and the present is no other than that of the "righteous sinner." There is danger and failure, as we have seen, when the concern of Christian inwardness is adopted. The concern of Christian activism of all kinds is no less serious and authentic because Thomas Münzer and Zwingli and Ignatius Loyola and Adolf Stöcker and John Mott and Leonhard Ragaz perhaps stand before us as rather horrifying examples. It may be that we will refuse to take this particular path. But again it will be very suspicious of us if in face of all the ancient and modern enthusiasts of church history and world history we can engage only in the rigid rejection which characterized Ritschl and which certain genuine followers of the reformation today regard as the only sound course. On this side, too, we are *questioned*. We are asked what we understand by hastening, whether we do not feel too much at home in the present, and whether we are letting ourselves be too little summoned by the future, if we are so anxious not to be suspected of excessive enthusiasm (as though enthusiasm did not begin with prayer), if our waiting does not have the character of the courageous act and venture with which one exposes and commits oneself. Have we really heard the command of conscience if we are not really anointed with a single drop of enthusiastic oil, if what we do is only conservative and not also revolutionary? |

We have now discussed the extreme possibilities of human waiting and hastening. Between these two poles there is a whole range of

---

[22]Münster; cf. p. 389, n. 40.

less-pronounced or mixed possibilities. We must all work these out for ourselves. The content of the pronouncement of our conscience does at least lie between the extremes. It applies to us in some specific relation between them.

Even of the *form* of the pronouncement of conscience we have to say that it is wholly conditioned by the fact that its subject is primarily God, and if it is secondarily, of course, the human I, it is this, not in the present reality of this I, but in its future reality as this moves from the eternity of God's will for man into his temporal present. The form of the divine claim as it is made upon man corresponds to the eschatological content of conscience which, as we have seen, gives to its word, as to God's Word, the distinctive character of the transcendent, of that which reaches across the limits of the situation of man as a creature and as a "righteous sinner," and which makes obedience to this word impossible for those who want to avoid at all costs any suspicion of mysticism or enthusiasm. Necessarily, we have the knowledge of the command of God that is mediated through conscience very differently from the way in which we have random ethical convictions or principles. As we have seen, we have a conscience as we have God, and therefore we have it in the same way as we have God. We thus have what conscience says to us as we have what God says to us, although with the more precise definition that here it is we ourselves who tell ourselves what God tells us. Yet what we tell ourselves is wholly conditioned by the fact that it is only what God tells us. Hence we cannot tell it to ourselves as we might tell other things. Even in the form of the pronouncement of conscience we cannot control the Word of God as though its power as God's Word were transferred to our human word and the power of God's Word were proper to this human word of ours. I speak here, but I do so as the child of God that has a share in the knowledge of God and therefore does not err but speaks universally valid and unequivocal truth. But I also listen here and form and express a thought on the basis of what I hear, being in this regard only a man of the present, a mere creature and "righteous sinner." As I begin to take control—and it is inevitable that I should— the pronouncement of conscience enters into the dialectic of my present existence, and its divine and future character asserts itself in the fact that we do not have it with exalted and extraordinary, let alone absolute, certainty and force, but rather, in relation to all the other axiomatic or experiential knowledge that we might have, with a defenselessness and weakness that again are not absolute but relatively extraordinary. If we are as certain of what we have heard as the pronouncement of our conscience as we are of what we have told ourselves in it; if the thought and word in which we have apprehended it and controlled it has the unbroken force of God's Word, this is not in virtue of our apprehension and control but in virtue of the voice and inspiration of the Holy Spirit, by the miracle of God himself, which, if it seems plainly to have taken place to us, we know to be finally hidden from us, we being in no position to lay our hands upon it. As regards our own knowledge of the pronouncement of our conscience, we are not absolutely defenseless or impotent but relatively very highly so. Which of the various judgments of which we are capable do we find to be so vague, so obscure in their epistemological and ontological basis, so ambiguous to ourselves and nonnormative for others, as the judgments of our conscience, and the more so, the more we have to do with pure judgments of conscience which cannot be made intelligible to ourselves or others except as such? We cannot make a great parade of our co-knowledge of God's truth, as we have it in conscience, in the present in which it is given to us. The possibility of conscience, real ability to introduce it as a power, and then necessarily as a power superior to all other powers, the powers of our own present and of that of others—this prophetic possibility is a real one, but not for us, for it does not lie in our own power but is the possibility of the miracle of God. If we ignore this possibility we are forced to say that conscience is one of the lesser and even the least things in our present. We can obey it, and, if this is part of obedience, tell others about it, only with the defenselessness and weakness with which alone the eternal future, because it is eternal, can be the present. Whenever we act or speak in any other way in the name of conscience, namely, with the power of the present, and therefore imperiously, imposingly, unequivocally, and impressively; whenever conscience acquires present breadth—I say breadth because it will always have some present extension—with what it says to someone and through this person perhaps to others, then with the prophetic possibility, upon which we will not cease to count, there always arises the question whether the strong vitality of the person concerned, or the independent force of his thoughts and words, does not have just as much or more to do with the development of that breadth than does conscience itself as God's own voice. A true and visible triumph of this voice would at all events mean the end of all things, i.e., the swallowing up of the present by the future of the eternal kingdom. We can reasonably count on the signs and wonders of this coming kingdom only as such, and not as possibilities[23] which will be realized if only we desire it with the right inwardness, or defiance. Normally we can listen to conscience only in the hiddenness in which we have it, and especially when we speak to others on the basis of conscience we cannot be aware enough of the modesty which is commanded with this hiddenness. Three points are to be noted particularly in relation to this hiddenness of conscience.

1. We all have conscience only as our *own* conscience, and therefore we all have what it says to us only as what it says to *us*. To be sure, it says it to us with the majesty of the truth of God which as such is valid truth for all. In itself the claim is justified that what my conscience says to me

[23]Barth originally had another *solchen* before possibilities, but the editor deleted this because it clashed with the preceding *solchen* ("such").

ought to be heard by others too. Our consternation is also justified when we are forced to say that we are not understood by others in a judgment which is for us a matter of conscience, and we perhaps find ourselves alone among many or even all others. The truth that is manifest in conscience comes to us with a drive for expansion. The attitude of a person whose conscience has spoken is quite uncapriciously a missionary attitude. On the basis of conscience, we think we are in the position of having something to say to others. Something of the explosive vehemence with which revelation forces the prophets to speak forces in some measure those who have heard the voice of conscience and who, as its hearers, confront another or others. This is all well and good. It would not be the voice of conscience if the "wait and hasten" which summons us did not in some sense become a message, if it did not become the movement or position of a fellowship, if it did not even lay claim openly or secretly to a certain universality. But precisely in this respect modesty is enjoined. God's speaking to me does not give me God's power over others. Unity in God with others is not put in my hands. I have to realize that God himself must seek and find others through their own consciences if this unity is to be true. It is on the concept of freedom of conscience that concrete light is shed here. I cannot urge upon others even the most urgent message that is laid upon me in the way that God imposes his Word upon them. The greater the urgency with which we address others in the name of conscience, the more we have to consider the alternative that, while this might be an appeal to the miracle of God, it might also be the illegitimate expansion of a decidedly human reality. Violation of freedom of conscience, no matter how well intentioned, always means that the others upon whom I force myself with the claim of my conscience no longer hear their own. To that extent they are devoid of conscience, for they cannot hear mine either. The limit of the task that I may have is marked by my being able to give them occasion to hear their own consciences. In this way alone will they hear God, and it is God that they ought to hear and not me. We have also to consider positively that conscience as that of each individual primarily and supremely makes each individual responsible as such. Prior to expansion and mission comes one's own obedience to conscience, which should not ask whether we have companions in what is commanded or forbidden us, but whose test is that we must dare sometimes to be completely alone. Pressuring the consciences of others often has its fatal basis in ourselves, in our seeking the consolation of companionship, of the support of those around us for doing what we are commanded to do. The more anxious and narrow are some movements of conscience, or the more it seems to be of the essence of the matter to bind others, the more similar the compulsion that the one exerts on the other seems to be to supremely secular compulsions and pressures, and the more there is cause to ask whether some part might not be played by the effort to escape personal responsibility by the formation of a group. Where the voice of conscience is truly heard, there, not to the detriment of a missionary attitude, a concern for freedom of conscience will also be present simply because there will be no inclination to shuffle off the responsibility of hearing on others. The individuality of conscience, however, is a mark of its defenselessness and weakness in the present and therefore indirectly of its eschatological character. Its freedom does not go well with the present power that we would like it to have. But we should strive for that power of conscience in which we know it as the voice of God. We should thus be concerned that each has only his or her own conscience. We must realize that in no case can we do more than this. God can. But if we try, we shall simply end up by being disobedient to his voice and by causing others to be disobedient to it too. To be obedient, we must dare to be obedient to it in the defenselessness and weakness in which it is the voice of the eternal future in the temporal present.

2. Connected with this is what I have referred to in the thesis as the strictly occasional nature of conscience as our co-knowledge of God's truth. What I mean is this: what conscience tells us relates, strictly speaking, only to the present in the strict sense, only to the given moment. Like God's command in general—and on the basis of conscience one may say this of God's command in general—it is a Word that God speaks personally. It is thus an event and not a thing. It does not exist; it takes place. Even the most authentic pronouncement of conscience cannot be stored and then unthinkingly brought out and proclaimed as the truth the next day or twenty years later because it was once so authentic and powerful. Here again we are reminded of the manna that was given to the Israelites in the wilderness, which had to be eaten at once, because even on the second day it would infallibly become spoiled and inedible if stored up [cf. Ex. 16:19f.]. The pronouncement of conscience—this, too, is part of its eschatological character—is truly bread from heaven which cannot be laid in store. It rings forth afresh each unrepeatable today—a today which as such is related to the eternal now, but which cannot be unrolled into a sequence. If there is a sequence here, as there is, it is that of the divine addresses, each of which must be heard as such and with completely new attention, unburdened so far as possible by any real or supposed preunderstanding. In this light one can use the concept of "conscientiousness" only with great caution. Conscientiousness might mean that we think we possess a store of verdicts of conscience on which we need only draw industriously to be obedient to conscience. As conscience, however, is not a kind of organ but the event in which we have to tell ourselves something as the children of God, so there is no store of hoarded truths of conscience. There can be a store only of our own ethical convictions and principles. This is a good thing, but it cannot be what we have to consider when we are referring to God's command. God's command may even be hampered if we confuse it with this; if we

forget, in face of our perhaps very distinguished morality, that at every moment conscience has in principle something new to say to the whole sum of our morality. Conscientiousness, then, has to mean being on the watch against the ever threatening danger of godlessness in the good, i.e., of confusing the real pronouncement of conscience with the mere recollection of such a pronouncement which then causes us to miss the real one. Conscientiousness has to mean fundamental openness and willingness to be guided by conscience. The pronouncement of conscience may be very different today from what it was yesterday, just as today is not yesterday. Today, today, he wants to be heard without hardening of heart [cf. Ps. 95:7f.; Heb. 3:7f.; 4:7] and to find obedience. This is undoubtedly part of the defenselessness and weakness of conscience in the present. Present power would obviously be possessed very differently by a conviction or principle from the way in which it is proper to the event of a real pronouncement of conscience in its strict contingency. Again, it is only too understandable why we should try to escape this contingency and constantly try to hoard up the bread from heaven. The history of movements of conscience would look very different from this standpoint if, as *movements*, they had not flourished on forgetfulness of this strict contingency. They thought—and which movement of conscience did not?—that they could save themselves in the present only by substituting a more practical and palpable present character for the future nature of the Word to which they owed their origin. The result was always a surrender of their birthright for a mess of pottage [cf. Gen. 25:29–34]. "What does it profit a man . . .?" [cf. Mark 8:36 par]. is also applicable here. How true this is may be seen in the tragedy of the fact that all these movements have had their time, but only their time, and finally they have had no more future in time but have had to be replaced by different and perhaps opposing movements, which have progressed according to the same law to their rise and probably their fall too. Again everything depends on being obedient to conscience precisely in the defenselessness and weakness in which it is God's own voice.

3. A final part of the eschatological determination of conscience is that what is called a good conscience, according to a fine observation of A. Ritschl,[24] is not another phenomenon of conscience which is experienced alongside a bad conscience or in alternation with it, but is rather something negative, an expression for the absence of a bad conscience, the latter filling up the total possible range of phenomena that offer themselves for observation. To the extent that conscience speaks into our present, how can it come as anything but a disruption, a warning, and a criticism, and how can a good conscience really signify anything other than a cessation of this disruption? If things were different, this voice would not come from where it does nor would it direct itself to

---

[24]A. Ritschl, *Über das Gewissen. Ein Vortrag*, Bonn 1876, p. 13.

where it does. Conscience is the great disruption also and precisely for the righteous sinner, we have said. It is a reminder that there can be no question of our remaining in a state of comforted despair. Hence all movements of conscience are in some way movements of opposition. Even in detail, conscience will constantly assert itself against us in our status as men and Christians. Necessarily, if God has something to say to us, he will call us to order. He will do so by putting what we do and fail to do in context, by measuring it against the coming perfection of his kingdom. But in this way he will call us to order. Everything depends on whether we accept this call to us who tarry in a distant and foreign land. Obviously we would like it to be different even in this context. We would like to have a good conscience and have it in a fully positive sense. But we can have it only as the reverse of a bad conscience, and again in present weakness and defenselessness. We do not like this. And it is again understandable that not just individuals but also the great historical movements of conscience have constantly had to fight the temptation to change the reality of the address of conscience, to make a position out of its opposition, i.e., to secure the strengthening of their own position. We can do this. It has been done innumerable times. One can only say that we ought not to do it if we are not to lose conscience itself, a good conscience, along with the hiddenness in which we may have a conscience, a good conscience. Here, again, the saying is true that "whosoever loses his life for my sake will save it." [cf. Mark 8:35].

§17

GRATITUDE

God's command always means a liberation of my action. It claims me. It claims me, and I have to listen, as it wins me not only for the commanded orderliness and humility but also for the God to whom I owe my existence, my salvation, and my final relationship to him.

1

In the preceding section we have learned to find in the concept of conscience the place where God's command comes to us as that of the Redeemer, i.e., the place where we have to stand according to this command. We might also say that we have answered again the question: "What shall *we* do?", the question of the noetic basis of the divine command. We have now to investigate its content for a third time, with the emphasis on: "What *shall* we do?" It is plain that in answering this question we must advance a standpoint that has not been considered thus far, inasmuch as we now start with the fact that the divine command is also that of the Father whose children we are, and that it comes to us as those who are partakers of the divine nature [cf. 2 Pet.

1:4]. What does it mean for our conduct, what character does it impress
upon this conduct, that we hear in our conscience the command of
promise, that the command of the Redeemer relates our conduct to the
future kingdom of God, that we [are] now so close to the God who is so
lofty when he confronts us as Creator and so holy, even in his mercy,
when he confronts us as Reconciler, [that] he speaks to us in the
encounter of immediacy which is encounter in a final unity with him?
We cannot be too careful in seeing things step by step from this
standpoint. We have to be aware that what is at issue is the encounter
between God and man in a *final* unity between them. If we were to
regard it as a first unity, we should have to begin with the standpoint
with which we now end and we should have to engage in some
presumptuous idealistic and mystical speculation even though we did it
with an appeal to Christ. We have to be aware, then, that, even in this
final unity, what is at issue is an *encounter* between God and man. We are
and remain God's children; we do not become secretly and ultimately
the Father himself. We must accept the distance that separates man and
his Creator and man and his Reconciler even though it is included and
removed (though not negated) in the new and final distance between
children and Father. We must also be aware that the special encounter
between God and man in this final unity of both is not an intrinsic or an
attained possession of man but a most actual affair of the divine giving.
It rests in God, not in us. It is to be sought in God, not asserted by us
against God. For this reason it is a *final* unity and for this reason it always
means *encounter* in unity.

Recollection of this final and comprehensive proviso points us to the
special determination which must obviously be proper to the command
of God from this specific standpoint, with regard to what it enjoins upon
us as obligatory. Older Protestantism spoke of a third use of the law in
which it rules the life of the regenerate by teaching.[1] We obviously have
to do with the life of the regenerate when we understand the encounter
between God and man as encounter in the unity of Father and children.
We must not confuse this with eternal life in the consummation itself.
When the present is swallowed up in the future, in eternity itself there
will no longer be any command. Hence the Formula of Concord (VI)
rightly relates the third use of the law to the regenerate, not in so far as
they are righteous, but in so far as they are sick and frail.[2] The command
has this third and final form and significance for man living here and now
in time, though for this man as he is born again of the Word of God and a
partaker of the promise of eternal life. What form and significance? If we
keep to the proviso made in asserting the unity between God and man,
then the command obviously has the form and significance that we are

[1]Cf. (K. A. von Hase) *Hutterus redivivus oder Dogmatik der evangelisch-lutherischen Kirche*,
Leipzig (1829) 1862[10], p. 310.
[2]Ibid., p. 310, n.7. Barth is not quoting exactly from the Formula.

referred to the pure gift of God which ultimately is given to us also and precisely as we are born again and are already partakers here and now in an unbreakable relationship to him who first encountered us as Creator and Reconciler, though in both cases in grace. By this relationship we obviously live already as his creatures, for how could we understand our life in distinction from him as a reality if in this life we did not participate in his own reality which is the content of his eternal promise to us? And by this relationship again we live as righteous sinners, for how again could we understand our righteousness as sinners if revelation and reconciliation in Christ did not mean that God in Christ gives us in promise a share in his own reality, but in this promise a real share? Hence the fact that we are regenerate is the promised meaning, too, of our encounter with God the Creator and the Reconciler.

When we look particularly at this meaning of our standing before God in the previous sense, our encounter with God is an encounter with God the Redeemer, and the command of God is given as we are directed to the promise, to the promise which is to the effect that we belong to God, that no one and nothing can pluck us out of his hand [cf. John 10:28f.], that in our creatureliness as the righteous sinners as which we find ourselves in the present we are one with God as children are with their father. We live by this. Here and now, and not just in the future, we live by the fact that it is promised to us in all the hiddenness of future truth. As we live by the fact that it is promised to us, we are pointed to God's *gift*, and what is required of us, the measure by which our conduct is measured from this third standpoint, is *gratitude*. In Question 86 the Heidelberg Catechism asks why we should do good works, and it answers that we should do them because Christ, after purchasing us with his blood, has renewed us in his image by his Holy Spirit, so that with our whole lives we should show ourselves thankful to God for his goodness, and he should be praised by us.[3] Here again the command of God is issued to us, and is to be received by us, as a claim. Here again its content means that we must recognize how we stand with God, that we must confess our situation before him, that we must honestly be what we are. From the standpoint of creation this meant that we must recognize God's order (§9). From that of reconciliation it meant that we must be ready to be humble (§13). From that of redemption it now means that we must be grateful. Certainly we would not really be orderly or humble if we were not so in gratitude. Nevertheless, beyond orderliness and humility, gratitude means specifically that I am *gladly*, i.e., voluntarily and cheerfully, ready for what God wills of me in acknowledgment of what is given to me by God and as my necessary

---

[3]Heidelberg Catechism, 1563, pt. 3: Of Thankfulness, Qu. 86: "Since, then, we are redeemed from our misery by grace through Christ, without any merit of ours, why must we do good works?" Answer: "Because Christ, having redeemed us by his blood, renews us also by his Holy Spirit after his own image, that with our whole life we may show ourselves thankful to God for his blessing . . ."

response to God's gift. This responsive "gladly" is not necessarily contained in the concepts of orderliness and humility. Orderliness might be grudging and humility forced, although naturally, in such cases, they could not be claimed as a fulfillment of the divine command. Gratitude, however, is this responsive "gladly" which by going beyond them makes all orderliness and humility right and complete. If God commands gratitude this means that by my own choice, although wholly in response to his act, he wants to win me for himself. He orders from me what I might try to escape as only apparently his servant or only apparently a member of the people in whom his honor dwells, namely, that I should be voluntarily and joyfully for him. In a word, he expressly and unequivocally wants me myself. We could not complete the chapters on creation and reconciliation without coming back to this "me myself" as the point of the demand made upon us. Here, in gratitude, this point of the requirement is itself required as such.

Now, for two reasons, we must show why it is only in an eschatological context that this gratitude, this "me myself," can be conceptually possible as the content of the divine command. First, how does it come about that of myself I myself am won for God as the command requires? From the standpoint of creation and reconciliation we obviously arrive only at the conclusion that God wills to win me for himself with power as the Lord of my life and the Savior of my life. In this light the winning of man is God's act upon him. But is not a final point missing here if we are to understand God's act as having really taken place and really been accomplished? That I *myself am* won for God can be shown neither from the concept of the grace of creation nor that of reconciliation in such a way that the "I am" is really perspicuous. "The hanged person also has to be there" (Luther).[4] Where is the hanged person? Do we not get the impression that the question of this person, even as a secondary character, is in some way dealt with too summarily, or completely ignored, in discussions of the great problem of obedience? The possibility that this might be reasonably required of us, that I might obey gladly, i.e., that I might obey in the strict sense, obviously rests on the eschatological reality of our divine sonship in which the Word of God constantly addresses us and which it brings about in so doing. Eschatologically considered, our human reality does not exhaust itself in our present being as creatures or as sinners saved by grace. Even if only in the present and obviously within the limits denoted by our sickness and frailty, man is now the new and future man of God. As this new and future man of God I *am* won for God. To me as such it may be meaningfully said: "Be what you are," i.e., not just: "Live in the order

---

[4]The editor has been unable to find this saying in Luther's works, but for material parallels cf. WA 39, I, 209, 29–32; 447, 8ff. Cf. also the same thought in Luther's mentor Johann von Staupitz (1469?–1524), *Sämmtlich Werke*, ed. J K. F. Knaake, vol. 1: *Deutsche Schriften*, Potsdam 1867, pp. 39f.

of your Creator or in humility before your Reconciler," but: "Live in gratitude. It is given to you to belong to God. You live in and by the fact that you are the child of God, that you already stand at his side, triumphing over the contradiction and the limits of your existence. Accept the fact that this is given to you. Act as one who lives in and by this gift. Know that your whole conduct is measured by the fact that it must be this confession and can be good only if it is." How else can we be won for God except on the basis of the future I which encounters us and which in conscience claims us for God's kingdom, for God's being "all in all" [cf. I Cor. 15:28]? To the extent that this voice speaks to us and we hear it, this voice in which God's word has come into our own word and with which we tell ourselves what we have to be told, to this extent we come to be and are won for God. Rightly, then, the Heidelberg Confession reminds us in the passage just quoted[5] that gratitude is conditioned by the fact that in addition to reconciling us to God—in a true event and fulfillment of reconciliation—Christ has also by his Holy Spirit renewed us in his image. This "also" denotes the eschatological reality of our divine sonship in which the "I am" is possible, and therefore gratitude makes sense as a demand upon us. On this basis it may be said to me, indeed, I must say it to myself as a true hearer of the Word: "You are"; "I am." On this basis I am summoned to that "gladly," to that willingness and cheerfulness in which I let myself be won for God. On what basis can I really be summoned, and know that I am summoned, except on the basis of myself? Gratitude cannot be commanded. I must really command it of myself. But how can I issue this command if I do not confront myself as I do when seen from the standpoint of eternity in my divine sonship, in my participation in the divine nature? It is in the Holy Spirit, without whom the Word of God would not come to me, that this commanding of self by the self, of the self as the one that has to be commanded here, is an actual event.

Second, in our thesis we have described the process of grateful action as a *liberated* action. God's command *frees* me by winning me for God the Redeemer. Our action in relation to God's command is not freed or liberated insofar as it is considered simply as that of the creature or of the sinner saved by grace, insofar as it is considered in its pure, self-resting, present character. It may well be good to the extent that it is orderly and humble but these concepts do not make it *freely* good. What is required still confronts us as the command of order, even though the order be that of our own life, or opposes us as the command of humility, even though this be the humility of Christ our Reconciler. That we should affirm this requirement which confronts and opposes us as something that we ourselves require of ourselves is what is ordered by the command of gratitude. To the extent that our conduct goes beyond orderliness and

[5]See p. 499, n.3.

humility and is also grateful conduct, its goodness is free. We are forced to say that even the goodness of orderly and humble conduct stands under this final question whether it is also free goodness. Christian freedom does not mean that we no longer stand under the command, that our conduct is no longer obedience. It means that we stand under the command that we ourselves affirm, that our obedience is our own will. Redemption or liberation is the redemption or liberation of ourselves as people who confront and even oppose God's command as enemies, the redemption or liberation of our own work as a work which in some way competes with the work that God has commanded. It is our placing in the home of the good. Hence the command of the Redeemer, inasmuch as it demands not only orderliness and humility but also gratitude, inasmuch as it demands that we be won for God because he grants us relationship to himself, is the law of freedom. As it comes to us it brings loosening, release, and relaxation. If this last door does not open, our present means imprisonment, bondage, and confinement, for all the relationship to God in which we find ourselves in this present, and even in this relationship. In the I-ness which confronts the command of God and even opposes it as an enemy, in the work of self which competes with the work of God, even as hearers of the Word we can only sigh, never being sure for a moment that the despair in comforted despair might not overpower the comfort.[6] "If for this life only we have hoped in Christ, we are of all men most to be pitied," Paul said in 1 Corinthians 15:29 to some Christians who had no time for the eschatological reality of the Christian, for the resurrection of the dead. Yet it is on this basis, and only on this basis, that the command of the Redeemer brings loosening, release, and relaxation into the present.|

I avoid saying "redemption" here (*Erlösung* instead of *Lösung*) because it says both too much and too little. Redemption is the fulfillment of the promise. What comes into our present with the command, however, is not the fulfillment and therefore not redemption itself. It is the promise, and therefore and therewith it is loosening (*Lösung*). In the present we are still sick and frail. We are still imprisoned, bound, and confined. Note that not only in Romans 7 but also at the climax of Romans 8 [vv. 19ff.] Paul fully confesses the sighing of creation and the yearning expectation of divine sonship. Nevertheless—here is the point—there is a release and relaxation even in this sighing, even in the despair which often enough does overpower the comfort. One should not overestimate this, nor expect too lofty, and especially not absolute things from it. One should not think that with increasing age it will become increasingly predominant, or that on our deathbed it will be manifested in some minor glory such as is usually depicted in pietistic biographies. The difference between redemption and release, which we can overlook and

---

[6]Here Barth uses *vorschlagen* intransitively for "overpower," "have the upper hand over," "outweigh" (*vorwalten*).

transcend only at the risk of very serious disillusionment and very dangerous temptation, is that Christian release, i.e., what we can experience and have as Christian freedom in the present, is itself sick and frail, being implicated and entangled in all the uncertainty, provisional nature, and vulnerability of our present existence, not visible and perceptible like a possession, like a constantly burning light which can be comfortably and with heartfelt conviction proclaimed by pastors as the special privilege of being a Christian, but probably shining forth only like lightning in a dark sky, a charisma which it is best not to grasp but rather to rejoice in when it is there and not to be surprised when it is not, and which, even when it is there, does not allow us to dispense for a single moment with the necessary vigilance of those who are commanded to watch and to hasten. There is such a thing as this Christian relaxation, this relaxation of man as such, of his whole present being as a creature. There is such a thing as a "walk in heaven" (Luther's not wholly inaccurate translation of πολίτευμα in Philippians 3:20)—in heaven where God's command is transcended as law because it can no longer be described as the opposite of what we ourselves will. The gratitude required of us, as the winning of ourselves for God, means at any rate an attack upon us inasmuch as we are not yet won for God, a thrust against the center of the misery of our present, an attack and a thrust which are not just made in some way against us but in which we ourselves participate and which we are summoned to undertake. Only in this light can one see the significance of the unheard-of Pauline imperatives to put off the old man and put on the new, to mortify one's members on the earth, to dedicate the same members to the service of righteousness [Eph. 4:22−24; Col. 3:5; Rom. 6:19]. Who is being addressed here? Undoubtedly my coming I as I am in Christ, dead, buried, and raised with him. But undoubtedly I myself, for as this future I it is in the present that I find myself addressed in God's Word. Hence I cannot *syschematizesthai tō aiōni toutō*. I am in process of change [Rom. 12:2]. There is an obedience that consists in letting go here and now in time, in growing up to be the child of God that I am, and there is a disobedience that consists in confirming and strengthening myself in my present which is condemned to destruction. It is a requirement and a task that our action should be liberated action, just as it is a charisma when it is. It is a requirement inasmuch as I myself must summon myself, really summon myself, to perform it. It is a charisma inasmuch as this summons comes into being when I am the child of God by the Holy Spirit and therefore the future I that issues the summons.

2

At this point, where we understand the required character of our action to be gratitude, it is in place to consider the bold thesis that our conduct bears the mark of good, of what is pleasing to God, when it is not done in earnest but in *play*. This is in truth a thesis which can be understood correctly only from an eternal standpoint, which cannot and must not be advanced except in this context, and against whose careless or too direct application we cannot give too much warning. Ultimately, in the last resort, our life is truly only a game. Asserted too hastily and casually, this thesis can only too easily mean that we overlook our being claimed by God's command, the validity of the command, and the seriousness of our situation as those who refuse to obey it; that we despise the riches of the mercy of God by which we are upheld in all our opposition to the command, and finally also the miracle that God calls us his children; that it would be more profitable for us, instead of rejoicing in the character of our existence as a game, to wake up finally out of sleep and see what it really means to be before God's face, i.e., to move each moment into God's judgment. If we still dare to adopt this thesis and thus to say that what is ultimately demanded of us is that our action should be play, we remember in so doing that our reference here is to the release of which we have just spoken and of which we have said that it is both a task and a charisma and that its presupposition is the Holy Spirit. The freedom of the Spirit, of the Holy Spirit in us, is the only thing that can be meant here, and if our action is really to be play we always have reason to consider whether it might not be the flesh that is liberated rather than the spirit—the flesh which is not meant to be promoted but is in fact disadvantaged by the work of gratitude, by the received, accepted, and self-activated release to which we refer.

Having said this, we should not fail to say that as God's children we are in fact released from the seriousness of life and can and should simply play before God. A question—I almost said a very serious question—which is put to our conduct is whether it has also the character of play or whether it is *only* serious, in which case it cannot really be good. For three reasons the term "play" is in truth appropriate for good conduct, the conduct that is required of us, when this is considered in the present context.

1. We are not only permitted but commanded to find the concept of our essential relationship to God in the promise that we are his children in the sense of his *little* children. We have said that the distance between God and us does not disappear even in the relationship of father and child. We must not play the part, then, of adult sons and daughters of God who gradually come to be on a level with their father. We must not try to view our work as a solemnly serious cooperation with God on the part of those who will be or are already becoming his colleagues. We are always, in fact, his little children, and our work in relation to his is more play than work, obedient play, play in the peace of the father's house that is waiting for us, yet still play. Play corresponds to what we said about the symbolical character of sacrifice in the section on humility.[7]

---

[7]Cf. pp. 405ff.

When we realize that even and precisely in our most serious action, e.g., as responsible politicians or theological dogmaticians and ethicists, we are God's little children at play, this serves precisely to keep us in the necessary fear of God and thus to call us back again and again to the point. One can walk before God in full seriousness only when one realizes that God alone is fully serious.

2. Our participation in the promises characterizes our action as provisional, as preceding our true action as those who live eternally in God's kingdom. God speaks with us. In this action of ours in time he judges us in relation to his will for us in eternity. We cannot anticipate by what we do here and now that which he wills for us, our eternal existence and conduct before him. We can understand this only as something that is promised to us. Hence we cannot allot final seriousness to what we do here and now. We do it under the divine patience which gives us time, but not with the significance of eternal action which, from the standpoint of the here and now, we may regard as God's action and not our own. From this angle, too, we can regard our action only as play. Children play before growing up. Even the greatest people still have to grow up. We do not have to become like children artificially, as some Anabaptists tried to do in the sixteenth century.[8] We have simply to realize that we are children, and will be so to the very end, in whatever we do, because the perfect has still to come beyond all that we do now. This makes it clear to us that whatever we do at least lacks the necessary purposefulness. We cannot be more grimly in earnest about life than when we resign ourselves to the fact that we can only play.

3. We have described gratitude as an action in which we act gladly, voluntarily, and cheerfully. It means that we ourselves are really present and claimed by ourselves. It is to be freed from the opposition or drive of the I-ness which does not want to be open but rather to be self-enclosed. Insofar as we are grateful to God, the strangeness of his command and the hostility with which it confronts us drop away. Related to this strangeness and hostility is the final constricting seriousness with which we often think that we can save ourselves—save ourselves from the fact that we know only too well that we are not those whom God has accepted, that inwardly we are still God's enemies for all the supposed and ostensible orderliness and humility of our conduct. This seriousness would not be necessary if only we would keep to the promise and let ourselves be told that we are the children of God. If only we would do this, then the rigidity of our obedience which is no true obedience, the strictness and anxiety with which we observe, watch, and harass ourselves and others, sincerely supposing it to be for the best, the hardness of thought, speech, and will which now usually characterize what are thought to be the best of people, the far too self-conscious and

---

[8]Cf. A. Ritschl, *Geschichte des Pietismus*, vol. 1: *Geschichte des Pietismus in der reformierten Kirche*, Bonn 1880, p. 26.

self-assertive attitude of those who want to be Christians in earnest[9]—all this, if it would not become nothing and certainly would not change into its opposite, would at least become inwardly very different, because good Christians would be what they are voluntarily and joyfully, and their obedience, attitude, work, relation to others, and whole responsibility to God would be like children's play. Need I say that repentance before God and service to one's neighbor are possible only on this basis, in the light of eschatological reality of our existence? Without this light we always take ourselves much too seriously to be ready to seek forgiveness of our sins from God and to forgive others their sins from our hearts. To be obedient and not just to seem to be so obviously have to be engaged in that change, in that putting off of the old man and putting on of the new [cf. Eph. 4:22–24]. But what does this mean except that what we ought to do we now want to do? What can it mean except that we play instead of trying to work with the seriousness which is appropriate only in face of that strange and hostile command? How can we obey if we will not learn that before God we can only play?

In conclusion, the insight that, from the eternal standpoint, the good action required of us has the character of play brings to light two special possibilities of life which theological ethics can only now consider, but now has to consider. I have in mind art on the one side and what I might call humor on the other.

In theological ethics, art must be considered in an eschatological context because it is the specific external form of human action in which this cannot be made intelligible to us except as play. In this connection, which we can understand only as a final one, humor has to be set alongside it and yet also contrasted with it as the universal and inner form of human action. When we speak of art, we do not have everything and all things in view but a specific human action in which we are not merely aware of the playful character of human action, as in humor, but this is brought to expression in concentrated, hypostatic, and explicit form, asserting itself in acts of a particular nature. Art and humor have in common that, strictly and exactly, only the children of God are capable of them. Art and humor define human action as something that is done gladly, voluntarily, and cheerfully; they define obedience as an inner necessity. But this is true of us only in the light of our eschatological reality. There is good reason, then, to regard art as a special gift of the deity to particular favorites. Since we have understood divine sonship to be man's uncontrollable future in his present, this cannot be equated with the so-called genius of the artist, and it will not surprise or disturb us—we now have the doctrine of justification to back us—that the greatest artists, notoriously, have not always been the best of men.

---

[9]Cf. For this phrase Luther's *Deutsche Messe und ordnung Gottis diensts* (1526), WA 19, 75, 5.

Similarly, to have real humor—unless by humor we mean a particular type of rancor—we have to be children of God, the shining of true humor in a person being necessarily a manifestation of that uncontrollable future of his in the present. Those who have hope of Christ only in this life cannot laugh (cf. 1 Cor. 15:19). In virtue of this common origin, art and humor also have in common that they would not be what they are if, precisely as joyful action, they were not sustained by an ultimate and very profound pain. Humor that is not grim humor, humor that laughs through tears [Kutter],[10] is not real humor. Nor is art that is not born of sorrow, even though conceived of joy, real art. Why is this so? Why does it have to be so? Obviously because the children of God, and they precisely, know that it does not yet appear what they shall be [cf. 1 John 3:2], because they precisely suffer with groaning creation in this present in which the future is present only as the future and whose corruptibility they cannot overlook or ignore even as they joyfully accept it for the sake of the future that is present. In autumn, when the shadows lengthen and the leaves begin to fall, these fruits ripen. Only those who have knowledge of the future resurrection of the dead really know what it means that we have to die.|

Being borne and born by pain is particularly the lot of art because this is by nature an expression, a special action which introduces special works, an action whose alien character as play cannot be concealed or diminished in the midst of the seriousness of the present. The artist's work is homeless in the deepest sense even though it is also real work alongside scholarship and church and state. Art does not come within the sphere of our work as creatures or our work as sinners saved by grace. As pure play it relates to redemption. Hence it is at root a nonpractical and lonely action. It belongs to the empty sphere of the uncontrollable future in the present. Its greatness and its fate are as Schiller depicted them in his *Teilung der Erde:* "Very late, when the distribution had already taken place, the poet drew near from the far distance and alas! there was nothing to be seen anywhere and everything had an owner." But he knew how to vindicate himself before Zeus: " 'I was with you,' said the poet, 'my eye was fixed on your countenance and my ear on the harmony of your heaven. Pardon the spirit which, intoxicated by your light, lost what is earthly.' " And it is consoling to hear what Zeus finally promises him: "If you want to live with me in my heaven, it will be open to you as often as you come.' "[11] This consolation ultimately means

---

[10]Cf. H. Kutter, *Reden an die deutsche Nation,* Jena 1916, p. 98; cf. also pp. 113, 225.

[11]F. Schiller, *Die Teilung der Erde* (1795); "Ganz Spät, nachdem die Teilung längst geschehen Naht der Poet, er kam aus weiter Fern;/Ach, da war überall nichts mehr zu sehen, Und alles hatte seinen Herrn./"Ich war," sprach der Poet, "bei dir./ Mein Auge hing an deinem Angesichte,/ An deines Himmels Harmonie mein Ohr;/ Verzeih' dem Geiste, der, von deinem Lichte/ Berauscht, das Irdische verlor!" "Willst du in meinem Himmel mit mir lebel:/ So oft du kommst, er soll dir offen sein."

homelessness, the least part of which may be that art has to pay its way;[12] that its works are so unequivocally characterized as play and play alone; that they are possible only as signs of the promise; that precisely in their strange and rootless isolation from all the works of present reality they live so totally *only* by the truth of the promise; that among others the artist must appeal to their openness to the ultimate if with his unusual language he is to be able to count on a hearing and understanding; that he must put to others a question without being able to reckon on an answer, the success of an answer involving the occurrence of a miracle which is the distinctive greatness but also the distinctive tragedy of art. For the nature of artistic creation and artistic enjoyment (which is a subsequent and concurrent creation) is that we are rigorously placed under the saying in Isaiah 65:17: "For behold, I create new heavens and a new earth; and the former things shall not be remembered or come into mind." In art we venture not to take present reality with final seriousness in its created being or in its nature as the world of the fall and reconciliation. Along with this we try to create a second reality which is only paradoxically possible, since we cannot break free from the first. Artistic creation will always aim at the unheard of, at that which has never been, at giving shape to the impossible, at impossible shaping. In principle all artistic creation is *futuristic*. It will always have to come back to reality in order to create *it* anew and see *it* changed and show it to be so—the reality that was created by God and has been reconciled to him, but this as redeemed reality in its sensed and anticipated perfection, hence, a clarified and purified reality, although much more is undoubtedly involved than clarification, which cannot be expressly understood as the working out of what is true and ultimate and definitive in reality. True aesthetics is the experiencing of real and future reality. Art is creation on the basis of this experience. To this extent art *plays* with reality. It does not let it be a last word in its present existence and nature. It transcends it with its own word. It thinks it can know it better and make it better. It transcends human words with the eschatological possibility of poetry, in which speech becomes, in unheard-of fashion, an end in itself, then to a higher degree—although we are still dealing only with the sound and tone of the human voice—with the eschatological possibility of song, and then—still with the intention of penetrating to what is true and ultimate, of proclaiming the new heaven and the new earth, but now using the voices of the rest of creation—with the eschatological possibility of instrumental music. In novels and plays it seeks to achieve and demonstrate in pure form the true and final meaning of the reality of human life and society, of human sin and forgiveness, of the whole dialectic of church and state in the broadest sense of the terms, the meaning which is obviously only concealed, as

---

[12]"Nach Brot gehen muss," a 16th-century proverb; cf. G. E. Lessing, *Emilia Galotti* (1772), Act I, Scene 2.

the future, in reality itself. As painting and sculpture it ventures to look at the outward form of present man and present nature as we can apparently see these only with our present eyes, but with the intention of seeing them with very different eyes and therefore of creating them anew in a better way, so that always and necessarily it sees them futuristically. |

In all this the true artist always proclaims himself as well, to the extent that as a child of God he has eyes to see the future in the present, and to the extent that a God must have given it to him to say what he suffers.[13] Since this is not just a matter of imagination—by itself the most lively imagination does not make an artist—but a matter of imaginative acting and creating and shaping and fashioning, play is itself work here, and the better the play the harder the work. It is thus true that what is serious is true enjoyment.[14] This is why there are laws and rules of esthetics, variable though these may be. This is why there is a distinctive artistic objectivity which is no less rigorous than scientific objectivity, though entirely different. Nevertheless, art is always play, and if its tragedy is that its work can never be serious in relation to the present, that the artist is at home in heaven and not on earth, its danger, the great danger of the whole esthetic possibility, is that its character as a final word and last and boldest climax of human activity will be overlooked, that with its help a supposed heaven will be set up on earth when all along the line all that can be done is the erection of a sign of the promise. We can forget that the Muse knows how to accompany ("geleiten") but not to lead ("leiten").[15] We can make art a constitutive principle of life. We can want to see and shape the future before and without taking seriously the problems of the present and achieving a truly realistic view of them. This is the root of the onlooker approach to life which has been touched on so often because it is so fateful, especially in theology. The onlooker thinks that he can escape decision with the calm of the supposed artist because he regards the standpoint of the artist, the standpoint from which, with his own objectivity, the artist sees men and things and himself other than they are, as a possible place from which one may not only paint or compose poetry or music but also live, live in that different relationship, and, e.g., do theology. This is not possible. We do not stand any less in decision because the content of our decision is ultimately play, because finally we can also, and perhaps must, paint and compose poetry and music. When play is taken seriously—and when it is not we have no true art—it takes upon itself the character of decision, and the problems of the present are taken seriously precisely

---

[13]Cf. J. W. Goethe, *Torquato Tasso* (1787–1789), Act V, Scene 5: "Und wenn der Mensch in seiner Qual verstummt,/ Gab mir ein Gott, zu sagen, wie ich leide."

[14]A. L. Seneca (4 BC–AD 65), *Epistolae morales* 23, 3f.: "Disce gaudere . . . Mihi crede, res severa est verum gaudium."

[15]Cf. J. W. Goethe, *Für junge Dichter* (1831): "Jüngling, merke dir in Zeiten,/ Wo sich Geist und Sinn erhöht,/ Dass die Muse zu *begleiten*,/ Doch zu *leiten* nicht versteht."

because they are seen in their limitation and are basically transcended in esthetics.|

This positive significance of art as the proclaimer of the possibility of a basic transcending of present reality—a significance in which it may be regarded as in some sense a counterpart to conscience—makes not only possible but also necessary some participation of our activity in that of art. It is a feeble view of art that isolates it as a sphere of its own for those who find it amusing. The word and command of God demand art, since it is art that sets us under the word of the new heaven and the new earth [cf. Isa. 65:17]. Those who, in principle or out of indolence, want to evade the anticipatory creativity of esthetics are certainly not good. Finally, in the proper sense, to be unesthetic is to be immoral and disobedient. To be sure, we are here on the margin or outer edge of what must be regarded as good and commanded, but this margin is part of the matter, and on it everything may be at issue. To be unesthetic is fundamentally to reject the signs that point beyond the present, the very nonpractical but very significant signs that art sets up. This will not do, any more than it will do to try to view the signs as more than signs. We cannot raise here the big question of the church and art, and especially art and the liturgy. But it ought to be clear that the church's activity, as human activity, ought to include this marginal possibility, though it should not be overlooked that, as an example of human action in obedience, as a human answer to the divine summons, it does belong on the necessary margin of divine service, it falls under the concept of the community that responds to God's Word, and it must not be confused with proclamation, which is enjoined upon the church in relation to the divine action. Participation in art is thus a general element in what is demanded of us, for as the children of God—and it is only as such that we are really and finally claimed by the command of God—we cannot avoid acting in play too. Play is not the opposite of serious decision. It is decision taken gladly, willingly, and cheerfully along the lines of the command and in opposition to the present reality in which we stand.|

If we think less of the specific action called art and more of the attitude that is ultimately demanded in all that we do, than we come up against the other concept that calls for notice here, namely, that of humor. Humor is fluid, its antithesis being that which is dry and frozen. Humor means being flexible, not rigid. Insofar as we are dealing here with what is good and commanded, this consists of the flexibility which our action acquires and has, because it is done in time but from the standpoint of eternity. Humor arises when the contrast between our existence as the children of God and our existence as the children of this eon is perceived and vitally sensed in what we do. Humor concerns the present as such with its strange connections and involvements. We are in these; we cannot slough them off; we have to suffer under them. To a high degree we have to take them seriously. We cannot change the future into the present and the present into the future. We must persevere as best we can. We have humor when we do this. Humor makes concrete the saying in Romans 8:18: "I consider that the sufferings of this present time are not worth comparing with the glory that is to be revealed in us," and the further saying in Romans 8:28: "We know that all things work together for good to those who love God." Like art, humor undoubtedly means that we do not take the present with ultimate seriousness, not because it is not serious enough in itself, but because God's future, which breaks into the present, is more serious. Humor means the placing of a big bracket around the seriousness of the present. In no way does it mean—and those who think it does do not know what real humor is—that this seriousness is set aside or dismissed. Humor arises, and can arise only, when we wrestle with this seriousness of the present. But above and in this wrestling, we cannot be totally serious as the children of God. As the future of God declares itself in one way in conscience, and then explicitly in art, so it declares itself implicitly as laugher amid tears, as the "gladly, voluntarily, and joyfully" with which we look beyond the present, endure it, and take it seriously within the bracket, because it already carries the future within itself. It is a liberated laughter that derives from the knowledge of our final position—in spite of appearances to the contrary—within present reality. Of humor, too, one may say that it is genuine when it is the child of suffering. Behind it, if it is authentic, stands all the distress of sighing under pain, under all the terrible unredeemedness of our present, all the questionability of our creaturely existence, all the invalidity of our existence as sinners who live by mercy. Those who do not know this, those who do not know that we have nothing to laugh about, how can they laugh as they must be able to laugh as the children of God? We shall always have cause to see that precisely those with whom everything goes well, who close their eyes to the riddles of existence, who for some reason feel very much at home in the present, and who are perfectly satisfied with their role, are those who have *no* humor. On the other hand, humor is to be sought among the assaulted, among those who, as Luther says, have been through the wringer,[16] among those who suffer from blows such as those that smote Job and Ecclesiastes. True humor may be distinguished from false, i.e., from that of the carnival, by the fact that it presupposes rather than excludes the knowledge of suffering, and quite unequivocally by the fact that its favorite target is oneself rather than others, since it sees the bracket in which the self stands, the question mark and exclamation point that must be placed against its own perhaps very important and serious heavenly existence. For this reason and in this way it has the significance of a liberation and release rather than poison and gall, even when directed at others. When we have first laughed at ourselves we can then laugh at others, and we can stand cheerfully the final test of being laughed at by them—a test which many

[16]Cf. WA 17 I, 236, 14ff.; 36, 514, 18ff.

supposedly humorous people ignominiously fail. The seriousness of real joy applies here no less than in art. The total seriousness of decision in face of God's command can reach a climax in our having to laugh and not just cry and gnash our teeth, in our having to make the best of a bad job. A serious problem one might have with Calvin is that he seems not to have been able to laugh, or to do so only bitterly. For much of his life, of course, he was a sick man. All the same, what we have here is an eschatological possibility. Humor, like art, is not a standpoint. We cannot begin with it; we can only end with it. We are commanded to do so, just as in another context we are commanded to be totally serious and to become increasingly so.

§18

HOPE

The commandment of God is fulfilled by me, i.e., my work is good, it is obedience to the command of promise, and is conscientious and grateful work, to the extent that I am told, and let myself be told, that it is done in unity with the will of my Redeemer. That this is told me, and that I let it be told me, is, as the work of the Holy Spirit, the reality of hope.

1

Thus far in the fourth chapter, drawing an innermost circle in the sphere of ethical problems, we have reached some mutually supplementary and elucidatory criteria of good and sanctified action which is obedient to the command of God: openness to the promise under which we are placed as hearers of the Word, conscientiousness, and, finally, gratitude. Here again, however we must not evade the question of action in itself and as such. We realize, of course, that what makes action good in itself and as such does not lie at our disposal but is enclosed in the righteous judgment of God whose good pleasure we cannot anticipate or enforce with any of our own intentions about criteria, however good. The assurance of the children of God would not be such did it not submit joyfully to the mystery of the twofold *election* of divine grace, in virtue of which alone our work can be called, and can be, good in a serious sense. But the divine verdict and the divine choice concern our existence and therefore our acts. It is not finally a special doctrine of James that man is justified or not by his works [cf. James 2:14–26]. Paul can and must say the same: God will give to all of us according to our works (Rom. 2:6); at the judgment seat of Christ we will all receive according what we have done in life, whether good or bad (2 Cor. 5:10). Fulfilling the command is no less a concern of ours, of our conduct, because it is God's concern alone to say whether our conduct is really a fulfillment. If there can be no question of trying to imagine or present the goodness of human action in abstraction from the divine decision, here again there is a need to point out expressly that the object of the divine decision is our action as such. This means that for a third time, in conclusion, we must search for a concept, which on the one side denotes a definite mode of human action, but on the other clearly expresses divine control of its ultimate quality. We concluded the preceding chapters with discussions of the concepts of·faith and love. The concept which suggests itself now, in this innermost eschatological circle of ethical reflection—and obviously with the Pauline triad of 1 Corinthians 13 [v. 13] in view—is that of *hope*.

2

Again we begin by asking what it must mean that my conduct as a child of God is good at this moment, that it is now a fulfillment of the command of promise, that I am now obedient to my conscience, that I am now truly grateful in what I do. But again, here, too, we have reason to consider that what is meant is no other than what is called, in the third petition of the Lord's Prayer, the doing of God's will on earth as it is done in heaven [cf. Matt. 6:10], so that the limit and distinction which this petition denotes cannot be removed. To be sure, what is now denoted is not the boundary which distinguishes the creature from the Creator nor that within which alone we can walk as reconciled people before the face of the God of mercy. Nevertheless, the fact that we are God's children in this temporality, in the present, also involves a limit and distinction, and it is indeed only in the nearness of the children of God to their Father that we can see the other boundaries in and with their final sharpness and severity. In any case, then, we can do God's will, we can be good, only *on earth*, only *on this side* of the coming perfection. Only with this proviso can I say, with the clarity that is reserved for God alone, that my conduct is at this moment good. Only with this proviso can I understand it as the conduct of the children of God that it is. In the second chapter we described the relation between an obedient human will and God's will as agreement,[1] while in the third chapter we called it commitment.[2] In this innermost circle we must not be afraid to use the term unity, which for good reason we have avoided thus far. Unity with God's will is what shows the will of God's children to be a good will. But unity is not identity. The father does not cease to be the Father, nor the child a child, even at this climax of the relationship to God which is in fact ascribed to us by his Word. Even now I will not speak about the unifying of man's will with God's in obedience, because the unity of the will of the child with that of the Father does not rest on, nor consist in, a uniting of the child's will with

[1]Cf. pp. 249ff.
[2]Cf. pp. 453ff.

that of the Father, but rather upon the fact that the will of the Father, in the final sense of the Word which he speaks to man, makes man his child, and therefore fundamentally unites his will with man's in order that he—and not we—may unite man's will with his. In *hope* we are the children of God and therefore capable of true and supreme obedience in the unity of our will with God's. But in hope means primarily in God's Word which is spoken to us. As the Word comes to us we come to ourselves as God's children. How could we boast of the goodness of our conduct except in the light of this future of ours, of the Word which always remains God's Word, and which we have always to understand as the Word that comes to us? How could we do so but in hope?

Again we are ineluctably referred to prayer if we are even to be able to think of any possibility of that unity between our will and God's. Hope is the orientation of our thought and will beyond the present to the perfect that is coming. In hope, we are citizens of the future world in the midst of the present. For this reason the voice of conscience has its basis in hope. In hope, we can and indeed we must be grateful. But hope might only be folly. It might only be a fanatical dreaming of our way into a suprareality to which we can have no relation in our present all-too-certain present. To be the children of God and therefore to be good in hope, if it were merely an orientation and nothing more, might be a wicked and highly impractical arrogance. But when we pray, confessing that we have no control of our own over this future of ours, but that we have to seek it, and that we have to seek it, not just anywhere or in any way, but with God, hope becomes wisdom. *Praying* in hope we confess once again the third petition of the Lord's Prayer with its explicit and restrictive "on earth." If it can be a matter only of doing God's will on earth as it is done in heaven, with all the distinction that there is between earth and heaven, then plainly we have that unity of our will with God's only as we seek it with God, since at every moment we have to *receive* it from God. Christian hope, then, is this prayerful seeking *with God* for our own future and for the goodness of our conduct therein enclosed. Like faith and love, hope bridges the gap between God and man without removing it, but rather in such a way as to affirm it and thus to give the glory to God and not to man. What is done in hope is well done because hope reaches out for the good, the only good which is God's. As we are children of God in hope, we affirm that God is the Lord, as in the kingdom of grace, so also in the kingdom of glory. Distinguishing between what is ours and what is the Lord's we emphasize: "*Thy* kingdom come! *Thy* will be done! Hallowed be *thy* name!" [Matt. 6:9, 10]. Faith does this too. Love does it too. In this regard faith and love and hope are in and with each other the obedience that is required of us. But if faith does it with respect and love with hot necessity, hope does it with what has already secretly become the present felicity, which runs: "It is *good* for me to cling fast to the Lord."[3]

To repeat, the hoping person looks gladly, willingly, and joyfully beyond the present and away from himself. Why? Because he has been born again to a living hope [cf. 1 Pet. 1:3], because he practices his own new existence as one who hopes, because here he lives in this new existence of his only as in a tent which will have to be folded up, while his house is that which is being built by God in heaven, for which he cannot cease to long even if he wanted to [cf. 2 Cor. 5:1f.]. Naturally this being born again to divine sonship, this glad and willing and joyful seeking of God and praying to God and giving God the glory, this being caught up truly in a work of hope, is not something that we think we have or think we know by being engaged in all kinds of works of hope. We cannot think that we read off from this that we may be aware of obeying conscience in certain ways or that our action perhaps gives some evidence of that fine freedom of the play of God's children. We cannot misuse even prayer as a means of giving ourselves self-certainty. This could only be deception. To rely on this would finally be to rely again on self. In none of it could we get past the disquiet of our own spirit. The basis of hope, as of faith and love, is negatively, without doubt, a nonbasis, a not-finally-relying on ourselves, on the seriousness or obedience of our conscience, on our ability to play, or even on our prayer. It is not for nothing that with *elpis*, as with *pistis* and *agapē*, Paul denotes less, or not at all, the act of the person concerned, but more, or totally, its object, the work of God as the Redeemer, as the Lord and Giver of that for which the person hopes. We said at the outset that at this final climax of our deliberations the only term that can serve to describe good human conduct is one that denotes a human mode of action but also clearly expresses divine control of the final quality of this mode of action. As faith is real faith only by being finally transcended in demonstration of the faithfulness of God, and as love is the good work of faith only inasmuch as we are loved by God before we ever love him [cf. 1 John 4:19], so the question whether we really hope can be answered with ultimate clarity and certainty only as we give up the dignity of being subjects and admit that we can hope only in and by God himself, and that the overwhelming certainty and clarity of Christian hope rests upon its being hope not at all on the basis of its own hope, but wholly and utterly for the sake of what is hoped for. Only *par elpida ep elpidi* can we really hope, as is said of Abraham in Romans 4:18: "Hoping against hope." Yet we do not plunge into an abyss here, for if we want to stand, then again we finally have to lose all ground beneath our feet save the one. Like faith and love, hope rests in the Word which is spoken to us

[3]Augustine, *Confessions* VII, 11.

and which here, because the subject of hope is our own future, is to be understood specifically as the Word of the Holy Spirit, as the pledge which God has given to us, as the Paraclete in a presence in which we may be certain of the coming Lord as such. In this Word that is spoken to us we are the children of God, and we have the divine hope in the light of which alone there can be human hope.

Even in this closing moment we cannot abandon or conceal the circular movement which we have followed these two semesters and which has to be followed in theology if it is true to its theme. Even now we have to say paradoxically but, for the sake of sharpness, quite openly that we can have certainty only insofar as we are ready to be certain of God in our own uncertainty. It is in this hope from above, from God, that we are saved [cf. Rom. 8:24] and do what is good, and not otherwise. Even in this last form, then, the question what shall we *do*, what is the good, leads back to that other question with which all ethics must begin, the question who we are, whether we are those who have heard the Word, i.e., to whom it has been told and who have let it be told them. If we are, then how can we fail to tell it to ourselves and thus answer the problem of ethics by pointing to the internal testimony of the Holy Spirit?[4] We confess to be those who have heard this testimony. And this answer will prove to be legitimate by the fact that we can make no other use of it than that of at once acting in such hope that the question of the criteria of the good can only become acute again, leaving us no option but in prayer to seek afresh what has been given to us and what has to be given to us again and again. It will prove to be legitimate by making impossible any mere consideration of the ethical problem, by pointing us beyond the reflection which is, of course, necessary, by plunging us into life itself, into the responsibility which we must always carry after having reflected. Yet the distinctive thing about Christian or theological ethics is that we do not have to do any carrying without remembering that we *are* carried. Precisely to the extent that that happens, theological ethics can and must claim and occupy its true place in life itself.

[4]Cf. J. Calvin, *Inst.* I, 7, 4, 5.

Theses on Church and State[1]

I. Church

1. The humility required of us, as repentance before God, means concretely that our action takes place in the order of the church and confirms the order of the church. The correlation between repentance and the church rests on the incarnation of the Christ who summons us to repentance; in this the church has its basis.
2. The church is not an order of creation. It is an order of grace relating to sin. It is not to be confused with the "barest, purest, and simplest religion" (Luther, EA, o.e. 1.1, 133)[2] of the lost state of innocence. Nor, according to Revelation 21:22, will there any longer be a church in the consummation.
3. The church is the order, sanctified by the actual presence of the Word and Spirit of God, in which, by the grace of God, the message of man's reconciliation with God through Christ is proclaimed, where, by the grace of God, the right answer is given to this by man, i.e., the act of repentance, and where, again by the grace of God, the fellowship of men takes place in this hearing and answering, the only possible and real fellowship.
4. In virtue of the actual presence of God and to his glory, the church is the one order, holy and infallible, which is binding on all men, outside which there is no salvation,[3] and which is the legitimate bearer and recipient of the prophetic and apostolic witness. But this actual presence of God as the ontic and noetic ground of these qualities has to be continually given to it, and therefore believed in it and acknowledged as grace in the act of repentance before God.
5. As a human work, and therefore in all its reality apart from the grace of God, the church has a share in the folly and wickedness of man, whose sin has been forgiven but has not ceased to be sin. It cannot ignore, then, the improper nature of that which is actively or passively done by men in it. It will not be led astray by the opposition of the rest of the world to its task and promise, but it will also be constantly reminded by this of its own worldliness and therefore of its starting-point, allowing itself to be referred back to the grace of God. It cannot abandon its fundamental and concrete attitude of humility before the World and Spirit of God that constitute it, in favor of a disposable plenitude of truth and power inherent either in its offices or in the whole community. Even as the bride of Christ, it cannot for a single moment or in any respect cease to be his handmaid. It knows that it can only be *led* into all truth [cf. John 16:13].
6. The human work of the church is thus the service of God in the broadest sense, because it can never act effectively except under the proviso of the grace of God. It is the setting up of the symbol of proclamation and repentance whose reality is God's

---

[1]Based on a copy of the first draft (1928/29) of § 13, 4; cf. pp. 440, n. 31.
[2]WA 42, 80, 41−81, 1 (LW, 1, 106).
[3]Cf. Cyprian *Ep.* 73, 21.

work alone. The symbol of this symbol is divine service in the narrower sense of the word (worship). This is the characteristic function of the church as such (in distinction from other human orders and societies which are not intrinsically the church).

7. The decisive elements of divine service in the narrower sense are as follows:

  a. personal, commissioned, and responsible transmission of the biblical witness to Christ in preaching and the administration of the sacraments as necessary recollection of the givenness of this witness which is not tied to human speech and hearing;

  b. all the other cultic possibilities which have their inner and outer criterion in whether or not they are commanded and responsible as expressions of repentance before God and to that extent as means of edification.

8. With the task of divine service in the broader and narrower senses the following special tasks are assigned to the church:

  a. individual pastoral care, which is not possible without energetic physical care of every type;

  b. the acts of individual members of the church as such, as these are characterized by repentance before God, namely, their participation and cooperation in the word of preaching oriented to the biblical witness;[4]

  c. Christian education of youth, whose Christian nature can be basically only a human question and a divine answer;

  d. evangelization and missions as a necessary expression of the church's life and its responsible proclamation to the rest of the world, which is alien to it but with which it must reckon in humility before God;

  e. theology, i.e., the never unnecessary critical self-reflection of the church on its origin, on the promises and warnings of its history, on its nature, and on its central and also its peripheral task.

9. The task and promise of this human work is fundamentally given to the church as such, i.e., to all its members. The holders of its special offices (the offices of pastor, deacon, theologian, and administrator) are no less servants of Christ, if God gives them grace, because they are also and as such separated servants of the community. The exalting of a special episcopal office above that of the pastor, being a disruption of the created balance of leadership and equality, is a poor symbol of the fact that in the community, as all serve the sovereign God, so each can only serve the other.

II.   The State

1. As service of the neighbor the humility required of us means concretely that our action takes place in the order of the state and confirms the order of the state. The correlation between service and the state also rests on the incarnation of Christ, which is the basis of the possibility of people being for one another—not merely living with one another before God, but also living for one another among one another. This living for one another among one another is the purpose of the state.

2. The state, too, is not an order of creation. Even more palpably than the church, it is an order of grace relating to sin. It is particularly an order of the patience of God which finds its limit and end in the eternal consummation. It is "a necessary remedy for corrupt nature" [Luther, EA, o.e. 1.1, 130].[5]

3. The state, too, is the order, sanctified by the actual presence of the Word and Spirit of God, in which, by the grace of God, the rules are set up and upheld for common

---

[4]The looser original, here emended by the Swiss editor, ran as follows: "b. participation and cooperation in the word of preaching oriented to the biblical witness and through the acts of individual members of the church as such as these are characterized by repentance before God."

[5]WA 42, 79, 7ff. (LW, 1, 104).

life, all being also made responsible for each and each for all, i.e., placed in mutual service. Thus the final and true purpose of the state can only be the Christian one, that on the basis of mutual forgiveness we should be not only with one another but also for one another.

4.   Insofar as the state, too, is established and upheld by the actual presence of God, it is in every possible form a minister in God's place [cf. Rom. 13:4], and it is Christian obedience to render to Caesar what is Caesar's [cf. Matt. 22:21]. The divine dignity of the state, too, is ultimately a matter of revelation and faith, so that in the age of the Reformation it was rightly made an object of church confession.[6] This means, of course, that where the actual presence of God in the reality of the state cannot possibly be believed, i.e., where it is not at all visible, God is to be obeyed rather than men [cf. Acts 5:29] to the extent that even the service of others, which is the purpose of its reality, can sometimes be turned into its opposite.

5.   As a human work, and therefore in all its reality, the state too, and even more palpably than the church, has a share in the corruption in which man, far from forgiving sin, with cunning and force pursues his own ends in the struggle for existence. The dignity of the individual state, and the respect that is owed and paid it, can for the following reasons be called service of the neighbor only in an improper sense:

   a.   because each individual state (contrary to its true nature) orders the common life of man and man on the assumption that the right of each must be protected and on the other hand each must be charged with his sins;

   b.   because the decisive means of existence of each individual state in relation to its members (contrary to its true nature) is brute force;

   c.   because each individual state (contrary to its true nature) is only one among others in relation to which it relies more or less on the right of might to maintain its existence. All this shows that the existing order of the state, more palpably than that of the church, is a relative order whose establishment and maintenance is service of the neighbor only insofar as it takes place in repentance before God, i.e., in the belief that God will make good what we cannot help but do badly.

6.   The human work of the state is thus service of the neighbor because it, too, can act effectively only under the proviso of the grace of God. It is the setting up of the symbol of fellowship whose reality is God's work alone. The symbol of this symbol is the setting up and upholding of this rule of law in an ethnographically and geographically defined territory by which a particular state is distinguished from other states and from other entities (economic, cultural, and ecclesiastical) in and outside its sphere of sovereignty.

7.   The decisive functions of the state are:

   a.   legislation, whose fundamental purpose is the creation of fundamentally equal rights in all questions of social life;

   b.   government, i.e., provision for the sure, complete, impartial, and objective observance of all existing laws;

   c.   justice as a system of applying the laws fairly in cases of dispute.

8.   The tasks of legislation and government always include:

   a.   a concern to provide and protect national labor;

   b.   protection of all who temporarily or permanently have a part in the organization of labor;

   c.   promotion of free learning;

   d.   concern for popular education and culture;

[6]Cf. CA XVI, 1; Apol. XVI, 53; CA XXVIII, 18; Small Catechism; Large Catechism; Geneva Catechism and Confession of Faith (24); Belgic Confession XXXVI; Second Helvetic Confession XXX. (Cf. T.G. Tappert, *The Book of Concord*, pp. 37, 81 ff., 222 f., 343, 384 f.; P. Schaff, *Creeds of Christendom* III, pp. 167, 75, 305, 433.)

e. concern for the freedom of action and expression of individuals, groups, and parties to the extent that this can be understood as an affirmation of the purpose of the state;

f. public acknowledgment and support of the church in particular as the society in which recollection of the ultimate purpose of the state particularly resides.

9.   The task and promise of this work are fundamentally for all, and in particular they are fundamentally for men and women equally. Christians especially realize that they are personally responsible for the life of the state and its activity. Here, too, leadership and office have to be, and can only be, a commission and ministry and not an intrinsic distinction of individuals or of certain families, ranks, or classes. Insofar as office is held by fallible people on the basis of fallible laws, it is open to criticism, and insofar as its exercise rests on force, one cannot rule out, as a last resort, in opposition to it, violent revolution on the part of the rest of the citizens.

III.   Church and State

1.   As Boniface VIII (bull *Unam Sanctam*, 1302) rightly presupposed, church and state, as two expressions of one and the same temporally though not eternally valid divine order, are the two swords of the one power of Jesus Christ.[7] The dualism of this order is conditioned and demanded by the dualism of man reconciled to God as a sinner saved by grace. Christian humility will in the same way recognize the relativity of the distinction and the necessity of the relative distinction. It will not reckon, then, either with an absolutizing of the distinction (the metaphysical differentiation of a religious and a secular sphere of life) or a one-sided removal of it (caesaropapism or "theocracy").

2.   There is no equality of rank between church and state but a superiority in favor of the church. "The one sword then should be subject to the other, and temporal authority subject to spiritual" (Boniface VIII).[8] The temple is prior to the home and above it (Luther EA o.e. 1.1, 130).[9] State and church coinhere. Yet the church is not first in the state, but the state in the church, for repentance before God establishes but does not presuppose service of the neighbor, whereas service of the neighbor presupposes but does not establish repentance before God. In all circumstances, then, the Christian is first of all a member of the church and only then and as such a citizen.

3.   If the responsible representatives of the church are not to lose their humility, the church can assert its principial superiority to the state only to the glory of God as Lord of both church and state, and not to its own glory, and it can do so only with the means that have been given to it, the proclamation of the Word and repentance, and not, with Boniface VIII, by the direct or indirect uniting of the two swords in its hands, or by the exercise of quasi-political authority in competition with that of the state.[10]

4.   The church, to the extent that it acts as such, renounces not only the appeal to the individual instinct of self-preservation and the assertion of the distinction between

[7]Cf. *Unam Sanctam*, Nov. 18, 1302: "Of this one and holy church there is one body and one head, not two heads like a monster, namely, Christ, and Christ's vicar is Peter, and Peter's successor . . . In this church are two swords, the spiritual and the temporal . . . Both are in the power of the church, the spiritual sword and the material. But the latter is to be used for the church, the former by her; the former by the priest, the latter by kings and captains, but at the will and by the permission of the priest. The one sword, then, should be under the other, and temporal authority subject to spiritual. . . ." Denz. no. 468f.

[8]See n.7.

[9]WA 42, 79, 7 (LW, 1, 104).

[10]Cf. n. 7.

right and wrong, and not only the use of external compulsion within or force without, but fundamentally also the setting up and upholding of any rigid rule of law. Canons and dogmas are not legal but spiritual norms, and are to be applied only as such. Church law in the strict sense can be only the church-recognized law of the state that exists even in the church. As an inevitable change into another genre the formation of special church law can be understood only as an incidental and doubly improper function of the church, and it comes under the rule: "The less of it, the better!"

5. As one society among others, the church in practice adjusts and subordinates itself to the state as the guardian of the rule of law. In relation to the national differentiation of states, things being as they are the church will accept as nonessential its necessary distinction and characterization over against other parts of the church.[11] The freedom and superiority which it maintains precisely in so doing are not tied to the amount of independence of leadership and organization in relation to the state, nor to the presence of a visible supranational church unity, but to the measure of certainty with which, as a fellowship of the proclamation of the Word and repentance, it maintains itself over against the justifiable and unjustifiable claims of the state as the bearer of its materially transcendent, and in fact united and therefore international, task. A state church that knows and is true to its cause, and to the unity of this cause, is to be preferred to even the freest of churches as a symbol of the ultimate unity of church and state.

6. The church acknowledges and promotes the state insofar as service of the neighbor, which is the purpose of the state, is necessarily included in its own message of reconciliation and is thus its own concern. In relation to the activity of the state, it will adopt a restrained attitude to the extent that the state diverges from this purpose or that it cannot accept co-responsibility for it as the church. Finally, with the means at its disposal, it will move on to protest against the state if the latter's activity becomes a denial of its purpose and it is no longer visible or credible as the order of God. Either way it will always confess positively the purpose of the state and therefore the national state itself.

7. If the representatives of the state are not to lose their humility, the state can assert its practical superiority over the church only to the glory of God as Lord of both church and state and not to its own glory—and it can do so only in its own field as the guardian of the rule of law, not as the herald of a philosophy or morality conformable to its own *raison d'être*, nor with the desire for a special civil Christianity. It gives the church freedom to fashion its own worship, dogma, and constitution and to practice its own preaching and theology.

8. The state for its part cannot be tied in principle to any specific form of the church. It recognizes and supports the church insofar as its own purpose is grounded and included in that of the church. Thus far it is neither nonreligious nor nonconfessional. But it is supraconfessional insofar as it is tolerant in face of the confessional division of the church, in principle assuring the same freedom to all church bodies within the framework of law.

9. In practice, however, without intolerance to others, and as an expression of the specificity with which it is conscious of its own purpose, the state may address and claim a specific form of the church in a special way as *the* form of the church in accordance with the recognition of the specific national state which the church does not withhold. As a symbol of the ultimate unity of church and state, the qualified recognition and support of the church is, even from the state's point of view, more appropriate than the system of a real organizational separation of church and state.

---

[11]An allusion to the lively debate in Germany after 1918 whether the borders of the state should also be those of the church; cf. O. Dibelius, *Das Jahrhundert der Kirche*, Berlin 1926, 1927[2], pp. 98f.

I

Scripture References

II

Names

(Numbers in italics indicate the individual named is cited only in the footnotes on that page)

Adam, Alfred, *210*
Adam, Karl, 484
Aesop, *348, 396*
Aksakov, Constantine, 104
Althaus, Paul, 475–76
Altweg, Wilhelm, *95*
Ambrose, Aurelius, 6
Anselm of Canterbury, 98, 315
Aristotle, 6, 12, 29, 33, *314, 323*
Augustine, 11, 14, 29, 33, *388, 389, 433,* 445, *465, 515*

Bacon, Francis, *136*
Barth, Heinrich, *19, 410*
Barth, Karl, *8, 17, 19, 33, 38, 51, 56, 65, 75, 90, 111, 114, 170, 181, 193, 211,* 218, *221, 230, 253, 269, 273, 275, 276, 279, 291, 298, 303, 304, 316, 346, 357, 365, 366, 376, 400, 410, 420, 421, 425, 440, 462, 464, 466, 467, 473, 475, 493, 498, 502*
Barth, Peter, *410*
Basil of Caesarea, 6
Baum, Wilhelm (Guilielmus), *273*
Bebel, August, 221
Beck, Johann Tobias, 276, 278
Beck, L.W., *36*
Bellarmine, Robert, 484
Benedict of Nursia, 6
Bentham, Jeremy, 4
Beriger, Leonhard, *142*
Beyreuther, Erich, *334*
Bismarck, Otto von, 137, *430*
Björnson, Björnstjerne, *94*
Blumhardt, Christoph, Jr., *475*
Boecking, Eduard, *131*
Böhme, Franz Magnus, *358*
Bohnenblust, Gottfried, *95*
Bolin, Wilhelm, *4*
Bolland, Johannes, *341*
Boniface VIII, 449, 520, 521
Brenz, Johannes, *210, 273*
Brunner, Emil, *51, 421*
Brutus, Marcus Junius, 149
Bubnoff, Nicolai von, *104*
Büchmann, Georg, *152*
Bultmann, Rudolf, 8, 17, 421
Burckhardt, Jacob, 135, 136, 137
Buridan, Johannes, 314

Caesar, Gaius Julius, 149
Calixt, George, 7
Calvin, John, 7, 17, 90, 91, 99, 111, 149–50, 225, 250, 273, 274, 277–78, 281, 289, 290, 313, *389, 404,* 445–46, 512, *516*
Cassius, Gaius, 149
Cathrein, Victor, *421*
Celsus, Publius Juventius, *205*
Chomiakov, Alexei, 104, *250*
Cicero, Marcus Tullius, 6, 12, 32, *381*
Clauren, Heinrich (Carl Heun), *156*
Clausewitz, Carl von, *154*

Clement of Alexandria, *341*
Clerc, François, *150*
Cohen, Hermann, 4, 195
Colli, Giorgio, *4*
Cunitz, Eduard, *273*
Cyprian, *341, 517*

Danaeus, Lambert, 7
De Wette, Martin Leberecht, 9, 21, 25, 46
Decatur, Stephen, *157*
Denzinger, Heinrich, *389, 408, 409, 411, 412,* 449, *520*
Dibelius, Otto, *450, 521*
Diem, Hermann, *17*
Dorner, August, *25*
Dorner, Isaak August, 25, 26, 27
Dostoievski, Feodor Mikhailovich, 146, 418

Ebermayer, Ludwig, *149*
Ehmann, Karl C. Eberhard, *125*
Ehrenberg, Hans, *104*
Elert, Werner, 195
Elias, Julius, *94*
Ellis, Robert Leslie, *136*
Enders, Ernst Ludwig, 273, 403
Epstein, Klaus, *149*
Erasmus of Rotterdam, 318–19
Erk, Ludwig, *358*
Erzberger, Matthias, 149

Fabricius, Cajus, *177*
Faesi, Robert, *95*
Fairweather, E.R., *315*
Feti, Domenico, *334*
Feuerbach, Ludwig, 4
Fèvre, Justinus, *484*
Fichte, Johann Gottlieb, 36, 86, *445*
Fitzmaurice, J., *171*
Flacius Illyricus, Matthias, 261
Florenski, Pavel Alexandrovich, 250
Forsthoff, Heinrich, *179*
Fouillée, Alfred, 120
Franklin, Benjamin, 170
Frederick the Great, 156, 385
Frederick William III of Prussia, *156*
Frei, Gottfried, *218*
Freiligrath, Ferdinand, *164*
Freystein, Johann Burchard, *75*

Gass, Wilhelm, 7
Gaudig, Hugo, *365*
Geibel, Emanuel, *193*
Gerhard, Johann, 9
Gerhard, Wilhelm, *386*
Gerhardt, Paul, 489, *490*
Glockner, Hermann, *445*
Goebel, Max, *489*
Goethe, Johann Wolfgang, *64,* 95, *132, 133,* 184, *197, 198, 302, 304,* 305, 306, *312, 387, 391,* 416, *422, 457, 509*

Gogarten, Friedrich, 8, 44, *179,* 238, 311, 421, 470, 471, 478
Gregory the Great, 6
Grotius, Hugo, *430*
Guyau, Jean-Marie, 120

Haarmann, Fritz, 153
Haeckel, Ernst, 4, 120
Haering, Theodor, 11, 46–47, 151
Hagenbach, Karl Rudolf, 21, 25
Hallinger, Kassius, *473*
Hardenberg, Friedrich von, *335*
Harnack, Adolf von, *142,* 225, *304*
Hase, Karl August von, *498*
Hausherr, Irénée, *473*
Hausrath, Adolf, *232*
Heath, Douglas Denon, *136*
Heermann, Johann, *160*
Hegel, Georg Friedrich Wilhelm, 314, 445
Heidelberg Catechism, 58, 97, 255, 373, *432,* 499, 501
Heim, Karl, 114
Herrmann, Wilhelm, 8, 21, 24, 46, 47, 120, 121
Herzog, Johann Jacob, *489*
Heun, Carl. See Clauren, Heinrich
Hinneberg, Paul, *29, 379*
Hirsch, Emanuel, 8
Höffding, Harald, 4
Hoffmann von Fallersleben, August Heinrich, *448*
Hofmann, Johann Christian Konrad von, 46, 47
Holl, Karl, *81,* 276, 277, 278, 281, 282, 284
Horace, *95*
Horn, Fritz, *179*
Hünefeld, Günther Ehrenfried Freiherr von, *171*
Hüssy (textile manufacturers), *170*
Hutten, Ulrich von, 131

Ihering, Rudolf von, 379, 381

Jaeger, Werner, *372*
Jaspert, Bernd, *8*
Jodl, Friedrich, *4*
Joël, Karl, *305*
Jonas, Ludwig, *10*
Juvenal, *332*

Kägi, Werner, *135*
Kähler, Martin, 8
Kant, Immanuel, 27, 36, 76, 78, 80, 86, 131, 296–97, 302, 303, 305, 309, 314
Kerschensteiner, Georg, *365*
Key, Ellen, *241*
Kierkegaard, Sören, 8, 17, 166, *269, 303*
Kirn, Otto, 11, 25, 46, 47
Kleist, Heinrich von, *381*
Knaake, Joachim Karl Friedrich, *500*
Knak, Gustav, 231–32

525

III

Subjects